The United States Government Internet Directory 2018

The United States Government Internet Directory 2018

Edited by Mary Meghan Ryan

Bernan Press

Lanham • Boulder • New York • London

Published by Bernan Press
An imprint of The Rowman & Littlefield Publishing Group, Inc.
4501 Forbes Boulevard, Suite 200, Lanham, Maryland 20706
www.rowman.com
800-865-3457

Unit A, Whitacre Mews, 26-34 Stannary Street, London SE11 4AB

ISBN: 978-1-59888-996-3

eISBN: 978-1-59888-997-0

ISSN: 1547-2892

∞™ The paper used in this publication meets the minimum requirements of American National Standard for Information Sciences Permanence of Paper for Printed Library Materials, ANSI/NISO Z39.48-1992.

Printed in the United States of America

Table of Contents

Quick Guide to Primary Government Websites and Finding Aids vii
Preface xi
About the Editors xiii
Introduction xv
What Can You Find at Agency Websites? xix
Freedom of Information Act (FOIA) Webpages xxi
Organization Charts xxiii

1 Finding Aids 1
2 Agriculture, Fishing, and Forestry 5
3 Business and Economics 21
4 Culture and Recreation 55
5 Defense and Intelligence 89
6 Demographics and Sociology 129
7 Education 137
8 Employment 169
9 Energy 183
10 Engineering and Technology 195
11 Environment and Nature 209
12 Government and Politics 245
13 Health and Safety 275

14 International Relations 323
15 Law and Law Enforcement 339
16 Legislative Branch 371
17 Presidency 385
18 Science and Space 391
19 Social Welfare 423
20 Transportation 441
21 Beyond the Federal Web—Nongovernmental Websites 453

Appendix A: List of Members of the 115th Congress 479

Appendix B: Congressional Committees 501

Appendix C: U.S. Embassies Abroad 509

Appendix D: Foreign Embassies in the United States 519

Index 527

Quick Guide to Primary Government Websites and Finding Aids

U.S. Congress	
House of Representatives	https://www.house.gov/
Senate	https://www.senate.gov/
THOMAS	https://www.congress.gov/
U.S. Judiciary	
Supreme Court of the United States	https://www.supremecourt.gov/
Administrative Office of the U.S. Courts	http://www.uscourts.gov/
U.S. Presidents	https://www.whitehouse.gov/about-the-white-house/presidents/
U.S. Vice President	https://www.whitehouse.gov/people/mike-pence/
Cabinet and Cabinet-Level Offices	
Agriculture	https://www.usda.gov/
Commerce	https://www.commerce.gov/
Council of Economic Advisers	https://www.whitehouse.gov/cea/

Defense	https://www.defense.gov/
Education	https://www.ed.gov/
Energy	https://www.energy.gov/
Environmental Protection Agency	https://www.epa.gov/
Health and Human Services	https://www.hhs.gov/
Homeland Security	https://www.dhs.gov/
Housing and Urban Development	https://portal.hud.gov/hudportal/HUD
Interior	https://www.doi.gov/
Justice	https://www.justice.gov/
Labor	https://www.dol.gov/
Office of Management and Budget	https://www.whitehouse.gov/omb /
State	https://www.state.gov/
Transportation	https://www.transportation.gov/
Treasury	https://home.treasury.gov/
U.S. Mission to the UN/New York	https://usun.state.gov/
U.S. Trade Representative	https://ustr.gov/
Veterans Affairs	https://www.va.gov/

Major Libraries, Catalogs, and Data Sources

Bureau of Labor Statistics	https://www.bls.gov/
Census Bureau	https://www.census.gov/
Data.gov	https://www.data.gov/
Government Publishing Office	https://www.gpo.gov/
Library of Congress	https://www.loc.gov/
National Agricultural Library	https://www.nal.usda.gov/
National Archives and Records Administration	https://www.archives.gov/
National Institutes of Health	https://www.nih.gov/
National Library of Medicine	https://www.nlm.nih.gov/

National Technical Information Service	https://www.ntis.gov/

U.S. Government Finding Aids

FDsys	https://www.gpo.gov/fdsys/
USA.gov	https://www.usa.gov/

Preface

Due to its massive online presence, federal government-related information can be difficult to find, even with an Internet search engine. *The United States Government Internet Directory* is intended to lead its users to valuable government information that could otherwise be overlooked. The *Directory* organizes selected government and nongovernment Web sites into subject-themed chapters, covering topics such as Transportation and Energy, with an additional chapter for organizations and agencies that are either privately funded or funded significantly by entities beyond the U.S. government. This subject-based approach allows users to narrow their searches to solely encompass their fields of interest; this type of directed and specifically aimed method streamlines and tailors results for quick and efficient use. This book has been designed to help meet the research needs of businesses, teachers, students, and citizens in the United States and around the world. It also provides a resource that more casual users can employ to discover the breadth and depth of government-related information and services available online.

The *Directory* features entries for approximately 1,800 government and nongovernment websites. Each site was chosen for its value individually and as a part of the whole publication. Each site is described to help users define its role and its value as a resource. Website descriptions can include information about the sponsoring agency, useful or unique aspects of the site, and, when pertinent, lists of some of the publications hosted on the site. Appendixes provide Internet addresses for individual members of Congress, standing and joint committees, and embassies of the United States abroad and foreign countries within the United States.

Special features in the directory include a "Quick Guide" to the websites of major federal agencies, libraries, and data sources, as well as organizational charts for federal, congressional, and Cabinet-level agencies.

The authors and site maintainers of the websites listed in this book provide a valuable service for writers, editors, students, and researchers alike—without them, this book would not be possible.

About the Editors

Mary Meghan Ryan is a senior research editor for Bernan Press. She has also been the editor for *State Profiles: The Population and Economy of Each U.S. State*; *Employment, Hours, and Earnings: States and Areas*; and *Vital Statistics of the United States: Births, Life Expectancy, Deaths, and Selected Health Data*. In addition, she serves as the associate editor for *Business Statistics of the United States: Patterns of Economic Change*.

Introduction

The United States Government Internet Directory is a guide to the multitude of websites from the Executive, Judicial, and Legislative branches of the U.S. federal government. As the federal Internet evolves slowly, the new entries and revised descriptions in the book reflect general trends. These trends are shaped by changes in both federal policies and how people use the Internet.

The *Directory* does not make a separate entry for every agency blog but does often mention them in the site descriptions. Separate entries are provided for blogs that exceed the scope of the related website. A comprehensive list of government blogs can be found on USA.gov. The online presence of agencies on popular social media sites like Facebook and Twitter has become common. Mobile sites and applications are not listed individually in the *Directory*; USA.gov provides a list at https://www.usa.gov/mobile-apps.

USING *THE UNITED STATES GOVERNMENT INTERNET DIRECTORY*

Web-based government information can be difficult to find, as the offerings are diverse, decentralized, and not uniformly indexed by search engines. The *Directory* presents some key advantages to sifting through this massive amount of information. It provides the context that is rarely found in an alphabetical list of agency links or in the nebulous results of a search engine query. It offers websites of value and identifies noteworthy resources, such as online publications and databases, within large sites.

Search engines are most helpful when a researcher is confident that certain information exists somewhere on the Internet and can construct a search that produces the desired website within the first few pages of the search results. Even then, information may be missed because search engines cannot and do not find everything online. The *Directory* offers complementary and overlapping approaches to browsing for government information, as it helps users discover new resources and quickly locate established resources that cannot be described via keyword search.

SCOPE

The *Directory* focuses on United States federal government information and services accessible online. The majority of the websites described in this book are the products of federal government agencies. The book also includes sites from some interagency groups, international organizations, federal advisory boards and commissions, private organizations established by congressional legislation, and quasi-governmental organizations, as well as websites produced by outside organizations with federal agency sponsorship or partnerships. In addition, the *Directory* covers selected sites created by nongovernmental organizations to help researchers find federal government information; an excellent example of this type of site is the CyberCemetery, an online archive maintained by the University of North Texas Libraries to preserve the websites of defunct federal agencies and commissions. Specific CyberCemetery URLs are provided where appropriate. Also included are a number of websites either nominally or not at all funded by the government; these organizations have been included in order to supplement the governmental sites with those that provide related, yet additional, information.

The sites included in the *Directory* span a broad range of subjects and serve an equally broad range of audiences. The government websites selected for this publication are designed to meet the information needs of citizens, consumers, businesses, librarians, teachers, scientists, students, and others. For the most part, only sites that do not require payment or registration, or otherwise limit public access, are included. Exceptions to this policy are noted. Some sites are publicly accessible but block portions of their content; when significant, this is also noted.

Each entry typically represents one website or a distinct section of a site. In some cases, complementary or companion sites are described in the same entry. Due to the networked nature of the Internet, it is sometimes difficult to define where one website ends and another begins. Some component databases, publications, or services considered to be of high value for researchers have been given their own entries.

ORGANIZATION

The *Directory*'s table of contents provides a start for browsing websites by topic. The table of contents shows the starting page numbers for the subject-oriented chapters and the sub-topic breakdown within those chapters.

Featured in the *Directory* is a "Quick Guide" to major federal websites, which can be found just after the table of contents. The Quick Guide includes URLs for frequently used government websites. Chapter 1 of the book, Finding Aids, is also a good starting point for researching information.

The book's introductory pages include organization charts for U.S. government agencies. Charts are provided for each Cabinet-level department and agency and for an overview of the U.S. government. The charts come from the *United States Government Manual*, the official handbook of the federal government. These organizational charts are not intended to represent the complete or formal organization of government entities, but instead to provide a strong overview of their structure and a tool for locating government sources online.

Other material in this introduction consists of an overview of government agencies' use of social media websites, a list of the types of information typically found on an agency website, and information on the Freedom of Information Act (FOIA)—a tool for obtaining government information not publicly accessible.

Arranged alphabetically, the chapters are further divided by sub-topic. The Finding Aids chapter includes sites that encompass many subject areas. The book sections covering libraries and kids' pages also include many subject areas.

Individual entries are organized in the following manner:

Site Name: Leading each entry is a site name or title for the resource. For the purposes of this work, several sources are used to identify the site name: agency press releases referring to the site, the name given to the site in the HTML tag, or the name in initial heading or graphic. Because names of websites are subject to ambiguity and change and do not always uniquely identify a site, names are just one way to refer to a resource. The Uniform Resource Locator, or URL, is the best way to uniquely identify a resource, although even this is subject to change.

Primary URL: The web address or URL indicates the location that should be entered in to retrieve the website.

Description: The resource description explains a site's organization, principal features, menu items, and significant links. When pertinent, a brief description of the agency's mission is included to help delineate the site's subject coverage.

Subject(s): The subject terms describe the primary focus or focuses of the entry. Some of the subject terms contain subheadings to more accurately represent the topic.

Two appendixes at the end of the book list web addresses for members of the House and Senate and for congressional committees.

At the back of the book, an index lists every website referenced.

HOW TO USE THIS BOOK

If You Want . . .	Consult . . .
Major department or agency website	U.S. government organization charts
Websites on a specific topic	Table of contents, with chapters and chapter subtopics, or the index
Website for which the name, but not the URL, is known	Index
Specific congressional contact information	Congressional appendixes
Embassy and ambassador information	Ambassadorial appendixes

What to Watch for in 2018

Web sites will undoubtedly continue to change under the Trump administration as they do under every administration. Most notably, the Environmental Protection Agency is updating its webpages "to reflect the EPA's priorities under the leadership of President Trump and Administrator Pruitt".

What Can You Find at Agency Websites?

Executive Branch departments and agencies and related organizations vary widely in the amount and type of information they provide online, but some standard content can typically be found at these sites. A list of the type of content or features one might find at federal agency sites is provided here.

- Advisory council information
- Agency history
- Agency leadership biographies
- Agency leadership speeches and congressional testimony
- Budgets, annual reports, and strategic plans
- Business opportunities in the areas of agency acquisitions, contracting, and technology transfer programs
- Databases related to the regulatory, research, education, or outreach mission of the agency
- Education resources, career information, and pages designed for kids
- E-mail forms for submitting comments or questions
- Employment, fellowships, and/or internship opportunities
- Forms for program applications, regulatory requirements, and/or other purposes (many agencies have automated their program application or regulatory filing processes)
- Freedom of Information Act (FOIA) information and copies of popular documents previously requested via FOIA
- Frequently asked questions (FAQs) sections on programs or services
- Granting and funding information
- Information and reports from the agency's Office of the Inspector General

- Laws and regulations under which the agency operates or which they are responsible for enforcing
- Legal or administrative decisions, rulings, or guidance issued by the agency
- Links to nongovernmental websites on topics relevant to the agency's work
- Links to related federal, state, and tribal agencies
- Links to the agency's presence on social media sites such as Facebook or Twitter
- Links to the webpages for the agency's departments, divisions, or regional offices
- Mobile applications that allow smartphone users access to the sites' contents
- Official documents, publications, and publication catalogs
- Press releases, media kits, fact sheets, and digital photos related to agency operations
- Program descriptions and mission statements
- Program information or publications in Spanish and/or additional languages
- Site search features and site indexes
- Statistics on programs or populations served
- User services including e-mail alerts, RSS news feeds, blogs, online video, and webcasts

Required Information for Executive Branch Agency Websites:

Agencies are required to provide certain online content, such as information on their organizational structure and their Freedom of Information Act procedures. The list above includes, but is not limited to, required content.

In June 2015, the White House Office of Management and Budget signed a memorandum requiring all publicly accessible federal websites and web services to provide service through a secure protection by December 31, 2016. As a result of this, most government websites now begin with HTTPS or Hypertext Transfer Protocol Secure. The previously used HTTP or Hypertext Transfer Protocal was vulnerable to manipulation and alteration. HTTPS helps guard against imposter websites. Many private websites mentioned in this book have also converted from http to https.

Freedom of Information Act (FOIA) Webpages

The Freedom of Information Act (FOIA) grants public access to U.S. federal executive agency records, unless the records requested meet specific FOIA exemption criteria. Under FOIA, federal executive agency websites are required to include information about how to request records from the agency. Many agency websites also contain "Electronic Reading Rooms," or similar features, to fulfill FOIA requirements. These types of pages contain copies of frequently requested documents. Before submitting a FOIA request to an agency, be sure to check for current information and instructions, which are usually available on the agency's FOIA page.

The central unit responsible for guiding agency compliance with FOIA is the Department of Justice's Office of Information Policy (OIP). Its website is https://www.justice.gov/oip/.

For citizens, FOIA.gov is the government's comprehensive FOIA website. It offers information about FOIA and can be used to find records that are already available online and to learn how to make a FOIA request. The site also features a comprehensive directory of FOIA websites and contacts for each government agency: https://www.foia.gov/report-makerequest.html

In late 2012, the FOIAOnline website (https://foiaonline.regulations.gov) was formed to serve as a device for making multi-agency requests.

FOIA WEBSITES FOR CABINET LEVEL DEPARTMENTS AND AGENCIES

- Department of Agriculture: https://www.dm.usda.gov/foia/

- Department of Commerce: http://www.osec.doc.gov/omo/FOIA/FOIA-Website.htm
- Department of Defense: http://www.esd.whs.mil/FOID/Defense-Agencies/
- Department of Education: https://www2.ed.gov/policy/gen/leg/foia/foia-toc.html
- Department of Energy: https://energy.gov/management/office-management/operational-management/freedom-information-act
- Environmental Protection Agency: https://www.epa.gov/foia
- Department of Health and Human Services: https://www.hhs.gov/foia/
- Department of Homeland Security: https://www.dhs.gov/freedom-information-act-and-privacy-act
- Department of Housing and Urban Development: https://portal.hud.gov/hudportal/HUD?src=/program_offices/administration/foia
- Department of the Interior: https://www.doi.gov/foia/
- Department of Justice: https://www.justice.gov/oip
- Department of Labor: https://www.dol.gov/general/foia
- Department of State: https://foia.state.gov/
- Department of Transportation: https://www.transportation.gov/foia/
- Department of the Treasury: https://www.treasury.gov/foia/Pages/index.aspx
- Department of Veteran Affairs: https://www.oprm.va.gov/foia/

Organization Charts

THE GOVERNMENT OF THE UNITED STATES

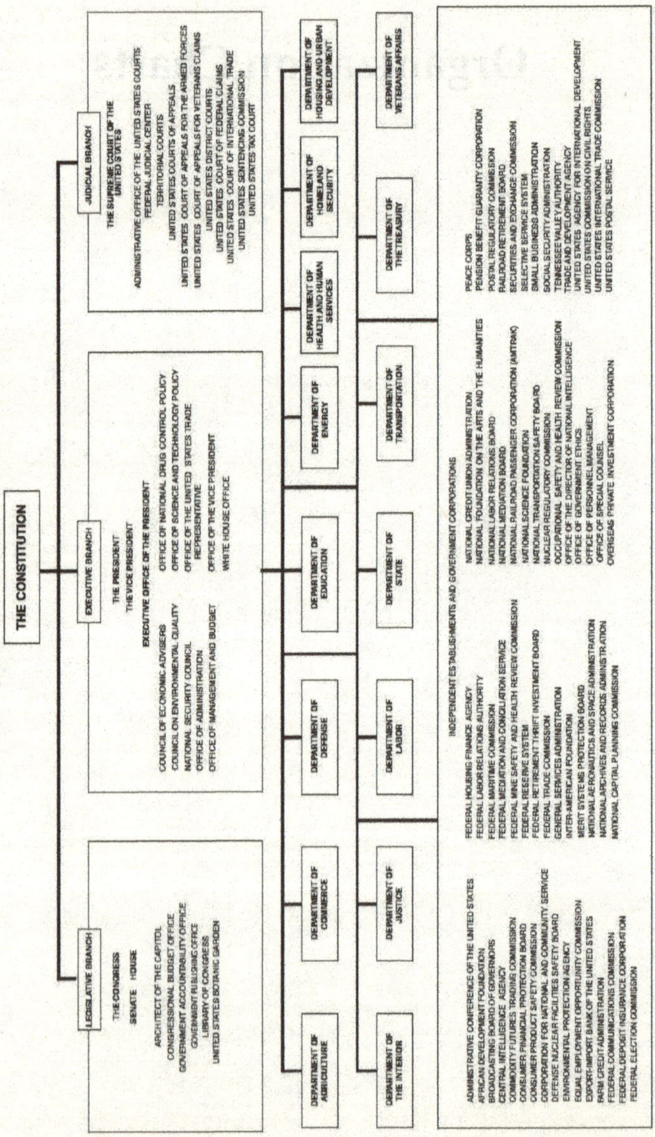

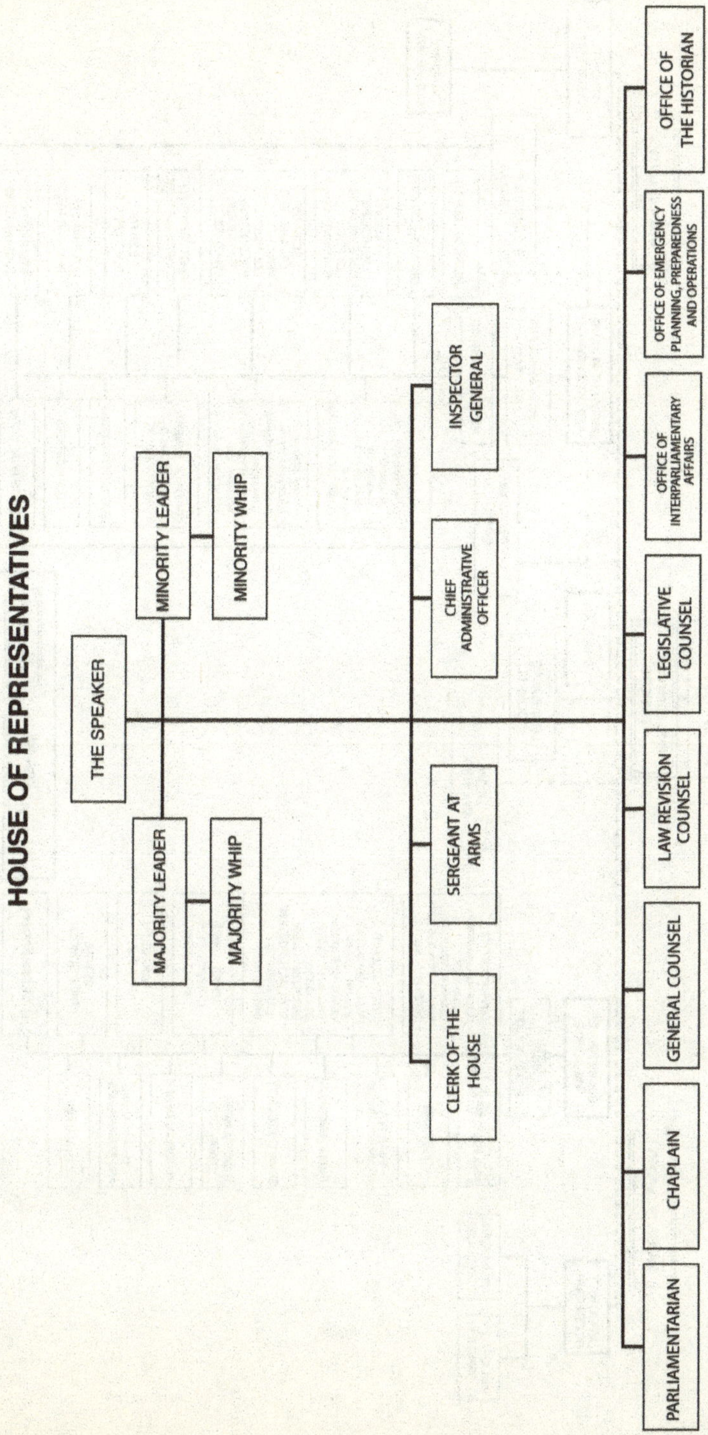
HOUSE OF REPRESENTATIVES
THE SPEAKER
MAJORITY LEADER
MAJORITY WHIP
MINORITY LEADER
MINORITY WHIP
CLERK OF THE HOUSE
SERGEANT AT ARMS
CHIEF ADMINISTRATIVE OFFICER
INSPECTOR GENERAL
PARLIAMENTARIAN
CHAPLAIN
GENERAL COUNSEL
LAW REVISION COUNSEL
LEGISLATIVE COUNSEL
OFFICE OF INTERPARLIAMENTARY AFFAIRS
OFFICE OF EMERGENCY PLANNING, PREPAREDNESS AND OPERATIONS
OFFICE OF THE HISTORIAN

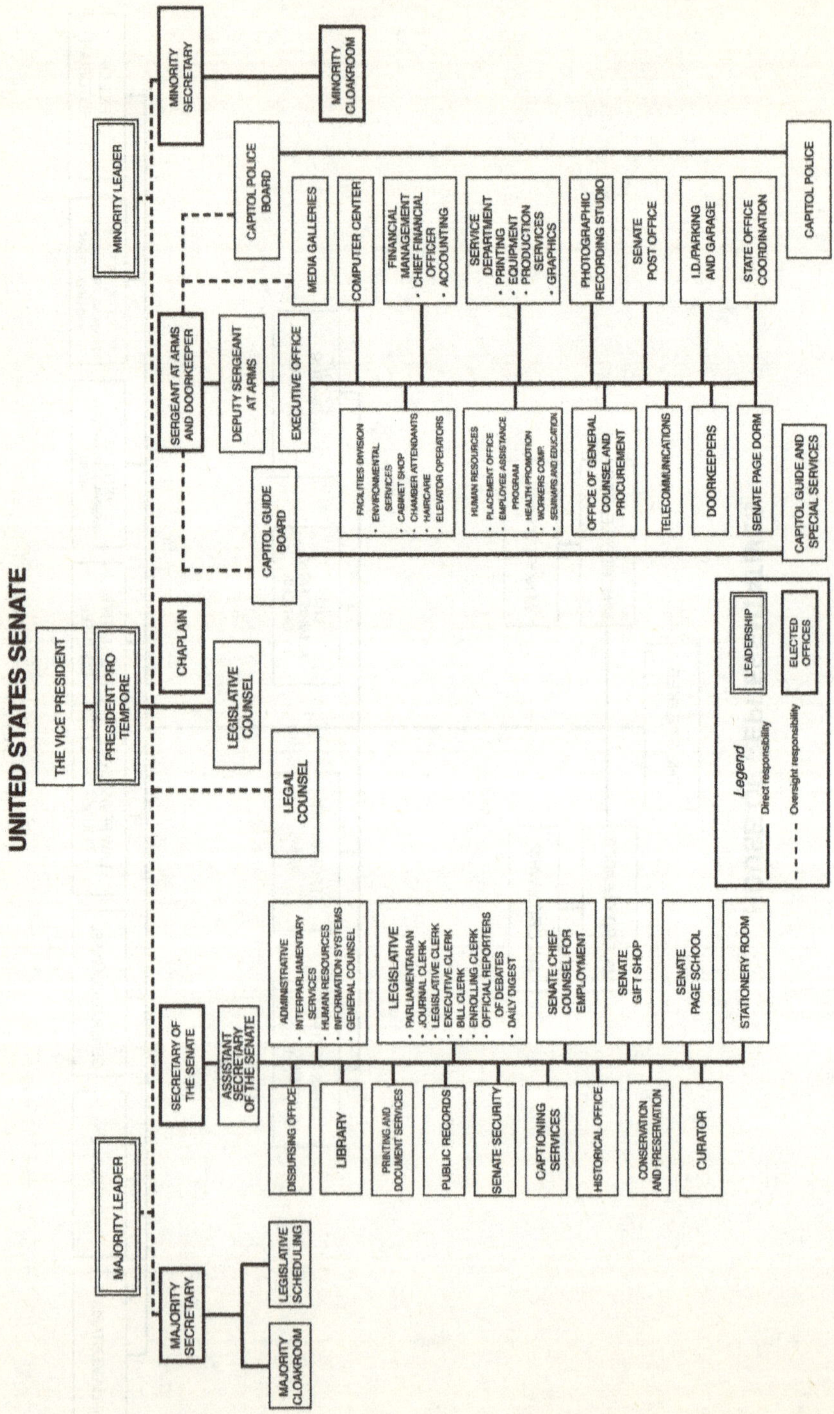
UNITED STATES SENATE
THE VICE PRESIDENT
PRESIDENT PRO TEMPORE
MAJORITY LEADER
MINORITY LEADER
MAJORITY SECRETARY
MAJORITY CLOAKROOM
LEGISLATIVE SCHEDULING
SECRETARY OF THE SENATE
ASSISTANT SECRETARY OF THE SENATE
DISBURSING OFFICE
LIBRARY
PRINTING AND DOCUMENT SERVICES
PUBLIC RECORDS
SENATE SECURITY
CAPTIONING SERVICES
HISTORICAL OFFICE
CONSERVATION AND PRESERVATION
CURATOR
ADMINISTRATIVE
• INTERPARLIAMENTARY SERVICES
• HUMAN RESOURCES
• INFORMATION SYSTEMS
• GENERAL COUNSEL
LEGISLATIVE
• PARLIAMENTARIAN
• JOURNAL CLERK
• LEGISLATIVE CLERK
• EXECUTIVE CLERK
• BILL CLERK
• ENROLLING CLERK
• OFFICIAL REPORTERS OF DEBATES
• DAILY DIGEST
SENATE CHIEF COUNSEL FOR EMPLOYMENT
SENATE GIFT SHOP
SENATE PAGE SCHOOL
STATIONERY ROOM
LEGAL COUNSEL
LEGISLATIVE COUNSEL
CHAPLAIN
CAPITOL GUIDE BOARD
CAPITOL GUIDE AND SPECIAL SERVICES
SERGEANT AT ARMS AND DOORKEEPER
DEPUTY SERGEANT AT ARMS
EXECUTIVE OFFICE
FACILITIES DIVISION
• ENVIRONMENTAL SERVICES
• CABINET SHOP
• CHAMBER ATTENDANTS
• HAIRCARE
• ELEVATOR OPERATORS
HUMAN RESOURCES
• PLACEMENT OFFICE
• EMPLOYEE ASSISTANCE PROGRAM
• HEALTH PROMOTION
• WORKERS COMP.
• SEMINARS AND EDUCATION
OFFICE OF GENERAL COUNSEL AND PROCUREMENT
TELECOMMUNICATIONS
DOORKEEPERS
SENATE PAGE DORM
MEDIA GALLERIES
COMPUTER CENTER
FINANCIAL MANAGEMENT
• CHIEF FINANCIAL OFFICER
• ACCOUNTING
SERVICE DEPARTMENT
• PRINTING
• EQUIPMENT
• PRODUCTION SERVICES
• GRAPHICS
PHOTOGRAPHIC RECORDING STUDIO
SENATE POST OFFICE
I.D./PARKING AND GARAGE
STATE OFFICE COORDINATION
CAPITOL POLICE BOARD
CAPITOL POLICE
MINORITY SECRETARY
MINORITY CLOAKROOM
Legend
Direct responsibility
Oversight responsibility
LEADERSHIP
ELECTED OFFICES

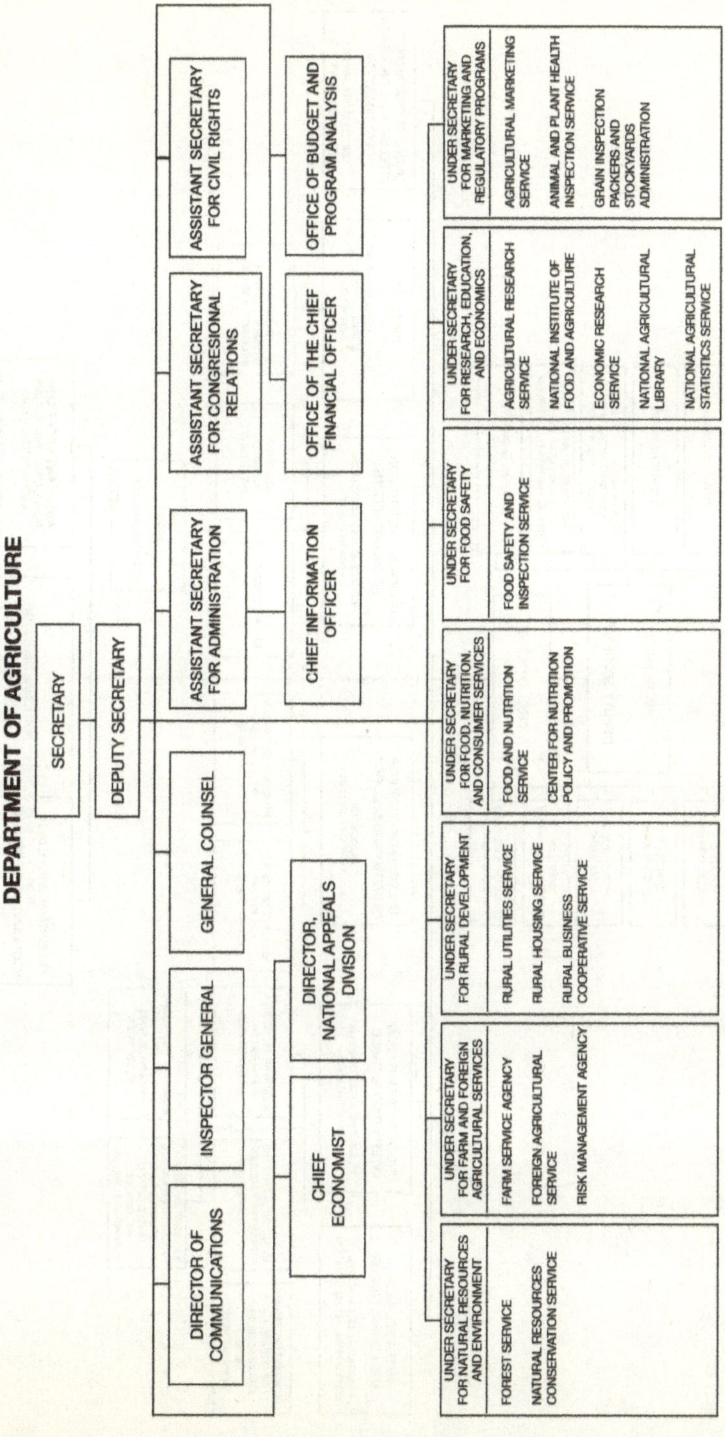
DEPARTMENT OF AGRICULTURE
SECRETARY
DEPUTY SECRETARY
DIRECTOR OF COMMUNICATIONS
INSPECTOR GENERAL
GENERAL COUNSEL
ASSISTANT SECRETARY FOR ADMINISTRATION
ASSISTANT SECRETARY FOR CONGRESIONAL RELATIONS
ASSISTANT SECRETARY FOR CIVIL RIGHTS
CHIEF ECONOMIST
DIRECTOR, NATIONAL APPEALS DIVISION
CHIEF INFORMATION OFFICER
OFFICE OF THE CHIEF FINANCIAL OFFICER
OFFICE OF BUDGET AND PROGRAM ANALYSIS
UNDER SECRETARY FOR NATURAL RESOURCES AND ENVIRONMENT
FOREST SERVICE
NATURAL RESOURCES CONSERVATION SERVICE
UNDER SECRETARY FOR FARM AND FOREIGN AGRICULTURAL SERVICES
FARM SERVICE AGENCY
FOREIGN AGRICULTURAL SERVICE
RISK MANAGEMENT AGENCY
UNDER SECRETARY FOR RURAL DEVELOPMENT
RURAL UTILITIES SERVICE
RURAL HOUSING SERVICE
RURAL BUSINESS COOPERATIVE SERVICE
UNDER SECRETARY FOR FOOD, NUTRITION, AND CONSUMER SERVICES
FOOD AND NUTRITION SERVICE
CENTER FOR NUTRITION POLICY AND PROMOTION
UNDER SECRETARY FOR FOOD SAFETY
FOOD SAFETY AND INSPECTION SERVICE
UNDER SECRETARY FOR RESEARCH, EDUCATION, AND ECONOMICS
AGRICULTURAL RESEARCH SERVICE
NATIONAL INSTITUTE OF FOOD AND AGRICULTURE
ECONOMIC RESEARCH SERVICE
NATIONAL AGRICULTURAL LIBRARY
NATIONAL AGRICULTURAL STATISTICS SERVICE
UNDER SECRETARY FOR MARKETING AND REGULATORY PROGRAMS
AGRICULTURAL MARKETING SERVICE
ANIMAL AND PLANT HEALTH INSPECTION SERVICE
GRAIN INSPECTION PACKERS AND STOCKYARDS ADMINISTRATION

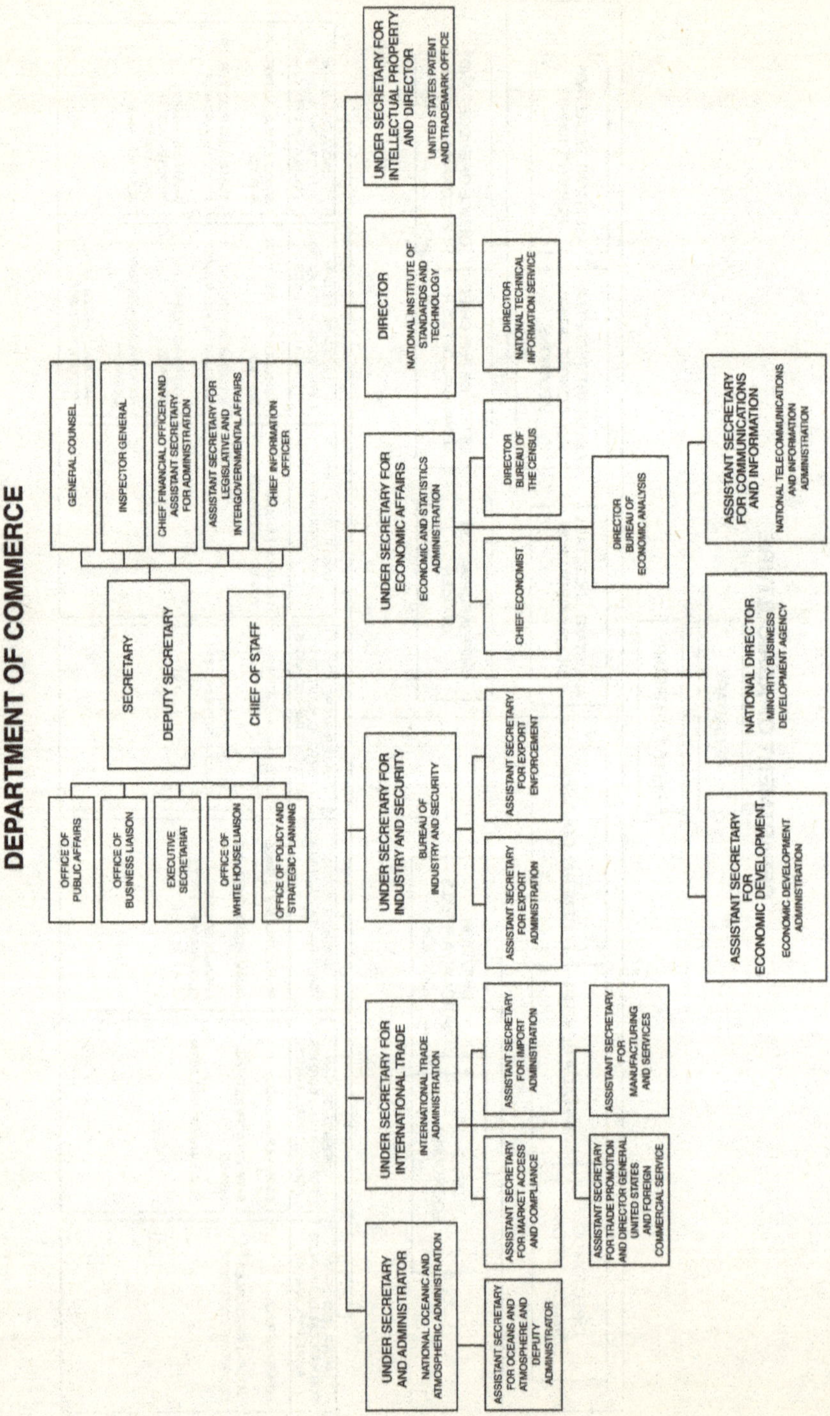
DEPARTMENT OF COMMERCE
SECRETARY
DEPUTY SECRETARY
CHIEF OF STAFF
GENERAL COUNSEL
INSPECTOR GENERAL
CHIEF FINANCIAL OFFICER AND ASSISTANT SECRETARY FOR ADMINISTRATION
ASSISTANT SECRETARY FOR LEGISLATIVE AND INTERGOVERNMENTAL AFFAIRS
CHIEF INFORMATION OFFICER
OFFICE OF PUBLIC AFFAIRS
OFFICE OF BUSINESS LIAISON
EXECUTIVE SECRETARIAT
OFFICE OF WHITE HOUSE LIAISON
OFFICE OF POLICY AND STRATEGIC PLANNING
UNDER SECRETARY FOR INTELLECTUAL PROPERTY AND DIRECTOR
UNITED STATES PATENT AND TRADEMARK OFFICE
DIRECTOR
NATIONAL INSTITUTE OF STANDARDS AND TECHNOLOGY
DIRECTOR NATIONAL TECHNICAL INFORMATION SERVICE
UNDER SECRETARY FOR ECONOMIC AFFAIRS
ECONOMIC AND STATISTICS ADMINISTRATION
DIRECTOR BUREAU OF THE CENSUS
CHIEF ECONOMIST
DIRECTOR BUREAU OF ECONOMIC ANALYSIS
UNDER SECRETARY FOR INDUSTRY AND SECURITY
BUREAU OF INDUSTRY AND SECURITY
ASSISTANT SECRETARY FOR EXPORT ENFORCEMENT
ASSISTANT SECRETARY FOR EXPORT ADMINISTRATION
UNDER SECRETARY FOR INTERNATIONAL TRADE
INTERNATIONAL TRADE ADMINISTRATION
ASSISTANT SECRETARY FOR IMPORT ADMINISTRATION
ASSISTANT SECRETARY FOR MARKET ACCESS AND COMPLIANCE
ASSISTANT SECRETARY FOR MANUFACTURING AND SERVICES
ASSISTANT SECRETARY FOR TRADE PROMOTION AND DIRECTOR GENERAL UNITED STATES AND FOREIGN COMMERCIAL SERVICE
UNDER SECRETARY AND ADMINISTRATOR
NATIONAL OCEANIC AND ATMOSPHERIC ADMINISTRATION
ASSISTANT SECRETARY FOR OCEANS AND ATMOSPHERE AND DEPUTY ADMINISTRATOR
ASSISTANT SECRETARY FOR COMMUNICATIONS AND INFORMATION
NATIONAL TELECOMMUNICATIONS AND INFORMATION ADMINISTRATION
NATIONAL DIRECTOR
MINORITY BUSINESS DEVELOPMENT AGENCY
ASSISTANT SECRETARY FOR ECONOMIC DEVELOPMENT
ECONOMIC DEVELOPMENT ADMINISTRATION

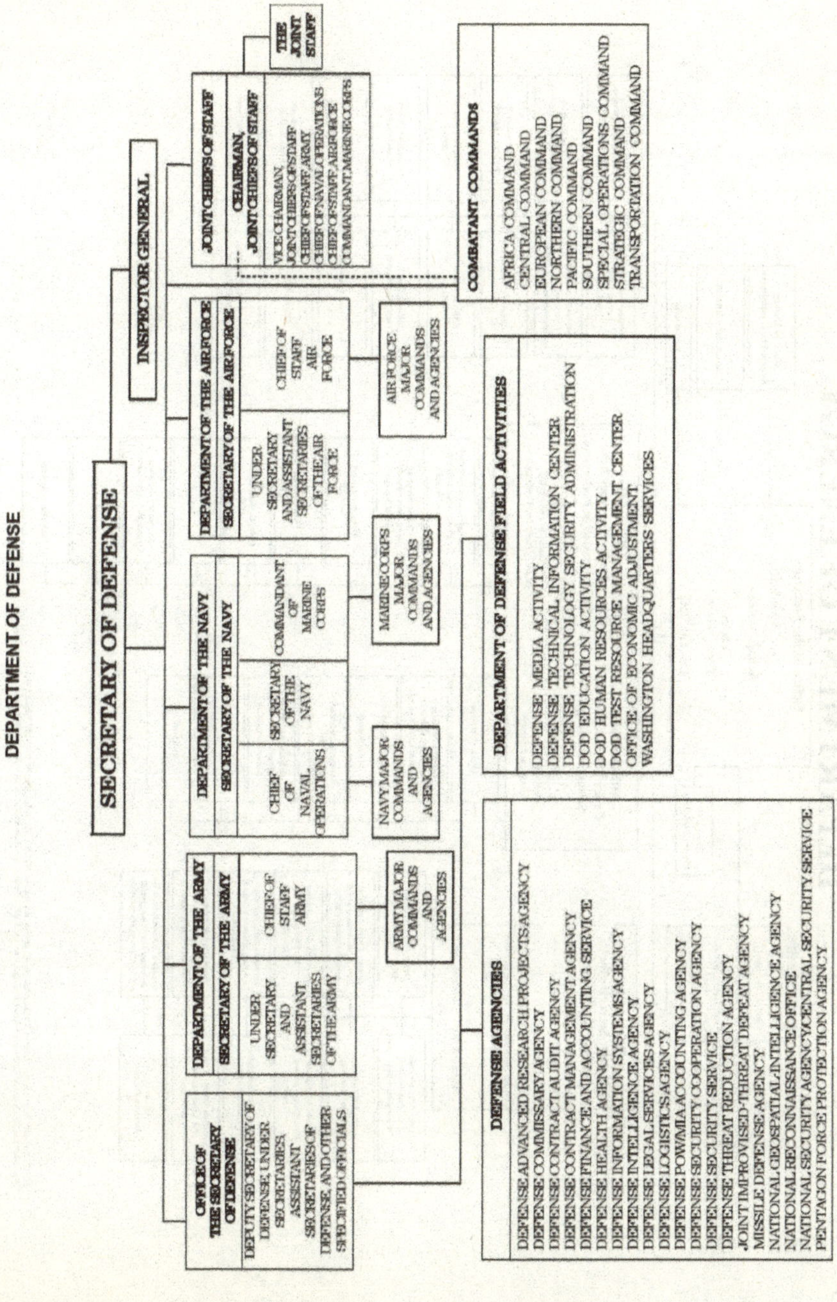
DEPARTMENT OF DEFENSE
SECRETARY OF DEFENSE
INSPECTOR GENERAL
OFFICE OF THE SECRETARY OF DEFENSE
DEPUTY SECRETARY OF DEFENSE, UNDER SECRETARIES, ASSISTANT SECRETARIES OF DEFENSE, AND OTHER SPECIFIED OFFICIALS
DEPARTMENT OF THE ARMY
SECRETARY OF THE ARMY
UNDER SECRETARY AND ASSISTANT SECRETARIES OF THE ARMY
CHIEF OF STAFF ARMY
ARMY MAJOR COMMANDS AND AGENCIES
DEPARTMENT OF THE NAVY
SECRETARY OF THE NAVY
CHIEF OF NAVAL OPERATIONS
SECRETARY OF THE NAVY
COMMANDANT OF MARINE CORPS
NAVY MAJOR COMMANDS AND AGENCIES
MARINE CORPS MAJOR COMMANDS AND AGENCIES
DEPARTMENT OF THE AIR FORCE
SECRETARY OF THE AIR FORCE
UNDER SECRETARY AND ASSISTANT SECRETARIES OF THE AIR FORCE
CHIEF OF STAFF AIR FORCE
AIR FORCE MAJOR COMMANDS AND AGENCIES
JOINT CHIEFS OF STAFF
CHAIRMAN, JOINT CHIEFS OF STAFF
VICE CHAIRMAN, JOINT CHIEFS OF STAFF
CHIEF OF STAFF, ARMY
CHIEF OF NAVAL OPERATIONS
CHIEF OF STAFF, AIR FORCE
COMMANDANT, MARINE CORPS
THE JOINT STAFF
COMBATANT COMMANDS
AFRICA COMMAND
CENTRAL COMMAND
EUROPEAN COMMAND
NORTHERN COMMAND
PACIFIC COMMAND
SOUTHERN COMMAND
SPECIAL OPERATIONS COMMAND
STRATEGIC COMMAND
TRANSPORTATION COMMAND
DEFENSE AGENCIES
DEFENSE ADVANCED RESEARCH PROJECTS AGENCY
DEFENSE COMMISSARY AGENCY
DEFENSE CONTRACT AUDIT AGENCY
DEFENSE CONTRACT MANAGEMENT AGENCY
DEFENSE FINANCE AND ACCOUNTING SERVICE
DEFENSE HEALTH AGENCY
DEFENSE INFORMATION SYSTEMS AGENCY
DEFENSE INTELLIGENCE AGENCY
DEFENSE LEGAL SERVICES AGENCY
DEFENSE LOGISTICS AGENCY
DEFENSE POW/MIA ACCOUNTING AGENCY
DEFENSE SECURITY COOPERATION AGENCY
DEFENSE SECURITY SERVICE
DEFENSE THREAT REDUCTION AGENCY
JOINT IMPROVISED-THREAT DEFEAT AGENCY
MISSILE DEFENSE AGENCY
NATIONAL GEOSPATIAL-INTELLIGENCE AGENCY
NATIONAL RECONNAISSANCE OFFICE
NATIONAL SECURITY AGENCY/CENTRAL SECURITY SERVICE
PENTAGON FORCE PROTECTION AGENCY
DEPARTMENT OF DEFENSE FIELD ACTIVITIES
DEFENSE MEDIA ACTIVITY
DEFENSE TECHNICAL INFORMATION CENTER
DEFENSE TECHNOLOGY SECURITY ADMINISTRATION
DOD EDUCATION ACTIVITY
DOD HUMAN RESOURCES ACTIVITY
DOD TEST RESOURCE MANAGEMENT CENTER
OFFICE OF ECONOMIC ADJUSTMENT
WASHINGTON HEADQUARTERS SERVICES

DEPARTMENT OF ENERGY

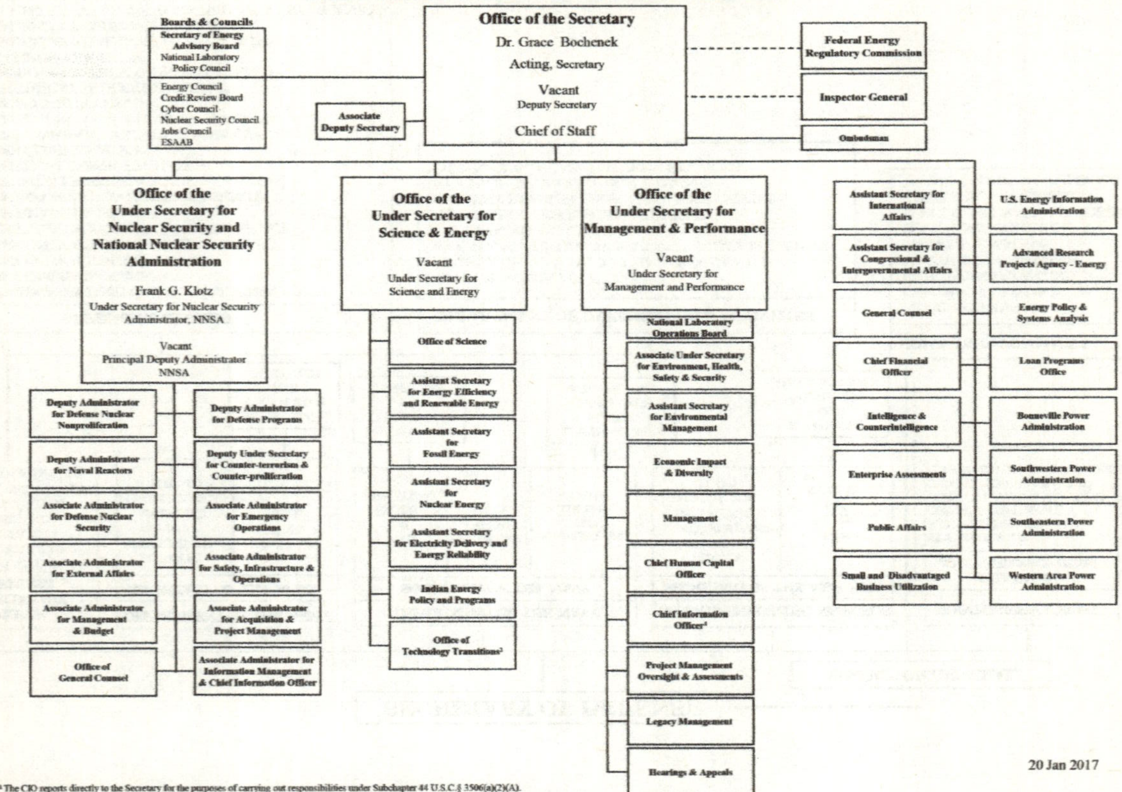

[1] The CIO reports directly to the Secretary for the purposes of carrying out responsibilities under Subchapter 44 U.S.C.§ 3506(a)(2)(A).
[2] The director of the Office of Technology Transitions also serves as DOE's Technology Transfer Coordinator who reports to the Secretary of Energy

DEPARTMENT OF EDUCATION

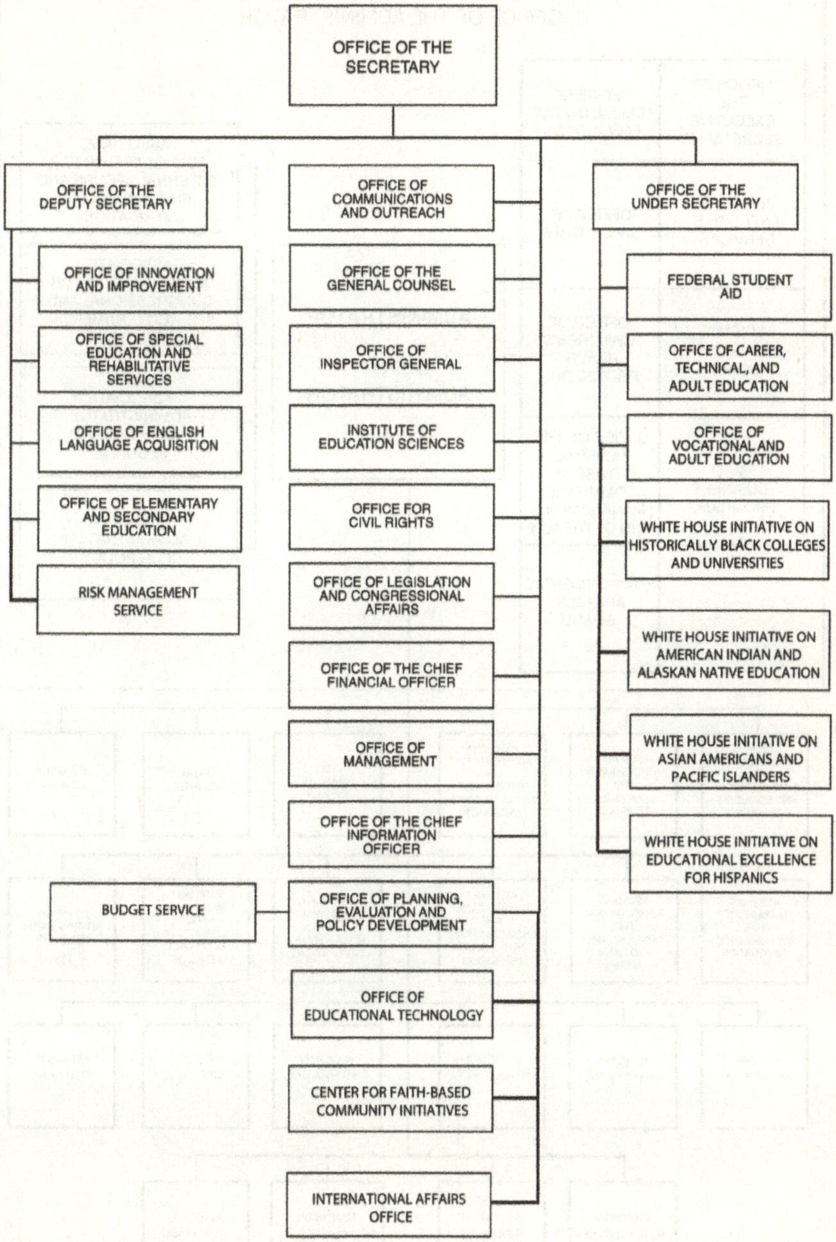

ENVIRONMENTAL PROTECTION AGENCY

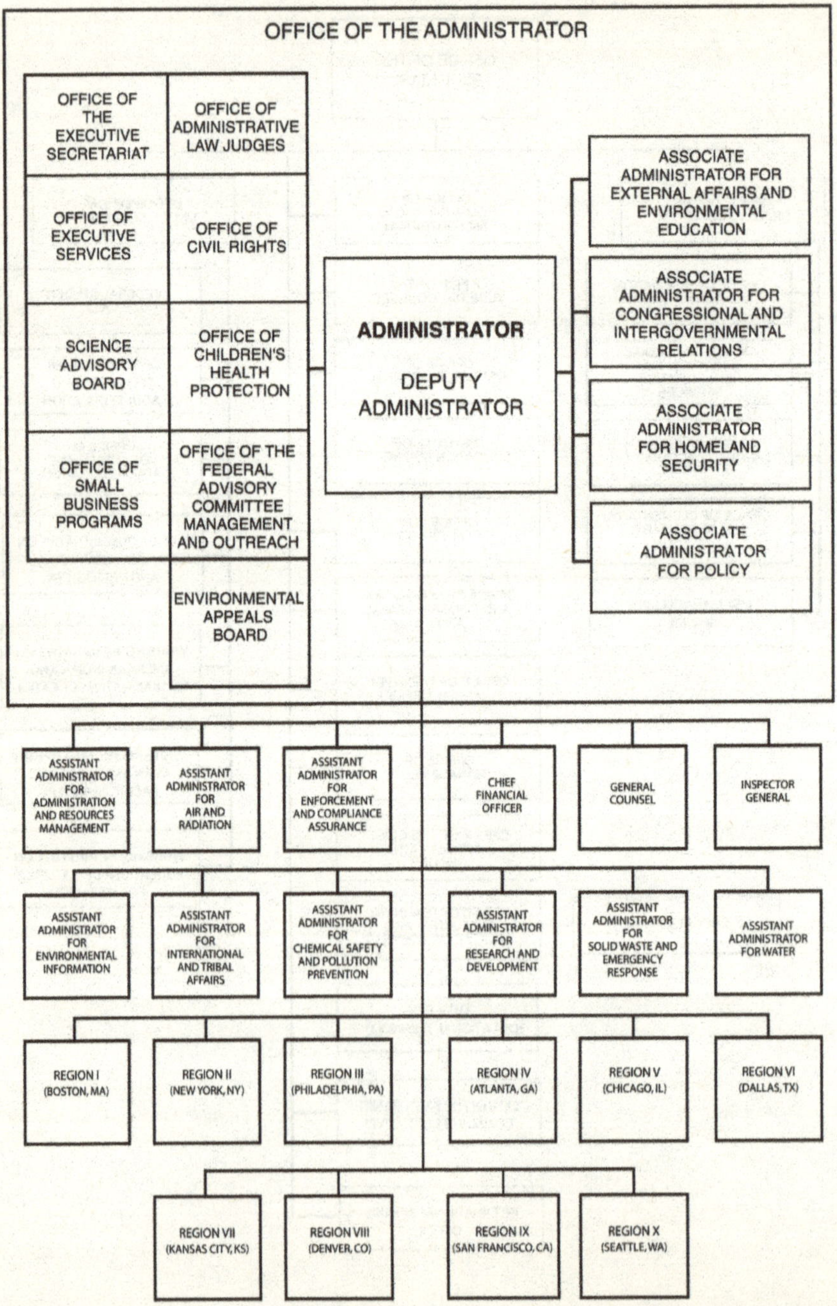

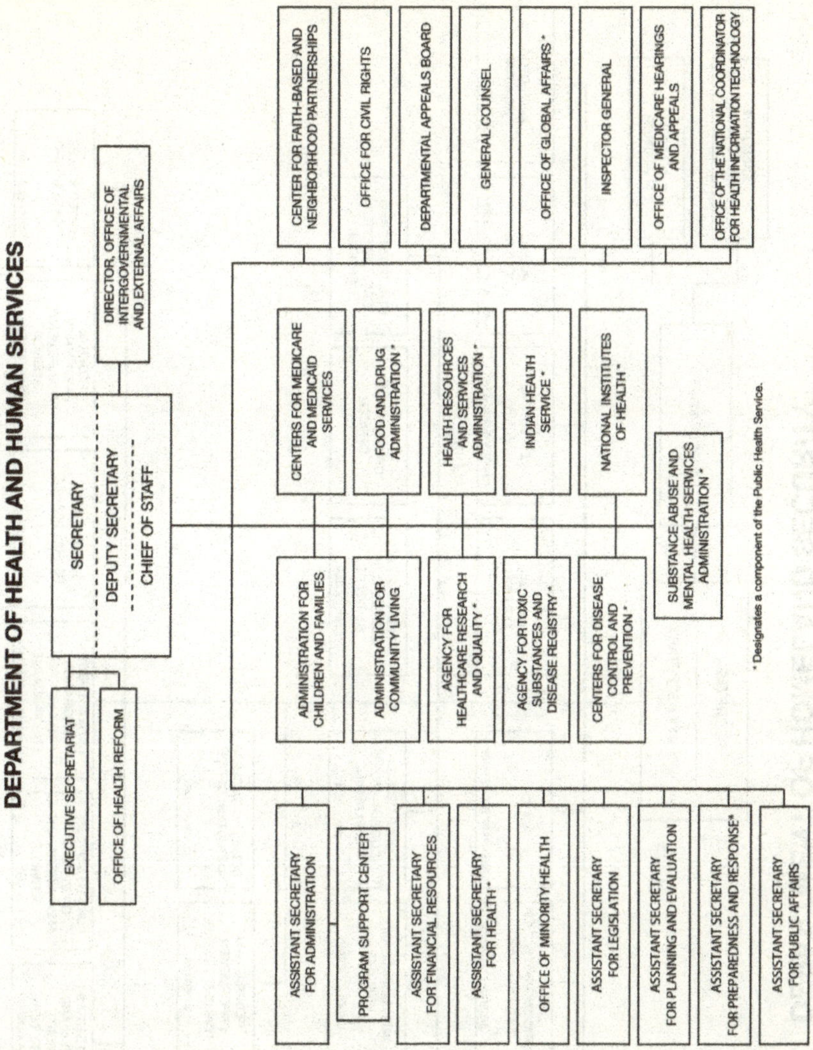
DEPARTMENT OF HEALTH AND HUMAN SERVICES
EXECUTIVE SECRETARIAT
OFFICE OF HEALTH REFORM
SECRETARY
DEPUTY SECRETARY
CHIEF OF STAFF
DIRECTOR, OFFICE OF INTERGOVERNMENTAL AND EXTERNAL AFFAIRS
ASSISTANT SECRETARY FOR ADMINISTRATION
PROGRAM SUPPORT CENTER
ASSISTANT SECRETARY FOR FINANCIAL RESOURCES
ASSISTANT SECRETARY FOR HEALTH *
OFFICE OF MINORITY HEALTH
ASSISTANT SECRETARY FOR LEGISLATION
ASSISTANT SECRETARY FOR PLANNING AND EVALUATION
ASSISTANT SECRETARY FOR PREPAREDNESS AND RESPONSE*
ASSISTANT SECRETARY FOR PUBLIC AFFAIRS
ADMINISTRATION FOR CHILDREN AND FAMILIES
ADMINISTRATION FOR COMMUNITY LIVING
AGENCY FOR HEALTHCARE RESEARCH AND QUALITY *
AGENCY FOR TOXIC SUBSTANCES AND DISEASE REGISTRY *
CENTERS FOR DISEASE CONTROL AND PREVENTION *
SUBSTANCE ABUSE AND MENTAL HEALTH SERVICES ADMINISTRATION *
CENTERS FOR MEDICARE AND MEDICAID SERVICES
FOOD AND DRUG ADMINISTRATION *
HEALTH RESOURCES AND SERVICES ADMINISTRATION *
INDIAN HEALTH SERVICE *
NATIONAL INSTITUTES OF HEALTH *
CENTER FOR FAITH-BASED AND NEIGHBORHOOD PARTNERSHIPS
OFFICE FOR CIVIL RIGHTS
DEPARTMENTAL APPEALS BOARD
GENERAL COUNSEL
OFFICE OF GLOBAL AFFAIRS *
INSPECTOR GENERAL
OFFICE OF MEDICARE HEARINGS AND APPEALS
OFFICE OF THE NATIONAL COORDINATOR FOR HEALTH INFORMATION TECHNOLOGY
* Designates a component of the Public Health Service.

DEPARTMENT OF HOMELAND SECURITY

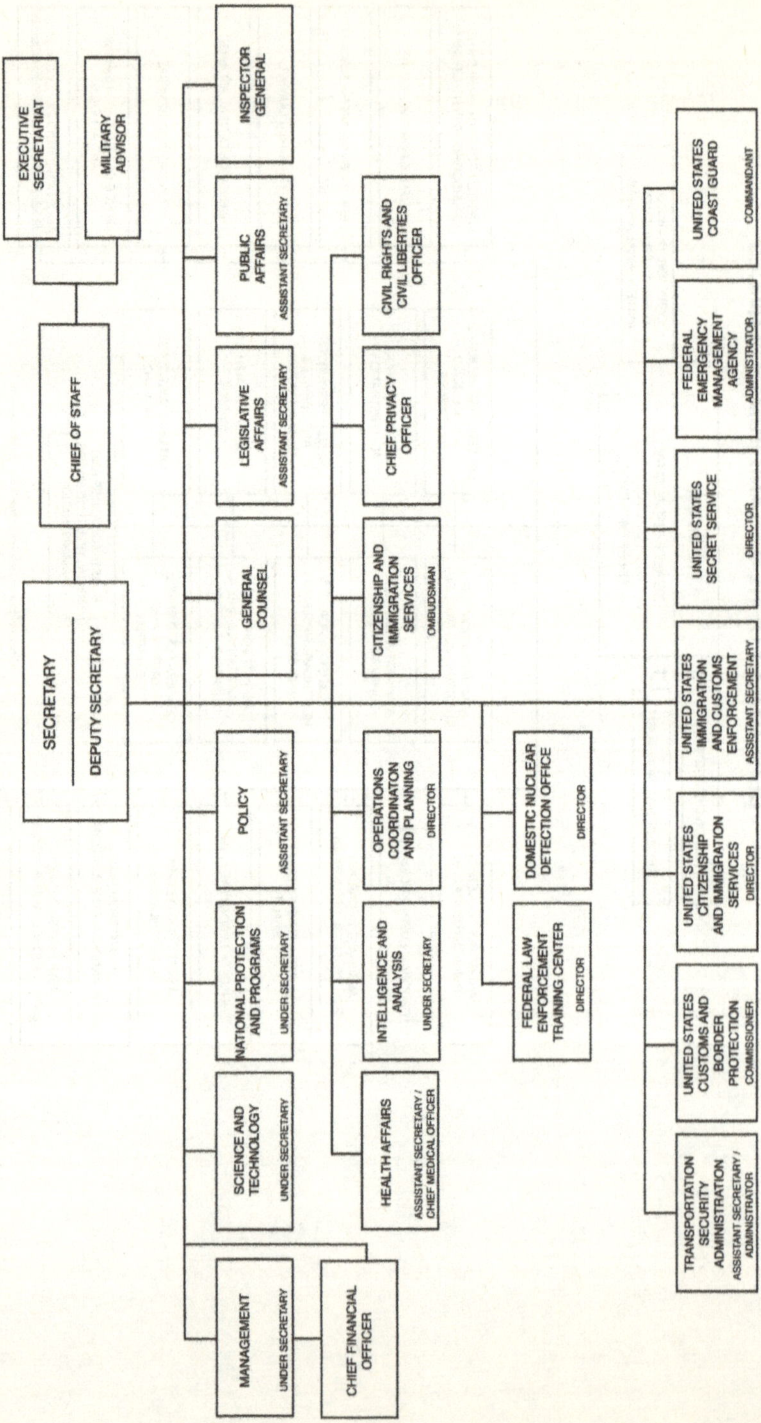

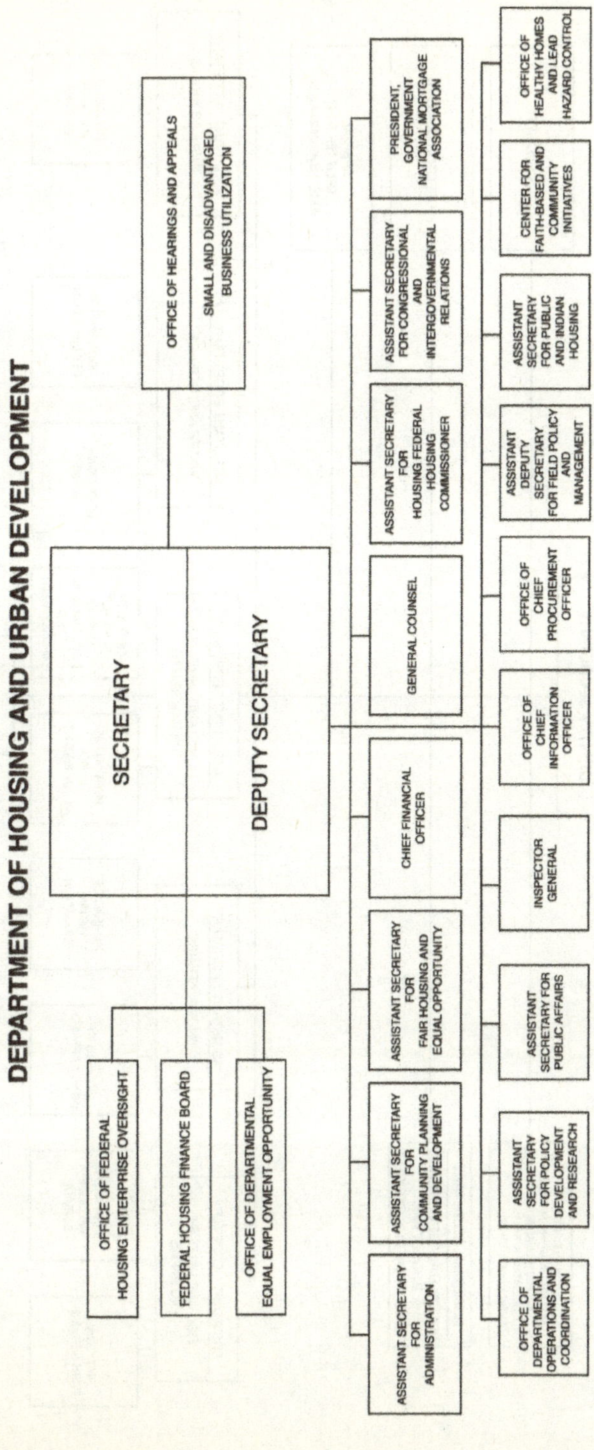
DEPARTMENT OF HOUSING AND URBAN DEVELOPMENT
SECRETARY
DEPUTY SECRETARY
OFFICE OF HEARINGS AND APPEALS
SMALL AND DISADVANTAGED BUSINESS UTILIZATION
OFFICE OF FEDERAL HOUSING ENTERPRISE OVERSIGHT
FEDERAL HOUSING FINANCE BOARD
OFFICE OF DEPARTMENTAL EQUAL EMPLOYMENT OPPORTUNITY
ASSISTANT SECRETARY FOR ADMINISTRATION
ASSISTANT SECRETARY FOR COMMUNITY PLANNING AND DEVELOPMENT
ASSISTANT SECRETARY FOR FAIR HOUSING AND EQUAL OPPORTUNITY
CHIEF FINANCIAL OFFICER
GENERAL COUNSEL
ASSISTANT SECRETARY FOR HOUSING FEDERAL HOUSING COMMISSIONER
ASSISTANT SECRETARY FOR CONGRESSIONAL AND INTERGOVERNMENTAL RELATIONS
PRESIDENT, GOVERNMENT NATIONAL MORTGAGE ASSOCIATION
OFFICE OF DEPARTMENTAL OPERATIONS AND COORDINATION
ASSISTANT SECRETARY FOR POLICY DEVELOPMENT AND RESEARCH
ASSISTANT SECRETARY FOR PUBLIC AFFAIRS
INSPECTOR GENERAL
OFFICE OF CHIEF INFORMATION OFFICER
OFFICE OF CHIEF PROCUREMENT OFFICER
ASSISTANT DEPUTY SECRETARY FOR FIELD POLICY AND MANAGEMENT
ASSISTANT SECRETARY FOR PUBLIC AND INDIAN HOUSING
CENTER FOR FAITH-BASED AND COMMUNITY INITIATIVES
OFFICE OF HEALTHY HOMES AND LEAD HAZARD CONTROL

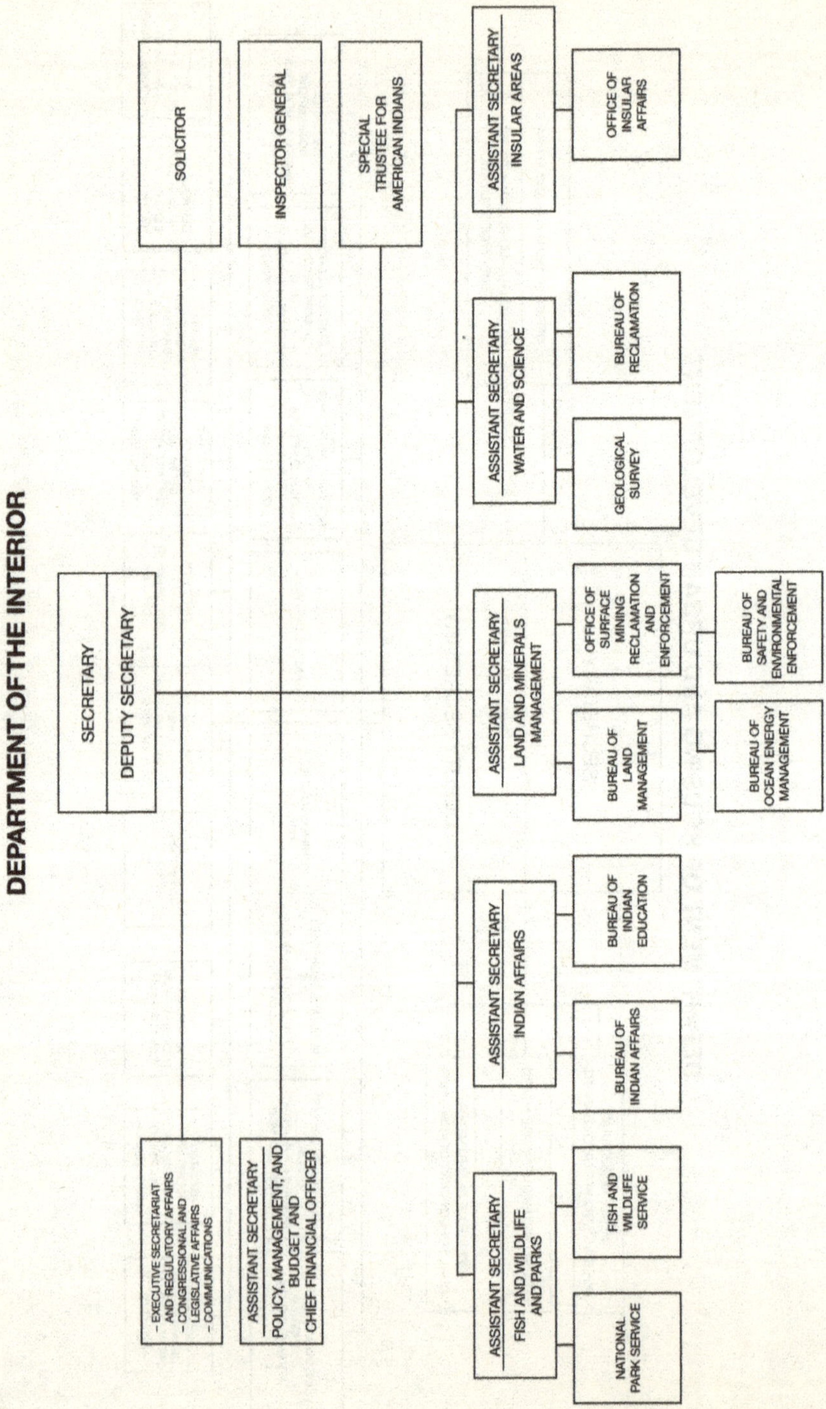
DEPARTMENT OF THE INTERIOR
SECRETARY
DEPUTY SECRETARY
SOLICITOR
INSPECTOR GENERAL
SPECIAL TRUSTEE FOR AMERICAN INDIANS
- EXECUTIVE SECRETARIAT AND REGULATORY AFFAIRS
- CONGRESSIONAL AND LEGISLATIVE AFFAIRS
- COMMUNICATIONS
ASSISTANT SECRETARY POLICY, MANAGEMENT, AND BUDGET AND CHIEF FINANCIAL OFFICER
ASSISTANT SECRETARY FISH AND WILDLIFE AND PARKS
NATIONAL PARK SERVICE
FISH AND WILDLIFE SERVICE
ASSISTANT SECRETARY INDIAN AFFAIRS
BUREAU OF INDIAN AFFAIRS
BUREAU OF INDIAN EDUCATION
ASSISTANT SECRETARY LAND AND MINERALS MANAGEMENT
BUREAU OF LAND MANAGEMENT
OFFICE OF SURFACE MINING RECLAMATION AND ENFORCEMENT
BUREAU OF OCEAN ENERGY MANAGEMENT
BUREAU OF SAFETY AND ENVIRONMENTAL ENFORCEMENT
ASSISTANT SECRETARY WATER AND SCIENCE
GEOLOGICAL SURVEY
BUREAU OF RECLAMATION
ASSISTANT SECRETARY INSULAR AREAS
OFFICE OF INSULAR AFFAIRS

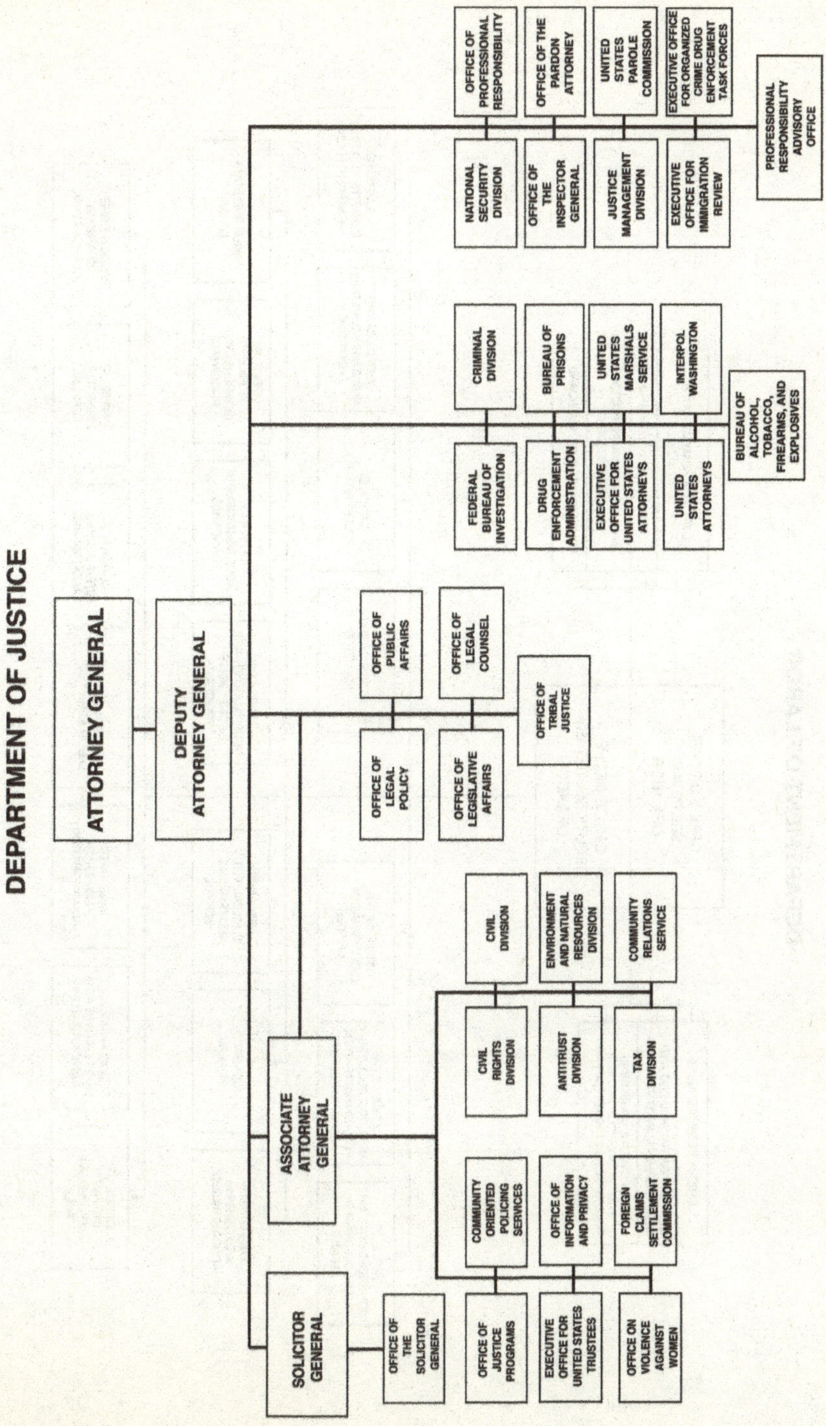
DEPARTMENT OF JUSTICE
ATTORNEY GENERAL
DEPUTY ATTORNEY GENERAL
SOLICITOR GENERAL
OFFICE OF THE SOLICITOR GENERAL
ASSOCIATE ATTORNEY GENERAL
OFFICE OF JUSTICE PROGRAMS
EXECUTIVE OFFICE FOR UNITED STATES TRUSTEES
OFFICE ON VIOLENCE AGAINST WOMEN
COMMUNITY ORIENTED POLICING SERVICES
OFFICE OF INFORMATION AND PRIVACY
FOREIGN CLAIMS SETTLEMENT COMMISSION
CIVIL RIGHTS DIVISION
ANTITRUST DIVISION
TAX DIVISION
CIVIL DIVISION
ENVIRONMENT AND NATURAL RESOURCES DIVISION
COMMUNITY RELATIONS SERVICE
OFFICE OF LEGAL POLICY
OFFICE OF PUBLIC AFFAIRS
OFFICE OF LEGISLATIVE AFFAIRS
OFFICE OF LEGAL COUNSEL
OFFICE OF TRIBAL JUSTICE
FEDERAL BUREAU OF INVESTIGATION
CRIMINAL DIVISION
DRUG ENFORCEMENT ADMINISTRATION
BUREAU OF PRISONS
EXECUTIVE OFFICE FOR UNITED STATES ATTORNEYS
UNITED STATES MARSHALS SERVICE
UNITED STATES ATTORNEYS
INTERPOL WASHINGTON
BUREAU OF ALCOHOL, TOBACCO, FIREARMS, AND EXPLOSIVES
NATIONAL SECURITY DIVISION
OFFICE OF PROFESSIONAL RESPONSIBILITY
OFFICE OF THE INSPECTOR GENERAL
OFFICE OF THE PARDON ATTORNEY
JUSTICE MANAGEMENT DIVISION
UNITED STATES PAROLE COMMISSION
EXECUTIVE OFFICE FOR IMMIGRATION REVIEW
EXECUTIVE OFFICE FOR ORGANIZED CRIME DRUG ENFORCEMENT TASK FORCES
PROFESSIONAL RESPONSIBILITY ADVISORY OFFICE

DEPARTMENT OF LABOR

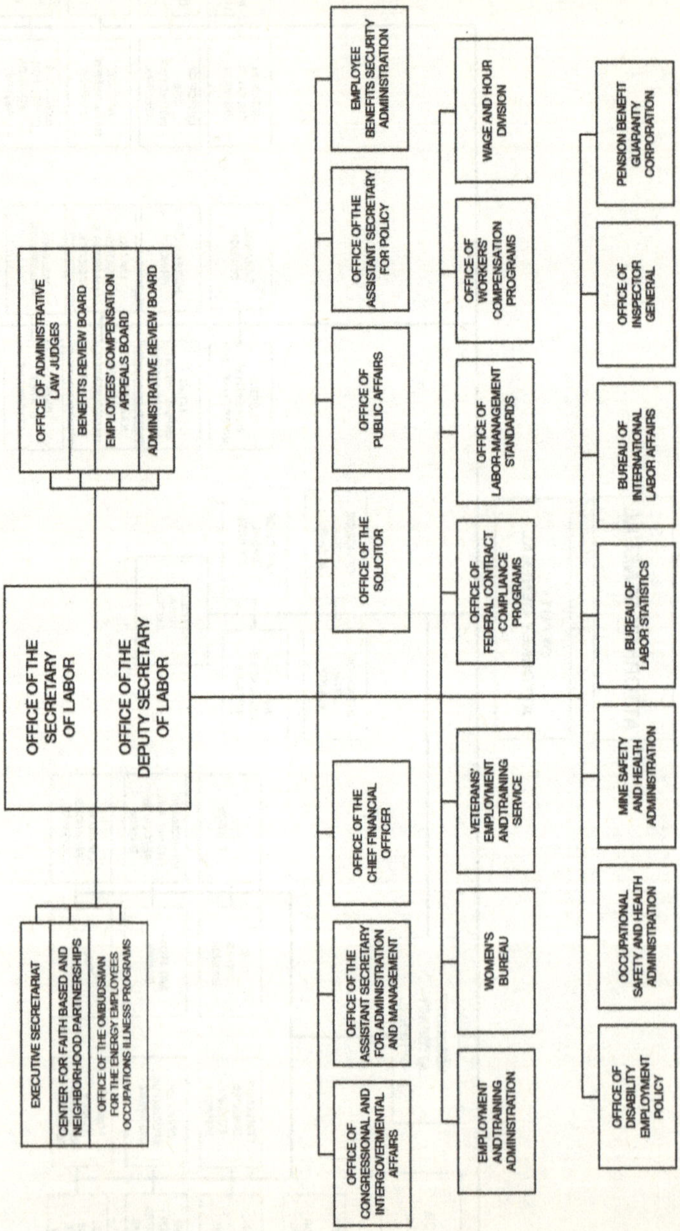

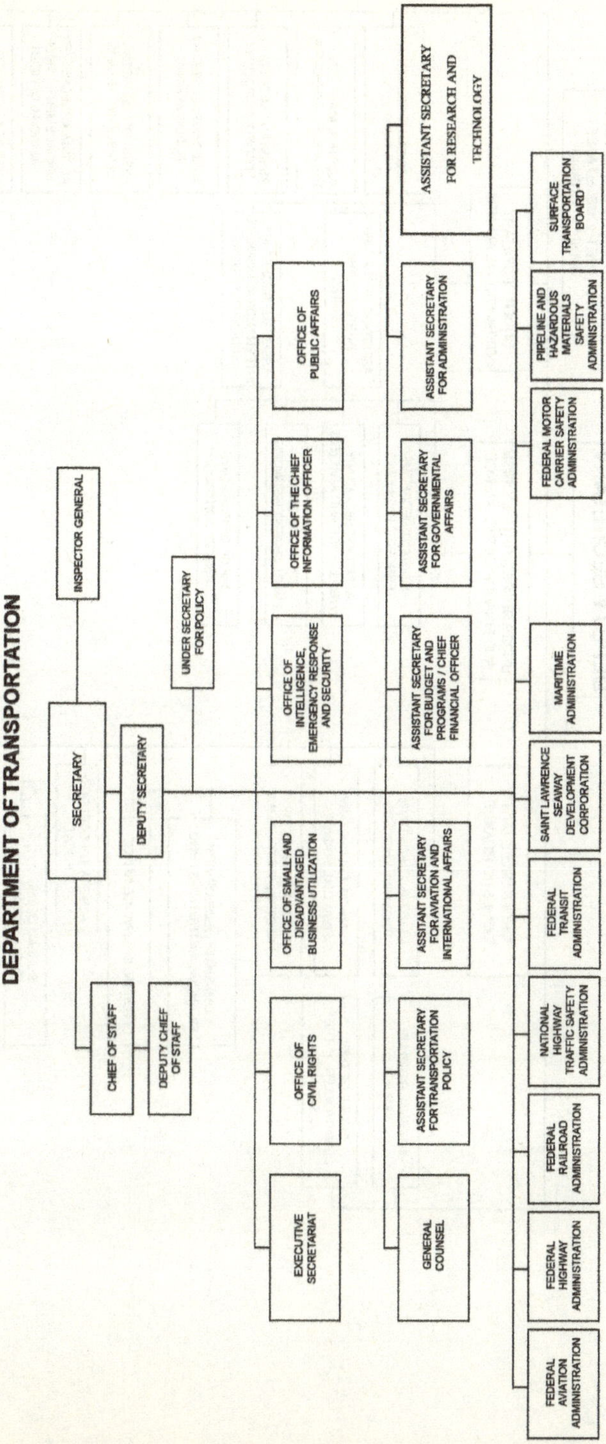
DEPARTMENT OF TRANSPORTATION
SECRETARY
INSPECTOR GENERAL
DEPUTY SECRETARY
CHIEF OF STAFF
DEPUTY CHIEF OF STAFF
UNDER SECRETARY FOR POLICY
EXECUTIVE SECRETARIAT
OFFICE OF CIVIL RIGHTS
OFFICE OF SMALL AND DISADVANTAGED BUSINESS UTILIZATION
OFFICE OF INTELLIGENCE, EMERGENCY RESPONSE AND SECURITY
OFFICE OF THE CHIEF INFORMATION OFFICER
OFFICE OF PUBLIC AFFAIRS
GENERAL COUNSEL
ASSISTANT SECRETARY FOR TRANSPORTATION POLICY
ASSISTANT SECRETARY FOR AVIATION AND INTERNATIONAL AFFAIRS
ASSISTANT SECRETARY FOR BUDGET AND PROGRAMS / CHIEF FINANCIAL OFFICER
ASSISTANT SECRETARY FOR GOVERNMENTAL AFFAIRS
ASSISTANT SECRETARY FOR ADMINISTRATION
ASSISTANT SECRETARY FOR RESEARCH AND TECHNOLOGY
FEDERAL AVIATION ADMINISTRATION
FEDERAL HIGHWAY ADMINISTRATION
FEDERAL RAILROAD ADMINISTRATION
NATIONAL HIGHWAY TRAFFIC SAFETY ADMINISTRATION
FEDERAL TRANSIT ADMINISTRATION
SAINT LAWRENCE SEAWAY DEVELOPMENT CORPORATION
MARITIME ADMINISTRATION
FEDERAL MOTOR CARRIER SAFETY ADMINISTRATION
PIPELINE AND HAZARDOUS MATERIALS SAFETY ADMINISTRATION
SURFACE TRANSPORTATION BOARD*

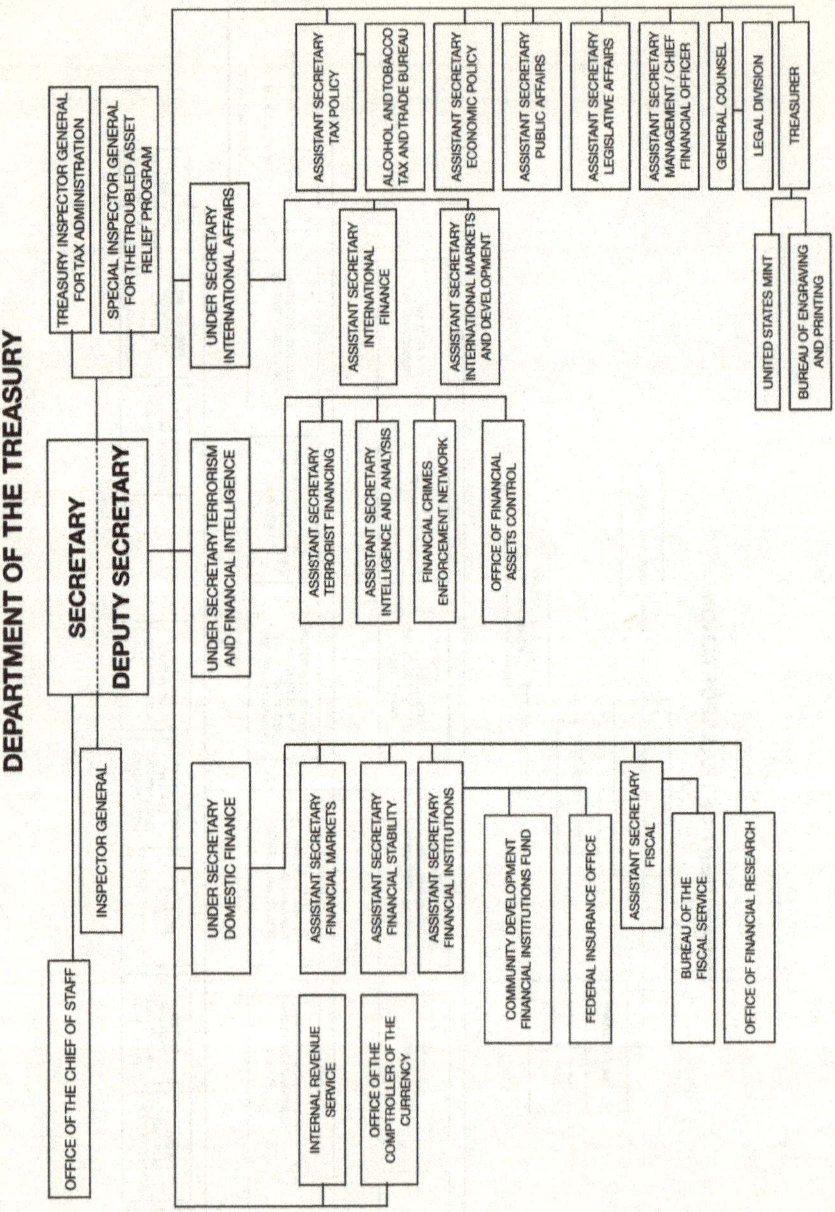
DEPARTMENT OF THE TREASURY
SECRETARY
DEPUTY SECRETARY
OFFICE OF THE CHIEF OF STAFF
INSPECTOR GENERAL
TREASURY INSPECTOR GENERAL FOR TAX ADMINISTRATION
SPECIAL INSPECTOR GENERAL FOR THE TROUBLED ASSET RELIEF PROGRAM
UNDER SECRETARY DOMESTIC FINANCE
INTERNAL REVENUE SERVICE
OFFICE OF THE COMPTROLLER OF THE CURRENCY
ASSISTANT SECRETARY FINANCIAL MARKETS
ASSISTANT SECRETARY FINANCIAL STABILITY
ASSISTANT SECRETARY FINANCIAL INSTITUTIONS
COMMUNITY DEVELOPMENT FINANCIAL INSTITUTIONS FUND
FEDERAL INSURANCE OFFICE
ASSISTANT SECRETARY FISCAL
BUREAU OF THE FISCAL SERVICE
OFFICE OF FINANCIAL RESEARCH
UNDER SECRETARY TERRORISM AND FINANCIAL INTELLIGENCE
ASSISTANT SECRETARY TERRORIST FINANCING
ASSISTANT SECRETARY INTELLIGENCE AND ANALYSIS
FINANCIAL CRIMES ENFORCEMENT NETWORK
OFFICE OF FINANCIAL ASSETS CONTROL
UNDER SECRETARY INTERNATIONAL AFFAIRS
ASSISTANT SECRETARY INTERNATIONAL FINANCE
ASSISTANT SECRETARY INTERNATIONAL MARKETS AND DEVELOPMENT
ASSISTANT SECRETARY TAX POLICY
ALCOHOL AND TOBACCO TAX AND TRADE BUREAU
ASSISTANT SECRETARY ECONOMIC POLICY
ASSISTANT SECRETARY PUBLIC AFFAIRS
ASSISTANT SECRETARY LEGISLATIVE AFFAIRS
ASSISTANT SECRETARY MANAGEMENT / CHIEF FINANCIAL OFFICER
GENERAL COUNSEL
LEGAL DIVISION
TREASURER
UNITED STATES MINT
BUREAU OF ENGRAVING AND PRINTING

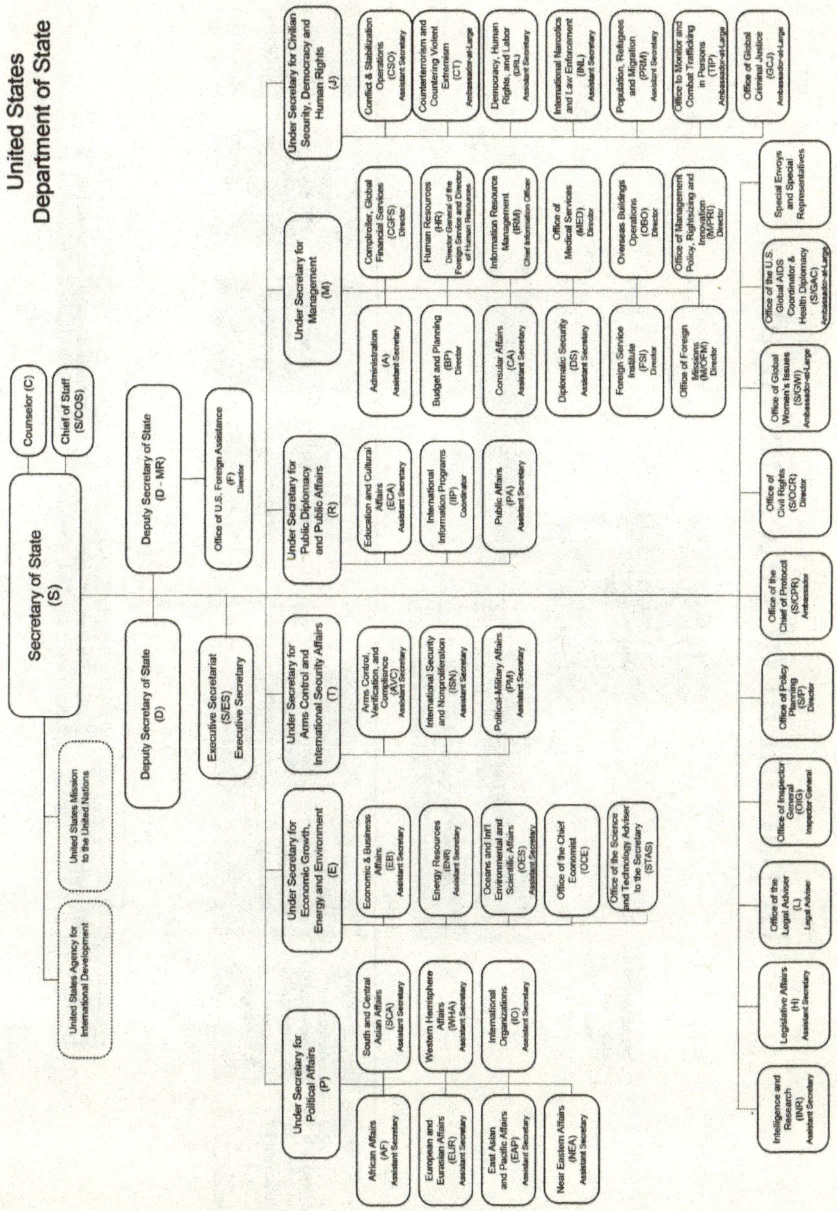
United States Department of State
Secretary of State (S)
Counselor (C)
Chief of Staff (S/COS)
United States Mission to the United Nations
United States Agency for International Development
Deputy Secretary of State (D)
Deputy Secretary of State (D - MR)
Executive Secretariat (S/ES) Executive Secretary
Office of U.S. Foreign Assistance (F) Director
Under Secretary for Political Affairs (P)
African Affairs (AF) Assistant Secretary
European and Eurasian Affairs (EUR) Assistant Secretary
East Asian and Pacific Affairs (EAP) Assistant Secretary
Near Eastern Affairs (NEA) Assistant Secretary
South and Central Asian Affairs (SCA) Assistant Secretary
Western Hemisphere Affairs (WHA) Assistant Secretary
International Organizations (IO) Assistant Secretary
Under Secretary for Economic Growth, Energy and Environment (E)
Economic & Business Affairs (EB) Assistant Secretary
Energy Resources (ENR) Assistant Secretary
Oceans and Int'l Environmental and Scientific Affairs (OES) Assistant Secretary
Office of the Chief Economist (OCE)
Office of the Science and Technology Adviser to the Secretary (STAS)
Under Secretary for Arms Control and International Security Affairs (T)
Arms Control, Verification, and Compliance (AVC) Assistant Secretary
International Security and Nonproliferation (ISN) Assistant Secretary
Political-Military Affairs (PM) Assistant Secretary
Under Secretary for Public Diplomacy and Public Affairs (R)
Education and Cultural Affairs (ECA) Assistant Secretary
International Information Programs (IIP) Coordinator
Public Affairs (PA) Assistant Secretary
Under Secretary for Management (M)
Administration (A) Assistant Secretary
Budget and Planning (BP) Director
Consular Affairs (CA) Assistant Secretary
Diplomatic Security (DS) Assistant Secretary
Foreign Service Institute (FSI) Director
Office of Foreign Missions (M/OFM) Director
Comptroller, Global Financial Services (CGFS) Director
Human Resources (HR) Director General of the Foreign Service and Director of Human Resources
Information Resource Management (IRM) Chief Information Officer
Office of Medical Services (MED) Director
Overseas Buildings Operations (OBO) Director
Office of Management Policy, Rightsizing and Innovation (M/PRI) Director
Under Secretary for Civilian Security, Democracy and Human Rights (J)
Conflict & Stabilization Operations (CSO) Assistant Secretary
Counterterrorism and Countering Violent Extremism (CT) Ambassador-at-Large
Democracy, Human Rights, and Labor (DRL) Assistant Secretary
International Narcotics and Law Enforcement (INL) Assistant Secretary
Population, Refugees and Migration (PRM) Assistant Secretary
Office to Monitor and Combat Trafficking in Persons (TIP) Ambassador-at-Large
Office of Global Criminal Justice (GCJ) Ambassador-at-Large
Intelligence and Research (INR) Assistant Secretary
Legislative Affairs (H) Assistant Secretary
Office of the Legal Adviser (L) Legal Adviser
Office of Inspector General (OIG) Inspector General
Office of Policy Planning (S/P) Director
Office of the Chief of Protocol (S/CPR) Ambassador
Office of Civil Rights (S/OCR) Director
Office of Global Women's Issues (S/GWI) Ambassador-at-Large
Office of the U.S. Global AIDS Coordinator & Health Diplomacy (S/GAC) Ambassador-at-Large
Special Envoys and Special Representatives

Department of Veterans Affairs

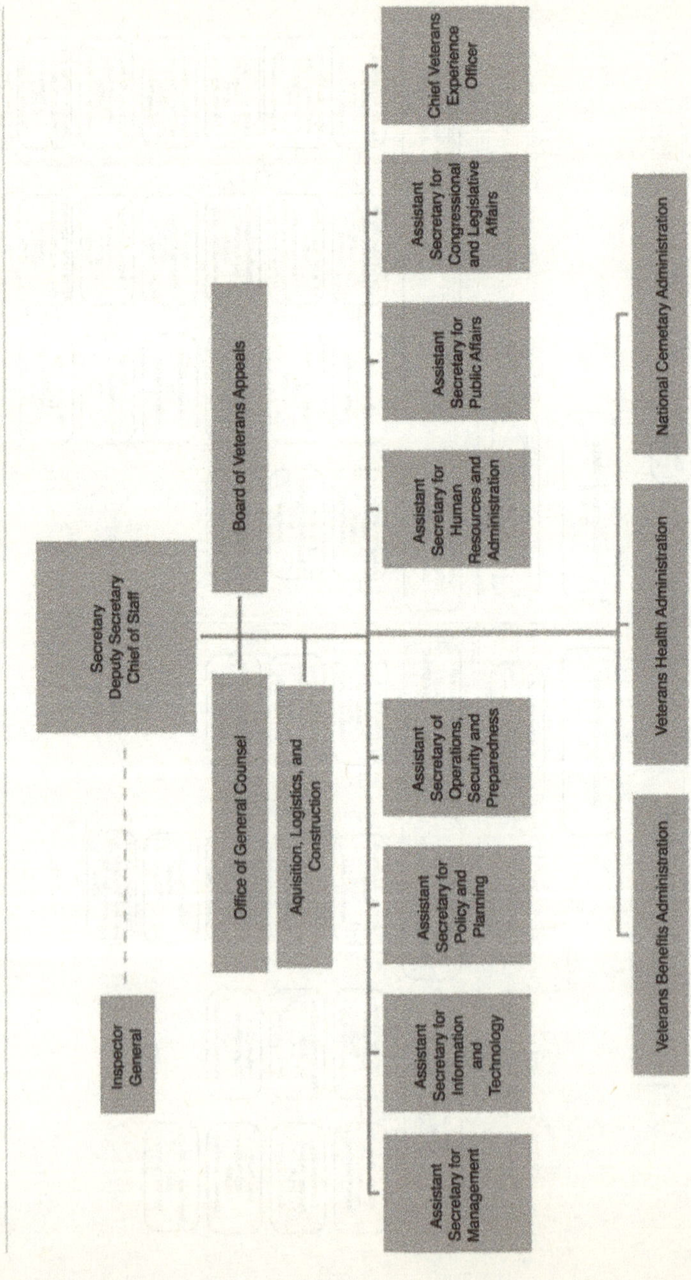

Chapter One

Finding Aids

The websites described in this chapter are designed specifically to help people find U.S. federal government information. These sites organize access to government grants, forms, press releases, publications, statistics, and more. When searching for government information, they can be much more effective tools than general search engines.

The two subsections of this chapter describe, first, finding aids developed by the U.S. government and, second, those developed by nongovernment organizations.

GOVERNMENT SOURCES

Catalog of U.S. Government Publications (CGP)

https://catalog.gpo.gov

Description: The CGP is a catalog of both print and electronic government publications from the Executive, Legislative, and Judicial branches of the U.S. government. The records provide bibliographic information and link to a copy of the cited publication if one is available online. Use the advanced search option to take full advantage of the CGP's features, such as limiting searches by year or format.

The CGP serves as the National Bibliography of U.S. Government Publications, and is the online version of the now discontinued *Monthly Catalog of United States Government Publications*. The CGP is not a sales catalog. Sales publications can be found online at the GPO's U.S. Government Bookstore at https://bookstore.gpo.gov/.

Subject(s): Publications

Contact Your Government

https://www.usa.gov/elected-officials/

Description: This section of the USA.gov site features contact information for many federal and state government offices and legislators and toll-free hotline numbers. Links are organized by elected official, topic, and agency.

Subject(s): Contact Information

Find Government Forms

https://www.gsa.gov/reference/forms#GSA

Description: This portal site provides "one-stop shopping" for forms commonly needed for federal government services. Locate forms by agency or by quick links to frequently used forms.

Subject(s): Forms

GobiernoUSA.gov

https://gobierno.usa.gov/

Description: This Spanish-language website is not a word-for-word translation of the English-language USA.gov site; instead, it is customized for those more likely to use it, with features such as a section for recent immigrants. The search engine allows users to search for words in Spanish and retrieve federal and state government web results that are in Spanish. Users can also complete some government transactions online in Spanish.

Subject(s): Finding Aids; Government Information

Grants.gov

https://www.grants.gov/

Description: Grants.gov is the federal government portal for finding and applying for competitive grant opportunities from federal grant-making agencies, including grants available under the Recovery Act. Users can search the full text of grants and refine searches by specifying certain agencies, topics, dates, or types of grants. Applications can be downloaded and completed offline. Completed grant application packages can then be submitted online. In addition to using the grants search feature, researchers can subscribe to receive e-mail notification of grant opportunities in their areas of interest.

Subject(s): Grants

Registry of U.S. Government Publication Digitization Projects

https://registry.fdlp.gov/

Description: The Registry of U.S. Government Publication Digitization Projects describes and links to online collections of digitized U.S. government publications. The collections are from government agencies, universities, and other institutions.

Subject(s): Publications

U.S. Government Photos and Images

https://www.flickr.com/groups/usagov/pool/

Description: Part of the USA.gov website, this resource links to collections of photos and graphics on federal agency websites. The images are arranged by agency or photo collection name. Many but not all of these photos and graphics are freely available for use in the public domain; check the specific disclaimers posted at each source.

Subject(s): Multimedia; Photos

U.S. Government YouTube Channel

https://www.youtube.com/user/USGovernment

Description: The official YouTube channel of the U.S. federal government, launched in May 2009, provides a single point of access for videos from numerous government agencies.

Subject(s): Government Information; Videos

USA.gov

https://www.usa.gov/

Sponsor(s): General Services Administration (GSA)

Description: Labeled "Government Made Easy," USA.gov is an Executive branch initiative that offers multiple routes to government information on the Internet. The USA.gov homepage is organized most prominently by the following topics: Benefits, Grants, and Loans; Health, Housing and Community; Jobs and Unemployment; Money and Shopping; and Travel and Immigration.

USA.gov also has an A–Z index of government agencies, and provides quick links to the main websites for state, local, and tribal governments. A special USA.gov search engine searches federal, state, and local government websites.

A Spanish-language version of USA.gov, GobiernoUSA.gov, is described elsewhere in this chapter.

USA.gov does an excellent job of serving multiple audiences and helping users find basic government information faster. The design is particularly well suited for browsing and finding information and services when the responsible agency is unknown.

Subject(s): Finding Aids; Government Information

OTHER SOURCES

CyberCemetery

http://govinfo.library.unt.edu

Description: As described on the site, the CyberCemetery is "an archive of government websites that have ceased operation (usually websites of defunct government agencies and commissions that have issued a final report)." Links to the archived sites are organized by branch of government, by date of the office's expiration, and by name; the sites can also be searched by keyword. Archived sites include those of the Citizens' Health Care Working Group, Coalition Provisional Authority for Iraq, and National Commission on Terrorist Attacks Upon the United States (also known as the 9/11 Commission). The CyberCemetery is operated under a partnership between the GPO and the University of North Texas Libraries, and it is an affiliated archive of the National Archives and Records Administration (NARA).

The policies, processes, and technologies for systematic archiving of electronic government information—and for providing access to and preservation of that information—are being actively developed by federal agencies. In the meantime, the CyberCemetery is providing a commendable service to researchers with straightforward access to resources that might otherwise be lost.

Subject(s): Digital Libraries; Government Information

Chapter Two

Agriculture, Fishing, and Forestry

This chapter describes websites covering agricultural practices, science, marketing, statistics, and related areas. Websites concerning food and nutrition can be found in the Health and Safety chapter. This chapter also includes websites about fishing (and aquaculture) and forestry; additional resources on fish and forests can be found in the Environment and Nature chapter.

Subsections in this chapter are Agriculture, Fishing, and Forestry.

AGRICULTURE

Agricultural Marketing Service (AMS)

https://www.ams.usda.gov/

Description: AMS supports the marketing, testing, regulation, and efficient transportation of agricultural commodities and issues marketing orders that establish basic minimum prices for commodities. The agency also runs the National Organic Program, and the site links to information about how to get a product certified as organic. AMS programs described on the site concern cotton, dairy, poultry, fruits and vegetables, livestock and seed, tobacco, commodity purchasing, grading and certification, and agricultural transportation. Additional sections cover farmers markets and local food marketing, science and research, federal rulemaking developments, and AMS services in the global marketplace. The Publications section provides regularly updated *Market News* reports for numerous agricultural commodities.

Subject(s): Agriculture Information

Agricultural Research Service (ARS)

https://www.ars.usda.gov/

Description: ARS leads the USDA's research projects in agriculture, nutrition, technology, and the environment. The ARS website presents information about its national research programs. The Research section of the site includes a database of ARS research projects and detailed information on the agency's national and international research programs.

Links in the Newsroom section include Latest News, Magazine (ARS's *AgResearch*), and Podcasts. The TEKTRAN database of pre-publication notices of recent ARS research results can be found in the Research section. This section also provides software and datasets of interest to scientists working in agricultural research areas.

The ARS website will primarily be of interest to agricultural researchers and research institutions.

Subject(s): Agricultural Research

Agriculture – EPA

https://www.epa.gov/agriculture

Description: The EPA's Agriculture site is a portal to information about regulatory compliance and environmental stewardship for the agricultural community. The site has an A–Z index that features specific topics, such as animal feeding operations, nutrient management and fertilizer, pesticides, and water. The Regulatory Requirements section organizes law and regulations by farm activity, EPA statute/laws, and upcoming and recent compliance dates.

Subject(s): Agricultural Regulation

Agriculture Network Information Collaborative (AgNIC)

https://www.agnic.org/

Description: AgNIC's website links to agricultural information on the Internet as selected by the National Agricultural Library (NAL), land grant universities, and other institutions. AgNIC is a distributed network that provides access to agriculture-related information, subject area experts, and other resources. From the site's homepage, users can perform a simple search with its information database or browse its contents by subject. A calendar of events lists conferences, meetings, and seminars in various agricultural fields.

AgNIC is not a government organization but is supported in part by the NAL.

Subject(s): Agriculture Information

Alternative Farming Systems Information Center (AFSIC)

https://www.nal.usda.gov/afsic

Description: The Alternative Farming Systems Information Center is an online portal to information on sustainable and alternative agricultural systems, crops, and livestock. Topics include alternative crops and plants, farm energy options, organic production, aquaculture, ecological pest management, and sustainability in agriculture.

Subject(s): Sustainable Agriculture

Amber Waves

https://www.ers.usda.gov/amberwaves/

Description: *Amber Waves*, a USDA online magazine published monthly, features information and economic analysis about food, farms, natural resources, and rural community issues. *Amber Waves* began publication in February 2003, replacing *Agricultural Outlook*, *Food Review*, and *Rural America.*

Subject(s): Agricultural Economics

Animal Disease Traceability

https://www.aphis.usda.gov/aphis/ourfocus/animalhealth/

Description: This Animal and Plant Health Inspection Service (APHIS) webpage explains the agency's new approach to animal disease traceability, which was announced in February 2010. The most current modification became effective in March 2013.

Subject(s): Animal Regulation

Animal and Plant Health Inspection Service (APHIS)

https://www.aphis.usda.gov/aphis/home/

Description: APHIS's mission is to protect the animal and plant resources of the United States from agricultural pests and diseases. Major sections of its website cover animal and plant health, biotechnology, emergency preparedness and response, wildlife damage management, animal welfare, and importing and exporting concerns. The Animal Health section includes a wealth of information, ranging from emergency management and major animal health monitoring to surveillance programs, traceability, and veterinary accreditation. The site also has information about reporting a pest or disease and tips on traveling with a pet.

Subject(s): Animal and Plant Regulation; Veterinary Medicine

Animal & Veterinary – Center for Veterinary Medicine (CVM)

https://www.fda.gov/animalveterinary/

Description: The Center for Veterinary Medicine regulates the manufacture and distribution of drugs and feed additives intended for animals. Its website provides information on the drug approval process, approved drugs, and recalls. For consumers, it has information on feeding and caring for pets. Resources on the site include the *Green Book (*FDA Approved Animal Drug Products*)*.

Subject(s): Veterinary Medicine

Beltsville Agricultural Research Center (BARC)

https://www.ars.usda.gov/northeast-area/beltsville-md-barc/beltsville-agricultural-research-center/

Description: BARC performs research in a variety of agricultural science disciplines, working on such topics as plant diversity, bioenergy, and food safety. The BARC site describes research coming out of the center's many laboratories. Major sections include Research Projects, Publications, and News.

Subject(s): Agriculture; Nutrition; Plants; Research

Carl Hayden Bee Research Center (CHBRC)

https://www.ars.usda.gov/pacific-west-area/tucson-az/honey-bee-research

Description: The mission of the CHBRC is "to conduct research to optimize the health of honey bee colonies, through improved nutrition and control of Varroa mites in order to maximize production of honey bee pollinated crops." (from the website) The site's Research section describes current and future research, and includes peer reviewed research articles. The Software section features research and beekeeping software.

Subject(s): Beekeeping; Entomology

Crop Explorer

https://ipad.fas.usda.gov/cropexplorer/

Description: Crop Explorer is an interactive web tool for mapping global crop condition information based on satellite imagery and weather data. For major crop-growing areas around the world, Crop Explorer displays thematic maps of conditions such as precipitation, temperature, and soil moisture. The site also provides frequently updated satellite data and imagery, regional growing season profiles, and narrative reports. Crop Explorer has its own mapping view and a Google Maps view.

Crop Explorer is designed to assist in forecasting production, supply, demand, and food assistance needs. The site has a well-designed interface and a rich library of current data.

Subject(s): Global Agriculture

Department of Agriculture (USDA)

https://www.usda.gov/

Description: The main USDA website provides efficient and uncluttered access to department information. The front page of the site contains current news, event announcements, quick task-based links (such as "Know Your Farmer, Know Your Food" and "Civil Rights"), information about administration initiatives, and a link for emergency preparedness and response. Major topical sections include Topics, Programs and Services, Newsroom, and Blog. The Newsroom section provides speech transcripts, radio and television broadcasts, and agency publications.

As the umbrella site for a large department, the USDA site provides a page of links to the websites for its agencies, services, and programs. It also reports on the department's activities related to the Open Government Initiative and the Recovery Act. The site features a Spanish-language version, which contains news, program information, and educational material.

This is a well-organized site with a simple, consistent interface. It serves as a gateway to the organization of the department and its major programs and publications.

Subject(s): Agriculture

Department of Agriculture (USDA)—Census of Agriculture

https://agcensus.usda.gov/index.php

Description: The Census Bureau took a census of agriculture every 10 years from 1840 to 1920, since 1925, this census has been roughly once every five years. The Census of Agriculture is a complete count of U.S. farms and ranches and the people who operate them. It looks at land use and ownership, operator characteristics, production practices, income and expenditures. Census of Agriculture data are used by all those who serve farmers and rural communities—federal, state and local governments, agribusinesses, trade associations and many others

Economic Research Service (ERS)

https://www.ers.usda.gov/

Description: The Economic Research Service produces key economic indicators and detailed data on the economics of food, farming, natural resources, and rural development. The ERS website provides multiple ways of accessing its information by topic. Popular topics are prominently linked on the home page. The New Releases and Events calendar on the home page includes a dated list of ERS releases. The Data section includes statistics on food pricing, farm economics, international food trade, and other topics. Many data sets can be downloaded in spreadsheet format with the option of creating a tailored report.

Subject(s): Agriculture; Economics; Rural Development; Statistics

Economics, Statistics, and Market Information System (ESMIS)

http://usda.mannlib.cornell.edu

Description: Hosted by Cornell University's Mann Library, this website features a collection of nearly 2,500 reports and data sets from USDA's economics agencies, including the Agricultural Marketing Service (AMS),

Economic Research Service (ERS), National Agricultural Statistics Service (NASS), and World Agricultural Outlook Board (WAOB). It includes current and historical data and reports on national food and agricultural developments; it also forecasts the effects of changing conditions and policies on domestic and international agriculture.

Users may search the entire database or a combination of its components for reports or datasets. They may also browse by topic, with available topics including agricultural baseline projections; commodities; economics and management; livestock, dairy, and poultry; specialty agriculture; trade and international; weather; and market news. In addition, information may be browsed alphabetically by agency through the links toward the top of the home page.

Materials cover both U.S. and international agricultural topics. Most reports are presented as PDF or ASCII text files. Most datasets are in spreadsheet format and include time-series data that are updated annually.

While some of these reports are available in full from USDA websites, the value of this Cornell University website lies in its standard interface, centralized access, and historical back files.

Subject(s): Agriculture; Economics; Statistics

Farm Credit Administration (FCA)

https://www.fca.gov/

Description: As stated on the website, "FCA's mission is to ensure a safe, sound, and dependable source of credit and related services for agriculture and rural America. Our agency was created by a 1933 Executive order of President Franklin D. Roosevelt. Today the Agency derives its authority from the Farm Credit Act of 1971, as amended." The website includes extensive information about the Farm Credit System (FCS), a "government-sponsored nationwide network of cooperatively organized banks and associations that are owned and controlled by their borrowers." (from the website) The Reports & Publications section of the FCA website has financial reports on the FCS. The Law & Regulations section includes rules and regulatory guidance. The FCS Information section includes details on FCS institutions and Federal Agricultural Mortgage Corporation (Farmer Mac) programs.

Subject(s): Agricultural Programs

Farm Service Agency (FSA)

https://www.fsa.usda.gov

Description: The Farm Service Agency assists farmers in income stabilization, resource conservation, credit services, and disaster recovery. The website links to state FSA offices and information about their services and provides online services and forms for FSA customers. Specific programs and topics covered by the website include aerial photography, commodity operations, disaster assistance, farm loan programs, and price support.

Subject(s): Agricultural Programs

Foreign Agricultural Service (FAS)

https://www.fas.usda.gov/

Description: The Foreign Agricultural Service represents U.S. interests in foreign markets. Its website includes information about commodities and products, trade policy, export assistance programs, market development, buying U.S. products, and food security. Also featured on the site is an extensive list of FAS programs, including the Emerging Markets Program (EMP), Quality Samples Program (QSP), Facility Guarantee Program (FGP), and Wool Apparel Manufacturers Trust Fund. News releases and congressional testimony are available in the Newsroom section, and the Data & Analysis section provides access to FAS databases and reports.

Subject(s): Global Agriculture; International Trade; Statistics

Germplasm Resources Information Network (GRIN)

https://www.ars-grin.gov/

Description: The National Genetic Resources Program is responsible for acquiring, characterizing, preserving, documenting, and distributing scientific information about germplasms of all life forms important for food and agricultural production. Its website features GRIN, which has germplasm information for plants, animals, microbes, and invertebrates within the NGRP. Information from the National Genetic Resources Advisory Council (NGRAC) is also available.

This site will primarily be of interest to users researching the germplasm of plants, animals, microbes, and invertebrate.

Subject(s): Agricultural Genetics

GrainGenes

https://wheat.pw.usda.gov/GG3/

Description: GrainGenes is a genetic database for *Triticeae* and *Avena*, providing "molecular and phenotypic information for wheat, barley, rye, and other related species, including oat." (from the website) Access to the data is available through an alphabetical browse feature (by category and name) and by a variety of keyword searches. The site also has information about related news, projects, data, publications, and other resources.

The GrainGenes database contains a substantial amount of genetic information and many links to other genome databases. The interactive and collaborative capabilities of the Internet are used to good advantage, as researchers can submit data for entry into the database and browse through data that has already been included.

Subject(s): Agricultural Genetics; Grains

Grain Inspection, Packers & Stockyards Administration (GIPSA)

https://www.gipsa.usda.gov/

Description: GIPSA facilitates the marketing of grains, livestock, poultry, and meat for the overall benefit of consumers and U.S. agriculture. GIPSA's Federal Grain Inspection Service (FGIS) establishes standards and regulations for grains, and its Packers and Stockyards Program (PSP) investigates fraud, unfair competition, and deception in the livestock, meat, and poultry industries. Target audiences for the agency's website include grain inspectors, livestock producers, poultry growers, and international governments and customers. The Newsroom section includes GIPSA news and publications, as well as FGIS and PSP information and reports.

Subject(s): Grain; Livestock; Regulation

Green Book (FDA Approved Animal Drug Products)

https://www.fda.gov/AnimalVeterinary/Products/ApprovedAnimalDrugProducts/

Description: The *Green Book* is available online in searchable form. The printed publication is issued annually with monthly updates published online. The online book includes FDA Approved Animal Drug Database files that support production of the book, all chapters of the printed book itself, and a searchable archive of the monthly updates.

Subject(s): Veterinary Medicine

Joint Agricultural Weather Facility (JAWF)

https://www.usda.gov/oce/weather/

Description: JAWF collects global weather and agricultural information to determine the impact of weather conditions on crop production around the world. This official JAWF webpage features U.S. Agricultural Weather Highlights, Major World Crop Areas and Climatic Profiles, and the *Weekly Weather and Crop Bulletin*.

Subject(s): Global Agriculture; Weather

***Journal of Extension* (*JOE*)**

https://www.joe.org/

Description: *JOE*, a peer-reviewed journal for the Cooperative Extension System (CES), is published six times a year and only in electronic format. The print version ceased publication in 1994. Issues from 1963 through the present are available on the site.

JOE is an easy-to-use online journal, with supplemental material about the journal, its peer review procedures, and usage statistics.

Subject(s): Agriculture; Extension Services

NAL Catalog (AGRICOLA)

https://agricola.nal.usda.gov/

Description: The NAL Catalog, also called AGRICOLA, is a large bibliographic database covering literature from all areas of agriculture and related fields. It indexes journal articles, short reports, book chapters, and other materials. The database was created in 1970 but also contains content from prior years. Users of AGRICOLA on the Internet can search the book collection of the NAL separately or in combination with AGRICOLA. Cited materials are not available online through AGRICOLA in full-text format. The site describes document delivery options; most remote users will need to find the materials through their local libraries.

Due to its quality, size, scope, and historical coverage, AGRICOLA is a key resource for conducting literature searches on topics related to agriculture.

Subject(s): Agriculture

NAL Digital Collections (NALDC)

https://naldc.nal.usda.gov/naldc/home.xhtml

Description: NALDC is a collection of digitized agriculture documents from past years. The collection can be browsed or searched by keyword.

Subject(s): Agriculture

National Ag Safety Database (NASD)

http://nasdonline.org

Description: The National Ag Safety Database is an online clearinghouse for a diverse array of materials related to agricultural health, safety, and injury causes and prevention. Its long list of topics includes chemicals/pesticides, hearing conservation, lightning, personal protective equipment, and supervising for safety. Safety videos and interactive training are available for online use. Many brochures are available in Spanish.

NASD provides easy access to practical guides that may also be of use to nonfarm industries. Due to the diversity of these materials, users may want to check the source and date provided at the bottom of each document.

Subject(s): Agricultural Safety

National Agricultural Law Center

http://www.nationalaglawcenter.org

Description: The National Agricultural Law Center is funded by the USDA and operated by the University of Arkansas School of Law. The center conducts original research into areas of agricultural and food law. Its website presents this research alongside research material from other sources. The Research by Topic section organizes information by topic, including biotechnology, country of origin labeling, marketing orders, and international agricultural law and organizations. Other highlights on the site include an agricultural law glossary, legislative histories of past farm bills, general reference links, and digests of federal regulations and court cases concerning agricultural law.

The National Agricultural Law Center site is an excellent starting point for legal, legislative, and government documents research on agricultural policy topics.

Subject(s): Agricultural and Food Law

National Agricultural Statistics Service (NASS)

https://www.nass.usda.gov/

Description: NASS publishes a broad range of national and state statistics on crops, livestock, and farming. Users are able to browse NASS data by state or subject, including Crops and Plants, Demographics, Economics and Prices, Environmental, and Livestock and Animals. The site has searchable data from the *Census of Agriculture*, which is conducted every five years. The Data and Statistics section features the Quick Stats database for searching national, state, and local data by commodity, state, or year. The Newsroom section provides NASS news releases and executive briefs.

Subject(s): Crop Production; Livestock; Statistics

National Arboretum

http://www.usna.usda.gov

Description: The National Arboretum's website is more than an online brochure for those planning to visit its gardens in Washington, D.C. The site has information of interest to the general gardening public, including horticultural facts, pest management, new hybrid plant releases, lists of state trees and flowers, and a plant hardiness map depicting the lowest expected temperatures throughout the United States. Information for researchers includes a directory of National Arboretum scientists and their specialties.

Subject(s): Gardening and Landscaping; Trees

National Institute of Food and Agriculture (NIFA)

http://nifa.usda.gov

Description: NIFA was established in 2009 and replaced the former Cooperative State Research, Education, and Extension Service (CSREES). The agency helps fund research at the state and local levels in a variety of areas, such as farm economics, wildlife and fish, animal and plant breeding, pest management, nutrition, and food safety. Its website has information for research grant seekers and recipients.

Subject(s): Agriculture; Food; Research Grants

National Organic Program (NOP)

https://www.ams.usda.gov/about-ams/programs-offices/national-organic-program

Description: This website presents USDA regulations and policies concerning growing, labeling, and marketing farm produce as organic. It includes the National List of Allowed and Prohibited Substances, which identifies the synthetic substances that may be used and the non-synthetic substances that cannot be used in organic production and handling operations. It also has a section on the National Organic Standards Board (NOSB).

This informative site should be of practical benefit to producers, retailers, and consumers of organic food.

Subject(s): Organic Food Certification

NRCS Soils

https://www.nrcs.usda.gov/wps/portal/nrcs/site/soils/home/

Description: The NRCS Soils website is part of the National Cooperative Soil Survey, a cooperative federal-state-academic project. The site has a broad range of scientific, applied, and educational information about soils. The centerpiece of the site is the Soil Survey, which has survey maps, soil characterization data, and soil climate data. The site's homepage links to Soil Data Access, a service that enables the user to download custom spatial and tabular soil data. Other major sections on the site provide images of soil, information about soil use, classification standards, current research topics, and resources for teachers and students.

Subject(s): Soil Surveys

Office of Public Health Science (OPHS)

https://www.fsis.usda.gov/wps/portal/informational/aboutfsis/structure-and-organization/ophs/

Description: The Office of Public Health Science provides scientific analysis and recommendations on public health and science topics of concern to USDA's Food Safety and Inspection Service. The OPHS website describes the agency's major departments and programs, including the Food Emergency Response Network (FERN) and Applied Epidemiology Staff. It also links to a directory of the FSIS Regulatory Field Services Laboratories.

Subject(s): Food Safety; Public Health; Research

Plants & Animals – NRCS

https://www.nrcs.usda.gov/wps/portal/nrcs/main/national/plantsanimals/

Description: This site focuses its resources on the acquisition, development, integration, quality control, dissemination, and access of plant and animal information. Its website features the fully searchable PLANTS Database and detailed fact sheets on selected trees and plants. Its areas of focus are fish and wildlife, insects and pollinators, invasive species and pests, livestock, and plants.

Subject(s): Animals; Plants

PLANTS Database

https://plants.usda.gov/java/

Description: The PLANTS Database features standardized information about the plants found in the United States and its territories. It includes names of plants, checklists, automated tools, identification information, species abstracts, distributional data, crop information, plant symbols, plant growth data, plant materials information, plant links, and references. The database can generate reports such as lists of endangered and threatened plants, invasive and noxious plants, wetlands plants, and state-specific lists of plants. The site includes a gallery of over 50,000 plant images.

This database is an excellent source for verifying plant names and other plant information.

Subject(s): Plants

Production, Supply and Distribution (PSD) Online

https://apps.fas.usda.gov/psdonline/app/index.html#/app/home

Description: The PSD online database has current and historical USDA data on the production, supply, and distribution of agricultural commodities for the United States and selected producing and consuming countries. The site offers predefined tables and the opportunity to download the raw data in comma-separated value format. Users can also perform custom queries by searching for a specific commodity, type of statistic, country, or year.

Subject(s): Agricultural Commodities; Statistics

Risk Management Agency (RMA)

https://www.rma.usda.gov

Description: RMA manages the Federal Crop Insurance Corporation (FCIC) and other risk management programs for agricultural producers. The site features extensive information and data to support farm risk planning. It also has a directory of insurance agent and company locators, an annual list of insurable crops, and other program information.

Subject(s): Crop Insurance; Disaster Assistance

State Fact Sheets – ERS

https://www.ers.usda.gov/data-products/state-fact-sheets/

Description: The State Fact Sheets website contains basic demographic and farm statistics for each state. These statistics are also available for the United States as a whole and include population, employment, income, organic agriculture, farm characteristics, top agriculture commodities, top agriculture exports, and farm financial indicators. Data are updated as new information becomes available.

This is a simple service for basic demographic and agricultural profiles of the states. Researchers looking for more detailed data can click on the links provided throughout each fact sheet to consult more extensive data tables. Agency contacts are also provided.

Subject(s): Agriculture; Demographics; Statistics

World Agricultural Outlook Board (WAOB)

https://www.usda.gov/oce/commodity/

Description: The WAOB coordinates analysis from many USDA agencies to produce the monthly *World Agricultural Supply and Demand Estimates* (*WASDE*) report, and it houses the Joint Agricultural Weather Facility (JAWF). This webpage, part of the larger USDA Office of the Chief Economist website, provides information about the WAOB and copies of publications.

Subject(s): Global Agriculture; Economics

FISHING

Atlantic States Marine Fisheries Commission (ASMFC)

http://www.asmfc.org/

Description: The ASMFC, a group made up of the 15 Atlantic coastal states, was formed by an interstate compact approved by Congress. These states work together through the ASMFC to manage the Atlantic fisheries. The ASMFC website includes news, research and statistics, law enforcement compliance reports, links to other fisheries organizations, educational resources, and information about pending actions open for public input.

Subject(s): Fisheries

Fish and Aquatic Conservation

https://www.fws.gov/fisheries/

Description: The DOI's Fish and Wildlife Service maintains this webpage as a portal to FWS division and program websites concerned with fisheries and habitat conservation. Topics include invasive species, pollution, restoration, and climate change. FWS programs linked to include the National Fish Hatchery System (NFHS) and Fish and Wildlife Conservation Offices (FWCOs).

Subject(s): Fisheries; Natural Resource Conservation

FishWatch

https://www.fishwatch.gov

Description: FishWatch provides consumers with information on the health and sustainability of U.S. seafood fisheries. The site explains what is meant by "sustainable" and supplies detailed sustainability, management, and nutrition profiles for over 30 types of fish. Other information details fisheries management, fishing vessels, U.S. seafood trade, and health and nutrition information.

FishWatch is an excellent consumer-oriented site that provides quick access to information written for the general public, as well as significant detail for those who wish to learn more.

Subject(s): Fisheries; Seafood; Sustainability

Gulf States Marine Fisheries Commission (GSMFC)

https://www.gsmfc.org

Description: The GSMFC is a Congress-authorized organization concerned with Gulf fisheries and made up of the five Gulf of Mexico states (Texas, Louisiana, Mississippi, Alabama, and Florida). Its website includes sections with information on programs, publications, databases, and regulations.

Subject(s): Fisheries

NOAA Fisheries

https://www.fisheries.noaa.gov/welcome

Description: The National Marine Fisheries Service, also known as NOAA Fisheries, is the component of NOAA charged with conserving, protecting, and managing living marine resources. The website covers issues related to overfishing, domestic fisheries, highly migratory species, seafood inspection, and laws such as the Magnuson-Stevens Fishery Conservation and Management Reauthorization Act (also known as the Magnuson-Stevens Act). The Regions and Science Centers sections of the site group content into regional and local areas. The Science and Technology section, under Programs, includes fisheries statistics and economic information, along with reports on the work of NOAA Fisheries science centers and research vessels. The Law Enforcement subsection describes the work of NOAA Fisheries special agents and enforcement officers. The website also has information on aquaculture and on the NOAA Seafood Inspection Program.

Although it sports an uncluttered and fun look, the NOAA Fisheries site contains broad and deep coverage of its topics. Users can easily navigate the NOAA divisions to find science, research, statistics, regulations, and other information related to NOAA's marine resources activities.

Subject(s): Fisheries; Marine Mammals

NOAA Office of Aquaculture

https://www.fisheries.noaa.gov/topic/aquaculture

Description: The aquaculture program at NOAA seeks to support an economically sound industry, provide safe seafood, and promote a healthy marine ecology. The website provides an overview of aquaculture in the United States. It also identifies competitive grant programs and financial assistance available from NOAA and other federal agencies.

Subject(s): Aquaculture

Northwest Fisheries Science Center (NWFSC)

https://www.nwfsc.noaa.gov/

Description: The Northwest Fisheries Science Center is an NMFS research center. Its website describes the center's mission and research and includes extensive image and video libraries of marine life and marine research. This site has a wide variety of information, primarily in the Research and Publications sections.

Subject(s): Fisheries

Pacific States Marine Fisheries Commission (PSMFC)

http://www.psmfc.org

Description: The PSMFC, authorized by Congress in 1947, is one of three interstate commissions dedicated to resolving fishery issues. It serves as a forum for discussion of fishery issues in California, Oregon, Washington, Idaho, and Alaska. Its website has information about current projects, including fisheries data projects, events, grants and contracts, and workshop proceedings.

Subject(s): Fisheries

FORESTRY

Ecosystem Management Coordination (EMC)

https://www.fs.fed.us/emc/

Description: The EMC Office is concerned with information and analysis to support USFS planning. Its website includes information about USFS's environmental appeals and litigation, information related to the National Environmental Policy Act (NEPA) and Environmental Impact Statements (EISs), and planning documents related to the National Forest Management Act (NFMA).

Subject(s): Environmental Policy; Forestry

Forest Service (USFS)

https://www.fs.fed.us/

Description: USFS manages public lands in national forests and grasslands. The website features a forest and grassland locator, and includes sections such as Know Before You Go, Maps, Natural Resources, Learn, Plants & Animals, People & Forests, and Working with Us. A variety of guidebooks, field guides, and reports can be found in the Publications section, and the Managing the Land section provides specialized resources for state and local governments, nonprofit organizations, educational institutions, and other groups.

Subject(s): Forestry

Forestry Technical Resources

https://www.nrcs.usda.gov/wps/portal/nrcs/main/national/landuse/forestry/

Description: This webpage serves as a central point for links to USDA and other federal agencies that provide information about forestry. Web links cover topics from forest farming and alley cropping to silvopasture and windbreaks.

Subject(s): Forestry

Forests and Rangelands

https://www.forestsandrangelands.gov/

Description: The Forests and Rangelands website is a portal to information about the National Cohesive Wildland Fire Management Strategy and related initiatives. The site provides reports, news, and documents relating to wildfires. The Resources section includes a wildland firefighting glossary.

Subject(s): Environmental Policy; Forest Fires

National Agroforestry Center (NAC)

https://www.fs.usda.gov/nac/index.shtml

Description: Agroforestry combines forestry, agriculture, land conservation, and sustainable development practices. NAC is a partnership of the USDA's Forest Service (USFS) and National Resource Conservation Service (NRCS). The NAC website provides research publications, analytical tools, guides, and other material related to agroforestry practices. Special topics include riparian forest buffers, silvopasture, and forest farming. The site's Multimedia section provides a collection of videos and presentations.

Subject(s): Forestry; Research

Chapter Three

Business and Economics

The federal government both regulates and supports U.S. businesses, and it monitors and influences the national economy. These roles drive much of the business and economic information published by the government, which has long been an important, authoritative source of industry and finance data. While this chapter has broad coverage, it does not feature labor-related information (see the Employment chapter) or government finance and taxation (see the Government and Politics chapter).

Subsections in this chapter are Business and Industry, Consumer Information, Economics, Federal Reserve System, Finance, International Trade, and Money.

BUSINESS AND INDUSTRY

Alcohol and Tobacco Tax and Trade Bureau (TTB)

https://www.ttb.gov/

Description: The TTB was created by the Homeland Security Act (HSA) of 2002, which moved the law enforcement functions of the Bureau of Alcohol, Tobacco, and Firearms (ATF) from the DoT to the Department of Justice (DOJ). The act established the TTB as manager of ATF functions that remained at the DoT. The TTB administers and enforces the federal laws and tax code provisions related to the production and taxation of alcohol and tobacco products. The bureau also collects all excise tax on the manufacture of firearms and ammunition.

The TTB website is divided into industry sections covering beer, wine, distilled spirits, other alcohol, tobacco, firearms, and ammunition. Information is also organized by topic, including labeling, permits, taxes/filings, imports/exports, and forms/publications. Information for industry about the

TTB and compliance is available in Spanish, French, and Chinese. The site has a search engine and A–Z index to help researchers locate specific information.

Subject(s): Alcohol; Guns; Regulation; Taxation; Tobacco

Baldrige Performance Excellence Program (BPEP)

https://www.nist.gov/baldrige

Description: The Malcolm Baldrige National Quality Award, sponsored by the DOC, is the centerpiece of the BPEP. This award recognizes performance excellence and focuses on an organization's overall performance management system. The award may be presented to manufacturers; service companies; small businesses; or nonprofit/government, education, or health care organizations. The BPEP website presents detailed information about the award, the award process, performance criteria, and past winners.

Subject(s): Awards

Business Center – FTC

https://www.ftc.gov/tips-advice/business-center

Description: This section of the FTC website is a central point for finding compliance information and fraud protection advice for businesses. Topics include advertising and marketing, credit, identity theft, and information security.

Subject(s): Business Compliance; Fraud Protection

Business & Industry – Census Bureau

https://www.census.gov/econ/

Description: This webpage provides a central access point for business and industry data from a variety of Census Bureau programs. It provides an overview of the survey programs and finding aids. The site's sidebar organizes links to Census Bureau data by sector (such as construction) and topic (such as business dynamics, small business, and historical data).

Subject(s): Business Statistics

Business Tools – STOPfakes.gov

https://www.stopfakes.gov/welcome

Description: This website is part of the PTO campaign to educate small businesses about the effects of piracy, counterfeiting, and intellectual property theft. It includes basic information about patents, trademarks, copyright, and the government's anti-piracy campaign.

Subject(s): Counterfeiting; Intellectual Property; Piracy; Small Business

Business USA

https://www.usa.gov/business

Description: Business USA provides plentiful resources for businesses and entrepreneurs, including help with starting and growing a business, exporting goods, and finding funding opportunities.

Subject(s): Business Development; Entrepreneurship

Center for Verification and Evaluation (CVE)

https://www.vetbiz.gov/

Description: The CVE works to promote veteran-owned businesses. Its website provides information about verification for Service-Disabled Veteran-Owned Small Businesses and Veteran-Owned Small Businesses (SDVOSBs/VOSBs).

Subject(s): Veteran-Owned Businesses

Committee on Foreign Investments in the U.S. (CFIUS)

https://www.treasury.gov/resource-center/international/pages/committee-on-foreign-investment-in-us.aspx

Description: The Committee on Foreign Investments in the U.S., an interagency committee chaired by the Secretary of the Treasury, reviews notices of potential foreign acquisitions of U.S. companies and may investigate on behalf of the President if such acquisitions could threaten national security. This DoT webpage links to regulations, guidance, and legislation.

Subject(s): Foreign Investment; National Security

Competition and Real Estate

https://www.justice.gov/atr/competition-and-real-estate-0

Description: This special website from the Antitrust Division of the DOJ focuses on the real estate brokerage industry. The site examines laws and practices that increase prices and suggests alternative models. Contact information and links to additional sites are provided.

Subject(s): Real Estate Brokerage

Department of Commerce (DOC)

https://www.commerce.gov/

Description: The DOC website is an excellent starting point for finding government information related to the world of business. It links to the sites for the department's various bureaus that deal with different aspects of commerce; these include the Bureau of Economic Analysis (BEA), International Trade Administration (ITA), Patent and Trademark Office (PTO), and National Oceanic and Atmospheric Administration (NOAA). The DOC site's homepage features current news and the department's blog.

Most substantive program information can be found at the individual websites of the DOC's bureaus.

Subject(s): Business; Foreign Trade

E-Stats: Measuring the Electronic Economy

https://www.census.gov/programs-surveys/e-stats.html

Description: E-Stats is a central clearinghouse for reports and data from the Census Bureau that define and measure e-commerce across multiple economic sectors. The E-Stats website has quarterly reports on online retail sales and annual reports comparing e-commerce sales to total sales. In May 2015, the 2013 e-commerce multi-sector "E-Stats" report was released.

Subject(s): E-commerce

Federal Trade Commission (FTC)

https://www.ftc.gov/

Description: The Federal Trade Commission enforces federal antitrust and consumer protection laws. Its website is organized into sections according to the FTC's roles. The For Consumers section includes guides for businesses and individual consumers dealing with unfair or fraudulent business practices. The Commission Actions section provides documents such as FTC advisory opinions, adjudicative opinions of the commission, advocacy filings, public comments on proposed regulations, and commission and staff reports. Other sections provide FTC news, economic reports, and congressional testimony.

On the consumer side, the FTC site offers many fact sheets and guides, an online complaint form, and links to federal consumer websites on specific topics such as identity theft and internet scams. The FTC also has a version of the site available in Spanish, which focuses on providing news and consumer protection information.

This website serves a valuable public function by presenting clear and timely information. The multiple ways provided to access information ensure that both consumers and antitrust researchers will be able to find what they need.

Subject(s): Antitrust Law; Business Regulation; Consumer Information; Consumer Protection

Manufacturing.gov

https://www.manufacturing.gov/

Description: Manufacturing.gov serves as an information and resource portal for advanced manufacturing in the United States. The website features the National Network for Manufacturing Innovation (NNMI), which "provides a manufacturing research infrastructure where U.S. industry and academia collaborate to solve industry-relevant problems." (from the website) The Publications page is organized into sections including Reports & Guidance, Speeches & Testimony, Articles & Blog Posts, and Legislation. The website also provides links to NNMI Institutes and associated federal initiatives.

Subject(s): Advanced Manufacturing

Manufacturing & Construction Statistics – Census Bureau

https://www.census.gov/mcd/

Description: This Census Bureau gateway website compiles all census-related information about manufacturing, mining, and construction into one page. Data primarily come from the *Annual Survey of Manufactures* (*ASM*), *Current Industrial Reports* (*CIR*), and *Economic Census*. Construction statistics include new residential construction, sales, and building permits. The Manufacturing section includes the latest releases on manufacturers' shipments, inventories, and orders. The site also links to a service, called Just the Facts, for tailoring your own statistical reports.

Subject(s): Construction Industry; Manufacturing; Mining; Statistics

Minority Business Development Agency (MBDA) Web Portal

https://www.mbda.gov/

Description: The Minority Business Development Agency's mission is to promote the growth and competitiveness of American minority business enterprises of all sizes. The agency funds business development centers throughout the United States. The MBDA website has agency news and announcements; a directory of regional offices; contract opportunity announcements; and background information about federal contracting, business development, and finance. The Business Tools section of the site offers a variety of online business tools, such as an interactive business plan writer. These tools can be used after setting up a free account.

Subject(s): Business Development; Minority Business Enterprise

National Women's Business Council (NWBC)

https://www.nwbc.gov/

Description: The National Women's Business Council is a federal advisory council that provides advice and policy recommendations to the President, Congress, and Small Business Administration (SBA) on issues relevant to female business owners. Its website features reports, an events calendar, and referrals to counseling and training programs. The Issues & Research section includes reports pertaining to women and entrepreneurship. Fact sheets are also available on the site.

Subject(s): Business Development; Women in Business

North American Industry Classification System (NAICS)

https://www.census.gov/eos/www/naics/

Description: NAICS is the official industry classification system used by U.S. statistical agencies. Adopted in 1997, NAICS replaced the Standard Industrial Classification (SIC) codes that had been used in government reports since the 1930s. This website is the central location for NAICS news and documentation. It includes information about the current edition of the *NAICS Manual*, just released this year, and previous editions. A NAICS Search section allows keyword and NAICS code number searching of the 2017, 2012, and 2007, editions of the *NAICS Manual*, along with links to display the code's hierarchy and description.

Subject(s): Industry Classification

Office of Women's Business Ownership

https://www.sba.gov/offices/headquarters/wbo/

Description: According to the website, "The Office of Women's Business Ownership's mission is to enable and empower women entrepreneurs through advocacy, outreach, education, and support." The Resources section provides a directory of Women's Business Centers. Funding and financial assistance information is available in the Loans & Grants section.

Subject(s): Business Development; Women in Business

Patent and Trademark Office (PTO)

https://www.uspto.gov/

Description: Information, guides, and online applications pertaining to patents and trademarks, as well as searchable patent and trademark databases, are readily available on PTO's website. The office's official journal, the *Official Gazette* (*OG*), and *Federal Register Notices* are available in the Learning and Resources section, as is an online glossary of intellectual property terminology. A directory of Patent and Trademark Resource Centers (PTRCs) can also be found in that section.

While the PTO website also offers thorough resources to address the complex fields of patent and trademark law, it is able to serve both novices and patent and trademark professionals.

Subject(s): Intellectual Property Law; Patents; Trademarks

Small Business Administration (SBA)

https://www.sba.gov/

Description: The mission of the SBA is to assist and protect the interests of small business. Its website defines the parameters of a small business in the Getting Started section under Contracting. The Starting & Managing section links to information about writing a business plan, business counseling, and growing a business. Forms can also be found in this section. Financial information is contained in the Loans & Grants section.

As of 2011, Business.gov's content moved to the SBA website. Business.gov provided one-stop access to practical business resources and services from federal and state agencies and other organizations.

Subject(s): Business Development; Small Business

CONSUMER INFORMATION

Aviation Consumer Protection Division

https://www.transportation.gov/airconsumer/

Description: The Aviation Consumer Protection Division of the DOT receives the general public's complaints about airline consumer issues and works with the aviation industry to improve compliance with consumer protection requirements. Complaints about air travel safety and security and airline service, as well as disability or discrimination claims, can be made through the site. The Most Popular Services section includes the following links: File an Aviation Consumer Complaint, Air Travel Consumer Reports, Aviation Enforcement Orders, Guidance on Aviation Rules and Statute, and Air Travel Tips.

Subject(s): Airlines; Consumer Information; Consumer Protection

Consumer and Governmental Affairs Bureau (CGB) – FCC

https://www.fcc.gov/consumer-governmental-affairs

Description: The Consumer and Governmental Affairs Bureau is responsible for developing and implementing the FCC's consumer policies. The bureau handles consumer inquiries and complaints and informs consumers on telecommunications issues, such as charges on phone bills, Internet access, disability access, the regulation of indecency and obscenity on broadcasts, and telecommunications fraud and scams. CGB also works with other government agencies to formulate telecommunications policy.

Subject(s): Consumer Protection; Telecommunications Regulation

Consumer Information – FTC

https://www.consumer.ftc.gov/

Description: This website hosts a blog with FTC consumer information. Also featured are informational sections for Money & Credit, Homes & Mortgages, Health & Fitness, Jobs & Making Money, and Privacy & Identity. A Spanish-language version of the site is available.

Subject(s): Consumer Information; Consumer Protection

Consumer Product Safety Commission (CPSC)

https://www.cpsc.gov/

Description: The Consumer Product Safety Commission develops and enforces standards to reduce the risk of injury or death from consumer products. The CPSC website highlights recent product recall news and features a database of previous recall announcements organized by date, product category, and company. Also available on the site are a variety of CPSC publications, including its *Annual Report* and *Injury Statistics Reports*. The Research & Statistics section features the National Electronic Injury Surveillance System (NEISS) database of emergency hospital visits involving injuries associated with consumer products.

The Business & Manufacturing section of the site includes regulatory guidance, information on how to report a potentially hazardous product, and a directory of testing labs by product. Some portions of the CPSC website, consumer guides and alerts in particular, are available in Spanish, Chinese, and Vietnamese.

This is a useful site for consumers, who can use it to report defective consumer products and check to see which products have been recalled. Consumers may also wish to visit the federal recalls website at https://www.recalls.gov/.

Subject(s): Consumer Protection; Product Recalls; Product Safety

econsumer.gov

https://www.econsumer.gov/#crnt

Description: econsumer.gov is a collaborative effort of 34 nations and an initiative of the International Consumer Protection and Enforcement Network (ICPEN); the FTC is primarily in charge of U.S. participation. The site was developed in response to the international nature of Internet fraud. It provides general information about consumer protection in all of the countries that belong to ICPEN, contact information for consumer protection authorities in those countries, and an online complaint form. The site can be viewed in English, Spanish, French, German, Chinese, Korean, Polish, and Turkish.

Subject(s): Consumer Protection; Internet Fraud

HelpWithMyBank.gov

https://www.helpwithmybank.gov/

Description: HelpWithMyBank.gov is designed for customers of national banks and federal savings associations. It addresses common consumer questions about topics such as bank accounts, credit cards, insurance, mortgages, and asset management. The site's "Need More Help?" section discusses how to determine if a financial institution is a national bank and how to file a banking complaint. The site's top menu links to a dictionary of financial terms. Some information is available in Spanish.

Subject(s): Banking; Personal Finance

MyMoney.gov

https://www.mymoney.gov/Pages/default.aspx

Description: Aimed at the individual consumer, this website provides tips on financial planning, credit, saving, home ownership, retirement, and other personal finance topics.

Subject(s): Financial Literacy; Personal Finance

National Consumer Protection Week

https://www.consumer.ftc.gov/features/national-consumer-protection-week

Description: This one-stop government website provides links to information about National Consumer Protection Week, which took place from March 4 through 10 in 2018. Some content is available in Spanish.

Subject(s): Consumer Protection

National Do Not Call Registry

https://www.donotcall.gov/

Description: The National Do Not Call Registry is managed by the FTC and allows individuals to block most telemarketing calls to their phones. Consumers can use this website to register their phone numbers; they can also file complaints about violations of the "do not call" rules or about scammers posing as members of the registry. The site also links to compliance information for telemarketers. A Spanish-language version of the site is available.

Subject(s): Consumer Protection; Telemarketing; Telephone Registry

OnGuard Online

https://www.consumer.ftc.gov/features/feature-0038-onguardonline

Description: OnGuard Online presents tips for securing personal computers and personal information. Topics covered on its website include wireless security, laptop security, computer disposal, online scams, and kids' online safety. The File a Complaint link at the bottom of the page directs users to appropriate agencies. A Spanish-language version of the site is also available.

Subject(s): Computer Security; Consumer Protection; Internet Security; Online Safety

SaferProducts.gov

https://www.saferproducts.gov/

Description: According to the website, "the U.S. Consumer Product Safety Commission is charged with protecting the public from unreasonable risks of injury or death from thousands of types of consumer products under the agency's jurisdiction." SaferProducts.gov allows users to search recalls and reports and to file reports about unsafe products. Registered businesses can respond to the complaints. The website's About section also provides information about the Consumer Product Safety Improvement Act (CPSIA) of 2008.

Subject(s): Consumer Protection; Product Safety

ECONOMICS

ALFRED®: Archival Federal Reserve Economic Data

https://alfred.stlouisfed.org/

Description: ALFRED® is an economic database that allows researchers to analyze historical decisions made based on the data that were available at the time (prior to revisions and updates). This "vintage" data, as they are called on ALFRED®, can be downloaded as compressed spreadsheets or as tab-delimited text files. Data is available for 292,006 series in nine categories, including Academic Data; Money, Banking, & Finance; National Accounts; Population, Employment, & Labor Markets; Production & Business Activity; Prices; International Data; Greenbook Projections; and U.S. Regional Data.

ALFRED® is intended for academic professionals and other advanced economics researchers.

Subject(s): Economic Data

Annual & Quarterly Services – Census Bureau

https://www.census.gov/services/index.html

Description: According to the website, "The Quarterly Services Survey (QSS) and the Service Annual Survey (SAS) work together to produce the most comprehensive data available on service activity in the U.S." Service sectors covered include Information; Finance and Insurance; Professional, Scientific, and Technical; Health Care and Social Assistance; Administrative and Support; and Arts, Entertainment, and Recreation.

Subject(s): Economic Data

Bureau of Economic Analysis (BEA)

https://www.bea.gov/

Description: The Bureau of Economic Analysis provides comprehensive statistics on the U.S. economy that are used in important government decisions impacting monetary policy, tax and budget projections, and business investment plans. BEA focuses on national income and product accounts (NIPAs) statistics, which include gross domestic product (GDP) and related measures of the national economy. The BEA homepage features the latest economic releases and an annual schedule for all BEA releases. BEA also publishes exclusively online the monthly *Survey of Current Business*. (Issues from 1921 to 2013 are available from the Federal Reserve Bank of St. Louis website at http://fraser.stlouisfed.org/publications/SCB/.)

BEA organizes links to its data under Regional, National, International, and Industry sections. Regional data includes Gross Domestic Product (GDP) by state and metropolitan area. National data includes GDP, Personal Income and Outlays, and Corporate Programs. International Data includes

Balance of Payments and Trade in Goods and Services. Industry data includes GDP by industry and sector. BEA Regional Fact Sheets (*BEARFACTS*) are available by state, county, and metropolitan statistical area (MSA).

The BEA website presents important national economic statistics, with multiple access points and several convenient downloading options. The site design makes it easy to access current or historical data.

Subject(s): Economic Statistics; National Accounts Statistics

Economic Census

https://www.census.gov/programs-surveys/economic-census.html

Description: Every five years, the *Economic Census* profiles the U.S. economy from the national to local level. This census tabulates the number of business establishments (or companies), the number of employees, payroll, and measures of output (such as sales and receipts); data are reported by industry sector and by geography. The *Economic Census* also surveys business owner characteristics such as race, age, and education. Data and reports from the *Economic Census* are available from this website and via the Census Bureau's American FactFinder (described elsewhere in this book). The website also supplies a number of guides to using the data.

The release of the 2012 *Economic Census* began in early 2014. The 2007 *Economic Census* releases occurred from 2009 through 2011.

Subject(s): Economic Statistics; Industry Statistics

Economic Indicators

https://www.gpo.gov/fdsys/browse/collection.action?collectionCode=ECONI

Description: The monthly publication *Economic Indicators* is prepared by the Council of Economic Advisors for Congress's Joint Economic Committee (JEC). *Economic Indicators* is hosted online by the Federal Digital System (FDsys) of the Government Publishing Office (GPO). Analyzed indicators include gross domestic product (GDP), sources of personal income, unemployment rates, productivity, producer prices, consumer prices, federal receipts and outlays, and more. *Economic Indicators* issued from 1995 forward are available at this site. For earlier data, the Federal Reserve's FRASER® website (described elsewhere in this chapter) makes available economic indicators back to 1948.

Economic Indicators is a convenient compilation for reference use. However, as it is a monthly publication, researchers should check elsewhere to see if an indicator has recently been updated. *Economic Indicators* notes the source of each indicator and makes it easy for users to check the website of the issuing agency, such as the Bureau of Labor Statistics (BLS).

Subject(s): Economic Statistics

Economics & Statistics Administration (ESA)

http://www.esa.doc.gov

Description: ESA delivers economic data, analyses, and forecasts. Its website links to information from its better-known component agencies, including the Census Bureau and Bureau of Economic Analysis (BEA). ESA periodically conducts its own studies, and these are available in the Reports section.

Subject(s): Economic Statistics

FRASER®: Federal Reserve Archival System for Economic Research

https://fraser.stlouisfed.org/

Description: FRASER® provides copies of historical economic statistical publications and releases in PDF format. Key documents include *All-Bank Statistics, United States, 1896–1955*, which was published by the Federal Reserve Board of Governors (FRB) in 1959, and *Banking and Monetary Statistics* for the periods 1914–1941 and 1941–1970. Other statistical series include the *Annual Statistical Digest* (1976–2000), *Productivity and Costs* (1971–2004), and the *Business Statistics* supplement to the *Survey of Current Business*. The site also features digitized documents reflecting the Fed's history.

By providing resources that were previously only available in printed form, FRASER® helps researchers compile uninterrupted historical data series. FRASER® also allows researchers to obtain data as they were reported in preliminary, revised, and final releases.

Subject(s): Economic Research; Economic Statistics

FRED®: Federal Reserve Economic Data

https://fraser.stlouisfed.org/

Description: FRED® is a database of U.S. economic data available as time series. FRED® data can be downloaded in spreadsheet or text formats or viewed as charts. Data series are grouped by source and under categorical headings such as Money, Banking, & Finance; National Accounts; Population, Employment, & Labor Markets; Production & Business Activity; Prices; International Data; and U.S. Regional Data.

Subject(s): Economic Data

GeoFRED®: Geographical Federal Reserve Economic Data

https://geofred.stlouisfed.org/

Description: GeoFRED® can be used to create thematic maps of U.S. economic data for states, counties, metropolitan statistical areas (MSAs), and other geographic areas. The data available to be mapped depend upon the geographic area selected. Custom maps can be printed or saved as PDF files,

GeoFRED® can create a web link for the map, and the data can be downloaded. The site also offers tutorials and lessons plans for educators based on GeoFRED®.

GeoFRED® puts simple thematic mapping of economic data into the hands of the general public. For important background information and instructions, see the Help link.

Subject(s): Economic Data; Economic Geography; Mapping

Office of Economic Policy

https://www.treasury.gov/about/organizational-structure/offices/Pages/Economic-Policy.aspx

Description: DoT's Office of Economic Policy analyzes domestic and international economic issues and the financial markets. The office's website includes economic policy reports, reports on key economic indicators, and annual reports of Total Taxable Resources (TTR). It also contains the *Social Security Trustee Report* and the *Medicare Trustee Report*.

Subject(s): Economic Policy

Page One Economics®

https://research.stlouisfed.org/publications/page1-econ/

Description: *Page One Economics®* is a newsletter that covers timely economic topics, as well as personal finance, for the layman. Each issue is released with a corresponding Classroom Edition, which includes questions for students and an answer key. Newsletters back to 2007 are available on the website.

Subject(s): Economics Education

FEDERAL RESERVE SYSTEM

Board of Governors of the Federal Reserve System (FRB)

https://www.federalreserve.gov/

Description: The Federal Reserve, the central bank of the United States, hosts this website with sections including About the Fed, Monetary Policy, Banking Information & Regulation, Payment Systems, Economic Research & Data, Consumer Information, Community Development, and Publications. Some consumer-level information is also available in Spanish.

The Economic Research & Data section has a special Data Download tool for custom downloads of the Fed's statistical releases. In the Monetary Policy section, the site has information on the Federal Open Market Committee (FOMC), which announces targets for the federal funds rate. The Monetary Policy section also links to the Fed's *Summary of Commentary on Current Economic Conditions by Federal Reserve District*, commonly known as the

Beige Book. The Publications section includes articles from the *Federal Reserve Bulletin* (no longer available in print), bank supervision manuals, news releases and historical data for interest rates, foreign exchange rates, consumer credit, and other related topics.

This website offers a substantial body of information and statistics from the FRB. It serves as a good starting point for users seeking information about the system as a whole. However, valuable data are also available from the individual Federal Reserve Banks. One limitation of this main site is that its links to the member bank websites are several clicks away; they can be found in the About the Fed section.

Subject(s): Banking Regulation; Federal Reserve; Monetary Policy

CASSIDI®: Competitive Analysis and Structure Source Instrument for Depository Institutions

https://cassidi.stlouisfed.org/

Description: The CASSIDI® database has geographic and deposit information for all U.S. bank holding companies, banks, thrifts, and their branches. It also has tools to compare market concentrations across banking markets. The site is intended to help those in the banking and finance industries examine how potential mergers or acquisitions could affect market structures and competition.

Subject(s): Banking

Fed in Print

https://www.fedinprint.org/

Description: Fed in Print is an index to Federal Reserve economic research. Sponsored by the St. Louis Fed, it covers Federal Reserve publications from all of the system's banks and the Board of Governors (FRB). The search form supports searches by keyword, author, bank, publication type, and date range.

Subject(s): Economic Research

Federal Reserve Bank of Atlanta

https://www.frbatlanta.org

Description: The Atlanta Fed encompasses banking institutions in the Sixth Federal Reserve District, which is made up of Alabama, Florida, and Georgia, and portions of Louisiana, Mississippi, and Tennessee. The main sections of the Atlanta Fed's website are About the Fed (including information about the Atlanta Fed and the Federal Reserve System); Banking, Research, & Data; Economy Matters; News & Events; Education; and Community Development. The website features the quarterly magazine *EconSouth*®, which focuses on the economy of the Southeastern United States. Blogs and podcasts with regional economic commentary are also available on the website.

Subject(s): Banking Regulation; Monetary Policy

Federal Reserve Bank of Boston

https://www.bostonfed.org/

Description: The Boston Fed serves the First Federal Reserve District, which includes the six New England states: Connecticut (excluding Fairfield County), Massachusetts, Maine, New Hampshire, Rhode Island, and Vermont. Along with full information from the Federal Reserve System, local information includes the website for the Federal Reserve Banks' New England Public Policy Center (NEPPC); the monthly *New England Economic Indicators* publication; and banking, economic, and government finance profiles for the region. Online publications include *Communities & Banking*.

Subject(s): Banking Regulation; Monetary Policy

Federal Reserve Bank of Chicago

https://www.chicagofed.org/

Description: The Chicago Fed's website features a wide range of banking information for the Seventh Federal Reserve District, which comprises all of Iowa and most of Illinois, Indiana, Michigan, and Wisconsin. The main sections of the site include Research, Banking, Markets, and Education. Online periodicals include the bank's *Annual Report* and *Chicago Fed Letter*, as well as *AgLetter* and *Economic Perspectives*. Regional information for the Midwest economy includes the Chicago Fed Midwest Manufacturing Index and National Activity Index.

Subject(s): Banking Regulation; Monetary Policy

Federal Reserve Bank of Cleveland

https://www.clevelandfed.org/

Description: The Cleveland Fed serves the Fourth Federal Reserve District, which is made up of Ohio, western Pennsylvania, eastern Kentucky, and the northern panhandle of West Virginia. Major topical sections on the site include Our Research, Community Development, and Banking Oversight. The Our Region subsection under Our Research provides local demographic, business, and economic statistics.

Subject(s): Banking Regulation; Monetary Policy

Federal Reserve Bank of Dallas

https://www.dallasfed.org/

Description: The Dallas Fed covers the 11th Federal Reserve District, which includes Texas, northern Louisiana, and southern New Mexico. It has branches in El Paso, San Antonio, and Houston. Regional economic data is available in the Research & Data section, including the DataBasics introduction to Texas economic indicators. The website links to the Globalization and Monetary Policy Institute, which was founded by the Dallas Fed in 2007.

The Dallas Fed website is a good resource for information on economic factors affecting the 11th District, such as the impacts of the oil industry and trade with Mexico.

Subject(s): Banking Regulation; Monetary Policy

Federal Reserve Bank of Kansas City

https://www.kansascityfed.org/

Description: The Kansas City Fed serves the 10th Federal Reserve District, which comprises Colorado, Kansas, Nebraska, Oklahoma, Wyoming, northern New Mexico, and western Missouri. The website includes sections that cover financial services, banking, community development, consumer help, and education. Regional economy information under Research & Data includes regional economic indicators and the Kansas City Financial Stress Index, and the online newsletter *The Main Street Economist* can be found under Publications.

Subject(s): Banking Regulation; Monetary Policy

Federal Reserve Bank of Minneapolis

https://www.minneapolisfed.org/

Description: This website features a variety of resources for the Ninth Federal Reserve District, which includes Montana, North Dakota, South Dakota, Minnesota, the Upper Peninsula of Michigan, and northwestern Wisconsin. Publications online include the *fedgazette*, *The Region*, and *Community Dividend*. Data on the site include regional economic data and forecasts, agricultural credit conditions, and manufacturing surveys.

Subject(s): Banking Regulation; Monetary Policy

Federal Reserve Bank of New York

https://www.newyorkfed.org/

Description: The New York Fed is responsible for the Second District: New York State, the 12 northern counties of New Jersey, Fairfield County in Connecticut, Puerto Rico, and the U.S. Virgin Islands. Research and data on the geographical region can be found throughout the site but are most readily available in the Economic Research and Outreach & Education sections. Second District publications include *Current Issues in Economics and Finance*, *Second District Highlights*, and *Upstate New York Regional Review*. In addition to the regional economic research and data, the site's Outreach & Education section is rich with information for all levels of learners.

Subject(s): Banking Regulation; Monetary Policy

Federal Reserve Bank of Philadelphia

https://www.philadelphiafed.org/

Description: The Philadelphia Fed is responsible for the Third Federal Reserve District, specifically eastern Pennsylvania, southern New Jersey, and the state of Delaware. The website's Payment Cards Center (PCC) is part of the bank's larger focus on economic and financial literacy. The PCC "provides meaningful insights into developments in consumer credit and payments that are of interest not only to the Federal Reserve but also to the industry, other businesses, academia, policymakers, and the public at large." (from the website) The PCC includes pertinent studies, legislative information, and consumer information. Other sections of the site include Research & Data, Bank Resources, Community Development, and Education. Along with specialist literature, the Publications page features more practical information for the general public in its Consumer Publications and Economic Education sections.

Subject(s): Banking Regulation; Consumer Credit Research; Economics Education; Monetary Policy

Federal Reserve Bank of Richmond

https://www.richmondfed.org/

Description: The Richmond Fed serves the Fifth Federal Reserve District, which includes the District of Columbia, Maryland, Virginia, North Carolina, South Carolina, and most of West Virginia. Its website features Research, Banking, Publications, Community Development, and Education sections. Regional data can be found in both the Research section and in *Region Focus*, the Richmond Fed's economics magazine.

Subject(s): Banking Regulation; Monetary Policy

Federal Reserve Bank of San Francisco

https://www.frbsf.org/

Description: The San Francisco Fed serves the 12th Federal Reserve District, which is comprised of Alaska, Arizona, California, Hawaii, Idaho, Nevada, Oregon, Utah, and Washington, as well as the territories of American Samoa, Guam, and the Northern Mariana Islands. The website features prominently the Center for Pacific Basin Monetary and Economic Studies, which the San Francisco Fed founded in 1990, and which works to "promote cooperation among central banks in the region and enhance public understanding of major Pacific Basin economic policy issues." (from the website) The site also hosts a blog with articles on timely economic topics.

Subject(s): Banking Regulation; Monetary Policy

Federal Reserve Bank of St. Louis

https://www.stlouisfed.org/

Description: The St. Louis Fed represents the Eighth Federal Reserve District, which comprises all of Arkansas and portions of Illinois, Indiana, Kentucky, Mississippi, Missouri, and Tennessee. The site hosts a Financial Crisis Timeline at http://timeline.stlouisfed.org/. The Research & Data section of the website provides numerous research resources not available on other Fed sites. For example, the site's FRED® database provides easy access to U.S. economic time series. Another database, FRASER®, provides historical economic statistical publications. The ALFRED® database has archival economic data. These resources from the St. Louis Fed are described in separate entries in this book.

The innovative resources in the Research & Data section make the St. Louis Fed website one of the more interesting regional sites for national-level research.

Subject(s): Banking Regulation; Economic Research; Monetary Policy

Federal Reserve Education

https://www.federalreserveeducation.org/

Description: This website organizes the many educational resources from the Federal Reserve Banks by audience (K–4, 5–8, 9–12, College, and Adult). The site's purpose is to promote economic and financial literacy to students of all levels and the general public.

Subject(s): Economics Education

Federal Reserve System Online

https://www.federalreserveonline.org

Description: This web directory site provides links to the websites of the individual Reserve Banks and to system-wide sites such as the Fed's online publications catalog and consumer help page.

Subject(s): Federal Reserve

National Information Center (NIC) – Federal Reserve

https://www.ffiec.gov/nicpubweb/nicweb/nichome.aspx

Description: The NIC website serves as a "central repository of data about banks and other institutions for which the Federal Reserve has a supervisory, regulatory, or research interest, including both domestic and foreign banking organizations operating in the United States" (from the website). The Institution Search and USBA Search enable searches by institution name, location, or type.

Subject(s): Banking

FINANCE

Commodity Futures Trading Commission (CFTC)

https://www.cftc.gov/

Description: The CFTC is an independent agency regulating commodity futures and options markets in the United States. The Market Reports section of the website includes *Commitments of Traders* (*COT*) reports in short and long formats, *Bank Participation Reports*, and other reports. The Consumer Protection section includes Reparations Programs and Fraud Case Status Reports.

The About the CFTC section includes commissioner biographies, the CFTC organization chart, advisory committee information, and CFTC history. The Industry Oversight section links to the exchanges designated by the CFTC as contract markets and derivatives clearing organizations registered with the CFTC. The site also features an Education Center with basic information on how futures markets work and consumer protection advice for those investing in futures markets.

Subject(s): Securities and Investments Regulation

Community Development Financial Institutions (CDFI) Fund

https://www.cdfifund.gov/Pages/default.aspx

Description: The CDFI Fund assists community development financial institutions (CDFIs) to promote economic revitalization in underserved and low-income areas. The site has information for applicants and for recipients of CDFI Fund awards. Under the Awards heading, the site has a database of awards made from 1996 to the present.

Subject(s): Economic Development

EDGAR: Securities and Exchange Commission Filings & Forms

https://www.sec.gov/edgar.shtml

Description: EDGAR stands for Electronic Data Gathering, Analysis, and Retrieval. The EDGAR database holds reports and documents submitted by publicly traded companies and others required by law to file forms with the SEC. The filings provide information on company finances, management, legal proceedings, and more. The EDGAR search page includes options for finding companies and their current associated filings and searching archived EDGAR documents. In 2006, the SEC added the capability to search the full texts of filings. The About EDGAR section provides essential information about the database's scope and coverage. The EDGAR website also has a tutorial, a guide to SEC filings, and file transfer capability.

The filings available through EDGAR are a standard source of information about publicly traded companies. Many researchers supplement EDGAR with commercial, for-fee database subscriptions that provide the same data but with enhanced search and report features. There are also free commercial websites for EDGAR filings, such as SEC Info (http://www.secinfo.com/).

Subject(s): Business Law and Regulation; Companies and Enterprises

FDIC and Financial Regulatory Reform

https://www.fdic.gov/regulations/reform/

Description: This section of the FDIC website explains the FDIC's work in implementing financial regulatory reform measures. Speeches, press releases, and related FDIC documents are also available here.

Subject(s): Banking Regulation; Financial Regulation

Federal Deposit Insurance Corporation (FDIC)

https://www.fdic.gov/

Description: The FDIC was created during the Great Depression to insure deposits in banks and thrift institutions in the United States. Major topical sections of the FDIC website are Deposit Insurance, Consumer Protection, Industry Analysis (bank statistics, a directory of FDIC-insured institutions, and a failed banks list), Regulations & Examinations, and Institution & Asset Sales (from failed banks). The site organizes content by audience, with separate pages for Bankers, Consumers & Communities, Analysts, and Regulators.

The FDIC website's offerings will be appealing to both professionals and consumers. For professionals, the detailed statistics and various full-text reports provide opportunities for research into banking trends and specific institutions. For consumers, the site offers advice, referrals to rating services, and statistics on individual institutions.

Subject(s): Banking Regulation; Financial Regulation

Federal Financial Institutions Examination Council (FFIEC)

https://www.ffiec.gov/

Description: The FFIEC is "a formal interagency body empowered to prescribe uniform principles, standards, and report forms for the federal examination of financial institutions by the Board of Governors of the Federal Reserve System (FRB), the Federal Deposit Insurance Corporation (FDIC), the National Credit Union Administration (NCUA), the Office of the Comptroller of the Currency (OCC), and the Consumer Financial Protection Bureau (CFPB), and to make recommendations to promote uniformity in the supervision of financial institutions." (from the website) Information about the FFIEC's supervisory framework, as well as FFIEC reports, are available on the site. Links to enforcement and orders pages at council members' websites can be found in the Enforcement Actions section.

The FFIEC's Uniform Bank Performance Reports (UBPRs), technical reports intended for use by banks and bank supervisors, have been made available on the FFIEC Central Data Repository (CDR) Public Data Distribution (PDD) website at https://cdr.ffiec.gov/. CDR makes FFIEC data available for searching and for bulk download.

Subject(s): Banking Regulation; Financial Regulation

Financial Crisis Inquiry Commission (FCIC)

http://fcic.law.stanford.edu

Description: The FCIC was created by the Fraud Enforcement and Recovery Act (FERA) of 2009. The commission investigated 22 areas of public interest related to potential fraud, risk, and enforcement problems in the mortgage industry, lending practices, the credit rating system, derivatives and unregulated financial products, corporate governance, and the performance of federal and state financial regulators. The website includes commission reports and testimony before the commission.

Subject(s): Banking Regulation; Financial Regulation

Financial Crisis Timeline

https://www.stlouisfed.org/financial-crisis/

Description: This site provides news, data, and government reports related to the 2008–2009 financial crisis. The site is organized around a timeline starting in February 2007. Each event on the timeline links to the related source document.

Subject(s): Banking and Finance; Economic Conditions

Investor.gov

https://investor.gov/

Description: Investor.gov has information on saving, investing, and protecting money. The site covers managing investments, transitioning into retirement, and fraud prevention, and provides SEC investor alerts and bulletins.

Subject(s): Consumer Investing; Personal Finance

Joint Board for the Enrollment of Actuaries

https://www.irs.gov/tax-professionals/enrolled-actuaries/

Sponsor(s): Treasury Department — Internal Revenue Service (IRS)

Description: The Joint Board for the Enrollment of Actuaries sets the qualification standards and certification process for individuals who perform actuarial services as required under the Employee Retirement Income Security Act (ERISA) of 1974. Its website provides information on the board and its qualification and renewal processes.

Subject(s): Actuary Certification

Money Services Businesses (MSBs)

https://www.fincen.gov/money-services-business-definition

Description: MSBs are nonbank financial institutions defined as such for purposes of the Bank Secrecy Act (BSA) of 1970. This website features a list of the conditions that define an MSB.

Subject(s): Financial Regulation; Money Laundering

National Credit Union Administration (NCUA)

https://www.ncua.gov

Description: NCUA is an independent federal agency that supervises and insures credit unions. Information for credit unions includes regulatory information and credit union financial data. Information for consumers includes educational information about credit unions and a list of recently closed credit unions. Documents available from the NCUA website include relevant laws, rules, and regulations; statistical reports; and *NCUA Letters to Credit Unions*. The Credit Union Analysis section has a searchable credit union directory. A Spanish version of the site is available.

Subject(s): Credit Unions; Regulation

Office of the Comptroller of the Currency (OCC)

https://www.occ.treas.gov/

Description: An independent bureau of DoT, the OCC charters, regulates, and supervises all national banks and supervises the federal branches and agencies of foreign banks. The OCC website features information about banking regulations, banker education, community development investments of national banks, consumer rights, electronic banking, and other topics. The Corporate Activities subsection features the *Weekly Bulletin*, a record of the actions by the OCC on all applications involving national banks for new banks, branches, mergers, conversions, changes in bank control, fiduciary powers, domestic subsidiaries, relocations of main offices and branches, and information on notices such as changes in corporate titles and branch closings. The News and Issuances section consists of news releases, consumer advisories, congressional testimony, alerts, and OCC Bulletins. The OCC website is clearly organized by topic, both general and specific, to help users find information easily.

Subject(s): Banking Regulation; Consumer Protection

Office of Domestic Finance

https://www.treasury.gov/about/organizational-structure/offices/pages/domestic-finance.aspx

Description: The Office of Domestic Finance has broad policy and oversight roles in areas relating to banking, financial institutions, financial markets, financial regulation, and government finance. The office's website provides detailed descriptions of their programs and links to commissions, bureaus, and resources.

Subject(s): Economic Policy; Financial Regulation

Office of Financial Stability

https://www.treasury.gov/initiatives/financial-stability/Pages/default.aspx

Description: This site provides news and information on the administration's Financial Stability Plan. It describes the Troubled Assets Relief Program (TARP) established under the Emergency Economic Stabilization Act (EESA) of 2008. TARP includes the Capital Assistance Program (CAP), Consumer and Business Lending Initiative (CBLI), Making Home Affordable® Program (MHA), Public-Private Investment Program (PPIP), Capital Purchase Program (CPP), Asset Guarantee Program (AGP), Targeted Investment Program (TIP), and Automotive Industry Financing Program (AIFP). The site provides *TARP Transaction Reports*, *Tranche Reports*, and other reports.

Subject(s): Banking and Finance; Economic Conditions

Office of the Special Inspector General for the Troubled Asset Relief Program (SIGTARP)

https://www.sigtarp.gov/Pages/Home.aspx

Description: SIGTARP coordinates audits and investigations of the purchase, management, and sale of assets under the Troubled Asset Relief Program (TARP). The website includes SIGTARP organizational information, press releases, updates on audits and investigations, and quarterly reports to Congress. Citizens can report suspected TARP waste, fraud, or abuse via the website or through a toll-free number.

Subject(s): Financial Crimes; Financial Regulation

Securities and Exchange Commission (SEC)

https://www.sec.gov/

Description: The Securities and Exchange Commission, which is led by five presidentially appointed commissioners, regulates the securities markets. The SEC website features both financial information for investors and information for the securities industry that it oversees. A major offering is the EDGAR database of corporate filings, which is described elsewhere in this chapter.

Toward the bottom of the homepage information is arranged by audience group (Investors, Broker-Dealers, Accountants, Small Businesses, Funds and Advisers, and International). The Investors link leads to the SEC's Office of Investor Education and Advocacy webpage, which contains the bulk of the online publications, with some consumer education publications available in Spanish. In the News section, the SEC provides webcasts of its open meetings, forums, and other public events. The daily *SEC News Digest* in the same section is available online back to 1956.

Subject(s): Securities and Investments Regulation

StopFraud.gov

https://www.stopfraud.gov/

Description: The StopFraud.gov website explains the work of the Financial Fraud Enforcement Task Force, established in 2009. The Task Force is a coalition of federal and state fraud enforcement agencies. The website has a page for reporting fraud by type, such as identity theft, mass marketing/telemarketing fraud, tax fraud, Medicare fraud, mortgage fraud, and loan scams. It also has news of financial fraud convictions and information on how to protect oneself from fraud.

Subject(s): Financial Crimes

Treasury International Capital (TIC) System

https://www.treasury.gov/resource-center/data-chart-center/tic/Pages/index.aspx

Description: The TIC System tracks the flow of investment funds between U.S. residents and foreign residents. Data are released on a quarterly, monthly, and annual basis, and are accessible from this site.

Subject(s): International Finance Statistics

XBRL.sec.gov

https://www.sec.gov/structureddata/osd-inline-xbrl.html

Description: This site will be most useful to publicly traded companies and other entities that file reports with the SEC. It provides information about eXtensible Business Reporting Language (XBRL), one of the SEC's data reporting standards.

Subject(s): Companies and Enterprises; Securities and Investments

INTERNATIONAL TRADE

African Growth and Opportunity Act (AGOA)

https://www.trade.gov/agoa/

Description: AGOA was signed into law in 2000, and its implementation is designed to offer incentives for African nations to maintain open economies and free market practices. Under the act, eligible sub-Saharan African countries may export certain products to the United States with no import duty. The AGOA website describes the original legislation and its subsequent amendments. The site includes AGOA reports to Congress, lists of eligible countries and products, African trade statistics, and information from the annual AGOA Forum.

Subject(s): Africa; International Economic Development; Trade Agreements

Automated Export System Direct (AESDirect)

https://www.census.gov/foreign-trade/aes/transitiontoace/index.html

Description: AESDirect allows shippers to file Electronic Export Information (EEI) online to the Automated Export System (AES). Its website offers user guides, registration information, and online training. It also offers links to related sites.

Subject(s): Export Regulations; Shipping

Bureau of Industry and Security (BIS)

https://www.bis.doc.gov/

Description: BIS regulates the export of sensitive goods, such as weapons technologies and encryption software, as well as exports to certain countries in accordance with U.S. policy. BIS also enforces U.S. antiboycott laws, the Fastener Quality Act (FQA), and the reporting provisions of the Chemical Weapons Convention (CWC). The BIS website links to major regulations, export licensing guidelines, news, and training courses on export restrictions. The primary audience for the site is the U.S. exporter community.

The site links to the Freedom of Information Act (FOIA) webpage for BIS with selected documents available in full. The Policy Guidance section provides general and specific information about export control. Other sections include Licensing, Enforcement, Reform, and Data.

While geared toward the practical needs of exporters, the BIS website is also a good source for general research on U.S. export controls.

Subject(s): Export Regulations; International Trade

Commercial Service

https://www.trade.gov/cs/

Description: The Commercial Service promotes U.S. exports to global markets. This website provides basic information on the organization's leadership, structure, and mission. The Commercial Service uses another website to promote its services; that site, Export.gov, is described elsewhere in this chapter.

Subject(s): Exports; International Trade

Commercial Service in China

https://2016.export.gov/china/

Description: This website provides information for U.S. companies seeking to do business with China. It provides information on trade policy initiatives and China's business laws and regulations. The site also has sections on market research on China, trade leads from China, trade and industry news, and links to other useful sites.

Subject(s): China; Exports; International Trade; International Trade Law

Defense Technology Security Administration (DTSA)

http://www.dtsa.mil

Description: DTSA's primary mission is to preserve critical U.S. military technological advantages through the monitoring and control of "international transfers of defense-related goods, services, and technologies." (from the website) The site has sections describing the work of DTSA's Licensing, Policy, Space, and Technology Directorates.

Subject(s): Arms Control; Export Regulations; Military Technology

Directorate of Defense Trade Controls (DDTC)

https://www.pmddtc.state.gov

Description: The DDTC website provides information about the rules governing U.S. exports of defense materials and services. The site has information on registration and compliance for relevant manufacturers, exporters, and brokers. The site also has a chart of country policies and embargoes linking to information published in the *Federal Register*.

Subject(s): Arms Control; Export Regulations

Enforcement and Compliance (E&C)

https://www.trade.gov/ia/

Description: E&C enforces laws and agreements to prevent unfairly traded imports. Its website provides E&C documents, including reviews and determinations on anti-dumping and countervailing duties (AD/CVD). The Highlights and News section provides notice of E&C actions with links to related documents. The site provides guidance for U.S. businesses encountering unfair trade practices and information on E&C programs such as the Foreign-Trade Zones (FTZs) Program and the Steel Import Monitoring and Analysis (SIMA) System.

Subject(s): Duties and Tariffs; Trade Laws and Regulations

Export.gov

https://www.export.gov/welcome

Description: Export.gov is a portal for information relevant to U.S. exporters. The site covers export basics, trade leads, trade events, export finance, market research, trade data, and trade problems (such as trade barriers and unfair practices). Under Opportunities, the Market Research section includes a step-by-step guide for researching markets using government websites and other resources.

As with other subject-oriented government web portals, this website provides one-stop access to resources available from a variety of government agencies. While it is intended for those in the export business, it also serves as a useful entry point and reference resource for international trade researchers.

Subject(s): Exports; International Trade

Export Administration Regulations (EAR)

https://www.bis.doc.gov/index.php/regulations/export-administration-regulations-ear/

Description: This is the online version of the legally official text of the EAR, which is available in the *Federal Register*. The EAR features a compilation of official regulations and policies governing the export licensing of materials, technology, and information.

Subject(s): Export Regulations

Export-Import Bank of the U.S. (EXIM)

https://www.exim.gov/

Description: The Export-Import Bank offers export financing for U.S. businesses. The What We Do section of its website features information about EXIM's services, such as its working capital financing, credit insurance, loan guarantees, and direct loans. Broker and lender locators, as well as applications and forms, are provided in the Tools for Exporters section, and how-to videos, webinars, publications, and newsletters are available under Learning Resources.

Subject(s): Banking; Finance; International Trade

Export USA

https://www.think.global/

Description: This website features the online version of *Export USA*, the official export promotion magazine of DOC. The magazine and website are designed to assist importers from around the world in their efforts to locate certain American products and services, and to help American sellers find buyers and distributors abroad for their products and services.

Although an official publication of DOC, this magazine is managed by a private company and accepts advertising.

Subject(s): Exports; International Trade

Foreign Trade Statistics

https://www.census.gov/foreign-trade/index.html

Description: The Foreign Trade Division (FTD) of the Census Bureau is "the official source of U.S. export and import statistics and responsible for issuing regulations governing the reporting of all export shipments from the

United States." (from the website) The site's two major sections correspond to these functions: The Data section features FTD's compilation and reporting of trade statistics and the Automated Export System (AES) section captures export shipping data.

Information available in the Data section includes reports on individual countries and their balance of trade with the United States, historical series back to 1960, product-specific statistics, a monthly list of top U.S. trading partners, and state export data. Current and past issues of the *U.S. International Trade in Goods and Services* report (also known as the *FT900)*, which is the major monthly update of U.S. trade in goods and services, are available in the same section.

Subject(s): Trade Statistics

Industry & Analysis (I&A)

https://www.trade.gov/industry/

Description: I&A, a division of ITA, offers services to promote U.S. exports and has special expertise in U.S. manufacturing and service sectors. Content on the sector pages varies, but most provide links to industry reports and information on industry-specific export programs. The site also has a directory of industry experts on staff.

Subject(s): Exports

Interactive Tariff and Trade DataWeb

https://dataweb.usitc.gov/

Description: DataWeb is a tariff and trade database designed by the USITC. The data comes from the Census Bureau, Customs Service, and the USITC itself. The system is free of charge but requires registration. DataWeb offers a number of options for custom-tailoring search results, as well as report options that include downloading to a spreadsheet format. DataWeb also generates prepared summary tables for commonly requested information, such as U.S. trade by geographic region or partner country. A separate tariff database presents tariff treatment information and links to trade data.

DataWeb is a flexible and relatively sophisticated system for U.S. trade data. For regular trade and tariff data users, it can be a very useful tool; new users may first wish to see if the site's prepared trade data tables can answer their questions.

Subject(s): International Trade Statistics

International Trade Administration (ITA)

https://www.trade.gov/

Description: ITA promotes U.S. exports and U.S. companies seeking to export. Most information about the agency is included in the About ITA and Press sections of its website. The site features information on the President's

Export Council; a Frequently Asked Questions section about importing and exporting; and Tradeology, the official ITA blog.

Subject(s): Exports

International Trade Commission (ITC)

https://www.usitc.gov/

Description: ITC is an independent federal agency that examines unfair trade practices and the impact of imports on U.S. industries. The ITC website's Investigations section, under Popular Topics, includes major case news and documents regarding antidumping and countervailing duty (AD/CVD) and intellectual property investigations, as well as recent petitions and complaints. The Tariff Affairs section includes the *Official Harmonized Tariff Schedule of the U.S.* (*HTS*), which describes all goods in trade for duty, quota, and statistical purposes. The Industry/Economic Analysis section contains detailed reports on products, services, and regions. The site also features DataWeb, ITC's international trade statistics and U.S. tariff database.

The availability of the *HTS* and DataWeb statistical tool makes this site a core resource for international trade information.

Subject(s): Duties and Tariffs; International Trade

Market Research Library

http://www.buyusainfo.net

Description: The Market Research Library is a full-text database of reports from the Commercial Service about foreign markets. The database can be searched by industry sector, country, and other criteria. It includes the *Country Commercial Guides* series prepared by Commercial Service trade specialists working in over 80 countries.

Subject(s): International Market Research

Subject(s): Exports; International Business; Middle East; North Africa

Notify U.S.

https://tsapps.nist.gov/notifyus/data/index/index.cfm

Description: This free e-mail subscription service provides "U.S. entities (citizens, industries, and organizations) an opportunity to review and comment on proposed foreign technical regulations that may affect their businesses and their access to international markets." (from the website) The United States receives notice of these proposed regulations as a member of the World Trade Organization (WTO).

Subject(s): International Trade Law

Office of Commercial and Business Affairs (CBA)

https://www.state.gov/e/eb/cba/

Description: CBA works within the Department of State to support and coordinate trade and investment by U.S. firms overseas. CBA's webpage links to Export.gov's extensive Market Research page and provides information on the DOS's commercial diplomacy efforts and business-related visas.

Subject(s): International Business

Office of Textiles and Apparel (OTEXA)

https://otexa.trade.gov/

Description: The OTEXA website provides information on exporting U.S.-made textiles and apparel products. The site provides detailed trade data, information on trade agreements and trade preferences, *Federal Register* notices, and export requirements. It also has country-specific information on textile import tariffs with links to the website of the foreign government office responsible for tariff administration.

Subject(s): Exports; Textile Industry; Trade Statistics

Office of Trade Agreements Negotiations and Compliance (TANC)

https://tcc.export.gov/

Description: TANC monitors foreign compliance with trade agreements and helps U.S. businesses overcome unfair trade practices. The TANC website features the following sections: Report a Trade Barrier, Defining a Trade Barrier, Removing Barriers, and Our Office.

The Trade Agreements subsection links to TANC's Trade and Related Agreements Database (TARA). TARA covers active, binding agreements between the United States and its trading partners concerning manufactured products and services (excluding agriculture). TANC's Agreements Guides, available on the same page as TARA, have concise explanations of a variety of trade agreements.

Subject(s): Trade Agreements; Trade Laws and Regulations

Office of Trade Policy & Analysis (TP&A)

https://www.trade.gov/mas/ian/

Description: TP&A develops trade and economic data products and provides analysis on issues affecting the competitiveness of U.S. manufacturing and services. The website provides trade statistics published by TP&A, covering topics including National U.S. Trade, U.S. Exporting Companies, and Jobs Supported by Exports. The site also links to the quarterly updated TradeStats Express™ database.

Subject(s): Trade Statistics

Office of the U.S. Trade Representative (USTR)

https://ustr.gov/

Description: The USTR is responsible for developing and coordinating U.S. international trade, commodity, and direct investment policy and for overseeing trade negotiations with other countries. This website presents information on negotiations, treaties, and issues in sections organized by trade agreement, world region, and issue area. The News section includes the agency blog, press releases, and reports.

Subject(s): International Trade Policy; Trade Agreements

Overseas Private Investment Corporation (OPIC)

https://www.opic.gov/

Description: OPIC is an independent U.S. government agency that assists U.S. companies investing in emerging economies around the world. For these companies, OPIC provides financing, political risk insurance, and investment funds. Its website has sections describing each of these services. The Media section contains links to annual reports, press releases, and the OPIC blog.

Subject(s): International Business; International Economic Development

Resources on Strategic Trade Management and Export Controls

https://www.state.gov/strategictrade/

Description: This website is sponsored by the Export Control and Related Border Security (EXBS) Program, a U.S. government interagency program designed to help other countries improve their export control systems to prevent "the proliferation of weapons of mass destruction and destabilizing accumulations and irresponsible transfers of conventional weapons." (from the website) The site has an overview of the U.S. export control program and describes its best practices. The Resources section directs users to information from the European Union (EU), non-governmental organizations (NGOs), and other sources.

Subject(s): Arms Control; Export Regulations

Special American Business Internship Training (SABIT) Program

https://www.trade.gov/sabit/

Description: SABIT assists U.S. companies and organizations working in Eurasian countries by funding training programs for managers in that region. The program is intended to facilitate U.S.-Eurasian business partnerships. Its website describes the program and links to a Russian-language SABIT website.

Subject(s): Emerging Markets; Eurasia; International Business

STOPfakes.gov

https://www.stopfakes.gov

Description: STOPfakes.gov is a multiagency product of the government's campaign against the piracy and counterfeiting of U.S. goods. Its website describes the campaign, provides resources for assistance, and includes links to relevant information at the websites of the Patent and Trademark Office (PTO) and the Customs and Border Protection (CBP).

This website is particularly helpful, as it brings together intellectual property information distributed across the websites of many agencies.

Subject(s): Counterfeiting; Intellectual Property; Trade Laws and Regulations; Piracy

Trade and Development Agency (USTDA)

https://www.ustda.gov

Description: The USTDA is an independent federal agency that provides assistance to developing countries for economic and infrastructure improvements and promotes opportunities for U.S. businesses abroad. This website has information on USTDA projects by world region and industry sector. Tools for businesses wishing to pursue USTDA contracts include a database of consultants and, in the Reports and Resources section, feasibility studies to support large infrastructure projects in developing markets abroad.

Subject(s): International Business; International Economic Development

TradeStats Express™

http://tse.export.gov/tse/

Description: TradeStats Express™ delivers annual U.S. trade data in the form of basic world maps, pie charts, and data tables. Its website is divided into sections for National Trade Data and State Export Data. For national trade, researchers can find U.S. exports, imports, and trade balances for all countries for a given commodity, or they can find data on all products traded between the United States and another country. For state exports, researchers can find data on a state's or U.S. region's exports to one or all countries or world regions, or they can view a state-by-state profile of U.S. exports to a given country.

TradeStats Express™ meets its goal of being easy to use. However, the trade data are complex enough that researchers should review the online manual via the Help link.

Subject(s): International Trade Statistics

MONEY

Advanced Counterfeit Deterrence (ACD) Program

https://www.moneyfactory.gov/about/advancedcounterfeitdeterrence.html

Description: The ACD program was established by the Department of Transporttaion in July 1982 to monitor counterfeit deterrence concerns. Its website provides information on the program and on counterfeit detection and links to the Bureau of Engraving and Printing (BEP) for details on current currency design and security features.

Subject(s): Counterfeiting

Bureau of Engraving and Printing (BEP)

https://www.moneyfactory.gov/

Description: BEP's website features information about the bureau, bureau tours, U.S. currency production, and anti-counterfeiting measures. The history behind each U.S. banknote can be found in the U.S. Currency section, and Collector Information, Production Reports, and Laws and Regulations are some of the pages available in the Resources section. The site also has an online shop called the BEP Store, which sells collectible products and souvenirs.

Subject(s): Money

Foreign Exchange Rates

https://www.federalreserve.gov/releases/h10/current/

https://www.federalreserve.gov/releases/g5/current/

Description: The first URL listed above links to *Foreign Exchange Rates H.10*, a weekly report of the average exchange rates for the previous week. The second URL links to *Foreign Exchange Rates G.5*, for monthly data on foreign exchange rates.

Subject(s): Exchange Rates

U.S. Mint

https://www.usmint.gov/

Description: The U.S. Mint produces and distributes U.S. coins; protects national gold and silver assets; and produces and sells platinum, gold, and silver bullion coins. The Mint's website has information about Mint facilities and tours, how coins are made, the Mint Police, and coin programs, as well as a product schedule, coin production and sales figures, and news releases. The site also has general information about coin collecting and a section for children and their teachers. An online store sells coins, commemoratives, medals, and other Mint products.

Subject(s): Coins; Money

Chapter Four

Culture and Recreation

Culture, for the purposes of this chapter, can be broadly defined to include the arts, humanities, and preservation of human heritage. The federal government has various roles in each of these areas, and in the promotion of recreational opportunities on federal lands. Many of the websites in this chapter are designed for the general public; others, particularly some of the federal libraries listed in the Libraries section, are for a far more limited and specialized audience. The federal library listings cover all subject areas, from the humanities to the sciences and engineering.

Subsections in this chapter are Arts, Culture, History, Libraries, Museums, Recreation, and Reference.

ARTS

Indian Arts and Crafts Board

https://www.doi.gov/iacb/

Description: The Indian Arts and Crafts Board enforces the legal requirement that products advertised as "Indian made" must indeed be made by American Indians. The board also promotes American Indian and Alaska Native arts and crafts and operates three regional museums. Its website includes an online version of the *Source Directory of American Indian and Alaska Native Owned and Operated Arts and Crafts Businesses*.

Subject(s): Arts; American Indians

National Endowment for the Arts (NEA)

https://www.arts.gov/

Description: NEA is an independent federal agency that promotes and provides funding for the arts and arts education. Its website has information on how to apply for a grant and lists recent grant recipients. It also highlights winners of NEA's national awards: the Jazz Master Fellowships, Opera Honors, National Heritage Fellowships, and National Medal of Arts. A Partnerships section lists state and regional arts organizations. The Home section includes NEA's quarterly magazine, *NEA ARTS*, and information on the advisory National Council on the Arts. NEA offers a wide range of publications on its site, covering such topics as arts education, accessibility in museums, and city design.

Subject(s): Arts; Grants

National Film Preservation Board (NFPB)

https://www.loc.gov/programs/national-film-preservation-board/about-this-program

Description: The National Film Preservation Board serves as a public advisory group to the librarian of Congress on matters related to motion picture preservation. According to its website, the board assists the librarian each year in selecting up to 25 "culturally, historically or aesthetically significant films" to add to the National Film Registry. The Library of Congress then works to ensure that these films are preserved. The board's website includes the Complete National Film Registry Listing dating back to 1989, a year after the NFPB was established by the National Film Preservation Act. The site also links to the National Film Preservation Foundation (with which it is associated) and to film institutes and associations from around the world.

Subject(s): Movies; History

Poetry and Literature Center of the Library of Congress

http://www.loc.gov/poetry/

Description: The Poetry and Literature Center is home to the Poet Laureate Consultant in Poetry, who is named by the librarian of Congress. As of press time, Juan Felipe Herrera was the current Poet Laureate. The center also administers the Rebekah Johnson Bobbitt National Prize for Poetry and the Witter Bynner Fellowships for poets. This website offers webcasts and podcasts of poetry readings at the Library of Congress and further information about the center.

Subject(s): Literature; Poetry

U.S. Commission of Fine Arts (CFA)

https://www.cfa.gov/

Description: CFA is an independent agency that advises the federal government and the District of Columbia government on matters of art and architecture that affect the appearance of the nation's capital. Its website includes the legislative and regulatory history of the commission, public meeting agendas and minutes, and information about the National Capital Arts and Cultural Affairs (NCACA) program.

Subject(s): Architecture, public buildings

CULTURE

American Folklife Center

http://www.loc.gov/folklife/

Description: The Library of Congress's American Folklife Center is charged with preserving and presenting American folklife. The center is responsible for the library's Archive of Folk Culture, a repository for American folk music and other materials. Its website offers a number of online collections, and featured projects include the Veterans History Project, Civil Rights History Project, and StoryCorps—an oral history project. Many of the center's publications, guides to researching the collections, and resources for teachers are available on the site.

Subject(s): Folklife Studies; Music

Archeology Program

https://www.nps.gov/archeology/

Description: The NPS Archeology Program website provides information about archeological investigations at national parks. It links to NPS regional archeological centers and offices. The site also carries the NPS Archeology Guide, which details responsible management of archeological resources under the stewardship of NPS. Other sections cover the Federal Archeology Program, National Historic Landmarks (NHLs), and topics such as preventing looting and vandalism and caring for collections.

Subject(s): Archeology

Center for the Book in the Library of Congress

http://www.read.gov/cfb/

Description: The Center for the Book promotes books, reading, libraries, and literacy. It is affiliated with the state book centers that conduct local activities for the same purpose. Its website has information about and links to the center's themes and projects, literary events (including the National Book Festival), publications, and affiliate programs.

Subject(s): Literacy

Corporation for Public Broadcasting (CPB)

https://www.cpb.org//

Description: CPB is a private, nonprofit corporation that was created by Congress in 1967. It receives partial funding through annual congressional appropriations and, in turn, funds public television and radio programming. The About CPB section of this website includes leadership profiles, CPB's annual reports, and financial information. The Programs & Projects section has a directory of CPB-funded programs for television, radio, and the Internet. More than 70 percent of CPBs funding is districuted to locally owned public radio and television stations.

Subject(s): Public Networking

Cultural Heritage Center

https://eca.state.gov/cultural-heritage-center/

Description: The Cultural Heritage Center serves as the DOS's center of expertise on global cultural heritage protection issues. The center supports U.S. compliance with laws and agreements on the import, export, and transfer of ownership of cultural property. The website also provides information from the U.S. Ambassadors Fund for Cultural Preservation (AFCP) and the Iraq Cultural Heritage Initiative.

DOS's Cultural Heritage Center website is an essential resource for those interested in the international sale, transfer, or repatriation of antiquities and other cultural artifacts.

Subject(s): Cultural Heritage

Institute of Museum and Library Services (IMLS)

https://www.imls.gov/

Description: IMLS is an independent federal agency that provides funding in support of all types of museums, libraries, and archives. The IMLS website has separate sections for grant applicants, grant reviewers, and grant recipients. Other sections cover IMLS programs for state-library administrative agencies and statistical reports from IMLS's surveys of public libraries and state-library agencies.

Subject(s): Libraries—Grants; Museums—Grants

John W. Kluge Center at the Library of Congress

http://www.loc.gov/loc/kluge/

Description: The Kluge Center hosts humanities scholars at the Library of Congress and presents the John W. Kluge Prize for Achievement in the Study of Humanity. The center offers Kluge Chairs to selected accomplished scholars in such areas as world cultures, American law and governance, and modern culture. The website has information on the Kluge Chairs, Fellowships, and Partnerships, as well as on the Kluge Prize, Resident Scholars, and the Scholars Council.

Subject(s): Humanities

National Archeological Database (NADB)

https://www.nps.gov/archeology/tools/nadb.htm

Description: The NADB online system is maintained through a cooperative agreement between NPS and CAST. NADB has two components: The Permits section contains a database of permits issued by the DOI under the Antiquities Act of 1906 and the Archaeological Resource Protection Act (ARPA) of 1979. The MAPS (Multiple Attribute Presentation System) section is a graphical application that contains a variety of maps in GIS format; these maps show the national distribution of cultural and environmental resources across the United States at the state and county levels.

Subject(s): Archaeology

National Capital Planning Commission (NCPC)

https://www.ncpc.gov/

Description: NCPC coordinates all planning activities for federal land and buildings in the National Capital Region (NCR), which includes Washington, D.C., and surrounding communities in Maryland and Virginia. The NCPC website provides information on current planning and public opportunities to comment.

Subject(s): Civil Planning

National Center for Preservation Technology and Training (NCPTT)

https://www.ncptt.nps.gov/

Description: As part of NPS, NCPTT is concerned with the art and science of preservation in areas such as archeology and historic architecture. The center's grants program focuses on the training, technology, and basic research aspects of preservation and conservation. The site provides information on the center's grants as well as on its programs in the areas of Archeology & Collections, Architecture & Engineering, Historic Landscapes, and Materials Conservation. It also covers cemetery conservation and disaster recovery projects.

Subject(s): Preservation; Architecture

National Endowment for the Humanities (NEH)

https://www.neh.gov/

Description: According to its website, "The National Endowment for the Humanities is an independent federal agency created in 1965. It is one of the largest funders of humanities programs in the United States." The site provides guidance on applying for and managing NEH grants, and the Grants section has information about the awards process. The About NEH section includes a staff directory, links to State Humanities Councils, and information on the Jefferson Lecture in the Humanities and the National Humanities Medals.

Subject(s): Grants; Humanities

National Native American Graves Protection and Repatriation Act (NAGPRA) Program

https://www.nps.gov/nagpra/

Description: As part of the NPS National Center for Cultural Resources (NCCR), National NAGPRA develops regulations and guidance for implementing the Native American Graves Protection and Repatriation Act. National NAGPRA also provides training and grants. Its website is a resource for information on the act, which delineates a process for museums and federal agencies to return certain Native American cultural items. The Online Databases section includes the Native American Consultation Database (NACD) of consultation contacts for Indian tribes, Alaska Native villages and corporations, and Native Hawaiian organizations.

Subject(s): Historic Preservation—Native Americans

National Recording Preservation Board (NRPB)

https://www.loc.gov/programs/national-recording-preservation-board/about-this-program

Description: According to its website, the NRPB advises the Library of Congress on the selection of culturally, historically, or aesthetically important sound recordings to be added to the National Recording Registry. These selections may include music, non-music, spoken word, or broadcast sound. The website includes information about the registry, the nomination process, and the board's preservation planning work. It also links to websites for other sound archives.

Subject(s): Historic Preservation—Sound

Preserve America

http://www.preserveamerica.gov

Description: Preserve America is a White House initiative carried out in cooperation with multiple federal agencies. The initiative is intended to encourage federal agencies to integrate heritage preservation and economic development, bolster local heritage preservation efforts, and promote intergovernmental and public-private partnerships to help accomplish these goals. The website includes information on the Preserve America Grants and the Preserve America Presidential Awards. It also has a list of designated Preserve America communities and neighborhoods, and in the Clearinghouse section there are links to related information from state governments and federal agencies.

Subject(s): Preservation—Community

Read.gov

http://read.gov

Description: The Center for the Book in the Library of Congress, discussed elsewhere in this section, uses this website to encourage reading at all levels. The site has sections for kids, teens, adults, and parents and educators. Read.gov has a wide variety of information, including booklists, online versions of children's classics, webcasts featuring prominent authors, and a directory of local book projects.

Subject(s): Reading

Smithsonian Center for Folklife and Cultural Heritage

https://folklife.si.edu/

Description: On its website, the Smithsonian Center for Folklife and Cultural Heritage describes itself as "dedicated to the collaborative research, presentation, conservation, and continuity of traditional knowledge and artistry with diverse contemporary cultural communities in the United States and around the world." The site has information about the center's major endeavors, including the annual Folklife Festival. The website also features online exhibits, educational resources, and the *Smithsonian Folkways Magazine*.

Subject(s): Folklife Studies

Smithsonian Institution

https://www.si.edu/

Description: The main Smithsonian Institution website links to all other Smithsonian museum sites and to information about the Smithsonian's research facilities, archives, and other centers. The site includes information about the history of the Smithsonian, hours and locations of the Smithsonian museums, and links to Smithsonian affiliate museums across the United States. The Smithsonian also has a number of blogs available via the Connect section on the home page. See the Explore section to link to the Encyclopedia page; it is organized by topic, including Art and Design, History and Culture, and Science and Technology, and provides links to high-quality online resources across the network of Smithsonian websites.

Subject(s): Museums

Smithsonian Institution Research Information System (SIRIS)

https://siris.si.edu/

Description: SIRIS consolidates links and finding aids for the many specialized databases and image collections on the network of Smithsonian websites. It links to searchable libraries, archives, and research catalogs and to collections that can be browsed online. SIRIS also links to the combined search engine for all collections.

Subject(s): Arts—Research; Museums

Smithsonian Magazine

https://www.smithsonianmag.com/

Description: This online version of *Smithsonian* includes articles and images from the print version, plus web-only features. The archive section has issues back to 1995.

Subject(s): Culture and Recreation

HISTORY

Access to Archival Databases (AAD)

https://aad.archives.gov/aad/

Description: AAD provides the public with access to a selection of historic databases and other electronic records maintained by the National Archives. This site includes nearly 85 million historic electronic records created by more than 30 federal agencies. The electronic records vary widely in subject matter, but all of them identify specific persons, geographic areas, organizations, or dates—making them useful as finding aids. Information includes several files on war casualties and prisoners of war, the Japanese-American Internee File for 1942–1946, the Work Stoppages Historical File for 1953–1981, and the Central Foreign Policy Files for 1973–1975.

First-time users should consult the Getting Started Guide for instructions on how to search AAD and for an explanation of what records are included on the site. The records in AAD represent only a small fraction of the electronic records holdings of NARA. For the most part, AAD does not include digitally scanned images of paper records and other non-electronic records.

Subject(s): Archives; Databases

Advisory Council on Historic Preservation (ACHP)

http://www.achp.gov

Description: The ACHP is an independent federal agency and the major policy adviser to the federal government in the field of historic preservation. The website contains an overview of the National Historic Preservation Program, including directories of federal, state, and tribal preservation officers and preservation-related websites. The site also has the full text of, and compliance guidance for, Section 106 of the Code of Federal Regulations, which concerns the protection of historic properties.

Subject(s): Historic Preservation

America's Historical Documents

https://www.archives.gov/historical-docs

Description: This website is an online exhibit of documents selected from the National Archives collections. Document images in the exhibit include the Declaration of Independence, the Louisiana Purchase Treaty, the check written for the purchase of Alaska, Edison's patent for the light bulb, and the Apollo 11 flight plan. The site links to similar exhibits, such as The Charters of Freedom, and to material on teaching with primary documents.

Subject(s): Government Publications—History

American Memory

http://memory.loc.gov/ammem/

Description: The Library of Congress's American Memory website provides online versions of distinctive historical Americana materials from the library's collections. These include digitized photographs, manuscripts, rare books, maps, recorded sound, and moving pictures. The diverse collections include Civil War photographs, the papers of Thomas Jefferson, nineteenth-century American sheet music, and late eighteenth-century maps of North America. The collections can be accessed in a number of ways, such as browsing by topic, historical time period, or the material's original format type. A popular "Today in History" feature links information on event anniversaries to items from the American Memory collection. The site also provides a section for teachers with guides to using primary source materials in the classroom.

Subject(s): Digital Libraries; History

General Land Office (GLO) Records Automation – BLM

https://glorecords.blm.gov/default.aspx

Description: This site provides access to federal land conveyance records, as well as to the initial transfer of land titles from the federal government to individuals, for certain states and time periods. It can be of use to genealogists tracking the location of individuals in the past.

According to the website, "Due to organization of documents in the GLO collection, this site does not currently contain every Federal title record issued for the Public Land States."

Subject(s): Genealogy; Public Lands—History

The Civil War

https://www.nps.gov/civilwar/index.htm

Description: The NPS has designed this website for the sesquicentennial anniversary of the American Civil War, which was observed from 2011 to 2015. It provides information on the 70-plus parks with resources related to Civil War history, programs related to the protection of historic battlefields, and the role of African Americans in the Civil War. The site also links to the NPS's Civil War Soldiers and Sailors System (CWSS), a database of servicemen from both sides during the Civil War.

Subject(s): Civil War (United States); National Parks and Reserves—History

Discover History and Historic Preservation

https://www.nps.gov/history/index.htm

Description: The Discover History and Historic Preservation website is a portal to the cultural information available from NPS websites and publications. Dropdown menus on the homepage allow users to find a program or grant by topic. The site also has extensive information on tax credits and other programs to encourage the preservation of cultural resources.

This website is a useful and well-designed portal for exploring the wide range of resources available through the NPS. Several of its resources are described in separate entries in this book.

Subject(s): Historic Sites; National Parks and Reserves—History

A Guide to the War of 1812

http://www.loc.gov/rr/program/bib/1812/

Description: This Library of Congress website presents an online compilation of material on the War of 1812. Materials include presidential papers, online exhibitions, information from the Prints & Photographs Online Catalog (PPOC), and links to external websites. Bibliographies for adults and children are also present.

Subject(s): War of 1812

Heritage Documentation Programs (HDP)

https://www.nps.gov/hdp/

Description: HDP administers the Historic American Buildings Survey (HABS) and its companion programs, the Historic American Engineering Record (HAER) and Historic American Landscapes Survey (HALS). The site also carries the standards and guidelines for HDP's historical documentation drawings.

This website links to the database of the program's architectural, engineering, and landscape documentation at the Library of Congress, which can be found at http://www.loc.gov/pictures/collection/hh/. Information is provided about a wide range of structures, including the Pueblo of Acoma, windmills, one-room schools, and the Golden Gate Bridge.

Subject(s): Architecture—History; Civil Engineering—History

JFK Assassination Records

https://www.archives.gov/research/jfk

Description: The President John F. Kennedy Assassination Records Collection Act of 1992 requires that all records related to his assassination in 1963 be housed in a single NARA collection. This website provides descriptions and finding aids for the physical collection of records, which can be viewed in NARA's College Park, MD, research rooms. Online finding aids include the JFK Collection Register, which lists all of the records in the collection at the general series level, and the JFK Database Search, which is an index of many of the documents in the collection.

Subject(s): Archives; President—History

Military Resources: War of 1812

https://www.archives.gov/research/military/war-of-1812

Description: The bicentennial commemoration of the War of 1812 began in 2012. NARA has provided this website of relevant military records information; sections include Genealogical Records of the War of 1812, War of 1812 Discharge Certificates, Genealogical Fallout from the War of 1812, and Records About Impressed Seamen, 1793–1814. The site also links to outside pages, which discuss such topics as "The Star-Spangled Banner" and its role in the war.

Subject(s): Military History; War of 1812

National Historical Publications and Records Commission (NHPRC)

https://www.archives.gov/nhprc

Description: NHPRC is a NARA grant-making affiliate whose purpose is to help identify, preserve, and provide public access to records, photographs, and other materials that document American history. Its website has directories of commission members, staff, and state coordinators, along with information about the projects funded by the commission and how to apply for and administer a grant.

Subject(s): Archives—Grants

National Register of Historic Places (NRHP)

https://www.nps.gov/nr/

Description: On its website, the National Register describes itself as "the official list of the Nation's historic places worthy of preservation." The site provides information about how to get a property listed on the National Register and what a listing means for the property owner. The site features a database of places listed in or determined eligible for the National Register, as well as a weekly list of new properties. The Publications section has bulletins and brochures about the National Register process, including a basic brochure about the program available in English and Spanish.

Subject(s): Historic Sites

Naval History and Heritage Command (NHHC)

https://www.history.navy.mil/

Description: The Naval Historical Center (NHC) was renamed the Naval History and Heritage Command in 2008. The NHHC collects, preserves, and makes available artifacts, documents, and art related to U.S. Navy history. The NHHC website links to information from Navy libraries, Navy museums, art collections, archives, and the underwater archaeology program under its management. Its website contains numerous online collections, exhibits, publications, and guides to information on U.S. Navy history and traditions.

Subject(s): Military History

Social Security History

https://www.ssa.gov/history/

Description: The Social Security History website provides extensive information and documentation on both the SSA and the Social Security program. It includes transcripts and audio files of presidential statements and conversations, oral history interviews, and legislative history documents, as well as a photo gallery, chronology, and other resources.

Subject(s): Social Security—History

State-Level Lists of Fatal Casualties of the Korean War and the Vietnam War

https://www.archives.gov/research/military/korean-war/casualty-lists

Description: NARA's Electronic Records Archives (ERA) has indexed the records for U.S. military casualties from the Korean War and the Vietnam War. For the Korean War, the database includes records for persons who died as a result of hostilities during the 1950–1954 period, including those who died while missing or captured. For the Vietnam War, the database includes records for persons who died during the 1956–2006 period as a result of hostile or nonhostile occurrences in the Southeast Asian Combat Area, including those who died while missing or captured. Full casualty records may be retrieved online through the Access to Archival Databases (AAD) system at http://aad.archives.gov/aad/.

Subject(s): Korean War; Vietnam War

U.S. Army Center of Military History (CMH)

https://history.army.mil/index.html

Description: The Center of Military History site offers full-text military history books, documents, and a museum display of army art. The majority of the collection can be found in the Resources/Research section. The Unit History section features the Army Lineage Series. The FAQ section addresses questions such as finding official unit records and the origin of the 21-gun salute. The site has a Medal of Honor citations list and a directory of Army museums. It also features a series of guides about researching military history, including information on oral history techniques, and a separate section about the history of military history.

Subject(s): Military History

U.S. Army Heritage and Education Center (USAHEC)

http://ahec.armywarcollege.edu/index.cfm

Description: USAHEC encompasses the Military History Institute (USAMHI), Army Heritage Museum (AHM), Historical Services Division (HSD), and Army War College (USAWC) Library; there is also a visitor and education center. The site has a catalog of the USAHEC collections, digitized photographs and documents, and research guides including numerous Civil War bibliographies. The site also presents multimedia exhibitions on several topics, including a profile of General Omar Bradley.

Subject(s): Military History

Veterans History Project

http://www.loc.gov/vets/

Description: The Veterans History Project collects, presents, and preserves firsthand accounts of U.S. veterans from wars, including World War I, World War II, the Korean War, the Vietnam War, the Persian Gulf War, the Iraq War, and the current war in Afghanistan. The accounts include letters, photographs, and oral histories in audio and video formats. Records describing the collections can be searched in a database, and digitized collections can be viewed or listened to online. The site also includes information on how to submit veterans' stories to the collection.

Subject(s): Veterans—History

Vietnam-Era Prisoner-of-War (POW) / Missing-in-Action (MIA) Database

http://lcweb2.loc.gov/pow/

Description: This database indexes government documents related to U.S. military personnel who were listed as unaccounted for in Southeast Asia during American involvement in Vietnam. Most of the documents are available to view online. The formal title of the collection is "Correlated and Uncorrelated Information Relating to Missing Americans in Southeast Asia."

Subject(s): Prisoners of War

Web Archiving

http://www.loc.gov/webarchiving/

Description: This website is the Web Archiving homepage for the Library of Congress. In 2000, the library established a pilot project to select, save, and catalogue historical information that had previously appeared exclusively on websites and might otherwise have been lost to future researchers. The collections were built around events such as the September 11, 2001, terrorist attacks and the presidential election of 2000. The success of that project, called MINERVA (Mapping the Internet Electronic Resources Virtual Archive), led to the creation of the library's Web Archive Collections, which is linked to from the site above but can be accessed directly at http://loc.gov/websites/collections/.

Subject(s): Digital Libraries; World Wide Web—History

LIBRARIES

Air University Library Index to Military Periodicals (AULIMP)

http://libguides.lib.msu.edu/AULIMP

Description: AULIMP is a website database of citations to journal, magazine, and trade paper articles on the topics of defense and aeronautics. The index goes back to 1988 and can be searched by author, subject, article title, journal title, and date range. Search results do not link to the full-text versions of the articles, but the Air University Library provides a list of indexed periodicals with online editions.

Subject(s): Defense Research

Archives Library Information Center (ALIC)

https://www.archives.gov/research/alic

Description: ALIC serves National Archives staff and researchers, both on site and online. The ALIC website links to the center's collection catalog, full-text versions of NARA publications, and finding guides for NARA records. The Reference at Your Desk section organizes web links for researching such topics as records management, genealogy, Congress, presidents, diplomacy, and military history. Some commercial databases linked on the ALIC page are only available to staff or on-site researchers.

Subject(s): Archives—Research; Genealogy

Bureau of Land Management Library

https://www.blm.gov/learn/blm-library

Description: The BLM Library website links to current and archival BLM publications and to a page of links to online resources on such topics as forests, plants, and weeds. The BLM library is in the process of building a new website, which will include our comprehensive range of services, including access to the extensive library catalog, publications, journals, databases, and subject guides.

Subject(s): Public Lands—Research

Conservation Library —USFWS

https://nctc.fws.gov/resources/knowledge-resources/

Description: The Conservation Library primarily serves the staff and students of the National Conservation Training Center (NCTC), where it is located. The library website links to a number of conservation-related periodicals online.

Subject(s): Conservation (Natural Resources)

D'Azzo Research Library

https://www.afit.edu/library/

Description: The D'Azzo Research Library supports the Air Force Institute of Technology (AFIT) and the Air Force Research Laboratory (AFRL). The library's website offers public access to its online library catalog, but many of the resources are available for use only by the authorized researchers that the library supports.

Subject(s): Scientific and Technical Information

Department of the Interior Library

https://www.doi.gov/library/

Description: The DOI Library website is primarily intended for use by DOI staff and library visitors. The library's collections include books and journals on such topics as public lands, Native Americans, wildlife conservation, mining, and Earth sciences. In the Guides to the Internet section the site offers some publically accessible resources on subjects including archeology, climate change, plants, water supply, and animals and wildlife.

Subject(s): Public Lands—Research

Department of Justice Libraries

https://www.justice.gov/jmd/ls

Description: The libraries of the Justice Department primarily serve Justice employees. The libraries are open to the public by appointment only for access to government depository items or unique titles.

Subject(s): Law Libraries

Engineer Research and Development Center (ERDC) Library

http://www.erdc.usace.army.mil/library.aspx

Description: The ERDC Library's website provides access to its online catalog and ERDC online publications.

Subject(s): Civil Engineering—Research

EPA National Library Network

https://www.epa.gov/libraries

Description: This website links to all the libraries in the EPA National Library Network, as well as to the National Service Center for Environmental Publications (NSCEP). Also accessible from the site is the EPA National Library Catalog, which is searchable by library, keyword, title, author, OCLC number, and report/call number.

Subject(s): Environmental Protection—Research

Subject(s): Law Enforcement—Research

Federal Bureau of Prisons Library

https://bop.library.net/

Description: This website is primarily a web interface for the library catalog. The site also includes a description of the library, a periodicals list, and a video list.

Subject(s): Prisons—Research

Federal Depository Library Program (FDLP)

https://www.fdlp.gov/

Description: To facilitate public access to federal government information, FDLP provides print and electronic government publications to over 1,000 designated depository libraries open to the public throughout the country. This webpage provides an explanation of the program and a searchable directory of the federal depository libraries.

Subject(s): Federal Depository Library Program

Federal Library and Information Network (FEDLINK)

http://www.loc.gov/flicc/

Description: FEDLINK and FLICC provide service and guidance to federal libraries and information centers. The website's resources will be of interest primarily to librarians, particularly federal librarians, and to vendors specializing in the federal library market.

Subject(s): Libraries

Fermi National Accelerator Laboratory (Fermilab) Library

http://ccd.fnal.gov/library/

Description: The Fermilab Library website features access to its online catalog, journal list, and documents and preprints from the lab. Some databases on the site are only available to Fermilab staff.

Subject(s): Physics—Research; Preprints

Geological Survey (USGS) Libraries Program

https://library.usgs.gov/

Description: The USGS Libraries Program is headquartered in Reston, VA, and has an additional four branches throughout the country. The program's website offers access to its catalog and under the Maps, Imagery, and Publications headline has an extensive set of web links on map topics.

Subject(s): Geology—Research; Maps and Mapping

Goddard Library Repository

https://gsfcir.gsfc.nasa.gov/

Description: The Goddard Library Repository is an online storehouse that was developed and is managed by the Goddard Library. The Repository's purpose is to "store, distribute, and preserve the digital resources of NASA GSFC." (from the website) On the Search All Collections page, the site allows users to search through the repository's digital collections. The library's audio and video collections of, as well as information about, colloquia and seminars going back to 1967 are available in the Colloquia Collection section.

Subject(s): Scientific and Technical Information

GOVDOC-L

http://govdoc-l.org

Description: This is the oldest (and still the primary) e-mail list for government documents librarians. While it is neither hosted nor sponsored by the federal government, the discussions, questions, and announcements relate directly to government information and the practice of government documents librarianship.

Previously, the Government Publishing Office (GPO) used GOVDOC-L for its official announcements to depository libraries. GPO now has its own announcements e-mail service through the Federal Depository Library Program (FDLP)—those interested can sign-up at https://www.fdlp.gov/news-and-events/.

Subject(s): Federal Depository Library Program; Email Lists

Ike Skelton Combined Arms Research Library (CARL)

https://usacac.army.mil/organizations/cace/carl/

Description: CARL, according to its website, "is the research center for the CGSC and the Combined Arms Center (CAC). It also serves other Training and Doctrine Command (TRADOC) installations as well as military scholars and researchers throughout the United States and overseas." Its Digital Library section has several digitized and indexed collections, such as the World War II Operational Documents and School of Advanced Military Studies Monographs.

Subject(s): Military Information

Library of Congress

https://www.loc.gov/

Description: As the largest library in the world, it is only fitting that the Library of Congress website should be one of the most extensive and information-packed governmental library websites. Its American Memory section, with scanned images, movies, audio files, and other reproductions of historic documents, is a leading example of the how the Internet is being used to make rare collections available to the public. The site's Exhibitions section has digital versions of major library exhibitions, past and present. A section called "Especially For..." organizes information by audience, including researchers, librarians, teachers, publishers, and kids and families. The section for researchers includes links to the websites for the library's special reading rooms, such as the Hispanic Area Studies, Science and Technology, and the Recorded Sound Reference Center. The library also provides links to its blogs, podcasts, webcasts, and presence on third-party sites such as Facebook and Twitter.

The main Library of Congress online catalog contains approximately 18 million records representing books, serials, computer files, manuscripts, cartographic materials, music, sound recordings, and visual materials. The library also has an online catalog for its special Prints and Photographs and Sound Recordings collections.

The library site links to the legislative information service THOMAS, the Copyright Office, the National Library Service for the Blind and Physically Handicapped, and more. The websites for some of the specialized collections and services are described in more detail elsewhere in this publication.

While the website offers only a small fraction of the material available at the library itself, it does provide a significant collection of free online material as well as detailed information about the library's collections and services. This is a large and well structured website that offers substantial resources of interest to librarians, teachers, researchers, publishers, lawyers, Congress, and the general public.

Subject(s): Digital Libraries; Libraries; United States History

Library of Congress Blog

https://blogs.loc.gov/loc/

Description: Managed by the public affairs office, the Library of Congress blog covers news about the institution's collections, events, and policies. Comments are permitted.

Subject(s): Blogs

Library of Congress Online Catalog

https://catalog.loc.gov/

Description: The Library of Congress Online Catalog is a database of over 18 million records representing books, serials, computer files, manuscripts, cartographic materials, music, sound recordings, and visual materials in the collections. The Online Catalog also provides cross-references, notes, and circulation status as well as information about materials still in the acquisitions stage. Additional information on the catalog is provided in the Frequently Asked Questions section. The Online Catalog page also links to online catalogs maintained for the Library of Congress Prints & Photographs Division and the Recorded Sound Reference Center.

Subject(s): Library Catalogs

Library of the Marine Corps (LoMC)

http://grc-usmcu.libguides.com/friendly.php?s=library

Description: This website includes some publicly available resources, such as research links and reading lists. While the LoMC's emphasis is on amphibious warfare, it also covers other aspects of and related to the military, including military history, geography, regional and area studies, and technology.

Subject(s): Marine Corps—Research

Library Statistics Program

https://nces.ed.gov/surveys/libraries/

Description: NCES publishes survey data on academic libraries and school media centers. In addition to reading the survey reports, researchers can download the data at this site.

Subject(s): Libraries—Statistics

Los Alamos National Laboratory Research Library

http://www.lanl.gov/library/

Description: The general public can search the LANL Library catalog, but most resources on this website are restricted to authorized LANL users.

Subject(s): Scientific and Technical Information

Military Educational Research Library Network (MERLN)

http://ndu.libguides.com/merln/

Description: MERLN is a resource-rich website maintained by a consortium of military education research libraries. The site's Digital Collections section features military education research materials digitized by MERLN participants. The site also has digitized White Papers from foreign ministries of defense. Military Policy Awareness Links (MiPALs) are MERLN web bibliographies on such topics as Afghanistan, North Korea, and Terrorism; they are particularly helpful for reference and research. The Publications section provides a convenient collection of annotated links to journals and publications available from MERLN member sites.

Subject(s): Military Information

Mine Safety and Health Administration (MSHA) Library Information

https://arlweb.msha.gov/training/library/library.htm

Description: The Technical Information Center and Library of the National Mine Health and Safety Academy is located in West Virginia. The physical collection includes current publications, the Accident Investigation File Archive, historic photographs, archival material from the former Bureau of Mines, and materials relating to major mine disasters in the United States from 1840 to the present. Online, the library site provides access to its catalog and the MSHA Digital Library, which is divided into sections for accident reports, research material, photographs, and moving images.

Subject(s): Mining—Research

Muir S. Fairchild Research Information Center (MSFRIC)

http://www.airuniversity.af.mil/MSFRIC/

Description: Many of the resources available through this Air University library website are restricted to AU users. However, the site provides public access to online bibliographies compiled by the library staff about topics such as leadership, unmanned systems, and terrorism.

Subject(s): Military Information; Bibliographies

NASA Headquarters Library

https://www.hq.nasa.gov/office/hqlibrary/

Description: The NASA Headquarters Library serves NASA staff and provides information online for the public. The library catalog and selected other resources on the library website are only available to staff. For the public, the library's site provides online bibliographies, links to NASA documents databases, and links to NASA video and imagery sites. The Browse Topics section of the site organizes bibliographies and web links under such topics as aerospace, engineering, science, and NASA itself.

Subject(s): Space—Research

National Agricultural Library (NAL)

https://www.nal.usda.gov/

Description: The National Agricultural Library is a major source for national and international agricultural information. The NAL website acts as a gateway to the library's resources and associated institutions. The NAL Catalog, also known as AGRICOLA, is an extensive database of published agriculture information. NAL Collections include the National Agricultural Library Digital Collections (NALDC). The website also links to the NAL's *Agricultural Thesaurus*, an online vocabulary look-up tool for agricultural and biological terms, and a glossary of over 4,000 terms related to agriculture. The thesaurus and the glossary are available in both English and Spanish. The site can be browsed by audience, with sections for USDA employees, librarians, and kids and teens.

This site can be used as an excellent starting point for finding agricultural information. NAL helpfully organizes its many resources by topic, such as Animals and Livestock, Food and Human Nutrition, and Rural Development.

Subject(s): Agriculture Information; Libraries

NARA Locations Nationwide

https://www.archives.gov/locations

Description: The National Archives operates research facilities across the United States, including NARA regional facilities and presidential libraries. This website provides collections and location information for each facility. The NARA regional facilities typically offer genealogy resources, archived federal agency records from the region, and federal courts records including bankruptcy cases. NARA Presidential Library websites, linked from this site, are described in a separate entry in this section.

Subject(s): Archives; Genealogy—Research

National Defense University (NDU) Library

http://www.ndu.edu/libraries.aspx

Description: The NDU Library resources available online include the library catalog, professional military reading lists, digitized collections, special commission reports on national defense, and related topics. The site also hosts the Military Education Research Library Network (MERLN), described elsewhere in this section.

Subject(s): Military Information

National Institute of Corrections (NIC) Library

https://nicic.gov/library-overview

Description: The NIC Library collects published and unpublished material on the topics of correctional operations and policies, offender programs, and special offender issues. The library staff provides research assistance, giving priority for custom research to corrections professionals. The library website organizes and links to a wealth of studies, documents, statistical reports, online videos and other content covering corrections topics.

Subject(s): Prisons—Research

National Institute of Environmental Health Sciences (NIEHS) Library

https://www.niehs.nih.gov/research/resources/library/

Description: The NIEHS Library serves the scientific and administrative staff of NIEHS but also provides limited services to the public.

Subject(s): Health and Safety—Research

National Institute of Standards and Technology (NIST) Virtual Library

https://www.nist.gov/nist-research-library

Description: Beyond general information about the library and its services, the NIST Virtual Library website offers its online catalog, standards and patent information, and publications. Many of the resources on the site are restricted to NIST staff.

Subject(s): Scientific and Technical Information

National Library of Education (NLE)

https://ies.ed.gov/ncee/projects/nle/

Description: NLE, though established in 1994, has roots going back to the 19th century. Its collections are intended for use by the general public, the education community, and government agencies. The site links to the library's catalog, as well as to the Education Resources Information Center (ERIC) and the What Works Clearinghouse (WWC).

Subject(s): Libraries

National Library of Medicine (NLM)

https://www.nlm.nih.gov/

Description: As a leading center for health sciences information, the National Library of Medicine offers a wealth of resources through its website. The site's homepage provides quick links to major NLM databases—such as PubMed and MedlinePlus—and to information for NLM client groups: the general public, health care professionals, researchers, librarians, and publishers. Links to NLM's social media pages are provided.

The homepage shows the full scope of the website's content. It organizes links under Explore NLM; Research at NLM; NLM for You; and Find, Read, Learn: Health Information, Library Catalog & Services (includes NLM publications), History of Medicine, Online Exhibitions & Digital Projects, Human Genome Resources, Biomedical Research & Informatics (which includes the UMLS/Unified Medical Language System), Environmental Health & Toxicology, About NLM, Grants & Funding, Training & Outreach, Network of Medical Libraries, and Health Services Research & Public Health.

The NLM website is a gateway to the various programs and information resources offered by the library. Many of the specific online resources created by NLM are described elsewhere in this book.

Subject(s): Libraries; Medical Information

National Library Service for the Blind and Physically Handicapped (NLS)

https://www.loc.gov/nls/

Description: NLS administers a free library program that circulates Braille and recorded materials to eligible borrowers through a network of cooperating libraries. The Learn section of its website has information on how NLS works, how to sign up, and where NLS network libraries are located. The website provides access to the online catalog of Braille and audio books, the *Braille Book Review*, and other bibliographies. The NLS/BPH Publications section of the site includes NLS fact sheets, bibliographies, circulars, and directories of libraries and resources related to reading material for the blind and physically handicapped. It also includes information on digital talking books and Web-Braille.

The NLS site is designed for text-based browsers, such as Lynx, that are frequently used by blind readers. See the About This Site section for more information.

Subject(s): Libraries; Vision Disorders

National Network of Libraries of Medicine (NN/LM)

https://nnlm.gov/

Description: NN/LM is coordinated by the National Library of Medicine (NLM) with the goal of improving access to medical information for both health professionals and the public. The website has a directory of member libraries, information on each regional component of NN/LM, training schedules and modules, and funding opportunities. The site also has a section about finding and using health information on the Internet.

Librarians and health educators are the intended audiences for much of the information on this site. General public users interested in medical libraries and information systems may also find helpful material.

Subject(s): Libraries; Medical Information

NIH Library

https://nihlibrary.nih.gov/Pages/default.aspx

Description: The NIH Library website features information about the library and services. Most information is restricted to authorized users; however, some information and social media links are available to the public.

Subject(s): Medical Information

NOAA Central Library

https://library.noaa.gov/

Description: The NOAA Central Library and regional libraries provide information and research support to NOAA staff and the public on topics such as atmospheric sciences, oceanography, and cartography. The NOAA Library website links to their many digital collections, including the NOAA Photo Library, digitized historical documents on U.S. fisheries, and the old Weather Bureau. The Subject Guides link in the Research Tools section of the website points to the WINDandSEA Internet Guide of over 1,000 links to websites concerned with oceanic and atmospheric issues. The site also has a number of other specialized web bibliographies and subject guides for researchers.

The NOAA Central Library is one of over 30 specialized NOAA libraries across the nation; the website links to all NOAA Libraries sites. Disciplines covered by the libraries include weather and atmospheric sciences, oceanography, ocean engineering, nautical charting, marine ecology, marine resources, ecosystems, coastal studies, aeronomy, geodesy, cartography, and mathematics and statistics.

Subject(s): Atmospheric Sciences—Research; Oceanography—Research

NOAA Seattle Library

https://www.wrclib.noaa.gov/

Description: This regional NOAA library serves NOAA agencies in the West. The site's Environmental Data Sources section is particularly useful. It provides a portal to data sets from the government and educational institutions, organized by subject, region, and provider.

Subject(s): Atmospheric Sciences—Research

National Radio Astronomy Observatory (NRAO) Library

http://library.nrao.edu

Description: This website features the library's catalog and the NRAO-Papers database of published papers and preprints for staff and visitor works. Some sections of the site are restricted to NRAO staff.

Subject(s): Astronomy—Research; Preprints

National Transportation Library (NTL)

https://ntl.bts.gov/

Description: NTL serves federal, state, and local governments. NTL's website also links to transportation information and reference services for the general public. Publicly available databases include the NTL catalog, the *Transportation Research Thesaurus* (*TRT*), and the cooperatively produced Transportation Research International Documentation (TRID) online database of published transportation research from around the world. The site's Research/Tools section links to numerous reference sources, such as transportation statistics, directories of transportation-related organizations, and transportation glossaries.

Subject(s): Transportation—Research

Naval Academy Nimitz Library

https://www.usna.edu/Library/

Description: The Nimitz Library website features information about the library and its services. Most resources are accessible to Naval Academy faculty and students only. Under Digital Collections, several online historical exhibitions can be accessed by the public, including one on the annual Army-Navy football game which dates back to 1890.

Subject(s): Engineering Research

Naval Observatory James Melville Gilliss Library

http://www.usno.navy.mil/usno/library/

Description: This site provides access to the United States Naval Observatory Library's online catalog and collection of historical photos of the observatory, astronomers, telescopes, and astronomy texts.

Subject(s): Astronomy—Research

Northwest and Alaska Fisheries Science Centers Library

https://lib.nwfsc.noaa.gov/

Description: This library supports the centers and field stations located in the Pacific Northwest and Alaska that serve NOAA's National Marine Fisheries Service, also known as NOAA Fisheries. Its website links to information on fisheries, maps, and charts, with an emphasis on the Pacific region.

Subject(s): Fisheries—Research

Patent and Trademark Resource Centers (PTRCs)

https://www.uspto.gov/learning-and-resources/support-centers/patent-and-trademark-resource-centers-ptrcs

Description: The PTO designates qualified libraries throughout the country to act as PTRCs. These libraries receive printed materials and electronic access from the PTO to assist the general public with researching patent and trademark information. The website provides links to depository and partner library websites, and lists the core publications and databases available through these libraries.

Subject(s): Libraries; Patent Law; Trademarks

Pentagon Digital Library

http://www.whs.mil/library

Description: The Pentagon Digital Library website provides access to numerous resources, including bibliographies, digitized historic materials, and military documents.

Subject(s): Libraries; Military Information

Presidential Libraries and Museums

https://www.archives.gov/presidential-libraries

Description: This National Archives webpage provides general information about the presidential libraries system, as well as guides for doing research in presidential materials. Links to each of the presidential libraries websites are provided, as is information on presidential library museum exhibits. The presidential library system currently includes 13 libraries, one for each president from Herbert Hoover to George W. Bush.

Subject(s): Presidential Documents

Ralph J. Bunche Library

https://www.state.gov/m/a/ls/

Description: This website offers a description of the main DOS library. The library's mission is to support the research needs of State Department personnel, and it offers few services to the public. The site calls this State Department's library "the oldest Federal Government library...founded by the first Secretary of State, Thomas Jefferson, in 1789."

Subject(s): Foreign Policy—Research

Scientific Library at the National Cancer Institute (NCI) at Frederick

https://ncifrederick.cancer.gov/scientificlibrary/

Description: The NCI Scientific Library's website offers public access to its online catalog and links to publications of its researchers. The site also links to PubMed.

Subject(s): Medical Information

Smithsonian Libraries

https://library.si.edu

Description: The 20 Smithsonian libraries support research in areas as wide-ranging areas as space exploration, art and design, tropical biology, and American history. Major resources on the site include the Smithsonian Institution Research Information System (SIRIS) combined catalog of the library collections, a database of images from books and manuscripts in the collections, and information on the Smithsonian special collections.

Subject(s): Libraries

Staff College Automated Military Periodicals Index (SCAMPI)

https://www.lib.umn.edu/indexes/moreinfo?id=6953

Description: SCAMPI indexes defense-related magazines and journals, such as Military Review and the Armed Forces Journal, from 1985 to the present.

Subject(s): Military Information

USAID Knowledge Management (KM) Support

https://www.usaid.gov/what-we-do/global-health/knowledge-management-services-kms-%E2%80%93-examples-products

Description: According to the website, "The focus of USAID's Knowledge Management Program is to connect people to the processes and technology that will help them to work effectively with partners to accomplish

USAID's mission." The website links to the USAID Library catalog and offers economic and social data related to USAID and development.

Subject(s): International Economic Development—Research

Wirtz Labor Library

https://www.dol.gov/oasam/wirtzlaborlibrary/

Description: The Department of Labor's Wirtz Labor Library has a website with the library's online catalog and links to online labor research resources. The site also has a digital library of historical labor publications and an archive of past Labor Department websites.

Subject(s): Libraries; Employment Law

MUSEUMS

Anacostia Community Museum

http://anacostia.si.edu

Description: The Smithsonian Institution's Anacostia Community Museum focuses on the history and culture of the African American community and family. It is located in the historic Washington, D.C., neighborhood of Anacostia, the former home of abolitionist Frederick Douglass. The museum's website has information on its collections and exhibits as well as on its educational resources and visiting the museum.

Subject(s): History; Museums

Cooper Hewitt, Smithsonian Design Museum

https://www.cooperhewitt.org/

Description: Cooper Hewitt, in New York City, concentrates on historic and contemporary design. Its website has information on the museum, its education programs, and the annual National Design Awards.

Subject(s): Arts—Awards and Honors; Museums

Hill Aerospace Museum

http://www.hill.af.mil/Home/Hill-Aerospace-Museum

Description: Located at Hill Air Force Base in Utah, the Hill Aerospace Museum collection includes a wide variety of military aircraft and missiles, munitions and weapons, ground vehicles associated with aircraft and missiles, and thousands of other historical artifacts. Its website provides information about visiting, museum activities and exhibits, and base history.

Subject(s): Aviation—History

Holocaust Memorial Museum (USHMM)

https://www.ushmm.org/

Description: The United States Holocaust Memorial Museum became an independent establishment of the U.S. government under Public Law 106-292. The museum's website provides information about the museum as well as extensive resources on Holocaust education, research, and history. It features a multimedia "Introduction to the Holocaust" and an online Holocaust encyclopedia in 14 languages beyond English. The site includes numerous online exhibitions, a section on Days of Remembrance, and information on contemporary genocide.

Subject(s): Museums; War Crimes—History

Museum Management Program

https://www.nps.gov/museum/

Description: The Museum Management Program supports policy and technical standards for the management of NPS museum collections, including natural, cultural, archival, and manuscript materials. The website has NPS museum collection profiles and information on current exhibits. For museum professionals, it features a calendar of professional events and a listing of laws and regulations relevant to NPS museum administration, archeology, records, and archives. The site also has a section that covers teaching with museum collections. The Virtual Museum Exhibits section is of general interest, with digitized images of objects from the NPS collections.

Subject(s): Museums

National Air and Space Museum (NASM)

https://airandspace.si.edu/

Description: The National Air and Space Museum offers information about the museum and its programs, including the Steven F. Udvar-Hazy Center in Virginia, which features an exhibition hangar, theater, and classrooms. In addition to visitor information, the website has digital images of objects in its collections, an extensive research section, and educational resources.

Subject(s): Aviation; Museums

National Gallery of Art (NGA)

https://www.nga.gov/

Description: On the NGA website, the Visit section includes information about the gallery's location and hours, as well as maps and information about how the NGA is organized and funded. The Collection section offers searches of the collections by artist, title, or subject; searches can also be limited to items for which online images are available.

Subject(s): Museums; Visual Arts

National Museum of African American History and Culture (NMAAHC)

https://nmaahc.si.edu/

Description: Authorized by law in 2003, the National Museum of African American History and Culture is currently organizing traveling exhibitions. The museum building in Washington, D.C., is scheduled to be completed in 2016. In the meantime, the website provides a wealth of online images and information from its collections, as well as information about the gallery at the National Museum of American History.

Subject(s): African Americans—History; Museums

National Museum of African Art

https://africa.si.edu/

Description: The National Museum of African Art website has information about its exhibits, programs, collections, library, and archives. The Collection section has a collections catalog that can be searched by artist or cultural group. The Radio Africa section has African music from the Smithsonian Institution. The site also has a section of activities for children.

This is a colorful, multimedia-providing site that makes use of high-quality photographs, sound, and images.

Subject(s): Museums; Visual Arts; Africa

National Museum of American History

http://americanhistory.si.edu

Description: The National Museum of American History website provides images, online exhibits, and research information related to American history. The site has a large and diverse collection of online exhibitions.

Subject(s): Museums; United States—History

National Museum of the American Indian (NMAI)

http://www.nmai.si.edu

Description: This website describes the Smithsonian NMAI facilities in New York City and Washington, D.C. Major sections include Visit, Explore, Support, Connect, and Shop.

Subject(s): Museums; American Indians

National Museum of Health and Medicine (NMHM)

http://www.medicalmuseum.mil

Description: The National Museum of Health and Medicine's main focus is on American military medicine. Its collections include anatomical specimens and medical devices, many of which are from the Civil War era, when the museum was established. This website has online guides to the museum's collections and photographs of many of its exhibits.

Subject(s): Medicine and Medical Devices—History; Museums

National Museum of Natural History

https://naturalhistory.si.edu/

Description: This website presents information about the National Museum of Natural History's exhibits, collections, programs, and research. The Research & Collections section features a collections database, bibliographies, and links to the museum's various Science Departments (Anthropology, Botany, Entomology, Invertebrate Zoology, Mineral Sciences, Paleobiology, and Vertebrate Zoology). The Explore a Topic section presents material from the museum organized into broad themes, such as "The Evolving Earth," "The Diversity of Life," and "The Human Connection."

Subject(s): Museums; Natural History

National Postal Museum

https://postalmuseum.si.edu/

Description: The National Postal Museum is funded by the U.S. Postal Service, the Smithsonian Institution's federal appropriation, and private gifts. The museum's collections include stamps, vehicles used to transport the mail, mailboxes, postage meters, and greeting cards. Major sections of its website include Exhibits, Collection, Education, Stamp Collecting, Research, Get Involved, and Activities (for both kids and adults).

Subject(s): Postage Stamps; Postal Service—History

Naval Undersea Museum

http://www.navalunderseamuseum.org

Description: The Naval Undersea Museum in Washington State presents submarines, torpedoes, diving equipment, and other artifacts related to naval undersea history, science, and operations. This website includes information about exhibits, volunteering, and visiting the museum.

Subject(s): Museums; Underwater Warfare—History

Smithsonian American Art Museum (SAAM)

https://americanart.si.edu/

Description: This website features an illustrated narrative overview of the museum's collections, and information about its current exhibits and events. The Luce Center on the site (under Collections) provides images of more than 3,000 items in SAAM's collection. The SAAM site also has information about the Renwick Gallery, which specializes in American crafts and decorative arts.

Subject(s): Arts; Museums

United States Botanic Garden (USBG)

https://www.usbg.gov/

Description: The USBG website has information about its gardens, production facility, and conservatory on the National Mall. The site offers visitor information, a virtual tour, and a description of the Botanic Garden's plant collections and work in plant conservation. Under the Grow heading, USBG provides gardening tips and a Plant Hotline.

Subject(s): Botany

RECREATION

America's Byways®

https://www.fhwa.dot.gov/byways

Description: The Department of Transportation has designated certain roads as National Scenic Byways, or All-American Roads, based on their archaeological, cultural, historic, natural, recreational, and scenic qualities. This website provides information about the designated roads or byways. It offers maps and descriptions of noteworthy sites along the routes.

Subject(s): Highways and Roads

Corps Lakes Gateway

https://corpslakes.erdc.dren.mil/visitors/visitors.cfm

Description: Corps Lakes Gateway describes outdoor recreation opportunities at lakes managed by the Army Corps of Engineers. The site has a clickable U.S. map for finding Corps lakes and related information.

Subject(s): Lakes; Outdoor Recreation

Fishing

https://www.fws.gov/fishing/

Description: This FWS website focuses on recreational fishing. The site describes the agency's work to improve fisheries and links to other organizations that provide information for recreational fishers. It features national and state fishing statistics from the National Survey of Fishing, Hunting, and Wildlife-Associated Recreation as well as hunting and fishing license statistics back to 1975.

Subject(s): Fishing

Forest Service (USFS) Recreational Activities

https://www.fs.fed.us/recreation/

Description: The Forest Service offers this website as an overview of the recreational opportunities on, and the guidelines for the use of, the National Forests and Grasslands. The forests and grasslands can be found by using a clickable map or by browsing by state or site name. Other sections provide information about passes, permits, travel advisories, and volunteer opportunities.

Subject(s): National Forests

National Avalanche Center (NAC)

https://avalanche.org/

Description: This Forest Service site provides detailed avalanche awareness information and interactive guides for snowmobilers, skiers, snowboarders, snowshoers, and others exploring the steep and snowy backcountry.

Subject(s): Outdoor Recreation; Avalanches

National Park Service (NPS)

https://www.nps.gov/index.htm

Description: The official NPS website is the primary source for information about America's national parks. It includes information about national memorials, national battlefields, national seashores, national historic sites, and other related sites. The Find a Park section links to information on each of the NPS locations by name, state, or topic (such as Civil War, fossils/dinosaurs, or geysers/hot springs). Individual parks have their own webpages, which contain printable travel guides, maps, and background information. The Discover History section of the site describes significant people, places, and events associated with the national parks. It offers learning programs and information about historic preservation grants. The Explore Nature section organizes a wealth of information related to science and environmental practices in the parks, under the Air Resources, Biological Resources, Geologic Resources, Natural Sounds & Night Skies, and Water Resources categories. The About Us section has information on laws, regulations, policy, budget, and publications. The site's news section compiles daily news from a number of NPS sources. Elsewhere on the site, there is a section for kids and teachers, information on volunteering at the parks, links to social media, and video features about the parks and NPS.

With its broad approach to the resources and heritage of the national parks system, the NPS website is relevant for many audiences, including travelers, scientists, history buffs, and teachers.

Subject(s): Historic Preservation; National Parks and Reserves

National Trails System

https://www.nps.gov/ncrc/programs/nts/

Description: The National Trails System is a network of scenic, historic, and recreational trails administered by the Department of the Interior and the Department of Agriculture in partnership with other agencies and organizations. Its website includes a trail system map, information about designating national scenic and national historic trails, and a link to the nonprofit Partnership for the National Trails System organization's website.

Subject(s): Outdoor Recreation

National Zoological Park

https://nationalzoo.si.edu/

Description: The National Zoo's website features information and photos for visitors and researchers. The Giant Pandas section (under the Animals heading) features Panda Cams, a panda photo gallery, and giant panda facts. Live cams are available for other animals as well. The Education section includes field trip guides, classroom resources, and information on further education and training opportunities. The Science section covers zoological medicine, land and aquatic ecosystems, biodiversity, and endangered species science, and links to information from the specialized research centers of the Smithsonian Conservation Biology Institute.

Subject(s): Animals; Conservation Biology; Zoos

The Presidio

https://www.presidio.gov/

Description: The Presidio, a former U.S. Army installation in San Francisco, is now a National Historic Landmark District (NHLD). The Presidio Trust, a federal agency established by Congress in 1996, manages it. This website provides information about the management of the Presidio and visiting the park.

Subject(s): Historic Sites

Recreation.gov

https://www.recreation.gov/

Description: Recreation.gov is designed to be a one-stop portal for learning about and getting permits and reservations for activities on public lands. The website is an interagency project, with information about recreation opportunities on land managed by the Army Corps of Engineers, Bureau of Land Management, Bureau of Reclamation, Forest Service, and National Park Service. Users can find recreation locations by state or activity (such as boating, camping, fishing, or hiking) or by a clickable U.S. map. For locations requiring a reservation, the website has an online reservation system.

Subject(s): Outdoor Recreation

Your Guide to Fishing on National Wildlife Refuges

https://www.fws.gov/refuges/fishingguide/

Description: This interactive online guide displays wildlife refuge information by state and by type of fish available. The Special Features section includes tips about catch and release as well as invasive aquatic species.

Subject(s): Fishing

REFERENCE

Official U.S. Time

https://www.time.gov/

Description: This website provides the current time in all U.S. time zones, including the time zones for the U.S. Pacific territories.

Subject(s): Time

Plain Language

https://www.plainlanguage.gov/

Description: The Plain Language website promotes the improvement of communications from the federal government to the public. The idea is to use "plain language" that can be understood at first reading. Government agencies are the intended audience. The site includes relevant examples, guidelines, and resources. The site is managed by the federal employees group Plain Language Action and Information Network.

While this site is intended for government writers, other writers will also find it to be a useful reference as well.

Subject(s): Writing

Popular Baby Names

https://www.ssa.gov/oact/babynames/

Description: This database of trends in baby names is compiled from names listed on Social Security card applications. Users can search for the most popular baby names by year and by state, track the popularity of a name over time, or look up popular names for twins.

Subject(s): Families

Chapter Five

Defense and Intelligence

The national defense, homeland security, and intelligence operations of the United States are all represented to varying degrees on the Internet. The Department of Defense (DoD) and the nation's armed forces, in particular, maintain numerous publicly accessible websites. These sites cover topics ranging from current military operations, to advanced research, to administrative and acquisitions matters. This chapter concludes with a Military Morale and Welfare section covering many of the services available for veterans, service members, and their families.

Researchers may also wish to check the International Relations chapter for information on arms treaties, the Education chapter for information on the educational activities managed by the DoD and the armed forces, and the Business and Economics chapter for sites on defense trade controls.

Subsections in this chapter are Armed Forces, Defense Operations, Defense Research, Homeland Security, Intelligence, and Military Morale and Welfare.

ARMED FORCES

Air Education and Training Command (AETC)

http://www.aetc.af.mil

Description: AETC is responsible for Air Force programs in military, technical, and flight training, as well as education programs at many levels. This website provides information on Air Force career opportunities, basic military training, and technical training. It also links to the Air Force Academy, Air Force ROTC, and Officer Training School.

Subject(s): Military Training and Education

Air Force

http://www.af.mil

Description: The emphasis of this central Air Force website is on current news. Along with a wealth of articles, the site features Air Force TV and has links to related social media sites. In addition to current news, the site has information about and from Air Force senior leadership.

The site has convenient links for headquarters, major commands, field operating agencies, bases, and deployed locations.

Subject(s): Air Force; News Services

Air Force Materiel Command (AFMC)

http://www.afmc.af.mil

Description: AFMC equips and supplies the Air Force through supply management, depot maintenance, systems testing and evaluation, information services, and combat support. The AFMC website has current news and background on the command's organization and programs. The Units section links to AFMC field operating agencies, test centers, laboratories, and other establishments.

Subject(s): Military Logistics; Military Supplies

Air Force Personnel Center (AFPC)

http://www.afpc.af.mil

Description: This public website from the Air Force Personnel Center has information for and about military and civilian Air Force personnel. The Library section includes demographic profiles of military and civilian personnel. The site also has personnel news and career information.

Subject(s): Air Force; Civilian Defense Employees

Air Force Reserve Command (AFRC)

http://www.afrc.af.mil

Description: The Air Force Reserve Command website features news, pay information, leadership biographies, fact sheets, and photos. The Join the Air Reserve section links to the official recruiting page.

Subject(s): Military Reserves

Air Force Space Command (AFSPC)

http://www.afspc.af.mil

Description: The Air Force Space Command leads the Air Force's space and cyberspace missions. The website has current news, photos, fact sheets, and a directory of unit websites. The Library section has biographies and fact sheets.

Subject(s): Air Force; Military Computing; Rockets

Air Mobility Command (AMC)

http://www.amc.af.mil

Description: AMC's mission is to provide airlift, air refueling, special air missions, and aeromedical evacuation for U.S. forces. Its public website provides current news, unit information, fact sheets, and biographies of AMC leadership.

Subject(s): Airlifts; Military Logistics

Air Reserve Personnel Center (ARPC)

http://www.arpc.afrc.af.mil

Description: The AFRC Personnel Center website has information about assignments, mobilization, training and education, retirement, separations and discharges, re-enlistments, and other related topics.

Subject(s): Military Reserves

AirForce.com

https://www.airforce.com/

Description: This Air Force recruitment website offers information for prospective recruits at all levels. The site also has a live chat feature.

Subject(s): Military Recruiting

Army Live

Army Publishing Directorate (APD)

https://armypubs.army.mil/

Description: The Publishing Directorate is the Army's agency for publishing and distributing information products. The Publications sections features a variety of publications organized into the following categories: Administrative, Technical and Equipment, Doctrine and Training, Engineering, and Medical. Also available on the site are a variety of forms under the Forms heading. The Order Pubs/Forms section links to information for users with and without accounts. The Search section allows for text and proponent searches.

Subject(s): Military Information

Blue Angels

https://www.blueangels.navy.mil/

Description: This website provides information about the choreographed flying of the Navy's Blue Angels squadron, including biographies of the squadron's officers and enlisted team. The site also features show information and a schedule.

Subject(s): Military Aircraft; Navy

Center for Army Lessons Learned (CALL)

https://usacac.army.mil/organizations/mccoe/call

Description: According to its website, "Since 1882, CAC and its predecessor organizations have been engaged in the primary mission of preparing the Army and its leaders for war. At present, this mission is divided between preparing the Army for the Global War on Terrorism and transforming it to meet future threats."

Subject(s): Military information

Coast Guard

https://www.uscg.mil/

Description: The Coast Guard is part of the Department of Homeland Security, but in wartime or when directed by the president it operates under the Secretary of the Navy. The breadth of information on the Coast Guard's website reflects its multiple roles. Its mission includes national defense and homeland security, as well as maritime search and rescue, International Ice Patrol (IIP) operations, polar and domestic waterway icebreaking, bridge administration, navigation assistance, recreational boating safety, vessel traffic management, at-sea enforcement of living marine resource laws and treaty obligations, and at-sea drug and illegal migrant interdiction.

In the About Us section, the site has fact sheets on Coast Guard aircraft, cutters, and boats. It also contains a History subsection with information on lighthouses, information on the Coast Guard Museum, historic photographs, and more. The Our Organization section links to each of the regional Coast Guard districts. The Coast Guard maintains a separate site about boating safety at http://www.uscgboating.org/.

The Coast Guard also has a major website called Homeport at https://homeport.uscg.mil/. It provides more technical and much more in-depth coverage.

Subject(s): Coast Guard; Homeland Security

GoArmy.com

https://www.goarmy.com/

Description: Established as a recruitment site for both the Army and the Army Reserve, this website features information likely to be of interest to prospective members. It includes sections on careers, benefits, and soldier life, and also provides an extra section for parents.

Subject(s): Military Recruiting

Navy Personnel Command (NPC)

http://www.public.navy.mil/bupers-npc/

Sponsor(s): Navy — Bureau of Naval Personnel (BUPERS)

Description: The Navy Personnel Command website serves current officers and enlisted personnel by providing information about pay, benefits, career progression, and quality of life services. It also includes information for retirees. The Reference Library section provides Navy personnel forms, manuals, and regulations, as well as links to various publications, such as *Shift Colors*.

The site will primarily be of interest to people in the Navy. Some sections are only open to authorized, registered users.

Subject(s): Defense Administration

Joint Chiefs of Staff (JCS)

http://www.jcs.mil

Description: The JCS website provides information about the chairman of the Joint Chiefs of Staff, the Joint Chiefs, Joint Staff, and the combatant commands. It also provides links to news, speeches, interviews, and photos.

Subject(s): Military Leadership

Los Angeles Air Force Base

http://www.losangeles.af.mil

Description: The Los Angeles Air Force Base hosts the Space and Missile Systems Center, part of the Air Force Space Command. SMC manages the acquisitions programs for military satellites and space systems. Organizations at the base are described in the website's Units section; they include the Military Satellite Communications (MILSATCOM) Systems Directorate and the 61st Air Base Group. The Library section has leadership biographies and fact sheets on satellite programs and space-based systems.

Subject(s): Air Force Bases; Space Technology

Marine Corps Forces Reserve (MARFORRES)

http://www.marforres.marines.mil

Description: The MARFORRES website has a directory of Reserve units with links to the unit websites. It also has news, photos, and information about joining the Reserves and staying in the Reserves.

Subject(s): Marine Corps

Marine Recruiting

https://www.marines.com/

Description: This website is the Marine Corps recruiting site. The site includes background information on service in the Marine Corps, recruiting contacts, and a companion section for parents and mentors. For general information about the Marines, see the official Marine Corps website at http://www.marines.mil/.

Subject(s): Marine Corps; Military Recruiting

Marines Corps Manpower and Reserve Affairs (M&RA)

https://www.manpower.usmc.mil/webcenter/portal/

Description: The Marines Corps M&RA website is organized into sections for the Active Marine, Reserve Marine, Veteran Marine, Civilian Marine, and Family. Frequently used sections of the site deal with the Wounded Warrior Regiment, awards, promotions, and assignments. Some online systems are limited to eligible, registered users who must log in to receive access.

Subject(s): Marine Corps

National Guard

http://www.nationalguard.mil

Description: The National Guard website provides news and information about the National Guard, its leadership, and Joint Staff organization. The Resources section includes links to National Guard state websites.

Subject(s): National Guard

Naval Network Warfare Command (NETWARCOM)

http://www.public.navy.mil/fltfor/nnwc/Pages/default.aspx

Description: NETWARCOM is concerned with network and information technology, intelligence, information operations, and space systems. The website provides basic information on the command, its leadership, and its core functions.

Subject(s): Military Computing; Military Intelligence

Naval Sea Systems Command (NAVSEA)

http://www.navsea.navy.mil

Description: NAVSEA develops, acquires, modernizes, and maintains affordable ships, ordnance, and systems for the Navy. The NAVSEA website has information on headquarters and leadership and it links to the websites for NAVSEA field activities. Other sections of the site include News, Resources (with a NAVSEA Instructions Library), and Business Partnerships.

Subject(s): Military Ships; Military Technology

Naval Warfare Centers (NWCs)

http://www.navsea.navy.mil/home/warfarecenters.aspx

Description: The Navy's Warfare Centers perform research, development, and testing and evaluation for the Navy's ships and systems. The website provides in-depth information about the Warfare Center Enterprise—which is comprised of the Naval Surface Warfare Center (NSWC) and the Naval Undersea Warfare Center (NUWC)—as well as basic information about each of its ten divisions.

Subject(s): Navy

Navy Reserve (USNR)

https://www.navy.com/about/about-reserve.html

Description: The website includes information about joining the Navy Reserve. It includes links about life in the Navy, joining the Navy, and careers and jobs in the Navy.

Subject(s): Military Reserves

Navy.com

https://www.navy.com/

Description: This is the primary Navy recruiting site. The Careers & Jobs section covers the many fields of specialty for officers or the enlisted. The site also has a Spanish-language version at http://www.navy.com/advisors/en-espanol.html.

Subject(s): Military Recruiting

Office of the Assistant Secretary of the Army for Acquisition, Logistics, and Technology (OASA[ALT])

https://www.army.mil/asaalt/

Description: OASA(ALT) leads Army acquisitions and research and development to support military readiness. The website provides organizational information and links to related sites.

Subject(s): Military Procurement

Office of the Assistant Chief of Staff for Installation Management (OACSIM)

http://www.acsim.army.mil

Description: The Army's Office of the Assistant Chief of Staff for Installation Management is the Army's proponent for military bases and the soldiers, civilians, and families who live on them. The website has information on leadership, staff, and OACSIM division operations.

Subject(s): Army Installations

Redstone Arsenal

http://www.militarybases.us/army/redstone-arsenal

Description: The Redstone Arsenal in Alabama is home to the U.S. Army Aviation and Missile Command (AMCOM) and the Space and Missile Defense Command (SMDC). The website has news and information about these and other units at Redstone. Redstone played an early role in U.S. rocket research and Cold War activities.

Subject(s): Army Bases; Missile Defense; Rockets—History

Soldiers

http://soldiers.dodlive.mil

Description: This is the website for the well-known print publication, *Soldiers*, the official magazine of the Army. The site features selected articles from the magazine going back to 2011.

Subject(s): Army

Space and Naval Warfare Systems Command (SPAWAR)

http://www.public.navy.mil/spawar/Pages/default.aspx

Description: SPAWAR's mission is to acquire, develop, and maintain integrated command, control, communications, computer, intelligence, and surveillance systems. Major sections of this website include Careers, Products & Services, and Support.

Subject(s): Military Technology

Today's Military

https://www.todaysmilitary.com/

Description: Today's Military is an overall guide to the benefits of joining the U.S. armed forces, with information from each military service branch. A special section is tailored to parents and educators.

Subject(s): Military Recruiting

U.S. Africa Command (AFRICOM)

http://www.africom.mil

Description: The U.S. Africa Command, or AFRICOM, was created in 2007. The website includes the command's posture statement, leadership biographies, news, and speech transcripts, and it links to the websites for AFRICOM's subordinate commands. The site is also available in French, Portuguese, and Arabic.

Subject(s): Unified Combatant Commands

U.S. Air Force Live

http://airforcelive.dodlive.mil

Description: This official blog of the United States Air Force is maintained by the Air Force Public Affairs Agency. The blog carries news and stories by those serving in the Air Force. Comments meeting the posted guidelines are accepted. Links to the blog's Facebook and Twitter pages are provided.

Subject(s): Air Force; Blogs

U.S. Air Force Recordings

http://www.music.af.mil/

Description: This site contains a list of active duty bands, air national guard bands and most requested recording. The user is able to choose from several different genres of music are including ceremonial, classical, country, holiday, jazz, and pop and rock.

Subject(s): Air Force; Music

U.S. Army

https://www.army.mil/

Description: This is the central website for the U.S. Army. The site links to Army news services, videos and images, and publications, such as Army strategic documents. Under the Info heading, the Organization section connects users to major commands and units; it also links to installations and facilities, including airfields, barracks, camps, libraries, medical centers, institutes, museums, and more. Other sections under Info cover Army history and heritage, career management, veterans' service organizations, and community outreach; the A–Z section provides a helpful alphabetical listing of Army websites.

This well-organized site should be one of the first stopping points for anyone seeking information about the Army, its bases, or related news. It is also a good resource for active service members, reservists, and those who have retired from the Army.

Subject(s): Army

U.S. Army Cyber Command

http://www.arcyber.army.mil/Pages/ArcyberHome.aspx

Description: "United States Army Cyber Command directs and conducts integrated electronic warfare, information and cyberspace operations as authorized, or directed, to ensure freedom of action in and through cyberspace and the information environment, and to deny the same to our adversaries." It is composed of a professional team defending army networks and providing full-spectrum cyber capabilities.

U.S. Central Command (CENTCOM)

http://www.centcom.mil

Description: CENTCOM is one of the Unified Combatant Commands assigned operational control of U.S. combat forces. Its area of responsibility spans a region from the Horn of Africa to Central Asia and includes Iraq, Afghanistan, and Syria. Its website features current and past news articles and press releases about U.S. involvement in that region going back to 2007. The site also provides photos, leadership information, command history, and links to related military websites. Information is available in Arabic, Russian, Farsi, and Urdu.

Subject(s): Afghanistan; Iraq; Syria; Unified Combatant Commands

U.S. European Command (EUCOM)

http://www.eucom.mil

Description: EUCOM is a Unified Combatant Command (UCC) headquartered in Stuttgart, Germany. EUCOM's area of responsibility includes 51 nations and territories extending from Greenland east to include all of Europe, Turkey, Israel, and Russia. The website carries current news about EUCOM, leadership biographies, an organizational directory, a recommended reading list, and links to the sites for U.S. armed forces in Europe and the George C. Marshall European Center for Security Studies. The site also has a blog and links to the EUCOM presence on social media.

Subject(s): Unified Combatant Commands

Marine Corps

http://www.marines.mil

Description: The official Marine Corps website focuses on current news, featuring articles written by marines. Major sections provide information about USMC Headquarters and links to individual units' webpages. The site connects to other Marine Corps sites of interest on recruiting, careers, community relations, and quality of life issues.

Subject(s): Marine Corps

Navy

http://www.navy.mil

Description: The official website of the Navy features Navy news, leadership biographies, photos, videos, and policy documents such as the Secretary of the Navy's Posture Statement. Under the About heading, the site provides Status of the Navy statistics and links to fun facts and a Command Directory. This section also has organizational information, profiles of current and past Navy ships, and fact sheets on Navy aircraft, weapons systems, submarines, missiles, ships, and other topics. Under Media, the site has archived digitized copies of all issues of the Navy magazine *All Hands* going back to its start in 1922.

Subject(s): Navy

U.S. Northern Command (NORTHCOM)

http://www.northcom.mil

Description: NORTHCOM was established in 2002 to counter threats and aggression aimed at the United States and its territories. The command's geographic area of responsibility includes North America, Puerto Rico, the U.S. Virgin Islands, and their respective air, land, and sea approaches. The command's website provides news and leadership information. The Educational section includes information for students about homeland defense.

Subject(s): Homeland Security; Unified Combatant Commands

U.S. Pacific Command (PACOM)

http://www.pacom.mil

Description: PACOM is one of the Unified Combatant Commands (UCCs) assigned to oversee operational control of U.S. combat forces. Headquartered in Hawaii, the command's geographic area of responsibility is the Asia-Pacific region, including China, Japan, India, Indonesia, and Australia. The website includes command news, leadership information, and a Photo Archive.

Subject(s): Unified Combatant Commands; Asia

U.S. Southern Command (SOUTHCOM)

http://www.southcom.mil

Description: SOUTHCOM, one of the Unified Combatant Commands (UCCs), is headquartered in Miami. According to the website, "SOUTHCOM is responsible for providing contingency planning, operations, and security cooperation in its assigned Area of Responsibility, which includes Central America, South America, and the Caribbean (except U.S. commonwealths, territories, and possessions). The command is also responsible for the force protection of U.S. military resources at these locations. SOUTHCOM is also responsible for ensuring the defense of the Panama Canal." The command's website includes information about its mission, activities, and components. The News section includes Fact Files, topical one-page websites with links to related news.

Subject(s): Unified Combatant Commands

U.S. Strategic Command (STRATCOM)

http://www.stratcom.mil

Description: STRATCOM is one of the Unified Combatant Commands (UCCs). It holds responsibility for missions in the areas of space operations; information operations; integrated missile defense; global command and control; intelligence, surveillance, and reconnaissance; global strike; and strategic deterrence. Its website has information about the command's organization and leadership. The Organization section has links to the command's functional and service components, information on STRATCOM's history, and fact sheets on missile systems, military space forces, and strategic computer and communications networks.

U.S. Cyber Command (CYBERCOM) was established in 2009 as a Subordinate Unified Command of STRATCOMM. CYBERCOM centralizes command of cyberspace operations, with its responsibilities including the protection of Defense Department information networks and the military cyberspace infrastructure.

Subject(s): Electronic Warfare; Unified Combatant Commands; Missile Defense

U.S. Transportation Command (TRANSCOM)

https://www.ustranscom.mil/

Description: TRANSCOM provides strategic mobility support for the Defense Department and the combatant commands. The site has information on TRANSCOM's organization, component units, leadership, news, and history.

Subject(s): Airlifts; Military Logistics; Unified Combatant Commands

Wright-Patterson Air Force Base

http://www.wpafb.af.mil

Description: This is the main public website for the Wright-Patterson Air Force Base, where missions include logistics management, research and development, and flight operations. The site has information on the base's history, the 88th Air Base Wing, Air Force research laboratories, and other units hosted at the base.

Subject(s): Air Force Bases

DEFENSE OPERATIONS

Army Financial Management

https://www.asafm.army.mil/

Description: Manuals, documents, and other information about Army accounting and financial management practices make up the bulk of this site. Sections include Army Budget, Financial Information Management, and Cost & Economics. The Army Budget section contains detailed materials on the current fiscal year.

The primary target audience for this fairly technical site is Army's budget and resource management staff.

Subject(s): Army; Defense Administration

Combating Terrorism Technical Support Office (CTTSO)

https://www.cttso.gov/

Description: CTTSO facilitates the development and acquisition of counterterrorism technology to support the Defense Department, State Department, other federal agencies, and domestic law enforcement organizations. Major sections of the site are Vendors, Transition and Innovation, Recent Awards, and International Partners. The site also describes the

CTTSO programs, namely the Technical Support Working Group, the Explosive Ordnance Disposal/Low-Intensity Conflict Program, and the Irregular Warfare Support Program. CTTSO operates as a program office under the Assistant Secretary of Defense for Special Operations/Low-Intensity Conflict.

Subject(s): Defense Contracting; Military Technology

Defense Civilian Personnel Advisory Service (DCPAS)

https://www.cpms.osd.mil/

Description: DCPAS provides centralized management and policy support for the department's civilian personnel programs. The homepage links directly to the site's topical sections, which include Employment Verification, Initiatives & Services, and Events & Training.

Subject(s): Civilian Defense Employees; Defense Administration

Defense Finance and Accounting Service (DFAS)

https://www.dfas.mil/

Description: DFAS handles pay for all Department of Defense military and civilian employees, retirees, and annuitants, plus major contractors and vendors. They also make travel payments, process contractor invoices, manage military retirement trust funds, and manage other aspects of military accounting. Major sections on the homepage are Military Members, Retired Military & Annuitants, and Civilian Employees.

Subject(s): Accounting; Defense Administration

Defense Information Systems Agency (DISA)

https://www.disa.mil/

Description: DISA develops information technology systems and provides communications solutions for the military. Some information on the site can only be accessed by authorized users. The site's About section covers the agency's mission, history, and organization. The site also has information on contracting opportunities and features the full text of the DSN Telephone Directory. (Defense Switched Network, or DSN, is used for voice communications between Department of Defense offices.)

Subject(s): Military Computing; Communications Technology

Defense Logistics Agency (DLA)

http://www.dla.mil

Description: DLA is the central supply and distribution agency for the military; it provides goods such as weapons parts, fuel, uniforms, food rations, and medical supplies. The Organizations section under the About DLA heading links to the websites of major DLA offices. The What DLA Offers section features DLA information by topic. The site also has a section on business operations as well as one for DLA news.

Subject(s): Military Logistics

Defense Logistics Agency (DLA) Energy

http://www.dla.mil/energy.aspx

Description: DLA Energy acquires, stores, and distributes fuel for the military. The About DLA Energy section includes information about the agency's organization, mission, and history, as well as agency news. The Doing Business With Energy section includes contact information for customers and vendors, access to the Contract Information System, and information on Energy's Small Business Program. The Publications subsection under the Library heading features the *DLA Energy Fact Book*, with statistical information on the agency's business operations, and DLA Energy's *Energy Source* magazine.

Subject(s): Military Logistics

Defense Media Activity (DMA)

https://www.dma.mil/

Description: According to its website, "DMA keeps Department of Defense audiences around the world informed. It presents news, information, and entertainment through media outlets, including radio, TV, Internet, print media, and emerging media technologies." The website describes DMA's work in more detail and links to related services.

Subject(s): Military Information

Defense Prisoner of War (POW) / Missing in Action (MIA) Accounting Agency

http://www.dpaa.mil

Description: This website covers the federal government's efforts to account for missing persons from all wars. The site includes Defense Department policies and procedures, information on archival research, and information specifically for families of POWs/MIAs. The site also features lists from missing personnel databases for the Iraq Theater & Other Conflicts, the Cold War, the Vietnam War, the Korean War, and World War II.

Subject(s): Prisoners of War

Defense Procurement and Acquisition Policy (DPAP)

https://www.acq.osd.mil/dpap/

Description: DPAP is responsible for all acquisition and procurement policy matters in the Department of Defense. The Defense Acquisition Regulations System (DARS) section of the site includes the Defense Federal Acquisition Regulation Supplement (DFARS), essentially a database of DoD acquisition regulations. Other content on the site includes the Contract Pricing Reference Guides, e-business and purchase card program information, and sections on contract policy, international contracting, and strategic sourcing. The Policy Vault section has acquisition policy documents available for dissemination to the public.

Subject(s): Defense Contracting—Policy; Government Procurement—Policy

Defense Security Service (DSS)

http://www.dss.mil

Description: DSS conducts personnel security investigations and operates programs in industrial security and security training. The DSS website describes its programs or those it participates in, including the National Industrial Security Program (NISP) and the Defense Security Service Academy (DSSA).

Much of the information at this site is for DSS customers, who are federal agencies and private industry and universities carrying out government contracts or conducting research and development.

Subject(s): Military Intelligence; National Security

Department of Defense (DoD)

https://www.defense.gov/

Description: The official Department of Defense website features armed forces news, leadership biographies and speeches, defense-related reports of current interest, an FAQ section, and much else. The website serves the media at large with information in the form of photos and videos, transcripts, news and press releases, and reports.

The DoD Sites section organizes links to the numerous DoD websites alphabetically and by category, and it has a search engine specifically for Defense Department sites. As with other Cabinet-level departments, the Defense website features an Open Government section and a Recovery Act section.

This site is an excellent starting point for users looking for U.S. military websites or current DoD news.

Subject(s): Military Information; Finding Aids

DoD Dictionary of Military Terms

http://www.jcs.mil/Portals/36/Documents/Doctrine/pubs/dictionary.pdf

Description: This is the online version of the *DoD Dictionary of Military and Associated Terms*. It provides brief explanations of terms such as "unconventional assisted recovery" and "reserved obstacles." The dictionary may be used online or downloaded in PDF or XML format.

Subject(s): Military Information; Reference

Joint Electronic Library (JEL)

http://www.jcs.mil/Doctrine/

Description: JEL is the source for joint doctrine and training information for the U.S. military forces. The website provides access to Joint Publications, Interorganizational Documents, and information on training and education. The site also includes the Joint Doctrine Hierarchy Chart, historical publications, and research publications. Some sections of the site are restricted to military users.

Subject(s): Military Doctrine

Office of the Under Secretary of Defense for Acquisition, Technology, and Logistics (OUSD[AT&L])

https://www.acq.osd.mil/

Description:This website is for authorized use only. This is the official website for the Office of the Under Secretary of Defense for Acquisition, Technology, and Logistics. The Offices section of the site presents a large menu of OUSD(AT&L) component offices and directorates, with links to their sites as well as to other Defense components.

Subject(s): Defense Administration; Military Procurement

Office of the Under Secretary of Defense (Comptroller) (OUSD[C])

http://comptroller.defense.gov

Description: The OUSD(C) website provides an extensive set of Department of Defense budget documents, such as the *DoD Agency Financial Report (AFR) / Performance and Accountability Report (PAR)*.

Subject(s): Defense Administration

Overseas Basing Commission

http://govinfo.library.unt.edu/osbc/

Description: The full name of the Overseas Basing Commission was the United States Congress Commission on Review of Overseas Military Facility Structure of the United States. The commission was charged with making recommendations to Congress and to the president regarding overseas military facilities. The commission closed after having made its final report in 2005. The website has been archived by the University of North Texas Libraries' CyberCemetery project, described in another chapter of this book.

Subject(s): Military Bases and Installations

Pentagon Force Protection Agency (PFPA)

http://www.pfpa.mil

Description: PFPA is responsible for security at the Pentagon and other Department of Defense facilities and activities in the Washington, D.C., area.

It performs standard police work and criminal investigations and is also concerned with terrorist, chemical, biological, and nuclear threats. The PFPA website has basic information about the agency, its component organizations, and employment opportunities.

Subject(s): Homeland Security; Police

Selective Service System (SSS)

https://www.sss.gov/

Description: The SSS website features information about the agency and the military draft and can be used to register online or check a registration. The site includes such sections as About, Registration, Public Affairs, FAQs, and Change of Information. The site also features historical draft statistics, a guide to requesting archival records of draft registrants, and a general history of the draft in the United States. The Reports section contains current and past editions of the agency's *Annual Report to Congress* and its newsletter *The Register*.

Subject(s): Military Draft

DEFENSE RESEARCH

Air Force Office of Scientific Research (AFOSR) – Wright-Patterson Air Force Base

http://www.wpafb.af.mil/afrl/afosr/

Description: AFOSR directs the Air Force's basic research program, with research concerning aerospace and materials sciences, chemistry and life sciences, mathematics and information sciences, and physics and electronics. Its website includes current news, research opportunity announcements, and information about its technology directorates. The site also has information about AFOSR educational, outreach, and special programs.

Subject(s): Military Research Laboratories

Air Force Research Laboratory (AFRL) – Wright-Patterson Air Force Base

http://www.wpafb.af.mil/afrl/

Description: AFRL conducts basic and applied research to improve the Air Force's fighting capabilities. AFRL is headquartered at Wright-Patterson Air Force Base in Ohio, and its website is part of the base's site. The site has fact sheets on the Small Business Innovation Research (SBIR) Program, the Technology Transfer (T2) Program, and partnership opportunities with AFRL.

Subjects(s): Military Research Laboratories

Army Research Laboratory (ARL)

http://www.arl.army.mil

Description: ARL's website provides information about its organization, research, and collaborative alliances. ARL's research directorates include computational and information sciences, sensors and electron devices, survivability/lethality analysis, weapons and materials research, human research and engineering, and vehicle technology. Research and analysis programs include robotics, precision guided missiles, tactical communications, and battlefield weather research. Each is described in more detail on the website. A separate section provides information about doing business with ARL.

Subject(s): Military Computing; Military Research Laboratories; Weapons Research

Combating Terrorism Center (CTC) at West Point

https://ctc.usma.edu/

Description: CTC conducts education, research, and policy analysis on such topics as terrorism, counterterrorism, homeland security, and weapons of mass destruction. Along with information about its programs of study, the CTC website has current news and publications, as well as information about the Downing Scholars Program and the Harmony Program. Also featured is the *CTC Sentinel*, a monthly publication that reflects the center's mission.

Subject(s): Terrorism—Research

Defense Advanced Research Projects Agency (DARPA)

https://www.darpa.mil/

Description: DARPA, founded in 1958 as the Advanced Research Projects Agency (ARPA), manages research and development to promote the technological superiority of the U.S. military. DARPA's website features an overview and history of the agency, with extensive information about and links to the websites of its component offices. The Work With Us section has information on DARPA solicitations as well as small business funding opportunities.

Subject(s): Military Technology—Research

Defense Forensics & Biometrics Agency (DFBA)

http://www.dfba.mil/

Description: The Defense Forensics & Biometrics Agency was established as a permanent organization within the Army in September 2012. DFBA maintains the Defense Department's authoritative biometric database in support of the National Security Strategy (NSS). The field of biometrics consists of the tools used to verify the identity of an individual based on distinct and measurable physiological characteristics, such as fingerprints. This website has information about the agency and about biometrics, including a basic tutorial, a glossary, and news stories on the topic. This site is for authorized use only.

Subject(s): Biometrics—Research

Defense Science Board (DSB)

https://www.acq.osd.mil/dsb/

Description: DSB advises the Department of Defense leadership on matters relating to science, technology, research, engineering, manufacturing, and the acquisition process. DSB accomplishes much of its work through special task forces. The DSB website lists current task forces and their missions; it also has PDF copies of past task force reports. This site is for authorized use only.

Subject(s): Military Technology; Defense Research

Defense Systems Information Analysis Center (DSIAC)

https://www.dsiac.org/

Description: Part of the DoD's Information Analysis Center Program. DSIAC serves as a resource of information for DoD and the greater Defense Systems community by engaging a network of subject matter experts and by providing access to the DoD Scientific and Technical Information Program (STIP). As listed on the website, DSIAC focuses on the following subject areas: Advanced Materials; Autonomous Systems; Directed Energy; Energetics; Military Sensing; Non-lethal Weapons; Reliability, Maintainability, Quality, Supportability, Interoperability (RMQSI); Survivability and Vulnerability; and Weapons Systems.

Subject(s): Information Analysis Centers; Weapons Research

Defense Technical Information Center (DTIC)

http://www.dtic.mil/dtic/

Description: DTIC is a DoD Field Activity for scientific, research, and engineering information services. It offers the Defense community, including contractors and DoD-funded researchers, a broad range of services for locating and delivering technical reports, research summaries, summaries of independent research and development, and other relevant publications. DTIC's website also offers publicly accessible databases.

In the search drop-down menu, the Technical Reports menu option searches technical reports generated for and by DoD; this database, which was formerly known as Public STINET, can be accessed directly at http://www.dtic.mil/dtic/search/tr/tr.html.

Subject(s): Scientific and Technical Information; Databases

Foreign Military Studies Office (FMSO)

https://community.apan.org/wg/tradoc-g2/fmso/

Description: According to its website, the Foreign Military Studies Office "provides translated selections and analysis from a diverse range of foreign articles and other media that our analysts believe will give military and security experts an added dimension to their critical thinking about the Operational Environment." Many of FMSO's analytical products are available online, organized by world region and by topic (e.g., border security, energy security, and terrorism).

Subject(s): Military Intelligence; Defense Research

High Performance Computing Modernization Program (HPCMP)

https://www.hpc.mil/

Description: HPCMP provides supercomputer services, high-speed network communications, and computational science expertise for the research, development, and test activities of DoD laboratories and test centers. Its website provides information about the program and related high-performance computing activities.

While focusing on military high-performance computing, this site will be of interest to others in the high-performance computing community.

Subject(s): High Performance Computing; Military Computing

Information Analysis Centers (IACs)

http://iac.dtic.mil

Description: This site serves as a central directory for homepages of the Department of Defense and other military Information Analysis Centers (IACs). IACs establish databases of historical, technical, scientific, and other data and information on a variety of technical topics. Information collections include unclassified, limited distribution, and classified information. IACs also provide analytical tools such as models and simulations. Most IAC home pages describe the databases they maintain, although they rarely provide public access.

The Defense Department IACs include AMMTIAC (Advanced Materials, Manufacturing, and Testing IAC), HDIAC (Homeland Defense and Security IAC), and DSIAC (Defense Systems IAC). The military IACs include APMIAC (Airfields, Pavements, and Mobility IAC), CEIAC (Coastal Engineering IAC), and CRSTIAC (Cold Regions Science and Technology IAC).

Many of the resources from the IACs will only be of interest to the defense community due to access restrictions. However, there are a few databases that have unclassified material available.

Subject(s): Information Analysis Centers; Military Information; Scientific and Technical Information

Institute for National Strategic Studies (INSS)

http://inss.ndu.edu

Description: INSS conducts policy research and analysis for senior U.S. military decision-makers and for decision-makers in the Executive branch and in Congress. This website has information on INSS, its centers, research programs, reports, and symposia. The Publications section includes papers and policy briefs, as well as books published by NDU Press.

Subject(s): Defense Research

Naval Research Laboratory (NRL)

https://www.nrl.navy.mil/

Description: This is the main page for the many directorates and divisions of NRL. The laboratory's research focus is broad, including specialties within the areas of materials science, ocean and atmospheric science, and space technology. NRL also has a Nanoscience Institute. The site provides information on NRL accomplishments in these areas, business opportunities, and career and student opportunities.

Subject(s): Navy—Research; Research Laboratories

Military Sensing Information Analysis Center (SENSIAC)

https://www.gtri.gatech.edu/locations

Description: SENSIAC focuses on sensing technologies for military use, such as infrared sensors, laser systems, radar, underwater acoustics, and seismic sensors. Only the most general information is available free of charge on this website.

Subject(s): Military Technology

U.S. Army Medical Research Institute of Infectious Diseases (USAMRIID)

http://www.usamriid.army.mil

Description: USAMRIID researches and develops medical solutions to protect troops from biological threats. Its website has information about the institute's achievements and technology transfer opportunities, as well as current news. The Scientific Publications section provides a bibliography of staff-authored journal articles. The Reference Materials section includes downloadable copies of textbooks and manuals. This site is for authorized use only.

Subject(s): Bioterrorism; Military Medicine

HOMELAND SECURITY

Center for Homeland Defense and Security (CHDS)

https://www.chds.us/c/

Description: NPS's Center for Homeland Defense and Security provides educational programs for government and military leaders. Its website has information on the programs, an index of faculty published papers, and the full text of master's theses from the CHDS Master's participants. The center's online Homeland Security Digital Library section is open to federal, state, local, and tribal government officials; homeland security researchers and academics; U.S. military personnel; but not to the general public. Eligible users must register for access. The center's Homeland Security Affairs journal is publicly available on the site.

Subject(s): Homeland Security—Research; Military Training and Education

Civil Air Patrol (CAP)

https://www.gocivilairpatrol.com/

Description: CAP is a nonprofit corporation that operates as the all-volunteer civilian auxiliary of the U.S. Air Force when performing services for the federal government. CAP assists federal, state and local authorities in performing various reconnaissance, emergency services, disaster relief, and homeland security missions. Its website describes these core operations, CAP aerospace education and cadet programs, and joining CAP. Since 2009, CAP's annual *Report to Congress* has been consolidated with its annual *Financial Report*, which can be found in the Media Center section under the News heading.

Subject(s): Civil Air Patrol

Defense Nuclear Facilities Safety Board (DNFSB)

https://www.dnfsb.gov/

Description: DNFSB is responsible for independent, external safety oversight of the Department of Energy (DOE) nuclear weapons complex. Its website offers information about the board's members and organizational structure. The Board Activities section organizes DNFSB documents by type, with links to Recommendations and Reports as well as information on public hearings.

Subject(s): Nuclear Weapons

Defense Threat Reduction Agency (DTRA)

http://www.dtra.mil

Description: The full name of this website is Defense Threat Reduction Agency & USSTRATCOM Center for Combating WMD & Standing Joint Force Headquarters for WMD Elimination. These entities' names are abbreviated DTRA, SCC-WMD, and SJFHQ-E, respectively, and they work closely together. DTRA addresses the threat of weapons of mass destruction (chemical, biological, radiological, nuclear, and high yield explosives) with combat support, technology development, threat control, and threat reduction. SCC-WMD coordinates counter-WMD activities at U.S. military locations around the world. SJFHQ-E supports WMD elimination operations through planning and training as well as direct participation in such operations. The Missions section provides detailed information on DTRA's broad but focused work. The website includes current information on DTRA research grants and business opportunities. The site also has information on the Nuclear Test Personnel Review (NTPR) Program, which assists veterans who received doses of radiation while participating in U.S. atmospheric nuclear tests during the Cold War era.

Subject(s): National Defense; Radiation Exposure

Department of Homeland Security (DHS)

https://www.dhs.gov/

Description: DHS was formed in January 2003 by consolidating many existing agencies and agency divisions whose missions related to domestic defense. The DHS website organizes information into major sections under the Topics link, including Preventing Terrorism, Border Security, Cybersecurity, Civil Rights and Civil Liberties, and Immigration Enforcement. Each of these sections has publications, grants, laws, program links, and background information as appropriate. A complete list of links to component agencies and offices is provided in the About DHS section, along with budget information, an organizational chart, and guidance on major laws and regulations.

Information is also organized on the home page (under "How Do I?"), with links to issues including "Find Overseas Travel Alerts" and "Report Cyber Incidents". As Cabinet departments are required to do, DHS maintains an Open Government page.

Researchers may also want to check the websites of DHS component agencies for detailed information. Many DHS component agencies are described elsewhere in this publication.

Subjects(s): Homeland Security

FBI National Security Branch (NSB)

https://www.fbi.gov/about/leadership-and-structure/national-security-branch

Description: NSB was established in 2005 to combine the bureau's counterterrorism, counterintelligence, and intelligence resources; a consolidated Weapons of Mass Destruction Directorate was added in 2006. The NSB website has news and background information about the branch, a member of the U.S. Intelligence Community. The Counterterrorism Division page has a most wanted list and a form for reporting tips. The site also provides information on the National Counterterrorism Center and the Terrorist Screening Center.

Subject(s): Homeland Security; Terrorism

Homeland Security Advisory Council (HSAC)

https://www.dhs.gov/homeland-security-advisory-council

Description: The Homeland Security Advisory Council provides advice and recommendations to the secretary of DHS. The council includes members from state and local government, academia, and the private sector. Its website contains member information, meeting minutes, and completed task force reports on topics such as the Southwest border and community resilience.

Subject(s): Homeland Security

Homeland Security Digital Library (HSDL)

https://www.hsdl.org/c/

Description: HSDL provides access to open source resources on homeland security policy, strategy, and organizational management. The extensive database of full text resources can be searched or browsed by topic. The site's On the Homefront blog announces significant new reports and documents on homeland security issues.

HSDL is maintained to support the information needs of homeland security officials in the government and military, academic researchers, and qualified homeland security researchers. This primary audience can request an ID to access the full HSDL collection. The general public has access to a smaller collection, which includes federal government documents as well as papers written at federal academic institutions, such as the Naval Postgraduate School and the Army War College. Some Federal Depository Libraries provide public access to the full collection; to find the depository library nearest to you, see http://www.gpo.gov/libraries/.

Subject(s): Homeland Security—Research

Information Sharing Environment (ISE)

https://www.dni.gov/index.php/who-we-are/organizations/ise/about-the-ise

Description: ISE was established by the Intelligence Reform and Terrorism Prevention Act of 2004. ISE works to promote information sharing between all levels of government and with the private sector and foreign partners. Its website links to documents relevant to the establishment and operation of ISE and describes ISE privacy guidelines. The site also describes ISE work with state, local, and tribal governments including information fusion centers and the Joint Counterterrorism Assessment Team (JCAT).

Subject(s): Law Enforcement Policy; Terrorism

Missile Defense Agency (MDA)

https://www.mda.mil/

Description: MDA is charged with developing an integrated missile defense system. The Ballistic Missile Defense Organization (BMDO) became the MDA in 2002, elevating the organization to agency status. The agency's website explains the basics of missile defense and budget information and features a guide to doing business with MDA. The News & Resources section includes images and videos of missile defense systems, fact sheets, environmental impact documents, and congressional testimony.

Subject(s): Missile Defense

National Commission on Terrorist Attacks Upon the United States

https://www.9-11commission.gov/

Description: The National Commission on Terrorist Attacks Upon the United States—also known as the 9-11 Commission—was an independent, bipartisan commission charged with investigating the September 11, 2001, terrorist attacks. The 9-11 Commission issued its final public report in July 2004 and closed in August 2004.

Documents on the site include the final report, video and transcript archives of the twelve public hearings, and staff monographs on terrorist financing and terrorist travel. The Press section includes photos and press releases.

This site is archived and will not be updated further. It has been kept online in its archived state by the University of North Texas Libraries' CyberCemetery project. Transcripts of hearings can be accessed at http://govinfo.library.unt.edu/911/hearings/index.htm.

Subject(s): Homeland Security; Terrorism

National Homeland Security Research Center (NHSRC)

https://www.epa.gov/homeland-security-research

Description: Through NHSRC, the EPA develops expertise and technology to counter public health and environmental emergencies arising from terrorist incidents. The website has publications and background information on the center's research in such areas as water infrastructure protection and indoor and outdoor decontamination.

Subject(s): Public Health—Research; Terrorism

National Nuclear Security Administration (NNSA)

https://nnsa.energy.gov/

Description: NNSA, a semi-autonomous agency within the Department of Energy, officially began operations on March 1, 2000. Its mission is to carry out the national security responsibilities of the DOE, including the maintenance of nuclear weapons, promotion of international nuclear safety and nonproliferation, and management of the naval nuclear propulsion program. The website's section Our Programs, under About, describes the activities of NNSA. The Defense Programs subsection (under Our Programs) covers the Stockpile Stewardship Program. Other sections focus on nuclear nonproliferation, naval reactors, and nuclear security. The About section includes information about the agency's leadership, locations, and budget.

Subject(s): Nuclear Weapons

NIAID Biodefense and Related Programs

https://www.niaid.nih.gov/research/biodefense

Description: NIAID, in cooperation with other agencies, academia, and industry, is studying medical countermeasures against radiological and nuclear threats. This site has information on its work in the areas of biodefense and radiation and chemical countermeasures.

Subject(s): Biological Warfare—Research

Ready.gov

https://www.ready.gov/

Description: The Ready.gov website provides advice on preparing for potential terrorist attacks and other emergencies, including natural disasters and technological and accidental hazards. There is advice tailored to certain audiences, such as infants and young children, seniors, schools, and businesses. There is also information for military families, people with disabilities and special needs, and people with pets. Checklists and brochures can be downloaded in PDF format.

A Spanish-language version of the site is available at https://www.listo.gov/es. Ready.gov also has pages translated into Arabic, Chinese, French, Korean, Russian, Vietnamese, and more.

Subject(s): Disaster Preparedness; Homeland Security

SAFETY Act

https://www.safetyact.gov/

Description: The SAFETY Act, part of the Homeland Security Act of 2002, aims to "encourage the development and deployment of effective anti-terrorism products and services by providing liability protections." (from the website) The site provides information about the legislation and about applications for the SAFETY Act Designation or Certification for products.

Subject(s): Business—Regulations

Small Business Innovation Research (SBIR) Program

https://www.dhs.gov/science-and-technology/sbir

Description: DHS participates in the federal government's Small Business Innovation Research Program. This official website presents information about solicitations, proposal reviews, and awards. (The Small Business Administration has additional information about SBIR on its website. SBA is described elsewhere in this book.)

Subject(s): Grants; Homeland Security—Research; Small Business—Grants

Transportation Security Administration (TSA)

https://www.tsa.gov/

Description: TSA was established within the Department of Transportation (DOT) in response to the terrorist attacks of September 11, 2001; it has since been transferred to the Department of Homeland Security. The agency has responsibility for transportation security nationwide. The TSA website provides current news about travel security and information on the agency's mission, organization, and operations. The Travel portion of the site includes lists of items prohibited in carry-on or checked luggage, tips for travelers with special needs, and information about privacy and risk-based security. The Press section has news, press releases, speeches, testimony, and fact sheets. TSA also maintains an active blog for travelers at http://blog.tsa.gov/ and has a mobile app called "My TSA."

Subject(s): Aviation Safety; Transportation Security

United States Secret Service (USSS)

https://www.secretservice.gov/

Description: The United States Secret Service was transferred in 2003 from the Department of the Treasury (DoT), where it was founded in 1865, to the Department of Homeland Security. The Secret Service has a role in protecting the president, vice president, former U.S. presidents, visiting foreign dignitaries, and other leaders, as well as investigating counterfeiting and other financial crimes. On the website, the Protection section covers the high-profile presidential security role. Under Investigations, the Know Your Money subsection provides details on how to detect counterfeit currency. Other sections cover Secret Service history and employment opportunities.

Although the Secret Service does not discuss details of its security operations, its website is designed to give clear answers to many of the questions the public might have. The Frequently Asked Questions section answers such questions as "Who is the Secret Service authorized to protect?" and "How long do former presidents receive Secret Service protection after they leave office?"

Subject(s): Counterfeiting; Homeland Security; Law Enforcement

DOJ National Security Division (NSD)

https://www.justice.gov/nsd

Description: NSD was created within the Justice Department in 2006 to combat terrorism and other threats to national security. It manages the administration and enforcement of the Foreign Agents Registration Act (FARA), and the website links to FARA registration and the FARA document database. The NSD Freedom of Information Act (FOIA) Library, within the NSD FOIA section, provides access to the *Annual Foreign Intelligence Surveillance Act (FISA) Report to Congress*. This annual document reports applications made by the government for authority to conduct electronic surveillance and physical search for foreign intelligence purposes under FISA.

Subject(s): National Security; Terrorism

Y–12 National Security Complex

https://www.y12.doe.gov/

Description: "The Y–12 National Security Complex is a premier manufacturing facility dedicated to making our nation and the world a safer place and plays a vital role in the Department of Energy's Nuclear Security Enterprise. Y–12 develops innovative solutions in manufacturing technologies, prototyping, safeguards and security, technical computing, and environmental stewardship." (from the website) The program's focal points are delineated in the Nuclear Deterrence, Global Security, and Naval Reactors sections. A news feed is available in the News section.

Subject(s): Security; Nuclear Weapons

INTELLIGENCE

Central Intelligence Agency (CIA)

https://www.cia.gov/index.html

Description: The CIA website has news, links to offices within the CIA, information on CIA careers, and information on CIA tours and the CIA Museum. Full-text, bibliographic and order information for CIA maps and publications are in the Library section. The full-text versions of two major reference publications, *The World Factbook* and *Chiefs of State and Cabinet Members of Foreign Governments*, are regularly updated on the site.

The Offices of CIA section includes information on the Directorate of Analysis, the Directorate of Support, and the Directorate of Science & Technology. The Library section includes information on the Center for the Study of Intelligence and the Kent Center, along with their publications. The Library section also contains the CIA's Freedom of Information Act (FOIA) Electronic Reading Room.

The availability of *The World Factbook* and *Chiefs of State and Cabinet Members of Foreign Governments* makes the CIA website an important reference source.

Subject(s): Foreign Countries; Intelligence Agencies

CIA Directorate of Operations (DO)

https://www.cia.gov/offices-of-cia/clandestine-service/

Description: The Directorate of Operations, also known as the Clandestine Service, is the undercover arm of the CIA. As stated on the website, the directorate's mission is "to strengthen national security and foreign policy objectives through the clandestine collection of human intelligence (HUMINT) and covert action." The site describes career and internship opportunities at the DO and has answers to frequently asked questions.

Subject(s): Intelligence

CIA Freedom of Information Act (FOIA) Electronic Reading Room

https://www.cia.gov/library/readingroom/

Description: This is the CIA's public gateway for access to agency documents through the Freedom of Information Act and the Electronic Freedom of Information Act. The centerpiece is a searchable database called the "25-Year Program Archive," a searchable database ("CREST") of declassified documents. The Frequently Requested Records section of the website has the full text of a small set of frequently requested documents such as the official Bay of Pigs report and Vietnam POW/MIA records. The Historical Collections sections includes documents related to former CIA director Richard Helms, documents from the National Intelligence Council (NIC) Collection, and other themed collections. The Your Rights section identifies the laws governing the release of documents.

The CIA Electronic Reading Room will answer the basic questions a researcher may have about FOIA and access to other declassified documents from the CIA. Researchers may also want to check the website of the private National Security Archive (https://nsarchive.gwv.edu), which maintains a repository of declassified documents obtained through FOIA.

Subject(s): Declassified Documents; Freedom of Information Act; Intelligence

Commission on the Intelligence Capabilities of the United States Regarding Weapons of Mass Destruction (WMD Commission)

http://govinfo.library.unt.edu/wmd/

Description: The WMD Commission closed its offices in May 2005 after making its final report. The website has been archived by the University of North Texas Libraries' CyberCemetery project. The site includes the final report and information about the WMD Commission and its members.

Subject(s): Intelligence Agencies

CREST: CIA Records Search Tool

https://www.cia.gov/library/readingroom/collection/crest-25-year-program-archive/

Description: This CIA site provides searchable access to the index of the CIA's CREST database. CREST's full text collection of declassified CIA documents can only be used in person at the main Maryland campus of the National Archives. The CIA refers to the index as the "25-Year Program Archive" because it is designed to include historically valuable records at least 25 years old. This index has citations to the full text documents but does not include the documents themselves. Citations include the ESDN tracking number to be used when submitting a FOIA request to the CIA.

Subject(s): Declassified Documents; Intelligence

Defense Intelligence Agency (DIA)

http://www.dia.mil

Description: DIA provides military intelligence to warfighters, defense planners, and defense and national security policymakers. Its website has information about DIA's organization and history, as well as employment and contracting opportunities with the agency. The site has an organizational chart, but does not provide much information on its centers and directorates. The National Intelligence University (NIU) has its own section on the site.

Subject(s): Intelligence Agencies; Military Intelligence

DOS

Bureau of Intelligence and Research (INR)

https://www.state.gov/s/inr/

Description: The State Department's Bureau of Intelligence and Research analyzes intelligence to support U.S. diplomacy. INR is a member of the U.S. Intelligence Community. Its website provides information about the Title VIII Grant Program, which supports advanced research, language, and graduate training programs conducted by U.S.-based organizations. The site also has INR's Independent States and Dependencies lists, which give the department's official short and long names and standard country codes for the independent countries and dependencies of the world.

Subject(s): Intelligence; Language Education—Grants

Intelligence Advanced Research Projects Activity (IARPA)

https://www.iarpa.gov/

Description: The Intelligence Advanced Research Projects Activity invests in cutting-edge research to advance U.S. intelligence capabilities. The website provides information about the organization, its programs, news, and events.

Subject(s): Intelligence—Research

In-Q-Tel

https://www.iqt.org/

Description: In-Q-Tel is a private, nonprofit enterprise originally associated with the Central Intelligence Agency (CIA). It was established to help apply new commercial information technologies to intelligence and analysis. In-Q-Tel's clients are the CIA and other members of the Intelligence Community. The In-Q-Tel website has information about the organization's history, partners, and leadership. The Portfolio section gives an overview of In-Q-Tel's focus in such areas as advanced analytics and digital identity.

Subject(s): Information Technology; Intelligence

Marine Corps Intelligence Department

http://www.hqmc.marines.mil/intelligence//

Description: The Marine Corps Intelligence Department is part of the U.S. Intelligence Community. The department's website has basic information about its mission, functions, and organization. Organizational acronyms link to further information from each of the department's branches.

Subject(s): Military Intelligence

National Counterintelligence and Security Center (NCSC)

https://www.dni.gov/index.php/ncsc-home

Description: NCSC is charged with improving the performance of U.S. counterintelligence efforts. This website has information about the center, its mission, and organization. Under the Resources heading, the site provides the text of counterintelligence laws and booklets with advice about economic espionage and protecting oneself while traveling abroad.

Subject(s): Intelligence Agencies

National Counterterrorism Center (NCTC)

https://www.dni.gov/index.php/nctc-home

Description: NCTC serves as the nation's central point for integrating and analyzing intelligence pertaining to terrorism and counterterrorism. The NCTC site provides background information about the agency and its role. According to the website, "through the Terrorist Identities Datamart Environment (TIDE), NCTC maintains a consolidated repository of information on international terrorist identities and provides the authoritative database supporting the Terrorist Screening Center and the U.S. government's watchlisting system." The site also features a Counterterrorism (CT) Calendar each year, which can be printed from a PDF file or used online in an interactive fashion. The calendar includes anniversaries of terrorist incidents and profiles of terrorist groups and individuals.

Subject(s): Terrorism

National Geospatial-Intelligence Agency (NGA)

https://www.nga.mil/Pages/Default.aspx

Description: NGA is an intelligence and combat support agency with expertise in geospatial intelligence, imagery analysis, geodesy, cartography, and related disciplines. A section titled Products & Services explains the availability of NGA products and provides contact information. The same section also features NGA's *GEOnet Names Server (GNS)*, a database of standard names for places and geographic features around the world, excluding the United States and Antarctica. The NGA website also has information on careers with the agency.

Subject(s): Maps and Mapping; Military Intelligence

National Reconnaissance Office (NRO)

http://www.nro.gov

Description: As part of the U.S. Intelligence Community, the NRO designs, builds, and operates the nation's reconnaissance satellites. The website provides an agency overview, press releases, and contracting information. The History and Studies section features information, photos, and videos about CORONA, the first photoreconnaissance satellite system.

Subject(s): Intelligence Agencies

National Security Agency / Central Security Service (NSA/CSS)

https://www.nsa.gov/

Description: Specializing in cryptology, NSA works to protect U.S. information systems security and to produce foreign intelligence. CSS coordinates with the U.S. armed forces. The website's About NSA section includes leadership biographies, answers to frequently asked questions, and an overview of the Information Assurance and Signal Intelligence fields. A Cryptologic Heritage subsection has information on NSA history, the National Cryptologic Museum, and the Center for Cryptologic History. The Research section includes published staff work, technology transfer information, and a feature on security-enhanced Linux. The Public Information section links to press releases, congressional testimony, Freedom of Information Act (FOIA) releases, and information from NSA's own declassification initiatives.

Subject(s): Cryptography and Encryption; Intelligence Agencies

National Security Archive

https://nsarchive.gwu.edu/

Description: The National Security Archive is a private, independent research institute and library located at George Washington University in Washington, D.C. Despite the official-sounding name, it is not a government agency. The archive collects and publishes declassified documents acquired through the Freedom of Information Act (FOIA). Only a fraction of the archive's holdings are online; nevertheless, the online offerings are significant.

The Documents section of the site includes Electronic Briefing Books (EBBs) and collections of scanned declassified documents along with National Security Archive analysis. The collections are grouped by topic, such as nuclear history. These online briefing books are free; other formal collections and analysis are available for purchase. The FOIA section of the site includes the downloadable guide *Effective FOIA Requesting for Everyone* and information on document classification.

The National Security Archive provides a valuable research service offline, with its archive of declassified U.S. documents obtained through FOIA and its own print and microform publications. The online collections meet some popular information needs and present documents with contextual commentary identifying relevant people and events.

Subject(s): Declassified Documents; Foreign Policy—Research; Freedom of Information Act

Publication(s):

Effective FOIA Requesting for Everyone

National Virtual Translation Center (NVTC)

https://www.fbi.gov/about/leadership-and-structure/intelligence-branch/national-virtual-translation-center

Description: NVTC is an interagency enterprise supported by agencies in the defense and intelligence communities. NVTC acts as a clearinghouse for facilitating interagency use of translators, and it partners with government, academia, and private industry to identify translator resources and engage their services. The NVTC website discusses its mission and employment opportunities. The Customers section offers an explanation of the services provided and an FAQ area.

Subject(s): Foreign Languages; Language Education

Office of the Director of National Intelligence (ODNI)

https://www.dni.gov/index.php

Description: The Office of the Director of National Intelligence (ODNI) was established by the Intelligence Reform and Terrorism Prevention Act of 2004, following a recommendation of the 9-11 Commission. The director is the principal adviser to the president on intelligence, separate from the Central Intelligence Agency (CIA). The website includes an organization chart and sections on major ODNI offices and centers, including the Information Sharing Environment, National Counterterrorism Center, the National Intelligence Council, and the National Counterintelligence and Security Center.

Subject(s): Intelligence Agencies

Office of Naval Intelligence (ONI)

http://www.oni.navy.mil

Description: This website has basic information about ONI, its leadership, news, and employment opportunities. The Proud History section, under the This Is ONI heading, provides a brief illustrated history of ONI since its founding in 1882.

Subject(s): Intelligence Agencies; Military Intelligence

Open Source Center (OSC)

https://www.opensource.gov

Description: The Open Source Center website is only available to registered, qualified government and military employees and government contractors. It provides English translations of news and information from a wide array of unclassified international sources. The Open Source Center was established as part of the CIA in late 2005; it absorbed the Foreign Broadcast Information Service (FBIS), which previously published English-language translations of foreign broadcasts and printed news.

Subject(s): Intelligence—International; News Services

OpenNet

https://www.osti.gov/opennet/

Description: According to the site, "OpenNet is a website supported by the Department of Energy's Office of Classification to provide easy, timely access to recently declassified documents and other related information, in support of the national Openness Initiative. In addition to DOE documents declassified and determined to be publicly available after October 1, 1994, citations to older agency document collections are included." The documents concern nuclear weapons testing, studies of the effects of radiation, and related activities of the United States and other governments. The site's Advanced Search function includes the ability to search full-text documents, as well as limit searches by declassification status, document location, and other factors. The Information Resources section of the website links to DOE's *Reports to Congress on the Inadvertent Releases of Restricted Data and Formerly Restricted Da*ta *under Executive Order 12958* and other of the department's Openness Initiative products.

Subject(s): Declassified Documents; Nuclear Weapons—History

Twenty-Fifth Air Force (25 AF)

http://www.25af.af.mil/

Description: The Twenty-Fifth Air Force, formerly known as the Air Force Intelligence, Surveillance, and Reconnaissance Agency (AFISRA), is headquartered at Lackland Air Force Base in Texas. 25 AF has the mission of providing intelligence, surveillance, and reconnaissance (ISR) for military operations. The website features news, leadership biographies, and unit information.

Subject(s): Intelligence Agencies; Military Intelligence

U.S. Army Intelligence and Security Command (INSCOM)

https://www.inscom.army.mil/

Description: INSCOM conducts intelligence, security, and information operations for military commanders and national decision makers. The central INSCOM website links to its major subordinate commands (MSCs). The site also has information on business opportunities with INSCOM.

Subject(s): Military Intelligence

MILITARY MORALE AND WELFARE

Air Force Bands

http://www.bands.af.mil

Description: This site provides extensive information on the Air Force Bands and Air National Guard Bands, including performance schedules, song recordings, requests for performances, and position openings in the bands.

Subject(s): Military Bands; Music

Air Force Medical Service (AFMS)

http://www.airforcemedicine.af.mil/

Description: The Air Force Medical Service's mission is "to enable medically fit forces, provide expeditionary medics, and improve the health of all we serve to meet our nation's needs." (from the website) The website provides information on the AFMS as well as news, photos, and history.

Subject(s): Air Force; Military Medicine

America's Heroes at Work (AHAW)

https://www.dol.gov/vets/ahaw/

Description: The America's Heroes at Work project is designed to provide support for employers of returning service members living with traumatic brain injury (TBI) or post-traumatic stress disorder (PTSD). The site includes answers to frequently asked questions, fact sheets, and training presentations to inform audiences about TBI and PTSD. The site also includes AHAW success stories.

Subject(s): Veterans

Arlington National Cemetery

https://www.arlingtoncemetery.mil/

Description: The official website for Arlington National Cemetery is organized into the following sections: Plan Your Visit, Funeral Information, Explore the Cemetery, Events, and News. The site is rich in historical information on such topics as famous memorials, famous individuals buried at Arlington, the origins of "Taps" and the 21-gun salute, and the history of the Tomb of the Unknowns. The Photo Gallery section includes photographs of military burial ceremonies. The Funeral Information section provides information about eligibility requirements for interment or inurnment at the cemetery.

Subject(s): Military History; Veterans' Cemeteries

Armed Forces Retirement Home (AFRH)

https://www.afrh.gov/

Description: The Armed Forces Retirement Home consists of two campuses, one in Washington, D.C., and one in Gulfport, MS. The site has information about both facilities and how to apply for residence.

Subject(s): Veterans

Army & Air Force Exchange Service (AAFES)

https://www.shopmyexchange.com/

Description: AAFES serves active duty military members, retirees, reservists, and their dependents by providing goods and services through a corporation and central store with a wide range of consumer products. While AAFES's physical facilities are located on military bases, its online presence provides access to its services to any eligible person with Internet access. The AAFES website features online shopping, store locations, business opportunities, and information about AAFES, with some sections open only to authorized users. It also has an option for sending gift certificates or prepaid phone cards to deployed troops.

This site caters to the active and retired military community authorized to shop at Army and Air Force exchanges. Others may find useful information in the About The Exchange section, which explains the history and operations of military base exchanges and provides information for suppliers or manufacturers wanting to do business with AAFES.

Subject(s): Military Morale and Welfare

Department of Defense Education Activity (DoDEA)

https://www.dodea.edu/

Description: This is the official Internet presence of the K–12 schools operated by the Department of Defense. The schools are located overseas and in the United States. The Data Center section of the website (under DoDEA HQ) features school contact information, school enrollment data, and standardized test results. Employment information can be found in the Human Resources section (also under DoDEA HQ).

Subject(s): Elementary and Secondary Education; Military Morale and Welfare

Department of Veterans Affairs (VA)

https://www.va.gov/

Description: Major sections of the VA website include Health, Benefits, and Burials & Memorials. The site has direct links to topics in demand, such as prescriptions, VA forms, and careers at the VA. The site also has a directory of VA locations and a link to online services. The About VA section has organization information, congressional testimony, and budget information.

More institutional information is provided in the News Room section. Because it is a Cabinet-level department, the VA also has an Open Government section on its website.

This site should prove useful to veterans and people involved in assisting them. Using the site map will help to uncover all of the available information.

Subject(s): Veterans

Employer Support of the Guard and Reserve (ESGR)

https://www.esgr.mil/

Description: ESGR works to facilitate the relationship between Reserve Component Service members and their civilian employers. The Reserve is comprised of all National Guard members and Reserve forces from all branches of the military. This website has information about the Uniformed Services Employment and Reemployment Rights Act (USERRA), ESGR incentive programs for employers, and local employer support volunteers. It also provides tips and fact sheets for employers and for members of the Reserve forces.

Subject(s): Labor-Management Relations; Military Reserves; National Guard

eVetRecs

https://www.archives.gov/veterans/military-service-records

Description: This site provides instructions on requesting information from military records and is intended for veterans or the next of kin of a deceased former member of the military. The site also links to guidance on requests from the general public, which require a different procedure. The eVetRecs site includes information on how the National Archives protects the privacy and security of veterans' records.

Subject(s): Veterans

National Resource Directory

https://www.nrd.gov/

Description: The subtitle of the National Resource Directory website is "Connecting Wounded Warriors, Service Members, Veterans, Their Families, and Caregivers with Those Who Support Them." The Departments of Defense, Labor, and Veterans Affairs maintain the site. It links to information on benefits and compensation, education and training, employment, health care, family and caregiver support, and other topics. The linked information is from federal, state, and local government agencies, veterans' service and benefit organizations, non-profit community-based and faith-based organizations, academic institutions, professional associations, and philanthropic organizations.

Subject(s): Veterans; Military Medicine

Nationwide Gravesite Locator

https://gravelocator.cem.va.gov/

Description: The Nationwide Gravesite Locator has burial records from many sources. It includes the burial locations of veterans and their family members in VA National Cemeteries, state veterans cemeteries, and other military and Department of Interior (DOI) cemeteries, as well as the locations of veterans buried in private cemeteries (1997 to present) when the grave is marked with a government grave marker. Researchers can search the database by name, birth or death date, and cemetery name.

Subject(s): Veterans' Cemeteries

Navy and Marine Corps Public Health Center (NMCPHC)

http://www.med.navy.mil/sites/nmcphc/

Description: The Navy and Marine Corps Public Health Center aims to ensure Navy and Marine Corps readiness through leadership in the prevention of disease and the promotion of health. The site covers such topics as deployment health, environmental and occupational health, and preventive medicine. Sections also link to the center's field activities and leadership information. An alphabetical index assists in finding information on this expansive site. Some sections may be closed to all but registered users.

Subject(s): Preventive Health Care; Military Medicine

Navy Medicine

http://www.med.navy.mil

Description: The Navy's Bureau of Medicine and Surgery provides health care to active duty Navy and Marine Corps members, retired service members, and their families. This site primarily provides information and services for those working in the Navy medical system and for the sailors they serve. The site carries the texts of Navy Medicine Policies and Navy Medicine Directives. It also has a list of links to the websites of Navy medical facilities around the world.

Subject(s): Military Medicine

Returning Service Members (OEF/OIF/OND)

https://www.oefoif.va.gov/

Description: This VA website provides information on benefits and transition assistance available for Operation Enduring Freedom, Operation Iraqi Freedom, and Operation New Dawn veterans.

Subject(s): Veterans; Military Medicine

Servicemembers and Veterans Initiative

https://www.justice.gov/servicemembers

Description: This website explains the major laws that support the rights of servicemembers and veterans: the Uniformed Services Employment and Reemployment Rights Act (USERRA), the Uniformed and Overseas Citizen Absentee Voting Act (UOCAVA), and the Servicemembers Civil Relief Act (SCRA). The site has brochures about protecting servicemember rights and returning servicemembers with disabilities.

Subject(s): Military Forces—Laws; Veterans—Laws

U.S. Army Music

http://www.music.army.mil

Description: The website has links to the Army's various bands, news, and performance schedules. The Music section includes the lyrics of the official Army song and sheet music for the Army's many bugle calls.

Subject(s): Military Bands; Music

U.S. Navy Band

http://www.navyband.navy.mil/

Description: The Navy Band's website has information about each of the Navy's bands and ensembles. The site includes concert schedules, a discography, history, resources for music educators, and the *Fanfare* newsletter. The site also has information on the Navy Hymn, "Eternal Father, Strong to Save," and the Navy Service Song, "Anchors Aweigh."

Subject(s): Military Bands; Music

USA4 Military Families

http://usa4families.militaryonesource.mil

Description: USA4 Military Families is a Defense Department initiative to educate and encourage state policymakers, non-profits, businesses, and others to adopt policies that have a positive effect on military families. It outlines and provides the status of ten quality of life issues, such as military consumer protections and licensure and academic credit for separating service members.

Subject(s): Armed Forces—Policy

Veterans Benefits Administration (VBA)

https://benefits.va.gov/benefits/

Description: The VBA website is part of the larger VA website. Major sections of the site cover education benefits, home loans, compensation and pensions, survivors' benefits, vocational rehabilitation, employment, and life insurance. The site links to forms, manuals, publications, and benefits fact sheets.

Subject(s): Veterans

Wounded Warrior Regiment

http://www.woundedwarrior.marines.mil/

Description: Established in 2006, the Marine Corps Wounded Warrior Regiment "serves Marines who are wounded in combat, fall ill, or are injured in the line of duty. This includes active duty, reserve, and veteran Marines." (from the website) The site has information for both marines and their families.

Subject(s): Marine Corps; Veterans

Chapter Six

Demographics and Sociology

Much of the statistical information about the U.S. population comes from the Commerce Department's Bureau of the Census. This chapter includes Census websites presenting demographic data, websites from other agencies producing demographic data, and those from academic institutions that play a role in making Census data available online. Information on other types of federal government statistics, such as education statistics, can be found in the relevant subject chapter, such as the Education chapter.

Subsections in this chapter are Census and Statistics, and Demographic Groups.

CENSUS AND STATISTICS

American Community Survey (ACS)

https://www.census.gov/programs-surveys/acs/

Description: The Census Bureau's American Community Survey is a survey sent to a sample of the U.S. population. Whereas the decennial *United States Census* consists of a short-form, the ACS is ongoing and consists of a long-form. The focus of the ACS is to provide the government with data more current and more detailed than those from the decennial Census in order to provide the government guidance in administering federal programs, distributing funding, and planning future projects.

The website describes how to access, use, and understand ACS data, which is integrated into the Census Bureau's American FactFinder interface and available for downloading. An explanatory brochure about the ACS is provided in Arabic, Chinese, Korean, Polish, Russian, Spanish, and other languages.

Subject(s): Census Techniques

American FactFinder

https://factfinder.census.gov/faces/nav/jsf/pages/index.xhtml

Description: American FactFinder allows researchers to create simple reports, custom tables, and reference maps using Census Bureau data. The main search box retrieves quick fact sheets for a single geographic area or topic.

The Guided Search section of American FactFinder is straightforward and menu driven. Users can refine queries by topics, geographies, and racial and ethnic groups. Each data set page offers a detailed description of the offering.

American FactFinder accesses enough data and has enough functionality to make it the first and last stop for many users, especially those looking for population and housing statistics. Consult the What We Provide section for guides to using American FactFinder.

Subject(s): Census; Economic Statistics; Population Statistics

***Census 2000* Gateway**

https://www.census.gov/main/www/cen2000.html

Description: This site provides information from *Census 2000* by serving as a starting point for finding associated products, data sets, news, documentation, and other information. There are three main approaches to the data itself. The American FactFinder section provides tables and maps of *Census 2000* data for all geographies, from the nation as a whole to the block level. The QuickFacts section has summaries of the most requested data for states and counties, as well as for cities and towns with populations of 5,000 or more. The Data Highlights section links to a variety of information at the state, county, and place level, including American FactFinder tables and maps, FTP access to data sets, technical documentation, news releases, state data center contacts, redistricting data, and other related statistics. Other data reports include rankings and comparisons, briefs and special reports, and selected historical Census data. The Census in Schools section includes teaching resources and lesson plans.

For access to current Census Bureau data on multiple topics, see the bureau's American FactFinder database at https://factfinder.census.gov/.

Subject(s): Census; Population Statistics

Census 2010

https://www.census.gov/2010census/

Description: The site contains the most relevant information from *Census 2010*, the most recent *United States Census*. Items under the Data heading include *2010 Census Summary Files*, *2010 Census Demographic Profiles*, and briefs on such topics as the American Indian and Alaska Native population and population distribution and change.

Subject(s): Census

Census Bureau

https://www.census.gov/

Description: According to the website, "the U.S. Census Bureau conducts more than 130 surveys each year" to produce data about the American people and economy. The bureau is most well-known for its decennial census, the *United States Census*. The site's home page offers multiple routes to the wide variety of information from and about the bureau. Major categories include Topics, Library, Data, Geography, Newsroom, and About Us. The Data Tools & Apps section (under Data) links to online data tools, software, and databases; the prominent data tool American FactFinder is described elsewhere in this chapter. The Publications link (under Library) provides other avenues to the data. Information about the Census Bureau itself is provided in the About Us section. Important resources within the Census Bureau website are described separately in this and other chapters in the book.

Overall, the Census Bureau website offers one of the largest collections of readily accessible statistical data and recent statistical press releases on the Internet. This should be one of the first sites checked by users looking for demographic and economic statistics.

Subject(s): Census; Economic Statistics; Population Statistics; Databases

Census Bureau Regional Offices

https://www.census.gov/regions/

Description: This website uses a clickable image map and alternative text list to link to the websites of the Census Bureau's six regional offices. Each office's page provides local contact information and information about regional resources.

Subject(s): Census

DataFerrett

https://dataferrett.census.gov/

Description: DataFerrett is a software tool that allows enhanced viewing and manipulation of selected government data sets. The website includes a users' guide and tutorial, as well as a section on frequently asked questions.

Subject(s): Statistics

International Programs Center (IPC) – Census Bureau

https://www.census.gov/programs-surveys/international-programs.html

Description: IPC, part of the Census Bureau's Population Division, offers a variety of international population statistics at its website, including a U.S. and World Population Clock, a second-by-second simulation of U.S.

and world population growth. IPC's International Database has extensive information on world demographics. IPC also produces the HIV/AIDS Surveillance Database, a compilation of information from small-scale surveys of developing countries. The IPC website has information and software products related to its work in assisting developing countries with census administration.

Subject(s): Vital Statistics—International

IPUMS USA: Integrated Public Use Microdata Series

https://usa.ipums.org/usa/

Description: The Integrated Public Use Microdata Series consists of Census microdata for social and economic research. It is a project of the University of Minnesota that is partially funded by federal grants. IPUMS offers population and household data samples from the U.S. decennial Censuses from 1850 forward and data from the American Community Survey (ACS) starting in 2000. Variables have been given consistent names across time, and other data fields have been harmonized across data sets. Users can download the IPUMS data by either extracting custom files or downloading entire data sets. The series is free but registration is required before extracting data.

The IPUMS tools are intended for expert researchers running statistical studies using sample data. The data itself cannot be browsed online and extracted files are very large. IPUMS does, however, offer an online data analysis system.

Subject(s): Census

My Congressional District

https://www.census.gov/mycd/

Description: This website was designed for use by members of Congress and their staff, but it is available to the general public. The site's emphasis is on access to Census Bureau data by congressional district. Searches by congressional district locate basic population, housing, and economic statistics with the data mapped to the district boundaries. The homepage also links to congressional district maps and other popular Census Bureau products.

Subject(s): Congressional Districts—Statistics

Selected Historical Decennial Census Counts

https://www.census.gov/population/www/censusdata/hiscendata.html

Description: The full title of this webpage is "Selected Historical Decennial Census Population and Housing Counts." It compiles links to past Census reports. The actual decennial reports are online in PDF format for every decade from 1790 through 2000, along with corresponding historical notes. The page also links to tabulations of data items across the years. For example, it links to a table comparing urban and rural populations for 1790 through 1990 and to historical Census statistics on the foreign-born population for the 1850–1990 period. Histories and questionnaires from past Censuses are also provided.

Subject(s): Census—History; Population Statistics

State Data Center (SDC) Program – Census Bureau

https://www.census.gov/about/partners/sdc.html

Description: The Census Bureau's SDC Program functions to disseminate "data produced by the Census Bureau to state and local governments and the data users within their communities." (from the website) The Program Guidelines PDF on the website provides basic contact information for the lead data center in each state, as well as detailed information about the program. It also links to related sites, such as those for the Census Information Center (CIC) Program and the Census Depository Library (CDL) Network.

Subject(s): Census

U.S. and World Population Clock

https://www.census.gov/popclock/

Description: This webpage features two population clocks that give second-by-second population estimates for the U.S. and for the world. New features show population data by day and year, country or U.S. region and year, and age and sex and year; there are also lists of the most populous and the most densely populated countries as well as U.S. states, counties, and cities. The U.S. Population Clock estimates the resident population of the United States by the second and gives the criteria for how the estimate is derived; historical estimates and documentation are also available. The World Population Clock estimates the world's population second-by-second and lists monthly estimates.

These clocks are useful for demonstrating the rate of change in population for both the United States and the world. However, before citing the estimates, users should read the documentation on how those estimates are reached and revised.

Subject(s): Population Statistics

QuickFacts

https://www.census.gov/quickfacts/

Description: QuickFacts offers simple access to frequently requested national, state, and county data from various Census Bureau programs, as well as data for cities and towns with more than 5,000 residents. In 2015, a revamped version of the website was made available. Users can choose a state from a list or from the clickable U.S. map and then select a county or city. Information at each geographic level is presented for three topics: people, business, and geography. At the state level, statistics are given for the state versus the country as a whole; at the county and city levels, county and city statistics are compared to the statewide numbers. Each state and county data table also has a link to more data sets for that location. The additional data sets include historical population counts, congressional district statistics, and tables from the American Community Survey (ACS), Economic Census, County Business Patterns, and Consolidated Federal Funds Reports, among other resources.

This site serves as both a quick reference tool and a resource locator. By clicking on the information icon next to each data heading, users link to a page that presents the source, definition, scope, and methodology for that heading, along with a list of relevant links.

Subject(s): Census; Population Statistics

TIGER Products

https://www.census.gov/geo/maps-data/data/tiger.html

Description: TIGER (Topologically Integrated Geographic Encoding and Referencing) is the name given to the Census Bureau's digital mapping system for the decennial census and other data. The TIGER home page offers TIGER-based digital geographic products, documentation and metadata, and information about the system. The TIGER/Line files are the primary public product created from the data in the TIGER database. The files comprise a database of geographic features, such as roads, railroads, and rivers. They can be used with the mapping or geographic information system (GIS) software that can import TIGER/Line files.

The TIGER Page is the central place to check for updates to the TIGER/Line files and related products. Explanatory material is available for both the newcomer and the experienced community of digital geographic data users.

Subject(s): Census Mapping; Geographic Information Systems (GIS)

DEMOGRAPHIC GROUPS

AgingStats.Gov

https://agingstats.gov/

Description: The Federal Interagency Forum on Aging-Related Statistics is made up of 15 federal agencies that produce or use statistics on aging. Their website, AgingStats.gov, is a finding aid for these statistics. The site links directly to aging-related statistics on its members' websites, including relevant data at the Census Bureau, Department of Veterans Affairs (VA), National Center for Health Statistics (NCHS), and Social Security Administration (SSA). The Contacts section provides the names, areas of expertise, and contact information for federal agency experts. The site also carries the full text of *Older Americans 2012: Key Indicators of Well-Being* and *Data Sources on Older Americans*.

Subject(s): Senior Citizens—Statistics

American Indian and Alaska Native Resources

https://www.census.gov/aian

Description: This Census Bureau webpage serves as a portal to Census information on American Indian and Alaska Native communities. In addition to population data, maps, and tribal information, the site includes statistical policy background and a link to the website for the Census Advisory Committee on the American Indian and Alaska Native (AIAN) Populations. The site links to available information from *Census 2010*.

Subject(s): American Indians—Statistics; Alaska Natives—Statistics

ChildStats.gov

https://www.childstats.gov/

Description: This website provides access to federal and state statistics and reports on children and their families across a range of concerns, including family and social environment, economic security, health, behavior, and education. The Federal Interagency Forum on Child and Family Statistics offers several reports on the site, the most prominent of which is the annual *America's Children: Key National Indicators of Well-Being*.

Subject(s): Child Welfare—Statistics

National Center for Veterans Analysis and Statistics (NCVAS)

https://www.va.gov/vetdata/

Description: This site provides current and projected veterans demographics at the national, state, county, and congressional district level. It also provides data on Veterans Administration expenditures by geographic area and links to other surveys and statistics on the veteran population.

Subject(s): Veterans—Statistics

Chapter Seven

Education

The Education Department is, naturally, the leader in publishing federal government education information on the Internet. This chapter includes many of the online resources made available by the department, but it also includes information on military education activities, federally sponsored scholarships, and some education-related social service programs. The Kids' Pages section of this chapter includes over 50 websites designed for a younger audience and covering a wide variety of subject areas.

Subsections of this chapter are Adult Education, Curriculum, Early Childhood Education, Education Funding, Education Policy, Education Research and Statistics, Elementary and Secondary Education, Higher Education, International Education, Kids' Pages, and Teaching.

ADULT EDUCATION

DANTES: Defense Activity for Non-Traditional Education Support

http://www.dantes.doded.mil

Description: DANTES provides support for the Department of Defense's off-duty, voluntary education programs. Its website has information about counselor support, distance learning, and tuition assistance. It also has a section about the Troops to Teachers (TTT) program, which assists military personnel interested in beginning a second career as a public school teacher.

Subject(s): Servicemembers—Education

Office of Career, Technical, and Adult Education (OCTAE)

https://www2.ed.gov/about/offices/list/ovae/index.html

Description: This site provides information about Office of Career, Technical, and Adult Education programs, grants, events, legislation, and resources concerning the fields of adult education and vocational education. Key sections are Adult Ed and Literacy, Career and Technical Ed, and Community Colleges.

Subject(s): Adult Education; Literacy; Vocational Education

USA Learns

https://www.usalearns.org/

Description: USA Learns provides free, online lessons to help adults learn English and improve basic reading, writing, and speaking skills. The website was developed with funding from the U.S. Department of Education and the California Department of Education. Currently, the Sacramento County Office of Education retains full ownership rights for the USA Learns website. See the About Us section for further details.

Subject(s): Language Education

Curriculum

Agriculture in the Classroom (AITC)

https://www.agclassroom.org/

Description: The USDA's Agriculture in the Classroom program coordinates state education programs designed to teach children about the role of agriculture in the economy and in society. The site includes a directory of state programs, a directory of educational materials about agriculture, information on the National Agriculture in the Classroom conference, and the online magazine *AgroWorld* for high school educators and students.

Subject(s): Agricultural Education; Educational Resources

ArtsEdge: The Kennedy Center's Arts Education Network

http://artsedge.kennedy-center.org/educators.aspx

Description: ArtsEdge, from the Kennedy Center, is a major arts resource for educators and students. The site includes lesson plans and content standards for grades K–12.

This well-designed site should be a primary starting point for users involved in arts education. The Kennedy Center is a federal government building, but its programs are privately funded. The Kennedy Center holds the copyright to all of the content on the site.

Subject(s): Arts Education; Lesson Plans

Bureau of Land Management (BLM) – Learning Landscapes

https://www.blm.gov/wo/st/en/res/Education_in_BLM/Learning_Landscapes.html

Description: This BLM website has information and activities for students and teachers. The Teachers section has information about field programs (mostly in the Western states), websites, resources, and classroom activities. Online resources for teachers and learners cover such areas as archeology, fire ecology, and energy on public lands.

Subject(s): Environmental Education; Science Education

DocsTeach

https://www.docsteach.org/

Description: The tagline of DocsTeach is "Bring history to life for your students." The site provides resources for using documents in the classroom, with links to thousands of primary source documents, such as illustrated family records from the 18th and 19th centuries and photos of John F. Kennedy's inauguration.

Subject(s): Education; History

EDSITEment

https://edsitement.neh.gov/

Description: The EDSITEment website's tag line is "the best of the humanities on the Web." It provides a cataloged selection of lesson plans built around high-quality, freely accessible material available on the Internet. The lesson plans are organized into sections including Art & Culture, Literature & Language Arts, Foreign Language, and History & Social Studies. Lessons are sortable by grade range. Each detailed lesson plan is labeled with the subject area, time required, and skills taught.

Subject(s): Lesson Plans; Humanities

Energy Education and Workforce Development

https://www.energy.gov/eere/education/education-homepage

Description: The Energy Education and Workforce Development website links to numerous resources for students, teachers, and adults pursuing energy or green energy jobs. For teachers, the site has a database of lesson plans and activities on energy efficiency and renewable energy for grades K–12. It also has information on internships and fellowships for teachers and students, as well as a section called "Green Your School." For others, the site has a section on clean energy jobs and education and training for these jobs.

Subject(s): Science Education; Jobs

Environmental Health Science Education: Teachers

https://www.niehs.nih.gov/health/scied/teachers/

Description: This NIEHS webpage provides curricular material and lesson resources on environmental health topics. The lessons are aligned with the National Science Education Standards and designed for grade levels K–12 and beyond.

Subject(s): Environmental Education

GLOBE Program

https://www.globe.gov/

Description: The GLOBE (Global Learning and Observations to Benefit the Environment) program is designed to promote science education at the primary and secondary school levels. GLOBE is sponsored by NASA and the National Science Foundation. The GLOBE program's primary objective is to involve students in taking environmental measurements. More than 28,000 schools in 116 countries are participating. The data they collect is accessible to anyone and there is information on how new schools can register to be included in the program. The site also has a teacher's guide and a schedule of teacher workshops. Much of the content is available in Spanish and other non-English languages such as Arabic, Chinese, and French.

With participating schools from all over the world, this kind of collaborative project demonstrates how the Internet can be used in a K–12 environment.

Subject(s): Environmental Protection; Science Education

Learning Registry

https://www.learningregistry.org/

Description: The Learning Registry's goal is to assist educators and education administrators in finding digital learning resources and integrating them into their classrooms. This online registry is a multi-agency initiative headed by the Departments of Defense and Education. The site features an Educators section that serves as a user's guide for teachers, as well as a Publishers section for those looking to share their digital content with the registry.

Subject(s): Digital Libraries

National Archives – Teachers' Resources

https://www.archives.gov/education

Description: This National Archives site features history lesson plans and teaching activities correlated to the National History Standards and the National Standards for Civics and Government. It focuses on teaching with the primary documents available on the Archives' site. The site links to information on teacher training, videoconferences, workshops, and other educational services from the National Archives. The site also links to education programs at the presidential libraries and resources for National History Day.

Subject(s): Lesson Plans; Social Studies Education

NASA – Education

https://www.nasa.gov/offices/education/about/index.html

Description: The NASA Education website provides information about the education programs that NASA offers to K–12 educators and students, as well as those offered to undergraduate and graduate students and faculty at universities. The site also features educational resources for all levels.

Subject(s): Science Education

National Marine Sanctuaries – Education

https://sanctuaries.noaa.gov/education/

Description: The National Marine Sanctuaries Education website features lesson plans, free materials, information on workshops, and other items of interest to science or environment teachers. The section specifically for teachers includes information on the NOAA Ocean Data Education (NODE) Project, which is developing curriculum for grades 5–8 designed to help teachers and students use real scientific data.

Subject(s): Lesson Plans; Science Education

National Science Foundation – Classroom Resources

https://www.nsf.gov/news/classroom/

Description: This website provides organized links to classroom resources on the Internet. The site describes its intended audience as students, their families, and teachers. Links are organized into science topics such as biology, computing, Earth and environment, mathematics, and physics. The linked sites are from a variety of educational organizations and institutions.

Subject(s): Science Education

NOAA – Education Resources

http://www.noaa.gov/education

Description: The NOAA Education Resources site has opportunity announcements and materials for both teachers and students that cover subjects including weather, climate change, oceans and coasts, weather satellites, and space environments. The Educator Opportunities link (under Education Opportunities) on the front page features up-to-date information on in-person workshops, online training, field experiences, and conferences. The Student Opportunities link under that same heading lists scholarships, internships, and fellowships.

Subject(s): Environmental Education

Office of English Language Acquisition (OELA)

https://www2.ed.gov/about/offices/list/oela/index.html

Description: The full title of this office is the Office of English Language Acquisition, Language Enhancement, and Academic Achievement for Limited English Proficient Students. As stated on the website, OELA's mission is "to provide national leadership to help ensure that English learners and immigrant students attain English proficiency and achieve academically." To this end, under Title III of the Elementary and Secondary Education Act (ESEA), OELA administers grant programs, supports research studies to inform policy, and disseminates information about language instruction. Information about applying to these and other grant programs is available on the site. OELA's website also features an *English Learner Tool Kit* and an *Early Learning Tool Kit*.

Subject(s): Language Education—Grants

Picturing America

https://picturingamerica.neh.gov/

Description: The Picturing America project provides schools with American art images and educational resources to facilitate teaching American history and culture. The website has information about the program, a gallery of Picturing America images, and downloadable materials such as a guide to using the images in a preschool curriculum.

Subject(s): Arts Education

Statistics in Schools

https://www.census.gov/schools/

Description: The Statistics in Schools program's website has materials for teachers (lesson plans, teaching ideas) and sections for kids and teens. It also has a section specifically for *Census 2010* materials.

Subject(s): Census; Social Studies Education

U.S. Geological Survey (USGS) – Science Education

https://education.usgs.gov/

Description: The USGS education website covers topics of concern to USGS scientists, including geography, geology, biology, and water resources. Educational resources are organized for grades K–6, grades 7–12, and undergraduate education. Resources include online lectures, science videos, satellite imagery, guides to teaching with maps, and educational products from the USGS online store. The site also covers USGS careers, internships, and postdoctoral fellowships.

Subject(s): Science Education; Kids' Pages

EARLY CHILDHOOD EDUCATION

Early Childhood Learning and Knowledge Center (ECLKC)

https://eclkc.ohs.acf.hhs.gov/hslc/

Description: The Early Childhood Learning and Knowledge Center provides extensive information on Head Start and Early Head Start programs and on topics such as early childhood development, dual language learners, parenting, and professional development for program grantees. It includes an online directory of Head Start programs. ECLKC also provides information on Head Start regulations and policy, performance standards, and program monitoring. Most information is available in Spanish.

Subject(s): Education—Early Childhood

Head Start

https://www.acf.hhs.gov/ohs

Description: The Office of Head Start administers grants for local public and private non-profit and for-profit agencies that provide child development services for low-income children and their families. The website has information on the program and relevant laws and regulations. The site also links to research on outcomes for both Head Start (preschool) and Early Head Start (infant to three years).

Subject(s): Early Childhood Education

EDUCATION FUNDING

Bureau of Indian Education (BIE)

https://www.bie.edu/

Description: BIE oversees 183 elementary and secondary schools and two post-secondary schools for American Indian tribes and Alaska Native Villages. The BIE website has a directory of the schools, annual ratings of the schools, and performance reports on special education programs (the latter two in the Reports section). The site also has resources for teachers at the schools.

Subject(s): American Indians

CyberCorps®: Scholarship for Service (SFS)

https://www.sfs.opm.gov/

Description: OPM's Scholarship for Service program funds the education expenses of undergraduate and graduate students in information assurance fields in exchange for an obligation to work for the federal government for an agreed-upon term. The program is designed to strengthen the federal government's expertise in information assurance (the security of computer and communication networks and the information they carry). This website has further details about the program and a list of participating higher education institutions.

Subject(s): Computer Science; Scholarships

Education Finance Statistics Center (EDFIN)

https://nces.ed.gov/edfin/

Description: The EDFIN website provides finance information on public elementary and secondary education. The site provides charts and data on per-pupil expenditures for public elementary and secondary education, the distribution of expenditures for public elementary and secondary education by function, and similar measures.

Subject(s): Education Funding—Statistics

FAFSA4caster

https://fafsa.ed.gov/FAFSA/app/f4cForm

Description: The FAFSA4caster website is for those planning for higher education but not yet ready to apply for financial aid. The site provides an orientation to the financial aid process and an estimate of eligibility for aid.

Subject(s): Financial Aid to Students

Federal Student Aid

https://studentaid.ed.gov/sa/

Description: This website is a portal and service center for federal student aid information and programs, designed for students and their parents or advisers. The site is available in both English and Spanish, and features information on applying for student aid, the types of student aid available, eligibility requirements, and repayment management, as well as a comprehensive section on preparing for college, The site links to the Free Application for Federal Student Aid (FAFSA) online.

Subject(s): Education Funding; Student Loans

Federal Student Aid Gateway

https://studentaid.ed.gov/sa/redirects/federal-student-aid-ed-gov

Description: This site provides information, referrals, and links for students, parents, financial aid professionals, and those doing business with the Federal Student Aid Office. It also provides program data, such as loan default rates.

The Federal Student Aid Gateway serves a broad audience. Other financial aid websites listed in this section are more specialized.

Subject(s): Financial Aid to Students

Free Application for Federal Student Aid (FAFSA)

https://fafsa.ed.gov/

Description: FAFSA's website makes it possible to apply online for federal financial aid for college. The site provides guidance on applying for aid, guidance on the application process, and information on deadlines.

Subject(s): Financial Aid to Students

Education and Training – Department of Veterans Affairs (VA)

https://www.benefits.va.gov/gibill/

Description: This VA website provides information on the range of education benefits for active duty and reserve servicemembers, veterans, survivors, and dependents. The site outlines the steps for applying for these benefits and provides tools, such as benefits comparison tools, to encourage informed planning. The site has a history of the original G.I. Bill, formally the Servicemembers' Readjustment Act of 1944, which preceded the current benefits framework.

Subject(s): Military Training and Education; Veterans

Information for Financial Aid Professionals (IFAP)

https://ifap.ed.gov/ifap/

Description: IFAP is an extensive electronic library for financial aid professionals. The site provides publications, information on regulations, and guidance regarding the administration of Title IV federal student aid. It also features online tools, worksheets, and schedules related to the various federal student aid programs.

Subject(s): Financial Aid to Students

EDUCATION FUNDING

Department of Education

https://www.ed.gov/

Description: The Department of Education website features current news, the department's blog, and links to high-profile initiatives. Major sections of the site include Student Loans, Grants, Laws, and Data. As a Cabinet-level department, Education also provides Recovery Act and Open Government Initiative information on its site.

Subject(s): Education—Policy; Educational Resources; Financial Aid to Students

Directorate for Education and Human Resources (EHR) – National Science Foundation (NSF)

https://www.nsf.gov/dir/index.jsp?org=ehr

Description: The Directorate for Education and Human Resources provides leadership in the effort to improve science, technology, engineering, and mathematics education in the United States. Its website includes links to descriptions of the EHR divisions—the Division of Graduate Education (DGE), Division of Undergraduate Education (DUE), Division of Research on Learning in Formal and Informal Settings (DRL), and Division of Human

Resource Development (HRD)—and the types of projects they sponsor. The site provides directorate reports and notices of funding opportunities.

This site will be of assistance to science and engineering students and educators at all levels who are interested in pursuing grants or scholarships.

Subject(s): Science Education—Grants

Every Student Succeeds Act (ESSA)

https://www.ed.gov/esea/

Description: The Every Student Succeeds Act was signed into law by President Barack Obama in 2015, replacing the No Child Left Behind (NCLB) Act of 2001. ESSA serves as the policy framework for the country's K–12 public education system. The site features accessible information about ESSA, including an informative fact sheet describing how it was drafted to address the many criticisms of No Child Left Behind.

Subject(s): Legislation—Education

Office of Innovation and Improvement (OII)

https://innovation.ed.gov/

Description: OII administers discretionary grant programs, coordinates public school choice and supplemental educational efforts, and works with the nonpublic education community. The website's Office of Non-Public Education (ONPE) section includes a private school locator and statistics on private education in the United States.

Subject(s): Elementary and Secondary Education—Education Policy

White House Initiative on Educational Excellence for Hispanics

https://sites.ed.gov/hispanic-initiative/

Description: The website for the White House Initiative on Educational Excellence for Hispanics provides a history of the initiative first established in 1990. The site has information on current activities and staff for the initiative.

Subject(s): Educational Resources; Hispanic Americans

EDUCATION RESEARCH AND STATISTICS

Division of Research on Learning in Formal and Informal Settings (DRL)

https://www.nsf.gov/div/index.jsp?div=drl

Description: DRL is concerned with teaching and learning in science, technology, engineering, and mathematics at all age levels. The division's website has information on programs and funding opportunities for research in these areas, along with division news and events.

Subject(s): Science Education—Grants

ED Data Express

https://eddataexpress.ed.gov/

Description: ED Data Express provides access to data on elementary and secondary schools in the U.S. Data is collected by the Department of Education from U.S. states and territories, specifically coming from ED*Facts*, Consolidated State Performance Reports (CSPR), State Accountability Workbooks, the National Center for Education Statistics (NCES), the National Assessment of Education Progress (NAEP), the College Board, and the Department's Budget Service office. The State Snapshots section provides profiles for each state, and in the Data Element section, data can be narrowed down by category and group.

Subject(s): Education Research and Statistics

ERIC: Educational Resources Information Center

https://eric.ed.gov/

Description: ERIC is a database and information system funded by the Department of Education to provide organized access to a wide array of published and unpublished material about education. It generally references education literature from 1966 to the present, although some earlier sources are available, and is a standard resource for educational research. Many of the indexed documents are available in full text.

The ERIC search interface has basic and advanced versions. Searchable fields include title, author, ERIC number, identifier, ISBN, ISSN, publisher, sponsoring agency, thesaurus descriptor, and date range. Searches can be limited by type of material cited (e.g., journal article, non-print media, or dissertation) and full-text availability. The ERIC Thesaurus is linked to the search interface; users can also browse and search the thesaurus separately.

Subject(s): Educational Resources; ERIC

Institute of Education Sciences (IES)

https://ies.ed.gov/

Description: IES was established in 2002 to focus on education research. It includes the National Center for Education Research (NCER), the National Center for Education Statistics (NCES), the National Center for Education Evaluation and Regional Assistance (NCEE), and the National Center for Special Education Research (NCSER). The website has information on IES and its grants and component programs.

Subject(s): Education Research

National Center for Education Statistics (NCES)

https://nces.ed.gov/

Description: NCES collects and analyzes data concerning education in the United States and other nations. NCES is a primary source for education statistics for all educational levels and for data on educational assessment, libraries, and international educational outcomes. The website describes NCES surveys and programs and provides advanced data tools for accessing them. The center's major annual reports are available in PDF and Web versions; the reports are *The Condition of Education*, *Digest of Education Statistics*, *Trends in High School Dropout and Completion Rates in the United States*, *Indicators of School Crime and Safety*, and *Projections of Education Statistics to 2019*. Use the Publications & Products section and its subject index to locate other NCES reports. The Fast Facts section highlights frequently requested information on a range of topics from assessments to postsecondary education. The site also includes a searchable directory of private and public schools, colleges, and public libraries.

For users searching for statistics related to any form of education, this site should be the first place to visit.

Subject(s): Education Statistics

National Center for Education Statistics (NCES)—Common Core of Data (CCD)

https://nces.ed.gov/ccd/

Description: The Common Core of Data (CCD) is a program that collects data about all public schools, public school districts, and state education agencies in the United States on an annual basis. The CCD contains three categoresi of information: general descriptive information on schools and school districts; data on students and staff; and fiscal data This site provides detailed information on the CCD.

ELEMENTARY AND SECONDARY EDUCATION

Computers for Learning (CFL)

https://computersforlearning.gov/

Description: The Computers for Learning website is designed for public, private, parochial, and home schools serving the K–12 student population, as well as other nonprofit educational organizations. The service allows these groups of students and nonprofit organizations to request donations of surplus federal computer equipment. The site includes program and eligibility information and sections on how to give and receive computers.

Subject(s): Educational Technology; Surplus Government Property

Emergency Planning – Department of Education (ED)

https://www2.ed.gov/admins/lead/safety/emergencyplan/index.html

Description: The Emergency Planning website provides school leaders with information to plan for emergencies such as natural disasters or violent incidents. The site includes instructional webcasts, a crisis planning guide, information on pandemic flu preparedness, and links to related assistance programs from the Education Department.

Subject(s): Disaster Preparedness; School Buildings

NAEP Data Explorer (NDE)

https://www.nationsreportcard.gov/ndecore/landing

Description: The NAEP Data Explorer allows researchers to analyze data from the National Assessment of Educational Progress, the testing program administered to fourth, eighth, and twelfth graders that measures skills in reading, math, science, and other subjects. The Data Explorer includes assessment results in 10 subject areas for the nation and participating states. It enables state and school district comparisons and also has trend data on national mathematics and reading results dating from the 1970s. Users can create custom tables and charts and export data in several formats including as spreadsheets. The site provides a tutorial and quick reference guide.

Subject(s): Educational Assessment—Statistics

Nation's Report Card

https://nces.ed.gov/nationsreportcard/

Description: This is the online home of the National Assessment of Educational Progress (NAEP), an ongoing national assessment for student achievement in grades 4, 8, and 12. It provides background information on the history and current operations of the NAEP. Current results are available in the form of state profiles. Users can also construct custom data tables and get reports at the national level or by state, region, or major urban district. The Other Studies section links to information about special studies on, for example, student achievement in private schools and charter schools.

Subject(s): Educational Assessment; Elementary and Secondary Education

Office of Elementary and Secondary Education (OESE)

https://www2.ed.gov/about/offices/list/oese/index.html

Description: The OESE website has information on its programs, office contacts, and reports. The Laws, Regs & Guidance section is largely concerned with the Every Student Succeeds Act (ESSA). The Standards/Accountability and the Flexibility sections also cover areas of ESSA. The Consolidated State Info section features the Consolidated State Performance Report (CSPR), the required annual reporting tool for states on their accomplishments and other education-related data. The site is searchable through the Topics A–Z index, useful in uncovering all of the information at this site.

Much of the information on the site is intended for elementary and secondary education professionals and officials who need to comply with the Every Student Succeeds Act or who are interested in its documents.

Subject(s): Education Standards; Educational Assessment; Elementary and Secondary Education

Office of Safe and Healthy Students (OSHS)

https://www2.ed.gov/about/offices/list/oese/oshs/index.html

Description: OSHS's major programs come under the categories of Safe and Supportive Schools; Health, Mental Health, Environmental Health, and Physical Education; Drug-Violence Prevention; Character and Civic Education; and Homeland Security, Emergency Management, and School Preparedness. Many of the programs are for the elementary and secondary level, although some programs also apply to higher education. Under Reports & Resources, links can be found to OSHS's webcasts, annual reports, and other publications.

Subject(s): Drug Control; School Safety

Office of Special Education Programs (OSEP)

https://www2.ed.gov/about/offices/list/osers/osep/index.html

Description: OSEP has the primary responsibility of administering programs and projects relating to the education of all children, youth, and adults with disabilities, from birth through age 21. The website covers OSEP's programs and initiatives, reports, news, and office contacts. The site also includes offices within OSEP, the National Institute on Disability and Rehabilitation Research (NIDRR) and the Rehabilitation Services Administration (RSA). The site has extensive information on the Individuals with Disabilities Education Act (IDEA), which authorizes OSEP programs.

Subject(s): Special Education—Grants

Presidential Scholars Program

https://www2.ed.gov/programs/psp/index.html

Description: The Presidential Scholars Program was established to recognize and honor some of the nation's most distinguished graduating high school seniors. This website includes information on the program, the application process, and frequently asked questions.

Subject(s): High Schools—Awards and Honors

School District Demographics System (SDDS)

https://nces.ed.gov/programs/maped/

Description: This site presents demographic and geographic data for school districts from the United States Census and the American Community Survey (ACS). The Map Viewers section features the MapED application that allows users to view state or individual school district maps. Users can also download school district data from the American Community Survey in spreadsheet file format.

Subject(s): Census; Elementary and Secondary Education—Statistics

State Contacts – Department of Education (ED)

https://www2.ed.gov/about/contacts/state/index.html

Description: This Education Department website features a database of state organizations that provide education-related resources. This information is updated annually. It includes organizations such as the department of education in each state, state literary resource centers, state directors of adult education, curriculum materials centers, and education libraries. Each organization's entry has complete contact information and a description of its services.

Subject(s): Educational Resources

USA Science and Engineering Festival

https://usasciencefestival.org/

Description: The mission of the USA Science and Engineering Festival, which will take place in April 2016 in Washington, D.C., is "to stimulate and sustain the interest of our nation's youth in science, technology, engineering and math (STEM) by producing and presenting the most compelling, exciting, and educational festival in the world." (from the website) The festival is sponsored by a variety of companies, organizations, and educational establishments. The About section includes information about the festival's sponsors, partners, and advisors, as well as information about the festival's congressional host committee. A science blog, press releases, and newsletters are available in the Newsroom section.

Subject(s): Science Education

HIGHER EDUCATION

Air Force Institute of Technology (AFIT)

https://www.afit.edu/index.cfm

Description: A component of Air University, AFIT is the Air Force's graduate school of engineering and management and its institute for technical professional continuing education. The website provides information on each of AFIT's schools and centers.

Subject(s): Air Force; Military Training and Education

Air University (AU)

http://www.airuniversity.af.mil/

Description: Air University, located at Maxwell Air Force Base, conducts professional military education, graduate education, and professional continuing education for officers, enlisted personnel, and civilians. This site links to each of the component schools that make up AU and to its research centers, including the Air Force Institute of Technology, Air Force Research Institute, and School of Advanced Air and Space Studies. The site also provides information on the university's history and mission.

Subject(s): Air Force; Military Training and Education

Army Logistics University (ALU)

http://www.alu.army.mil

Description: The Army Logistics Management College became the Army Logistics University in 2009. ALU is the center for military and Defense Department logistics leader education. The website links to a course catalog, the ALU Library, and an online version *of Army Sustainment* magazine (formerly *Logistician*).

Subject(s): Army; Military Training and Education

Barry Goldwater Scholarship Program

https://goldwater.scholarsapply.org/

Description: Goldwater Scholarships are awarded for undergraduate education in the fields of mathematics, science, and engineering. The Goldwater Foundation was established by Congress to encourage study in these fields. The website has scholarship application information and lists of past award recipients.

Subject(s): Higher Education; Scholarships

College Navigator

https://nces.ed.gov/collegenavigator/

Description: College Navigator is a database of information on colleges, universities, community colleges, technical colleges, and similar institutions. The database can be searched by institution name, location, type of school, programs offered, tuition and enrollment ranges, and other criteria. For each institution, the database typically supplies phone numbers, a URL, average costs, and basic background information. Colleges can also be compared for such factors as estimated student expenses and graduation rates.

College Navigator is a useful reference for college-bound students as well as for those simply looking for a college's phone number or URL. Note that the site states that an institution's inclusion in the database does not constitute a recommendation by the Department of Education.

Subject(s): Higher Education

Defense Language Institute Foreign Language Center (DLIFLC)

http://www.dliflc.edu

Description: DLIFLC is the primary foreign-language training institution within the Department of Defense. Programs are for U.S. military personnel and select agency staff. The website has information on the history of the center and its current language programs. Some resources on the site are available only to authorized users, but many online cultural and language tutorials are open to the public.

Subject(s): Language Education; Military Training and Education

Harry S. Truman Scholarship Foundation

https://www.truman.gov/

Description: Truman Scholarships are awarded to outstanding undergraduate students who wish to pursue graduate study and careers in government or public service. This website has information about the Truman Foundation and its scholarship program, with sections for candidates, faculty, and current Truman scholars.

Subject(s): Public Policy; Scholarships

Marine Corps University (MCU)

https://www.usmcu.edu/

Description: The Marine Corps University's website provides information about its programs, history, and faculty.

Subject(s): Military Training and Education

National Defense University (NDU)

http://www.ndu.edu

Description: The NDU website provides an online course catalog and links to the university's component colleges and schools: the Joint Forces Staff College, the National War College, the Dwight D. Eisenhower School for National Security and Resource Strategy (The Eisenhower School), the Information Resources Management College (iCollege), and the College of International Security Affairs. NDU Research Centers online include the NDU Research Council and the Institute for National Strategic Studies. The site also links to NDU's regional centers, such as the Asia-Pacific Center for Security Studies, and special components, such as the Center for Joint and Strategic Logistics.

Subject(s): Military Training and Education; National Defense—Research

Naval Postgraduate School (NPS)

http://www.nps.edu

Description: NPS emphasizes education and research programs relevant to the Navy, defense, and national and international security interests. The website links to information from each of the NPS component schools: Business and Public Policy, Engineering and Applied Sciences, Operations and Information Sciences, and International Graduate Studies. The Research section includes archives of technical reports and abstracts from theses.

Subject(s): Military Training and Education

NSF Division of Graduate Education (DGE)

https://www.nsf.gov/div/index.jsp?div=dge

Description: The programs of the NSF's Division of Graduate Education promote the early career development of scientists and engineers by offering support at critical junctures of their careers. This website describes the division's research and teaching fellowships for graduate students in the sciences. Major programs described on the site include the Graduate Research Fellowship Program (GRFP) and the National Science Foundation Research Traineeship (NRT) Program.

Subject(s): Fellowships; Science Education

NSF Division of Undergraduate Education

https://www.nsf.gov/div/index.jsp?div=due

Description: The NSF's Division of Undergraduate Education focuses on improving undergraduate education in science, technology, engineering, and mathematics. The division awards funds to scholarship programs at educational institutions; they do not award scholarships directly to students. The division also funds programs for teacher education and curriculum development. The website has information on the programs, deadlines, and awards.

Subject(s): Science Education

Office of Postsecondary Education (OPE) – Department of Education (ED)

https://www2.ed.gov/about/offices/list/ope/index.html

Description: In the Programs/Initiatives section, this website provides a guide to the postsecondary-related education programs administered by the OPE. Initiatives include programs for improving educational institutions, supporting international education, funding teacher training, and reaching out to students from disadvantaged backgrounds. The Reports & Resources section of the site includes the *Federal Campus-Based Programs Data Book* and other statistical reports on OPE programs, including the Federal Pell Grant Program and the Federal Student Loan Program. The Accreditation section of the site explains the accreditation of educational institutions and has a directory of the numerous accrediting agencies. The OPE website has an A–Z subject index for finding information on specific topics.

This is a useful site with a substantial body of information sources of interest to students, educators, and financial aid offices.

Subject(s): Financial Aid to Students; Higher Education; International Education

Smithsonian Office of Fellowships and Internships (OFI)

https://www.si.edu/ofi

Description: The Office of Fellowships and Internships has applications, lists of fellowship and internship opportunities, and announcements of recipients.

Subject(s): Fellowships

U.S. Air Force Academy

http://www.usafa.af.mil

Description: The United States Air Force Academy website provides information for cadets, staff, and faculty. It includes visitor information and sections on admissions, academics, and athletics. Information about the academy's libraries and research centers is also included.

Subject(s): Air Force; Military Training and Education

U.S. Army Command and General Staff College (CGSC)

https://usacac.army.mil/organizations/cace/cgsc/

Description: The U.S. Army Command and General Staff College is focused on leadership development within the Army. This site offers information on the college, its training programs, and its organizations.

Subject(s): Army; Military Leadership; Military Training and Education

U.S. Army War College

https://www.armywarcollege.edu/

Description: The U.S. Army War College website provides information on the college, its library, and publications. The site includes information on affiliated centers, including the Center for Strategic Leadership, the Strategic Studies Institute, the Peacekeeping and Stability Operations Institute, and the U.S. Army Heritage and Education Center. The site's homepage features news and summaries of timely studies in national defense. The site also carries the quarterly *Parameters*, the Army's senior professional journal.
Subject(s): Army; Military Training and Education

U.S. Merchant Marine Academy

https://www.usmma.edu/

Description: The Merchant Marine Academy website has information about admissions, academics, and other activities. In the Academics section, the site links to information about the academy's curriculum and majors.

Subject(s): Military Training and Education; Shipping

U.S. Military Academy at West Point

https://www.usma.edu/SitePages/Home.aspx

Description: The West Point website has information for prospective and current students, alumni, visitors, and the West Point community. Sections include Admissions, Academics, Military, Athletics, Leadership, Community, and News. A brief section on USMA history, found in the About Us section, includes a timeline and list of notable graduates.

Subject(s): Army; Military Training and Education

U.S. Naval Academy

https://www.usna.edu/homepage.php

Description: This site contains information on the Naval Academy, mainly for students, prospective students, and midshipmen. The About section links to information about the academy's history and notable graduates.

Subject(s): Navy—Recruitment

White House Initiative on Historically Black Colleges and Universities

https://sites.ed.gov/whhbcu/

Description: The White House Initiative on Historically Black Colleges and Universities was established by executive order in 1981 and has since been renewed. This website has information on the initiative's work, conferences, scholarships, fellowships, and grants. It also has a list of Historically Black Colleges and Universities (HBCUs) by state and type of institution, with Web addresses provided for each institutions.

Subject(s): African Americans, Higher education

INTERNATIONAL EDUCATION

Bureau of Educational and Cultural Affairs (ECA)

https://exchanges.state.gov/

Description: The Bureau of Educational and Cultural Affairs website has information about its many international exchange and education programs. For U.S. citizens, the site has information on English-language teaching abroad, hosting a study abroad student, and other opportunities. For the audience abroad, the site has information about studying in the United States and a range of programs and exchanges from the high school level up to the academic scholar and professional level. Use the exchange program search feature to look through a database of international exchange programs.

Subject(s): Cultural Exchanges; International Education

EducationUSA

https://educationusa.state.gov/

Description: The State Department's EducationUSA program functions to assist international students who would like to study in the United States. The website's main sections include The Experience of Studying in the USA, Your 5 Steps to U.S. Study, and Find an Advising Center. EducationUSA maintains a global network of more than 400 advising centers in more than 170 countries.

Subject(s): International Education

International Activities Program (IAP)

https://nces.ed.gov/surveys/international/

Description: This website is NCES's central page for the international education statistics that it collects. The site links to information on the Trends in International Mathematics and Science Study (TIMSS), Program for International Student Assessment (PISA), Progress in International Reading Literacy Study (PIRLS), and other studies. The site offers prepared statistical tables and reports on the data. The site's International Data Explorer allows researchers to create their own custom tables and reports.

Subject(s): Educational Assessment–International

International Affairs Office – Department of Education (ED)

https://sites.ed.gov/international/

Description: The International Affairs Office coordinates the Education Department's international programs and works with international agencies such as the United Nations Educational, Scientific, and Cultural Organization (UNESCO). The website provides a directory of Education Department programs that have an international aspect. It also describes the office's activities, such as the U.S. Network for Education Information (USNEI).

Subject(s): Education—International

National Committee on Foreign Medical Education and Accreditation (NCFMEA)

https://sites.ed.gov/ncfmea/

Description: NCFMEA reviews the standards used by foreign countries to accredit medical schools and determines whether those standards are comparable to standards used to accredit medical schools in the United States. The website provides information on the review process and lists countries the NCFMEA has found to have comparable standards.

Subject(s): Medical Schools—International

STEM: Science, Technology, Engineering, and Math

https://2009–2017.state.gov/e/oes/stc/stem/exhibit/index.htm

Description: This website contains data that was released online from January 20, 2009 through January 20, 2017. The content in this site will no longer be updated. STEM was the focus of this State Department Website under the Obama administration. It promoted the advancement of science, technology, engineering, and math in American schools, universities, government, and industry. According to the site, science diplomacy is key to issues such as ocean mapping, nuclear disarmament, passport safety, and cybersecurity. The website provides links to information about STEM careers in the department; the Virtual Student Foreign Service; and the Networks of Diasporas in Engineering and Science (NODES), which is an effort between the DOS, the American Association for the Advancement of Science (AAAS), the National Academy of Sciences (NAS), and the National Academy of Engineering (NAE).

Subjects(s): Education; Science

U.S. Network for Education Information (USNEI)

https://www2.ed.gov/about/offices/list/ous/international/usnei/edlite-index.html

Description: USNEI is an interagency and public-private partnership set up to provide official information for anyone researching U.S. education. It also provides U.S. citizens with authoritative information about education in other countries. The site covers all levels of education, with topics including visas, accreditation, professional licensure, and teaching abroad (or in the United States).

Subject(s): International Education

Youth and Education

https://www.state.gov/youthandeducation/

Description: Designed as the student website for the State Department, this site is largely written for students at the secondary school level. The site explains the work of the department, international exchange opportunities available to students, and the nature of careers within the DOS.

The site also includes a substantial amount of information relating to diplomacy, U.S. diplomatic history, country information, international exchange programs, and educational outreach activities.

Subject(s): Career Information; Diplomacy

KIDS' PAGES

Admongo.gov

https://www.consumer.ftc.gov/admongo/

Description: Admongo is a game designed to teach kids ages 8 to 12 to be savvy about advertisers' claims. The main site, which includes a section for parents and one for teachers with lesson plans and sample ads, also has a text version available.

Subject(s): Consumer Information; Kids' Pages

America's Story from America's Library

http://www.americaslibrary.gov

Description: This Library of Congress website is designed for children and their families. It uses digitized images from the library's collection, accompanied by text and graphics, to create educational pages about American history and culture. Sections include Explore the States, Jump Back in Time, and Meet Amazing Americans.

Subject(s): History; Kids' Pages

Ben's Guide to U.S. Government

https://bensguide.gpo.gov/

Description: With a cartoon version of Benjamin Franklin as a guide, this GPO site for children covers topics such as the U.S. Constitution, how laws are made, the branches of the federal government, and citizenship. It features sections for specific age groups, plus a special section for parents and educators.

Subject(s): Civics—Kids

BLS Career Information

https://www.bls.gov/k12/

Description: This BLS Career Information page for youth uses a graphical interface to match kids' interests with potential careers. A Teacher's Desk section refers teachers to additional information available from BLS. The site is most appropriate for upper elementary grades and high school students.

Subject(s): Career Information; Kids' Pages

Choose MyPlate for Kids

https://www.choosemyplate.gov/kids/

Description: The Choose MyPlate kids' page, designed for elementary school children, contains games, activity sheets, and videos that teach children about nutrition and diet.

Subject(s): Nutrition; Kids' Pages

CIA Kids' Zone

https://www.cia.gov/kids-page/

Description: The CIA Kids' Zone has sections for students in grades K–5 and 6–12 and for parents and teachers. It also has a separate games section and links to the kids' pages at other intelligence agency websites. Kids' activities include learning about the CIA seal, CIA history, and working for the CIA. Parent and teacher materials include lesson plans and guidance on topics such as Internet safety and helping children avoid drug abuse.

Subject(s): Intelligence Agencies; Kids' Pages

CryptoKids®

https://www.nsa.gov/resources/everyone/digital-media-center/publications/cryptokids/

Description: This site has games, activities, and background information about NSA's specialty, cryptography. The Student Resources section has NSA career information for high school and college students.

Subject(s): Kids' Pages

EIA Energy Kids

https://www.eia.gov/kids/

Description: The Department of Energy's Information Administration provides this educational page. Sections include What is Energy?; History of Energy; Energy Sources; Using & Saving Energy; and Games & Activities. The section for teachers has lesson plans and teacher guides.

Subject(s): Energy; Kids' Pages

FBI Kids' Page

https://www.fbi.gov/fbi-kids

Description: The FBI website provides pages for kids in kindergarten through fifth grade, such as the About Our Dogs section, and pages for those in grades 6–12, such as the How We Investigate section.

Subject(s): Crime Detection; Kids' Pages

FCC Kids Zone

https://www.fcc.gov/kidszone-site-archive

Description: The FCC Kids Zone site was formerly a popular feature of the FCC website. It has since retired but an archive of the site is still available. It included information on the history of communications technology, online games, and a section about satellites. It also had special sections about communications technology designed for grades K–3, 4–8, and 9–12.

Subject(s): Telecommunications; Kids' Pages

FDA Kids' Site

https://www.fda.gov/ForConsumers/ByAudience/ForKids/default.htm

Description: This webpage links to FDA or related kids' websites, including sites on health and nutrition and the kids site from the FDA's Center for Veterinary Medicine (CVM).

Subject(s): Adolescents; Health Promotion; Kids' Pages

Inside the White House

https://obamawhitehouse.archives.gov/blog/2010/11/09/you-re-invited-inside-white-house

Description: This website was maintained under the Obama administration but it is not currently being updated. It features sections on past presidents and presidential trivia. An Interactive Tour feature shows floor plans of the White House, allowing users a peek inside the famous structure. The West Wing Tour section provides additional information about the White House. A section on art and decor is also available.

Subject(s): White House (Mansion); Kids' Pages

Kids.gov

https://kids.usa.gov/

Description: Kids.gov is a portal to U.S. federal and state government web pages designed for children. The site groups web links in sections for grades K–5 and grades 6–8. Links are then organized by topic, such as online safety, science, and government. A section for educators provides links organized in the same categories.

Kids.gov provides an easy way for children (as well as teachers and parents) to find kid-friendly information on the Internet.

Subject(s): Government Information; Finding Aids; Kids' Pages

Kids and Families – Social Security

https://www.ssa.gov/people/kids/

Description: This SSA website includes a Kids' Place and a Parents' Place. The Kids' Place offers tales about saving for the future and an introduction to the Social Security card. On the main page, there is also a link to information for the families of youth with disabilities.

Subject(s): Social Security; Kids' Pages

Kids in Parks

https://www.nps.gov/kids/index.cfm

Description: This website includes information for children about the national parks. Children can learn about topics such as the junior ranger and bark ranger program. There is also a site for teachers to obtain lesson plans on language, math, science, and social studies.

Subject(s): Kids' Pages

Kids in the House

https://kids-clerk.house.gov/

Description: The House Clerk's website is divided into parallel sections for young learners, grade school, middle school, and high school. Each section provides age-appropriate information on Congress, how bills are made into law, and the art and architecture of the U.S. Capitol. The site also has a For Teachers section with resources and lesson plans.

Subject(s): Legislative Procedure; Kids' Pages; Civics Education

Let's Go Outside!

https://www.fws.gov/letsgooutside/kids.html

Description: Connecting people with nature is this Fish and Wildlife Service website's stated mission. The site has information for several audiences (Kids, Families, Educators, and Youth Group Leaders). The Kids page is organized into the following sections: Play Outdoors in Nature!; Discover Online Games; Explore Wildlife & Photos; Help Fish & Wildlife; Conservation Careers; and Volunteer.

Subject(s): Endangered Species; Kids' Pages

NASA for Students

https://www.nasa.gov/audience/forstudents/index.html

Description: The NASA for Students page has sections for students in grades K–4, 5–8, 9–12, and postsecondary levels. It also features a NASA Kids' Club site with games and graphics. The NASA Education website at http://www.nasa.gov/offices/education/about/ provides comprehensive information for educators about the many NASA educational initiatives and opportunities.

Subject(s): Space; Kids' Pages

NASA

Space Place

https://spaceplace.nasa.gov/spacepl.htm

Description: Space Place is full of games, projects, and animations relating to earth and space science. The site has a Spanish-language version available at http://spaceplace.jpl.nasa.gov/sp/kids/.

Subject(s): Space; Kids' Pages

NCEH Kids Page

https://www.cdc.gov/nceh/kids/

Description: This site discusses how the environment can affect health and how the agency researches those environmental effects. It includes brief sections on asthma, emergency response, global health, lead poisoning, and other topics. The site's Fun Activities section features word games and puzzles.

Subject(s): Health Promotion; Kids' Pages

NGAkids Art Zone

https://www.nga.gov/education/kids.html

Description: This National Gallery of Art kids' page includes plenty of interactive activities, such as the Art Zone, where interactive art can be created.

Subject(s): Arts Education; Kids' Pages

NIEHS Kids' Pages

https://kids.niehs.nih.gov/

Description: This Kids Page offering from NIEHS has sections such as Discover & Explore, "What's That Word?", Scientific Kids, and Fun & Games.

Subject(s): Environmental Education; Health Promotion; Kids' Pages

NRO Jr.gov

http://www.nrojr.gov

Description: The NRO kids' page features information and activities with a satellite and space theme. The site has sections for students in grades K–5 and 6–12, as well as for teachers and parents.

Subject(s): Space; Kids' Pages

Peace Corps Kids World

https://www.peacecorps.gov/kids/

Description: The Peace Corps kids' page is a "Peace Corps Challenge" game simulating a volunteer experience in the fictional village of Wanzuzu.

Subject(s): Geography; Kids' Pages

The Student Corner – NRC

https://www.nrc.gov/reading-rm/basic-ref/students.html

Description: The NRC student's website explains everything from what nuclear energy is to emergency planning to radioactive waste. It also has a section for teachers containing lesson plans and classroom activities.

Subject(s): Science Education; Kids' Pages

A Student's Guide to Global Climate Change

https://www3.epa.gov/climatechange/kids/

Description: This site is in the process of being updated to reflect EPA's priorities under President Trump and Administrator Pruitt.

Subject(s): Environmental Education; Kids' Pages

Sci4Kids

https://www.ars.usda.gov/oc/kids/index/

Description: With a colorful all-graphics menu, Sci4Kids shows how scientific research affects many areas of life. The site includes information about careers in science, as well as a section for science projects.

Subject(s): Science Education; Kids' Pages

Science Education

https://energy.gov/science-innovation/science-education

Description: The Department of Energy's Science Education page provides resources for energy education. The home page links to the Energy Literacy video series as well as a guide for energy educators called the Energy Literacy Framework.

Subject(s): Education; Science Education

Smithsonian Education: Students

http://www.smithsonianeducation.org/students/

Description: The Smithsonian website for kids and students features themed IdeaLabs called Sizing Up the Universe, Walking on the Moon, and Digging for Answers. The At the Smithsonian section links to pages of interest to kids from many Smithsonian websites. More activities are organized under the topics of Everything Art, Science & Nature, History & Culture, and People & Places. Links in the upper right corner lead to Smithsonian content for educators, students, and families.

Subject(s): Kids' Pages

State Facts for Students

https://www.census.gov/schools/facts/

Description: A map of the United States serves as a menu for basic Census statistics, history, and trivia concerning each of the states, Puerto Rico, and the District of Columbia. It includes a lesson plan for teachers.

Subject(s): Geography; Kids' Pages

StopBullying.gov

https://www.stopbullying.gov/

Description: This site has extensive information and a variety of activities for kids about dealing with bullying behavior. There is also information for parents and educators about bullying, responses, and interventions.

Subject(s): Children; Kids' Pages

Students for the Environment

https://www.epa.gov/students

Description: This EPA website serves as a portal to information about the environment for a variety of educational levels and has special sections for students and for educators and parents. The site also provides news, homework resources, and deadlines for contests.

Subject(s): Environmental Education; Kids' Pages

ToxMystery

https://toxmystery.nlm.nih.gov/

Description: ToxMystery is an interactive game designed to teach kids about dangerous household substances. The site includes sections for parents and teachers, and has a version in Spanish.

Subject(s): Kids' Pages; Environmental Health

United States Mint's Site for Kids: H.I.P. Pocket Change™

https://www.usmint.gov/kids/

Description: This site features games and activities to teach children about the history of coins, coins around the world, and coin collecting. The site links to information for teachers, including activities and lesson plans.

Subject(s): Coins; Kids' Pages

USPTO Kids

https://www.uspto.gov/kids/

Description: The Patent and Trademark Office's kids' page features both online and DIY activities for kids, including instructions on how to make your own model rocket and flip book. There are also sections for teens, parents, and educators.

TEACHING

Ames Educator Resource Center (ERC)

https://www.nasa.gov/centers/ames/education/ERC/

Description: This site is almost exclusively descriptive of the ERC, which is located at NASA's Ames Research Center in Moffett Field, California. It serves educators in the western states (Alaska, northern California, Hawaii, Idaho, Montana, Nevada, Oregon, Utah, Washington, and Wyoming). This page provides contact information, hours, and a listing of the kinds of educational materials available—only a few of which are available online.

The Ames Educator Resource Center website is most useful for those who want to visit or contact the center.

Subject(s): Educational Resources; Science Education

Library of Congress Teacher Resources

http://www.loc.gov/teachers/

Description: This website serves as an entry point for Library of Congress online resources relevant to teachers, with an emphasis on teaching with the primary sources available in the Library's online collections. The site has information on classroom materials and information on professional development opportunities for teachers. Classroom materials include lesson plans, activities, and themed sets of primary sources to use. For educators, the site has presentations that can be used to lead others in professional development and online training modules for individual use.

Subject(s): Educational Technology; Lesson Plans; Social Studies Education

James Madison Graduate Fellowships

https://www.jamesmadison.gov/

Description: James Madison Graduate Fellowships are for teachers at the secondary school level who wish to enhance their knowledge of the U.S. Constitution. The fellowships are for graduate study leading to a master's degree. The James Madison Memorial Fellowship Foundation, the sponsor of these fellowships, is an independent agency within the Executive branch.

Subject(s): Constitution of the United States; Fellowships; Civics Education

NCELA: National Clearinghouse for English Language Acquisition

https://ncela.ed.gov/

Description: NCELA, known in full as the National Clearinghouse for English Language Acquisition and funded by the Department of Education, is concerned with the education of linguistically and culturally diverse learners in the United States. The NCELA website provides direct access to a wealth of information on research, resources, statistics, funding, and programs to assist those working with English-language learners.

Subject(s): Language Education

Teach.org

https://www.teach.org/

Description: This site provides information and encouragement to those considering a career in teaching. The site's sections include Why Teach, Become a Teacher, Community, and Find a Job, which includes portfolio tips and interview hints. The site also includes a blog.

Subject(s): Teachers; Teaching

What Works Clearinghouse (WWC)

https://ies.ed.gov/ncee/wwc/

Description: WWC collects and reviews studies of the effectiveness of educational programs and practices. It is intended to be a "central and trusted source of scientific evidence for what works in education." (from the website) In addition to reports and guides, the site provides a database of education program evaluators and technical information on evaluating education programs.

Subject(s): Educational Assessment

Chapter Eight

Employment

The federal government has a role in employment law, in regulating workplace conditions, in measuring employment and promoting jobs growth, and also—to a degree—in labor-management relations. All of these areas are reflected in the following websites. Many of the sites covering the government's role as an employer, however, are in the Government and Politics chapter.

Subsections in this chapter are Employment Law, Employment Statistics, Jobs, Labor-Management Relations, and Workplace Conditions.

EMPLOYMENT LAW

Benefits Review Board (BRB)

https://www.dol.gov/brb/welcome.html

Description: The BRB rules on appeals of worker's compensation claims that arise under the Longshore and Harbor Worker's Compensation Act and the Black Lung Benefits amendments to the Federal Coal Mine Health and Safety Act of 1969. Its website has the text of BRB published and unpublished opinions and lists of case citations for Longshore and Black Lung cases.

Subject(s): Labor—Compensation

Davis–Bacon and Related Acts

https://www.dol.gov/whd/govcontracts/dbra.htm

Description: This website provides guidance for construction contractors complying with the Davis–Bacon Act. (The Davis–Bacon Act concerns wage rates for laborers working on public buildings or public works projects.) The site has fact sheets, forms, All Agencies Memoranda (AAMs), and the Davis–Bacon work site poster. It also has information, in Spanish and English, on requirements for Recovery Act contracts and links to the online Prevailing Wage Resource Book used in training conferences.

Subject(s): Construction Industry—Regulations; Wages—Regulations

Department of Labor (DOL)

https://www.dol.gov/

Description: The Department of Labor home page provides one-click access to news, hot topics and features, frequently asked questions, Labor agencies and offices on the Internet, and economic indicators. The homepage browse menu helps researchers find information by topic (work hours, statistics, unemployment insurance) and has a feature for finding Labor services by state and ZIP code.

The department's blog highlights programs, services, and legislative and regulatory news. As a Cabinet department, the Labor Department also features information on their Recovery Act contracts and funding and on their Open Government Initiative plans. A Spanish-language version of the site is available.

This website provides effective access to Department of Labor information and to related websites by providing multiple paths for accessing information and by highlighting the most frequently consulted topics.

Subject(s): Employment; Labor Law; Labor Statistics; Labor-Management Relations

DOL Data Enforcement

https://enforcedata.dol.gov/homePage.php

Description: The Enforcement Data website provides a central location for searching and using data from the Labor Department's major enforcement agencies, such as the Mine Safety and Health Administration (MSHA), the Occupational Safety and Health Administration (OSHA), and the Wage and Hour Division (WHD).

Subject(s): Employment Law

elaws: Employment Laws Assistance for Workers and Small Businesses

https://webapps.dol.gov/elaws/

Description: The elaws Advisors are interactive tools designed to help employees and employers understand their respective rights and responsibilities under the laws and regulations administered by the Department of Labor. Each elaws Advisor provides information about a specific law or regulation. The Advisor imitates the interaction that an individual might have with an employment law expert. It asks questions, provides information, and directs the user to the appropriate resolutions based on the user's responses.

Featured expertise includes the Fair Labor Standards Act, Family and Medical Leave Act, Veterans' Preference, and Worker Adjustment and Retraining Notification (WARN) Act.

Subject(s): Labor Law

Employee Benefits Security Administration (EBSA)

https://www.dol.gov/agencies/ebsa

Description: EBSA is concerned with private retirement plans and private health and welfare plans. Its website explains pension rights and employer compliance programs. Major sections include COBRA Assistance, the Affordable Care Act, the Pension Protection Act, Information for Reservists, ERISA (Employee Retirement Income Security Act) Enforcement, Technical Guidance, Compliance Assistance, and Consumer Information. The main page highlights news, upcoming compliance assistance seminars, and frequently asked questions. The site also has forms, criminal enforcement news releases, EBSA publications (some available in Spanish), and links to relevant laws, regulations, and proposed regulations. Consumer information covers health plans, retirement plans, and retirement savings.

The EBSA website has material for both employee benefit specialists and consumers. The site design makes it easy for both audiences to find relevant content.

Subject(s): Health Insurance; Pensions

Equal Employment Opportunity Commission (EEOC)

https://www.eeoc.gov/

Description: EEOC coordinates federal equal employment opportunity regulations and investigates charges of employment discrimination. Its website provides information for employees, employers, small businesses, attorneys, and the public. The Discrimination by Type section has clear descriptions of laws related to age, disability, race/color, religion, and other areas. Statistics and additional information sources are provided for each area. A Laws, Regulations, Guidance, & MOUs section serves as a library for relevant legal documents. Other topics include enforcement and employment statistics, special information for federal agencies and employees, reports on litigation settlements, how to file a discrimination charge, training and outreach programs, publications and posters, and news. The Other Languages section has translations of fact sheets and basic information in Chinese, Arabic, Russian, Vietnamese, Korean, and Haitian Creole. A Spanish-language version of the website is also available.

The EEOC website provides a straightforward presentation of important content. The home page has a clean table-of-contents style that makes the lack of a site map much less critical. The site offers adjustable font size and a plain text version, making it even more accessible for users.

Subject(s): Employment Discrimination—Laws

E-Verify

https://www.uscis.gov/e-verify

Description: E-Verify allows participating employers to electronically verify the employment eligibility of their newly hired employees and the validity of their Social Security Numbers. The program is run by USCIS in partnership with the Social Security Administration. The website has information for employees, employers, and federal contractors. It includes text and videos guides to the E-Verify system. The site also has information on the Systematic Alien Verification for Entitlements (SAVE) program. USCIS has a Spanish version of its website, and the E-Verify information is available there as well.

Subject(s): Employment—Regulations; Immigrant Workers

Job Accommodation Network (JAN)

https://askjan.org/

Description: JAN is an Americans with Disabilities Act (ADA) information service sponsored by the Department of Labor and operated by West Virginia University. This website provides information on JAN's free consulting service for employers and on the employability of people with disabilities. The website has numerous fact sheets on accommodations for disabilities and on the ADA law, information about JAN, training webcasts and podcasts, and contacts for learning about JAN's offline information and training services. The site will be relevant to employers, employees, and other professionals concerned with accommodation of disabilities in the workplace.

Subject(s): Disability Employment

Office of Disability Employment Policy (ODEP)

https://www.dol.gov/odep/

Description: ODEP manages programs, policies, and grants to further its mission to increase employment opportunities for people with disabilities. The website links to further information on the programs and technical assistance centers that ODEP funds, sponsors, or otherwise participates in. The site's Newsroom section contains press releases and policy resources by topic.

Subject(s): Disability Employment

Office of Foreign Labor Certification (OFLC)

https://www.foreignlaborcert.doleta.gov/

Description: The Office of Foreign Labor Certification in the Department of Labor provides labor certifications to employers seeking to bring foreign workers into the United States. The site provides program news, employment verification information, and applications. The FAQs section covers questions about permanent, H1-B, H2-A, and other classifications, and about prevailing wages.

Subject(s): Immigrant Workers—Regulations; Wages—Regulations

Office of Special Counsel for Immigration-Related Unfair Employment Practices (OSC)

https://www.justice.gov/crt/immigrant-and-employee-rights-section

Description: The Office of Special Counsel for Immigration-Related Unfair Employment Practices investigates employers charged with national origin and citizenship status discrimination under the antidiscrimination provision of the Immigration and Nationality Act. This website provides guidance for both employers and employees and links to relevant laws and regulations. The site also has news of enforcement actions, updates on eligibility requirements for Temporary Protected Status (TPS), and information on the public education grant program.

Subject(s): Employment Discrimination—Immigrant Workers

Pension Benefit Guaranty Corporation (PBGC)

https://www.pbgc.gov/

Description: PBGC is a federal corporation created by the Employee Retirement Income Security Act of 1974. It insures and protects pension benefits in certain pension plans. The website explains what PBGC does and does not guarantee, as well as the legal limits on their guarantees. PBGC offers online transactions for tasks such as applying for pension benefits and designating a beneficiary; instructions for doing these tasks by phone are also provided. Information is categorized for Workers & Retirees and for Practitioners (pension plan professionals). In the Workers & Retirees section, the Find an Unclaimed Pension section is a searchable directory of people known to be entitled to a pension from a company that went out of business or ended its defined benefit pension plan, but who have not yet claimed their pension. The Practitioners section includes interest rates, mortality tables, premium filing instructions, laws, regulations, appeals board decisions, and opinion letters.

This website offers well-organized content and online services. It should prove useful to anyone seeking information on one of the PBGC-insured pension plans.

Subject(s): Pensions; Retirement

Railroad Retirement Board (RRB)

https://www.rrb.gov/

Description: RRB is an independent agency that administers retirement-survivor and unemployment-sickness benefit programs for railroad workers and their families. The website provides benefits information, forms, and online services for railroad employees and beneficiaries as well as for employers. The section for the general public, titled Public, serves as a central location for RRB legal opinions and decisions, financial statistics, and organizational information. Due to frequent requests, this section also has useful information for people seeking former railroad employee records for genealogical research. The RRB site also has a collection of videos for online briefings, a listing of railroad job vacancies, and a ZIP code locator for finding the nearest RRB office.

Subject(s): Railroads; Retirement

Veterans' Employment and Training Service (VETS)

https://www.dol.gov/vets/aboutvets/regionaloffices/map.htm

Description: This site from the Department of Labor provides a listing of VETS offices by state. It also provides information on hiriing a veteran, resources for veterans, and programs s and services for veterans

Subject(s): Veterans

Wage Determinations OnLine.gov

https://www.wdol.gov/

Description: This website, intended for federal contracting officials, provides Service Contract Act (SCA) and Davis–Bacon Act (DBA) wage determinations. It is also open to labor organizations, contractor associations, employees, and the general public. SCA determinations can be searched by state and county. Archived SCA wage determinations can be retrieved by number. Users can also browse a list of determinations due to be revised. DBA wage determinations can be browsed by state, searched by number, or searched by a combination of state, county, and construction type. Archived DBA wage determinations and a list of determinations due to be revised are also online. The Library section links to the Federal Acquisition Regulations and other websites related to federal contracting.

Subject(s): Construction Industry—Regulations; Government Contracts; Wages—Regulations

Wage and Hour Division (WHD)

https://www.dol.gov/whd/

Description: The Department of Labor's Wage and Hour Division administers some of the best-known labor laws in the United States. These include the Fair Labor Standards Act (which concerns minimum wage and overtime), the Family and Medical Leave Act, the Migrant and Seasonal Agricultural Worker Protection Act, worker protections provided in several temporary visa programs, and the prevailing wage requirements of the Davis–Bacon Act. Its website provides fact sheets, posters, opinion letters, and compliance information for these laws.

Subject(s): Wages—Laws; Employment Law

Youth at Work

https://www.eeoc.gov/youth/

Description: Youth at Work is targeted at working teens. It provides straightforward information on employment discrimination, employee rights, and employee responsibilities. The site is available in English and Spanish.

Subject(s): Adolescents; Employment Discrimination

YouthRules!

https://www.youthrules.gov/

Description: The Department of Labor's YouthRules! Program promotes safe work experiences for young workers. The website has information on federal and state laws and regulations governing child labor, including the "Final Rule," which is designed to protect working children from workplace hazards while also recognizing the value of safe work for children and their families. The main sections are centered on information pertaining to teens, parents, educators, and employers. The site includes some information in Spanish and other languages.

Subject(s): Adolescents—Regulations; Labor Law

EMPLOYMENT STATISTICS

Bureau of Labor Statistics (BLS)

https://www.bls.gov/

Description: The BLS website is a major source for employment, economic, and labor statistics. The home page features the latest key economic indicators from BLS, including the Consumer Price Index (CPI), unemployment rate, payroll employment, average hourly earnings, the Producer Price Index (PPI), the Employment Cost Index (ECI), productivity, and the U.S. Import Price Index.

BLS data and products are organized under the Subjects tab; subtopics include Inflation & Prices, Unemployment, and Pay & Benefits. For each subtopic, the site links to BLS news releases, databases, prepared tables, publications, and related documentation for its subsections. Online tutorials are available for the databases, along with tools and calculators to work with the data. The homepage links to "At a Glance" tables for the U.S., regions, states, and specific industries.

BLS helps researchers by providing multiple approaches to their data. The database tutorials are a welcome feature on the site.

Subject(s): Labor Statistics; Wages—Statistics; Employment Statistics

Current Population Survey (CPS)

https://www.bls.gov/cps/

Description: The CPS is the primary source of information on the labor force characteristics of the U.S. population. The Census Bureau surveys a sample of households to get the data for BLS. Estimates obtained from the CPS include employment, unemployment, earnings, hours of work, multiple jobholders, union membership and other statistics. The monthly CPS news release, the *Employment Situation*, is widely quoted for details on the current national unemployment rate.

The CPS homepage links to CPS data in news releases, publications, databases, and prepared tables. Researchers can also download the entire database or subsets.

Subject(s): Employment Statistics

Income – Census Bureau

https://www.census.gov/topics/income-poverty/income.html

Description: The Census Bureau's webpage for income data provides reports, briefs, and research in addition to aggregated data and microdata. It links to the income data from the Current Population Survey, American Community Survey, Decennial Census, Small Area Income and Poverty Estimates, Survey of Income and Program Participation, and other Census programs. Data tables include median state income and historic income inequality. The site provides detailed information on the data sources and links to other income data programs online.

Subject(s): Wages—Statistics

Longitudinal Employer-Household Dynamics (LEHD)

https://lehd.ces.census.gov/

Description: This website describes the LEHD project and provides access to the data. LEHD involves a Census Bureau partnership with the states, combining federal and state administrative data on employers and employees while ensuring confidentiality. Most of the site is concerned with Local Employment Dynamics (LED), which provide data on local labor market conditions. LED's Quality Workforce Indicators (QWI) include data for employment, job creation, wages, worker turnover, and other factors at state, county, and city levels. The site includes the QWI Explorer, OnTheMap (which maps work and home locations with other workforce data), and the LED Extraction Tool.

LEHD provides an extensive library of information, documentation, and research for social scientists, economic development specialists, and those familiar with the data; other users will face a learning curve. Most, but not all, states participate—the site has a list of participating states.

Subject(s): Employment Statistics

JOBS

Employment and Training Administration (ETA)

https://www.doleta.gov/

Description: ETA supports workforce training programs and job placement through employment services. The ETA website offers information about its services for businesses and industry, job seekers, and workforce professionals. The site has a Grants section and links to regional and state resources. Grants information is also displayed on the home page. Other information on the site includes a research publications database, relevant laws and regulations, ETA advisories, and links to information on ETA programs. Major programs include Foreign Labor Certification, Migrant and Seasonal Farmworkers Program, and the Dislocated Worker Program.

Many employment and training programs operate at the state level. The ETA website provides information and links to find state information in addition to federal guides and programs.

Subject(s): Job Training

Intelligence Careers

https://www.intelligencecareers.gov/

Description: This website is dedicated to describing the Intelligence Community (IC) to the general public and to job seekers. Its Careers section allows users to explore different positions and find jobs within the Intelligence Community.

Subject(s): Jobs; Intelligence

O*NET OnLine: Occupational Information Network

https://www.onetonline.org/

Description: O*NET is a database system with comprehensive information on job requirements and worker competencies. It is aligned with the Standard Occupational Classification (SOC) system. The website has a Find Occupations section to browse or search the database by keyword and other criteria, and a Skills search tool, under Advanced Search, that allows users to select from a list of skills and match them to occupations. It also features a Crosswalks search between the O*NET classifications and other classifications, such as the Military Occupation Classification. O*NET has also added a section highlighting the Green Economy.

Subject(s): Job Skills; Occupations

Occupational Outlook Handbook

https://www.bls.gov/ooh/

Description: The *Occupational Outlook Handbook* profiles job and career options and describes the work involved and the training or education needed for each career. It is updated every two years. Each entry is available in HTML or PDF format. The *Handbook* is also available for purchase in print. BLS also offers Spanish-language descriptions for 100 occupations.

Occupation profiles can be found with a keyword search or through the site's A–Z index. Occupations can also be browsed by category, such as median pay and on-the-job training. The website links to supporting material, including a teacher's guide, *Career Outlook*, and an overview of trends in job opportunities for the future.

This website contains an excellent online implementation of a standard reference source. The links to definitions and related occupations make the *Handbook* easy to browse online. The latest version of the occupational outlook handbook was released in October 2017.

Subject(s): Career Information; Occupations; Workforce

Standard Occupational Classification (SOC) System

https://stats.bls.gov/soc/

Description: The SOC system is used by federal statistical agencies to classify workers into occupational categories for the purpose of collecting, calculating, and disseminating data. This website allows users to browse or search the classification system, or to order a copy of the printed edition of the *SOC Manual*. Related reference material is provided, including the *SOC User Guide*. The SOC was updated in 2010. The 2000 version and related materials are archived at this site.

Subject(s): Occupations

Student and Recent Graduate Jobs – USAJOBS

https://www.usajobs.gov/Help/working-in-government/unique-hiring-paths/students/

Description: This website is a clearinghouse of information about the Pathways Program, which matches students and recent graduates with federal internships and career development opportunities. A Federal Occupations by College Major page lists degrees matched to occupations found in the federal government.

Subject(s): Internships; Job Openings; Students

USAJOBS

https://www.usajobs.gov/

Description: The core of the USAJOBS website is a database of current federal government employment opportunities. These openings can be searched by keyword or by other criteria, including by agency, occupational grouping, salary, or state. Users can create and store a resume online for applying for federal jobs and set up a profile to receive automated job alerts. The site has special sections for veterans, students, senior executives, and individuals with disabilities.

Subject(s): Government Employees; Job Openings

Women's Bureau (WB)

https://www.dol.gov/wb/

Description: The Department of Labor's Women's Bureau was created in 1920 to promote profitable employment opportunities for women. Its website describes the bureau's current and past programs. The Data & Statistics section contains information from the Department of Labor, the Department of Commerce, and Congress's Joint Economic Committee.

Subject(s): Occupations—Statistics; Women—Policy

LABOR-MANAGEMENT RELATIONS

Federal Mediation & Conciliation Service (FMCS)

https://www.fmcs.gov/

Description: FMCS is an independent agency set up by Congress to promote sound and stable labor-management relations. One of the agency's major responsibilities is to mediate collective bargaining negotiations. The Services section on its website provides information about collective bargaining, alternative bargaining processes, arbitration, the FMCS grants program, and other topics. The site also describes the FMCS e-service, which is called Technology Assisted Group Solutions (TAGS); TAGS includes capabilities for online meetings, online voting, and other services. The Resources section has relevant forms and applications.

Subject(s): Labor-Management Relations; Mediation

Key Workplace Documents

https://digitalcommons.ilr.cornell.edu/keydocs/

Description: Cornell University's Catherwood Library, while not a government institution, offers an online archive of historical government reports, statistics, and public policy papers from various agencies and commissions. The subject focus is on the workforce and employer-employee relationships. Federal publications in the collection include many reports from the Congressional Research Service.

This collection is small but focused. It is a nongovernmental information source but provides an excellent service in maintaining access to government reports that might not otherwise be available on the Internet.

Subject(s): Child Labor; Labor-Management Relations—Policy; Workforce—Policy

National Labor Relations Board (NLRB)

https://www.nlrb.gov/

Description: NLRB conducts secret-ballot elections to determine whether employees want union representation; it also investigates unfair labor practices by employers and unions. The Rights We Protect section explains the National Labor Relations Act. The site also has NLRB decisions and memos, a weekly summary of new documents, and the CiteNet database for the Classified Index of NLRB Board Decisions and Related Court Decisions. The Reports & Guidance section includes NLRB manuals, regulations, annual reports, and some publications in Spanish.

Subject(s): Labor Unions

National Mediation Board (NMB)

http://www.nmb.gov

Description: NMB is an independent U.S. government agency whose principal role is to foster harmonious labor-management relations in the rail and air transport industries in order to minimize disruptions to the flow of interstate commerce. The NMB website's Mediation section includes information on Presidential Emergency Boards. The What's New section contains a weekly report on mediation, representation, and arbitration activity, as well as Freedom of Information Act links.

Subject(s): Airlines; Labor Mediation; Railroads

Office of Labor-Management Standards (OLMS)

https://www.dol.gov/olms/

Description: OLMS administers and enforces certain reporting, disclosure, and operational requirements for labor unions and union officers. The website has financial disclosure reports for labor unions, union officers, and union employees, as well as reports for employers and labor relations consultants. The scanned reports can be viewed in PDF format and are generally available from 2000 to the present. Data from the annual financial reports submitted by unions can also be searched by criteria, such as type of union, state or ZIP code, and the dollar range of assets, liabilities, receipts, and disbursements. The site also has compliance assistance information and notification of civil and criminal enforcement actions.

Subject(s): Labor Unions—Regulations

WORKPLACE CONDITIONS

Federal Occupational Health (FOH)

https://foh.psc.gov/

Description: FOH provides occupational health services to federal government managers and their employees. It is a quasi-governmental organization that must cover its operating costs with funds collected through the service provision. The FOH website includes information on topics such as worksite health centers, environmental health, safety, and health promotion.

Subject(s): Government Employees; Health Promotion

Mine Safety and Health Administration (MSHA)

https://www.msha.gov/

Sponsor(s): Labor Department

Description: MSHA is charged with enforcing mine safety and health standards to prevent accidents and minimize health hazards. The MSHA website makes a wealth of current information on mine safety available for multiple audiences. The site has extensive information about mine safety laws and regulations and guidance on compliance with the laws. It has statistics on mining accidents, injuries, and fatalities. MSHA also features the Mine Data Retrieval System (MDRS), a database with mine overviews, accident histories, violation histories, inspection histories, inspector dust samplings, operator dust samplings, and employment/production data. Use the A–Z index to locate specific information on the extensive MSHA site. A version of the site is available in Spanish.

Subject(s): Mining; Workplace Safety—Regulations

Nanotechnology at NIOSH

https://www.cdc.gov/niosh/topics/nanotech/

Description: This site is concerned with the occupational safety and health implications related to applications of nanotechnology. It describes NIOSH research and published scientific research from other institutions. The Guidance & Publications section provides fact sheets and links to other resources.

Subject(s): Nanotechnology; Workplace Safety

National Institute of Occupational Safety and Health (NIOSH)

https://www.cdc.gov/niosh/

Description: NIOSH is responsible for conducting research and making recommendations for the prevention of work-related injuries and illnesses.

Its website offers multiple points of access to the agency's publications, databases, program information, and other resources. Information is organized into major sections, including Industries & Occupations, Hazards & Exposures, Diseases & Injuries, Chemicals, Safety & Prevention, and Emergency Preparedness & Response. NIOSH databases on the site include the NIOSHTIC-2 Research Database, the Power Tools Database, the National Occupational Respiratory Mortality System (NORMS), the Work-Related Injury Statistics Query System (Work-RISQS), and the Work-Related Lung Disease Surveillance System (eWoRLD). It also links to the grant-supported Electronic Library of Construction Safety and Health (eLCOSH). The website includes a NIOSH Science Blog. The site has an A–Z subject index and a search engine. A smaller version of the site is available in Spanish.

Subject(s): Workplace Safety

Occupational Safety and Health Administration (OSHA)

https://www.osha.gov/

Description: OSHA's mission is to prevent work-related injuries, illnesses, and deaths. The OSHA website provides information on the agency and its regulations and educational and enforcement activities. The homepage links to sections covering worker rights, how to file a complaint, compliance assistance/outreach, record keeping, resources for small businesses, the OSHA workplace poster, and other popular topics. The Data & Statistics section provides multiple ways of searching OSHA inspection data. OSHA links to the Bureau of Labor Statistics for workplace injury, illness, and fatality statistics. OSHA also offers OSHA interpretations, Federal Register notices, and the *QuickTakes* newsletter.

This website includes a Spanish-language section designed for employers and employees.

Subject(s): Workplace Safety—Regulations

Chapter Nine

Energy

The federal government is both a regulator and producer of energy. The government sets energy policy, and it plays a role in the development of energy-related technologies. This chapter covers the varied federal websites that describe energy use and production, consumer energy issues, and energy statistics. Information on the work of the Department of Energy's research laboratories can be found in the Science and Space chapter. Information on some aspects of Energy's defense work can be found in the Defense and Intelligence chapter. The topic of transportation is covered in the Transportation chapter.

Subsections in this chapter are Alternative and Renewable Fuels, Energy Policy and Information, Fossil and Nuclear Fuels, and Utilities.

ALTERNATIVE AND RENEWABLE FUELS

Alternative Fuels and Data Center

https://www.afdc.energy.gov/

Description: Alternative fuels for vehicles is the singular theme of this Department of Energy website. The site describes fuels such as biodiesel, electricity, ethanol, hydrogen, natural gas, and propane. The Fuels & Vehicles section includes buying guides and explanatory material. The Locate Stations section includes an alternative fuel station locator for finding CNG, ethanol/E85, propane, biodiesel, LNG, hydrogen, and electric refueling stations. Another section details federal and state incentives for alternative fuel use.

Subject(s): Fuels

Bioenergies Technology Office (BETO)

https://www.energy.gov/eere/bioenergy/bioenergy-technologies-office

Description: The Energy Department's Bioenergies Technology Office "is focused on forming cost-share partnerships with key stakeholders to develop, demonstrate, and deploy technologies for advanced biofuels production from lignocellulosic and algal biomas." (from the website) The Research & Development section provides resources for students and educators, as well as information about fellowships and the BioenergizeME Infographic Challenge. The Information Resources section includes publications, state and regional program information, and audience-specific pages for industry, researchers, policymakers, consumers, and students. The site also has information about funding for basic and applied research for converting biomass resources to biofuels.

Subject(s): Biomass Fuels—Research

Biomass Research

https://www.nrel.gov/bioenergy/

Description: This website describes the biomass research activities of the National Renewable Energy Laboratory. Capabilities and projects discussed include biochemical conversion, thermochemical conversion, and microalgal biofuels. NREL also makes energy analysis information and tools available for researchers on the site.

Subject(s): Biomass Fuels—Research

Clean Cities

https://cleancities.energy.gov/

Description: The Clean Cities Program promotes alternative fuels and vehicles, fuel blends, fuel economy, hybrid vehicles, and a reduction in engine idle time for diesel vehicles. Clean Cities is a voluntary program that involves government, industry, and professional associations. Its website provides information about these coalitions and the program's accomplishments. The site also carries the quarterly *Clean Cities Now* newsletter.

Subject(s): Alternative Fuel Vehicles

Hydrogen and Fuel Cells Interagency Working Group

https://www.hydrogen.gov/

Description: The Hydrogen and Fuel Cells Interagency Working Group comprises a consortium of federal agencies that exchange information related to research and developments in hydrogen and fuel cell issues. The site provides an interagency action plan and a list of participating agencies, which include the Department of Agriculture, the Department of Homeland Security, the Office of Management and Budget, and the Environmental Protection Agency. Information about funding opportunities is also provided.

Subject(s): Alternative and Renewable Fuels—Research

National Renewable Energy Laboratory (NREL)

https://www.nrel.gov/

Description: NREL focuses on renewable energy and energy efficiency research and development. This website presents detailed information about each of NREL's major research areas. The Technology Transfer and Technology Development sections cover the laboratory's commercialization programs, technology licensing, technical assistance to state and local governments, and programs for universities. The Resources section of the site, in the right sidebar, includes educational resources, photographs, and renewable resource maps and data.

NREL also provides information and reports on their energy data analysis, market analysis and policy impact analysis, technological and sustainability analysis, and energy forecasting and modeling.

Subject(s): Renewable Energies—Research; Research Laboratories

Office of Energy Efficiency and Renewable Energy (EERE)

https://energy.gov/eere/office-energy-efficiency-renewable-energy

Description: EERE's mission is to enhance energy efficiency and productivity and bring clean, reliable, and affordable energy technologies to the marketplace. The EERE website describes their programs in energy efficiency (for homes, buildings, vehicles, industry, and government) and renewable energy sources (solar, wind, geothermal, and other sources). The site provides information on EERE technology commercialization, contract solicitations, and Recovery Act projects.

Subject(s): Energy Conservation; Renewable Energies

ENERGY POLICY AND INFORMATION

Building America

https://energy.gov/eere/buildings/building-america-bringing-building-innovations-market

Description: Building America is a partnership program between the Department of Energy and industry to research new solutions for more energy-efficient homes. Its website features a national, interactive map/database of homes constructed as a result of participation in Building America research projects.

Subject(s): Energy Conservation; Home Construction

Building Energy Codes Program (BECP)

https://www.energycodes.gov/

Description: The Building Energy Codes Program develops model commercial and residential energy codes and compliance assistance. This website provides information on federal rules and on state adoption of model codes. The content will be of most interest to state and local governments, builders, and suppliers to the construction industry.

Subject(s): Construction Industry—Regulations; Energy Conservation—Regulations

Energy and the Environment

https://www.epa.gov/energy

Description: This portal to EPA clean energy programs and information describes clean energy as including "energy efficiency and clean energy supply options like highly efficient combined heat and power as well as renewable energy sources." The site links to information on federal, state, and local programs and policy and links to specific programs such as the National Action Plan for Energy Efficiency and the Green Power Partnership. It features a Power Profiler tool that shows what types of power are used in any ZIP code and how the emissions compare to a national average. The site links to other online tools, including a Greenhouse Gas Equivalencies Calculator and the eGRID database of plant-specific emissions data for all U.S. electricity-generating plants.

Subject(s): Air Quality; Energy Conservation

Department of Energy (DOE)

https://www.energy.gov/

Description: The Department of Energy website's home page presents news and headlines, with links to popular topics such as Tax Credits, Rebates, and Savings; Heating & Cooling; and Appliances & Electronics. Each of these sections provides topical access to news and programs. The Offices section links directly to component organizations, laboratories, and technology centers. The Science & Innovation tab links to information on the department's Science & Technology, Science Education, Innovation, Energy Sources, and Energy Efficiency focuses. As with other Cabinet departments, Energy has a section on its website devoted to tracking its Recovery Act work and a section on Open Government.

Subject(s): Energy Policy

Energy Information Administration (EIA)

https://www.eia.gov/

Description: EIA provides data, forecasts, and analyses regarding energy and its interaction with the economy and the environment. The EIA website is divided into major topical areas under Sources and Uses, including Petroleum & Other Liquids, Natural Gas, Electricity, Coal, Nuclear & Uranium, and Electricity. Each section has data, reports, analyses, and forecasts. Other major sections focus on the environment, markets and finance, and projections and analyses.

EIA produces an extensive line of statistical publications and datasets. The home page links to a catalog of EIA reports and products and to the EIA e-mail update service. The Press Room section lists new and upcoming reports and testimony. For highly specialized information beyond the scope of the site, EIA provides a directory of its subject experts on a wide range of topics, including statistical methods, the environment, and electric power emissions; this directory is available under Contact Us link at the bottom of the page. The site also includes an energy glossary.

With its broad scope and multiple access points, the EIA website is the place to start when looking for energy-related data. Much of the data are at the national level, but state, regional, and international data are also available. An A–Z Index helps in locating specific information on this large site.

Subject(s): Energy—Statistics; Energy Prices and Costs; Databases

Energy Saver

https://energy.gov/energysaver/energy-saver

Description: This Energy Saver website includes tips for consumers on saving energy and reducing energy costs in house cooling and heating, water heating, lighting, windows, insulation, and other areas. The site also has information on tax credits and other financial incentives to save energy.

Subject(s): Energy Conservation

Energy Savers Blog

https://energy.gov/energysaver/listings/blog

Description: This blog focuses on energy-saving tips for consumers, covering topics such as energy-efficient appliances and weatherization.

Subject(s): Energy Conservation; Blogs

ENERGY STAR

https://www.energystar.gov/

Description: ENERGY STAR is a voluntary labeling program designed to identify and promote energy-efficient products. The core of this website is its extensive and detailed directory of qualified projects. Other sections cover energy-efficient home improvement projects, finding new homes that qualify for ENERGY STAR, and guidelines for energy-efficient commercial buildings.

Subject(s): Energy Conservation

Federal Energy Regulatory Commission (FERC)

https://www.ferc.gov/

Description: FERC is an independent regulatory commission, organized under the Department of Energy, with responsibilities in the areas of electricity, natural gas, oil, and hydroelectric power businesses. The About section of its website enumerates the responsibilities that are inside and outside FERC's jurisdiction. The site has extensive data and analysis of the electricity, gas, and other markets in the Market Oversight section. The site's eLibrary section serves as a central point for parties filing documents with FERC and for researchers seeking FERC documents. The Legal Resources section has current information about administrative litigation, court cases involving FERC, and the FERC Alternative Dispute Resolution process. Special sections provide guidance to regulated parties and other users on such topics as the Energy Policy Act of 2005 and open access transmission tariff reform. FERC has Market Oversight updates and Technical Conference notices.

Subject(s): Energy—Regulations

Saving Energy at Home

https://www.consumer.ftc.gov/topics/saving-energy-home

Description: This consumer-oriented website provides tips on reducing energy costs through the use of energy-saving appliances, compact fluorescent bulbs, better gas mileage in cars, and other household strategies. The site is also available in Spanish.

Subject(s): Energy Conservation

Weatherization and Intergovernmental Program

https://energy.gov/eere/wipo/weatherization-and-intergovernmental-programs-office

Description: The Weatherization and Intergovernmental Program works with regional and state energy offices to promote energy-efficient technologies and policies. This website outlines its major program areas and funding opportunities. Major programs include Energy Efficiency and Conservation Block Grants, the Weatherization Assistance Program, the State Energy Program, the Tribal Energy Program, and the Renewable Energy Production Incentive.

Subject(s): Energy Conservation—Grants

FOSSIL AND NUCLEAR FUELS

Blue Ribbon Commission on America's Nuclear Future

https://cybercemetery.unt.edu/archive/brc/20120620211605/http:/brc.gov/

Description: The Blue Ribbon Commission was established to review the processing, storage, and disposal of used nuclear fuel. The commission's website has information about its membership, videos of its meetings, and copies of relevant documents. The final commission report was released in January 2012 and the site has been archived by the University of North Texas.

Subject(s): Nuclear Fuels

Depleted UF6 Management Information Network

http://web.ead.anl.gov/uranium/

Description: The Depleted UF6 Management Information Network is a public information website about the Department of Energy's management of its depleted uranium hexafluoride inventory. The material is a product of the uranium enrichment process and must be managed to protect the environment and the safety of workers and the public. This site provides information about the material, its uses and risks, and the status of the management program. It includes environmental impact statements, program documents, and answers to frequently asked questions.

Subject(s): Nuclear Waste

Energy Resources Program

https://energy.usgs.gov/

Description: The USGS Energy Resources Program conducts research and provides scientific information and supply assessments for geologically based energy resources, such as oil, natural gas, and coal. Information, including maps and images, is organized by energy source. Other sections cover environmental and health issues, such as acid mine drainage and mercury emissions from coal, and USGS research in geochemistry and geophysics.

Subject(s): Fossil Fuels

fueleconomy.gov

https://www.fueleconomy.gov/

Description: The Department of Energy and the Environmental Protection Agency co-sponsor this website. The site features a database that can be used to find and compare gas mileage, greenhouse gas emissions, and air pollution ratings for various car and truck models. The site also has tips for improving gas mileage and explains why miles per gallon (MPG) rates can vary. The Find the Cheapest Gas section, under Save Money, links to gas price data from other sources and has information about related topics, such as gasoline taxes and regional variations in retail price. Other sections cover hybrid and alternative fuel vehicles. The annual *Fuel Economy Guide* compiles fuel economy values for the model year for gasoline and alternative fuel cars, as well as light trucks, minivans, and sport utility vehicles. A Spanish-language version of the site is also available.

Subject(s): Gasoline; Motor Vehicles—Statistics

Idaho National Laboratory (INL)

https://www.inl.gov/

Description: The Idaho National Engineering and Environmental Laboratory (INEEL) and the Argonne National Laboratory-West became the Idaho National Laboratory (INL) in February 2005. This website describes INL's research and development work in the nuclear energy, national security, and energy science and technology areas. It includes information about the Center for Advanced Energy Studies and the Next Generation Nuclear Plant projects.

Subject(s): Nuclear Energy—Research; Scientific Research

National Energy Technology Laboratory (NETL)

https://www.netl.doe.gov/

Description: NETL conducts research related to coal, natural gas, and oil. The website's Research section describes NETL's research capabilities in basic sciences, energy system dynamics, geological and environmental systems, and materials science. The same section also covers topics including oil and natural gas supply, carbon sequestration, and hydrogen as an energy source. Information about research grants and technology transfer is available in the Business section. The Newsroom section of the site links to numerous news articles, papers, presentations, reports, and other publications in NETL's areas of expertise, including carbon sequestration, coal and power systems, hydrogen and clean fuels, and oil and natural gas supply.

Subject(s): Fossil Fuels—Research

Nuclear Regulatory Commission (NRC)

https://www.nrc.gov/

Description: NRC is an independent agency charged with regulating civilian use of nuclear materials. Its website highlights current news, public meetings schedules, and current rulemakings. Much of the material explaining NRC regulations and responsibilities can be found under the Nuclear Reactors, Nuclear Materials, Radioactive Waste, and Nuclear Security headings. Of interest to the general public, the site has a section on public involvement in NRC regulatory activities, information about reporting a safety or security concern, a directory of operating nuclear facilities, a section on radiation protection, and the option to receive e-mail news notices. The Event Reports section gives a daily status of nuclear power reactors, and the For the Record section provides NRC responses to "information on controversial issues or to significant media reports that could be misleading." (from the website)

The NRC Library section organizes access to NRC public documents. It features the Agency wide Documents Access and Management System (ADAMS), a database that provides access to all image and text documents that the NRC has made public since November 1999, as well as bibliographic records made public by the NRC before that date. Other online document collections include NRC regulations, commission paper and orders, significant enforcement actions, NUREG-Series Publications, and Regulatory Guides.

Subject(s): Nuclear Energy—Regulations

Office of Fossil Energy (FE)

https://www.energy.gov/fe/office-fossil-energy

Description: The Department of Energy's Office of Fossil Energy organizes its website content into major sections, including Services, Science & Innovation, Mission, and About Us. Topical sections in Science & Innovation include Clean Coal, Carbon Capture and Storage, and Oil & Gas. News, a link to the office's blog, and social media page links are also included on the home page.

Subject(s): Fossil Fuels

Office of Nuclear Energy (NE)

https://www.energy.gov/ne/office-nuclear-energy

Description: The Office of Nuclear Energy is concerned with developing new nuclear energy generation technologies, managing the national nuclear infrastructure, and working to support university nuclear engineering programs. Programs include Fuel Cycle Research and Development, Generation IV Nuclear Energy Systems (Gen-IV), and International Nuclear Energy Policy and Cooperation (INEPC). The Document Library section includes budget information, reports to Congress, a Price-Anderson Indemnification section regarding insuring the public for damages from nuclear accidents, and a link to more publications.

Subject(s): Nuclear Energy—Research

Oil and Gas Industry Initiatives

https://www.ftc.gov/tips-advice/competition-guidance/industry-guidance/oil-and-gas

Description: As stated on the site, "this website describes the FTC's oversight of the petroleum industry, with special sections on our activities related to merger enforcement, anticompetitive nonmerger activity, and gasoline price data."

Subject(s): Antitrust Law; Petroleum

U.S. Petroleum Reserves

https://energy.gov/fe/services/petroleum-reserves

Description: This website provides profiles of the Strategic Petroleum Reserve and the much smaller Northeast Home Heating Oil Reserve and Naval Petroleum and Oil Shale Reserves. For the Strategic Petroleum Reserve, the site has data on the current inventory, the general locations of the secure storage sites, information on expanding the reserve, and information about when and why crude oil has been released from the reserve.

Subject(s): Petroleum

UTILITIES

Rural Utilities Service (RUS)

https://www.rd.usda.gov/about-rd/agencies/rural-utilities-service/

Description: RUS supports the expansion and maintenance of electric, telecommunications, water, and waste disposal utilities in rural areas. Information about the RUS website is divided into sections covering Electric Programs, Water and Environmental Programs, and Telecommunications Programs. Each major section includes program information and contacts.

Subject(s): Distance Learning—Grants; Rural Development; Rural Utilities; Telemedicine—Grants; Water Treatment

Southeastern Power Administration (SEPA)

https://energy.gov/sepa/southeastern-power-administration

Description: SEPA is responsible for marketing the electric power and energy generated at reservoirs operated by the U.S. Army Corps of Engineers in Georgia, Florida, Alabama, Mississippi, southern Illinois, Virginia, Tennessee, Kentucky, North Carolina, and South Carolina. Its website includes rate schedules, a system map, and information about how hydroelectricity works.

Subject(s): Hydroelectric Power

SmartGrid.gov

https://www.smartgrid.gov/

Description: A smart grid is an advanced version of the electrical grid network of technologies that delivers electricity from power plants to consumers in their homes and offices. SmartGrid.gov explains the technology basics. It describes government-funded projects for research, investment, and workforce training. The website also has a wealth of background information on the topic, as well as Recovery Act Smart Grid programs.

Subject(s): Electricity

Southwestern Power Administration (SWPA)

https://www.swpa.gov/

Description: The Southwestern Power Administration is responsible for marketing the hydroelectric power produced at 24 U.S. Army Corps of Engineers multipurpose dams. Its website has information about how the Southwestern Power Administration operates and its rate schedules, estimated power generation, and acquisitions information.

Subject(s): Hydroelectric Power

Tennessee Valley Authority (TVA)

https://www.tva.gov/

Description: TVA is a federal corporation and public power company. It operates fossil fuel and nuclear power plants and manages a system of dams. The Energy section of the site describes TVA's power sources, transmission system, and right-of-way lands. The Environment section includes environmental reviews of TVA projects under the National Environmental Policy Act (NEPA). The site also covers river management and TVA's recreational lakes. For information on TVA's role in encouraging economic development, the site links to TVA Economic Development at https://www.tva.com/Economic-Development.

Subject(s): Electricity; Utilities (Energy)

Western Area Power Administration (WAPA)

https://www.wapa.gov/

Description: WAPA markets and delivers hydroelectric power in the central and western United States. The Power Marketing and Transmission sections provide detailed background information. The About section has financial data and annual reports. The Energy Services section is designed for customers. The website also has information on WAPA's Electric Power Training Center, which is open to public enrollment. Other sections offer news, acquisitions information, Federal Register notices, and links to webpages for each WAPA region.

Subject(s): Hydroelectric Power; West (United States)

Chapter Ten

Engineering and Technology

Engineering and technology websites from the federal government cover a broad range of applications and goals, such as aerospace research and development, computer security, telecommunications regulations, technical assistance for manufacturers, industrial standards, and technology transfer and commercialization. Sponsors of these websites include the military, the Department of Energy, and the National Institute of Standards and Technology (NIST). Researchers may also want to check the Science chapter of the book, particularly the Scientific and Technical Information section and the Space section, for additional sites of interest.

Subsections in this chapter are Communications, Engineering, and Technology.

COMMUNICATIONS

FCC Enforcement Bureau

https://www.fcc.gov/enforcement/

Description: The FCC's regulatory enforcement arm implements rules regarding consumer protection, local competition enforcement, and public safety/homeland security. In the Investigative & Adjudicatory Areas section, the bureau explains its work on consumer telephone issues, local telephone competition enforcement, indecent or obscene broadcasts, wireless 911 violations, communications equipment marketing violations, and other areas. The bureau's website has instructions on filing complaints about amateur radio interference, indecent broadcasts, and other topics. The site also has current news and documents.

Subject(s): Broadcasting—Laws; Telecommunications—Laws

FCC International Bureau

https://www.fcc.gov/international/

Description: The International Bureau administers the FCC's international telecommunications policies and obligations. Its website includes information about bureau contacts and current FCC actions. The Applications section includes Earth Station Licensing information, fee filing guides, and a link to file pleadings. The Industry Information section contains news related to the World Trade Organization Basic Telecommunications Agreement and the annual circuit status reports for U.S. facilities-based international common carriers. The Resources section provides a long list of reference information, including foreign ownership guidelines, international agreements, rules for foreign carriers, and Significant Satellite Rulemakings.

Subject(s): Telecommunications—International

FCC Media Bureau

https://www.fcc.gov/media/

Description: The FCC Media Bureau manages policy and licensing programs relating to electronic media, including cable television, broadcast television, and radio. This website carries news on regulatory, licensing, and merger developments. The Official Documents section includes documents from the Media Bureau and from its recent predecessors, the Mass Media Bureau and the Cable Services Bureau. The site also provides quarterly tallies of broadcast stations, information on political programming rules, and a "Significantly Viewed" list of television stations. Media Bureau databases include CDBS (licensing information for radio and RV broadcast stations) and COALS (Cable Operations and Licensing System).

Subject(s): Broadcasting—Regulations

FCC Office of Engineering and Technology (OET)

https://www.fcc.gov/engineering-%26-technology

Description: OET is concerned with the policies and regulations for frequency allocation, spectrum usage, advanced communications technologies, and other matters related to communications engineering. Major sections of its website focus on information about radio frequency safety, radio spectrum allocation, and the authorization of equipment using the radio frequency spectrum. The OET Docket Information page provides access to FCC orders, notices, and press releases. It also links to mapping resources, technical documents, and a database of equipment authorizations.

Subject(s): Communications Technology—Regulations

FCC Office of Native Affairs and Policy (ONAP)

https://www.fcc.gov/general/native-nations

Description: This site describes FCC programs to overcome the lack of telecommunications availability and use on tribal lands. The site includes the FCC "Statement of Policy on Establishing a Government-to-Government Relationship with Indian Tribes." It also covers specific issues such as tower and antenna siting, tribal lands bidding credits for telecommunications services, and financial assistance.

Subject(s): Telecommunications—Policy; American Indians

FCC Public Safety & Homeland Security Bureau

https://www.fcc.gov/public-safety-and-homeland-security

Description: The FCC Public Safety and Homeland Security Bureau was established in 2006 to coordinate FCC activities related to public safety, homeland security, national security, emergency management and preparedness, and disaster management. The website covers topics such as the public safety communications spectrum, emergency communications planning, 911 call centers, and related advisory groups and safety groups. The site also has an online clearinghouse of public safety communications information.

Subject(s): Communications—Policy; Disaster Preparedness; Homeland Security

FCC Wireless Telecommunications Bureau

https://www.fcc.gov/wireless-telecommunications

Description: The Wireless Telecommunications Bureau handles FCC domestic wireless telecommunications programs and policies for cellular, paging, maritime mobile, and other wireless communications services. Its website includes statements, public notices, and other documents. Other sections within the site include Auctions, Licensing, and Wireless Services. The Wireless Services section links to FCC information for over 30 services, including amateur radio, Wireless Communications Service (WCS), and Broadband Radio Service (BRS).

Subject(s): Wireless Communications—Regulations

FCC's Parents' Place

https://www.fcc.gov/general/parents

Description: The FCC created this website to help parents understand and monitor their children's use of communications technology, including cell phones, television, and the Internet. The site includes sections on children's television programming, parental controls, online safety, blocking objectionable content on mobile devices, and more.

Subject(s): Communications Technology

Federal Communications Commission (FCC)

https://www.fcc.gov/

Description: The FCC regulates interstate and international communications by radio, television, wire, satellite, and cable. The FCC website provides centralized access to information about the commission and its work, along with biographies of its commissioners and links to the FCC bureaus, offices, and advisory committees. The home page also features current FCC news and a link to the online version of the *Federal Communications Commission Daily Digest*, which is also available via e-mail delivery. The *Daily Digest* is a synopsis of commission orders, news releases, speeches, public notices and all other FCC documents released each business day, with links to the full-text version of each document. Issues are archived and kept online from June 1994 onward. The FCC offers a variety of finding aids for its website and documents collections.

Subject(s): Telecommunications—Regulations

Institute for Telecommunication Sciences (ITS)

https://www.its.bldrdoc.gov/

Description: ITS is the research and engineering branch of the National Telecommunications and Information Administration (NTIA). The website's Programs section links to information on such projects as the Audio Quality Research, Video Quality Research, Wireless Networks, and Radio Frequency Interference Monitoring System projects. It also links to information about technology transfer and ITS cooperative research and development agreements (CRADAs). The Publications section offers access to a variety of NTIA reports.

Subject(s): Communications Technology—Research

National Broadband Plan

https://www.fcc.gov/general/national-broadband-plan

Description: In the context of the Internet, the word "broadband" in the most general sense refers to a network with transmission speeds and capacity better than today's average. The FCC's National Broadband Plan, the centerpiece of this website, proposes strategies for stimulating private sector competition to expand capacity and coverage of the nation's networks. The report was mandated by Congress in 2010. The FCC used a number of strategies, such as workshops, to gather input from across the United States.

The Broadband.gov website is also available in Spanish. The Executive Summary is available in Spanish, Chinese, Thai, Vietnamese, Korean, Tagalog, and Samoan.

Subject(s): Internet—Policy

National Telecommunications and Information Administration (NTIA)

https://www.ntia.doc.gov/home

Description: NTIA, an Executive branch agency within the Department of Commerce, is principally responsible for domestic and international telecommunications and information policy issues. The NTIA website has information about the administration, its publications, and its press releases. Much of the information on the site is found on the pages for NTIA's component offices, such as the page for Spectrum Management. The Grants section, under Topics, includes information on the Public Telecommunications Facilities Program (PTFP), Public Safety Interoperable Communications (PSIC), and other grant programs. The NTIA website also links to extensive information about the Broadband Technology Opportunities Program grants funded through the Recovery Act of 2009.

Subject(s): Internet—Policy; Telecommunications—Policy

USDA Telecommunications Program

https://www.rd.usda.gov/programs-services/all-programs/telecom-programs/

Description: The Rural Development Telecommunications Program assists with financing for rural America's telecommunications infrastructure. The program provides loans and grants in the areas including broadband connectivity, distance learning, and telemedicine. Program materials on the website include grant and loan applications and a list of materials acceptable for use on the telecommunications systems of borrowers.

Subject(s): Telecommunications

ENGINEERING

CADRE: Center for Aerospace-Defense Research and Engineering

https://www.erg.jhu.edu/

Description: CADRE, formally CPIAC (Chemical Propulsion Information Analysis Center) is a research center focused on chemical, electrical, and nuclear propulsion for missile, rocket, and space and gun propulsion systems. In the Products section, the website includes an archive of the *CPIAC Bulletin* (published from 1974 to 2011) and listings of current CADRE publications and databases. Database access is granted only to those that meet the eligibility requirements listed on the site. For the general public, the site offers propulsion news items from non-restricted sources.

Subject(s): Information Analysis Centers; Propulsion Technology; Rockets

Coastal and Hydraulics Laboratory (CHL)

http://www.erdc.usace.army.mil/Locations/CHL/

Description: The U.S. Army Corps of Engineers Coastal and Hydraulics Laboratory (CHL) conducts research and development in civil engineering related to shorelines, coastal structures, water flow, and waterways navigation. The CHL website provides information on its research programs, data and software publications research and development applications, research facilities, and organizational structure. CHL capabilities are organized by area of expertise, such as dredging, estuaries, flood control, and coastal structures.

Subject(s): Civil Engineering—Research; Waterways—Research

Construction Engineering Research Laboratory (CERL)

http://www.erdc.usace.army.mil/Locations/CERL/

Description: CERL conducts research in civil engineering and environmental quality to support sustainable military installations for the army. The website has information about CERL, its leadership, and its facilities and products.

Subject(s): Civil Engineering—Research

Engineer Research and Development Center (ERDC)

http://www.erdc.usace.army.mil

Description: ERDC specializes in engineering and environmental sciences in support of the military and for domestic projects. ERDC and its laboratories are concerned with the engineering and science aspects of coastal environments and hydraulics, flood control and storm damage reduction, cold regions, construction, engineering geology, environmental cleanup and restoration, information technology, geospatial systems, and military support. The website links to each of the ERDC laboratory websites.

Subject(s): Civil Engineering; Defense Research

Engineering at LLNL

https://engineering.llnl.gov/

Description: The website highlights the engineering projects underway at the Lawrence Livermore National Laboratory. Designed for potential clients and the general public, the site covers such LLNL specialties as biotechnology, materials engineering, and precision engineering,

Subject(s): Engineering Research; National Laboratories

Hollings Manufacturing Extension Partnership (MEP)

https://www.nist.gov/mep

Description: The Hollings Manufacturing Extension Partnership (MEP), named for Sen. Ernest Frederick "Fritz" Hollings, is a network of extension centers and experts who offer technical and business assistance to smaller manufacturers. Its website describes the program and offers a directory of participating extension centers.

Subject(s): Manufacturing

Engineering Laboratory

https://www.nist.gov/el

Description: The Engineering Laboratory at NIST focuses on measurements and standards issues in parts manufacturing. The laboratory's divisions are Materials and Structural Systems, Energy and Environment, Fire Research, Intelligent Systems, and Systems Integration, with the offices of the Smart Grid Program, Applied Economics, and National Earthquake Hazards Reduction Program (NEHRP). Each division provides information on the technology in its realm. The website also provides information by topics, such as disaster resilience, robotics and automation, and supply chain integration. The Products/Services section of the site has information on software products and guest researcher opportunities.

Subject(s): Manufacturing Technology

Manufacturing Technology Program (ManTech)

https://www.dodmantech.com/

Description: ManTech focuses on improved processes in the production of weapons systems. The site describes program activities in such areas as metals, composites, and electronics research. The site also includes information on the program's funding, relevant legislation, business opportunities, and achievements.

Subject(s): Manufacturing Technology

National Institute of Standards and Technology (NIST)

https://www.nist.gov/

Description: NIST, an agency within the Department of Commerce, seeks to promote economic growth by working with industry to develop and apply technology, measurements, and standards. One of its major projects is to develop standards to enable the nation's move to a "smart grid," a modernized electric power infrastructure; the work is discussed at https://www.nist.gov/smartgrid/. The NIST website provides information from the agency's ten specialized laboratories, including Building and Fire Research, Electronics and Telecommunications, and Information Technology. The site also organizes NIST's work by general topic, such as bioscience and health, energy, quality, and transportation.

The site also accesses the NIST online databases and NIST publications.

Subject(s): Research and Development; Research Laboratories; Standards and Specifications

Standards.gov

https://www.nist.gov/standardsgov

Description: Standards.gov provides background information on standards (including a legal definition of "standards" for the purposes of the website) and assistance in locating information about the use of standards in government. The site focuses on federal agency use of standards for regulatory and procurement purposes. The Federal Agency Info section links to agency websites about standards, the Interagency Committee on Standards Policy (ICSP), and federal standards-related laws, policies, and guidance.

Subject(s): Standards and Specifications

U.S. Army Corps of Engineers

https://www.usace.army.mil

Description: The U.S. Army Corps of Engineers provides engineering services for military construction and civil works projects in areas such as flood control and waterway navigation and emergency response. The Library section includes links to the USACE libraries, publication listings, and maps information. The Media section links to news releases, fact sheets, and videos and images. The website also has information on USACE locations and business opportunities, and a blog by the Commanding General of USACE.

The Army Corps of Engineers has an extensive network of websites. To discover the full range of content available, use the organizational and geographic district links in the About section.

Subject(s): Civil Engineering; Waterways

U.S. Army Corps of Engineers Cold Regions Research and Engineering Laboratory (CRREL)

http://www.erdc.usace.army.mil/Locations/CRREL.aspx

Description: CRREL conducts scientific and engineering research on cold temperature environments. A CRREL fact sheet is linked to on the home page. The sites main sections are Research Areas, Products and Services, Facilities, and Expertise.

Subject(s): Engineering Research; Research Laboratories

TECHNOLOGY

Biometrics

https://www.dhs.gov/biometrics/

Description: The site includes an extensive introduction to biometrics including the benefits of biometrics and links to the biometric missions of the

Department of Defense, Department of State, and Departmnet of Justice in addition to the Department of Homeland Security.

Subject(s): Biometrics

Biometrics Resource Center Website

https://www.nist.gov/itl/computer-security-division/biometrics-resource-center-website

Description: NIST is part of the government's Biometric Consortium. This website describes the biometrics research activities of NIST's Information Technology Laboratory and offers links to Biometric Consortium conference information and to related government websites.

Subject(s): Biometrics—Research

Digital Preservation

http://www.digitalpreservation.gov

Description: Digital Preservation is the website for the National Digital Information Infrastructure and Preservation Program (NDIIPP), a collaborative effort led by the Library of Congress to develop a national strategy to collect, preserve, and make available digital content. The website has information on NDIIP's over 300 partner institutions and their digital preservation initiatives. The website features access to many of the tools and services created by project partners, as well as reports, video presentations, and podcasts. The site also has a section on personal archiving for individuals who would like to preserve their own digital creations.

Subject(s): Archives; Digital Libraries; Information Technology

Digital Television

https://www.fcc.gov/general/digital-television

Description: This special FCC website was created to educate consumers about the 2009 switch from analog format to digital by full-power television broadcast stations. The site now has basic consumer information on digital television. It is also available in Spanish.

Subject(s): Television

Energy Science and Technology Software Center (ESTSC)

https://www.osti.gov/moved/estsc/

Description: ESTSC licenses and distributes federally funded scientific and technical software developed by the national laboratories, Department of Energy contractors, and other developers. This website serves as the central catalog and order site. The software available is highly technical and specialized, with titles such as "Unsaturated Groundwater and Heat Transport Model" and "Simulation Program for Non-isothermal Multiphase Reactive Geochemical Transport."

Subject(s): Software; Technology Transfer

Energy Sciences Network (ESnet)

http://www.es.net

Description: ESnet is a high-speed network, funded by the Department of Energy, that provides network and collaboration services in support of the agency's research missions. ESnet is used by researchers at national laboratories, universities, and other institutions and provides direct connections to all major DOE sites with high performance speeds. Major sections of the website include Network R&D (Research and Development) and News & Publications.

Subject(s): Internet—High-speed

Information Technology Laboratory (ITL)

https://www.nist.gov/itl

Description: This NIST laboratory develops the tests and test methods used by researchers and scientists to measure, compare, and improve information technology systems. Detailed information is available on its website, organized by research area: advanced network technologies, computer security, information access, applied and computational mathematics, software and systems, and statistical engineering. The site also has information on the laboratory's role as an ANSI standards developer.

Subject(s): Information Technology—Research

Information Technology Portal

https://www.nist.gov/topics/information-technology

Description: The NIST Information Technology Portal links to NIST research, news, and publications on a broad range of technologies. Topics covered by the portal include biometrics, computer forensics, computer security, conformance testing, and cybersecurity.

Subject(s): Information Technology

Nanotechnology at NIH

https://www.nih.gov/research-training/nanotechnology-nih

Description: This site provides basic information about nanotechnology and about the nanotechnology research and resources at NIH.

Subject(s): Nanotechnology—Research

NASA Advanced Supercomputing Division (NAS)

https://www.nas.nasa.gov/

Description: NAS provides research, development, and delivery of high-end computing services and technologies to facilitate NASA mission success. The website describes projects running on the NASA supercomputers and provides—under the Publications heading—links to NAS technical reports.

Subject(s): High Performance Computing

NASA Independent Verification and Validation Facility (IV&V)

https://www.nasa.gov/centers/ivv/home/index.html

Description: The IV&V Facility was established in 1993 to ensure the safety and reliability of the agency's mission-critical software and systems. The site has information about this process in the IV&V Services section. Other sections provide information about the facility's mission and organization, research, education programs, and annual workshop.

Subject(s): Software

NASA Strategic Partnerships Office

https://partnerships.gsfc.nasa.gov/index.html

Description: The Strategic Partnerships Office (SPO) is a connector – forging innovative partnerships that link NASA researchers at Goddard Space Flight Center (*internal inventors*) with corporations, startups, universities, and other government agencies (*external partners*). The SPO is responsible for three core program areas: technology transfer, SBIR/STTR, and partnerships.

Subject(s): Space Technology; Technology Transfer

NASA Technology Transfer Portal (T2P)

https://technology.nasa.gov/

Description: NASA's T2P highlights the NASA technologies that have commercial potential. A Success Stories section describes NASA spinoffs into the commercial sector.

Subject(s): Space Technology; Technology Transfer

Networking and Information Technology Research and Development (NITRD) Program

https://www.nitrd.gov/

Description: The National Coordination Office's support for the NITRD Program includes planning and technical expertise. According to the website, this program "provides a framework in which many federal agencies come together to coordinate their networking and information technology (IT) research and development (R&D) efforts." (from the website) The site has information on the work of the NITRD Program's interagency groups, including Cyber Security and Information Assurance, High End Computing, and Large Scale Networking. The site also has the annual *Supplement to the President's Budget*, which coordinates the information technology R&D plans of multiple agencies.

Subject(s): Information Technology—Research

National Energy Research Scientific Computing Center (NERSC)

http://www.nersc.gov

Description: NERSC provides high-performance computing services to scientists supported by the DOE's Office of Science. Its website provides information on NERSC computing resources, research projects, and publications. Although the computing resources of NERSC are limited to authorized scientists, the NERSC site provides some information for non-affiliated users interested in computational sciences and high-performance computing.

Subject(s): High Performance Computing; Scientific Research

National Geological and Geophysical Data Preservation Program (NGGDPP)

https://datapreservation.usgs.gov/

Description: NGGDPP was established to set up an archive of geography-related data, maps, well logs, and other information; to create a national catalog of this data; and to assist state geological surveys with their data. The website outlines the work being led by NGGDPP in these areas.

Subject(s): Data Storage; Geology

National Nanotechnology Initiative (NNI)

http://www.nano.gov

Description: NNI is a multi-agency effort to coordinate federal research and development in nanoscale science, engineering, and technology. The NNI website includes information on available funding opportunities for nanotechnology R&D, the areas of research focus for NNI, current research news, and information about nanotechnology safety issues. The site also describes educational outreach programs for various educational levels.

Subject(s): Nanotechnology—Research

National Vulnerability Database (NVD)

https://nvd.nist.gov/

Description: NVD provides current information about threats to computer security. NVD includes databases of security checklists, security related software flaws, misconfigurations, product names, and impact metrics. The website also has a statistics generation engine to graph and chart vulnerability characteristics.

Subject(s): Computer Security

NIST Computer Security Resource Center (CSRC)

https://csrc.nist.gov/

Description: CSRC is designed to collect and disseminate computer security information and resources to help users, systems administrators, managers, and security professionals better protect their data and comply with the Federal Information Systems Management Act (FISMA). Most of the information on the site can be found in the Projects/Research sections: Cryptographic Technology, Education & Outreach, FISMA & Cybersecurity Initiatives, Identity Management & Access Control, Security Automation & Vulnerability Management, Systems & Emerging Technologies, and Validation Programs & Testing. Publications on the CSRC site include Federal Information Processing Standards (FIPS) information. The Drivers section covers the legal and regulatory framework governing federal information security practices.

Subject(s): Computer Security

Section 508

https://www.section508.gov/

Description: Section 508 of the Rehabilitation Act requires federal agencies to make their electronic and information technology accessible to people with disabilities. This GSA-sponsored website provides explanations of Section 508 requirements to help both agencies and vendors comply with the law.

Subject(s): World Wide Web—Laws

Technology Innovation Program (TIP)

https://www.nist.gov/technology-innovation-program

Description: TIP supports high-risk, high-reward research in areas determined to be of critical national need. The website has information on the current competition for TIP funding and on past funded projects.

Subject(s): Research and Development—Grants

Usability.gov

https://www.usability.gov/

Description: According to the website, "Usability.gov is the leading resource for user experience (UX) best practices and guidelines, serving practitioners and students in the government and private sectors." The website is sponsored by NCI and is an excellent resource for people learning about or working in UX or related fields.

Subject(s): World Wide Web

US-CERT

https://www.us-cert.gov/

Description: US-CERT (United States Computer Emergency Readiness Team) is a partnership between the Department of Homeland Security and the public and private sectors that was established to protect the nation's Internet infrastructure. The site offers several security alert services deliverable by e-mail or RSS feed and excellent security publications for the average user.

Subject(s): Computer Security

Chapter Eleven

Environment and Nature

The Environmental Protection Agency, the Department of the Interior, and the Commerce Department's National Oceanic and Atmospheric Administration sponsors public websites with data, science, policy, and educational information related to the environment. Sites from these and other agencies are included in this section. Outdoor recreation information can be found in the Culture and Recreation chapter. Atmospheric sciences sites are in the Science and Space chapter.

Subsections in this chapter are Environmental Law, Environmental Policy, Environmental Protection, Environmental Science, Geography, Natural Resources, Pollutants and Waste, and Weather.

ENVIRONMENTAL LAW

Enforcement and Compliance History Online (ECHO)

https://echo.epa.gov/

Description: ECHO is an EPA information system that provides violation and enforcement information on approximately 800,000 facilities under key environmental statutes. From the home page, users can search by ZIP code or address to find regulated facilities and display their inspection and enforcement history. The More Search Options button enables additional search criteria, including facility name, EPA region, county, and state. Searches can be filtered by a number of characteristics, such as whether the facility has had violations, is on Indian land, is near the U.S.-Mexico border, or has a certain percentage of minority population within a three-mile radius. Specific types of data, such as compliance on hazardous waste or compliance with water rules, can also be searched separately. Facilities identified in search results can be located on Google maps.

The EPA provides detailed document and guides to the data, and the data fields on tables link to helpful descriptions.

Subject(s): Environmental Law

Environmental Appeals Board

https://yosemite.epa.gov/oa/EAB_Web_Docket.nsf

Description: The Environmental Appeals Board handles administrative appeals under all of the major environmental statutes administered by the EPA. The website carries published decisions and lists of decisions reviewed by the federal courts or pending federal court review. It includes guidance documents and *A Citizens' Guide to EPA's Environmental Appeals Board.*

Subject(s): Environmental Law

Environmental Appeals Board Practice Manual

EPA Laws & Regulations

https://www.epa.gov/laws-regulations

Description: This EPA page links to information on environmental regulations organized by environmental topic and business sector. The page also links to significant regulatory guidance documents and to the major federal laws and executive orders that the EPA administers. Background information includes sections on how the EPA writes regulations, how to comment on proposed regulations, and how the EPA enforces environmental laws.

Subject(s): Environmental Protection—Regulations

National Environmental Policy Act (NEPA)—CEQ

https://ceq.doe.gov/

Description: This site provides news and information from the Council on Environmental Quality (CEQ) related to the implementation of NEPA. The site has statutes, regulations, executive orders, and regulatory guidance concerning NEPA. The Legal Corner section has NEPA-related case law and litigation statistics. The site also provides NEPA reports and publications, including *The Citizen's Guide to the National Environmental Policy Act*.

Subject(s): Environmental Impact Statements; Environmental Law

National Environmental Policy Act (NEPA)—EPA

https://energy.gov/nepa/office-nepa-policy-and-compliance

Description: This website summarizes the Department of Energy's activities related to NEPA. Documents available on the site include relevant Records of Decision, Notices of Intent, and NEPA Annual Planning Summaries. The site also provides environmental impact statement schedules, a public meeting calendar, information for NEPA contractors, and the *Lessons Learned* quarterly report. The site also covers NEPA compliance guidance. A notice on the site regarding secure documents advises: "Categorical exclusions are categories of actions that the DOE has determined, by regulation, do not individually or cumulatively have a significant effect on the human environment and for which, therefore, neither an environmental assessment nor an environmental impact statement normally is required." These restricted-access documents can be requested in hard copy format.

Subject(s): Environmental Law

Regulatory Development and Retrospective Review Tracker (Reg DaRRT)

https://yosemite.epa.gov/opei/RuleGate.nsf/

Description: This website includes rules that have not yet been proposed, those that are open for public comment, those for which the EPA is working on a final rule, and those that have been recently finalized. Researchers can find rules with an advanced search, or sort them by topic, rulemaking phase, or effect. Under Get Alerts, the site provides over a dozen RSS newsfeeds, including for new rules added to the Gateway, newly opened comment periods, and notice of the final rule.

Subject(s): Environmental Law

ENVIRONMENTAL POLICY

American Indian Tribal Portal

https://www.epa.gov/tribal

Description: This website serves as a central access point for EPA information specifically relevant to tribal governments. The site links to EPA Indian policies, EPA tribal programs, and agency tribal contacts. It also links to general information on environmental grants, laws, and regulations.

Subject(s): American Indians

Bureau of Oceans and International Environmental and Scientific Affairs (OES)

https://www.state.gov/e/oes/

Description: OES coordinates U.S. foreign policy related to science, the environment, and the world's oceans. The website presents remarks, reports, and press releases related to topics such as climate change, biodefense, science and technology cooperation, sustainable development, fisheries, polar affairs, and water issues. The site also links to webpages for the State Department's regional environmental hubs located in selected U.S. embassies around the world. Links to the bureau's Facebook, Twitter, and Flickr pages are displayed on the homepage.

Subject(s): Oceans—Policy; Science and Technology Policy—International; Environmental Policy—International

Bureau of Safety and Environmental Enforcement (BSEE)

https://www.bsee.gov/

Description: As of October 2011, the former Bureau of Ocean Energy Management, Regulation, and Enforcement (BOEMRE) was reorganized and replaced with the Bureau of Ocean Energy Management (BOEM) and the Bureau of Safety and Environmental Enforcement (BSEE).

According to the website, "BSEE works to promote safety, protect the environment, and conserve resources offshore through vigorous regulatory oversight and enforcement." The Inspections & Enforcement section includes information about programs and civil penalties and appeals. The Technology & Research section has links to information about the National Offshore Training Center and OHMSETT—The National Oil Spill Response and Renewable Energy Test Facility. Procurement business opportunities can be found in the About BSEE section.

Subject(s): Safety; Environmental Policy

Council on Environmental Quality (CEQ)

https://www.whitehouse.gov/ceq/

Description: CEQ coordinates federal environmental efforts and oversees federal agency implementation of the environmental impact assessment process. The CEQ website has been expanded under the new administration. It includes press releases, a FOIA page, and information on CEQ initiatives such as Gulf Coast Ecosystem Restoration, America's Great Outdoors, and the Climate Change Adaptation Task Force. The Initiatives section also includes information on the administration's update of Principles and Guidelines for Water and Land Related Resources Implementation Studies.

Subject(s): Environmental Protection—Policy; National Environmental Policy Act

DENIX: DoD Environment, Safety, and Occupational Health Network and Information Exchange

https://www.denix.osd.mil/

Description: DENIX is a centralized resource for environment, safety, and occupational health policy and guidance information for the entire Department of Defense. Topical sections on the website are Programs, Performance, and Conferences & Training. The site also provides information on international agreements and on policies from the armed services.

Some sections of the website may be available only to authorized users.

Subject(s): Defense Administration; Environmental Protection—Policy; Historic Preservation

The EPA Blog

https://blog.epa.gov/blog/

Description: The official blog of the EPA is written by a variety of EPA employees. Topics range from consumer issues, such as asthma or recycling, to the scientific, such as radiation monitoring, and also cover policy and environmental education issues. Comments in accordance with their posted comment policy are encouraged and an RSS subscription feed is available.

Subject(s): Environmental Policy; Blogs

Federal Advisory Committees at EPA

https://www.epa.gov/faca

Description: EPA's Federal Advisory Committees are subject to the Federal Advisory Committees Act (FACA) and gather advice on a range of environmental issues. The website provides information and documents from each of the committees.

Subject(s): Environmental Policy

National Center for Environmental Economics (NCEE)

https://www.epa.gov/environmental-economics

Description: NCEE conducts economic research and analysis related to environmental issues, such as economic incentives for protecting the environment and the benefits and costs of environmental policies and regulations. The site has information on NCEE's reports and working papers, seminars and workshops, grants and funding, and an extensive catalog of websites concerning environmental economics.

Subject(s): Economics; Environmental Protection—Policy

Office of Federal Sustainability Council on Environmental Quality

https://sustainability.gov/

Description: The Office of Federal Sustainability (OFS) coordinates policy to promote energy and environmental sustainability across Federal Government operations, which encompasses 330,000 buildings, 660,000 vehicles, and $470 billion in purchased goods and services annually, including more than $21 billion for energy. It works closely with agencies and other White House components on policies and initiatives that improve energy efficiency, promote deployment of efficient technologies, and modernize federal facilities and operations through sound use of taxpayer dollars.

Subject(s): Recycling

Office of Natural Resources Revenue (ONRR)

https://www.onrr.gov/

Description: During the reorganization and renaming of the Minerals Management Service in 2010, ONRR took over the responsibilities of the Minerals Revenue Management (MRM) program. As stated on the website, the office "is a trustee of royalty assets from Indian trust properties and is an advocate for the interests of Indian mineral owners. In conjunction with the Bureau of Indian Affairs, ONRR provides revenue management services for mineral leases on American Indian lands. Money collected is returned—100 percent—to respective Indian tribes and individual Indian mineral owners through the Office of Trust Funds Management."

Subject(s): Natural Resources Management

Tribal Energy and Environmental Information Clearinghouse (TEEIC)

https://teeic.indianaffairs.gov/index.htm

Description: TEEIC provides information about the environmental effects of energy development on tribal lands. One section of the site offers impact, mitigation, regulatory, and case study information by type of energy, such as coal or wind. A second section focuses on guidance for conducting project-specific impact assessments and monitoring. The third section covers federal laws, regulations, and Executive Orders that may apply to energy development activities on tribal lands.

Subject(s): American Indians

Udall Foundation

https://www.udall.gov/

Description: The Morris K. Udall and Stewart L. Udall Foundation is an Executive branch agency created by Congress to honor Congressman Morris Udall's service in the House of Representatives. The foundation provides for internships, scholarships, and fellowships, most with a focus on public service, the environment, and Native Americans. The foundation also runs the U.S. Institute for Environmental Conflict Resolution. The website includes information on these and other Udall Foundation programs.

Subject(s): Environmental Education; American Indians; Scholarships

ENVIRONMENTAL PROTECTION

America's National Wildlife Refuge System

https://www.fws.gov/refuges/

Description: This Fish and Wildlife Service website has online visitor information for each of the National Wildlife Refuges. The site also provides information on the National Wildlife Refuge System, lands and planning, wildlife and habitat management, budget information, and relevant federal regulations.

Subject(s): Conservation (Natural Resources); Wildlife

Coastal Program

https://www.fws.gov/coastal/

Description: The Coastal Program works to conserve fish and wildlife and their habitats in the bays, estuaries, and watersheds around the U.S. coastline. The website has information about program activities, including the National Coastal Wetlands Conservation Grants.

Subject(s): Coastal Ecology

Earth Day

https://www.epa.gov/earthday

Description: This site is a portal for government information on Earth Day, celebrated every April 22nd. The site has information on Earth Day activities, environmental practices, and links to environmental volunteer opportunities. It features a number of links to EPA lesson plans.

Subject(s): Environmental Education

Environmental Protection Agency (EPA)

https://www.epa.gov/

Description: The central EPA website provides information resources on science and policy related to the environment, environment-related health issues, climate, ecosystems, pollution, hazardous substances, water quality, and more. The major sections of the site are: Learn the Issues, Science & Technology, Laws & Regulations, and About EPA. Click on the A–Z Index link in the upper right corner of the homepage to use the helpful index and other finding aids, such as links to the most popular topics, links to EPA's regional websites, and a list of EPA databases and software.

The homepage features EPA news and the site's blog, Greenversations. The Science & Technology section organizes EPA research areas by topic. The Laws & Regulations section has environmental laws and regulations, information on how to comment on regulations, and regulatory guidance and enforcement information.

As with other Cabinet-level agencies, EPA provides a Recovery Act section and an Open Government section its site. The EPA website has Spanish, Chinese, Vietnamese, and Korean versions.

Subject(s): Environmental Protection

Estuary Education

https://coast.noaa.gov/estuaries/

Description: This educational website explains the environmental importance of estuaries. It includes a section for students and provides curriculum guides for teachers.

Subject(s): Coastal Ecology; Environmental Education

Estuary Restoration Act & NOAA

https://www.fisheries.noaa.gov/national/habitat-conservation/estuary-restoration-act

Description: NOAA is one of five federal agencies serving on an interagency council charged with implementing the Estuary Restoration Act (ERA). This site provides information on project funding and the Estuary Habitat Restoration Strategy. It also has information on the law and on the Estuary Habitat Restoration Council.

Subject(s): Wetlands

Marine Protected Areas of the United States

https://oceanservice.noaa.gov/facts/mpa.html

Description: This site provides a classification system for the various types of marine protected areas (MPAs), including their conservation focus and levels of environmental protection. The Multimedia section includes photos, infographics, and podcasts. The site also has organizational information on the National MPA Center and the Advisory Committee.

The MPA website provides multiple approaches to rich content on science, policy, regulation, enforcement and many other topics related to MPAs.

Subject(s): Coastal Ecology; Marine Life

Migratory Bird Conservation Commission

https://www.fws.gov/refuges/realty/mbcc.html

Description: The Migratory Bird Conservation Commission considers any recommendations by the Secretary of the Interior for the purchase or rental of land for the Fish and Wildlife Service. It also considers the establishment of any new waterfowl refuges. The website has information on the commission, its members, its annual report, the Migratory Bird Conservation Fund, and related topics.

Subject(s): Birds; Conservation (Natural Resources)

Migratory Bird Program

https://www.fws.gov/birds/

Description: This Fish and Wildlife Service program supports bird habitat conservation partnerships through the North American Wetlands Conservation Act grants program and other programs. The site has sections on the North American Waterfowl Management Plan, the U.S. Shorebird Conservation Plan, and other bird conservation plans.

Subject(s): Birds; Conservation (Natural Resources)—Grants

National Estuarine Research Reserve System

https://coast.noaa.gov/nerrs/

Description: Areas in the National Estuarine Research Reserve System are protected for long-term research, water-quality monitoring, education, and coastal zone management. The website has profiles of the designated areas and the programs offered under the Reserve System. Featured education programs include the National Estuarine Research Reserve System's Graduate Research Fellowships and the Coastal Training Program.

Subject(s): Environmental Education; Environmental Protection; Rivers and Streams

National Marine Sanctuaries

https://sanctuaries.noaa.gov/

Description: The National Marine Sanctuary System provides resource protection, coordinates scientific research on the sanctuaries, and facilitates multiple uses of the national marine sanctuaries. Its colorful website includes sections on marine expeditions, maritime heritage, visiting sanctuaries, and volunteer opportunities. The Management and Resource Protection section has relevant regulations, permit information, and an ocean etiquette guide. The Science section includes Condition Reports for each sanctuary, updated every five years, and the Conservation Series of published articles. The multimedia *Encyclopedia of the Sanctuaries* and sanctuary maps are in the Photos & Videos section.

Subject(s): Marine Sanctuaries

National Wild and Scenic Rivers System

https://www.rivers.gov/

Description: The Wild and Scenic Rivers Act is intended to protect selected rivers, keeping them free-flowing and preserving the general character of a river. This site describes the Scenic Rivers program and lists protected rivers. A kids' page is linked at the top of the home page.

Subject(s): Rivers and Streams

Natural Resources Conservation Service (NRCS)

https://www.nrcs.usda.gov/wps/portal/nrcs/site/national/home/

Description: NRCS provides expertise in conserving soil, water, and other natural resources. The site's Topics section points to information on such topics as air, soils, water, and energy. It includes Field Office Technical Guides (FOTGs) with soil and conservation profiles. The Programs section has an inventory of financial assistance programs for conservation of wetlands, farm and ranch lands, grasslands, and other purposes. It also provides information on program funding and allocations by state. The Newsroom section includes state program news and photos. A smaller version of the site is available in Spanish.

Subject(s): Conservation (Natural Resources); Environmental Protection

Office for Coastal Management

https://coast.noaa.gov/

Description: As stated on the website, "NOAA's Office of Ocean and Coastal Resource Management and the Coastal Services Center joined forces to become the new Office for Coastal Management." The office helps state and local coastal resource management programs by providing them with data, tools, training, and technical assistance. The website has information broken down by region, including Northeast & Mid-Atlantic, Great Lakes, West Coast, and Pacific Islands. Its programs include the National Estuarine Research Reserves, Digital Coast, Coral Reef Conservation, and Coastal Zone Management.

Subject(s): Coastal Ecology; Remote Sensing

Office of Response and Restoration (OR&R)

https://response.restoration.noaa.gov/

Description: OR&R provides scientific support for oil and chemical spill response and damage assessments in coastal waters. Their website has information for emergency responders, research institutions, the general public, and students and teachers. It links to closely related websites, such as its Damage Assessment, Remediation, and Restoration Program (DARRP) and the NOAA Restoration Center site. The OR&R website also links to its own portal, IncidentNews, which has news, photos, and other information about selected oil spills where OR&R provided support. IncidentNews contains information on thousands of historical incidents spanning 30 years.

Subject(s): Oceans; Oil Spills

Office of Protected Resources (OPR)

http://www.nmfs.noaa.gov/pr/

Description: The NOAA Fisheries Office of Protected Resources coordinates the protection, conservation, and restoration of marine mammals, endangered species, their habitats, and marine-protected areas. This website provides legal and regulatory information on the Marine Mammals Protection Act (MMPA) and the Endangered Species Act (ESA), and a listing of threatened and endangered species. The site also has program descriptions, permit information, and a section for educators and students.

Subject(s): Endangered Species; Marine Life; Marine Mammals

U.S. Coral Reef Task Force

https://www.coralreef.gov/

Description: The Coral Reef Task Force, established by Executive order, is an interagency task force co-chaired by the Interior Department and NOAA. This site has information about the responsibilities of the task force, its meetings, documents, working groups, and available grants.

Subject(s): Coral Reefs

U.S.-Mexico Border 2020 Program

https://www.epa.gov/border2020

Description: U.S.-Mexico Border 2020 Program is a U.S.-Mexico binational program focusing on cleaning the air, providing safe drinking water, reducing the risk of exposure to hazardous waste, and ensuring emergency preparedness along the U.S.-Mexico border. The website has information on regional and border-wide working groups and on measuring conditions and progress in the border region. The site is also available in Spanish, Chinese, Vietnamese, and Korean.

Subject(s): Environmental Protection; Mexico

ENVIRONMENTAL SCIENCE

Air Resources Laboratory (ARL)

https://www.arl.noaa.gov/

Description: The Air Resources Laboratory focuses on air quality and climate research. The site describes current research, work of the ARL divisions, and climate and meteorological data.

This site will be primarily of interest to atmospheric scientists for the data and information on atmospheric and air quality modeling.

Subject(s): Air Quality—Research; Atmospheric Sciences

Atlantic Oceanographic and Meteorological Laboratory (AOML)

http://www.aoml.noaa.gov

Description: AOML conducts research in oceanography, tropical meteorology, atmospheric and oceanic chemistry, and acoustics. The site provides online access to the lab's data sets. The Publications section provides a searchable catalog of AOML-authored publications dating back to 1985.

Subject(s): Hurricanes—Research; Meteorology—Research; Oceanography—Research

Bureau of Ocean Energy Management (BOEM)

https://www.boem.gov/

Description: As of October 2011, the former Bureau of Ocean Energy Management, Regulation, and Enforcement (BOEMRE) was reorganized and replaced with the Bureau of Ocean Energy Management (BOEM) and the Bureau of Safety and Environmental Enforcement (BSEE).

BOEM's mission is to explore and develop offshore resources. Key responsibilities include the assessment duties of the Five Year Outer Continental Shelf (OCS) Oil and Natural Gas Leasing Program, offshore renewable energy programs, environmental stewardship, and sand and gravel negotiated agreements. The Newsroom section links to fact sheets, congressional testimony, press releases, and speeches.

Subject(s): Energy—Regulations; Natural Gas; Natural Resources Management; Oceans

Climate Change

https://www.epa.gov/climatechange

Description: This page is in the process of being updated to reflect EPA's priorities under the leadership of President Trump and Administrator Pruitt.

Subject(s): Climatology; Climate Change

Coastal and Marine Geology Program (CMGP)

https://marine.usgs.gov/

Description: The Coastal and Marine Geology Program promotes understanding of marine and coastal geologic systems, addressing issues relating to environmental quality, public safety, and natural resources. The online newsletter *Sound Waves* has much of the current program information available at the site. Much of the rest of the content is organized as a database, allowing researchers to specify their topic or region of interest. The database includes research projects, educational material, photographs, movies, maps, publications, and data set. Topics include beaches, sediments, erosion, mapping, remote sensing, minerals, and oil and gas. The site also links to field centers in California, Florida, and Massachusetts.

Subject(s): Coastal Ecology; Geology

CSCOR: Center for Sponsored Coastal Ocean Research

https://coastalscience.noaa.gov/

Description: NOAA's Center for Sponsored Coastal Ocean Research manages a competitive research program to support the understanding of complex coastal systems. CSCOR research focuses on the causes of ecosystem change: climate change, extreme natural events, pollution, invasive species, and land and resources use. The website includes grants information and a database of sponsored research summaries. The Publications section includes fact sheets and the *Decision Analysis Series*.

Subject(s): Coastal Ecology—Grants

Earth Observatory

https://earthobservatory.nasa.gov/

Description: The Earth Observatory website is a NASA outreach effort to provide satellite imagery and scientific information about Earth to the public. The site is appropriate for the high school through undergraduate science levels, or for any non-specialist interested in the topic. The Earth Observatory provides NASA images and data mapped onto global image maps. (Check the image use policy link at the bottom of the page for information about copying images from the site.) The website also has feature articles and news, with a focus on the global climate and environmental changes.

Subject(s): Environmental Education; Remote Sensing

Global Change Research Program

https://www.globalchange.gov/

Description: The United States Global Change Research Program coordinates federal research on changes in the global environment and their implications for society. Multiple federal agencies participate in the program, which is run by a steering committee and overseen by the Executive Office of the President. The website describes the two research priorities, national climate assessment and human health. The site links to news from the program and international organizations, as well as to climate change coverage by news media around the world. The site also has an image gallery and materials for educators.

Subject(s): Climate Change

National Centers for Environmental Prediction (NCEP)

http://www.ncep.noaa.gov

Description: This site links to the websites for the component NCEP centers: the Aviation Weather Center, the Climate Prediction Center, the Environmental Modeling Center, the Ocean Prediction Center, the Space Weather Prediction Center, the Storm Prediction Center, the National Hurricane Center, and NCEP Central Operations. Each of these publishes images, data, and information related to its specialty.

Most maps and data presented at the Prediction Center sites may be beyond the scope of anyone who is not a professional meteorologist, but some of the sites—such as the Storm Prediction Center—carry information that will be of interest to a broader audience.

Subject(s): Meteorology; Weather Forecasts

National Environmental Satellite, Data, and Information Service (NESDIS)

https://www.nesdis.noaa.gov/

Description: NESDIS manages environmental satellites, disseminates the data they collect, and conducts related research. The About NESDIS, Satellites, Data Centers, and Resources sections of the NESDIS website have information on satellite operations and development.

Subject(s): Environmental Science; Satellites

National Ocean Service (NOS)

https://oceanservice.noaa.gov/

Description: NOS is the primary civil agency within the federal government responsible for the health and safety of the nation's coastal and oceanic environment. Topics include coral reef conservation, oil and chemical spills, coastal monitoring and observations, national estuarine research reserves, global positioning, and tides and currents. The Education section offers lesson plans and online tutorials on corals, tides and water levels, and related topics. The NOS website also links to the websites for other NOS offices and programs, such as the International Program Office and the Office of Coast Survey.

Subject(s): Oceanography

National Oceanic and Atmospheric Administration (NOAA)

http://www.noaa.gov

Description: With information on issues such as climate, fisheries, and the ocean, the NOAA website is a major resource for the environmental sciences. Beyond providing current news and agency information, this central NOAA site best serves as a finding tool for the substantive content on the sites of NOAA's component divisions and offices. Subject access is provided by links to Weather, Oceans, Climate, Coasts, Fisheries, Charting, Research, and Satellites. The NOAA In Your State section has a map of NOAA activities relevant to each U.S. state.

Subject(s): Atmospheric Sciences; Environmental Science; Oceanography

National Oceanographic Data Center (NODC)

https://www.nodc.noaa.gov/

Description: The National Oceanographic Data Center provides public access to global oceanographic and coastal data, products, and information. Click on "Access Data" on the home page to reach the Archived Data, CD-ROMs, Publications, and Online Store sections. Available data sets cover ocean currents, plankton, salinity, sea level, and more. The site features the popular "Coastal Water Temperature Guide," which reports near real-time temperature of the U.S. coastal regions and makes them available as RSS feeds or viewable on maps.

Subject(s): Oceanography

National Water and Climate Center

https://www.wcc.nrcs.usda.gov/

Description: The NRCS National Water and Climate Center provides water and climate information and technology to support natural resource conservation. The center's website supplies detailed water supply forecasts, snow data, and climate reports at the regional and local levels.

Subject(s): Climate Research; Water Supply

National Wetlands Inventory (NWI)

https://www.fws.gov/wetlands/

Description: NWI studies and reports on the nation's wetlands and deepwater habitats. NWI's website focuses on wetlands mapping standards, mapping tools, and geospatial wetlands digital data. The website features a Wetlands Mapper, under Wetlands Data, to support the integration of digital map data with other information. The Status and Trends section of the site includes NWI national, regional, and state reports on the status of wetlands.

Subject(s): Wetlands

NOAA Commissioned Officer Corps

https://www.omao.noaa.gov/learn/noaa-commissioned-officer-corps

Description: Members of the NOAA Corps are part of the United States uniformed services and may serve in the armed forces during times of war. Their usual occupations include operating NOAA ships, flying aircraft, managing research projects, conducting diving operations, and serving in staff positions. They are professionals in such fields as oceanography, meteorology, and fisheries science. This website provides information on NOAA Corps organization and operations along with recruiting information.

Subject(s): Environmental Science

NOAA Earth System Research Laboratory (ESRL)

https://www.esrl.noaa.gov/

Description: NOAA's Earth System Research Laboratory was formed in 2005 through the consolidation of six NOAA research organizations. "ESRL researchers monitor the atmosphere, study the physical and chemical processes that comprise the Earth system, and integrate those findings into environmental information products." (from the website) The site provides access to data sets and describes ESRL research at its labs, observatories, and field programs. A link beneath the site search box leads to a catalog of ESRL peer-reviewed publications.

Subject(s): Climate Research; Meteorology—Research

NOAA Research

https://research.noaa.gov/

Description: This site links to extensive information on NOAA research activities. NOAA Research includes internal research laboratories, programs for undersea research and ocean exploration, a grants program through the

Climate Program Office, and external research at Sea Grant universities and programs.

Subject(s): Environmental Science—Research

National Centers for Coastal Ocean Science (NCCOS)

https://coastalscience.noaa.gov/

Description: NCCOS conducts and supports research, monitoring, assessment, and technical assistance for managing coastal ecosystems. The website links to information from each of these centers. The site presents the centers' research, publications, and data. Research described on the site covers such topics as coral reefs, estuaries, pollution, and invasive species. Grants and funding information is provided in the Funding section.

Subject(s): Coastal Ecology; Oceans—Research

National Service Center for Environmental Publications (NSCEP)

https://www.epa.gov/nscep

Description: This site provides indexed access to free online and print publications from the EPA. The database can be searched and browsed.

Subject(s): Environmental Protection; Publications Catalogs

Pacific Marine Environmental Laboratory (PMEL)

https://www.pmel.noaa.gov/

Description: PMEL carries out interdisciplinary scientific investigations in oceanography and atmospheric sciences. The site has sections for Research, Publications, Data, Theme Pages, and Infrastructure. Theme pages explore such topics as the North Pacific Ocean, the Arctic, and ocean seismicity. Featured topics include tsunamis, acoustics, and engineering. The Publications page offers a search of PMEL publications by year, author, title, citation, abstract, division, and media type.

Subject(s): Atmospheric Sciences—Research; Oceanography—Research

Physical Oceanography Distributed Active Archive Center (PODAAC)

https://podaac.jpl.nasa.gov/

Description: The Physical Oceanography Distributed Active Archive Center is a component of the NASA Earth Observing System Data Information System (EOSDIS). The center is responsible for archiving and distributing satellite data relevant to the physical state of the ocean. The site has a data catalog and specialized data tools.

While most of the data is for the use of scientists, the site also has links to educational websites and products.

Subject(s): Oceanography

Smithsonian Tropical Research Institute (STRI)

https://stri.si.edu/

Description: The Smithsonian Tropical Research Institute is based in Panama. In addition to its own scientific staff, the institute hosts visiting scholars and students conducting research on the ecology and behavior of tropical plants and animals, and on man's impact in the tropics. The website has information on the institute's research, facilities, academic programs, and opportunities for visiting scientists. The institute's research data is available in the Bioinformatics section.

Subject(s): Environmental Science—Research

Upper Midwest Environmental Sciences Center (UMESC)

https://www.umesc.usgs.gov/

Description: UMESC is a river-related inventory, monitoring, research, spatial analysis, and information-sharing program. One of its main program areas is the Long-Term Resource Monitoring Program (LTRMP) of the Upper Mississippi River System and adjoining geographic areas. The Maps, Tools, and Databases section includes a variety of environmental datasets, photographs, and maps for the Mississippi River. The Science Programs section is organized into sections for aquatic sciences, river inventory and monitoring, invasive species, and terrestrial sciences. The Outreach and Education section has a variety of educational material on the Mississippi River.

This site provides access to a substantial amount of information for researchers on fish and wildlife, vegetation, invertebrates, water quality, water levels, sediments, contaminants, and nutrients, as well as access to aerial and satellite photography, software, scientific publications, and geographic information systems maps, quadrangles, and figures.

Subject(s): Rivers and Streams—Research

GEOGRAPHY

EarthExplorer

https://earthexplorer.usgs.gov/

Description: EarthExplorer is a system for finding and ordering satellite images, cartographic products, and high resolution scanned images from photographs through USGS. EarthExplorer provides cross inventory search capabilities and secured e-commerce support for product orders. Users may log in as guests or as registered users; registration is required to order and download data.

Subject(s): Geography—Satellite Imaging

Earth Resources Observation and Science (EROS) Center

https://eros.usgs.gov/

Description: The EROS Center is a data management, systems development, and research center for the U.S. Geological Survey's Climate and Land Use Change Mission Area. The website provides consolidated access to aerial photography, satellite, imagery, digital maps, land use data, and specialized data tools. The Science section provides research information related to climate change, landscape dynamics, hazards and disasters, and international activities. The site also links to extensive information and data from remote sensing programs.

Subject(s): Maps and Mapping; Remote sensing

Federal Geographic Data Committee (FGDC)

https://www.fgdc.gov/

Description: The Federal Geographic Data Committee is "an interagency committee that promotes the coordinated development, use, sharing, and dissemination of geospatial data on a national basis." (from the website) The FGDC coordinates the National Spatial Data Infrastructure (NSDI), which encompasses policies, standards, and procedures for organizations to cooperatively produce and share geospatial data. Website sections include Metadata, Standards, Policy & Planning, Training, and Grants. The Standards section covers FGDC standards projects, processes, and publications.

Subject(s): Geography

Geographic Names Information System (GNIS)

https://geonames.usgs.gov/domestic/

Description: The GNIS database has federally recognized names of physical and cultural geographic features in the United States and its territories. Geographic features are defined broadly and include populated places, as well as airports, cemeteries, mines, lakes, rivers, streams, schools, beaches, and parks. For each feature, GNIS provides the official name, geographic coordinates, state and county, and feature type. GNIS assigns each geographic feature a unique Feature ID "as the only standard Federal key for accessing, integrating, or reconciling feature data from multiple data sets." (from the website) Compressed files of the data can be downloaded from the site. The site also has an online form for proposing geographic name changes or new names.

Subject(s): Geography; Reference

GEONet Names Server (GNS)

http://geonames.nga.mil/gns/html/

Description: The GNS database is the official repository of foreign place names and undersea feature names, such as the Great Barrier Reef, approved by the U.S. Board on Geographic Names. (A notice on the site states, "The names, variants, and associated data may not reflect the views of the United

States Government on the sovereignty over geographic features.") GEONet covers place names for all areas of the world except the United States and Antarctica, which are maintained by the United States Geological Survey Geographic Names Information System (http://geonames.usgs.gov/).

Subject(s): Geography; Reference

GeoPlatform.gov

https://www.geoplatform.gov/

Description: GeoPlatform.gov is part of an interagency initiative to provide a open platform for geographic data, software, services, and applications. It is intended to provide dynamic mapping capabilities to governments at all levels and to the general public. GeoPlatform.gov was initially launched to provide mapping services related to the April 2010 BP oil spill.

Subject(s): Maps and Mapping; Oil Spills

National Geodetic Survey (NGS)

https://www.ngs.noaa.gov/

Description: NGS develops and maintains the National Spatial Reference System (NSRS), a national coordinate system that defines latitude, longitude, height, scale, gravity, and orientation throughout the United States, including how these values change with time. The website describes NGS services and programs, such as the Continuously Operating Reference Station (CORS) network and the Height Modernization Program.

Subject(s): Geodesy; Maps and Mapping

National Geospatial Program (NGP)

https://www2.usgs.gov/ngpo/

Description: NGP, established in 2004, is responsible for all USGS-led geospatial programs, such as The National Map and the Center of Excellence for Geospatial Information Science (CEGIS). NGP works to promote a National Spatial Data Infrastructure for consistent means to share geographic data between parties. The website has news and program information.

Subject(s): Maps and Mapping

National Map

https://nationalmap.gov/

Description: "The *National Map* is a collaborative effort among the USGS and other federal, state, and local partners to improve and deliver topographic information for the nation. It has many uses ranging from recreation to scientific analysis to emergency response. The *National Map* is easily accessible for display on the web, as products and services, and as downloadable data. The geographic information available from the *National Map* includes orthoimagery (aerial photographs), elevation, geographic names, hydrography, boundaries, transportation, structures, and land cover." (from the website) The *National Map* website includes a viewer for the data. The Products and Services section has information on current and planned future maps, images, and mapping services.

Subject(s): Maps and Mapping

Office of Coast Survey (OCS)

https://www.nauticalcharts.noaa.gov/

Description: The Office of Coast Survey is the official U.S. chart-making agency. It manages nautical chart data collections and information programs. The NOAA charts can be viewed at the site or ordered online. The Nautical Charts & Pubs section also links to explanatory information, historical maps and charts, and major data portals such as nowCOAST and Tides and Currents; GIS products are listed in a separate section. The site also covers development of new charting technologies, current hydrography projects, and data on submerged wrecks.

Subject(s): Maps and Mapping; Oceans—Research

NATURAL RESOURCES

Alaska Science Center

https://alaska.usgs.gov/

Description: The USGS Alaska Science Center conducts monitoring, research, and assessments of natural resources issues and natural hazards in Alaska and the region. Under Science, the site links to relevant information in the areas of biology, geography, geology, and water, among other features. The Products section has a publications catalog and a link to the Alaska Geospatial Data Clearinghouse.

Subject(s): Wildlife—Research; Alaska—Research

Animal Welfare

https://www.aphis.usda.gov/aphis/ourfocus/animalwelfare

Description: This APHIS website is concerned with the latest news about animal health and welfare. . The site includes publications, animal research facility reports, regulations, information on traveling with a pet, and a blog on various categories.

Subject(s): Animals—Regulations

Animal Welfare Information Center (AWIC)

https://www.nal.usda.gov/awic

Description: AWIC compiles links to information about the welfare of farm, lab, circus, and zoo animals, as well as companion animals (pets) to assist with regulatory compliance. The site has information on laws, policies, and guidelines, and links to related databases and websites. Linked resources come from both government and non-government sources. AWIC also maintains RSS feeds for news about animal welfare.

Subject(s): Animals

Bureau of Land Management (BLM)

https://www.blm.gov/

Description: BLM administers U.S. public lands, which are primarily in the Western states. The site's What We Do section links to BLM activities in the areas of energy, fire, grazing, and land use planning. The What We Do page also contains information on abandoned mine lands, cultural and paleontological resources, General Land Office records, law enforcement, the National Landscape Conservation System (NLCS), rights-of-way, and more. The Information Center section includes news, laws, regulations, policies, and publications. BLM's annual *Public Land Statistics* report provides statistics on federal lands, their commercial uses, recreational uses, conservation, and related topics. The Information Center's Online Services subsection has information on researching BLM records and on doing business with BLM or public lands. The site's home page features a clickable U.S. map as the interface to public lands information for states or regions.

Subject(s): Public Lands

Bureau of Reclamation

https://www.usbr.gov/

Description: The subtitle of this website is "Managing Water in the West." The Bureau of Reclamation manages dams and reservoirs in the western states and produces hydroelectric power. The website's Projects and Facilities Database includes information about Reclamation power plants, projects, and major Reclamation dams. The Resources & Research section of the site serves as an index to many other reclamation activities, including desalination, cultural resources management, hydroelectric research, and materials engineering and research. The Water Operations section links to the websites for BLM regional offices representing the Great Plains, Lower Colorado, Upper Colorado, the Mid-Pacific, and the Pacific Northwest. Each regional site has information on its dams, reservoirs, projects, news, and publications.

Subject(s): Hydroelectric Power; Water Supply

Department of the Interior (DOI)

https://www.doi.gov/

Description: The Interior Department's website serves primarily as a portal to the sites for the department's many component agencies, such as the Bureau of Indian Affairs, the National Park Service, the U.S. Fish and Wildlife Service, and the U.S. Geological Survey. The main page features news from Interior and its component agencies. Like other major departments and agencies, the Interior has a section for Recovery Act information and for Open Government Initiative information on its website.

The site is well organized and its multiple access points to various DOI resources make it easy to use.

Subject(s): Natural Resources; Public Lands

Endangered Species

https://www.fws.gov/endangered/

Description: This Fish and Wildlife Service site provides a broad collection of news and information on endangered species and the Endangered Species Act (ESA). The Endangered Species lists for animals and plants, as well as proposals for changes to the list, can be found in the Species section of the site. The Species section also has a map for finding endangered species by state and information on critical habitats. The site also provides extensive information in the For Landowners section. The Laws & Policies and Library sections have *Federal Register* notices and documents related to the Endangered Species Act. The website also has information on grants and a section for kids.

Subject(s): Endangered Species; Native Plants

EPA

Office of Water

https://www.epa.gov/aboutepa/about-office-water

Description: As the primary EPA agency overseeing regulatory issues relating to clean water, the Office of Water's website features a variety of resources related to drinking water, water pollution, watersheds, and wastewater management. OW's several offices, as well as its many programs and projects, are linked to toward the bottom of the home page.

Subject(s): Drinking Water; Water Pollution

Fish and Wildlife Service (FWS)

https://www.fws.gov/

Description: FWS aims to conserve, protect, and enhance fish, wildlife, plants, and their habitats. The website features current news on its varied programs and focuses, such as endangered species, the Federal Duck Stamp Program, and the National Wildlife Refuge System. Quick links lead to information on FWS coastal programs, environmental contaminants, fisheries and habitat conservation, grants, hunting, law enforcement, Native American issues, permits, policy and directives, wetlands, and more.

Subject(s): Birds; Conservation (Natural Resources)—Laws; Fisheries; Natural Resources Management; Wildlife

Fort Collins Science Center (FORT)

https://www.usgs.gov/centers/fort

Description: Scientists at this USGS biological science center study the ecosystems of the mountain, desert, and semi-arid western United States in support of land managers and natural resource decision makers. Programs described on the website include Invasive Species Science, Ecosystem Dynamics, Information Science, Trust Species and Habitat, and Policy Analysis and Science Assistance. The Products section has publications, software, and data.

Subject(s): Environmental Science—Policy; Wildlife—Research; West (United States)

National Interagency Fire Center (NIFC)

https://www.nifc.gov/

Description: NIFC in Idaho is the national support center for wildland firefighting. In addition to the Forest Service and relevant Interior Department agencies, Fire Center participants include the National Park Service, U.S. Fire Administration, and the nongovernmental National Association of State Foresters (NASF), in addition to other agencies. The website features current wildland fire news, wildland fire statistics, policies, and prevention and education information. It also links to wildland fire training programs.

Subject(s): Firefighting; Forest Fires

National Wild Horse and Burro Program

https://www.blm.gov/programs/wild-horse-and-burro

Description: The Bureau of Land Management manages wild horses and burros on public lands. The website outlines myths and facts about the program, program statistics, and current plans for funding and managing the program. The site includes information from the Wild Horse and Burro Advisory Board and about wild horse and burro adoption. The site also links to information on state-level wild horse and burro programs.

Subject(s): Wild Horses

National Wildlife Health Center (NWHC)

https://www.nwhc.usgs.gov/

Description: NWHC provides information, technical assistance, and research on national and international wildlife health issues. The website's home page features links to information on current issues, such as avian influenza and chronic wasting disease. The Disease Information section discusses major wildlife health concerns, with links to reports and online resources for each. NWHC publications online include fact sheets, quarterly wildlife mortality reports, and wildlife health bulletins.

Subjcct(s): Wildlife—Research

NOAA's Coral Reef Information System (CoRIS)

https://www.coris.noaa.gov/

Description: This portal to NOAA coral reef information and data products has a variety of data sets, reference resources, and information on coral reef biology and environmental threats. The home page offers access to NOAA's Coral Health and Monitoring Program (CHAMP) electronic discussion list. The Data & Publications section has a searchable catalog of coral ecosystem data sets and NOAA papers and reports along with links to other coral reef websites. The site also has information about coral reef biology, diseases, and hazards, and a glossary of coral reef terminology.

Subject(s): Coral Reefs

Northern Prairie Wildlife Research Center

https://www.npwrc.usgs.gov/

Description: Part of the USGS Biological Research Division, staff at the Northern Prairie Wildlife Research Center study the species and ecosystems of the Great Plains region. The Our Science section of this site contains information about the center's focuses, including Climate Change, Cranes, Grassland Birds, Honey Bees and Native Pollinators, and Prairie and Wetlands Management.

Subject(s): Conservation (Natural Resources)—Research; Wildlife—Research; Butterflies

NPS: Explore Nature

https://www.nps.gov/nature/index.htm

Description: This National Park Service site links to information on natural resource conservation and science activities in the parks. Extensive environment and science coverage is provided in sections on air resources, biological resources, geologic resources, natural sounds and night skies, water resources, and more. Special features include the Climate Change Response Program, the National Natural Landmarks Program, information on coral reefs in national parks, and the National Park Service Planning, Environment, and Public Comment (PEPC) site. The website also links to nature-focused sites hosted by individual parks.

Subject(s): Conservation (Natural Resources); Parks and Reserves

Office of Surface Mining Reclamation and Enforcement (OSMRE)

https://www.osmre.gov/

Description: OSMRE has the responsibility of reclaiming abandoned mines and protecting the environment and people during coal mining and reclamation. Major sections link to legal, regulatory, and science and technology information related to the missions of regulating coal mines; reclaiming abandoned mine lands; and applying sound science. The Resources section includes directives, grants, forms, FAQs, and other documents. The "How Do I?" section provides links for reporting an emergency, finding a regulator, and other OSMRE-related tasks.

Subject(s): Coal; Mining Reclamation

Patuxent Wildlife Research Center (PWRC)

https://www.pwrc.usgs.gov/

Description: PWRC, located in Maryland, is one of 17 research centers of the U.S. Geological Survey. The center focuses on coastal and wetlands ecology and on migratory birds and waterfowl. The center operates national wildlife inventory and monitoring programs and is responsible for the North American Bird Banding Program. The website addresses these topics and includes sections on research and education and a photo gallery of birds, animals, and habitats.

This site will be useful for anyone getting involved with an inventory and monitoring program as well as for those interested in some of the species for which monitoring programs are available.

Subject(s): Birds; Wildlife

Water Data for the Nation

https://waterdata.usgs.gov/nwis/

Description: Water Data for the Nation has current and historic data on the quantity, quality, distribution, and movement of surface and underground waters in the United States. Use the drop-down menu to view information for a particular state or territory.

Subject(s): Water Supply

Water Resources of the United States

https://www2.usgs.gov/water/

Description: As one of the major subject-oriented USGS websites, Water Resources of the United States covers USGS materials related to water use, surface water, ground water, and water quality. It links to the websites for USGS water resources programs. The primary divisions of this site include Data, Publications, Maps/GIS, Software, Multimedia, Education, and Programs. Information is organized by locale (state or territory) in the site's Water Science Centers feature on the home page.

Subject(s): Water

Wetland and Aquatic Research Center (WARC)

https://www.usgs.gov/centers/wetland-and-aquatic-research-center-warc/

Description: In October 2015, USGS's Southeast Ecological Science Center in Gainesville, Florida, and the National Wetlands Research Center is Lafayette, Louisiana, merged to form the Wetland and Aquatic Research Center. WARC was created as a "hub of ecological science in the southeast region that provides the Department of Interior and partners with a range of research capabilities from animals, to plants, to restoration of coasts and wetlands." (from the website)

Subject(s): Wetlands

POLLUTANTS AND WASTE

AirCompare

https://www3.epa.gov/aircompare/

Description: AirCompare enables U.S. county and state comparisons of air quality. It also provides air quality information for groups such as asthma sufferers and for the general population. Information is not available from all counties. An interagency group provides the data.

Subject(s): Air Quality

Contaminated Site Clean-Up Information (CLU-IN)

https://clu-in.org/

Description: The CLU-IN website provides information about innovative treatment technologies to the hazardous waste remediation community. The site has databases on Remediation and Characterization and Monitoring, as well as technology descriptions and selection tools in these areas. Users with a professional interest in environmental technology can subscribe to e-mail delivery of several newsletters including *Technology News and Trends* or receive an RSS feed of CLU-IN news. Major sections of the site include Contaminants, Issues (e.g., brownfields, mining sites), Strategies & Initiatives, Vendors & Developers, and Training & Events (including online seminars).

Subject(s): Environmental Cleanup

Department of Energy Hanford Site

https://www.hanford.gov/

Description: Hanford, formerly a plutonium production complex, is now one of the world's largest environmental cleanup projects. The project is being managed by the DOE as it explores ways of handling Hanford's tank waste retrieval, treatment, and disposal, as well as restoring the Columbia

River Corridor where the plant is located. The website includes the plant history, resources for reporters, a list of contractors, a calendar of public meetings, and official documents.

Subject(s): Environmental Cleanup; Nuclear Waste

DOE Office of Environmental Management

https://energy.gov/em/office-environmental-management

Description: The Energy Department's Office of Environmental Management manages the cleanup of radioactive, chemical, and other hazardous waste left after years of nuclear weapons production. The website lists current projects and links to completed projects.

Subject(s): Environmental Cleanup; Nuclear Waste

Envirofacts Data Warehouse

https://www3.epa.gov/enviro/

Description: Envirofacts provides a central location for access to major environmental databases from the EPA. Databases include the Toxics Release Inventory (TRI), Safe Drinking Water Information System, Permit Compliance System, Brownfields Management System, Compensation and Liability Information System (CERCLIS), and many others. Researchers can choose individual databases or search multiple databases at once. Searches are also organized by general topic, such as land, air, or water.

Subject(s): Pollutants; Databases

EPA Office of Air and Radiation (OAR)

https://www.epa.gov/aboutepa/about-office-air-and-radiation-oar

Description: The Office of Air and Radiation's website includes links to projects and programs in the fields of fuel economy, Clean School Bus USA, the SmartWay Transport Partnership, the National Clean Diesel Campaign, and other issues. News releases and standards also are linked, and the Clean Air Act and the Atomic Energy Act are referenced.

Subject(s): Air Quality

Federal Remediation Technologies Roundtable (FRTR)

https://frtr.gov/

Description: FRTR is an interagency working group supporting collaboration among the federal agencies involved in hazardous waste site remediation. The website features a section on Remediation Optimization and a variety of tools, information, and case studies to help with selecting the best technology for remediation tasks. FRTR meeting information and publications are also online.

Subject(s): Environmental Cleanup

Green Vehicle Guide

https://www.epa.gov/greenvehicles

Description: This online guide rates the environmental performance of recent car models. Consumers can look up the score for a specific model and make of automobile or browse by type of vehicle, such as pickup or minivan. The best environmental performers earn the EPA SmartWay designation. The site includes explanations of the rankings and information on auto emissions.

Subject(s): Motor Vehicles

Environmental and Sustainable Programs

http://www.dla.mil/whatdlaoffers/environmentalandsustainableprograms.aspx

Description: The DLA's Environmental and Sustainable Programs provide guidance to Defense Department personnel on safely handling and transporting hazardous materials. The site is organized into the following sections: Disposal of Hazardous Waste, Green Products Inquiries, Hazardous Minimization, and Regulated Materials Helpline.

Subject(s): Hazardous Waste

EPA Office of Chemical Safety and Pollution Prevention (OCSPP)

https://www.epa.gov/aboutepa/about-office-chemical-safety-and-pollution-prevention-ocspp

Description: OCSPP is involved in protecting public health and the environment from potential risk from toxic chemicals. The office promotes pollution prevention and the public's right to know about chemical risks and evaluates pesticides and chemicals to safeguard children and other vulnerable members of the population, as well as threatened species and ecosystems. The office implements the Federal Insecticide, Fungicide, and Rodenticide Act (FIFRA), the Federal Food, Drug and Cosmetic Act (FFDCA), the Toxic Substances Control Act (TSCA), and the Pollution Prevention Act (PPA).

Subject(s): Pesticides; Toxic Substances

EPA Office of Land and Emergency Management (OLEM)

https://www.epa.gov/aboutepa/about-office-land-and-emergency-management

Description: OLEM provides policy, guidance, and direction for the EPA solid waste and emergency response programs. The site covers such topics as Superfund and federal facility cleanups, brownfields, landfills, underground storage tanks, safe waste management, grants and funding, and environmental emergencies.

Subject(s): Environmental Cleanup; Hazardous Waste

EPA Office of Pollution Prevention and Toxics (OPPT)

https://www.epa.gov/aboutepa/about-office-chemical-safety-and-pollution-prevention-ocspp#oppt

Description: OPPT has primary responsibility for administering the Toxic Substances Control Act and the Pollution Prevention Act. The site links to information on OPPT's work in assessment of new chemicals in the marketplace, regulation of High Production Volume (HPV) chemicals, and many other areas.

Subject(s): Toxic Substances

RadTown USA

https://www3.epa.gov/radtown/

Description: RadTown USA provides educational information about radiation. It uses an interactive graphic of a town to show everyday sources of radiation. Sections of Radtown discuss personal exposure, use of radioactive materials, radiation-treated materials, radioactive waste, natural radiation, and security applications of radiation.

Subject(s): Radiation

RestoreTheGulf.gov

https://www.restorethegulf.gov/

Description: RestoreTheGulf.gov is the official federal portal for information on the Deepwater BP oil spill response and recovery. The information is provided by multiple agencies, including the U.S. Coast Guard. The site has current news and health and safety, and assistance information.

Subject(s): Environmental Cleanup

Savannah River Site (SRS)

https://www.srs.gov/general/srs-home.html

Description: A former production site for weapons-grade nuclear materials, SRS is now focused on management of the nuclear stockpile and nuclear materials and on related environmental issues. The website's Programs section describes each program at SRS and provides related documents. The Documents & Publications section includes a library of environmental reports about SRS.

Subject(s): Nuclear Weapons

Superfund Program

https://www.epa.gov/superfund

Description: This EPA portal for the Superfund environmental cleanup program covers information about the program, the individual Superfund sites, law and policy documents, liability and enforcement, community involvement, training, regional contacts, databases, and the cleanup process. It also links to a clickable map (under Superfund Sites Where You Live). The website has a version available in Spanish.

Subject(s): Environmental Cleanup

Tox Town

https://toxtown.nlm.nih.gov/

Description: Tox Town is an educational site about toxic chemicals, designed for a general audience. The site uses a graphical pathway image to serve as an interface to toxicity information from such agencies as the National Institutes of Health and the Environmental Protection Agency. It has modules for a city, town, farm, shipping port, and the U.S.-Mexico border. Modified versions of the content are provided in Spanish and in a text-only version. Tox Town also has teaching resources and an alphabetical index of information on the site.

Subject(s): Toxic Substances

ToxFAQs™: Toxic Substances Portal

https://www.atsdr.cdc.gov/toxfaqs/index.asp

Description: ToxFAQs™ offers fact sheets on hazardous substances and the effects of exposure on human health. The information is excerpted from the ATSDR Toxicological Profiles and Public Health Statements. Much of the core material at the ToxFAQs™ site is also available in Spanish.

Subject(s): Hazardous Waste; Toxic Substances

TribalAIR

https://www.epa.gov/tribal-air

Description: This site from the EPA's Office of Air and Radiation provides information about air quality programs in Indian country. It includes regional contacts, training schedules, regulations, and success stories from tribal environmental professionals in the Tribe to Tribe section. The *Tribal Air Newsletter* is also available in full text.

Subject(s): Air Quality; American Indians

Technical Air Pollution Resources

https://www.epa.gov/technical-air-pollution-resources

Description: This site provides access to a collection of EPA resources with technical information about many areas of technology, regulation, and science.

Subject(s): Air Quality; Technology Transfer

U.S. Chemical Safety Board (CSB)

https://www.csb.gov

Description: CSB is an independent, scientific investigatory board that works to determine the causes of chemical accidents. CSB also investigates chemical hazards. The CSB website features current news and reports of current investigations. It also has reports of completed investigations and recommendations.

Subject(s): Chemical Industry; Industrial Accidents

WEATHER

AirNow

https://airnow.gov/

Description: AIRNow offers daily Air Quality Index (AQI) forecasts and real-time AQI conditions for over 300 cities across the United States. AirNow is an interagency website sponsored by the Environmental Protection Agency (EPA), the National Oceanic and Atmospheric Administration (NOAA), the National Aeronautics and Space Administration (NASA), the National Association of Clean Air Agencies, and the National Park Service (NPS), along with Canada and U.S. partner agencies in tribal, state, and local governments. Detailed local observations and forecasts on the site come from the partner agencies. The EnviroFlash feature provides e-mail notification of current air quality conditions in many cities and towns in the United States.

AQI data can be downloaded from AIRNow in Keyhole Markup Language (KML) format, allowing the data to be used in 3D viewers such as Google Earth. Some content is available in Spanish.

Subject(s): Air Quality

Aviation Weather Center (AWC)

https://aviationweather.gov/

Description: The Aviation Weather Center has forecasts, advisories, and observations for pilots. Observations include *Pilot Reports (PIREPs)*, *Meteorological Aviation Reports (METARs)*, and radar and satellite imagery. An Aviation Links section includes other aviation weather sites and Volcanic Ash Advisory Centers.

Subject(s): Aviation; Weather Forecasts

Climate Analysis Branch (CAB)

https://www.esrl.noaa.gov/psd/psd1/

Description: CAB, within NOAA's Earth System Research Laboratory, researches the causes of observed climate variations. CAB researches topics such as El Nino/La Nina and U.S. precipitation anomalies. Their website provides climate and weather data and interactive tools to chart or map the data.

Subject(s): Climate Research; El Nino

Climate Prediction Center

http://www.cpc.ncep.noaa.gov

Description: The Climate Prediction Center maintains a continuous watch on climate fluctuations and attempts to diagnose and predict them. This website provides climatological information, with highlights on long-term temperature and climate outlooks, U.S. Hazards Assessment, and U.S. Drought Assessment. The Outreach section has the center's publications, educational materials, and a climate glossary.

Subject(s): Climatology; El Nino; Weather Forecasts

Global Systems Division (GSD)

https://www.esrl.noaa.gov/gsd/

Description: NOAA's Global Systems Division conducts research to develop global environmental information and forecast technology products. After development, technologies are transferred to the National Weather Service, other government agencies, the commercial and general aviation communities, and others. The website describes Global Systems Division projects and products.

Subject(s): Meteorology—Research; Technology Transfer

Heat Island Effect

https://www.epa.gov/heat-islands

Description: The term "heat island" describes the phenomenon of urban and suburban temperatures that are two to ten degrees Fahrenheit hotter than nearby rural areas. This website provides information on the effect, research results, and energy use and health impacts. It also features a section on ameliorative measures, such as installing green roofing and planting trees.

Subject(s): Climate Research

National Centers for Environmental Information (NCEI)

https://www.ncei.noaa.gov/

Description: As the world's largest active archive of weather data, NCEI produces numerous climate publications and data sets and makes a wide variety of information available on this site. Users may search for weather station data for a particular location or use a clickable map interface.

NCEI presents various different catalogs and subsets of its products via links or online purchase. Some of the online data and publications require a paid subscription, with exemptions for education, military, and government use.

NCEI provides an enormous amount of information and data. The website manages to make it accessible by offering multiple well-designed approaches to the content.

Subject(s): Climatology; Data Products; Weather

National Data Buoy Center (NDBC)

http://seaboard.ndbc.noaa.gov

Description: The National Data Buoy Center site provides buoy-measured environmental data and an overview of the NDBC. Real-time meteorological and oceanographic data are available for locations along the coasts of North America, Hawaii, the Caribbean, Brazil, Chile, France, Great Britain, and the Western Pacific. Historical data are also available, grouped by station ID. Other sections of the site include Station Status and Observations, and information on the Dial-a-Buoy program that provides station information over the telephone. The site also provides RSS feeds of observation data and a page designed specifically for mobile phone access.

Subject(s): Oceans; Weather Forecasts

National Hurricane Center

https://www.nhc.noaa.gov/

Description: The Tropical Prediction Center website features data, graphs, and other information on tropical cyclones and hurricanes. Menu items on the home page include Marine Forecasts, Cyclone Forecasts, and Outreach & Education. This site covers conditions in the Atlantic and Eastern Pacific regions, and the latest forecasts are featured prominently, as are the site's Facebook and Twitter pages. It also links to tropical cyclone centers worldwide.

This is the key government website to consult during hurricane season.

Subject(s): Hurricanes

National Severe Storms Laboratory (NSSL)

https://www.nssl.noaa.gov/

Description: The NSSL site describes research and development work concerning forecasting, radar, and warnings. The Research Tools has a topical list of NSSL fields. The site also has an Education section with a "Severe Weather 101" primer and other content for children.

Subject(s): Tornadoes; Weather—Research

National Weather Service (NWS)

https://www.weather.gov/

Description: The National Weather Service collects weather data and provides forecasts for the United States and surrounding waters. The NWS homepage features a color-coded map of current weather warnings and advisories in the United States. A city/state name search box gives quick access to local short- and long-term weather forecasts, current conditions, and radar and satellite images. The Forecast section links to the forecasts available on NOAA websites, including hurricanes, fire, marine, aviation, and river flows. The Safety section takes a similar approach, linking to NOAA Weather Radio and to safety information related to storms, heat, lightning, hurricanes, tornadoes, rip currents, and floods. Publications designed for the general public are available online in HTML and PDF formats. Some forecast information is available in Spanish.

The Organization section, under About, has links to the websites for the many NWS regional offices and centers, each of which provides a wealth of local U.S. data.

While the NWS data repository is vast, this website makes the most popular data easily accessible.

Subject(s): Meteorology; Weather Forecasts

National Weather Service Marine Forecasts

http://www.nws.noaa.gov/om/marine/home.htm

Description: This gateway site links to marine weather forecast information. Shortcuts are provided to marine forecasts in text or graphic formats. Preparedness information on such topics as rip currents and thunderstorms is also provided.

Subject(s): Maritime Transportation; Weather Forecasts

NOAA Tides & Currents

https://tidesandcurrents.noaa.gov/

Description: Tides & Currents is the website for the Center for Operational Oceanographic Products and Services (CO-OPS). The center collects, analyzes, and distributes historical and real-time observations and predictions of water levels, coastal currents, and other meteorological and oceanographic data. The website features a zoomable data retrieval map and station list for finding all CO-OPS information by locale. CO-OPS programs include the Physical Oceanographic Real-Time System (PORTS®) that integrates observed and predicted data for mariners. CO-OPS also manages the National Current Observation Program (NCOP). Tide data and predictions are available on the site. The Education section includes lesson plans about tides.

Subject(s): Oceanography

NOAA Weather Radio (NWR)

http://www.nws.noaa.gov/nwr/

Description: NOAA Weather Radio (NWR) is a nationwide network of radio stations broadcasting continuous weather information that can be picked up by special radio receivers. This site has station listings, coverage maps, and consumer information on radio receivers. Other sections explain NWR's role as an "all hazards" radio network—broadcasting non-weather emergency information when requested by state or local officials. The site is also available in Spanish.

Subject(s): Disasters and Emergencies; Weather

Storm Prediction Center (SPC)

http://www.spc.noaa.gov

Description: Storm Prediction Center provides forecasts for severe thunderstorms and tornadoes over the contiguous United States. The SPC also monitors heavy rain, heavy snow, and fire weather events across the United States. Their website reports on and maps current storm, tornado, fire, and convective watches. The Outreach section features extensive information about tornadoes and derechos. The Organization section on the top menu bar links to regional centers with more detailed local information. SPC also provides RSS feeds for tornado and severe thunderstorm watches, fire weather outlooks, and other topics.

Subject(s): Tornadoes; Weather Forecasts

Tsunami

https://www.tsunami.noaa.gov/

Description: The NOAA Tsunami website is largely concerned with the agency's responsibility for the nation's Tsunami Warning System. The site provides detailed background information about how tsunamis occur and about NOAA's role in forecasting tsunamis. It includes sections on current tsunami observations and data, tsunami preparedness and response, and public education. The website also has photos and animations of tsunamis.

Subject(s): Oceans

Chapter Twelve

Government and Politics

This chapter covers some of the federal government's most familiar roles, such as tax collector, mail carrier, employer, purchaser, and provider of emergency relief.

Subsections in this chapter are Democracy, Government Administration, Government Business, Government Employees, Government Finance, Government Information, Government Services, Intergovernmental Relations, and Public Policy.

DEMOCRACY

Campaign Finance Reports and Data

https://www.fec.gov/disclosure.shtml

Description: The FEC's campaign finance retrieval system includes financial data for candidates, campaign committees, and political action committees (PACs). Data can be viewed online or downloaded. Images of the actual campaign finance disclosure filings are also online. The site provides data on "electioneering communications," a category of political broadcast advertisements that became regulated under the Bipartisan Campaign Reform Act (BCRA) of 2002 (also known as McCain-Feingold). The FEC has a Disclosure Data Blog on the site to report on content updates.

While the FEC site is easy to use, researchers may also want to try the nongovernment OpenSecrets.org, which downloads FEC data and adds value, with an emphasis on current data and newsworthy reports.

Subject(s): Campaign Funds; Elections

Civics and Citizenship Toolkit

https://www.uscis.gov/citizenship/organizations/civics-and-citizenship-toolkit

Description: The Civics and Citizenship Toolkit publication is the product of a project to assist U.S. immigrants and is overseen by USCIS. The kit is distributed through public libraries, which can request a single, free copy using the website.

Subject(s): Citizenship; Civics Education

Core Documents of U.S. Democracy

https://www.govinfo.gov/content/core-documents-our-democracy

Description: With input from government documents librarians, GPO has developed a selective list of important current and historical government publications to feature as having "free, permanent, public access" on the GPO website. Although GPO aims to provide the same access to many other documents, these have been selected as being essential to an informed democratic process. The selection includes the Constitution of the United States of America, the Bill of Rights, the Declaration of Independence, Supreme Court decisions, congressional bills and the Congressional Record, the United States Code, the Budget of the United States Government, the Federal Register, and the Code of Federal Regulations.

Subject(s): Government Publications

Democratic National Committee

https://www.democrats.org/

Description: The national Democratic Party website features news on politics and policy, a blog, and a directory of local party organizations throughout the United States. Interactive features focus on online voter registration, fundraising, volunteering, and interning. The site also has a version available in Spanish.

Subject(s): Political Parties

Election Assistance Commission (EAC)

https://www.eac.gov/

Description: The EAC was established by the Help America Vote Act of 2002 (HAVA) to provide guidance and funding to improve the administration of federal elections. Its website features information about HAVA and the competitive grant programs authorized by HAVA to improve the administration of elections. The Payments and Grants section has updates to the state HAVA plans originally filed in 2004. The EAC site also has information on the testing and certification of voting systems, resources for elections officials, the National Mail Voter Registration Form, and helpful information for voters. Information is available in Spanish, Vietnamese, and other languages.

Subject(s): Elections—Regulations

Electioneering Communications Database (ECD)

http://apps.fcc.gov/ecd/

Description: This website is intended to help political campaigns comply with a provision of the Federal Election Campaign Act of 1971, which requires candidates who spend more than $10,000 on an "electioneering communication" during any calendar year to file a statement with the Federal Election Commission. The database helps users determine if their broadcasts qualify as electioneering communications.

Subject(s): Elections—Regulations

Electoral College

https://www.archives.gov/federal-register/electoral-college/

Description: The National Archives oversees the Electoral College and provides this website to inform the public about how it works. The site features statistics and summaries of the votes in the Electoral College for every presidential election since the election of George Washington. Other features include the Make a Prediction tool and Frequently Asked Questions. Users can also view the states' certificates for their electors and for the electors' votes.

Subject(s): Electoral College

Federal Election Commission (FEC)

https://www.fec.gov/

Description: FEC is an independent regulatory agency whose mission is to disclose campaign finance information, enforce provisions of the law such as the limits and prohibitions on contributions, and oversee the public funding of presidential elections. The Campaign Finance Disclosure Portal section of the site provides finance data for candidates, campaign committees, and political action committees. The Enforcement Matters section has audit reports and a database of documents related to completed enforcement cases. The Law, Regulations, and Procedures section has FEC advisory opinions, information on FEC litigation, and information on major campaign laws. Other sections include Meetings and Hearings and Help with Reporting and Compliance. A section called Quick Answers discusses frequently asked-about issues that typically come from candidates, state party committees, researchers, and the general public.

Subject(s): Campaign Funds—Laws; Voting—Statistics

Federal Voting Assistance Program (FVAP)

https://www.fvap.gov/

Description: FVAP provides U.S. citizens worldwide with a broad range of nonpartisan information and assistance to facilitate their participation in the voting process, regardless of where they work or live. Located within the Department of Defense, FVAP is responsible for serving military personnel, their families, and other U.S. citizens residing outside the United States. The main page of the site is designed for U.S. voters who are overseas, but the site also has sections for local elections officials and voting assistance officers. The site includes instructions for civilian and military voters and supplies an online version of the federal postcard application for voter registration and absentee ballots.

Subject(s): Voting

Improving U.S. Voting Systems

https://www.nist.gov/itl/voting

Description: NIST is charged with advising the Election Assistance Commission on the development of technical guidelines for voting systems. This website provides news, background, and research reports related to the development of the technical guidelines.

Subject(s): Voting

Republican National Committee (RNC)

https://www.gop.com/

Description: The RNC website has sections on how to become active in supporting the party, how to register to vote online, and how to make contributions online. The site also has a directory of the Republican Party's state offices, blogs, and issue statements.

Subject(s): Political Parties

Tax Information for Political Organizations

https://www.irs.gov/charities-non-profits/political-organizations

Description: This IRS webpage focuses on reporting and disclosure requirements for political parties, campaign committees, and political action committees, which fall under section 527 of the Internal Revenue Code.

Subject(s): Campaign Funds

GOVERNMENT ADMINISTRATION

Administrative Conference of the United States (ACUS)

https://www.acus.gov/

Description: Established in 1968, the Administrative Conference was not funded by Congress between 1995 and 2010. Currently, ACUS develops recommendations to improve the fairness and effectiveness of rulemaking and other activities of federal agencies. The website provides information on the agency's activities and organization.

Subject(s): Regulatory Policy

Chief Information Officers (CIO) Council

https://cio.gov/

Description: The CIO Council is the principal interagency forum focused on federal agency management of information technology. The site provides information on council membership, meetings, and projects. It links to blogs written by members of different federal agencies.

Subject(s): Information Technology

Federal Executive Boards (FEBs)

https://www.feb.gov/

Description: FEBs coordinate many of the activities carried out by federal agency regional offices, which are located outside of Washington, D.C. Based in 28 cities and regions and with a large federal presence, FEBs operate under the direction of OPM and are concerned with coordination in such areas as management strategies, personnel programs, and community relations. This website provides background information about the boards and links to each of the local FEB websites.

Subject(s): Government Administration

General Services Administration (GSA)

https://www.gsa.gov

Description: GSA procures and manages federal office space, vehicles, technology, and supplies. The agency also sells off surplus government property. GSA's activities are described in this website's About Us section. The Policy & Regulations section covers GSA's role in setting rules for management of federal acquisitions, real property, travel, and more. The Technology section provides information on products and services, purchasing programs, government initiatives, and training. While GSA mostly works with federal agencies or government contractors, the site includes a section for citizens and consumers, including information on consumer issues and government surplus property sales. Other popularly requested information includes federal per diem rates, the Federal Acquisition Regulations, forms, and procurement information for vendors.

Because GSA is involved in a wide range of activities, first-time users may wish to browse the site map to become familiar with the variety of information available on the site.

Subject(s): Government Administration; Government Procurement; Public Buildings

IDManagement.gov

https://www.idmanagement.gov/IDM/s/

Description: IDManagement.gov provides news and background information on the security technology and procedures the federal government is applying to its operations. The website features sections on the Homeland Security Presidential Directive 12 (HSPD-12): Policy for a Common Identification Standard for Federal Employees and Contractors; Federal Public Key Infrastructure (FPKI); and other solutions.

Subject(s): Computer Security; Homeland Security

IGNET—Federal Inspectors General

https://www.ignet.gov/

Description: IGNET is a gateway site that serves the federal inspector general (IG) community, whose members are the offices of the inspectors general that conduct audits, investigations, and inspections. The site includes a directory of agency inspectors general, links to their websites, and information about the role of the IGs.

IGNET provides a broad range of materials for both IG employees and for whistleblowers interested in contacting one of the IG offices.

Subject(s): Inspectors General

Office of Government Ethics (OGE)

https://www.oge.gov/

Description: OGE coordinates activities in the Executive branch related to the prevention of conflicts of interest on the part of government employees and the resolution of conflicts of interest that do occur. The site features information for the general public, for international interests, and for the media. The Financial Disclosure section has subsections for public and confidential disclosure. The Laws & Regulations section provides the complete text of applicable executive orders, Federal Register issuances, employee standards of conduct, and statutes and regulations related to the Executive branch ethics program.

The OGE site also has substantial information about agency model practices, easily accessible by clicking on the Site Index link.

Subject(s): Ethics in Government; Government Employees—Regulations

Office of Government-wide Policy (OGP)

https://www.gsa.gov/about-us/organization/office-of-governmentwide-policy-overview

Description: OGP was created to consolidate all of GSA's government-wide policymaking activities within one central office. These activities include acquisitions, government travel, and internal management systems. The site links to OGP's component offices, such as the Office of Acquisition

Policy, the Office of Executive Councils, and the Office of Travel, Transportation, and Asset Management.

Subject(s): Government Administration—Policy; Government Procurement—Policy

Office of Management and Budget (OMB)

https://www.whitehouse.gov/omb/

Description: OMB assists the president in overseeing the preparation of the federal budget and supervises budget administration in Executive branch agencies. In addition, OMB oversees the administration's procurement, financial management, information, and regulatory policies. OMB's website covers each of these areas of responsibility.

Primary sections of the site include Budget, Management, Regulation & Information, Legislative, and OMBlog. The site includes *OMB Circulars*, the *OMB Bulletin*, OMB memoranda, and privacy guidance for executive agencies. Documents under the Budget section include budget supplementals and amendments. The Regulation & Information section includes information about federal statistical programs and standards, regulatory policy, information policy, and e-government.

OMB news releases, circulars, and *Statements of Administration Policy* are available as RSS feeds.

In addition to the collection of federal budget documents, this site is useful for the availability of the *OMB Circulars*, such as *OMB Circular A-130*, which establishes administration policy for the management of federal information resources, and *OMB Circular A-76*, which concerns federal policy for the competition of commercial activities. OMB's *Statements of Administration Policy*, found in the Legislative section, will be helpful to those tracking bills in which the administration has a strong interest.

Subject(s): Budget of the U.S. Government; Government Administration

OMB Blog

https://obamawhitehouse.archives.gov/omb/blog

Description: This website was maintained during the Obama administration but has not been updated by the Trump administration. The OMB Blog was written by the office's staffers. The blog discusses government budget policy, regulatory policy, and other topics within OMB's purview. It is not open for comments.

Subject(s): Budget of the U.S. Government—Policy; Blogs

Performance.gov

https://www.performance.gov/

Description: Performance.gov tracks the performance of federal agencies in regard to contract spending, proper and improper payments, real estate streamlining and downsizing, technological productivity, and personnel performance. The site includes information about the areas of focus, links to participating agencies, a frequently asked questions section, and a link to provide feedback.

Subject(s): Performance Evaluation

Treasury Inspector General for Tax Administration (TIGTA)

https://www.treasury.gov/tigta/

Description: TIGTA provides independent oversight of Internal Revenue Service (IRS) activities, serving in effect as an inspector general for the IRS. The TIGTA website explains the office's role and posts copies of its audit reports and congressional testimony. The site also has information about the TIGTA hotline and an online form for reporting any knowledge of IRS waste, fraud, or abuse.

Subject(s): Inspectors General; Taxation

United States Government Manual

https://www.usgovernmentmanual.gov

Description: The official, annual *United States Government Manual* is a descriptive directory of the Executive, Legislative, and Judicial agencies of the federal government. It also includes information on quasi-official agencies; international organizations; and boards, commissions, and committees. Content is available in text and PDF versions, but only the PDFs contain the agency organization charts and other graphics.

The strength of the *United States Government Manual* lies in the descriptions of the agencies, how they were established, what they do, and the nature of their primary divisions, as well as in the publication's helpful appendices. As with the print edition, users of the online version of this reference classic will want to check more frequently updated sources—such as agency websites—for current personnel and organizational information.

Subject(s): Federal Government; Directories

GOVERNMENT BUSINESS

AbilityOne

https://www.abilityone.gov/

Description: Through federal procurement policies, the AbilityOne program (formerly known as Javits-Wagner-O'Day or JWOD) generates jobs and training opportunities for people who are blind or have other severe disabilities. AbilityOne is administered by the Committee for Purchase From People Who Are Blind or Severely Disabled, an independent federal agency. Its website includes information about the committee, relevant laws and notices, a procurement list, program contacts, and information about how to participate.

Subject(s): Disabilities; Government Procurement—Policy

Acquisition.gov

https://www.acquisition.gov/

Description: Acquisition.gov is a central collection point for news, reference, and regulatory information needed by individuals and organizations involved in government contracting and procurement. It links to the *Federal Acquisition Regulation (FAR)* and to websites relevant to contractor performance evaluations, bid protests, individual agency procurement, and professional development for government contracting personnel.

Subject(s): Government Procurement; Military Procurement

Acquisition One Source

http://www.secnav.navy.mil/rda/onesource/pages/default.aspx

Description: Acquisition One Source provides authoritative acquisitions policy, regulations, and other information of interest to the Navy acquisitions and procurement community. Information is grouped under subjects such as Bridge Contract Policy, Business Opportunities, and Strategic Sourcing.

Subject(s): Military Procurement

Civilian Board of Contract Appeals (CBCA)

http://www.cbca.gsa.gov

Description: The CBCA hears and decides contract disputes between government contractors and executive agencies for all agencies except the Department of Defense, Army, Navy, Air Force, National Aeronautics and Space Administration (NASA), United States Postal Service, Postal Rate Commission, and Tennessee Valley Authority. The website has copies of the board's decisions and rules of procedure. It also carries decisions from the boards it superseded.

Subjects(s): Government Contracts

Commission on Wartime Contracting in Iraq and Afghanistan

https://cybercemetery.unt.edu/archive/cwc/20110929213815/http://www.wartimecontracting.gov/

Description: The Commission on Wartime Contracting in Iraq and Afghanistan, established by Congress, issued an interim report in 2009 and its final report in 2011. "The Commission is required to study, assess, and make recommendations concerning wartime contracting for the reconstruction, logistical support, and the performance of security functions in Iraq and Afghanistan. The Commission's major objectives include a thorough assessment of the systemic problems identified with interagency wartime contracting, the identification of instances of waste, fraud, and abuse, and ensuring accountability for those responsible." (from the website) The website has commission briefings, hearings, special reports, and a meetings schedule.

This website was archived in December 2011. It is hosted by the University of North Texas on behalf of the National Archives and Records Administration.

Subject(s): Military Procurement

Defense Logistics Agency (DLA) Disposition Services

http://www.dla.mil/dispositionservices.aspx

Description: Due to the launch of the We Are DLA initiative in 2010, the Defense Logistics Agency Disposition Services website was established. With headquarters in Michigan, the Disposition Services division is involved with the disposal of excess property from military services, selling DoD surplus property, and maintaining environmental conscientiousness. Sections include information on such topics as turn-in documentation; property searches for military, state, federal, and special programs; and property for sale to the public.

Subject(s): Surplus Government Property

DLA Land and Maritime

http://www.dla.mil/LandandMaritime/

Description: DLA Land and Maritime, a Department of Defense procurement and supply center, offers information about military procurement and about buying from and selling to the center. The site links to the DLA-EBS Internet Bid Board System (DIBBS) and to the DoD EMALL system.

Subject(s): Military Procurement

eSRS: Electronic Subcontracting Reporting System

https://www.esrs.gov/

Description: The Federal Funding Accountability and Transparency Act of 2006 requires subcontract award data to be included in the USAspending.gov database. (USAspending.gov is described in a separate entry.) The Electronic Subcontracting Reporting System, or eSRS, collects this data from federal government contractors.

Subject(s): Government Contracts

FedBizOpps.gov: Federal Business Opportunities

https://www.fbo.gov/

Description: FedBizOpps.gov is the central clearinghouse for information about federal government procurement notices in excess of $25,000. Vendors seeking government business opportunities on this site can search the full-text versions of notices and limit searches by agency, set-aside code, date range, and other criteria. The site provides subscribers with free e-mail notification of procurement announcements. Online videos demonstrate how to use FedBizOpps.gov.

Subject(s): Government Contracts; Government Procurement

Federal Acquisition Jumpstation

https://prod.nais.nasa.gov/pub/fedproc/home.html

Description: The Federal Acquisition Jumpstation provides a simple list of links to federal agency web pages concerned with procurement, contracts, and grants.

Subject(s): Government Procurement

Federal Acquisition Regulation (FAR)

https://www.acquisition.gov/?q=browsefar

Description: This version of FAR provides access to HTML and PDF versions of the regulations. It includes PDF files of Federal Acquisition Circulars in both their looseleaf and Federal Register printing formats. There are also special sections for proposed rules and for Small Entity Compliance Guidelines. Users can subscribe to the Acquisition News e-mail service to receive news of circulars, proposed rules, and public meetings, as well as other information about FAR-related issues.

Subject(s): Government Procurement—Regulations

Federal Acquisition Service (FAS)

https://www.gsa.gov/portal/content/105080

Description: FAS was formed in late 2006 by combining the Federal Technology Service with the Federal Supply Service. FAS offers procurement services for federal government agencies. Its website has information about the organization and links to its component offices.

Subject(s): Government Procurement

Federal Laboratory Consortium for Technology Transfer

https://www.federallabs.org/

Description: The Federal Laboratory Consortium for Technology Transfer helps to move the federal laboratories' research and development into the U.S. private sector. On the website, the FLC's tool for locating technology allows users to request technical assistance and be partnered with the appropriate laboratory. The site also has a searchable directory of FLC laboratories, as well as a link to the FLC Facebook page.

Subject(s): Technology Transfer

Federal Procurement Data System—Next Generation

https://www.fpds.gov/fpdsng_cms/index.php/en/

Description: The Federal Procurement Data System—Next Generation (FPDS-NG) is the central repository of statistical information about federal Executive branch contracting. It contains detailed information about contract awards over $3,000. Free registration is required to search the data, which is also available free of charge. Selected reports and "top requests" (such as Recovery Act contracts) are available from the main page without signing in.

FPDS-NG, launched with fiscal year 2004 data, was designed to meet the need for faster reporting of contract actions. Since then, the federal government has launched the USAspending.gov website for both contracts and assistance (grants and loans) reporting. The USAspending.gov contract information is based on FPDS-NG data.

Subject(s): Government Contracts

GovSales.gov

https://www.govsales.gov/govsales/govsales/

Description: The tagline for GovSales.gov is "The Official Site to Find U.S. Government Property." The site has separate sections for each type of goods, including real estate, computers, and industrial. See the FAQs section on the top menu bar for important information about registering and bidding.

Subject(s): Government Auctions; Surplus Government Property

GSA Advantage!

https://www.gsaadvantage.gov/advantage/main/start_page.do

Description: This GSA website, for use by federal government agencies only, is an online shopping and supply site. Authorized users can use government credit cards to purchase products from the Federal Supply Service. Non-registered users can browse the products catalog.

Subject(s): Government Procurement

iEdison

https://era.nih.gov/iedison/iedison.htm

Description: Government grantees and contractors are required to report any government-funded inventions to the federal agency that made the award. Interagency Edison, or iEdison, is an online system designed to streamline the administrative tasks involved in complying with this requirement. It can be used to report to a number of agencies, including the Department of Energy and the National Institutes of Health.

Subject(s): Intellectual Property

NASA Acquisition Internet Service

https://prod.nais.nasa.gov/cgibin/nais/index.cgi

Description: The NASA Acquisition Internet Service website provides a central online point of contact for businesses interested in NASA acquisitions and procurement opportunities. The site includes the annual NASA acquisition forecasts and the NASA Procurement Data View (NPDV) system. The site also offers an e-mail alert system for news about NASA opportunities.

Subject(s): Government Procurement

SBIR and STTR Awards

https://www.sbir.gov/sbirsearch/award/all/

Description: The Small Business Innovation Research and Small Business Technology Transfer programs are competitive funding programs that encourage innovative research and development in small businesses and non-profit research institutions. They are offered by agencies with large research and development budgets and are coordinated by SBA. This website allows users to search the award listing and filter results by agency, year, ownership type, and state.

Subject(s): Small Business—Grants

Small and Disadvantaged Business Utilization (OSDBU)

https://www.dm.usda.gov/smallbus/index.php

Description: The mission of OSDBU is to assist small businesses with the Department of Agriculture's contracting process. Its website includes a directory of subcontracting opportunities, the USDA Forecast of Business Opportunities, and small business community events.

Subject(s): Government Procurement; Small Business

SUB-Net

https://eweb.sba.gov/gls/dsp_sbabanner.cfm

Description: This website was designed primarily as a place for businesses to post solicitations and notices. Prime contractors can use SUB-Net to post subcontracting opportunities. These may or may not be reserved for small business and they may include either solicitations or other notices, such as notices of sources sought for teaming partners and subcontractors on future contracts. Small businesses can use this site to identify opportunities in their areas of expertise. Major sections of the website are Search, Post, and Help.

Subject(s): Government Contracts

System for Award Management (SAM)

https://www.sam.gov/portal/SAM/#1#1

Description: The SAM website is a single point of access and registration for vendors who want to do business with the federal government. The site includes a section for user guides and helpful hints and space for news and announcements.

Subject(s): Defense Contracting; Government Procurement

UNICOR: Federal Prison Industries, Inc.

https://www.unicor.gov/index.aspx

Description: The UNICOR website allows the federal government and contractors to buy goods and services from Federal Prison Industries (FPI), Inc., whose primary mission is the productive employment of inmates. The site has an online product catalog with browsing and ordering capabilities. It also provides substantial background information on the Inmate Training Programs.

Subject(s): Government Procurement; Prisoners

USA.gov Buying from the U.S. Government

https://www.usa.gov/buy-from-government

Description: The USA.gov website section that deals with government sales and auctions describes it purpose as one that allows users to "buy new, seized, and surplus merchandise and real estate from the government." This portal to other government Internet resources is divided into the following sections: Auctions and Sales; Collectibles, Books, and More; and Surplus Sales by State.

Subject(s): Government Auctions; Surplus Government Property

USDA Procurement

https://www.dm.usda.gov/procurement/

Description: This procurement site from the Department of Agriculture provides guidance on the department's highly decentralized procurement activities. The site provides news, updates, the Acquisition Toolkit, information on policy and regulations, and links to related USDA information.

Subject(s): Government Procurement

GOVERNMENT EMPLOYEES

Federal Labor Relations Authority (FLRA)

https://www.flra.gov/

Description: FLRA is an independent agency responsible for administering the labor-management relations program for federal employees. Its website includes information about filing a case with FLRA and the types of cases it handles. It also carries the decisions made by FLRA and the statutes and regulations under which it does its work.

Subject(s): Government Employees; Labor-Management Relations

Federal Retirement Thrift Investment Board (FRTIB)

https://www.frtib.gov/

Description: The Federal Retirement Thrift Investment Board administers the Thrift Savings Plan (TSP) for federal employees. Its website includes a Reading Room with the board's annual TSP audit report and other frequently requested documents. The site also links to TSP contact information and publications.

Subject(s): Government Employees

FedScope

https://www.fedscope.opm.gov/

Description: FedScope is a central access point for data about the federal government's civilian workforce. Its website provides flexible retrieval of aggregate statistics extracted from OPM's Central Personnel Data File on topics including length of service, gender and age, pay grades, work schedules, and employment location. The Employment Statistics link on the top menu leads to electronic publications compiling historical trends and data. Data products are typically available in PDF and spreadsheet formats.

It may be particularly helpful for users to review the About Our Data and Data Source/Definitions sections before using the FedScope data in analyses.

Subject(s): Government Employees—Statistics

FedsHireVets.gov

https://fedshirevets.gov/

Description: FedsHireVets.gov is part of the Veterans Employment Initiative, established by executive order in 2009. The website is intended to be a central source for federal employment information for veterans, transitioning service members and their families, and federal hiring managers. The site has a section for individuals looking for a job and for agency human resources personnel looking to hire. It also has a directory of Veteran Employment Program Offices (VEPOs).

Subject(s): Veterans

Merit Systems Protection Board (MSPB)

https://www.mspb.gov/

Description: The MSPB serves as guardian of the federal government's merit-based system of employment, primarily by hearing and deciding appeals from federal employees concerning removals and other major personnel actions. The board also hears and decides other types of civil service cases, reviews significant actions and regulations of the Office of Personnel Management, and conducts studies of the merit systems. Its website includes additional descriptive information about the board, along with links to decisions, studies, and information on how to file an appeal.

Subject(s): Government Employees; Labor-Management Relations

National Personnel Records Center (NPRC)

https://www.archives.gov/st-louis

Description: NPRC in St. Louis is a central repository for federal civil service and military personnel records. Its website describes the collections and how to request information. The records themselves are not available online. A special site, eVetRecs, allows veterans and the next of kin of deceased veterans to request records online. The eVetRecs site is linked to on the following NARA webpage: https://vetrecs.archives.gov/.

Subject(s): Government Employees; Veterans

Office of Compliance

https://www.compliance.gov/

Description: The Office of Compliance is an independent agency that was established by the Congressional Accountability Act of 1995 to protect the safety, health, and workplace rights of covered employees in the legislative branch. Its website includes information about employee rights, the directives of the board of directors, regulations, and procedural rules.

Subject(s): Labor Law; Legislative Branch—Regulations

Office of Personnel Management (OPM)

https://www.opm.gov/

Description: As the federal government personnel office, OPM is a primary source for information about working for the federal government. OPM displays the current operating status of the federal government (for example, for holidays) and features sections for federal job seekers, federal employees, retirees, and human resources practitioners. The OPM website's homepage links directly to the most requested pages, including the USAJOBS employment website, the Feds Hire Vets site, forms, wages and salaries, and information on retirement benefits. Links to reports to the president and to Congress, to Inspector General reports, and to the OPM Publications database can be found under News. Use the site's helpful subject index to find additional information.

Subject(s): Government Employees; Personnel Management

Presidential Management Fellows Program

https://www.pmf.gov/

Description: The Presidential Management Fellows Program is designed to recruit for public service a variety of outstanding citizens interested in the leadership and management of public policies and programs. This site provides information on the program and how to apply.

Subject(s): Government Employees

Salaries and Wages

https://www.opm.gov/policy-data-oversight/pay-leave/salaries-wages/#url=2018

Description: This official OPM website for government-wide pay programs for federal employees has information about the General Schedule (GS), Law Enforcement Pay Schedules, and the Memorandum on Executive Order for 2018 Pay Schedules. It provides a variety of resources. Most of the schedules are presented in PDF format. The following schedules are available: General Schedule and Locality Pay Tables, Law Enforcement Officer (LEO) General Schedule Locality Pay Tables, Executive & Senior Level Employee Pay Tables, and Special Rate Tables.

Subject(s): Government Employees; Pay and Benefits

Telework.gov

https://www.telework.gov/

Description: Telework.gov provides guidance, policies, procedures, and studies related to telecommuting for federal government employees.

Subject(s): Government Employees—Policy

Thrift Savings Plan (TSP)

https://www.tsp.gov/index.html

Sponsor(s): Federal Retirement Thrift Investment Board

Description: TSP is a retirement savings plan for federal civilian employees and for uniformed services members. This site offers basic information about the service, participation, and retirement planning.

Subject(s): Government Employees

Office of Special Counsel (OSC)

https://osc.gov/

Description: OSC is an independent federal investigative and prosecutorial agency that is responsible for protecting federal employees and applicants from prohibited personnel practices, especially reprisal for whistleblowing. The agency is also concerned with adherence to the Hatch Act, which restricts political activity by federal government employees. Major sections of its website explain prohibited personnel practices, whistleblower procedures and protections, and Hatch Act rules. The site also covers the Uniformed Services Employment and Reemployment Rights Act (USERRA), which prohibits discrimination against persons because of their service in the Armed Forces Reserve, the National Guard, or other uniformed services. The site provides summaries of a variety of successful Special Counsel cases. The Resources section includes OSC publications and the Public Filing documents associated with recently closed whistleblower cases.

Subject(s): Government Employees—Laws; Hatch Act

GOVERNMENT FINANCE

Budget of the United States Government

https://www.whitehouse.gov/omb/budget/

Description: OMB provides the full-text version of the current U.S. budget, supporting documents, and additional information online. Most of the files are available in PDF format, with some tables available in spreadsheet format. The Government Publishing Office's FDsys.gov web service has copies of the budget online for the past several years, and provides the extra functionality of a word search; it can be accessed at https://www.gpo.gov/fdsys/.

Subject(s): Budget of the U.S. Government; Government Finance

Bureau of the Fiscal Service

https://www.fiscal.treasury.gov/

Description: The Bureau of the Fiscal Service was established in October 2012 through the merging of the Treasury's Bureau of the Public Debt and the Financial Management Service. The Bureau of the Fiscal Service operates the government's collections and deposit systems; uses the sale of Treasury bonds, notes, and bills to borrow the money needed to operate the government; provides access to TreasuryDirect (described in a separate entry), where Treasury securities can be purchased online; and offers administrative, reporting, and other finance-related managerial services. The site provides information about the bureau's reports, publications, and programs.

Subject(s): Government Finance

Department of the Treasury

https://home.treasury.gov/

Description: The Treasury Department's website provides current news and links to the issues handled by the department. The "Treasury For..." section links to information for the general public, business, financial institutions, and government. The Initiatives section provides information about such topics as Wall Street reform and housing finance reform. Data and charts can be found under Resource Center. The Treasury Notes blog can be found under Social Hub and on the right-hand side of the home page, while a link to Treasury auctions can be found on the home page.

Subject(s): Government Finance

Federal Accounting Standards Advisory Board (FASAB)

http://www.fasab.gov

Description: FASAB is a federal advisory committee responsible for establishing generally accepted accounting principles for federal entities. FASAB publishes the *FASAB Handbook of Federal Accounting Standards* *and Other Pronouncements, as Amended*, interpretations, and technical bulletins. Along with background information, its website has a newsletter that reports board meeting highlights.

Subject(s): Accounting

Federal Financing Bank (FFB)

https://www.treasury.gov/ffb/

Description: FFB is a government corporation that works under the general supervision of the secretary of the Treasury. FFB coordinates federal and federally assisted borrowing from the public with the overall financial and economic goals of the government. Its website includes information about FFB's operations, press releases, and financial statements.

Subject(s): Government Finance

Following the Money: GAO's Oversight of the Recovery Act

https://www.gao.gov/recovery/

Description: As they are required by the Recovery Act, the GAO reports on aspects of management and spending under the act. The site provides GAO's reviews of how Recovery Act funds are being spent in a sample of states and whether they are achieving the act's goals.

Subject(s): Government Finance

Internal Revenue Service (IRS)

https://www.irs.gov/

Description: The intended audience for the official website of the IRS is the average U.S. taxpayer. Special sections also lead to information for businesses, charities and nonprofits, government entities, tax professionals, and users concerned with retirement plans and tax-exempt bonds. A Spanish-language version of the site is available. The section for individuals includes instructions, forms and publications, and resources for electronic filing through the IRS e-file program. The site's News & Events section links to media contacts, IRS guidance, news, and information about tax scams.

The IRS site, one of the most heavily used federal websites, is well organized and provides multiple points of access to major sections and resources. The site map can help users find specific information.

Subject(s): Income Tax; Tax Forms; Taxation

Tax Statistics

https://www.irs.gov/statistics

Description: The Tax Statistics web page serves as a central access point for a variety of statistics about IRS operations that have been aggregated from filings with the IRS. Major sections include Business Tax, Charitable, Compliance, Individual Tax, and (Statistics) by Form. A special Tax Stats

Topics section includes statistics on estate and gift tax returns and research on taxpayer compliance.

Subject(s): Taxation—Statistics

Taxpayer Advocate Service

https://www.irs.gov/advocate

Description: The Taxpayer Advocate Service was created to ensure that taxpayer complaints not resolved through the normal channels could be resolved fairly and efficiently, and to recommend system changes based on the experiences that occur while reviewing these complaints. This website provides information about the service and how to use it. The site also has the taxpayer advocate's annual report to Congress, which details the most frequent taxpayer complaints and makes recommendations for improvement.

Subject(s): Income Tax

TreasuryDirect

https://www.treasurydirect.gov/

Description: TreasuryDirect has three separate sections: Individuals, Financial Institutions (institutional investors), and Government. The section for individuals allows customers to set up an account with the Department of the Treasury; purchase Treasury bills, bonds, and notes; participate in Treasury security auctions; convert paper savings bonds to electronic; and otherwise manage their accounts.

The section for institutional investing focuses on Treasury auctions, but also provides access to online account services and relevant information. The Government section describes programs specifically for government entities, such as the Federal Investments Program and the State and Local Government Series (SLGS) securities program.

Subject(s): Treasury Bills; Treasury Bonds; Treasury Notes

U.S. Chief Financial Officers Council (CFOC)

https://cfo.gov

Description: Members of the CFOC are the chief financial officers of the largest federal agencies and senior officials of the Office of Management and Budget and the Department of the Treasury. The CFOC website includes a membership list, council charter, news, documents, and meetings information. The Resources section links to the annual financial reports of the Cabinet departments and major agencies.

Subject(s): Government Finance

GOVERNMENT INFORMATION

CENDI

https://cendi.gov/

Description: CENDI is a working group of federal scientific and technical information (STI) managers. (It is named for the initial four entities that formed the group: the Department of Commerce, the Department of Energy, NASA, and the Defense Information Managers Group.) This website has CENDI publications, materials from CENDI workshops, and information from CENDI working groups. Topics covered include digital libraries, copyright, technology assessments, and current federal STI projects.

Despite CENDI's specialized mission and membership, the content available on this site may also be useful to digital library managers outside the realms of federal and scientific/technical information.

Subject(s): Digital Libraries; Government Information

Data.gov

https://www.data.gov/

Description: Launched in May 2009, Data.gov is a portal to more than 191,000 free federal government data sets. The site also links to online tools for data extraction, for porting data and information to websites through a widget, and for other data tasks. The Data section provides browsing capability for items from a number of sources.

Federal Digital System (FDsys)

https://www.gpo.gov/fdsys/

Description: The Federal Digital System, or FDsys, provides online access to federal documents and information produced by the Government Publishing Office. FDsys was launched in early 2009 as a replacement for the GPO Access website, and all content was transferred by the end of 2011.

As the official source for electronic formats of core U.S. government documents, FDsys is an essential resource.

Subject(s): Congressional Documents; Government Publications; Presidential Documents

Government Publishing Office (GPO)

https://www.gpo.gov/

Description: As stated on its website, GPO is "the Federal Government's official, digital, secure resource for producing, procuring, cataloging, indexing, authenticating, disseminating, and preserving the official information products of the U.S. Government." The site has information about GPO, its print and electronic information services for agencies, its network of federal depository library partners, new government publications, and contract opportunities for printing. It also links to the online *Catalog of U.S. Government Publications (CGP)*, the online bookstore, and GPO's Ben's Guide to U.S. Government for Kids.

GPO has migrated content from its original online database system, GPO Access, to the Federal Digital System (FDsys) at https://www.gpo.gov/fdsys. The GPO.gov site links directly to FDsys.

Subject(s): Government Publications

Information Security Oversight Office (ISOO)

https://www.archives.gov/isoo

Description: ISOO is responsible for policy and operations related to classifying, declassifying, and safeguarding national security information. ISOO's annual report compiles statistics on agency classification and declassification activities. Its website describes the scope of the office's authority and responsibilities and provides relevant policy documents, ISOO notices, and security forms. ISOO activities described on the site include the Interagency Security Classification Appeals Panel (ISCAP), the National Industrial Security Program (NISP), and the Controlled Unclassified Information (CUI) Office.

Subject(s): Information Policy; National Security—Regulations

National Archives and Records Administration (NARA)

https://www.archives.gov/

Description: NARA oversees the archival records of the executive, congressional, and judicial branches of the federal government. Its website describes these holdings and provides online access to selected digital collections. The Research Our Records section of the site offers an introduction to the archives' contents and explains how to search for materials. The web version of the *Guide to Federal Records in the National Archives of the United States* allows users to search the guide or enter a record group number directly. The site also has information for genealogists and in this section provides tips on researching census records, military records, immigration records (ship passenger lists), naturalization records, and land records. The site's alphabetical subject index provides quick links to specific collections. Links at the bottom of the home page lead to the information the site provides in Spanish, as well as relevant social media pages.

NARA's website explains the agency's varied responsibilities and includes equally varied content. For example, NARA houses the Office of the Federal Register, which is responsible for publishing public laws and the *Federal Register*, and also for coordinating the Electoral College. NARA's Information Security Oversight Office works with security classification policies for government and industry. NARA also oversees the Presidential Libraries. Aside from the Presidential Libraries, NARA has locations across the country; the site links to NARA Research Centers, regional archives, and affiliated archives located outside of Washington, D.C., in the Research Our Records section.

For archivists, the Records Managers section offers news and information pertaining to federal records management policy; a separate section covers document preservation. For educators and students, the site provides lesson plans, an introductory research activity, and more. The Archivist of the United States maintains a news blog, which links to other NARA blogs, at https://aotus.blogs.archives.gov/.

This site is unusual in the scope of materials available. While very little actual archival material is online, NARA has put selected high-interest items on the site.

Subject(s): Archives

National Declassification Center (NDC)

https://www.archives.gov/declassification

Description: NDC is part of the National Archives and works to improve the declassification process and to implement standard declassification training for records determined to have permanent historical value. The website includes key policy documents, information on declassification, and the center's bi-annual status report.

Subject(s): Declassified Documents

National Technical Information Service (NTIS)

https://www.ntis.gov/

Description: NTIS is one of the major government publishing agencies and features hundreds of thousands of publications related to scientific, technical, engineering, and business information that have been produced by or for the U.S. government. However, since NTIS is run on a cost recovery basis, many of its services require payment.

NTIS provides a search engine to find items in its large collection of reports for sale. The site's search box can be found in the navigation bar.

Subject(s): Government Publications; Scientific and Technical Information; Publication Catalogs

Office of Information and Privacy (OIP)

https://www.justice.gov/oip

Description: OIP manages the Department of Justice's responsibilities related to the Freedom of Information Act (FOIA) and the Privacy Act. These responsibilities include coordinating and implementing policy development and government-wide compliance for FOIA, compliance by the Justice Department for the Privacy Act, and the decisions on all appeals from denials of access to information under those acts by any component of the

Justice Department. Its website includes online access to reference documents, including the *DOJ Annual FOIA Report*.

Subject(s): Freedom of Information Act

Office of Information and Regulatory Affairs (OIRA)

https://www.whitehouse.gov/omb/information-regulatory-affairs/

Description: This website was still in the process of being updated as this book went to press. In addition to its important responsibilities in the area of regulatory policy, OIRA is concerned with government information collection and management. The site also has a section that provides information on federal government statistical programs and standards, including the schedule of release dates for principal federal economic indicators. The Information Policy section of the OIRA website covers information policy documents, federal website standards guidance, privacy guidance, the Government Paperwork Elimination Act, and the Freedom of Information Reform Act.

OIRA reviews draft federal regulations from federal agencies and articulates the administration's regulatory policy. Documents related to these activities can be found in the Regulatory Matters section of the OIRA site.

Subject(s): Government Information—Policy; Regulatory Policy

Office of the Federal Register

https://www.ofr.gov/

Description: The Office of the Federal Register prepares the official texts for federal regulatory materials, federal laws, presidential documents, and the *U.S. Government Manual*. The website serves as a portal linking to the government websites hosting the online version of these documents. The Public Inspection Desk section of the site provides access to the documents (notices, regulations, and other items) that will appear in the next day's *Federal Register* and selected documents scheduled for later issues.

The office has several other roles in addition to its responsibilities as an official legal information service. It administers and maintains the website for the Electoral College. It also compiles Privacy Act Issuances, through which federal agencies disclose any information system containing personally identifiable information and explain how individuals can access records about themselves. These issuances are available on the office's site.

Subject(s): Laws; Privacy—Regulations

Public Interest Declassification Board (PIDB)

https://www.archives.gov/declassification/pidb/

Description: PIDB advises the president and Executive Branch officials on issues related to the review and declassification of national security documents to serve the public interest and contribute to an accurate archival record. Its website includes the board's enabling legislation, meeting minutes, and recommendations.

Subject(s): Government Information—Policy; National Security

U.S. Government Bookstore

https://bookstore.gpo.gov/

Description: GPO's sales catalog can be searched by keyword or browsed by topic on this website. Documents can be ordered online. The site also features a list of government best sellers.

Subject(s): Government Publications; Publication Catalogs

United States Government Blog

https://blog.usa.gov/

Description: This blog highlights useful government information and services for Americans' everyday lives. Typical topics include history, nutrition, financial matters, and current events. Bloggers are employees of the General Services Administration (GSA). Comments are allowed, and entries can be Tweeted or liked on Facebook.

Subject(s): Government Services; Blogs

GOVERNMENT SERVICES

Citizens' Stamp Advisory Committee (CSAC)

http://about.usps.com/who-we-are/csac/

Description: CSAC is the mechanism by which subjects are selected to be featured on U.S. postage stamps. CSAC receives recommendations, then evaluates them and makes its own recommendations to the postmaster general. This U.S. Postal Service website has information about CSAC, a list of current committee members, and the formal criteria for stamp subject selection.

Subject(s): Postage Stamps

Federal Emergency Management Agency (FEMA)

https://www.fema.gov/

Description: The FEMA website features news and victim assistance information for any current disasters in the United States. The site also provides information about how to prepare for emergencies ranging from floods to terrorist threats, how to apply for disaster assistance, and how to keep safe and recover after a disaster. Audience-specific sections provide information and resources for businesses, emergency personnel, homeowners, livestock owners, volunteers, kids, and others. The About the Agency section has a leadership directory. Information about grants can be found in the Grants section. The site map is an alphabetical index providing quick access to resources, including FEMA programs such as the National Fire Academy, the National Fire Incident Reporting System, the National Flood Insurance Program, and urban search-and-rescue programs. The FEMA website is available in many languages, including Spanish, French, Arabic, Chinese, Korean, Polish, Russian, and Vietnamese.

Subject(s): Disaster Assistance

FloodSmart.gov

https://www.floodsmart.gov/

Description: FloodSmart.gov is currently under construction. It has consumer information on flood risk, preparing for flooding, and flood insurance. The website is sponsored by the National Flood Insurance Program (NFIP). The user should be able to find all the information they need at https://www.fema.gov/national-flood-insurance-program

Subject(s): Flood Insurance

GovLoans.gov

https://govloans.gov/

Description: GovLoans.gov is a central location for information about federal loan programs. Major sections cover topics such as agriculture, business, disaster relief, education, housing, and veterans' loans. The site is a cooperative effort between the Departments of Agriculture, Commerce, Education, Housing and Urban Development, and Veterans Affairs, as well as the Small Business Administration. It is hosted by the Department of Labor's GovBenefits.gov website. GovLoans.gov is also available in Spanish.

Subject(s): Government Loans

LEP.gov

https://www.lep.gov/

Description: The LEP.gov website was created by the Federal Interagency Working Group on Limited English Proficiency. The site offers information and guidance for language access to federal and federally assisted programs, with three major target audiences: federal agencies, recipients of federal funds, and community organizations. The site provides policy guidance, directories of translator and interpreter organizations, demographic data, and program news. Information in other languages, including Spanish, is available on the site.

Subject(s): Civil Rights—Regulations; Language Groups

Postal Regulatory Commission (PRC)

https://www.prc.gov/

Description: PRC is an independent regulatory agency that reviews Postal Service requests for changes in postal rates. The References and Reports/Data sections have statistical reports made by the Postal Service for the PRC on topics such as personnel, payroll, and productivity.

Subject(s): Postal Service—Regulations

U.S. Postal Service (USPS)

https://www.prc.gov/

Description: The USPS website provides information, such as a directory of post offices, and online services for the general public and businesses. Online services include stamp sales, a postage rate calculator, and package tracking. The site's Forms & Publications section, which is accessed through a link at the bottom of the page, has over 100 U.S. postal forms in PDF format.

USPS videos and press releases are available in the About USPS Home section. This section includes the annual report as well.

Subject(s): Postal Service

INTERGOVERNMENTAL RELATIONS

Advisory Commission on Intergovernmental Relations (ACIR)

http://www.library.unt.edu/gpo/acir/acir.htm

Description: ACIR was established by Congress in 1959 to study the relationships between federal, state, and local government. The commission was closed in 1996. The University of North Texas Libraries maintains this website to provide permanent public access to the electronic publications that were available on the ACIR website. It includes editions of *Significant Features of Fiscal Federalism*, a reference tool for data on state and federal revenues and expenditures and federal spending in the states. All serial publication volumes from 1976 through 1994 are available online, with other documents from the 1960s to the 1990s available as well.

The ACIR materials are accessible thanks to a partnership between the University of North Texas Libraries and the U.S. Government Publishing Office to provide permanent public access to the electronic websites and publications of defunct U.S. government agencies and commissions.

Subject(s): Intergovernmental Relations

Codetalk

https://portal.hud.gov/hudportal/HUD?src=/program_offices/public_indian_housing/ih

Description: Codetalk is an interagency website that was established to deliver electronic information from government agencies and other organizations to Native American communities. The name is based on the Native American Code Talkers, who were heroes of the two World Wars. The site is hosted on the Department of Housing and Urban Development website and includes detailed information about American Indian housing programs and federal program news.

Subject(s): American Indians

Federal, State, & Local Governments—Census Bureau

https://www.census.gov/govs/

Description: This website brings together information from Census Bureau programs that cover federal, state, and local governments and their finances. Featured data sources include the *Census of Governments* and *State Government Tax Collections Survey*. The site has survey forms, publications, summary reports, and press releases. Statistics are available under topical headings such as Government Employment & Payroll, Government Finance Statistics, Tax Statistics, and Federal Spending. There are options to view national or individual state data, and reports can be downloaded in spreadsheet format or as a flat ASCII file.

Subject(s): Government Employees—Statistics; Government Finance—Statistics; State Government—Statistics

Indian Affairs

https://www.indianaffairs.gov/

Description: The Indian Affairs website provides information from the Bureau of Indian Affairs (BIA) and the Bureau of Indian Education (BIE). BIA manages land held in trust by the United States for American Indian tribes and Alaska Natives. BIE provides education services to American Indian students. The website describes BIA's structure and mission, services, and current tribal consultations. The What We Do section of the site organizes BIA activities by topic, such as Economic Development, Education, Gaming, and Justice Services. The site's Document Library includes the *Tribal Leaders Directory*, the *Guide to Tracing Your American Indian Ancestry*, and the *FR Notice—Indian Entities Recognized and Eligible to Receive Services from the U.S. BIA*.

Subject(s): American Indians

Office of the Special Trustee for American Indians (OST)

https://www.doi.gov/ost

Description: OST was created by law in 1994 to improve the accountability and management of Indian funds held in trust by the federal government. The website provides current news, information for Indian Trust beneficiaries, and Trust documents. It has a special section on the Cobell v. Salazar legal settlement concerned with trust fund mismanagement.

Subject(s): American Indians

Office of Tribal Justice (OTJ)

https://www.justice.gov/otj

Description: The Office of Tribal Justice (OTJ) was established in 1995 with the purpose of increasing the responsiveness of the Department of Justice to the concerns of the American Indian Nations, individual Indians, and others interested in Indian affairs. The website's About the Office section has the *Department of Justice Policy on Indian Sovereignty* and related policy documents. The site's Federal Partners and Other Resources section links to information from the Justice Department and other federal agencies on American Indian legislation and other issues.

Subject(s): American Indians

Tax Information for Indian Tribal Governments

https://www.irs.gov/government-entities/indian-tribal-governments/

Description: This website is designed for use by tribes and is maintained by the IRS's office of Indian Tribal Governments (ITG). The site addresses topics such as employment taxes, casino issues, and fraud and abuse schemes. The site also includes news and compliance guidance.

Subject(s): American Indians

PUBLIC POLICY

John C. Stennis Center for Public Service

https://www.stennis.gov/

Description: The John C. Stennis Center for Public Service was created by Congress in 1988 to promote public service in the United States at all levels of government. The center is governed by a board of trustees appointed by the Democratic and Republican leaders in the U.S. Senate and House of Representatives. The website has information about the center's programs and its namesake. Programs described include the Emerging Congressional Staff Leaders Program, the Stennis Fellows Program, and the Stennis Student Congress.

Subject(s): Fellowships; Civics Education

Woodrow Wilson International Center for Scholars

https://www.wilsoncenter.org/

Description: The Wilson Center supports scholarship linked to public policy. The center offers fellowships and special opportunities for research and writing with a focus on history, political science, and international relations. As a public/private partnership, the center receives roughly one-third of its operating funds from federal appropriations. The website has information about current Wilson Center projects and publications, and audio files of its weekly radio program, “Dialogue.” The site also carries essays and other items from the center’s journal, *The Wilson Quarterly*. In the About section, the site offers information on applying for a fellowship or internship with the center.

Subject(s): Fellowships; Public Policy—Research; Social Science Research

Chapter Thirteen

Health and Safety

Government health sciences websites serve everyone from research scientists to clinicians and the general public. Health science professionals have used government websites to expand a tradition of disseminating research information. Government information on the Internet has also been a boon to the average citizen seeking authoritative medical information written in layman's terms. This chapter includes a full range of information on nutrition, safety, and health care finance.

Subsections in this chapter are Conditions and Treatment, Health Care Finance, Health Occupations, Health Policy and Promotion, Health Research, Medical Information, Medicine and Medical Devices, Nutrition, and Safety.

CONDITIONS AND TREATMENT

AIDSinfo

https://aidsinfo.nih.gov/

Sponsor(s): Health and Human Services Department

Description: AIDSinfo is a user-friendly website with well-designed sections on drugs, clinical trials, related health topics, and guidelines for prevention and treatment. The HIV/AIDS Health Topics section is a portal to information from government and a variety of other sources on all of these aspects of AIDS treatment. The Mobile Resources & Tools section provides a live chat feature and a place to order publications. Some publications are available in Spanish.

Subject(s): AIDS

Alzheimer's Disease Education and Referral (ADEAR) Center

https://www.nia.nih.gov/health/alzheimers

Description: The ADEAR Center is operated as a service of the National Institute on Aging. It is an information clearinghouse for health professionals, people with Alzheimer's disease, their families, and the general public. The website provides information on the disease and news of current research and clinical trials, with links to Alzheimer's research centers. The site also offers an e-mail service for news updates.

Subject(s): Alzheimer's Disease

Autism Information

https://www.hhs.gov/programs/topic-sites/autism/index.html

Description: The Autism Information page provides general information on autism spectrum disorders (ASDs) and links to more specific information on federal websites. The site covers topics such as signs and symptoms, screening and diagnosis, treatment options, causes and risk factors, and research and clinical trials. The page also links to publications from the Interagency Autism Coordinating Committee (IACC) at http://www.iacc.hhs.gov/.

Subject(s): Diseases and Conditions

Cancer Control P.L.A.N.E.T.

https://cancercontrolplanet.cancer.gov/

Description: Cancer Control P.L.A.N.E.T. is designed specifically for professional cancer control planners, program staff, and researchers. Its website is a portal to information needed in developing cancer control programs; it links primarily to information compiled by the federal government. The site is sponsored by the American Cancer Society and by Department of Health and Human Services agencies, including the National Cancer Institute and the Centers for Disease Control and Prevention.

Subject(s): Cancer; Public Health

Cancer Information Service (CIS)

https://www.cancer.gov/contact/contact-center

Description: CIS is a free, public service set up to answer individual questions about cancer. The LiveHelp link provides an instant messaging service. In addition to providing information about CIS, the site links to cancer news, resources, and publications. CIS also operates a toll free number, 1-800-4-CANCER.

Subject(s): Cancer

CDC Cancer Prevention and Control

https://www.cdc.gov/cancer/

Description: The CDC Cancer Prevention and Control website provides national and state statistics, fact sheets, program information, and publications related to cancer. The Prevention section has information about screening tests and risk reduction, while the Cancer Survivorship section has information for caregivers and survivors. The site also has a Spanish-language version available.

Subject(s): Cancer—Statistics

CDC National Prevention Information Network (NPIN)

https://npin.cdc.gov/

Description: NPIN focuses on control and prevention of HIV/AIDS, viral hepatitis, sexually transmitted diseases (STDs), and tuberculosis (TB). NPIN has databases of relevant organizations, conferences, and private and government funding opportunities for community-based and HIV/AIDS, STD, and TB service organizations. The site offers RSS feeds for daily news, conference announcements, and funding opportunity announcements and links to its Twitter, Facebook, LinkedIn, and Pinterest pages on the homepage.

Subject(s): AIDS; HIV Infections; Sexually Transmitted Diseases; Tuberculosis

Centers for Disease Control and Prevention (CDC)

https://www.cdc.gov/

Description: The CDC is concerned with public health, disease prevention and control, environmental health, and health promotion and education. Its main website has information about the agency with links to all of CDC's component centers, institutes, and offices. The site features current public health topics of interest. The Diseases & Conditions section is a gateway to extensive CDC information under categories such as ADHD, cancer, and diabetes. The Data & Statistics section brings together news and links for CDC's many statistical compilations, including pediatric growth charts. The Publications section includes the *Morbidity and Mortality Weekly Report (MMWR)* and the journals *Emerging Infectious Diseases* and *Preventing Chronic Disease*. The CDC website has a Spanish-language version.

CDC offers a version of its site for mobile Internet devices, as well as several apps, a news feed, Facebook and Twitter links, and numerous RSS feeds.

This main CDC page serves as a starting point for finding extensive information on various diseases, disease statistics, and disease prevention. The site offers an A–Z index, a search engine, dynamic links to the most-visited pages, and an entry point by audience type such as individuals, researchers, and businesses. The information is well organized and the pages are easy to navigate.

Subject(s): Diseases and Conditions; Epidemiology; Public Health

Diabetes Public Health Resource

https://www.cdc.gov/diabetes/

Description: This site communicates practical information on diabetes prevention and control. It includes a diabetes fact sheet, frequently asked questions, diabetes statistics, and information on state-based diabetes prevention and control programs. The Press & Social Media section has CDC statements, press releases, and congressional testimony related to diabetes. The site also has a Spanish-language version available.

Subject(s): Diabetes

Eldercare Locator

https://eldercare.acl.gov/Public/index.aspx

Description: According to the website, "The Eldercare Locator…is a nationwide service that connects older Americans and their caregivers with information on senior services." The site provides searches by topic or ZIP code, and in the Resources section features information about such topics as long-term care planning and benefits for older adults, caregivers, and professionals. Fact sheets and news are also available in this section, and links to relevant social media pages are also provided.

Subject(s): Senior Citizens

Flu.gov

https://www.cdc.gov/flu/

Description: Flu.gov is the main government interagency website, hosted by the Department of Health and Human Services, for the public to learn about influenza vaccination, prevention, and treatment. It has information for special populations, such as seniors. During flu season, the site has a national directory of flu shot providers. Flu.gov also provides planning and communications guides for schools, businesses, local governments, and others.

Subject(s): Diseases and Conditions; Public Health

Genetic and Rare Diseases Information Center (GARD)

https://rarediseases.info.nih.gov/

Description: GARD is concerned with research on rare, or orphan, diseases, defined as diseases or conditions affecting fewer than 200,000 persons in the United States. The website provides resources on research, clinical trials, conferences, patient support groups, and relevant genetics information for rare diseases. Information is also available in Spanish.

Subject(s): Diseases and Conditions—Research

GulfLINK

https://health.mil/Military-Health-Topics/Health-Readiness/Environmental-Exposures/GulfLINK/

Description: GulfLINK was established in August 1995 to provide online access to medical, operational, and intelligence documents from the 1990–1991 Gulf War. The Library section of the site includes Case Narratives, *Environmental Exposure Reports*, and RAND research reports. The site also has information on services for veterans and medical evaluation programs, as well as a summary of medical issues relating to symptoms among Gulf War veterans.

Subject(s): Gulf War Disease

HIV.gov

https://www.hiv.gov/

Description: HIV.gov is a portal to government HIV/AIDS information and resources. The site links to information on a wide range of resources on federal programs and policies, such as the Presidential Advisory Council on HIV/AIDS (PACHA), research, grants, and international issues. AIDS.gov also has an extensive HIV/AIDS Basics section discussing prevention and treatment. Some resources are available in Spanish.

HIV.gov makes extensive use of social media in its How to Use New Media section, providing a blog, podcasts, a Twitter feed, a Facebook page, and other outlets for AIDS information. The blog is described in a separate entry.

Subject(s): HIV, AIDS

HIV.gov Blog

https://blog.hiv.gov/

Description: The HIV.gov blog is intended to assist individuals, organizations, and government officers concerned with public health promotion and particularly with HIV and AIDS awareness. Comments are allowed, and articles can be shared via Twitter and Facebook.

Subject(s): HIV,AIDS

HIV/AIDS Surveillance Reports

https://www.cdc.gov/hiv/library/reports/hiv-surveillance.html

Description: These annual reports contain detailed statistics on the incidence of HIV and AIDS in the United States, including data by state, metropolitan statistical area, mode of exposure to HIV, sex, race/ethnicity, age group, vital status, and case definition category.

Subject(s): AIDS—Statistics; HIV Infections—Statistics

Influenza (Flu)

https://www.cdc.gov/flu/

Description: Seasonal flu is the single topic of this website. It provides information on the flu vaccine, antiviral drugs, and flu symptoms and treatment in general. The website has sections for health care professionals, parents, businesses, people at high risk, and other special groups. A link to CDC Flu's Twitter feed is also provided. This CDC website is available in a Spanish-language version.

Subject(s): Diseases and Conditions

National Center for HIV/AIDS, Viral Hepatitis, STD, and TB Prevention (NCHHSTP)

https://www.cdc.gov/nchhstp/

Description: The NCHHSTP website features current disease research news and data, with information for researchers, patients, public health professionals, and the public. The site provides extensive background information on specific Sexually Transmitted Diseases (STDs), HIV/AIDS, Viral Hepatitis, and Tuberculosis (TB). The State Health Profiles section of the site has statistics and program information about HIV/AIDS, Viral Hepatitis, STDs, and TB for all 50 states and the District of Columbia. The site also has information on global HIV/AIDS.

Subject(s): AIDS; HIV Infections; Sexually Transmitted Diseases

National Center for PTSD

https://www.ptsd.va.gov/

Description: The VA's National Center for Post-Traumatic Stress Disorder (PTSD) provides this website as an educational resource concerning PTSD and other consequences of traumatic stress. The primary audiences are veterans and their families, researchers, and mental health care providers. The website offers information on assessment, treatment, and VA services. In addition to combat stress, reactions to trauma caused by natural disasters, abuse, and other factors are discussed. The site offers free online access to PILOTS, a database indexing the literature on PTSD and other mental health consequences of exposure to traumatic events.

Subject(s): Mental Health; Veterans

National Diabetes Education Program (NDEP)

https://www.niddk.nih.gov/health-information/health-communication-programs/ndep/pages/index.aspx

Description: NDEP is a partnership of NIH, the Centers for Disease Control and Prevention (CDC), and over 200 public and private organizations to promote awareness of diabetes prevention and control. The site has a wealth of background information on diagnosis, prevention, and treatment. It includes resources for health, education, and business professionals. Publications can be ordered online for free in English, Spanish, and more than 15 other languages.

Subject(s): Diabetes

National Heart, Lung, and Blood Institute (NHLBI)

https://www.nhlbi.nih.gov/

Description: NHLBI organizes resources into sections for the public and for health professionals. The section for the public links to fact sheets and publications on heart and vascular diseases, lung diseases, and blood diseases. The site also links to educational material on high blood cholesterol, high blood pressure, overweight and obesity, and heart attack warning signs. Sections for professionals cover information including clinical practice guidelines, scientific reports, and continuing education. The site also carries announcements of technology transfer opportunities and clinical trials.

Subject(s): Heart Disease—Research

National HIV and STD Testing Resources

https://gettested.cdc.gov/

Description: The site features a nationwide database of testing locations for detecting HIV and other sexually transmitted diseases, along with information about the tests. It provides information in both English and Spanish.

Subject(s): HIV Infections

National Kidney Disease Education Program (NKDEP)

https://www.niddk.nih.gov/health-information/health-communication-programs/nkdep/Pages/default.aspx

Description: The NKDEP site has sections for patients and the public, health professionals, and laboratory professionals. Each section provides detailed information on different aspects of kidney disease diagnosis and care. The site also has a Spanish-language version.

Subject(s): Kidney Disease

NIH Senior Health

https://nihseniorhealth.gov/

Description: The NIH Senior Health website is a joint project of the National Institute on Aging and the National Library of Medicine to produce online content for seniors that is designed in an age-appropriate style. The site uses large print and breaks content into short segments. Topics include Arthritis, Exercise, Osteoporosis, Taking Medicines, and more. Some sections include short video clips with the option of reading the video transcript.

Subject(s): Alzheimer's Disease; Senior Citizens

Office of Cancer Survivorship

https://cancercontrol.cancer.gov/ocs/

Description: This website is designed for researchers, health professionals, advocates, and cancer survivors and their families. Topics include cancer survivorship research, possible late effects of treatment, and clinical practice follow-up guidelines. The site provides reports, fact sheets, information on research funding, news, and conference information.

Subject(s): Cancer

Organ Donation

https://www.organdonor.gov

Description: This Department of Health and Human Services website provides general information on the process of organ and tissue donation and information on how to sign up. It features a downloadable donor card and brochure. The site also covers transplantation basics and how to avoid the risk of needing a transplant. The sections entitled Materials & Resources and Legislation have information on research grants, the National Organ Transplant Act, and organ transplant policy.

Subject(s): Medical Information

President's Malaria Initiative (PMI)

https://www.pmi.gov/

Description: PMI is an interagency effort to fund malaria treatment and prevention in 15 counties in sub-Saharan Africa. It is led by USAID and includes the Department of Health and Human Services, the Department of State, the White House, and other agencies. Its website includes program information and statistical profiles of malaria conditions in the target countries, and information on topics such as mosquito nets and anti-malarial drugs.

Subject(s): Malaria

SAMHSA: Substance Abuse and Mental Health Service Administration Publication Ordering

https://store.samhsa.gov/

Description: The website for the SAMHSA National Clearinghouse provides a wealth of information resources on mental health, substance abuse, prevention, and treatment. Publications can be located by selecting the intended audience, drug name, treatment, or location. Some publications are available in Spanish.

Subject(s): Substance Abuse

HEALTH CARE FINANCE

Centers for Medicare & Medicaid Services (CMS)

https://www.cms.gov/

Description: CMS runs the Medicare program and oversees the federal portions of Medicaid and the Children's Health Insurance Program (CHIP). The CMS website has information on the programs it administers, which also include portions of the Health Insurance Portability and Accountability Act. The Regulations and Guidance section includes CMS program manuals, rulings, transmittals, regulatory updates, and extensive background on major laws. The extensive and varied information in the Research, Statistics, Data & Systems section includes Medicare enrollment tables, the Medicare Current Beneficiary Survey, national health expenditure data, program data sets, and the new Medicare & Medicaid Research Review journal. The site also provides administrative information by provider type, such as hospice or home health agency. The site's FAQs section has a searchable database of answers to common questions.

Much of the information on the CMS site is relevant to health care providers and program administrators. For consumer information on Medicare, see Medicare.gov at https://www.medicare.gov/. For consumer information on CHIP, see Insure Kids Now at https://www.insurekidsnow.gov/. For information on the Affordable Care Act, see https://www.healthcare.gov/. Each of these sites is listed elsewhere in this book.

Subject(s): Health Care Finance; Medicaid; Medicare

Children's Health Insurance Program (CHIP)

https://www.medicaid.gov/chip/chip-program-information.html

Description: The Children's Health Insurance Program (CHIP) is jointly financed by the federal and state governments and is administered by the states. This website has information on the Children's Health Insurance Program Reauthorization Act (CHIPRA) of 2009, CHIP dental coverage, and national CHIP policy.

This site is intended for program administrators. Consumer information on the program is available from the federal website Insure Kids Now at https://www.insurekidsnow.gov/

Subject(s): Health Insurance; Child Health and Safety

HealthCare.gov

https://www.healthcare.gov/

Description: HealthCare.gov is designed to help consumers navigate the health insurance market and learn about the Patient Protection and Affordable Care Act. The site has information on the new law as specifically applies to families with children, individuals, people with disabilities, young adults, and seniors. A section called Get Coverage links to specific health insurance plans based on your home state and demographic information, such as age range, employment or self-employment status, and presence of children. The site also covers preventative care and links to online tools to compare the quality of hospitals, nursing homes, and dialysis facilities.

Subject(s): Health Insurance

Insure Kids Now

https://www.insurekidsnow.gov/

Description: This site links to information on children's health insurance programs in each state and offers answers to a variety of questions about insurance for children. Sections include Medicaid & CHIP Basics, Learn About Programs in Your State, and Questions & Answers. A Spanish-language version of the site is available.

Subject(s): Health Insurance; Child Health and Safety

Medicare Payment Advisory Commission (MedPAC)

http://www.medpac.gov

Description: MedPAC is a nonpartisan congressional advisory body charged with providing policy advice and technical assistance for Medicare payment policies. Major sections of the website are About MedPAC, Public Meetings, Documents, and Research Areas. The home page includes a clickable calendar with upcoming events.

Subject(s): Medicare—Policy

Medicare.gov

https://www.medicare.gov/

Description: This official Medicare site for consumers features Medicare pamphlets and publications, news, and basic explanations of various aspects of Medicare. Sections cover information about Medicare enrollment, plan choices, the prescription drug plan, long-term care, preventive services, billing, and appeals. Under Forms, Help & Resources, the site offers online tools to help consumers find, compare, or evaluate services, such as doctors, nursing homes, Medigap policies, home health care, prescription drug plans, and dialysis facilities. The site features the annual consumer guide *Medicare & You*.

Medicare.gov has a Spanish-language version, a large-text version, and a printable version. The site also links to an access screen for MyMedicare.gov, a personal Medicare beneficiary portal.

Subject(s): Medicare; Nursing Homes

TRICARE: Military Health System

https://tricare.mil/

Description: TRICARE is the health care benefit for the military. This website provides information and documents for TRICARE beneficiaries and providers, including a directory of providers. TRICARE beneficiaries can also log into the TRICARE Online service to conduct transactions such as scheduling appointments.

Subject(s): Health Insurance; Military Medicine

Veterans Health Administration (VHA)

https://www.va.gov/health/

Description: The VHA website is part of the larger Veterans Affairs site. It provides consumer-oriented information and services, with sections on applying for care, refilling a prescription, or finding a VA health facility, as well as a crisis prevention hotline for veterans. In the A–Z index, the site links to VHA information on specific topics, such as dental care, prescriptions, prosthetics and sensory aids, health promotion, and VA medical research.

Subject(s): Veterans

HEALTH OCCUPATIONS

Bureau of Health Workforce (BHW)

https://bhw.hrsa.gov/

Description: The mission of the Bureau of Health Workforce (BHW) improves the health of underserved and vulnerable populations by strengthening the health workforce and connecting skilled professionals to communities in need. We manage the designation of Health Professional Shortage Areas (HPSA) and Medically Underserved Areas/Populations (MUA/P), which are used to determine eligibility for federal programs

Subject(s): Health Occupations—Grants; Medical Schools—Grants

Medical Reserve Corps (MRC)

https://mrc.hhs.gov/HomePage

Description: MRC consists of local units of volunteer medical and public health professionals organized to assist their communities during emergencies and to promote public health. The MRC website has information on volunteering, a directory of MRC units, program news, information on joining or forming a unit, and guidance for existing units.

Subject(s): Disaster Preparedness; Public Health

National Health Service Corps (NHSC)

https://nhsc.hrsa.gov/

Description: NHSC recruits primary care clinicians for medically underserved areas. It offers financial assistance to medical students who will practice in underserved areas, as well as work experience and residencies. The site has online applications and information about NHSC programs.

Subject(s): Health Care

National Practitioner Data Bank (NPDB)

https://www.npdb.hrsa.gov/

Description: NPDB compiles records of malpractice and other adverse reports filed against physicians, dentists, and other health care practitioners. The database is fully available to the general public. A modified version of the data bank file, containing selected information and no identification data, may be downloaded from the site. Under NPDB Resources, the site links to annual reports, the publicly accessible file, and summary statistics from NPDB.

Subject(s): Health Care—Regulations; Health Occupations—Regulations

Uniformed Services University of the Health Sciences (USUHS)

https://www.usuhs.edu/

Description: According to the website, USUHS's mission "is to train, educate and prepare uniformed services health professionals, officers, and leaders to directly support the Military Health System, the National Security and National Defense Strategies of the United States, and the readiness of our Armed Forces." This website provides basic information about the university and its School of Medicine, Graduate School of Nursing, and research.

Subject(s): Medical Schools; Military Medicine

HEALTH POLICY AND PROMOTION

Administration on Aging (AoA)

https://aoa.acl.gov/

Description: The AoA website features resources for the elderly, their families, and professionals who work with the elderly. The main page presents sections for aging statistics, AoA programs, and grant opportunities. The online Eldercare Locator is a nationwide directory assistance service designed to help older persons and caregivers locate local support services. Covered topics include benefits, long-term care, Medicare, and information resources. The Newsroom has social media features, information for the press, and other services related to the aging. The website also offers statistics on the aging population.

Subject(s): Senior Citizens

Adolescent and School Health

https://www.cdc.gov/healthyyouth/

Description: This site deals with both school practices to promote student health and health issues relevant to adolescents. It provides school health education resources, school health policies, statistics, and an evaluation and planning tool called School Health Index. Specific health topics include asthma, obesity, injury and violence, and sexual risk behaviors.

Subject(s): Adolescents; Health Promotion; School Safety

American Indian Health

https://americanindianhealth.nlm.nih.gov/

Description: The mission of this NLM-sponsored site is "to bring together health and medical resources pertinent to the American Indian population, including policies, consumer health information, and research." The site links to online resources from the federal government, academia, and health profession organizations. Information covered includes health care access, traditional healing, environmental health, and research. A Health Topics section points to similar specialized resources.

Subject(s): Health Promotion; American Indians

Center for Global Health

https://www.cdc.gov/globalhealth/index.html

Description: The CDC's Center for Global Health focuses on collaborating with other nations and international organizations to promote healthy lifestyles and to prevent high rates of disease, disability, and death in the global health arena. The website spotlights efforts focusing on AIDS, malaria, influenza, polio, and global disease detection. The site describes numerous other initiatives in such areas as environmental health, migration and quarantine, and foodborne infections. The site also has information on the International Health Regulations (IHR), global training opportunities, and global health funding.

Subject(s): Health Care—International

Chronic Disease Prevention

https://www.cdc.gov/chronicdisease/

Description: NCCDPHP works to reduce the incidence of such chronic diseases as diabetes, cancer, and heart disease. Chronic disease programs also address topics such as arthritis, tobacco use, nutrition and physical activity, and teen pregnancy. The agency's website describes its various programs, grants, research, and public health surveillance. The site has summary facts and graphs derived from its surveillance programs for behavioral risk factors, youth risk behavior, cancer registries, and pregnancy risks. On the homepage, a clickable map of the United States allows users to access state profiles that include information about programs and funding, as well as health indicators and other useful statistics and data.

Subject(s): Health Promotion; Preventive Health Care

Consumer Health Information

https://www.fda.gov/forconsumers/

Description: The FDA compiles a wide variety of consumer health information on this website. The site has consumer news, recalls, and product alerts, with an RSS news feed and e-mail service for updates. The news covers drugs, medical devices, cosmetics, food, and other products under FDA regulation. The site also has a section providing fraud alerts and guidance. The Consumer Information by Audience section has tips for patients, women, health educators, and others. Some online publications are available in both English and Spanish.

Subject(s): Consumer Information

Department of Bioethics

https://www.bioethics.nih.gov/home/index.shtml

Description: The Department of Bioethics is part of the NIH Clinical Center. According to the website it "conducts conceptual, empirical, and policy-related research into bioethical issues; offers comprehensive training to future bioethicists and educational programs for biomedical researchers and clinical providers; and provides high quality ethics consultation services to clinicians, patients, and families of the NIH's Clinical Center and advice to the NIH IRBs, investigators, and others on the ethical conduct of research."

Subject(s): Bioethics—Policy

Division of Community Health (DCH)

https://www.cdc.gov/nccdphp/dch/

Description: Through its Community Health Status Indicators (CHSI) online application, the DCH website presents over 3,000 county health status profiles representing each county in the United States excluding territories. Users can also make customized brochures with the county's health indicators and download the data for their own projects. CHSI is a project of the Health and Human Services Department and several nonprofit health associations.

Subject(s): Health Statistics

girlshealth.gov

https://www.girlshealth.gov/

Description: girlshealth.gov is designed to help adolescent girls learn about the health issues and social situations that they will encounter during their teen years. Sections provide information about fitness, nutrition, bullying, relationships, and other related topics. The site also has sections for parents, caregivers, and teachers.

Subject(s): Health Promotion; Kids' Pages

Health Resources and Services Administration (HRSA)

https://www.hrsa.gov/index.html

Description: HRSA works to expand health care access for the uninsured, underserved, and special needs populations. HRSA concerns include health care for uninsured people, people living with HIV/AIDS, maternal health, rural health, organ transplants and donations, and emergency preparedness. The site includes information on current and past grants and an online grant application process. Under the Data and Statistics heading, data about Shortage Areas, the Organ Transplantation Program, and the National Health Service Corps is available.

The HRSA website provides extensive information on the many programs they operate, providing information for administrators and users of health care, researchers, and policy makers.

Subject(s): Public Health

Health.gov

https://health.gov/

Description: This health gateway site consists of links to federal health initiatives information, government health agency sites, and other government-produced information. Site content is also available in Spanish.

Subject(s): Health and Safety

Healthy People 2020

https://www.healthypeople.gov/

Description: This site has information on the Healthy People 2020 national health promotion initiative. A major part of the effort is to establish metrics for measuring progress in the population's health. The Topics & Objectives section breaks down the program's goals by health topic.

Subject(s): Health and Safety—Statistics; Health Promotion

Health Center Program

https://www.bphc.hrsa.gov/

Description: The site describes HRSA's Bureau of Primary Health Care, whose Health Center Program is designed to provide primary health care services to medically underserved communities and vulnerable populations. The site has a directory of health care centers, information on how public and private nonprofit health care organizations may apply to receive funding under the program, and related policy and administrative information. The site's Uniform Data System has statistics on program operations, including information on health care for the homeless, migrants, and public housing residents.

Subject(s): Hospitals and Clinics—Grants

HRSA Telehealth

https://www.hrsa.gov/rural-health/telehealth/index.html

Description: This site describes telehealth as "the use of electronic information and telecommunications technologies to support long-distance clinical health care, patient and professional health-related education, and public health and health administration." The site features telehealth-related publications and grants information.

Subject(s): Telemedicine

Indian Health Service (IHS)

https://www.ihs.gov/

Description: IHS is the primary federal agency responsible for providing health care services to American Indians and Alaska Natives. Major sections of the IHS website include About IHS, Locations, For Patients, For Providers, Community Health, Career Opportunities, and Newsroom. The About IHS section includes legal and policy information, publications, and organizational overviews. The website includes a search engine, frequently asked questions, and an A–Z index.

IHS Fact Sheets can be accessed at https://www.ihs.gov/newsroom/factsheets. This is a user-friendly webpage with basic information on topics such as behavioral health, diabetes, Indian health disparities, and IHS budget planning with tribes.

Subject(s): Health Care; American Indians

Interagency Autism Coordinating Committee (IACC)

https://iacc.hhs.gov/

Description: IACC, a federal advisory committee, coordinates all aspects of Department of Health and Human Services involvement with autism spectrum disorders (ASDs). IACC meetings, which are open to the public, are summarized on the Meetings & Events page. The site also includes sections on the various IACC subcommittees, as well as reports and meetings from non-IACC sources.

Subject(s): Mental Health

National Committee on Vital and Health Statistics (NCVHS)

https://www.ncvhs.hhs.gov

Description: NCVHS is concerned with the quality of the health data and statistics that inform national health policy, including issues of privacy and confidentiality. Reports, recommendations, and meeting recordings from the full committee and its working groups are available on the website.

Subject(s): Medical Information—Policy

NIDA for Teens: The Science Behind Drug Abuse

https://teens.drugabuse.gov/

Description: NIDA for Teens is designed to provide adolescents ages 11 through 15 (as well as their parents and teachers) with science-based facts about how drugs affect the brain and body. The site includes fact sheets on specific drugs and classes of drugs, teens' questions, informative blog postings, and interactive online activities.

Subject(s): Adolescents; Drug Abuse

Office of the Assistant Secretary for Planning and Evaluation (ASPE)

https://aspe.hhs.gov/

Description: ASPE advises the secretary of HHS on policy development, strategic planning, policy research, and economic analyses. The main portion of the homepage is set up to perform literature searches on topics of concern to ASPE, such as child welfare, disability, insurance, and substance abuse. The In the Spotlight section covers topics such as Affordable Care Act research and poverty and income statistics. A section called Most Viewed links to the HHS Poverty Guidelines.

Subject(s): Health Care—Policy; Social Services—Policy

Office of Lead Hazard Control and Healthy Homes (OLHCHH)

https://www.hud.gov/program_offices/healthy_homes

Description: OLHCHH provides funding to state and local government entities in order to eradicate the threat of lead poisoning in homes. The site has links to associated programs and grants, information about such topics as lead and radon, and direct links to popular related posts.

Subject(s): Lead Poisoning

Office of National AIDS Policy (ONAP)

https://obamawhitehouse.archives.gov/administration/eop/onap

Description: The website contains archives from the Obama administration's White House Office of National AIDS Policy. It provided information on the National HIV/AIDS Strategy and maintained a blog reporting policy and program developments.

Subject(s): AIDS—Policy

Office of Population Affairs (OPA)

https://www.hhs.gov/opa/

Description: OPA operates programs concerned with reproductive health, family planning, and adolescent pregnancy. Its website offers sections on health topics, such as contraception, and on OPA activities, such as grant programs and funding. The Legislation Mandates section, under Title X Family Planning, has the full text of the statutes and regulations under which OPA operates.

Subject(s): Family Planning, Reproductive Health

Office of Science Policy—National Institutes of Health

https://osp.od.nih.gov/clinical-research/clinical-research-policy/

Description: According to the website, the office of Science Policy offers "various offices and programs work on a wide range of issues including biosafety, biosecurity, genetic testing, genomic data sharing, human subjects protections, the organization and management of the NIH, and the outputs and value of NIH-funded research. This is accomplished through a wide range of analyses and reports, commentary on emerging policy proposals, and the development of policy proposals for consideration by NIH, the Federal government, and the public."

Subject(s): Clinical research and bioethics

Office of Rural Health Policy (ORHP)

https://www.hrsa.gov/rural-health/index.html

Description: This website for ORHP provides information on federal government grants, policy, and research focused on improving health conditions in rural America. It also reports on HRSA's Border Health Initiative, which it manages. For further information, the site links to rural health publications and related websites.

Subject(s): Rural Health—Policy

Office of the Surgeon General

https://www.surgeongeneral.gov/

Description: The Surgeon General's website has current and historical information on the office, including portraits and biographies of all previous surgeons general. It contains speeches made by the surgeon general, testimony before Congress, and general information on public health priorities such as preventing childhood obesity. The site has the full texts of reports issued by the surgeon general.

The Priorities section provides information about the office's tobacco, prevention, breastfeeding support, and family health history reports.

Subject(s): Public Health—Policy

Office of the U.S. Global AIDS Coordinator

https://www.state.gov/s/gac/

Description: As stated on the website, "The U. S. Global AIDS Coordinator's mission is to lead implementation of the U.S. President's Emergency Plan for AIDS Relief (PEPFAR)." The site provides basic information on the office. For more information on the plan, see https://www.pepfar.gov/.

Subject(s): AIDS—International

President's Council on Physical Fitness, Sports & Nutrition

https://www.hhs.gov/fitness/index-a.html

Description: Established by executive order in 1956, the President's Council on Physical Fitness, Sports & Nutrition promotes physical fitness and good nutrition for Americans of all ages. The website has information on the history, mission, and membership of the council under the About PCFSN section. The Resource Center section includes the quarterly *Elevate Health*, a summary of the latest scientific information on issues relating to physical activity and diet.

Subject(s): Physical Fitness; Sports

President's Emergency Plan for AIDS Relief (PEPFAR)

https://www.pepfar.gov/

Description: PEPFAR involves strategic funding to combat HIV/AIDS in over 120 countries. The website includes information on participating countries, implementing agencies, policy guidance, reports to Congress, and PEPFAR reports. Links to PEPFAR social media pages are also provided.

Subject(s): AIDS—International; Foreign Assistance; HIV Infections—International

President's New Freedom Commission on Mental Health

http://govinfo.library.unt.edu/mentalhealthcommission/

Description: The President's New Freedom Commission on Mental Health was charged with studying the U.S. mental health service delivery system and advising the president on methods to improve it. The Commission presented its final report in July 2003. The commission's website has been archived at the address above thanks to a partnership between the University of North Texas Libraries and the U.S. Government Publishing Office.

Subject(s): Mental Health—Policy

Protecting Children's Environmental Health

https://www.epa.gov/children

Description: Children face special and increased risks from exposure to environmental pollutants. This website explains the risks and how to minimize them. Sections include What You Can Do to Protect Children, Children's Environmental Health Facts, and Pediatric Environmental Health Toolkit. The site also offers publications, regulatory information, data, and other extensive coverage of the topic.

Subject(s): Child Health and Safety; Environmental Health

Reports of the Surgeon General

https://profiles.nlm.nih.gov/NN/

Description: This site carries the full texts of all official surgeon general reports, beginning with *Smoking and Health* in 1964, the first report given. The National Library of Medicine has digitized these along with conference proceedings, pamphlets, photographs, and brochures from the Office of the Surgeon General. Historical information on the office and on U.S. public health supplements the reports.

Subject(s): Public Health—Policy

Smokefree.gov

https://www.smokefree.gov/

Description: NCI maintains this website to help smokers quit and to disseminate free anti-smoking materials. In the Methods That Work For You section, the site lists and describes a variety of different methods for quitting smoking,

Subject(s): Smoking

Specialized Information Services (SIS) Division

https://www.sis.nlm.nih.gov/

Description: The SIS Division of NLM is responsible for information resources and services in toxicology, environmental health, HIV/AIDS, drugs and household products, emergency preparedness and response, and topics in regard to special population groups. Its website features information products in each of these areas. The website also includes information from the SIS Outreach and Special Populations Branch, which focuses on improving access to quality health information in special populations.

Subject(s): Health Promotion; Environmental Health

Substance Abuse and Mental Health Services Administration (SAMHSA)

https://www.samhsa.gov/

Description: SAMHSA administers grants, programs, training, and public education campaigns to assist those working to combat substance abuse and mental illness. The website's Topics section organizes SAMHSA program information into subject areas, such as co-occurring disorders, health reform, suicide prevention, the SAMHSA Syringe Exchange Program, and National Children's Mental Health Awareness Day. The site also links to treatment center directories. The Data section offers reports and data from the National Survey on Drug Use and Health (NSDUH) and the Drug Abuse Warning Network (DAWN), and other sources. SAMHSA has RSS feeds for announcements of new publications and awareness campaigns. The site is also available in Spanish.

Subject(s): Mental Health; Substance Abuse

Women's health.gov

https://www.womenshealth.gov/

Description: This site from the Office of Women's Health from the U.S. Department of Health and Human Services provides information on a wide range of topics related to women's health care. It was established in 1991 to improve the health of U.S. women by advancing and coordinating a comprehensive women's health agenda. Its goals as stated on its website are to: inform and influence policies, educate the public, educate health professionals, and support innovative programs. Between September and October 2017, this website removed a page that contained comprehensive information about lesbian and bisexual health.

Subject(s): Women's health

Youth Tobacco Prevention

https://www.cdc.gov/tobacco/basic_information/youth/

Description: This CDC site links to an extensive list of resources about young people and smoking. Resources include research reports, content especially for children, and materials (such as videos and program guides) for adults responsible for organizing anti-smoking campaigns for children.

Subject(s): Smoking; Tobacco; Kids' Pages

HEALTH RESEARCH

Agency for Healthcare Research and Quality (AHRQ)

https://www.ahrq.gov/

Description: AHRQ supports research to improve the quality of health care and reduce its cost and broaden its access. Its website features a wide range of resources in sections including Health Care Information, For Patients & Consumers, Research Tools & Data, and Funding & Grants. Some consumer publications are available in Spanish.

Subject(s): Health Policy

Arctic Health

https://arctichealth.nlm.nih.gov/

Description: NLM's Arctic Health website is a central point for information on Arctic health and environment. The site has research and publications databases and covers such topics as diseases, traditional medicine, climate change, and telemedicine. Arctic Health, which defines the Arctic as encompassing all or portions of Alaska, Canada, Greenland/Denmark/Faroe Islands, Iceland, Norway, Sweden, Finland, and Russia, is built on the premise that the populations of these countries are subject to a unique set of health and environmental challenges. Along with NLM, the site is co-sponsored by University of Alaska Anchorage's Alaska Medical Library.

Subject(s): Arctic Regions

Armed Forces Medical Examiner System (AFMES)

https://health.mil/afmes/

Description: According to the website, AFMES "provides worldwide comprehensive medico-legal services and investigations." AFMES specializes in the areas of forensic pathology, forensic toxicology, DNA technology and identification, and mortality surveillance. The website contains contact information as well as a collection of service request forms.

Subject(s): Forensics; Toxicology (Medicine)

Cancer Research Network

https://crn.cancer.gov/

Description: The Cancer Research Network is a consortium funded by NCI to conduct research on cancer prevention, early detection, treatment, long-term care, and surveillance. The website identifies the participating health plans and research centers and describes the nature of the research. Research areas include prevention and screening, epidemiology of prognosis and outcomes, health care quality and cost, and communications and dissemination.

Subject(s): Cancer—Research

Cancer.gov Clinical Trials

https://www.cancer.gov/about-cancer/treatment/clinical-trials

Description: This NCI site provides information on cancer-related clinical trials. A database of trials can be searched by type of cancer, type of trial, and location of trial. The site also has educational materials about clinical trials and information from recent clinical trials.

Subject(s): Cancer; Clinical Trials

Center for Information Technology (CIT)

https://cit.nih.gov/

Description: According to the website, "In 1998 the Center for Information Technology (CIT) was formed, combining the functions of the Division of Computer Research and Technology (DCRT), the Office of Information Resources Management (OIRM), and the Telecommunications Branch." Major sections of the website for CIT, which is part of NIH, include CIT Service Catalog, Information Security, Support, Science, IT Policies, and About CIT. The Science Catalog includes a list of tools and resources and computational SIGs. The About CIT section includes sections with information for collaborators and partners, job seekers, scientists, staff, "techies," vendors, and visitors.

Subject(s): Information Technology

ClinicalTrials.gov

https://clinicaltrials.gov/

Description: NLM has developed this site to provide patients, family members, and the public with current information about clinical research studies sponsored privately and by the federal government. ClinicalTrials.gov currently contains over 200,000 trials with locations in every U.S. state and over 190 countries. Users may search the database by disease or condition, location of the trial, study type, and other criteria.

Subject(s): Clinical Trials—International

Environmental Health Perspectives: EHP Online

https://ehp.niehs.nih.gov/

Description: The EHP Online site provides free access to the NIEHS peer-reviewed journal *Environmental Health Perspectives* and its Chinese-language edition. Issues of the journal are online from 1972 to the present. EHP offers updates via e-mail alerts. Podcasts are also available. Paid subscriptions are required for the print version of the journal.

Subject(s): Environmental Health

Epidemic Intelligence Service (EIS)

https://www.cdc.gov/eis/

Description: EIS is a surveillance and response unit for all types of epidemics in the United States and throughout the world. EIS employs physicians and other health specialists seeking a postgraduate program of service and on-the-job training in the practice of epidemiology. The site includes information about EIS's work and program eligibility.

Subject(s): Epidemiology; Public Health—Research

Fogarty International Center (FIC)

https://www.fic.nih.gov

Description: FIC promotes international cooperation and advanced study in the biomedical sciences. It fosters research partnerships between American scientists and their foreign counterparts through research and training grants, fellowships, exchange awards, and international agreements. The website provides information on these activities and on FIC programs. The site also lists available grant opportunities.

Subject(s): Biological Medicine—Grants; Medical Research—International

National Cancer Institute (NCI)

https://www.cancer.gov/

Description: The NCI website provides information on over 100 types of cancer. It has a cancer drug dictionary. The site also includes sections on research programs, research funding, and clinical trials information, as well as others featuring statistics, news, and free informational booklets to download. Some information is available in Spanish. The About NCI section has links to NCI's main divisions, to its advisory boards, and to information on legislation and funding related to cancer research. The Cancer Statistics section (under About Cancer) has information on the public-use Surveillance, Epidemiology, and End Results (SEER) program, described elsewhere in this chapter. State cancer profiles, maps and graphs of cancer data, and online interfaces to query cancer data are also provided.

NCI's website is easy to navigate and is an important starting point for many cancer information needs.

Subject(s): Cancer

National Center for Advancing Translational Sciences (NCATS)

https://ncats.nih.gov/

Description: According to the website, "the mission of the National Center for Advancing Translational Sciences (NCATS) at the National Institutes of Health (NIH) is to catalyze the generation of innovative methods and technologies that will enhance the development, testing, and implementation of diagnostics and therapeutics across a wide range of human diseases and conditions." NCATS has three major program areas: Clinical and Translational Science, Rare Disease Research and Therapeutics, and Re-engineering Translational Sciences. Major sections include Research (with a program index), Funding & Notices, and News & Media.

Subject(s): Health Research

National Center for Complementary and Integrative Health (NCCIH)

https://nccih.nih.gov/

Description: NCCIH is concerned with health care practices that are outside the realm of conventional medicine as practiced in the United States. Its website describes research grant opportunities and priorities and the clinical trials it conducts. The Health Info section addresses popular topics, such as acupuncture and homeopathy. It also has information for the consumer on choosing alternative medicines or treatments. Some consumer information is available in Spanish.

Subject(s): Alternative Medicine

National Center for Toxicological Research (NCTR)

https://www.fda.gov/nctr/

Description: NCTR conducts peer-reviewed scientific research in support and anticipation of the FDA's regulatory needs. Initiatives include programs in food safety, bioinformatics, biostatistics, computational toxicology, and nanotechnology. NCTR research divisions include Biochemical Toxicology, Microbiology, Neurotoxicology, Bioinformatics and Biostatistics, Genetic and Molecular Toxicology, and Systems Biology.

Subject(s): Biotechnology—Research; Toxicology (Medicine)—Research

National Institute on Minority Health and Health Disparities (NIMHD)

https://www.nimhd.nih.gov/

Description: NIMHD supports programs involving basic and clinical research, training, and the dissemination of health information to reduce disparities in health for minority population groups. This site has information about the office and its programs, as well as news releases and an events schedule.

Subject(s): Medical Research—Policy; Minority Groups

National Council on Disability (NCD)

https://ncd.gov/

Description: NCD is an independent agency that works with Congress and the Executive Branch on disability-related policy. The NCD Policy Areas section, under About Us, details the wide variety of issues on which the agency works. Educational sources can be found in the Resources section.

Subject(s): Disability

National Eye Institute (NEI)

https://www.nei.nih.gov/

Description: NEI supports research to prevent and treat eye diseases and other vision disorders. The Health Information section includes fact sheets and guides written at the consumer level. These cover glaucoma, macular degeneration, diabetic eye disease, eye anatomy, and other topics. Many of the guides are also available in Spanish. The site also has information on research funding and on the public awareness campaigns supported by NEI.

Subject(s): Vision Disorders—Research

National Institute of Allergy and Infectious Diseases (NIAID)

https://www.niaid.nih.gov/

Description: NIAID supports and conducts basic research in immunology, microbiology, and infectious disease. On its website, users can explore research on AIDS, allergic diseases, asthma, biodefense, E. coli, hepatitis, influenza, malaria, tuberculosis, and more. Agency information on this site includes research grant announcements and NIAID laboratory profiles. On the research side, the site describes each research activity and related clinical trials, news, and resources. The website has a detailed A–Z index for its health and research topics.

Subject(s): AIDS—Research; Allergies—Research; Diseases and Conditions—Research; Medical Research—Grants

National Institute of Arthritis and Musculoskeletal and Skin Diseases (NIAMS)

https://www.niams.nih.gov/

Description: The NIAMS website features health information, information about basic research, clinical and epidemiologic research, research databases, and information on grant opportunities in the fields of rheumatology, orthopedics, dermatology, metabolic bone diseases, heritable disorders of bone and cartilage, inherited and inflammatory muscle diseases, and sports medicine. The Health Information section includes pamphlets on such conditions as acne, arthritis, back pain, fibromyalgia, gout, knee problems, lupus, osteoporosis, vitiligo, and sports injuries. The site also has a Spanish-language version available, as well as information in Chinese.

Subject(s): Arthritis—Research; Diseases and Conditions—Research; Medical Research—Grants

National Institute of Biomedical Imaging and Bioengineering (NIBIB)

https://www.nibib.nih.gov/

Description: NIBIB supports research to develop innovative technologies that improve health care. The website includes information on funding opportunities, training, and job vacancies. It also has a directory of NIBIB Biomedical Technology Resource Centers throughout the United States. A version of the site is also available in Spanish.

Subject(s): Biotechnology; Medical Computing

National Institute of Child Health and Human Development (NICHD)

https://www.nichd.nih.gov

Description: NICHD's full name is the Eunice Kennedy Shriver National Institute of Child Health and Human Development. It conducts research, clinical trials, and epidemiological studies related to the health of the human growth, development, and reproductive processes. The website has information about NICHD, its divisions, grants and contracts, intramural research, and fellowships. The Health & Research section has information on numerous child health and human development topics.

Subject(s): Reproductive Health—Research; Child Health and Safety—Research

National Institute of Dental and Craniofacial Research (NIDCR)

https://www.nidcr.nih.gov/

Description: The NIDCR website offers a substantial collection of documents and information on dental research. Major sections include Oral Health, Clinical Trials, Research, Grants & Funding, and Careers & Training. Under Research, the Tools for Researchers subsection links to specialized databases and research centers related to microbiology and immunology and to craniofacial development. The Oral Health section links to publications and resources on topics such as fluoride, smokeless tobacco, temporomandibular joint and muscle disorders, and oral complications of systemic diseases. The site also has sections for finding low-cost dental care, oral health statistics, and material in Spanish.

Subject(s): Dental Health—Research

National Institute of Diabetes and Digestive and Kidney Diseases (NIDDK)

https://www.niddk.nih.gov/

Description: The NIDDK website features information on disorders studied by the agency, including diabetes, digestive diseases, endocrine diseases, hematologic diseases, kidney diseases, and urologic diseases. Sections include Health Information, Research & Funding for Scientists, and News. Spanish-language pamphlets are also available.

Subject(s): Diabetes—Research; Medical Research—Grants; Kidney Disease—Research

National Institute of Environmental Health Sciences (NIEHS)

https://www.niehs.nih.gov/

Description: NIEHS, an institute for research on environment-related diseases, links to a wide variety of information for health researchers, the general public, and teachers. The site identifies diseases and conditions, such as asthma and lung disease, that may be strongly related to environmental exposures. It also describes NIEHS scientific and clinical research, research grants, and research databases. For teachers and students, the site has a Science Education section under Health & Education.

Subject(s): Toxicology (Medicine)—Research; Environmental Health—Research

National Institute of Mental Health (NIMH)

https://www.nimh.nih.gov/index.shtml

Description: NIMH conducts and funds research on mental and behavioral disorders, and works to educate the public on mental health topics. The site has information on NIMH grants and on its intramural research. The Health Topics section links to specific areas of NIMH research, such as autism spectrum disorder, eating disorders, and schizophrenia. For the public, the NIMH site also has information on medications, coping with traumatic events, getting help, and suicide prevention. For researchers, the site provides information on grants and research contracts. Some information is available in Spanish.

Subject(s): Brain—Research; Mental Health—Research

National Institute of Neurological Disorders and Stroke (NINDS)

https://www.ninds.nih.gov/

Description: NINDS supports biomedical research on disorders of the brain and nervous system. For researchers, the site has information on research funding, research plans, and the text of workshop and conference proceedings. The Disorders A–Z section of the site is an extensive guide to numerous neurological disorders, such as Alzheimer's disease, autism, epilepsy, multiple sclerosis, Parkinson's disease, and stroke. The site also has a Spanish-language version.

Subject(s): Brain—Research

National Institute of Nursing Research (NINR)

https://www.ninr.nih.gov/

Description: The NINR site features information on the broad range of nursing research. The site includes sections for About NINR, News & Information, Research & Funding, and Training. News & Information has NINR-supported investigator publications and summaries of NINR-supported research, as well as articles and podcasts. The Research & Funding section has grant information, information on NINR supported projects, and information about NINR intramural and extramural research. The Training section is designed for training researchers.

Subject(s): Nursing—Research

National Institute on Aging (NIA)

https://www.nia.nih.gov/

Description: NIA provides leadership in aging research (including Alzheimer's disease research), training, health information dissemination, and other programs related to aging. The site has information on research funding opportunities and research training support. The Research and Funding section offers further details on NIA research areas and funding opportunities. The Health and Aging section has publications and a directory of related organizations. Under About NIA, the site also has information on the National Advisory Council on Aging, which reviews applications for funding and training and makes recommendations to NIA regarding research plans. Some information is available in Spanish.

Subject(s): Medical Research—Grants; Senior Citizens

National Institute on Alcohol Abuse and Alcoholism (NIAAA)

https://www.niaaa.nih.gov/

Description: NIAAA conducts and supports research and education to reduce alcohol-related problems in the population. The NIAAA site features the sections About NIAAA, Publications & Multimedia, Research, Alcohol & Your Health, News & Events, and Grant Funding. Publications include the full text of the bulletin *Alcohol Alert*, along with pamphlets and research monographs.

Subject(s): Alcohol Abuse

National Institute on Deafness and Other Communication Disorders (NIDCD)

https://www.nidcd.nih.gov/

Description: NIDCD conducts and supports research about the normal and disordered processes of hearing, balance, smell, taste, voice, speech, and language. The website has information on the institute and its research grants programs. The section on NIDCD research describes its work in such areas as the biophysics and mechanics of sensory cells and gene structure and function. The Health Info section has resources for the general public on topics such as ear infections, hearing aids, balance disorders, dysphagia, and stuttering. Some resources in this section are available in Spanish.

Subject(s): Hearing Disorders—Research

National Institute on Disability, Independent Living, and Rehabilitation Research (NIDILRR)

https://acl.gov/programs/nidilrr/

Description: Through sponsoring disability and rehabilitation research, NIDILRR's mission is to improve the quality of life for people with disabilities. The Resources section of the site provides links to a variety of publications and databases. The Grant-Funding Programs & Awards section lists projects currently funded by NIDILRR.

Subject(s): Disabilities—Research

National Institute on Drug Abuse (NIDA)

https://www.drugabuse.gov/

Description: NIDA supports research and education to reduce drug abuse and addiction. The Drugs of Abuse section on the NIDA website provides fact sheets, statistics, and information on drug testing and treatment research. The site has a section for researchers with information on grants, funding, ongoing research, and clinical trials, as well as sections for medical and health professionals, parents and teachers, and students and young adults. It also provides extensive information in Spanish.

The NIDA website is easy to use and a recommended first stop for non-technical information on the science of drug abuse and addiction.

Subject(s): Drug Abuse

National Institutes of Health (NIH)

https://www.nih.gov/

Description: The NIH website is a key starting point for finding government-related health sciences information. Sections include Health Information, Grants & Funding, News & Events, Research & Training, Institutes at NIH, and About NIH. The About NIH section covers its mission, organization, leadership, staff, and budget. The Institutes at NIH section links to the many component NIH organizations. The Health Information section has resources for the general public on health topics, clinical studies, and drug information, with links to health databases and health hotlines.

The Grants & Funding section features NIH funding opportunities and application kits, grants policy, and award data. New funding announcements can be viewed online or sent automatically via e-mail or RSS feed. The Research & Training section covers NIH intramural research news, postdoctoral and clinical training opportunities, and laboratory research resources. The News & Events section has news, social media links, and podcasts. The site also has a Spanish-language version.

NIH is a significant health sciences and medical research institution. This central NIH site contains excellent information about NIH and its component organizations. More importantly, the site links to an important body of NIH resources in the health sciences for the general public, health science researchers, and health science professionals. Many of the NIH component websites are listed in this publication.

Subject(s): Diseases and Conditions—Research; Medical Research—Grants

National Institutes of Health Public Access

https://publicaccess.nih.gov/

Description: Peer-reviewed journal manuscripts based on NIH-funded research are required to be submitted to the NIH PubMed Central online repository. This site provides an explanation of the policy and instructions for compliance.

Subject(s): Publishing—Policy; Health Research—Policy

National Toxicology Program (NTP)

https://ntp.niehs.nih.gov/

Description: NTP is an interagency program conducting toxicity/carcinogenicity studies on agents suspected of posing hazards to human health. Hundreds of chemical studies are on file, and much of this information is available on the NTP website.

This site contains a significant amount of toxicological data for researchers and those interested in the scientific basis for the regulation of toxic chemicals.

Subject(s): Toxicology (Medicine)—Research

NCI at Frederick

https://ncifrederick.cancer.gov/Default.aspx

Description: NCI at Frederick is one of the main NCI cancer research centers. It focuses on direct research to help identify the causes of cancer, AIDS, and related diseases. Under the Our Science heading, the NCI at Frederick website links to its laboratories, branches, programs, and investigators. The site also has information on its support services and training and a visitor's guide.

Subject(s): Cancer—Research

NIH Center for Scientific Review

https://public.csr.nih.gov/pages/default.aspx

Description: The Center for Scientific Review receives all grant applications sent to NIH and organizes the peer review groups for a majority of the research grants. The website has a section with resources for grant applicants and a section for those serving in peer review study sections.

Subject(s): Grants Management; Health Research—Grants

NIH Clinical Center

https://www.cc.nih.gov/

Description: The NIH Clinical Center is a specialized research hospital at the National Institutes of Health. It is involved in a variety of clinical studies, and the website features a section about participating in these. For researchers and physicians, the site has information about research opportunities, information for referring physicians, summary information on research activities, and other resources.

Subject(s): Clinical Medicine

NIH Common Fund

https://commonfund.nih.gov/

Description: The NIH Common Fund is an effort by NIH to identify and pursue areas that the agency must address as a whole, rather than leaving them to be addressed by the individual institutes within NIH. The focuses of Common Fund programs include clinical research training, nanomedicine, and structural biology. The website provides background on the target areas and has information on funding opportunities, workshops, and news within the targeted research areas.

Subject(s): Health Research—Policy

NIH Office of the Director

https://www.nih.gov/institutes-nih/nih-office-director

Description: The director of NIH oversees the director's office and 27 institutes and centers. The Office of the Director website has information about the director, communications, policy, research, administration, and funding.

Subject(s): Health Policy

Office of Animal Care and Use

https://oacu.oir.nih.gov/

Description: This office provides oversight of animal care and use at NIH. The site is designed as an informational resource for NIH scientists and others at NIH involved in biomedical research. It includes information on NIH policy, guidelines, regulations, and standards, as well as information on health and safety issues.

Subject(s): Animals; Biological Medicine—Research

Office of Behavioral and Social Sciences Research (OBSSR)

https://obssr.od.nih.gov/

Description: OBSSR promotes research into how behavioral and social factors, such as family environment or cognitive issues, influence health. The website explains this field of research and lists opportunities for education and funding in the field.

Subject(s): Mental Health—Research; Social Science Research

Office of Disease Prevention (ODP)

https://prevention.nih.gov/

Description: ODP coordinates preventive medical research across NIH centers and with agencies and organizations outside NIH. The website has information about prevention research at NIH.

Subject(s): Preventive Health Care—Research

Profiles in Science

https://profiles.nlm.nih.gov/

Description: NLM's Profiles in Science website presents information on twentieth-century leaders in biomedical research and public health. For each profiled person, the site includes biographical information and a collection of digitized materials, such as manuscripts, journal articles, photographs, and video clips.

Subject(s): Biographies; Health Research—History

Research Portfolio Online Reporting Tools (RePORT)

https://report.nih.gov/

Description: RePORT provides reports and data on the research activities of NIH. The site has a searchable database of NIH reports and most frequently requested statistical reports, such as average research grant size. The site's Categorical Spending section reports total spending by topic, such as heart disease or genetics. The centerpiece of the website is RePORTER, which enables detailed searching of a repository of NIH-funded research projects and provides access to publications and patents resulting from NIH funding.

Subject(s): Health Research

Stem Cell Information

https://stemcells.nih.gov/

Description: This NIH site includes information on research and federal policy, and frequently asked questions, about stem cell research. The Current Research section provides an overview of research at NIH and non-NIH institutions. The General Information section offers substantial background information on stem cells and stem cell research, including a glossary and links to external websites that cover ethical issues of stem cell research. Another section covers related federal policy, statements, and legislation.

Subject(s): Biology—Research

MEDICAL INFORMATION

CDC WONDER

https://wonder.cdc.gov/

Description: CDC WONDER provides a single point of access to a variety of CDC reports, guidelines, and numeric public health data. The numeric databases can provide the numbers and rates for many diseases and health occurrences, including sexually transmitted diseases, cancer cases, and types of mortality and births in the United States. A list of topics covered on CDC WONDER is available by major area (such as communicable diseases) and in an alphabetical list.

Subject(s): Public Health—Statistics

Evaluating Internet Health Information

https://medlineplus.gov/webeval/

Description: This site provides a tutorial on evaluating the health information that can be found on the Internet. The tutorial can be viewed online or downloaded for use without an Internet connection.

Subject(s): Internet

healthfinder.gov

https://healthfinder.gov/

Description: healthfinder.gov is designed to assist consumers in finding government health information on the Internet. It links to selected publications, databases, websites, support and self-help groups, and government health agencies. The site has consumer health news available by e-mail or as an RSS newsfeed, in English and Spanish. A version of the site is also available in Spanish.

This site is an excellent starting point for finding health information and information about health services at the consumer level, rather than the more technical information available elsewhere for medical practitioners and researchers.

Subject(s): Health Care; Medical Information; Finding Aids

HealthIT.gov

https://www.healthit.gov/

Description: This umbrella site provides information on the efforts of federal and state government and private partnerships to implement electronic management of medical information. The site is a joint effort between the Office of the National Coordinator for Health Information Technology (ONC) and the Agency for Health Research and Quality (AHRQ); more agencies may also join. The site also states that it "makes it possible for health care providers to better manage patient care through secure use and sharing of health information." Major topics include health IT funding opportunities, programs, federal advisory committees, and regulatory guidance. It also has a blog called Health IT Buzz.

Subject(s): Medical Records

Lister Hill National Center for Biomedical Communications

https://lhncbc.nlm.nih.gov/

Description: Lister Hill specializes in health care communication, computing, and information sciences. The website features its work in biomedical informatics, multimedia visualization, knowledge and language processing, and other areas. The site carries related journal articles and technical publications.

Subject(s): Information Technology—Research; Medical Computing—Research

MedlinePlus

https://medlineplus.gov/

Description: MedlinePlus, the main NLM consumer health information website, presents information on hundreds of diseases and conditions, along with a guide to medications and supplements. The core of the site is the Health Topics section, a portal to a wide range of health issues. For each medical condition, MedlinePlus provides basic information and any other resources that may be useful to the public, such as surgery videos or interactive tutorials. For those who wish to go directly to the videos, there is a Videos & Tools section. The site also has a medical dictionary; directories of doctors, dentists, and hospitals; and health news. MedlinePlus also features RSS feeds and links to its Twitter feed.

MedlinePlus is an outstanding resource for current, non-technical information on diseases, health conditions, medication, health supplements, and other medical topics. The site's design and content are both exemplary.

Subject(s): Medical Information; Pharmaceuticals; Databases

***Morbidity and Mortality Weekly Report* (*MMWR*)**

https://www.cdc.gov/mmwr/index.html

Description: The *Morbidity and Mortality Weekly Report* (*MMWR*), along with its associated reports, is a standard and authoritative resource for detailed health statistics. The online version presents the full text of each issue of the *MMWR* from February 1982 (volume 31, issue 5) onward, with one issue from 1981 available. Individual components and issues of the *MMWR* series, such as the *Summary of Notifiable Diseases*, can be browsed in the Publications section. The weekly publication is also available as an RSS feed. Podcasts are also offered on the site.

The CDC has done a commendable job of converting this essential publication to an online format and organizing the website so that it is relatively easy to find current articles and back issues.

Subject(s): Diseases and Conditions—Statistics; Vital Statistics

National Center for Health Statistics (NCHS)

https://www.cdc.gov/nchs/

Description: NCHS is the lead agency for U.S. health statistics. Major sections of the site cover NCHS surveys and data collection, publications derived from the data, and downloadable data sets and data analysis tools. Major surveys conducted by NCHS include the *National Health Care Survey (NHCS)* and *National Health and Nutrition Examination Survey (NHANES)*. NCHS also maintains the National Vital Statistics System (NVSS).

NCHS website menus provide layered access to data and reports—from raw data to prepared fact sheets. The homepage makes it easy to find the most frequently used information.

Subject(s): Health and Safety—Statistics; Health Care—Statistics; Vital Statistics

National Health Information Center (NHIC)

https://health.gov/nhic/

Description: NHIC, a health information referral service, produces this website featuring health information for health professionals and consumers. The *Federal Health Information Centers and Clearinghouses* list includes about 1,600 organizations and government offices that provide health information upon request. NHIC also supports healthfinder.gov; health care consumers will want to check that site for additional information.

Subject(s): Health Promotion

National Rehabilitation Information Center (NARIC)

https://www.naric.com/

Description: Funded by NIDILRR, NARIC collects and disseminates the results of federally funded research projects in the area of disability and rehabilitation. The site tailors this information for three audiences: the general public, researchers, and NIDILRR grantees. The information for researchers includes REHABDATA, an extensive database of literature abstracts covering physical, mental, and psychiatric disabilities; independent living; vocational rehabilitation; special education; assistive technology; and other issues related to people with disabilities. REHABDATA also has the full text access of original research documents that are the direct result of government-funded research.

Subject(s): Disabilities—Research

NLM Gateway

https://gateway.nlm.nih.gov/

Description: The NLM Gateway has been all but retired. The About link on the page lists the NLM resources formerly contained in the NLM Gateway and the URLs at which they can be accessed. The only resource still provided by the Gateway is the Meeting Abstracts database (last updated in 2010), which contains abstracts from meetings and conferences on AIDS, health services research, and space life sciences.

Subject(s): Medical Information; Databases

PubMed

https://www.ncbi.nlm.nih.gov/pubmed/

Description: PubMed is part of the Entrez text-based search and retrieval system operated by NLM's National Center for Biotechnology Information (NCBI). It searches more than 25 million citations for biomedical literature. The citations are from MEDLINE and additional life science sources. Pub-

Med also includes links to sites providing full-text articles and other related resources. Other PubMed services include the MeSH (Medical Subject Headings) Database, Citation Matcher (single and batch), Clinical Queries (for physicians), and LinkOut, which links to a wide variety of relevant online resources.

PubMed is a central resource for searching life sciences literature.

Subject(s): Medical Information; Medline

PubMed Central (PMC)

https://www.ncbi.nlm.nih.gov/pmc/

Description: PMC is a free digital archive of biomedical and life sciences journal literature. Participating journals deposit their content with PMC, but copyright is retained by the journal or authors (as appropriate). A section on the site, as well as an RSS feed, provides news on new journals added to PMC.

Subject(s): Biological Medicine—Research; Life Sciences—Research

Surveillance, Epidemiology, and End Results (SEER) Program

https://seer.cancer.gov/

Description: The SEER program collects and publishes cancer incidence and survival data from a number of population-based cancer registries. Its data and publications are available on this website. The Cancer Statistics section provides an introduction to cancer statistics and access to simplified quick reference tools, such as Fast Stats and State Cancer Profiles. The Datasets & Software section links to the SEER data, statistical software resources, and supporting materials.

Subject(s): Cancer—Statistics

TOXNET

https://toxnet.nlm.nih.gov/

Description: TOXNET is a group of databases on toxicology, hazardous chemicals, and related areas. The site allows users to search the databases separately or together. Hosted databases include the Hazardous Substances Data Bank (HSDB), Chemical Carcinogenesis Research Information Service (CCRIS), International Toxicity Estimates for Risk (ITER), and the Developmental and Reproductive Toxicology Database (DART). The site also links to TOXMAP, an NLM service that maps the Environmental Protection Agency's (EPA) Toxics Release Inventory (TRI) data.

Subject(s): Chemical Information; Toxic Substances

U.S. Renal Data System (USRDS)

https://www.usrds.org/

Description: USRDS is a national data system that collects, analyzes, and distributes information about end-stage renal disease (ESRD) in the United States. The organization's work is funded by Department of Health and Human Services agencies—the National Institute of Diabetes and Digestive and Kidney Diseases and the Centers for Medicare and Medicaid Services. The site includes an annual data report on end-stage renal disease in the United States and the Renal Data Extraction and Referencing (RenDER) System database.

Subject(s): Kidney Disease—Statistics

Visible Human Project®

https://www.nlm.nih.gov/research/visible/

Description: NLM's Visible Human Project® has created digital image datasets of the normal male and female human body. The site includes detailed information on the project and on other projects based on the visible human data set. It provides information on how to obtain the data, including the license agreement. Translations are available in Finnish, German, Russian, and Belarusian.

Subject(s): Human Anatomy and Physiology; Medical Computing

VitalStats

https://www.cdc.gov/nchs/vitalstats/index.htm

Description: VitalStats is a central location for data on births and perinatal mortality.

Subject(s): Health Care—Statistics; Vital Statistics

MEDICINE AND MEDICAL DEVICES

DailyMed

https://dailymed.nlm.nih.gov/dailymed/

Description: DailyMed provides FDA-approved labels (package insert information) for more than 48,000 marketed drugs. Label information can be e-mailed from the site or all drug labels can be downloaded at once. DailyMed also has an RSS feed for notification of updates to the database.

Subject(s): Pharmaceuticals

Drug Information Portal

https://druginfo.nlm.nih.gov/drugportal/

Description: The Drug Information Portal serves as a starting point for finding information about prescription and over-the-counter drugs. It includes drugs from the time they are entered into clinical trials through to their entry in the U.S. market place. The site links to websites and databases for drug information from such government agencies as the National Institutes of Health and the Food and Drug Administration.

Subject(s): Pharmaceuticals

Drugs

https://www.fda.gov/drugs/

Description: This website provides information for consumers, medical professionals, and the pharmaceutical industry. It features a number of databases, including the *Orange Book* of approved drugs, the National Drug Code Directory, and the Adverse Event Reporting Program. The wealth of information on the site is organized into several major sections: Drug Approvals and Databases; Drug Safety and Availability; Development & Approval Process (Drugs); Guidance, Compliance & Regulatory Information; News & Events; and Science & Research (Drugs).

Subject(s): Pharmaceuticals

Drugs@FDA

https://www.accessdata.fda.gov/scripts/cder/daf/

Description: Drugs@FDA has information on U.S. approved and tentatively approved prescription and over-the-counter drugs intended for human use. It also has information on drugs removed from the U.S. market for reasons besides safety or effectiveness. (The website's FAQ section provides a more complete list of drug types that are included and excluded.) Drugs@FDA can be used to find labels for approved drugs, generic drug products for a brand name drug, therapeutically equivalent drug products for a brand name or generic drug product, consumer information for approved drugs, drugs with a specific active ingredient, and the approval history of a drug. The website also offers a downloadable file of the Drugs@FDA database.

Subject(s): Over-The-Counter Drugs; Pharmaceuticals

Electronic Orange Book

https://www.accessdata.fda.gov/scripts/cder/ob/

Description: This online version of *Approved Drug Products with Therapeutic Equivalence Evaluations*, known as the *FDA Orange Book*, includes information on prescription drugs, over-the-counter drugs, and discontinued drugs. Users can search by the following categories: Active Ingredient, Applicant Holder, Proprietary Name, Patent Number, or Application Number. The result categories include Active Ingredient, Dosage Form and Route, Applicant Holder, Proprietary Name, Strength, Application Number, and Reference Listed Drug. The Patent Search page can also display recently added patents and patent delistings.

This is a useful database for verifying FDA approval of a drug and for determining the length of time for which it has been approved. Read the Frequently Asked Questions section for important information about how often the database is updated.

Subject(s): Pharmaceuticals

FDA Notices of Judgment Collection 1908 to 1966

https://ceb.nlm.nih.gov/fdanj/

Description: The FDA Notices of Judgment website is currently unavailable due to maintenance. As described on the site previously, "The FDA Notices of Judgment Collection is a digital archive of the published notices judgment for products seized under authority of the 1906 Pure Food and Drug Act." The collection spans 1908 to 1966 and covers the legal document related to food, drugs, medical devices, and cosmetics.

Subject(s): Health Products—Laws; Medicine and Medical Devices—Regulations

Food and Drug Administration (FDA)

https://www.fda.gov/

Description: The FDA regulates the quality and safety of food, drugs, cosmetics, medical devices, biologics (such as vaccines), animal feed, veterinary drugs, radiation-emitting products (such as tanning lamps), and tobacco products. The FDA website features news, recalls and safety alerts, statutes and regulations, and a variety of paths to information on its regulated product areas. Press releases, recall notices, and alerts are available as RSS feeds. The site links to the specialized offices that make up the FDA, the FDA field offices, and the FDA advisory committees. Specific sections of the website are tailored to consumers, industry, health professionals, and state and local officials. Some consumer health publications are available in Spanish.

The FDA site is well designed, with multiple paths to find all of the information the agency provides online. Use the A–Z subject index to find specific information quickly.

Subject(s): Food—Regulations; Pharmaceuticals—Regulations

Medical Devices

https://www.fda.gov/medicaldevices/

Description: CDRH is concerned with the safety and regulation of medical devices and electronic products that produce radiation. Website sections include Products and Medical Procedures, Medical Device Safety, Device Advice: Comprehensive Regulatory Assistance, Science and Research (Medical Devices), News and Events (Medical Devices), and Resources for You (Medical Devices). The products profiled include LASIK eye surgery, surgical staplers, hearing aids, infusion pumps, home healthcare products, tanning devices, and medical devices for children.

Subject(s): Medical Devices—Regulations; Radiation—Regulations

MedWatch: The FDA Safety Information and Adverse Event Reporting Program

https://www.fda.gov/Safety/MedWatch/default.htm

Description: MedWatch provides information and alerts about the safety of medical products to both health care professionals and the public. MedWatch also allows both of these groups to report problems related to medical products to the FDA. Users can subscribe to receive MedWatch alerts by e-mail or RSS feed.

Subject(s): Medicine and Medical Devices—Regulations

Vaccines and Immunizations

https://www.cdc.gov/vaccines/index.html

Description: This CDC website provides information on immunization and vaccine safety for the general public, parents, travelers, health care professionals, local governments, immunization program managers, and others. It includes immunization schedules and information on vaccine safety and vaccination records. The site also has information on requirements and laws, and recommendations from the Advisory Committee on Immunization Practices. The Vaccination Coverage and Surveillance section has data from the National Immunization Survey and other sources. Publications include *Vaccine Information Statements* and the *Epidemiology and Prevention of Vaccine-Preventable Disease*s, known as the *Pink Book*.

This CDC site provides organized access to a tremendous amount of information on vaccines and immunizations. It should be a first stop for general research in this area.

Subject(s): Immunization

NUTRITION

Center for Food Safety and Applied Nutrition (CFSAN)

https://www.fda.gov/food/

Description: CFSAN is responsible for the safety and proper labeling of food and cosmetics. The site has information on national food safety programs, food facility registration, consumer advice, information for industry, and updates on food and cosmetics laws and regulations. Information on the site covers such topics as biotechnology, cosmetics, dietary supplements, food labeling and nutrition, foodborne illness, import and exports, pesticides and chemical contaminants, and seafood (including the *Regulatory Fish En-*

cyclopedia). The site links to information on inspections, compliance, enforcements, and recalls.

The CFSAN site provides relevant and practical content for consumers, industry, health professionals, legal experts, and others.

Subject(s): Food Safety; Cosmetics—Regulations

Center for Nutrition Policy and Promotion (CNPP)

https://www.cnpp.usda.gov/

Sponsor(s): Agriculture Department

Description: CNPP is the focal point within USDA for scientific research linked with the nutritional needs of the public. Project links include *Dietary Guidelines for Americans*, the *Healthy Eating Index*, and *Nutrient Content of the U.S. Food Supply*.

Subject(s): Dietary Guidelines; Nutrition

ChooseMyPlate.gov

https://www.choosemyplate.gov/

Description: ChooseMyPlate.gov is a federal initiative to provide the general public with nutritional guidance. The site provides an image of a plate and the proportions of fruits, vegetables, grains, and proteins that should be added to it. Other reference sources discuss such topics as weight management and physical activity. The SuperTracker tool allows users to plan and analyze their diet and activity choices.

Subject(s): Nutrition

Dietary Supplement Label Database (DSLD)

https://dsld.nlm.nih.gov/dsld/

Description: This database provides ingredient and health claim information from the product labels of over 7,000 selected brands of dietary supplements. The information can be searched or browsed by brand name, active ingredient, and manufacturer. The database also links to ingredient fact sheets (when available). The site links to warnings and recalls from the Food and Drug Administration (FDA) and provides helpful background information on dietary supplements.

Subject(s): Dietary Supplements

Food and Nutrition Information Center (FNIC)

https://www.nal.usda.gov/fnic

Description: The FNIC website says that the center "provides credible, accurate, and practical resources for nutrition and health professionals, educators, government personnel, and consumers." Topics include food safety, food labeling, dietary guidance, weight and obesity, and food composition. The site provides numerous resources and databases to further nutrition education. The site also has an RSS feed combining food and nutrition news from USDA and other federal government sources.

Subject(s): Nutrition

Healthy Meals Resource System

https://healthymeals.fns.usda.gov/

Description: This site has a wealth of resources on child nutrition and food safety. Materials discuss nutrition education, menu planning, resources for the HealthierUS School Challenge program, as well as professional and career resources.

While the site is designed for day care providers who participate in the USDA's Child and Adult Care Food Program (CACFP), parents and others will also find the recipes and educational activity ideas useful.

Subject(s): Child Care; Nutrition; Recipes

Nutrition.gov

https://www.nutrition.gov/

Description: Nutrition.gov is a portal website for government information on nutrition. It organizes links to nutrition information from many federal agencies into sections such as Smart Nutrition 101, Weight Management, Dietary Supplements, and Food Assistance Programs. The site serves consumers, nutrition educators, health providers, and researchers.

Subject(s): Nutrition

Office of Dietary Supplements (ODS)

https://ods.od.nih.gov/

Description: ODS promotes scientific research in the area of dietary supplements. The website describes ODS programs, research, and funding. ODS does not have granting authority but co-sponsors research with other institutes. In the Research & Funding section, the ODS website provides resources such as the Computer Access to Research on Dietary Supplements (CARDS) Database and the Dietary Supplement Ingredient Database (DSID). The Health Information section has information for the consumer, including information on health claims and labeling. The site also offers a newsletter and more than 60 fact sheets on specific dietary supplements, including botanical supplements, vitamins, and minerals.

This site provides extensive information for health professionals and consumers. The ODS booklet "How To Evaluate Health Information on the Internet: Questions and Answers" should be of assistance to many consumers—even beyond those with an interest in dietary supplements.

Subject(s): Dietary Supplements; Nutrition—Research

SNAP-Ed Connection

https://snaped.fns.usda.gov/

Description: The SNAP-Ed Connection website is designed for Supplemental Nutrition Assistance Program (SNAP) nutrition education providers, but it includes excellent resources for users looking for nutrition information. The Resource Library section has educational and training materials on topics such as dietary guidelines, meal planning, food purchasing, and weight control. The site also has a recipe database of recipes submitted by nutrition and health professionals. Other materials on the site, such as state program links and professional development materials, will primarily be of interest to the site's intended audience of nutrition educators.

Subject(s): Nutrition; Recipes

WIC Works Resource System

https://wicworks.fns.usda.gov/

Description: This site offers resources for state-based professionals facilitating the USDA's Special Supplemental Nutrition Program for Women, Infants, and Children (known as WIC). WIC Works is a clearinghouse for educational and promotional materials about nutrition for WIC program clients.

Subject(s): Nutrition

SAFETY

Air Force Rescue Coordination Center (AFRCC)

http://www.1af.acc.af.mil/Units/AFRCC.aspx

Description: AFRCC is the single federal agency responsible for coordinating search and rescue (SAR) activities in the continental United States. AFRCC also coordinates search and rescue agreements, plans, and policy. This website describes their structure and operations. The AFRCC SAR Links section includes links to other federal and private search and rescue organizations. AFRCC annual reports provide detailed reporting and statistics on the previous year's missions.

Subject(s): Search and Rescue

CDC Emergency Preparedness and Response

https://emergency.cdc.gov/

Description: This CDC portal site links to a broad range of practical information about health and safety emergencies. It includes sections including Resources for Emergency Health Professional, Protecting Yourself and Your Loved One, and the CDC A-Z index. Additionally, it includes information on recent topics that are news worthy.

Subject(s): Disaster Preparedness

Disaster Information Management Research Center

https://sis.nlm.nih.gov/dimrc.html

Description: The Disaster Information Management Research Center provides disaster health information resources and research to assist public health officials, healthcare providers, special populations, and the public. The site links to information from NLM and other websites about such topics as bioterrorism, earthquakes, and public health preparations for mass gatherings.

Subject(s): Disaster Assistance; Public Health

DisasterAssistance.gov

https://www.disasterassistance.gov/

Description: DisasterAssistance.gov is the federal government's portal to information about disaster assistance and services from federal and state government and from nongovernment sources. The site also has advice and referrals for Americans affected by disaster when in a foreign country.

Subject(s): Disaster Assistance

Food Safety

https://www.fns.usda.gov/ofs/food-safety

Description: This site compiles information on food safety and security related to the assistance programs administered by FNS. Resources include guidance for food service in schools and the latest food product recall information. The federal government also maintains a multi-agency food safety portal for consumers at https://foodsafety.gov/.

Subject(s): Food Safety

Food Safety and Inspection Service (FSIS)

https://www.fsis.usda.gov/wps/portal/fsis/home

Description: FSIS is the public health regulatory agency in the USDA responsible for ensuring that meat, poultry, and egg products are safe, wholesome, and accurately labeled. Major topics covered by the FSIS website include food safety education, food safety science, regulations and policies, FSIS recalls, and food defense and emergency response. The site has information on federal and state inspection programs and compliance assistance, as well as news on food safety issues in the United States. Background on the Codex Alimentarius Commission (the international mechanism for guarding safety in food trade) is provided on the site. The Recalls and Public Health Alerts section lists current food recalls, which are voluntary actions by a manufacturer or distributor, and information on how to report a food problem. The site has numerous fact sheets covering such topics as safe food handling, food labeling, and meat, poultry, and egg preparation. Other publications can be found in the FOIA Electronic Reading Room section, which is linked from the bottom of the page. The site is also available in Spanish.

For users concerned with food safety issues, this site offers easy access to relevant information.

Subject(s): Food Safety

FoodSafety.gov

https://www.foodsafety.gov/

Description: FoodSafety.gov is a gateway to selected food safety-related information on government websites. The site provides practical guidance on keeping food safe, seasonal food handling advice, types of food poisoning, and where to report a problem. The site also has information on inspections and compliance guidance for the food industry. The News & Features section includes product recall alerts and food safety news from multiple federal agencies concerned with different aspects of food safety.

Subject(s): Food Safety

Healthy Homes and Lead Hazard Control

https://www.hud.gov/program_offices/healthy_homes/leadinfo

Description: This HUD office works to eliminate lead-based paint hazards in privately owned and low-income housing. The site focuses on regulations, enforcement, grants information, technical training, and technical studies and guidelines. It also includes information on mold and moisture.

Subject(s): Home Maintenance; Lead Poisoning

Household Products Database

https://householdproducts.nlm.nih.gov/

Description: This database of thousands of household products provides information on the chemicals the products contain, any ill effects those chemicals may cause, and what first aid steps should be taken if necessary. It also provides the manufacturer's toll free number, the product's health and flammability ratings, and tips for handling and disposal. The database can be searched by product or ingredient. Product sections include Auto Products, Pesticides, Landscape/Yard, Pet Care, and more.

Subject(s): Chemical Information; Product Safety

Lead—EPA

https://www.epa.gov/lead

Sponsor(s): Environmental Protection Agency (EPA)—Pollution Prevention and Toxics Office (OPPT)

Description: This EPA website provides information on lead poisoning and where lead is likely to be a hazard. The site also has relevant regulations, guidelines for professionals who deal with lead-based paint, information on the National Lead Information Center hotline, and links to other EPA resources on lead hazards.

Subject(s): Lead Poisoning

National Center for Injury Prevention and Control (NCIPC)

https://www.cdc.gov/injury/

Description: NCIPC seeks to reduce morbidity, disability, mortality, and costs associated with injuries outside the workplace. Its website features data and statistics, fact sheets, research and funding information, and publications. Topical categories include Violence Prevention, Traumatic Brain Injury, Motor Vehicle Safety, Prescription Drug Overdose, and Home & Recreational Safety. In the Data & Statistics section the site's WISQARS™ (Web-based Injury Statistics Query and Reporting System) database provides customized reports of injury-related data. The same section also links to a national inventory of injury data systems.

Subject(s): Injuries; Safety

U.S. Fire Administration (USFA)

https://www.usfa.fema.gov/

Description: As part of FEMA, USFA works to reduce life and economic losses due to fire, arson, and related emergencies. The website features current fire news and information on firefighter fatalities, fire statistics, and the National Fire Department Census database. It also features a searchable database of hotels and motels that meet federal fire and life safety requirements. Major sections include Grants & Funding, Data Publications & Library, Operations Management & Safety, Fire Prevention & Public Education, and Training & Professional Development. A version of the site is available in Spanish.

Subject(s): Fire Prevention; Firefighting—Grants

Chapter Fourteen

International Relations

This chapter includes a number of websites from the State Department and other agencies whose work involves international assistance, immigration control, diplomacy, or other topics related to the U.S. role in the world. The field of international relations often intersects with those of defense and commerce. Researchers may want to check the Defense and Intelligence chapter and the International Trade section of the Business and Economics chapter for additional websites of interest. Also, the Education chapter has a section on International Education.

Subsections in this chapter are Arms Control, Country Information, Diplomacy, Foreign Policy, International Migration and Travel, and International Relations.

ARMS CONTROL

Bureau of Arms Control, Verification and Compliance (AVC)

https://www.state.gov/t/avc/

Description: AVC works to ensure compliance with international arms control, nonproliferation, and disarmament agreements and commitments. AVC reports to Congress on other nations' compliance. The bureau also reports in the Federal Register, noting any sanctions against countries providing controlled technology to particular countries of concern. The website has information on the New Strategic Arms Reduction Treaty (New START) and copies of other treaties and agreements concerned with nonproliferation and disarmament.

Subject(s): Arms Control; Nonproliferation

Chemical Weapons Convention Website

http://www.cwc.gov

Description: This website brings together background information, regulations, documents, and reports related to U.S. compliance with the Chemical Weapons Convention. The treaty affects U.S. private industries that produce, process, consume, import, or export dual-use chemicals that could be used to produce chemical weapons. The Declarations section of the site includes handbooks and forms to assist companies with compliance. More publications are available in the Outreach section.

Subject(s): Chemical Warfare

Nonproliferation and Disarmament Fund (NDF)

https://www.state.gov/t/isn/ndf/

Description: NDF was established to enable quick responses to stop the proliferation of nuclear, biological, and chemical weapons; weapons of mass destruction; and advanced conventional weapons. The NDF website provides basic information on the fund, its legal authority, and projects.

Subject(s): Arms Control; Nonproliferation

COUNTRY INFORMATION

Bilateral Relations Fact Sheets

https://www.state.gov/r/pa/ei/bgn/

Description:This popular series of brief country profiles comes from the Department of State. Each country's edition is consistently formatted and mostly contains facts and narrative on the political and economic relations between that country and the United States. However, be sure to check the date of the latest revision for each country; there may have been significant changes in a country since the last update.

Subject(s): Foreign Countries; History

Country Studies Series

https://www.loc.gov/collections/country-studies/

Description: The *Country Study Series* is a collection of books that provide detailed—if dated—information on other countries. Each publication in the series covers a particular foreign country, describing and analyzing its political, economic, social, and national security systems and institutions and examining the interrelationships of those systems and the ways they are shaped by cultural factors. Each study was written by a multidisciplinary team of social scientists. Intended as background material for the U.S. Army, the series includes such countries as North Korea and Kazakhstan but does not cover Canada, France, or the United Kingdom. This site offers full-text search capabilities across all or any combination of the available books. The series has not been updated since 1998 because the Army discontinued funding for the project.

Although these books have not been updated to reflect current events, they remain valuable reference tools for the cultural and historical information they provide. Each study also includes a selective bibliography for further research.

Subject(s): Foreign Countries; History

World Factbook

https://www.cia.gov/library/publications/the-world-factbook/

Description: The CIA's *World Factbook* is a standard reference for country information. Information and data on the site is updated throughout the year. For each country, the *World Factbook* provides a map, a color image of the national flag, and a profile that includes reference information about the country's geography, population, government, economy, communications, transportation, military, and transnational issues. The *World Factbook* has prepared tables ranking the countries on certain numerical data, such as total population. Appendices include an extensive list of international organizations and an acronyms and a conversion table for weights and measures.

Given its authority and frequent updates, the *World Factbook* website is a recommended online reference tool.

Subject(s): Foreign Countries

DIPLOMACY

Broadcasting Board of Governors (BBG)

https://www.bbg.gov/

Description: The Broadcasting Board of Governors is an independent federal agency responsible for all non-military, international broadcasting by the U.S. government. The board's website describes each of the international broadcasting services in operation: the Voice of America (VOA), Radio Free Europe/Radio Liberty (RFE/RL), the Middle East Broadcasting Networks (MBN), Radio Free Asia (RFA), and Radio and TV Marti. Each is assisted by the International Broadcasting Bureau (IBB), a division within the BBG. The website also has press releases and board meeting reports.

Subject(s): Broadcasting—International

Bureau of Diplomatic Security (DS)

https://www.state.gov/m/ds/

Description: The Bureau of Diplomatic Security (DS) is the security and law enforcement arm of the Department of State. DS manages the security programs that protect U.S. personnel working in U.S. diplomatic missions around the world. DS also assists foreign embassies and consulates in the United States with security and manages immunity issues for foreign diplomats in the United States. Additionally, the bureau investigates passport and visa fraud and manages the Department of State's personnel security clearance program. The website describes each aspect of the DS mission in detail and provides current information about its activities. The News and Information section includes fact sheets and press releases.

Subject(s): Terrorism

Department of State (DOS)

https://www.state.gov/

Description: The homepage of the Department of State website features current news, the department's latest Tweets, and videos of recent department events. Toward the bottom of the page, there is a link to a subject index of the content on the site. The website's main topical sections include Media Center, Travel, Careers, Business, Youth & Education, and About State. The Media Center section links to the *Daily Press Briefings*, videos, and press releases. The Travel section covers passports, visas, and international travel warnings. The Business section covers trade issues and State support for businesses. The Youth & Education section includes information on educational and cultural exchange programs, State Department and U.S. diplomatic history, and intercountry adoption. The About State section includes biographies of State Department officials, organizational information, department publications, and directories such as Key Officers at Foreign Service Posts and U.S. Embassies and Consulates. Other major sections of the site address the policy roles of the State Department in arms control, economics, democracy abroad, foreign aid, and additional issues.

This site provides a wealth of information about international issues.

Subject(s): Diplomacy; Foreign Policy

DipNote

https://blogs.state.gov/

Description: DipNote is the State Department's official blog. The term "DipNote" refers to a diplomatic note, a form for communication between national governments. Blog entries are regularly written by employees in many different sections of State, including foreign service offers posted abroad, ambassadors, and headquarters staff. Comments are permitted.

Subject(s): Diplomacy; Blogs

Frontline Diplomacy: **Foreign Affairs Oral History Collection**

https://www.loc.gov/collections/foreign-affairs-oral-history/about-this-collection/

Description: Part of the Library of Congress American Memory online collection, the full title of this set of interview transcripts is "Frontline Diplomacy: The Foreign Affairs Oral History Collection of the Association for Diplomatic Studies and Training." The interviews with State Department Foreign Service officers and other officials are mostly from the 1940s to the 1990s. The collection can be searched by word or browsed by topic or author.

Subject(s): Diplomacy—History

Japan-United States Friendship Commission (JUSFC)

https://www.jusfc.gov/

Description: JUSFC administers a trust fund for promoting scholarly, cultural, and public affair activities between the United States and Japan. Its website has information on JUSFC grants and fellowships and the U.S.-Japan Creative Artists Program.

Subject(s): Culture—Grants; International Education—Grants; Japan

Office of the Chief of Protocol

https://www.state.gov/s/cpr/

Description: This website details the varied responsibilities of the Department of State's chief of protocol and features information about major diplomatic events both in the United States and abroad. Reference material on the site, found in the Publications section, includes the *Diplomatic List*, a list of accredited diplomatic officers of foreign embassies in the U.S., and the *Foreign Consular Offices in the United States* directory.

Subject(s): Diplomacy

Open World Leadership Center

https://www.openworld.gov/

Description: The Open World Leadership Center, an independent entity in the legislative branch, enables emerging political and civic leaders from Russia and other former Soviet Union countries to work with their U.S. counterparts. Open World also sponsors a cultural program. This website provides information about program activities, grants for hosting organizations, countries authorized to participate, and program donors.

Subject(s): Cultural Exchanges; Russia

U.S. Agency for International Development (USAID)

https://www.usaid.gov/

Description: USAID is an independent agency that provides economic development and humanitarian assistance around the world. The USAID website has information about the agency, its work and locations, policy documents, press releases, contracting and acquisition opportunities, and agency employment. Its many program areas include HIV/AIDS treatment and prevention, democracy and governance training, Food for Peace, American Schools and Hospitals Abroad, literacy, microenterprise development, Women in Development, and the Denton Program for transporting humanitarian donations on U.S. military cargo planes. Information about these and other programs is provided in the What We Do section.

The site links to statistical sources such as *U.S. Overseas Loans & Grants Online* (also known as the *Greenbook*) and the *U.S. Official Development Assistance Database*. The site also features the Development Experience Clearinghouse, an online resource for USAID-funded technical and project materials.

Subject(s): Foreign Assistance

U.S. Diplomacy Center (USDC)

https://diplomacy.state.gov/

Description: USDC organizes exhibits, educational programs, and events to demonstrate the role of the State Department and both current and historic U.S. diplomacy. USDC draws from its collection of over 6,000 artifacts to create exhibits at its own facilities and at other U.S. and international sites; a selection can be viewed on the website. The Education Resources section includes classroom materials and content designed to inform students about the State Department and diplomatic careers.

Subject(s): Diplomacy—History; Museums

USEmbassy.Gov

https://www.usembassy.gov/

Description: This website provides information about U.S. embassies, consulates, and diplomatic missions abroad. The site is broken down by region for easy reference. Information about citizen services, visas, and travel warnings can also be accessed from this starting point.

Subject(s): Diplomacy; Embassies

U.S. Institute of Peace (USIP)

https://www.usip.org/

Description: USIP is an independent, nonpartisan federal institution created and funded by Congress to strengthen the nation's capacity to promote the peaceful resolution of international conflict. The website describes USIP programs such as the Center for Conflict Analysis and Prevention and the Center for Mediation and Conflict Resolution. The Issue Areas section of the site organizes USIP information by topic, such as economics and conflict education, post-conflict and peacekeeping activities, religion and peacemaking, and rule of law. The site also has information on USIP subject specialists, grants and fellowships, and education and training programs. Published material can be found in the Articles & Publications, USIP Library, and USIP Bookstore sections of the site.

Subject(s): International Relations—Research; Peace

U.S. Mission to the International Organizations in Vienna (UNVIE)

https://vienna.usmission.gov/

Description: UNVIE works with the cluster of UN and UN-related agencies headquartered in Vienna. These include the International Atomic Energy Agency (IAEA) and the Preparatory Commission for the Comprehensive Nuclear-Test-Ban Treaty Organization. The UNVIE website provides news and fact sheets, links to relevant documents, and UNVIE statements.

Subject(s): International Organizations

U.S. Mission to the OECD

https://usoecd.usmission.gov/

Description: The Organisation for Economic Co-operation and Development (OECD) in Paris works to foster cooperation among advanced market-based democracies. Along with information about the current U.S. ambassador to the OECD, this website summarizes U.S. goals and work in current issue areas. Current issues include energy, governance, and combating corruption.

Subject(s): International Economic Relations; International Organizations

U.S. Mission to the OSCE

https://osce.usmission.gov/

Description: The Organization for Security and Co-operation in Europe (OSCE) is a regional security organization with 57 participating nations from Europe, Central Asia, and North America and 11 additional partner countries. The website for the U.S. Mission to the OSCE in Vienna explains the work, history, and goals of the OSCE and the U.S. objectives in the organization. It includes U.S. statements to the OSCE Permanent Council.

Subject(s): International Relations; Europe—Policy; International Organizations

U.S. Mission to the United Nations (USUN)

https://usun.state.gov/

Description: The U.S. Representative to the United Nations, along with several deputies who serve with ambassador rank, represents the United States in meetings with the United Nations. This website provides information about the work of the ambassadors and staff in the U.S. mission to the United Nations, which uses the acronym USUN. The site provides official statements, press releases, blog entries, and background information on a wide range of foreign policy issues.

Subject(s): Diplomacy; International Organizations

Vietnam Education Foundation (VEF)

http://www.vef.gov/

Description: VEF provides opportunities for Vietnamese nationals to pursue graduate and postgraduate studies in science and technology in the United States and for American citizens to teach in the same fields of study in Vietnam. Its website provides news and information about the program.

Subject(s): International Education; Vietnam

Voice of America (VOA)

https://www.voanews.com/

Description: VOA is an international broadcasting service funded by the U.S. government. VOA programs, which cover U.S. news, information, and culture, are produced and broadcasted in English and nearly 50 other languages via radio, satellite, and the Internet. The VOA website highlights daily VOA newswire stories and broadcasts, and provides news in RSS feeds and webcasts. The Programs section lists the VOA's radio and TV offerings, and the site offers a pronunciation guide for international names and places in the news. Links to VOA's social media feeds are included on the homepage.

Subject(s): Broadcasting—International; News Services

FOREIGN POLICY

Bureau of African Affairs

https://www.state.gov/p/af/

Description: The Bureau of African Affairs is concerned with sub-Saharan Africa policy. In the Regional Topics section, the bureau's website has press releases and documents on such issues as the African Growth and Opportunity Act and AIDS relief. The site also has biographies of chiefs of mission and other senior State Department principals in Africa.

Subject(s): Africa—Policy

Bureau of Economic and Business Affairs

https://www.state.gov/e/eb/

Description: The Department of State's Bureau of Economic and Business Affairs is responsible for coordinating U.S. foreign economic policy. The bureau's website describes its work in supporting U.S. business in foreign markets, negotiating at economic summits and with international organizations, combating bribery in international commerce, coordinating economic sanctions policy, and making recommendations for national energy security. Material from the bureau and its component offices covers such specific topics as Internet freedom, conflict diamonds, Open Skies agreements, and free trade agreements.

Subject(s): International Economic Relations—Policy

Bureau of Near Eastern Affairs

https://www.state.gov/p/nea/

Description: The Bureau of Near Eastern Affairs is concerned with policy toward Algeria, Bahrain, Egypt, Iran, Iraq, Israel, Jordan, Kuwait, Lebanon, Libya, Morocco, Oman, Palestinian Territories, Qatar, Saudi Arabia, Syria, Tunisia, United Arab Emirates, and Yemen. The Regional Topics section of its website includes information on the Iran nuclear deal, Iraq, and the Middle East Partnership Initiative (MEPI).

Subject(s): Middle East—Policy

Bureau of South and Central Asian Affairs

https://www.state.gov/p/sca/

Description: The Bureau of South and Central Asian Affairs is concerned with policy toward the countries of Afghanistan, Bangladesh, Bhutan, India, Kazakhstan, Kyrgyzstan, Maldives, Nepal, Pakistan, Sri Lanka, Tajikistan, Turkmenistan, and Uzbekistan. The site provides news releases and biographies of the U.S. ambassadors in the region, along with links to the bureau's social media pages.

Subject(s): Asia—Policy

Bureau of Western Hemisphere Affairs

https://www.state.gov/p/wha/

Description: The Bureau of Western Hemisphere Affairs is concerned with policy toward the region including Canada, Mexico, Central and South America, and the Caribbean island nations. The website features sections on Hemispheric Security and the U.S. Mission to the Organization of American States. The Regional Topics section links to information on free trade agreements, the Caribbean Basin Security Initiative, the Summit of the Americas, and other initiatives.

Subject(s): North America—Policy; South America—Policy; Caribbean—Policy

DOS Office of the Historian

https://history.state.gov/

Description: "The Office of the Historian is responsible, under law, for the preparation and publication of the official documentary history of U.S.

foreign policy in the Foreign Relations of the United States series." (from the website) The website provides the *Foreign Relations of the United States* series online along with a wealth of other historical resources. Content includes biographies and records of official travel for all former Secretaries of State, U.S. visits by foreign heads of state from 1874 onward, foreign travels by former U.S. presidents, the status of U.S. diplomatic relations with each country of the world, and a guide to the diplomatic archives of other countries.

Subject(s): Foreign Policy—History

***Foreign Relations of the United States* (*FRUS*)**

https://history.state.gov/historicaldocuments

Description: The *Foreign Relations of the United States* (*FRUS*) series, published by the Department of State's Office of the Historian, is a compilation of U.S. foreign policy documents beginning with the Lincoln administration in 1861. Documents selected for inclusion come from the State Department and other sources, including the intelligence agencies and private papers. The Historical Documents section provides a description of the series, a list of all of its volumes, and information about print volumes sold by the Government Publishing Office and the status of its work on the series. The State Department also provides the full texts of volumes starting with the Truman administration; these are available in HTML format. Online volumes can be searched by keyword.

A *FRUS* digitization project at the University of Wisconsin–Madison Libraries can be accessed at https://uwdc.library.wisc.edu/collections/frus/. This site has scanned copies of the *FRUS* for 1861 through 1960 (with some gaps). The set can be browsed by volume or searched by keyword.

Subject(s): Foreign Policy—History

INTERNATIONAL MIGRATION AND TRAVEL

Bureau of Population, Refugees, and Migration (PRM)

https://www.state.gov/j/prm/

Description: PRM has primary responsibility for formulating policies on population, refugees, and migration, and for administering U.S. refugee assistance and admissions programs. The website includes background information and news releases. It also has funding information for nongovernmental organizations that carry out relief services overseas.

Subject(s): Refugees—Policy

CDC Travel Information

https://wwwnc.cdc.gov/travel

Description: This website provides health risk information by travel destination. It contains information about diseases and disease outbreaks, including avian influenza; vaccine recommendations; insect protection; special needs travelers; and cruise ship and air travel. The site also links to CDC's *Health Information for International Travel*, commonly called the *Yellow Book*. The site has travel notices for specific countries on its home page.

Subject(s): Diseases and Conditions—International; Tourism

Executive Office for Immigration Review (EOIR)

https://www.justice.gov/eoir

Description: EOIR conducts immigration court proceedings, appellate reviews, and administrative hearings in individual cases. This website contains information about the EOIR and its organization and activities. The site includes a national directory of immigration courts.

Subject(s): Immigration Law

Immigration Data and Statistics

https://www.dhs.gov/immigration-statistics

Description: This site compiles links to publications, data tables, and other sources of statistics related to migration to the United States. Statistics cover immigration, naturalization, refugees, asylum seekers, the undocumented immigrant population, applications for immigration benefits, and related topics. The main page of the site features new releases.

Subject(s): International Migration—Statistics

Office of Refugee Resettlement (ORR)

https://www.acf.hhs.gov/orr

Description: ORR provides assistance to people fleeing persecution in their homelands. Its website describes the programs, policy, grants, and funding of ORR and explains the legal definition of refugee status and who is eligible for benefits. It covers special programs such as those for unaccompanied refugee minors and has a directory of state-level refugee coordinators. A Refugee Arrival Data subsection reports on refugee arrivals by country of origin and by U.S. state.

Subject(s): Refugees

Travel.State.Gov

https://travel.state.gov/content/travel/en.html

Description: The Bureau of Consular Affairs, which maintains this website, is concerned with the safety of U.S. citizens in foreign countries. The bureau issues passports for U.S. citizens traveling abroad and visas for foreign citizens traveling to the United States. Travel.State.Gov has practical news, advice, and fact sheets about travel safety, applying for a passport, and

U.S. visa programs. The site supplies consular information sheets for each country, which summarize entry requirements, local health and safety information, customs regulations, and registering with the local U.S. embassy or consulate. It also contains official Travel Warnings and Public Announcements for specific countries or regions. The Legal Considerations section has clear explanations of legal issues related to Americans abroad (such as those pertaining to judicial assistance), citizenship and nationality, and law enforcement. The website also has a section on addressing international parental child abduction cases.

The Bureau of Consular Affairs site provides simple, straightforward access to essential travel information. The passport and visa information is particularly thorough and includes links to the necessary forms.

Subject(s): Passports; Visas

U.S. Citizenship and Immigration Services (USCIS)

https://www.uscis.gov/

Description: The responsibilities of USCIS include asylum and refugee processing, naturalization, special immigration status programs, and issuance of immigration documents. The website provides easy access to guidance, forms, legal information, online services, and current news. It links to the E-Verify system for employers who need to check the immigration status of job applicants. Major sections on the home page address the green card (permanent residency), citizenship, immigrant family issues, working in the United States, refugees and asylum, international adoption, and citizenship for members of the U.S. military. The site's Laws section has the text of relevant laws, regulations, administrative decisions, and policy memoranda. It also links to sources for free legal services. The USCIS site is available in Spanish.

Subject(s): Citizenship; Immigration Law

INTERNATIONAL RELATIONS

Bureau of Counterterrorism (CT) and Countering Violent Extremism

https://www.state.gov/j/ct/

Description: The Department of State's Bureau of Counterterrorism develops U.S. counterterrorism policy and coordinates U.S. efforts to improve counterterrorism cooperation with foreign governments. Its website includes statements on U.S. policy and describes the office's programs. The site also provides the annual publication *Country Reports on Terrorism*, the list of State Sponsors of Terrorism, and explanations of the terrorist designation lists.

Subject(s): Terrorism—Policy

Commission on Security and Cooperation in Europe (CSCE)

https://www.csce.gov/

Description: CSCE, better known as the U.S. Helsinki Commission, is an independent government agency created by Congress. It monitors and encourages compliance with the Helsinki Accords and other commitments of the countries participating in the Organization for Security and Co-operation in Europe (OSCE). The commission's website includes information about the CSCE and OSCE and the full texts of the commission's press releases, hearings, briefings, and statements.

Subject(s): Human Rights

Congressional-Executive Commission on China (CECC)

https://www.cecc.gov/

Description: CECC was established to monitor the human rights situation and development of the rule of law in China. Its website has information about the commission and records of its hearings and roundtables. It includes information on Chinese law, a directory of Chinese legal provisions, and a database of prisoners of conscience in China.

Subject(s): Human Rights; China—Policy

Defense Security Cooperation Agency (DSCA)

http://www.dsca.mil

Description: DSCA assists U.S. allies through foreign military sales, training, and technical and humanitarian assistance. The DSCA website provides background information on the agency and its organizational components and features announcements of major foreign military arms sales. The Publications section provides links to the key policy and legal documents on foreign military assistance.

While much of the DSCA website is technical in nature and written for a very specific audience, researchers will find it to be a valuable source for information on U.S. security assistance and arms transfer policy.

Subject(s): International Relations; National Defense—Policy

DOJ Activities in Iraq

https://www.justice.gov/archive/iraq/

Description: Justice Department employees serve throughout Iraq on projects to facilitate the rule of law. This website provides information on the projects and working groups, including the Office of the Rule of Law Coordinator (RoLC), the Major Crimes Task Force (MCTF), and the International Criminal Investigative Training Assistance Program (ICITAP). The site also lists job openings with the Iraq offices.

Subject(s): Iraq

Famine Early Warning Systems Network (FEWS NET)

https://www.fews.net/

Description: FEWS NET provides information and analysis on food security conditions in African nations, Central America, Haiti, Yemen, and other counties. FEWS NET is funded by USAID and implemented through a partnership with other federal and international organizations. Its website highlights food emergency announcements and warnings, drought and flood hazard assessments, market conditions, and remote-sensing imagery of rainfall and vegetation on the African continent. The site has versions in French, Spanish, and Portuguese.

Subject(s): Famine; Africa; Middle East; Central America; Caribbean

Foreign Agents Registration Act (FARA)

https://www.justice.gov/nsd-fara

Description: FARA requires that individuals and organizations lobbying on behalf of foreign business or foreign government interests register with the Department of Justice. The Foreign Agents Registration Unit, within Justice's National Security Division, has responsibility for administering the act. This website has information for those who need to register as well as for those interested in researching FARA registrations.

In 2007, Justice made FARA registrations available in an online, searchable database. Searchers should read the Document Search Help explainer and understand the FARA statute to use the database most productively.

Subject(s): Lobbyists—Regulations

House Democracy Partnership (HDP)

https://hdp.house.gov/

Description: As stated on the website, the mission of the House Democracy Partnership is "to support the development of effective, independent, and responsive legislative institutions." The site includes the commission's news and a list of "partner legislatures" participating in the program.

Subject(s): Democracy—International; Foreign Assistance

Inter-American Foundation (IAF)

https://www.iaf.gov/

Description: IAF is an independent agency that provides assistance to Latin America and the Caribbean by awarding grants directly to local organizations throughout the region. Its website features sections entitled About the IAF, Our Work, Apply for Grants, Resources, and Partners. The site is available in Spanish, Portuguese, and Creole.

Subject(s): Foreign Assistance; South America

Middle East Partnership Initiative (MEPI)

https://mepi.state.gov/

Description: MEPI supports reform in the areas of politics, economics, education, and women's issues in the Middle East. Its website provides background information and details about its organization and structure. The site also links to the websites for the Abu Dhabi and Tunis regional offices, as well as grant application information.

Subject(s): Foreign Assistance; Middle East

Millennium Challenge Corporation (MCC)

https://www.mcc.gov/

Description: MCC, a government corporation, works with countries to promote sustainable economic growth and reduce poverty through investments in areas such as agriculture, education, and private sector development. Countries are selected to receive aid based on their performance in governing justly, investing in their citizens, and encouraging economic freedom. The website provides information on MCC and its leadership, selection criteria, country activities, and business and procurement.

Subject(s): International Economic Development

Office of Global Criminal Justice (GCJ)

https://www.state.gov/j/gcj/

Description: As described on the website, GCJ, formerly the Office of War Crimes, "advises the Secretary of State and other elements of the United States government on the prevention of, and response to, atrocity crimes. The Office provides advice and expertise on transitional justice, including ways to ensure justice and accountability for genocide, crimes against humanity, and war crimes, as well as other grave human rights violations." The site provides information on recent war crimes tribunals, such as the International Criminal Tribunal for Rwanda.

Subject(s): War Crimes

Overseas Security Advisory Council (OSAC)

https://www.osac.gov

Description: OSAC was established to promote security cooperation and communication between the U.S. government and U.S. private sector companies and organizations that operate abroad. OSAC services are for registered constituent organizations and some website content is available only to registered constituents. The OSAC website provides unclassified information, such as daily news of foreign events and reports on topics such as crime and security trends in foreign countries. The Country Councils section of the site provides links to the web pages for each of the over 50 regional OSAC councils.

Subject(s): Terrorism; Crime Prevention—International

U.S.-China Economic and Security Review Commission (USCC)

https://www.uscc.gov/

Description: USCC was created to review the national security implications of trade and economic ties between the United States and the People's Republic of China. Its website has hearings schedules, congressional testimony, and annual reports. The site also has directories of the commissioners and staff and copies of research papers and trade data and analyses.

Subject(s): International Economic Relations; China—Policy

U.S. Commission on International Religious Freedom

http://www.uscirf.gov

Description: The Commission on International Religious Freedom is a federal government commission established to monitor the status of religious freedom in other nations and make policy recommendations to the president, secretary of state, and Congress. The commission issues an annual report on religious persecution around the world; current and past reports are available on its website. The commission maintains lists of Countries of Particular Concern and a country Watch List, both available online. The site also has additional information about the commission and its hearings, press releases, congressional testimony, and relevant legislation.

Subject(s): Human Rights

U.S. Mission to NATO

https://nato.usmission.gov/

Description: The Department of State and Department of Defense have a combined United States Mission to the North Atlantic Treaty Organization (NATO). This website has current speeches and statements from the U.S. ambassador to NATO and current news from the U.S. government on security issues.

Subject(s): International Agreements

Chapter Fifteen

Law and Law Enforcement

Websites concerning law and law enforcement are primarily sponsored by the Justice Department and the federal courts. The Justice Department in particular has a very broad role in legal matters, covering topics from legal practices to community policing to homeland security. This chapter has a similarly broad scope. However, some subject-specific websites, such as sites about environmental law, can be found in the relevant subject chapters in this book.

Subsections in this chapter are Areas of Law, Courts and the Judicial System, Crime and Enforcement, and Laws and Legal Information.

AREAS OF LAW

ADA Homepage—Information and Technical Assistance on the Americans with Disabilities Act

https://www.ada.gov/

Description: The Department of Justice's central website for the Americans with Disabilities Act (ADA) compiles a wide range of information for audiences such as the general public, businesses, and state and local governments. The site provides a catalog of publications about ADA regulations, technical assistance, information about ADA enforcement actions, information for state and local governments, and links to other federal agency websites with disability information. Some publications are available in Spanish. The Contact Us section lists the Justice Department's toll-free ADA hotlines, 800-514-0301 (voice) and 800-514-0383 (TTY).

New features on the site, found under the New on ADA.gov section, include recent settlement agreements, complaints, and consent degrees.

This site's broad scope will make it of interest to anyone concerned with ADA compliance and information.

Subject(s): Americans with Disabilities Act (ADA)

Administrative Decisions and Other Actions

https://guides.lib.virginia.edu/administrative_decisions

Description: This university website is a finding aid for administrative actions that fall outside the usual scope of the *Code of Federal Regulations* and the *Federal Register*. Its lengthy list includes links to items such as the advisory opinions from the Consumer Product Safety Commission, Department of Energy directives, Federal Labor Relations Authority decisions, Food and Drug Administration enforcement reports, and Postal Service administrative decisions.

Maintained at the University of Virginia Library's Government Information Resources site, this page fills an important niche for finding legal information online.

Subject(s): Administrative Law; Finding Aids

Alcohol Policy Information System (APIS)

https://alcoholpolicy.niaaa.nih.gov/

Description: APIS compiles detailed information on federal and state law and policy on alcohol topics. Issues covered include underage drinking, retail sales, alcoholic beverage control, taxation, and transportation laws. The site also tracks changes in laws and policies and provides a national summary of state laws and regulations related to underage drinking and access to alcohol. The Maps and Charts section contains comprehensive statistical data broken down by state on topics such as taxation, transportation, and blood alcohol concentration limits.

Subject(s): Alcohol—Laws

Antitrust Division

https://www.justice.gov/atr

Description: The Antitrust Division promotes competition through enforcing antitrust law. The division's website provides full-text antitrust cases and information about the division and its activities. The Public Documents section links to selected appellate briefs (back to 1993), international information, Economic Analysis Group Papers, policy statements and guidelines, and other publications. The Antitrust Case Filings page includes cases from December 1994 onward, which are arranged alphabetically. The site has a Report Violations section and a home page link to reporting possible antitrust violations.

Subject(s): Antitrust Law

Civil Rights Division

https://www.justice.gov/crt

Description: The Civil Rights Division of the Justice Department enforces federal statutes prohibiting discrimination. Pages for each of the division's organizational sections hold most of the content at the site. The organizational sections—under the About the Division heading—are Appellate, Criminal, Disability Rights, Educational Opportunities, Employment Litigation, Federal Coordination and Compliance, Housing and Civil Enforcement, Office of Special Counsel for Immigration-Related Unfair Employment Practices, Policy and Strategy, Special Litigation, and Voting. Each section's web page typically includes background material on the relevant area of practice, statutes enforced, and cases or briefs. The Publications section has material on a wide range of topics not covered elsewhere on the site, such as the pamphlet *Federal Protections Against National Origin Discrimination*, which is available in 16 languages.

Subject(s): Civil Rights—Laws

Comptroller General Decisions and Opinions

https://www.gao.gov/legal/

Description: The GAO comptroller general issues decisions regarding use of federal appropriations, government contract bid protests, and major federal regulations. This site provides access to summaries and full texts of recent decisions in HTML and PDF formats.

Subject(s): Government Contracts—Regulations

Copyright Office

https://www.copyright.gov/

Description: The U.S. Copyright Office website includes information on copyright law, searching existing copyright records, and registering a work for copyright protection. The site also highlights hot topics and provides an RSS feed of copyright news. The Publications section of the site has copies of the office's circulars, brochures, and forms. One-page fact sheets cover specific topics such as fair use, international copyright, and how to register specific types of works, such as books, music, and photographs. The site also has information on licensing, preregistration, and recording documents.

The About section includes basic information and an organizational chart.

Subject(s): Copyright Law; Intellectual Property

Copyright Royalty Board (CRB)

https://www.crb.gov/

Description: The Copyright Royalty Board (CRB) was created by the Copyright Royalty and Distribution Reform Act of 2004. The CRB consists of three permanent copyright royalty judges. The website has information on rate and distribution proceedings, CRB notices in the Federal Register, and forms for filing royalty fee claims for cable, satellite, and digital audio recording devices and media.

Subject(s): Copyright Law

Department of Justice (DOJ)

https://www.justice.gov/

Description: The central website for the Department of Justice links to the department's 50-plus component divisions and programs. Under Resources, the site brings together the department's publications, forms, and information on notable cases, such as *United States v. Bernard L. Madoff*. The News section includes videos and the department's blog. This central Justice website also has information on the department's grants, business opportunities, and careers.

The home page of the site features an Action Center with links such as Report a Crime; Locate a Prison, Inmate, or Sex Offender; Find Sales of Seized Property; and Report and Identify Missing Persons. As a Cabinet department, Justice also maintains information on its Recovery Act programs and Open Government Plan.

This well-organized site is easy to navigate.

Subject(s): Law and Law Enforcement

Disability Rights Section

https://www.justice.gov/crt/disability-rights-section

Description: The Civil Rights Division's Disability Rights Section is concerned with the enforcement of the Americans with Disabilities Act (ADA) and related federal law. The websites covers enforcement issues, compliance assistance, certification of building codes, and other regulatory topics.

Subject(s): Disabilities—Laws

Federal Mine Safety and Health Review Commission (FMSHRC)

http://www.fmshrc.gov/

Description: FMSHRC is an independent adjudicative agency that provides administrative trial and appellate review of legal disputes arising under the Federal Mine Safety and Health Act of 1977 (also known as the Mine Act). Sections featured on the site include About FMSHRC, Decisions, Review Commission Arguments & Meetings, The Mine Act & Procedural Rules, Reports & Budget Submissions, Cases on Review, and FOIA. The site also has information and cases related to the Mine Improvement and New Emergency Response Act of 2006.

Subject(s): Mining—Laws

Foreign Claims Settlement Commission (FCSC)

https://www.justice.gov/fcsc

Description: The Foreign Claims Settlement Commission is a quasi-judicial independent agency within the Department of Justice. The commission rules on claims of U.S. nationals against foreign governments. The website has information on the commission, special claims programs, and copies of the annual report.

Subject(s): International Law

Historical Publications of the United States Commission on Civil Rights

http://www.law.umaryland.edu/marshall/usccr/index.html

Sponsor(s): University of Maryland Thurgood Marshall Law Library

Description: This site provides access to PDF copies of Civil Rights Commission documents that are in the collection of the University of Maryland Thurgood Marshall Law Library. It includes a selection of documents dating back to the Civil Rights Act of 1957, which created the original Civil Rights Commission.

Subject(s): Civil Rights

Military Commissions

http://www.mc.mil

Description: The Office of Military Commissions website provides material related to operating military commissions, also called military tribunals, and the Military Commissions Act. As stated in the law, the Military Commissions Act "establishes procedures governing the use of military commissions." The website includes the *Manual for Military Commissions* and related press materials.

Subject(s): Military Justice

Military Legal Resources

http://www.loc.gov/rr/frd/Military_Law/

Description: This Library of Congress site provides access to a growing collection of historic, digitized military legal resources, including the *Military Law Review* (1958–2014, Geneva Conventions materials, the *Manuals for Courts-Martial*, and *The Army Lawyer* (1971–2015). Historical military legal documents are also grouped under headings for the Indian Wars Era, the Civil War Era, the World War II Era, the Korean War Era, and the Vietnam War Era.

Subject(s): Military History; Military Justice

National Indian Gaming Commission (NIGC)

https://www.nigc.gov/

Description: NIGC is an independent federal regulatory agency established by the Indian Gaming Regulatory Act of 1988. The Commission section includes an overview of the commission and the laws and regulations with which it is concerned. The site also features National Indian Gaming Commission decisions, enforcement actions, approved gaming ordinances, a list of tribal gaming locations, and more.

Subject(s): Gambling—Regulations; American Indians

Occupational Safety and Health Review Commission (OSHRC)

https://www.oshrc.gov/

Description: OSHRC is an independent federal agency created to decide contests of citations or penalties resulting from OSHA inspections. The commission functions as an administrative court, with established procedures for conducting hearings, receiving evidence, and rendering decisions by its administrative law judges. Its website has recent decisions by the commission and administrative law judges. Other sections include Rules, Publications, and Budget.

Subject(s): Labor Law; Workplace Safety—Laws

Office of Legal Counsel

https://www.justice.gov/olc

Description: The Office of Legal Counsel drafts legal opinions of the attorney general and provides legal advice for the White House and Executive branch agencies. The office also reviews draft executive orders and proclamations for legality. The website has the text of selected opinions and memoranda from the office from 1992 onward.

Subject(s): Legal Issues

Office of Privacy and Civil Liberties

https://www.justice.gov/opcl

Description: The mission of the Privacy and Civil Liberties Office is to ensure that the Justice Department is compliant with laws and policies regarding personal privacy and the protection of individual civil liberties. The website has information on the Privacy Act of 1974, including an updated guide. The Resources section of the site has the text of laws and Office of Management and Budget policies regarding privacy. The site also has completed DOJ Privacy Impact Assessments, conducted when an agency makes new plans to use information technology to collect or share content that may include personally identifiable information.

Subject(s): Privacy

Religious Freedom in Focus

https://www.justice.gov/crt/combating-religious-discrimination-and-protecting-religious-freedom-12

Description: *Religious Freedom in Focus* is a periodic newsletter about the Justice Department's Civil Rights Division's cases protecting religious liberty in such areas as education, employment, and housing. This DOJ site provides current and past editions of the newsletter as well as instructions on how to subscribe to it.

Subject(s): Civil Rights; Religion—Laws

U.S. Access Board

https://www.access-board.gov/

Description: The United States Access Board is an independent federal agency whose mission is to promote accessibility for people with disabilities. Its website has information on accessibility guidelines, standards, and enforcement of the Architectural Barriers Act (ABA). The Guidelines and Standards section includes information on relevant laws and policies.

Subject(s): Americans with Disabilities Act (ADA)

U.S. Commission on Civil Rights (USCCR)

http://www.usccr.gov

Description: USCCR investigates and reports on discrimination because of race, color, religion, sex, age, disability, or national origin. The USCCR website includes commission news, meeting transcripts, information on the commission's 51 State Advisory Committees, congressional testimony, and information on filing a complaint. Topics covered on the site include voting rights, educational opportunities, ending campus anti-Semitism, and access to health care.

Subject(s): Civil Rights

USDA Office of the Assistant Secretary for Civil Rights

https://www.ascr.usda.gov/

Description: The USDA Office of the Assistant Secretary for Civil Rights handles complaints regarding employment discrimination for USDA staff and program discrimination for those served by USDA programs. The website has information on how to file a complaint and has the full text of directives and regulations. The site is also available in Spanish.

Subject(s): Civil Rights; Employment Discrimination

COURTS AND THE JUDICIAL SYSTEM

Bankruptcy— United States Courts

http://www.uscourts.gov/services-forms/bankruptcy

Description: Federal courts have exclusive jurisdiction over bankruptcy cases. This website has an overview of bankruptcy and information on federal bankruptcy courts and copies of official bankruptcy forms. The site also provides information on credit counseling, filing fees, fee waivers, and filing for bankruptcy without an attorney.

Subject(s): Bankruptcy Court

Civil Division

https://www.justice.gov/civil

Description: The Civil Division represents the United States, its departments and agencies, members of Congress, Cabinet officers, and other federal employees in litigation. The website includes sections for each of the division's branches under the About the Division heading, including Appellate, Commercial Litigation, Consumer Protection Branch, Federal Programs, Immigration Litigation, and Torts. The Torts Branch section includes the Aviation and Admiralty Section, the Environmental Tort Litigation Section, the Federal Tort Claims Act Litigation Section, and the Constitutional and Specialized Torts Litigation Section.

Subject(s): Litigation

Court of Appeals, (01) First Circuit

http://www.ca1.uscourts.gov

Description: The First Circuit covers Maine, Massachusetts, New Hampshire, Puerto Rico, and Rhode Island. The court's official site has a database of its opinions and dockets. The site also features the court calendar, rules and procedures, forms and notices, and links to the websites of other courts in the First Circuit.

Subject(s): Federal Appellate Courts

Court of Appeals, (02) Second Circuit

http://www.ca2.uscourts.gov

Description: The Second Circuit covers Connecticut, Vermont, and New York. The court's official site has opinions issued within the past 30 days. Opinions can be browsed by date range or searched by case name or docket number. The official site also offers a court directory, forms, and the Federal Rules of Appellate Procedure and Local Rules of the Second Circuit.

Subject(s): Federal Appellate Courts

Court of Appeals, (03) Third Circuit

http://www.ca3.uscourts.gov

Description: The Third Circuit covers Delaware, New Jersey, Pennsylvania, and the Virgin Islands. At its official site, the court has its most current opinions, searchable by keyword. A much more comprehensive source is available at the Villanova University School of Law site at http://digitalcommons.law.villanova.edu/thirdcircuit/. Villanova has the full texts of the decisions from the Third Circuit from May 1994 to the present.

The court's site also has a Death Penalty Information section, listing the appeals status and history for individuals given a death sentence in courts within the Third Circuit.

Subject(s): Federal Appellate Courts

Court of Appeals, (04) Fourth Circuit

http://www.ca4.uscourts.gov

Description: The Fourth Circuit covers Maryland, North Carolina, South Carolina, Virginia, and West Virginia. The Court of Appeals site has its opinions online going back to 1996; it also offers an e-mail alert service for new opinions.

Subject(s): Federal Appellate Courts

Court of Appeals, (05) Fifth Circuit

http://www.ca5.uscourts.gov

Description: The Fifth Circuit covers Louisiana, Mississippi, and Texas. The official Fifth Circuit Court of Appeals website includes published and unpublished opinions released from 1992 to the present. The cases can be searched by date, docket number, and keyword. Researchers can sign up for an RSS feed or download opinions from recent years. The site also includes dockets, calendars, and a practitioner's guide.

Subject(s): Federal Appellate Courts

Court of Appeals, (06) Sixth Circuit

http://www.ca6.uscourts.gov

Description: The Sixth Circuit covers Kentucky, Michigan, Ohio, and Tennessee. The website has a database of published opinions issued since July 1999 and unpublished opinions issued since October 2004. The site also has dockets, forms, fee information, and links to the Sixth Circuit district courts.

Subject(s): Federal Appellate Courts

Court of Appeals, (07) Seventh Circuit

http://www.ca7.uscourts.gov

Description: The Seventh Circuit covers Illinois, Indiana, and Wisconsin. This site has searchable access to its opinions and oral arguments; searching is by case number or date. The Seventh Circuit provides an RSS feed for all new opinions or for opinions by a judge.

Subject(s): Federal Appellate Courts

Court of Appeals, (08) Eighth Circuit

http://www.ca8.uscourts.gov

Description: The Eighth Circuit covers Arkansas, Iowa, Minnesota, Missouri, Nebraska, North Dakota, and South Dakota. Online documents include opinions and oral arguments. The site also has the court calendar, rules, and publications. The Circuit Library section provides news and links to the Eighth Circuit courts.

Subject(s): Federal Appellate Courts

Court of Appeals, (09) Ninth Circuit

https://www.ca9.uscourts.gov/

Description: The Ninth Circuit covers Alaska, Arizona, California, Hawaii, Idaho, Montana, Nevada, Oregon, Washington, Guam, and the Northern Mariana Islands. Opinions can be browsed by date or case number. The site has added audio files of oral arguments before the Ninth Circuit; they are available online the day after the oral argument is made. The Ninth Circuit offers RSS feeds for its opinions, memoranda, cases of interest, and announcements. Other sections of the site include the court calendar, rules, and the status of pending cases.

Subject(s): Federal Appellate Courts

Court of Appeals, (10) Tenth Circuit

https://www.ca10.uscourts.gov/

Description: The Tenth Circuit covers Colorado, Kansas, New Mexico, Oklahoma, Utah, and Wyoming. This official site features information on the circuit, links to current opinions, and a link to the Bankruptcy Appellate Panel (BAP) of the Tenth Circuit. Opinions can be browsed back to 1995. Enhanced access to opinions is available at http://ca10.washburnlaw.edu/.

Subject(s): Federal Appellate Courts

Court of Appeals, (11) Eleventh Circuit

http://www.ca11.uscourts.gov

Description: The Eleventh Circuit covers Alabama, Florida, and Georgia. On the website, published opinions are available from 1995 to the present. The site has an RSS news feed that announces new published opinions. Unpublished opinions are online from April 2005 to present. The site also includes a fee schedule, court rules, and links to district and bankruptcy court sites within the Eleventh District.

Subject(s): Federal Appellate Courts

Court of Appeals, District of Columbia Circuit

https://www.cadc.uscourts.gov/internet/home.nsf

Description: The D.C. Circuit Court of Appeals hears appeals from the U.S. District Court for the District of Columbia and also for many federal administrative agencies. The court's website carries its opinions going back to 1997. Georgetown University's Law Library site, http://www.law.georgetown.edu/library/, carries the opinions going back to April 1995.

Due to the jurisdiction of the court, researchers will find this site useful for documents in high-profile cases involving the federal government.

Subject(s): Federal Appellate Courts

Court of Appeals, Federal Circuit

http://www.cafc.uscourts.gov

Description: The U.S. Court of Appeals for the Federal Circuit has nationwide jurisdiction to hear appeals in specialized claims cases, including patent cases. The website has background information on the court and its workload statistics. The court's site carries its opinions from 2004 to the present and posts recordings of its oral arguments. The Georgetown University's Law Library website, http://www.law.georgetown.edu/library/, has opinions available back to July 1995.

Subject(s): Federal Appellate Courts

Federal Judicial Center (FJC)

https://www.fjc.gov/

Description: The FJC conducts research on federal court operations and history, and it manages training programs for federal judges and court employees. The FJC publishes research, analysis, and training products on such topics as alternative dispute resolution, court management, federal judges, and probation and pretrial services. Many of these publications are available online. Educational materials online include an orientation site called "Inside the Federal Courts." The Federal Judicial History section includes biographies of federal judges since 1789 and a history of landmark legislation affecting the courts.

Subject(s): Federal Courts

FindLaw: Cases and Codes (Federal Courts of Appeals)

https://caselaw.findlaw.com

Description: FindLaw—a free, nongovernment website—offers this section with cases from all the circuit courts. Most are searchable by docket number, party name, or words in the text. The cases can also be browsed by date. FindLaw also provides a court directory for each circuit and a link to recent, related blog posts.

Like their Supreme Court database, FindLaw's circuit court site is an easy-to-use tool for searching for recent opinions. In addition, the site links to other websites that provide judicial opinions online.

Subject(s): Federal Courts; Finding Aids

FindLaw: Supreme Court Opinions

https://caselaw.findlaw.com/court/us-supreme-court

Description: FindLaw, a nongovernment finding aid for Internet law sources, features Supreme Court opinions in HTML format back to 1760. The opinions have links from references to other cases available through FindLaw.

This is an excellent, free source for Supreme Court opinions on the Internet.

Subject(s): Supreme Court

History of the Federal Judiciary

https://www.fjc.gov/history/home.nsf

Description: The History of the Federal Judiciary website presents basic reference information about the history of the federal courts and the judges who have served on them since 1789. Major sections on this site include Judges of the United States Courts, to search for judges by name or browse by alphabetical listing, and Courts, Caseloads, and Jurisdiction, which contains information on historical court caseloads.

Subject(s): Legal System—Federal

Legal Services Corporation (LSC)

https://www.lsc.gov

Description: LSC is a private, nonprofit corporation established by Congress to provide civil legal assistance to low-income people. The About LSC section explains how LSC operates and its various grant programs. State information can be found in the Find Legal Aid section.

Subject(s): Legal Assistances

Office of Legal Policy

https://www.justice.gov/olp

Description: The Office of Legal Policy develops and promotes the legal policy initiatives of the president and the Justice Department and reviews Justice Department regulations. The office also assists with filling certain judicial vacancies.

Subject(s): Judges; Laws—Policy

PACER: Public Access to Court Electronic Records

https://www.pacer.gov/

Description: "Public Access to Court Electronic Records (PACER) is an electronic public access service that allows users to obtain case and docket information online from federal appellate, district, and bankruptcy courts, and the PACER Case Locator. PACER is provided by the Federal Judiciary in keeping with its commitment to providing public access to court information via a centralized service." (from the website) The service is fee based and is financed through the collection of these user fees. Registration is required. The type of information available through case dockets on PACER includes a listing of all parties and participants in the case, a chronology of case events, appellate court opinions, and judgments or case status. The main sections include Register, Find a Case, E-File, and Quick Links.

Subject(s): Federal Courts; Databases

State Justice Institute (SJI)

http://www.sji.gov

Description: SJI is a federally funded organization established by Congress to award grants to improve the state court system. The website has information on available grants and news releases.

Subject(s): Court Administration—Grants

U.S. Court of Appeals for the Armed Forces

http://www.armfor.uscourts.gov

Description: The United States Court of Appeals for the Armed Forces has appellate jurisdiction over members of the armed forces on active duty and others subject to the Uniform Code of Military Justice. This site provides information about the court and access to online opinions. Opinions are available back to October 1996; access is by date. The site also has information on court history, jurisdiction, judges, rules, and scheduled hearings.

Subject(s): Military Justice

U.S. Court of Appeals for Veterans Claims

http://www.uscourts.cavc.gov

Description: The court reviews final decisions of the Board of Veterans' Appeals, which largely consist of cases concerning entitlement to benefits. The court's website has information on how to appeal, court rules, forms, and fees. Orders and opinions are online from 2000 to present, with archives for previous years. Audio files for oral arguments are online beginning with 2005.

Subject(s): Veterans

U.S. Courts: The Federal Judiciary

http://www.uscourts.gov

Description: The Administrative Office of the U.S. Courts maintains this site about the U.S. federal court system, including the U.S. Supreme Court, courts of appeals, district courts, and bankruptcy courts. A Court Locator is featured on the home page. The About Federal Courts section offers an excellent overview of and information on topics such as bankruptcy law, appointment of legal counsel, probation, and the jury service. The site also has information on federal judgeships, judicial vacancies, and judicial appointments, and statistics on court operations, bankruptcy proceedings, and wiretap approvals. Other sections cover court rules, forms, and fees, and a selection of educational resources for teachers and students.

The site includes press releases, *A Journalist's Guide to the Federal Courts*, and *Third Branch News*, the Judiciary's official source for news.

Subject(s): Court Administration

United States Attorneys

https://www.justice.gov/usao

Description: The United States Attorneys, working under the attorney general, conduct most of the trial work in which the United States is a party. The website has a directory of the 93 United States Attorneys stationed throughout the United States, Puerto Rico, the Virgin Islands, and Guam. The site describes the Executive Office for United States Attorneys, which serves as a liaison between the Department of Justice and the attorneys. The Executive Office for United States Attorneys includes the Crime Victims' Rights Ombudsman, with information on the Crime Victims' Rights Act and procedures for complaints under the Act. The website is also available in Spanish.

Subject(s): Litigation

U.S. Court of Federal Claims

http://www.uscfc.uscourts.gov

Description: The Court of Federal Claims is authorized to largely hear money claims founded upon the Constitution, federal statutes, executive regulations, or contracts with the United States. As described on the site, many of the cases before the court concern complex tax refund disputes, government contracts, natural resource issues, civilian and military pay, and Indian tribe and nation claims. Published and unpublished decisions are available on the website. The site also has information on rules, forms, fees, and the court's Office of Special Masters, which handles claims under the National Vaccine Injury Compensation Program.

Subject(s): Federal Courts

U.S. Court of International Trade

https://www.cit.uscourts.gov//

Description: The United States Court of International Trade handles litigation arising out of international trade disputes and within their jurisdiction of the United States. The court's website has sections for the weekly court calendar, court staff directory, rules and forms, and biographies of the judges. Slip opinions are online for 1999 forward.

Subject(s): Federal Courts; International Trade—Laws

U.S. Court Resources

http://www.washlaw.edu/uslaw/judicial.html

Description: United States Court Resources is a section of the website WashLaw: Legal Research on the Web. It links to the free sources of federal case law on the Internet and complementary information on the federal judiciary.

Subject(s): Federal Courts

U.S. Sentencing Commission (USSC)

https://www.ussc.gov/

Description: USSC was created by the Sentencing Reform Act of 1984 to reduce disparities in federal sentences. The commission is an independent agency in the Judicial Branch. In the Guidelines Manual section, the commission's website has the *United States Sentencing Commission Guidelines Manual* and its amendments, and the Research and Publications section provides federal sentencing statistics by state, district, and circuit. The site also has training materials for judges, attorneys, and others on the application of federal sentencing guidelines.

Subject(s): Sentencing

U.S. Tax Court

https://www.ustaxcourt.gov/

Description: The United States Tax Court, a federal court established by Congress under Article I of the Constitution, provides a judicial forum for affected persons to dispute "tax deficiencies" as determined by the Commissioner of Internal Revenue, prior to payment of the disputed amounts. The site has sections for Today's Opinions, Opinions Search, Forms, Rules, Fees/Charges, and general information about contacts and frequently asked questions. The Opinions Search section offers a search of past opinions by release date, petitioner's name, judge, and opinion type, and sorted by case name or release date. The Taxpayer Information section is a guide to the process for those who represent themselves before the court.

Subject(s): Federal Courts; Taxation—Laws

U.S. Trustee Program

https://www.justice.gov/ust

Description: The United States Trustee Program oversees the bankruptcy process to ensure legal and procedural compliance. The Trustee website provides basic information for individuals, including the *Bankruptcy Information Sheet*, which is available in 17 languages besides English, and a directory of Trustee Program offices nationwide. The site has information on the Bankruptcy Abuse Prevention and Consumer Protection Act of 2005, notice of any proposed regulations, and additional resources for practitioners. The Press & Public Affairs section includes bankruptcy fact sheets and bankruptcy statistics.

Subject(s): Bankruptcy

CRIME AND ENFORCEMENT

AMBER Alert

https://www.amberalert.gov/

Description: AMBER Alerts are local systems for alerting the public when a child has been abducted. This site includes program information, statistics, and answers to frequently asked questions. It also provides State AMBER Alert contacts and information on the wireless AMBER Alert service.

Subject(s): Kidnapping

America's Most Wanted Criminals

https://www.usa.gov/report-crime#item-36382

Description: USA.gov presents this compilation of links to most-wanted lists from eight U.S. and international sources.

Subject(s): Criminals

ATF: Bureau of Alcohol, Tobacco, Firearms and Explosives

https://www.atf.gov/

Description: As part of the Homeland Security Act of 2002, the Bureau of Alcohol, Tobacco, Firearms and Explosives (ATF) was transferred from the Treasury Department to the Justice Department in early 2003. Certain functions of the ATF remain with Treasury in the Alcohol and Tobacco Tax and Trade Bureau, or TTB. See the separate entry for the TTB website for more information.

ATF is a law enforcement organization charged with enforcing federal laws and regulations relating to alcohol, tobacco, firearms, explosives, and arson. The ATF website has a section for each topic discussing enforcement, regulations, and other information. The Publications section includes ATF circulars, bulletins, delegation orders, and fact sheets.

Subject(s): Law Enforcement; Wanted People

Bureau of Justice Assistance (BJA)

https://www.bja.gov/

Description: BJA supports local criminal justice agencies throughout the United States, offering grants, training, and technical assistance. The site offers information on funding and training opportunities. Program information is available in the Topics section under topical headings such as Adjudication, Corrections, Crime Prevention, and Justice Information Sharing.

Subject(s): Law Enforcement—Grants

Bureau of Justice Statistics (BJS)

https://www.bjs.gov/

Description: BJS collects and reports data on law enforcement, crime, and corrections at the federal, state, and local levels. The website provides downloadable data in multiple formats, such as prepared reports and statistical tables. Data products and publications are organized under topics including Corrections, Courts and Sentencing, Crime Type, Employment and Expenditure, Law Enforcement, and Victims.

BJS also supports grant programs for state, local, and tribal governments to assist with criminal justice statistics programs at those levels.

Subject(s): Criminal Justice—Statistics; Prisons—Statistics

Community Relations Service (CRS)

https://www.justice.gov/crs

Description: CRS was established by the Civil Rights Act of 1964 to help communities resolve serious racial or ethnic conflicts. The Resource Center has annual reports, training videos, and the *CRS Fact Sheet* in Spanish, Arabic, and Punjabi, as well as a frequently asked questions section. The About CRS section has a list of CRS regional and field offices. CRS is involved with such topics as hate crimes and police use of force.

Subject(s): Dispute Resolution; Mediation

Computer Crime and Intellectual Property Section (CCIPS)

https://www.justice.gov/criminal-ccips

Description: This website for the Justice Department's CCIPS reports on relevant policy developments, cases, guidance, laws, and documents in the areas of computer crime, intellectual property protection, and electronic evidence.

Subject(s): Computer Security; Intellectual Property

Coordinating Council on Juvenile Justice and Delinquency Prevention

https://www.juvenilecouncil.gov/

Description: The Coordinating Council on Juvenile Justice and Delinquency Prevention is an independent body within the Executive branch. It coordinates federal programs concerning juvenile delinquency prevention, programs and activities that detain or care for unaccompanied juveniles, and programs relating to missing and exploited children. Its website has information on the council, its members, its meetings, and links to relevant grant programs.

Subject(s): Child Welfare; Juvenile Delinquency; Juvenile Justice

COPS Office: **Grants and Resources for Community Policing**

https://cops.usdoj.gov/

Description: The Community Oriented Policing Services (COPS) Office makes grants to state and local law enforcement agencies to advance community policing. The website has information on the grants and training available. It also covers community policing topics such as gangs and school safety.

Subject(s): Police-Community Relations—Grants

Criminal Division

https://www.justice.gov/criminal

Description: The Department of Justice's Criminal Division enforces and prosecutes federal criminal law. Most of the information on the website can be reached via the About the Division section. The Sections/Offices subsection links to information on the Narcotic and Dangerous Drug Section, the Fraud Section, the Capital Case Section, the Organized Crime and Gang Section, among others. The Task Forces subsection links to information on special task forces, such as the Hurricane Katrina Fraud Task Force and the Organized Crime Drug Enforcement Task Forces. The Public Services subsection features other Criminal Division sections including the Child Exploitation and Obscenity Section and the Human Rights and Special Prosecutions Section.

Subject(s): Crime; Law Enforcement

Cyber Crime

https://www.fbi.gov/investigate/cyber

Description: The FBI is in-part concerned with stopping computer network intrusions, online sexual predators, online operations that target U.S. intellectual property, and organized criminal enterprises engaging in Internet fraud. The Cyber Crime website has FBI news and information on initiatives in these areas. It also carries advice to the public about protection from computer crime.

Subject(s): Computer Security

Dru Sjodin National Sex Offender Public Website

https://www.nsopw.gov/

Description: The National Sex Offender Public Website is a cooperative effort between the state agencies hosting public sexual offender registries and the federal government. It can be searched by name, county, city/town, and ZIP code. The site provides background information that should be consulted before using the database, covering what may legally constitute a sex offense and warning about the differences in registries from state to state. The site also has a lengthy "conditions of use" statement under the Search section that includes individual state, territory, and tribal conditions of use for the information.

The website was renamed the Dru Sjodin National Sex Offender Public Website in October 2006 in memory of Dru Sjodin, a college student who was murdered in North Dakota by a convicted sex offender.

Subject(s): Criminals

Drug Enforcement Administration (DEA)

https://www.dea.gov/index.shtml

Description: The DEA website focuses on information about current illegal drug threats and recent DEA enforcement actions. Topical sections include Prevention, Drug Info (including fact sheets), and Topics of Interest. The Operations section links to information about diversion control, training, and programs. The Press Room section includes links to speeches, testimony, and a multimedia resource library.

Subject(s): Drug Control; Law Enforcement

Federal Bureau of Investigation (FBI)

https://www.fbi.gov/

Description: For an overview of the FBI's work, see this site's What We Investigate header, which is in the About Us section. It links to substantial information on FBI programs in counterterrorism, counterintelligence, public corruption, civil rights, organized crime, white collar crime, art theft, and other areas. Other sections of the website cover crime prevention tips, the FBI's Most Wanted, laboratory services, information technology initiatives, agency history, and directories of FBI field and overseas offices. The site also has an online form for submitting tips about suspected criminal activity.

The Freedom of Information Act section, linked from the bottom of each page, can be accessed directly at https://www.fbi.gov/foia/. It has an index to the popularly requested FOIA documents in its Washington FOIA reading room, with links to those documents that have been digitized and put online. An Electronic Reading Room section, the Vault, has online documents organized alphabetically and by topic.

Because information is spread throughout the many sections of this site, first-time users may want to consult the site map.

Subject(s): Crime Detection; Law Enforcement; Wanted People

Federal Bureau of Prisons (BOP)

https://www.bop.gov/

Description: BOP is responsible for the federal prison system and federal inmates. The BOP website has the Inmate Locator database of federal inmates incarcerated from 1982 to present. It also has a Facility Locator and links to web pages for each of the facilities operated by the Bureau of Prisons. The Inmate Custody & Care section covers topics such as medical care, substance abuse treatment, preparation for release, and the Victim/Witness Notification Program. The site also has information on employment and acquisition opportunities.

Subject(s): Prisons

Federal Law Enforcement Training Centers (FLETC)

https://www.fletc.gov/

Description: FLETC is the federal government's centralized law enforcement training organization. Its website includes a list of locations and FLETC news. The FLETC site will be of interest primarily to those considering FLETC training.

Subject(s): Homeland Security; Law Enforcement

Financial Crimes Enforcement Network (FinCEN)

https://www.fincen.gov/

Description: FinCEN supports law enforcement investigations into domestic and international financial crimes and money laundering. The agency works with the law enforcement (local, national, and international), financial, and regulatory communities on information sharing in the network. The site has regulatory guidance on the Bank Secrecy Act (BSA) and the USA PATRIOT Act. FinCEN's *SAR Activity Review* of statistical data from the Suspicious Activity Report forms filed by various financial institutions is available, along with reports on suspected mortgage fraud. The FinCEN Advisory Publications, which often focus on financial transactions with specific countries, are also on the site.

The website has specific guidance sections for depository institutions, casinos, Money Services Businesses (MSBs), the insurance industry, securities and futures, and the precious metals/jewelry industry.

Subject(s): Financial Crimes; Money Laundering

Identity Theft

https://www.consumer.ftc.gov/features/feature-0014-identity-theft

Description: This site serves as a central point for government information on identity theft, which occurs when someone appropriates personal information without that person's knowledge to commit fraud or other crimes. The FTC provides detailed information for consumers, businesses, law enforcement, the media, and members of the military. Consumer information is available in Spanish.

Subject(s): Identity Theft

Immigration and Customs Enforcement (ICE)

https://www.ice.gov/

Description: ICE has investigation and law enforcement responsibilities within the Department of Homeland Security. ICE is concerned with such issues as illegal shipments, drug trafficking, and immigrant smuggling. Most information about the agency's operations is in the What We Do section. Topics include the detention and removal of illegal aliens, intelligence analysis, intellectual property rights, and combating human smuggling, trafficking in persons, and clandestine terrorist travel. The Newsroom section of the site includes links to fact sheets on ICE programs, federal regulation notices, and *The Cornerstone Report*. Basic information about ICE is available in Spanish.

Subject(s): Customs (Trade); Homeland Security; Immigration Law

Internet Crime Complaint Center (IC3)

https://www.ic3.gov/default.aspx

Description: The Internet Crime Complaint Center is a partnership between the FBI, the Bureau of Justice Assistance, and the National White Collar Crime Center. The website describes current Internet crime schemes and has a form for filing a complaint online. In the Press Room section, the center's annual *Internet Crime Report* provides statistics on complaints by state.

Subject(s): Fraud; Internet

INTERPOL Washington

https://www.justice.gov/interpol-washington

Description: INTERPOL Washington, or the U.S. National Central Bureau of Interpol, acts as the U.S. representative to the International Criminal Police Organization (INTERPOL) on behalf of the U.S. attorney general. Among its responsibilities, the bureau distributes INTERPOL notices on fugitives, lost persons, stolen art and cultural objects, organized crime groups, and other matters. The website has information on the bureau's mission, organization, and programs.

Subject(s): International Crimes; Wanted People

Justice Information Sharing

https://it.ojp.gov/

Description: This Justice Department site provides a central location for news, documents, funding information, data and technology standards, and policy related to sharing information and intelligence among law enforcement, public safety, and private sector officials at all levels. The National Initiatives section covers Fusion Centers and the National Information Exchange Model. The site also has information on privacy and civil liberties as related to justice information sharing.

Subject(s): Government Information; Law Enforcement Policy

JUSTNET: Justice Technology Information Network

https://www.justnet.org/

Description: JUSTNET is the website for the National Law Enforcement and Corrections Technology Center (NLECTC), which assists state and local law enforcement and corrections personnel with technology, equipment, and information systems. The website describes NLECTC programs in technology assistance, equipment testing and evaluation, and training assistance. Resources such as journal articles, government websites, and grants programs are organized by technology, including communications, crime mapping, explosives, forensics, and personal protective equipment.

Subject(s): Law Enforcement—Grants

National Center on Elder Abuse (NCEA)

https://ncea.acl.gov/

Description: NCEA serves as a national resource center on the prevention of elder mistreatment. The website provides federal, state, and community outreach information resources for families, caregivers, and communities. The site has a directory of elder abuse hotlines and adult protective services (APS) and information on state APS laws. The site also features a calendar with conferences, events, and training.

Subject(s): Senior Citizens

National Criminal Justice Reference Service (NCJRS)

https://www.ncjrs.gov/

Description: NCJRS compiles resource information from federal agencies involved in law enforcement research and policy. It responds to queries from law enforcement and corrections officials, lawmakers, judges and court personnel, and researchers. The NCJRS website houses numerous publications on a wide range of criminal justice and law enforcement topics. It also provides access to the NCJRS Abstracts Database with summaries of more than 220,000 justice and substance abuse publications.

Other topical links on the main page include Corrections, Courts, Crime, Crime Prevention, Drugs, Justice System, Juvenile Justice, Law Enforcement, and Victims. These topic sections include links to publications, Department of Justice seminars, and related resources. The NCJRS site also includes a list of federal grants relating to criminal justice.

The vast number of publications available from the NCJRS site makes it a leading source for criminal justice statistics and reports. Many of the publications are available directly from the individual agencies. NCJRS provides centralized access.

Subject(s): Criminal Justice

National Institute of Corrections (NIC)

https://nicic.gov/

Description: NIC provides training, technical assistance, information services, and program development assistance to federal, state, and local corrections agencies. Publications announcements are in the About Us section. The Library section provides access to many of NIC's digital resources and a directory of other corrections websites, as well as e-mail and RSS subscription options.

Subject(s): Criminal Justice; Prisons

National Institute of Justice (NIJ)

https://www.nij.gov

Description: NIJ supports research, evaluation, and demonstration programs, development of technology, and national and international information dissemination in the area of criminal justice. Program topics include biometrics, forensic DNA, communications technologies, body armor, and crime mapping. The website has information on the institute and its programs, funding opportunities, and publications.

Subject(s): Criminal Justice—Research

National Missing and Unidentified Persons System (NamUs)

https://www.namus.gov/

Description: NamUs is a national repository for the names of missing persons and the records of people who have died but have not been identified. A database for unclaimed persons lists decedents whose names are known but whose next of kin has not been identified. The database is made available to the general public and law enforcement to help solve cases. Registration is not required to search the database, but registered users can take advantage of advanced features. The site explains the issues of missing persons and unidentified decedents in an online video and in the About NamUs section.

Subject(s): Crime Detection; Missing Children

Office of the Attorney General

https://www.justice.gov/ag

Description: The attorney general is the head of the Justice Department and the chief law enforcement officer of the federal government. This site describes the office and has some biographical information on the current attorney general. It also provides links to speeches, testimony, annual reports, and the office's FOIA section.

Subject(s): Law Enforcement

Office for Victims of Crime (OVC)

https://ojp.gov/ovc/

Description: OVC was established by the 1984 Victims of Crime Act to oversee grants, training, and other programs that benefit victims of crime. Major sections include Grants & Funding, Help for Crime Victims, Library & Multimedia, News & Features, Providers/Community Leaders, Public Awareness, and Crime Victims' Rights. The Help for Crime Victims section directs users to resources, particularly nongovernment organizations and their websites, that can assist with such areas as child abuse, elder abuse, sexual abuse, white collar crime, and stalking. It also features an online directory of crime victim services.

Much of the funding and technical assistance information on the OVC website is for professionals and organizations that manage victim assistance programs. The Help for Victims section can be of direct interest to individuals.

Subject(s): Victims of Crime

Office of Child Support Enforcement (OCSE)

https://www.acf.hhs.gov/css

Description: Child support enforcement is conducted primarily at the state level. OCSE supports state and local efforts to locate participants in child support cases, collect child support payments, and enforce child support orders. The website has information on available grants, state child support websites, and services for finding participants in child support cases. Some materials, such as a handbook for the party seeking child support, are available in Spanish as well as English.

Subject(s): Child Support

Office of Justice Programs (OJP)

https://ojp.gov/

Description: OJP provides federal assistance to the nation's justice system. OJP and its program bureaus are responsible for collecting statistical data and conducting analyses, identifying emerging criminal justice issues, providing technical assistance and training, evaluating program results, and disseminating information to state and local governments. The website has sections on funding resources and on technical and training assistance. The OJP Topics section has detailed information on resources in specific areas such as juvenile justice and corrections.

Subject(s): Criminal Justice—Research; Law Enforcement—Grants

Office of Juvenile Justice and Delinquency Prevention (OJJDP)

https://www.ojjdp.gov/

Description: OJJDP supports states and communities in their work to prevent and control juvenile crime. Featured sections of the site include Topics, Funding, Programs, Publications, State Contacts, and Statistics. The Topics section organizes OJJDP publications, programs, funding opportunities, and events by subject. Topics include Child Protection, Corrections/Detention, Courts, Delinquency Prevention, Offenses/Offenders, and Schools. The publications catalog links to full-text publications on the National Criminal Justice Reference Service (NCJRS) site.

Subject(s): Juvenile Delinquency; Juvenile Justice

Office of Terrorism and Financial Intelligence (TFI)

https://www.treasury.gov/about/organizational-structure/offices/pages/office-of-terrorism-and-financial-intelligence.aspx

Description: TFI develops policies, regulations, and strategies to guard financial systems against illegal use and to target the use of financial systems by terrorists. Topics covered by the website include freezing terrorist assets and protecting charities from misuse by terrorist organizations.

Subject(s): Financial Crimes; Terrorism

Office of the Deputy Attorney General

https://www.justice.gov/dag

Description: This page features the deputy attorney general's speeches, congressional testimonies, and publications.

Subject(s): Law Enforcement Policy

Office on Violence Against Women

https://www.justice.gov/ovw

Description: The Office on Violence Against Women was established as a source for assistance to female victims of violence. The website links to resources and publications on help for victims (including hotline numbers), domestic violence, sexual assault, dating violence, and stalking. The site also has information on grant programs, federal laws, and the National Advisory Committee on Violence Against Women.

Subject(s): Domestic Violence; Victims of Crime

Office to Monitor and Combat Trafficking in Persons

https://www.state.gov/j/tip/

Description: The Office to Monitor and Combat Trafficking in Persons is concerned with preventing abusive smuggling of the men, women, and children across international borders. The website provides background information on the issue and details on U.S. laws on trafficking in persons and government-funded anti-trafficking programs.

Subject(s): International Crimes

Project Safe Childhood

https://www.justice.gov/psc

Description: Project Safe Childhood is designed to strengthen the investigation and prosecution of sexual exploitation crimes committed against children. The website provides detailed information on the program and news and reports related to the victimization of youth.

Subject(s): Children

Project Safe Neighborhoods

https://www.bja.gov/programdetails.aspx?program_id=74

Description: Project Safe Neighborhoods is a nationwide commitment to reduce gun and gang violence. Federal support comes in the form of funding, grants, law enforcement training, and technology. This website provides background information on the project and links to related publications and topics.

Subject(s): Guns; Crime Prevention

Sourcebook of Criminal Justice Statistics

https://www.albany.edu/sourcebook/

Description: The *Sourcebook of Criminal Justice Statistics* is a key Justice Department reference publication that presents over 600 tables of data from over 100 sources. This university site has made the *Sourcebook* available online and the data is continuously updated. Data tables are in PDF and spreadsheet formats. The *Sourcebook* is no longer issued in print; the site has an archive of past *Sourcebook* editions going back to 1994.

Subject(s): Criminal Justice—Statistics

U.S. Customs and Border Protection (CBP)

https://www.cbp.gov/

Description: "CBP takes a comprehensive approach to border management and control, combining customs, immigration, border security, and agricultural protection into one coordinated and supportive activity." (from the website) The agency's primary focus is, however, on preventing the entry of terrorists and their weapons into the country. The CBP website includes information on the agency's history and organization, as well as details on its day-to-day activities.

Subject(s): Homeland Security—International Borders

U.S. Marshals Service

https://www.usmarshals.gov/

Description: The U.S. Marshals Service, in existence since 1789, today has a range of duties including court security, fugitive investigations, and the sale of properties seized and forfeited by federal law enforcement agencies. The website emphasizes news of current fugitives and recent captures. Other sections of the site cover the agency's duties and its long and eventful history, the Asset Forfeiture Program (including current asset sales), prisoner transportation and custody issues, court and witness security, and service of process. The site also has career information, a detailed directory of local district offices, and an RSS feed for news releases.

Subject(s): Law Enforcement; Wanted People

U.S. Postal Inspection Service

https://postalinspectors.uspis.gov/

Description: The U.S. Postal Inspection Service is a federal law enforcement agency with the security and enforcement responsibilities for U.S. mail and U.S. Postal Service workers. Major sections of the website concern mail fraud, identity theft, mail theft, child exploitation, and dangerous mail (for example, hazardous substances). The site also has a list of the U.S. Postal Inspection Service's most wanted criminals with links to their wanted posters.

Subject(s): Postal Service; Wanted People

U.S. Park Police

https://www.nps.gov/subjects/uspp/index.htm

Description: This site describes the history, role, and activities of the United States Park Police, law enforcement officers with jurisdiction in National Park Service areas and certain government properties. The site describes the agency's field operations (including horse mounted police), icon protection branch (protecting the Golden Gate Bridge and other American cultural icons), and investigative branch. The site also features the Park Police Most Wanted List and phone numbers for their offices.

Subject(s): National Parks and Reserves; Police

U.S. Parole Commission

https://www.justice.gov/uspc

Description: The United States Parole Commission makes parole determinations in certain federal offender cases, District of Columbia Code violation cases, Uniform Code of Military Justice offender cases, and for certain state probationers and parolees who have been placed in the federal witness protection program. The site describes the commission and its specific jurisdiction. Sections include Victim Witness Program, USPC FOIA, News, and Resources. Questions such as "How does the Commission determine if someone is eligible for parole?" and "What happens at a parole hearing?" are addressed in the Frequently Asked Questions section.

Subject(s): Prisoners

VetoViolence

https://vetoviolence.cdc.gov/apps/stryve/

Description: VetoViolence is a comprehensive source for violence prevention. Its goal is to educate and empower communities to stop violence before it happens. Veto Violence has shared research, trends, and best practices gathered from all over the country in a newly relaunched site. National Youth Violence Protection week is March 19–23, 2018.

Subject(s): Violence

LAWS AND LEGAL INFORMATION

***Code of Federal Regulations* (*CFR*)**

https://www.gpo.gov/fdsys/

Description: As described by the Government Publishing Office (GPO), the *Code of Federal Regulations* (*CFR*) "is the codification of the general and permanent rules published in the Federal Register by the departments and agencies of the Federal Government. It is divided into 50 titles that represent broad areas subject to Federal regulation." The *CFR* on GPO's FDsys online system is a digital version of the printed edition. Content is updated annually when the print volumes are updated. Past editions, going back to 1996, are kept online.

GPO has also developed a complementary online version, called e-CFR. The e-CFR is available at https://www.ecfr.gov/. The e-CFR text is continually updated with new federal regulations.

Researchers using either version of the *CFR* should read the online background information to learn how the regulations are updated.

Subject(s): Legal Information—Regulations

Federal Register

https://www.gpo.gov/fdsys/browse/collection.action?collectionCode=FR

Description: The *Federal Register* is the official daily publication for rules, proposed rules, and notices of federal agencies and organizations, as well as Executive orders, presidential proclamations, and other presidential documents. At the website listed above, *Federal Register* issues are available on the Government Publishing Office's FDsys online system for 1994 to the present. The issues are compiled by the National Archives and put online by GPO.

The newer *Federal Register* website, FederalRegister.gov, which provides users with a more interactive interface, is listed in a separate entry.

Subject(s): Legal Information—Regulations

FederalRegister.gov

https://www.federalregister.gov/

Description: FederalRegister.gov features an unofficial and interactive edition of the *Federal Register* and is intended to make it easier to find and comment on federal regulations. Researchers can do a word search or browse regulations by the issuing agency's name. Researchers can also browse by topic and set up an RSS news feed of new items in that topic area.

The official version of the *Federal Register* is available through the GPO's FDsys online system is described in a separate entry.

Subject(s): Laws—Regulations

Global Legal Monitor (GLM)

http://www.loc.gov/law/foreign-news/

Description: GLM features international legal news by topic and by country. The Law Library of Congress introduced GLM, an online publication, in 2006. News updates are available as an RSS feed, and all news can be searched by topic, country, and date.

Subject(s): Legal Information—International

Office of the Law Revision Counsel

http://uscode.house.gov

Description: "The United States Code is a consolidation and codification by subject matter of the general and permanent laws of the United States. It is prepared by the Office of the Law Revision Counsel of the United States House of Representatives." (from the website) The Law Revision Counsel makes the U.S. Code available online for searching, browsing, or downloading. The site also features the office's classification tables, which show where recently enacted laws will appear in the U.S. Code and which sections of the code have been amended by those laws.

See also the separate entry for the U.S. Code website, which is sponsored by the Legal Information Institute.

Subject(s): Laws

Public and Private Laws

https://www.gpo.gov/fdsys/

Description: The GPO's FDsys website has a database of public and private laws enacted from 1995 to the present. Laws are available in both text and PDF formats. Most laws are Public Laws. Private laws are enacted to assist citizens that have been injured by government programs or who are appealing an executive agency ruling such as deportation.

Select "Public and Private Laws" from the FDsys menu or access it directly at https://www.gpo.gov/fdsys/browse/collection.action?collectionCode=PLAW.

Subject(s): Laws

Public Laws

https://www.archives.gov/federal-register/laws

Description: Public laws are published by the National Archive's Office of the Federal Register. This web page explains how laws are numbered and printed. Users can view a list of laws from the current session of Congress or sign up to receive automatic e-mail announcements of new public law numbers.

Subject(s): Laws

RegInfo.gov

https://www.reginfo.gov/public/

Description: RegInfo.gov is a finding aid for federal regulatory information and learning how to track regulations throughout the regulatory process. The site features the Regulatory Review Dashboard, an interactive graph for finding regulations currently under review. The site links to key online resources for regulatory information such as the *Federal Register* and the *Code of Federal Regulations*, Small Business Administration Regulatory Alerts, and the Unified Agenda of Federal Regulatory and Deregulatory Actions.

RegInfo.gov is a useful portal site for official regulatory documents and information on the federal regulatory process.

Subject(s): Regulatory Policy; Finding Aids

Regulations.gov

https://www.regulations.gov/

Description: Regulations.gov is intended to make it easier for the general public to participate in the federal regulations review process. The site is an interagency effort led by the EPA. Users can search by word, agency, and other facets to find proposed and final regulations currently open for comment. Search results include a docket ID, Federal Register citation and date for when the regulation was first published, and final date for comments. The results also have links to view the Federal Register announcement in text or PDF formats and a link to a web form for submitting comments. The full docket of materials includes the text of public comments in accordance with the policies of the individual agencies. Prepared searches to make it easy to find newly issued regulatory proposals and regulations with a comment period that is ending soon.

Subject(s): Regulatory Policy

U.S. Code

https://www.law.cornell.edu/uscode/text

Description: Cornell University's Legal Information Institute (LII) offers this popular and free interface for searching the *U.S. Code*. The code can be searched by word, by title and section number, or browsed. The site also features a table of popular names of laws, such as the Voting Rights Act and Railroad Retirement Act. Where these laws can easily be linked to one part of the code, LII does so.

The *U.S. Code* can also be accessed and browsed on GPO's FDsys system: https://www.gpo.gov/fdsys/browse/collectionUScode.action?collectionCode=USCODE

Subject(s): Laws

Chapter Sixteen

Legislative Branch

The United States Congress is comprised of two chambers, 535 member offices, over forty committees, various legislative and operational offices, and several major congressional support agencies. Most of these entities have their own website. In addition, many private and educational sites help to spread and interpret congressional information. This chapter describes major legislative branch websites and other useful finding aids for legislative information. The websites for individual members of Congress and congressional committees are listed in appendixes A and B at the end of this book.

Subsections in this chapter are Congress, Congressional Support Agencies, and Legislative Information.

CONGRESS

Biographical Directory of the United States Congress

http://bioguide.congress.gov/biosearch/biosearch.asp

Description: For over a century, the *Biographical Directory of the United States Congress* has provided valuable information about the more than 13,000 individuals who have served in the national legislature, including members of the Continental Congress, the Senate, and the House of Representatives, from 1774 to the present. Congress offers an online version of this historical resource that goes beyond the scope of the printed *Biographical Directory* by including images and extended information about research collections relating to each member. The online version is also continuously updated. The biographies may be searched by name, position (e.g., senator or Speaker of the House), party, and state.

Subject(s): Members of Congress; Biographies

Black Americans in Congress

http://history.house.gov/exhibitions-and-publications/baic/black-americans-in-congress/

Description: As described on the site, Black Americans in Congress features "biographical profiles of former African-American members of Congress, links to information about current black members, essays on institutional and national events that shaped successive generations of African Americans in Congress, and images of each individual member, supplemented by other historical photos." The Education section of the site includes lesson plans and fact sheets on African American congressional "firsts." It is based on the publication *Black Americans in Congress, 1870–2007*.

Subject(s): African Americans—History; Lesson Plans

Clerk of the House

http://clerk.house.gov

Description: The Clerk of the House is charged with a variety of procedural and administrative duties. The clerk's website includes information about the office itself, along with a wealth of congressional information associated with the clerk's duties. The site includes directories of members of Congress, leadership offices, committees, and subcommittees; House legislative activity schedules; legislative procedure information; roll call vote results; congressional history; congressional election statistics; and public disclosure information, such as members' financial disclosure reports and official foreign travel and expenditures reports. It also carries the official list of congressional office vacancies and current tallies of party alignment in the House and Senate.

Subject(s): Congressional Information; Legislative Procedure

Committee on House Administration

https://cha.house.gov/

Description: Although other congressional committees do not receive a separate entry in this section, the Committee on House Administration is featured here because of several reference resources available on the site. It provides a directory of Congressional Member Organizations, such as the Congressional Arts Caucus, the Law Enforcement Caucus, and the Military Veterans Caucus. The site also has information from the Commission on Congressional Mailing Standards, known as the Franking Commission, which regulates issues related to outgoing congressional mail.

Subject(s): House of Representatives

Congressional Directory

https://www.gpo.gov/fdsys/browse/collection.action?collectionCode=CDIR

Description: The *Congressional Directory*, the official directory of Congress, has been published since 1888. The Government Publishing Office has made it available online on their FDsys website for the 105th Congress (1997–1998) to the 113th Congress (2013–2014). Each edition of the *Congressional Directory* can be searched by keyword or browsed by section. The online edition is typically updated once before the next edition appears in print.

The following webpage provides tips from the GPO about searching for entries in the *Congressional Directory*:

https://www.gpo.gov/help/sample_searches_and_urls_for_congressional_directory.htm

The publishing schedule of the *Congressional Directory* makes it less valuable as a source of current contact information than as a source of historical reference. Useful lists in the Statistical Information section of each edition include: joint sessions of Congress for 1789 to present; House impeachments of judges, presidents, and members of Congress; and political divisions in the House and Senate from 1855 onward.

Subject(s): Congressional Information

Guide to House and Senate Members

https://memberguide.gpo.gov/

Description: The House of Representatives and the Senate each feature directory pages of members and committees on their websites. Among the various free congressional directories online, these naturally tend to be the most current and authoritative. In addition to the official listings and links to members' websites, the House directories page includes information on current vacancies and member addresses formatted as downloadable mailing labels. The Senate page features a list that can be sorted by name, state, or party. The Senate listing includes e-mail addresses. The House offers a Write Your Representative feature for finding and e-mailing your House member.

The data come from the *Pictorial Directory* and the *Congressional Directory*. These publications are available on the GPO's FDsys website at https://www.gpo.gov/fdsys.

Subject(s): Members of Congress; Directories

History of the United States Capitol

https://www.gpo.gov/fdsys/pkg/GPO-CDOC-106sdoc29/content-detail.html

Description: The full-text version of the *History of the United States Capitol: A Chronicle of Design, Construction, and Politics*, a 2002 book by architectural historian William C. Allen, is available in PDF format on this FDsys webpage. The book, which was sponsored by Congress and printed as a Senate document, includes numerous illustrations and photographs, as well as a bibliography.

Subject(s): Capitol Building—History

House Democratic Leader

https://www.democraticleader.gov/

Description: The website for House Democratic Leader Nancy Pelosi includes an Issues section, which is broken down into such topics as Jobs & Economy, Health Care, and Campaign Finance Reform. The site also includes a calendar (under Resources), a biography of Pelosi, and a Newsroom section with press releases, speeches, and reports.

Subject(s): House of Representatives

House of Representatives—Committees

https://www.house.gov/committees

Description: This webpage provides links to all of the House committee websites. The content of these sites can vary tremendously from one committee to the next. Most include a list of committee members and information on the committee's jurisdiction and schedule. Most provide live webcasts of hearings, but not all provide archives of past hearings. Each site, managed by the committee's majority party, typically links to a website for the committee's minority party members.

The House committee websites can be useful sources for current legislative information and of information about the programs within their jurisdiction. Many of the sites, however, could be improved with more timely provisions of hearings transcripts or availability of archived hearing webcasts.

Subject(s): Congressional Committees

House *Statement of Disbursements* (*SOD*)

https://www.house.gov/the-house-explained/open-government/statement-of-disbursements

Description: According to the website, "The Statement of Disbursements (SOD) is a quarterly public report of all receipts and expenditures for U.S. House of Representatives Members, Committees, Leadership, Officers and Offices." It is published by the Chief Administrative Officer of the House. It has been published in print since 1964 and has been published online since 2009. The website has the SOD for July 2009 forward.

This document is fairly technical and specific to House disbursements. Be sure to review the supporting documentation for help in reading the statements.

Subject(s): House of Representatives

Lobbying Disclosure—House

https://lobbyingdisclosure.house.gov/

Description: The House provides this website for those who must by law register with the House Clerk's Office and file regular reports on their lobbying activities.

Prior to 2008, the House did not make copies of the disclosure reports available online. Changes in the reporting system were brought about in compliance with the Honest Leadership and Open Government Act of 2007, described on this site. An alternative for lobbying data is the nonprofit OpenSecrets.org Lobby Database at http://www.opensecrets.org/lobby/.

Subject(s): Lobbyists

Lobbying Disclosure—Senate

https://www.senate.gov/pagelayout/legislative/g_three_sections_with_teasers/lobbyingdisc.htm

Description: For those who wish to lobby the Senate, this webpage provides access to filing forms and information about compliance with lobbying disclosure law. It also links to databases of lobbyists' disclosure filings. One database is for the standard (LD-1/LD-2) quarterly report; the other is for a relatively new semiannual report (LD-203) of payments for honorary contributions, event hosting costs, and other contributions. The disclosure filings search page can be directly accessed at https://www.senate.gov/pagelayout/general/one_item_and_teasers/file_not_found.htmAn alternative for lobbying data is the nonprofit OpenSecrets.org Lobby Database at http://www.opensecrets.org/lobby/.

Subject(s): Lobbyists

Majority Whip

https://www.majoritywhip.gov/

Description: The Majority Whip is responsible for marshaling the votes of members of the majority party in the House. The whip's website is used to keep members informed about upcoming legislation and floor votes; researchers can also use it for this purpose. In the Schedule section, the site features a daily schedule as well as a live stream of the House Floor, and a listing of legislation passed that month.

Subject(s): Legislation

Senate Majority Leader

https://www.mcconnell.senate.gov/public/

Description: Senator Mitch McConnell (R-Ky.) is the current majority leader of the Senate. This site includes a Leadership section with links to the pages of other Senate members who hold leadership roles.

Subject(s): Senate

Senate Minority Leader

https://www.schumer.senate.gov/

Description: The site for the Senate's minority leader, Senator Charles Schumer Reid (D-new York), includes information about the senator and his bills and actions in the Senate.

Subject(s): Senate

Speaker's Blog

https://www.speaker.gov/blog/

Description: The blog for the Speaker of the House links to analysis of congressional and presidential initiatives. Comments are permitted.

Subject(s): House of Representatives

Speaker.gov

https://www.speaker.gov/

Description: The website for the Speaker of the House, Rep. Paul Ryan (R-Wisc.), includes photos and video, a biography of Ryan, and information about legislative initiatives. Links to social media pages and a blog (described in a separate entry) are also available.

Subject(s): House of Representatives

U.S. House of Representatives

https://www.house.gov/

Description: The House of Representatives website includes a wealth of current legislative and policy information. The site provides quick links to House member websites, which typically have information about their House district and representational services for constituents of the district. The House site also links to individual House committee websites, which report on legislation within their jurisdiction. Links for finding and writing to local representatives are provided in the upper right-hand corner of the home page.

Other sections of the site link to House schedule information, sources for legislative and legal research, House members' voting information, information for kids and students, visitor information, and the websites for legislative branch agencies.

Subject(s): House of Representatives

U.S. Senate

https://www.senate.gov/

Description: The United States Senate website is a source for both current legislative news and historical Senate information. The major sections of the site are Senators, Committees, Legislation & Records, Art & History, Visitors, and Reference. As with the House site, the content of individual member and committee sites varies, and the committee sites typically carry hearings schedules and some form of testimony.

The Legislation & Records section links to Senate votes, schedules, lobbying disclosure reports, and guides to the legislative process. The Active Legislation subsection identifies currently active bills and labels them by topic. The Nominations section performs a similar role and includes lists of nominations by status, nominations withdrawn, and nominations failed or returned.

In the Reference section, the Senate Library offers a Virtual Reference Desk (VRD) with information about topics including filibustering, Senate traditions, congressional medals and honors, the Senate Page program, and women and minorities in the Senate. This section also has reference statistics and lists (including a list of the longest-serving senators), bibliographies, research guides, and a glossary. The Art & History section is particularly rich with historical information and images.

Subject(s): Senate

U.S. Senate: Committees Homepage

https://www.senate.gov/committees/committees_home.htm

Description: The Senate's homepage for its committees features direct links to the committees' websites, committee membership lists, and a schedule of upcoming committee hearings and meetings. It also provides background information about the committee system and offers links to related websites.

Subject(s): Congressional Committees

Women in Congress

http://history.house.gov/Exhibition-and-Publications/WIC/Women-in-Congress/

Description: The Women in Congress site features historical and current information about female members of the House and Senate. It includes biographical profiles, historical essays, and historical data such as a list of women who have been elected to party leadership positions. The Education section features lesson plans.

Subject(s): Lesson Plans; Women—History

CONGRESSIONAL SUPPORT AGENCIES

Architect of the Capitol (AOC)

https://www.aoc.gov/

Description: The Architect of the Capitol (AOC) is responsible for the maintenance, operation, development, and preservation of the United States

Capitol Complex, which includes the Capitol and its grounds, the congressional office buildings, the Library of Congress buildings, the Supreme Court building, the Capitol Power Plant, and other facilities. Major sections of this website include Who We Are, Architecture, For Visitors, and Multimedia.

The Architecture section provides extensive information about the history, art, and architecture of the Capitol Building, supplemented by historic and contemporary photographs and illustrations. The new Capitol Visitor Center has a small website of its own, http://www.visitthecapitol.gov/, with maps and information on booking a tour.

The detailed current and historical information on this site makes it a useful resource for reference or research. It will be of interest to tourists as well as students of history, government, art, architecture, and historical preservation.

Subject(s): Capitol Building

Congressional Budget Office (CBO)

https://www.cbo.gov/

Description: CBO provides Congress with the analyses needed for economic and budget decisions and with the information and estimates required for the congressional budget process. The CBO website has the full-text versions of its many publications, including economic forecasts, budget projections, analysis of the president's budget, CBO testimony before Congress, and cost estimates for bills reported by congressional committees. The Topics section has drop-down menus that allow users to browse publications by topic, congressional session, budget function, and publication type. The CBO website offers RSS feeds and the option to create a customized My CBO page.

CBO publications provide a wealth of information on the federal budget and on tax and spending proposals. Outside of its regular budget report series, CBO publishes special reports on policy and program topics such as funding for homeland security and the outlook for Social Security.

Subject(s): Budget of the U.S. Government; Congressional Support Agencies

Congressional Oversight Panel

https://cybercemetery.unt.edu/archive/cop/20110401223205/http:/ www.cop.senate.gov/

Description: The Congressional Oversight Panel, which ceased operation in early 2011, was established in 2008 by the Emergency Economic Stabilization Act. The panel's website, now archived in the University of North Texas Libraries' CyberCemetery, provided news, reports, and testimony related to congressional oversight of actions taken by the Treasury Department and financial institutions and their effect on the economy. The website also has biographies of the panel members, who were appointed by House and Senate minority and majority leadership.

Subject(s): Banking Regulation; Finance—Regulations

Congressional Research Service Employment Opportunities

http://www.loc.gov/crsinfo/

Description: The Congressional Research Service is a legislative support agency located within the Library of Congress. Its mission is to provide nonpartisan analysis and research services to Congress. The purpose of its website is to provide information about job openings, internships, and other employment options. Basic background and research information about CRS is also provided. Because CRS works exclusively for Congress, this employment page is its only official public site.

Subject(s): Congressional Support Agencies

CRS Reports—UNT Libraries

https://digital.library.unt.edu/explore/collections/CRSR/

Description: The goal of the CRS Reports project at the University of North Texas Libraries is to provide permanent public access to CRS Reports that have been available at a variety of different websites since 1990. The reports can be searched or browsed by topic. Subject indexing of the reports uses the CRS Legislative Indexing Vocabulary, supplemented with Library of Congress Subject Headings.

This University of North Texas website was launched at about the same time as the Open CRS Network website, which is also described in this publication. The Open CRS Network site is focused on expanding the number of CRS Reports in the public domain and lobbying for better public access to these reports. This UNT Libraries website brings greater historical coverage, search capabilities, subject indexing, and the goal of permanent public access to past CRS Reports.

Subject(s): Legislative Information

Government Accountability Office (GAO)

https://www.gao.gov/

Description: GAO is the investigative arm of Congress. It examines the use of public funds and evaluates federal programs and activities to help the Congress in oversight, policy, and funding decisions. Its website features the full-text versions of GAO Reports and Testimony and recent comptroller general decisions and opinions. E-mail alert lists and RSS news feeds are offered to notify subscribers when new reports or decisions are published. GAO's FraudNET service allows the public to report allegations of waste, fraud, abuse, or mismanagement of federal funds; the site provides an online form for reporting such allegations. The GAO website also features information from their biennial report to Congress on federal programs at high risk for waste, fraud, and abuse. In addition, GAO has a section explaining their role in Recovery Act oversight and to provide related reports.

Subject(s): Congressional Support Agencies; Government Administration

Office of Congressional Ethics (OCE)

https://oce.house.gov/

Description: As stated on the website, OCE is "an independent, nonpartisan entity charged with reviewing allegations of misconduct against members, officers, and staff of the United States House of Representatives and, when appropriate, referring matters to the House Committee on Ethics." OCE was established by House resolution in 2008. The website lists the members of the board of directors and provides copies of ethics rules documents, board meeting minutes, and reports. It also connects to OCE blog postings.

Subject(s): Ethics in Government

Office of Technology Assessment: The OTA Legacy

http://www.princeton.edu/~ota/

Description: After Congress terminated its Office of Technology Assessment (OTA) at the end of 1995, the official OTA website ceased. This Princeton University site makes archived OTA information available to the public. It provides the full text of OTA publications arranged by title, year, and topic, as they were on the official OTA site. The Technology Assessment and the Work of Congress section describes the history and operations of OTA, including speeches and news reports about its role.

Subject(s): Science and Technology Policy

U.S. Capitol Visitor Center

https://www.visitthecapitol.gov/

Description: The new U.S. Capitol Visitor Center, on the east side of the Capitol Building, hosts tours and exhibits. The website has information on planning a visit to the Capitol, with a special section for schools and teachers planning field trips. Information about Congress is also provided.

Subject(s): Capitol Building

LEGISLATIVE INFORMATION

A Century of Lawmaking for a New Nation: U.S. Congressional Documents and Debates, 1774–1875

http://memory.loc.gov/ammem/amlaw/lawhome.html

Description: Congressional documents, beginning with the Continental Congress through to 1875, are available to search, browse, and display on this website, courtesy of the Library of Congress and its Law Library. This digitized collection includes the *Journals of the Continental Congress* (1774–1789); the *Letters of Delegates to Congress* (1774–1789); *The Records of the Federal Convention of 1787*; *The Debates in the Several State Conventions on the Adoption of the Federal Constitution* (1787–1788), or *Elliot's Debates*; the journals of the House of Representatives (1789–1875) and the Senate (1789–1875), including the *Senate Executive Journal* (1789–1875) and the *Journal of William Maclay* (1789–1791); the debates of Congress as published in the *Annals of Congress* (1789–1824), the *Register of Debates* (1824–1837), the *Congressional Globe* (1833–1873), and the *Congressional Record* (1873–1875); the *Statutes at Large* (1789–1875); the *American State Papers* (1789–1838); and congressional bills and resolutions for selected sessions beginning with the 6th Congress (1799) in the House of Representatives and the 16th Congress (1819) in the Senate. It also includes selected documents from the *U.S. Serial Set* from 1833 through 1916.

The site provides tips on using, searching, and viewing the collection. A search button for "All Titles" leads to a search page with many options, including searching one specific title or a combination of several titles. Browse options are also presented on the search page. The title page for each document includes links to a citation guide and basic historical background on the document.

This collection provides substantial public access to the documentary history of American democracy.

Subject(s): Congress—History; Congressional Documents

Center for Legislative Archives

https://www.archives.gov/legislative

Description: The Center for Legislative Archives is the repository for historically valuable congressional records at the National Archives and Records Administration. The center, located in Washington, D.C., holds more than 170,000 cubic feet of records, dating from the first Congress to modern Congresses. The official records from the committees of the House of Representatives and the Senate—the standing, select, special, and joint committees, which Congress uses to accomplish the majority of its work—represent the core holdings of the center. It also holds some collections from legislative support agencies, such as federal government publications from the Government Publishing Office. The site provides various online finding guides, which can be searched by keyword.

Most of the holdings are not available online. A few have been digitized and are available in the Featured Document section (under Resources). The Other Congressional Collections section, also under Resources, links to a directory of congressional members' personal papers collections, most of which are held at archival institutions other than NARA. The website also links to information from the Advisory Committee on the Records of Congress.

Subject(s): Congressional Documents

Congress.gov

https://www.congress.gov

Description: Congress.gov, a service of the Library of Congress that acts under the direction of the Congress, makes U.S. legislative information freely available on the Internet. Legislation is available for the 93rd Congress (1973) to the present. The site tracks the action on each bill in Congress, provides links to the full-text version of the bill and related debate in the *Congressional Record*, and identifies its congressional sponsor or co-sponsor, amendments to the bill, and any related bills. Congress.gov also has a database of Presidential Nominations (from 1981 to the present) and Treaties (largely from 1975 to the present), both of which are handled by the Senate.

In addition to its core databases, Congress.gov links to a variety of legislative research tools and educational information about the legislative process.

This is one of the most widely used Internet sources for legislative information. While it does not yet deliver all the information that some users might desire, it does make a significant body of legislative documentation easily available to the public.

Subject(s): Legislation; Databases

C-SPAN

https://www.c-span.org/

Description: The cable television industry created C-SPAN (Cable-Satellite Public Affairs Network) in 1979 to provide live, gavel-to-gavel coverage of the House of Representatives. Senate coverage started in 1986, when the Senate began televising its proceedings. C-SPAN currently offers audio and video of floor proceedings and some hearings over the Internet. Online users can browse the schedules for C-SPAN's cable and radio stations and receive public affairs and congressional programming online.

C-SPAN has grown to include more educational and video material. The C-SPAN website includes the C-SPAN Classroom, the C-SPAN Video Library archives, and the First Ladies section. The Resources section includes links to numerous public affairs websites.

Subject(s): Congressional Information; Legislative Procedure

How Our Laws Are Made

https://www.congress.gov/resources/display/content/How+Our+Laws+Are+Made+-+Learn+About+the+Legislative+Process

Description: This classic guide provides a readable and non-technical outline of the numerous steps in the federal lawmaking process. It is available online as a single PDF file or as a chapter-divided HTML file.

The HTML version of this classic is organized to make it is relatively easy for users to read the entire work or browse relevant sections.

Subject(s): Legislative Procedure

Legislative Resources on FDsys

https://www.gpo.gov/fdsys/

Description: FDsys.gov is GPO's online system. FDsys provides access to many congressional documents, including House and Senate bills, congressional committee reports, the *Congressional Record*, the *Congressional Directory*, and the *Congressional Pictorial Directory*.

Subject(s): Congressional Documents; Databases

LLSDC's Legislative Source Book

http://www.llsdc.org/sourcebook/

Description: The Legislative Interest Section of the Law Librarians' Society of Washington, D.C., has compiled a variety of useful legislative research tools developed by its members. Many are unique to this website. They include a guide to researching federal legislative histories, an overview of the *Congressional Record* and its predecessor publications, and instructions for finding and establishing direct links to documents online at the Library of Congress's Congress.gov and GPO's FDsys (both described in this section).

This site will be of interest to government documents librarians and serious legislative researchers.

Subject(s): Congressional Documents; Legislation—Research

Chapter Seventeen

Presidency

The Trump Administration is the fourth presidential administration to maintain a White House website. It is the second to use the site to link to an official White House presence on such third-party social media sites as Facebook, Twitter, and Instagram. This chapter includes websites sponsored by the current presidential administration as well as finding aids for presidential documents from this and other administrations.

Subsections in this chapter are Current Administration and Presidential Information.

CURRENT ADMINISTRATION

Administration

https://www.whitehouse.gov/the-trump-administration/

Description: This website contains brief information about President Trump, Vice President Pence, contains a listing of the cabinet members, and provices links to the Executive Offices.

Subject(s): President, Vice President, Presidential Advisors

Council of Economic Advisers (CEA)

https://www.whitehouse.gov/cea/

Description: The CEA, which consists of one chairman and two members, advises the president of the United States on domestic and international economic policy and assists in the preparation of the *Economic Report of the President*. The CEA website describes the mission and operations of the council and links to current CEA publications and the text of the chairman's speeches. The Fact Sheets & Reports section includes the quarterly report on the economic impact of the American Recovery and Reinvestment Act of

2009. CEA publications include the monthly *Economic Indicators*, and the CEA website links to this document.

Subject(s): Economic Statistics; Economic Policy; Presidential Advisors

Domestic Policy Council

https://obamawhitehouse.archives.gov/administration/eop/dpc

Description: This page was maintained under the Obama administration but it is currently not being maintained. This website provides a brief description of the council's history and work and has a leadership biography.

Subject(s): Presidential Advisors; Public Policy

First Lady Melania Trump

https://www.whitehouse.gov/people/melania-trump/

Description: The First Lady's website provides a biography, a photographic portrait, and information on the First Lady's initiatives and her philanthropic work.

Subject(s): First Lady

National Security Council (NSC)

https://www.whitehouse.gov/nsc/

Description: The National Security Council is the president's forum for considering national security and foreign policy matters with his senior national security advisers and cabinet officials. The NSC website describes the NSC's role and history. It also includes sections on cybersecurity and transnational organized crime. This page was still in the process of being updated as this book went to press.

Subject(s): National Security—Policy; Presidential Advisors

Vice President Mike Pence

https://www.whitehouse.gov/people/mike-pence/

Description:

The vice president is authorized to nominate individuals to the U.S. Military, Naval, and Air Force Academies; the website links to information and an application form. The Vice President's website provides a biography and a photographic portrait

Subject(s): Vice President

White House

https://www.whitehouse.gov/

Description: The White House website combines current news and policy statements from the administration with historical information relating to both the building and the Executive Office of the Presidency. In addition to a White House blog, current content is provided in sections including Briefing

Room, Issues, and The Administration. The Briefing Room provides news releases and the text of press briefings; the president's weekly address; presidential Executive orders, memoranda, and proclamations; presidential speeches and statements; press briefings; the president's and vice president's daily schedules; legislation before the president; visitor access records; and a listing of the status of many of the presidential nominations and appointments. The Issues section summarizes the Obama Administration's policies on major topics, such as defense and health care. The Administration section has biographies of Cabinet members and leading White House staff.

The section titled 1600 Penn provides historical information about the White House and related buildings, biographies of past presidents and first ladies, information on White House tours and events, and more. The Our Government subsection under 1600 Penn provides an overview of the structure of American federal, state, and local government. The White House website includes a search engine and links to relevant social media pages.

The White House website should be the first stop online for users seeking current presidential news, statements, and documents; biographies of elected and appointed White House officials; and historical information about the White House and its occupants.

Subject(s): First Lady; Presidency; White House (Mansion)

White House 1600 Daily

https://www.whitehouse.gov/1600daily/

Description: This site is a daily blog described as "your morning summary of news, events, and updates. Anyone can enter their email address to receive the daily information.

Subject(s): President; Blogs

White House Fellows Program

https://www.whitehouse.gov/get-involved/fellows/

Description: The nonpartisan White House Fellows Program was established by President Lyndon B. Johnson in 1964 to provide early-career professionals with firsthand experience in governing the nation. Each fellow works full time for one year as a special assistant to a cabinet member or senior presidential adviser. This website provides information about the program, selection criteria, the application process, and the current class of fellows.

Subject(s): Fellowships; Public Policy

White House Military Office

https://obamawhitehouse.archives.gov/administration/eop/whmo

Description: This site was last maintained by the Obama administration.. The White House Military Office units include the White House Communications Agency, the Presidential Airlift Group, the White House Medical Unit, Camp David, Marine Helicopter Squadron One, the Presidential Food Service, and the White House Transportation Agency. The website explains the role and responsibilities of the White House Military Office, with a section about its history. This page was still in the process of being updated as this book went to press.

Subject(s): President

PRESIDENTIAL INFORMATION

American Presidency Project

http://www.presidency.ucsb.edu/

Description: Although it is an unofficial website, the American Presidency Project website provides a more complete collection of certain key presidential documents than can be found elsewhere on the Internet. The site contains the following: Public Papers of the Presidents (1929–2007 and 2011–present), State of the Union addresses (1790–present), inaugural addresses (1789–present), transcripts from presidential candidate debates (1960–present), and other related documents. The site also has presidential elections results from 1789 to the present, numerous presidential statistics (number of vetoes, job approval ratings, and more), and audio and video of presidents' speeches.

Subject(s): Presidential Documents

Codification of Presidential Proclamations and Executive Orders

https://www.archives.gov/federal-register/codification

Description: The Office of the Federal Register presents this online version of the *Codification of Presidential Proclamations and Executive Orders*, which covers proclamations and executive orders issued by presidents from April 13, 1945, through January 20, 1989. Documents that had no legal effect on January 20, 1989, are excluded. The Disposition Tables Numeric Index section lists all the documents back to 1945, noting whether the documents have been revoked or superseded, or have become otherwise obsolete. Earlier proclamations and executive orders are included if they were amended or otherwise affected by documents issued during the 1945–1989 period.

Subject(s): Executive Orders; Presidential Documents

Compilation of Presidential Documents

https://www.gpo.gov/fdsys/browse/collection.action?collectionCode =CPD

Description: The Compilation of Presidential Documents provides access to the text of presidential speeches, bill signing statements, executive orders, proclamations, communications to Congress, and other presidential materials released by the White House Press Secretary. It includes both the *Daily Compilation of Presidential Documents* and its predecessor, the *Weekly Compilation of Presidential Documents*. The Daily Compilation began on January 29, 2009. Copies of the Weekly Compilation are online from 1993 to January 20, 2009. The content is published by the National Archives and made available through the Government Publishing Office's FDsys system.

Subject(s): Presidential Documents

Executive Orders Disposition Tables

https://www.archives.gov/federal-register/executive-orders/disposition

Description: This website provides online citations and status information for executive orders issued by presidents from 1937 through the present. The Disposition Tables include the executive order number, signing date, Federal Register citation, title, amendments (if any), and current status (where applicable).

Subject(s): Executive Orders; Presidential Documents

First Ladies

https://www.whitehouse.gov/about-the-white-house/first-ladies/

Description: This page has traditionally presented brief biographies of all first ladies and was still in the process of being updated as this book went to press.

Subject(s): First Lady; Biographies

Office of the Pardon Attorney

https://www.justice.gov/pardon

Description: The Office of the Pardon Attorney reviews requests for presidential pardons for federal criminal offenses. Its website includes application forms, regulations, and background information relating to clemency petitions. The site also provides clemency statistics from 1900 onward and lists of clemency recipients from 1989 onward.

Subject(s): Pardons

Presidential Directives and Executive Orders

https://fas.org/irp/offdocs/direct.htm

Description: This website, maintained by a nonprofit research organization, focuses on intelligence-related presidential directives and executive orders from the Truman administration to the present. Copies of documents that are not still classified are available on this site. The site also links to helpful background information on presidential directives.

Subject(s): Intelligence; Presidential Documents

Public Papers of the Presidents of the United States

https://www.gpo.gov/fdsys/

Description: FDsys.gov hosts *Public Papers of the Presidents of the United States*, a printed volume series that compiles the messages and papers of the presidents, begins with the Hoover administration. GPO has put the series online beginning with the 1991 volume in the George H. W. Bush administration. Each volume in the series contains the papers and speeches of the president of the United States that were issued by the Office of the Press Secretary during the specified time period.

In the Browse section select "Public Papers of the Presidents of the United States" for access.

Subject(s): Presidential Documents

Chapter Eighteen

Science and Space

The federal government is involved in basic and applied science, in helping to disseminate scientific information, and in encouraging scientific research in academia and other research centers. Many websites in this chapter present highly specialized and technical information.

Subsections in this chapter include Life Sciences, National Laboratories, Physical Sciences, Science Agencies and Policy, Scientific and Technical Information, and Space.

LIFE SCIENCES

Computational Bioscience and Engineering Laboratory (CBEL)

https://dcb.cit.nih.gov/node/9

Description: CBEL's work addresses areas requiring high-performance parallel computing, with projects in areas such as biomedical imaging, human genetic linkage analysis, and computationally intensive statistical applications. Its website features links to the lab's divisions, job opportunities, and research studies.

Subject(s): Medical Computing—Research

DOE Joint Genome Institute (JGI)

https://jgi.doe.gov/

Description: JGI is a cooperative effort involving the Department of Energy's Lawrence Berkeley, Lawrence Livermore, Los Alamos, Oak Ridge, and Pacific Northwest National Laboratories, along with the Hudson Alpha Institute for Biotechnology. Operated by the University of California, the institute works on genetic sequencing research to further the Energy Department's missions related to clean energy generation and environmental characterization and cleanup. The website highlights current projects and links to specialized research sections on topics such as fungal genomics and plant genomics. The Education section describes higher education opportunities sponsored by JGI.

Subject(s): Energy—Research; Genomics—Research

Genome Integrity & Structural Biology Laboratory

https://www.niehs.nih.gov/research/atniehs/labs/gisbl/

Description: The lab's mission is to provide insights into the biological processes that impact human environmental health. The site has information on the lab's facilities and its scientists and their research focuses.

Subject(s): Molecular Biology—Research

genomics.energy.gov

https://genomics.energy.gov/

Description: genomics.energy.gov consolidates information on the genome programs of the Department of Energy's Office of Science. The site links to the Human Genome Project Archive, a genomics image gallery, and research highlights from the Office of Science.

Subject(s): Genomics—Research

Integrated Taxonomic Information System (ITIS)

https://www.itis.gov/

Description: ITIS is an excellent tool for looking up the taxonomic names and common names of the biota of North America. (Biota refers to all the plant and animal life in an area.) ITIS is a partnership of U.S., Canadian, and Mexican agencies, organizations, and taxonomic specialists that cooperate on the development of a scientifically credible list of biological names. The ITIS database can be searched by scientific name, common name, or taxonomic serial number (TSN). The records in the database include scientific name, common name, synonym, taxonomic serial number, author, and credibility rating. The full database, or custom reports from it, can be downloaded.

Subject(s): Biological Names

Laboratory of Neurosciences

https://www.nia.nih.gov/research/labs/lns

Description: The goal of basic research at the Laboratory of Neurosciences is to establish methods for preventing and treating age-related neurological disorders, such as Alzheimer's disease and Parkinson's disease. Links to information from each of the lab's research programs are at the bottom of the page, as are links to staff publications.

Subject(s): Neurology—Research

NASA Astrobiology

https://astrobiology.nasa.gov/

Description: Astrobiology is the study of the origin, evolution, distribution, and destiny of life in the universe. It uses multiple scientific disciplines and space technologies. The website's About Astrobiology section features a history of the field and information about its current status, including profiles of astrobiology projects on space exploration missions. The site also links to publications and education programs. *Astrobiology Magazine* is a NASA-sponsored online popular science magazine, and can be accessed at https://www.astrobio.net/.

Subject(s): Astrobiology

NASA Life Sciences Data Archive

https://lsda.jsc.nasa.gov/

Description: The Life Sciences Data Archive is a searchable collection of information and data sets from space flight experiments funded by NASA. The growing archive includes documentation from experiments flown since 1961 that include human, animal, or plant studies. The archive can be searched by mission, experiment, research area, and other parameters. The website also describes current and historical research. Online books in the reading room include *Biomedical Results of Apollo*.

Subject(s): Astrobiology—Research; Human Space Exploration—Research

National Center for Biotechnology Information (NCBI)

https://www.ncbi.nlm.nih.gov/

Description: NCBI conducts basic and applied research in computational molecular biology and maintains a variety of databases related to their work. This site describes and links to numerous NCBI databases and software tools. Literature databases include PubMed, PubMed Central, and Online Mendelian Inheritance in Man (OMIM). Molecular and genome databases include GenBank, Nucleotide, and BLAST. The site has an alphabetical index of all the linked databases and information resources. At the top of the page, researchers can use the search box to search one or all of the NCBI-provided databases.

This is an important site for genome and genetic sequence researchers. The site provides access to multiple databases with detailed help files to assist with database searches. NCBI gives multiple means of accessing the data.

Subject(s): Genomics—Research; Molecular Biology—Research; Databases

National Human Genome Research Institute (NHGRI)

https://www.genome.gov/

Description: NHGRI led the now-completed Human Genome Project, and currently focuses its genomic research on human health and disease issues. This site brings together news, research reports, and educational resources related to the institute's work. In addition to profiles of each research branch, the Research at NHGRI section has information about NHGRI clinical trials, online databases developed at the institute, and publications by NHGRI researchers. The Research Funding section links to information on current opportunities. The Health section has information on genetic and rare diseases, and educational information for health professionals. The Issues in Genetics section covers such topics as privacy, ethics, genetic discrimination, and policy issues.

Subject(s): Genomics—Research

National Institute of General Medical Sciences (NIGMS)

https://www.nigms.nih.gov/Pages/default.aspx

Description: NIGMS supports basic biomedical research that is not targeted at specific diseases, but instead lays the foundation for advances in disease diagnosis, treatment, and prevention. The website spotlights findings from NIGMS-funded research. Major sections of the site are Research Funding, Research Training, News & Meetings, Science Education, and About NIGMS. The Publications section, within the Science Education section, offers a number of science education booklets aimed at the general public.

Subject(s): Biological Medicine—Research

PubChem

https://pubchem.ncbi.nlm.nih.gov/

Description: PubChem contains the chemical structures of small organic molecules and information on their biological activities. The PubChem system consists of several information tools, including PubChem Compound, PubChem Substance, PubChem BioAssay, and a chemical structure similarity search tool.

Subject(s): Molecular Biology

NATIONAL LABORATORIES

Argonne National Laboratory (ANL)

http://www.anl.gov

Description: The Energy Department's Argonne National Laboratory, located just outside of Chicago, maintains a website with a mix of information on research, technology transfer, and career opportunities. Major sections include Energy, Environment, Security, User Facilities, and Science. Research at Argonne concerns basic science, energy resources, environmental management, and national security. The site provides links to Argonne's social media pages and YouTube channel.

Subject(s): Nuclear Energy—Research; Research Laboratories; Scientific Research

Brookhaven National Laboratory (BNL)

https://www.bnl.gov/world/

Description: BNL carries out and supports research in a multitude of scientific disciplines, including high energy physics, materials science, environmental sciences, and nonproliferation. Its website serves as a gateway to information on its many research projects, facilities (including the Relativistic Heavy Ion Collider), and divisional sites.

Because the BNL site includes so much information on so many projects and fields of science, the A–Z site index may be a helpful tool for discovering information on the site.

Subject(s): Particle Accelerators; Research Laboratories

Fermi National Accelerator Laboratory (Fermilab)

http://www.fnal.gov

Description: Fermilab is a research lab with a focus on high-energy physics and the fundamental nature of matter and energy. It is known for its particle accelerator, the Tevatron. The Science section summarizes the lab's accomplishments and major research areas, such as particle physics, neutrino physics, and the dark matter of the cosmos. The site also has information on the many educational programs offered at each level of learning.

Subject(s): Particle Accelerators; Physics—Research; Research Laboratories

Lawrence Berkeley National Laboratory (LBL)

http://www.lbl.gov

Description: The Berkeley Lab conducts basic research in a wide range of fields. Current areas of interest highlighted on the lab's website include energy efficiency, climate change, computational science, and energy bioscience. The site has profiles for each research division and for the national user research facilities. The site also has information on educational opportunities and technology transfer, and a creative video glossary featuring lab scientists explaining scientific terminology, such as "galactic emissions" and "cellular senescence." The website has an extensive A–Z index for its content.

Subject(s): Physics—Research; Research Laboratories

Lawrence Livermore National Laboratory (LLNL)

https://www.llnl.gov/

Description: LLNL research areas include nuclear sciences, defense technology, energy, computation, and materials sciences. The website links to research information under categories including Biosecurity, Counterterrorism, Defense, Energy, Intelligence, and Nonproliferation. The site's Publications section (under News) includes the lab's published research papers, reports, and periodicals, with issues of *Science and Technology Review* as far back as 1994 (when it appeared under its previous title, *Energy and Technology Review*).

The LLNL site provides a substantial amount of online full-text documents of interest to researchers. The site should be the starting point for anyone seeking more information about the lab's programs or its areas of expertise.

Subject(s): Nuclear Weapons—Research; Research Laboratories

Los Alamos National Laboratory (LANL)

http://www.lanl.gov

Description: Created to help in the development of nuclear weapons, the central mission of the Los Alamos National Laboratory is national security. It has stewardship of the nation's nuclear stockpile and conducts research related to this role. The lab website describes it work in sections on such areas as global security, environmental sciences, and strategic science. Publications on the site include *1663: Los Alamos Science and Technology Magazine*. Other sections on the site cover procurement, technology transfer, and educational opportunities.

Subject(s): Nuclear Weapons; Physics—Research; Research Laboratories

Oak Ridge National Laboratory (ORNL)

https://www.ornl.gov/

Description: Oak Ridge National Laboratory is a multiprogram science and technology laboratory. ORNL research focuses on neutron science, energy, high-performance computing, biological systems, and national security. The About ORNL section has information on organizational structure, leadership, procurement, and ORNL history since its founding in World War II.

Subject(s): Research Laboratories; Scientific Research

Pacific Northwest National Laboratory (PNNL)

https://www.pnnl.gov/

Description: PNNL conducts research in chemical and molecular sciences, biological systems sciences, climate change science, applied materials science and engineering, applied nuclear science and technology, and other areas. Work at the lab is described in the Research section of its website.

Other sections describe the lab's facilities, educational opportunities, staffing, business resources, and technology licensing program. The Publications section includes archived material from the lab's former magazine, *Breakthroughs*, and a database of materials published since 1998 by PNNL staff or by external researchers using PNNL facilities.

Subject(s): Research Laboratories

Sandia National Laboratories

http://www.sandia.gov

Description: Sandia focuses on research and development related to national security goals. Sections of the Sandia site discuss activities in areas such as nuclear weapons, energy, defense systems, and homeland security. The News section has links to news releases, corporate information, and Sandia publications.

Subject(s): Research Laboratories; Weapons Research

Savannah River National Laboratory (SRNL)

https://srnl.doe.gov/

Description: SRNL is the applied research and development laboratory at the Energy Department's Savannah River Site. The website describes the major areas of the lab's research focus: environmental stewardship, clean energy, and national security. Research capabilities in related technologies, such as hydrogen storage and radioactive chemical processing, are also described.

Subject(s): Energy—Research; Research Laboratories

PHYSICAL SCIENCES

Alaska Volcano Observatory (AVO)

https://avo.alaska.edu/

Description: AVO is a federal, state, and university partnership to monitor Alaska's volcanoes. The website describes the monitoring, hazard assessments, and volcano research conducted by AVO. The Volcano Information section features an interactive map of Alaskan volcanoes and a database of eruption events. The Current Volcanic Activity section includes webcams and volcano activity notifications.

This well-designed site has content for those with general interest in volcanoes and for those in the scientific and Alaskan regional communities.

Subject(s): Volcanoes

Cascades Volcano Observatory (CVO)

https://volcanoes.usgs.gov/observatories/cvo/

Description: CVO watches volcanoes and other natural hazards, including earthquakes, landslides, and debris flows in the western United States. The CVO website has current status reports and other reports on volcanoes in the Cascade Range, including Mount Rainier and Mount St. Helens. The site features maps, photos, hazard assessment reports, and information on living with volcanoes and visiting volcanoes. The Education section includes materials that will be of interest to students, teachers, and the general public, including seminar announcements.

Subject(s): Volcanoes

Chemoinformatics Tools and Services

https://cactus.nci.nih.gov/

Description: This collaborative website includes chemical information databases, software tools, and links to other chemistry-related databases. It features a Chemical Structure Lookup Service (CSLS) for discovering whether a structure occurs in any of the public and commercial databases the service has checked. The National Cancer Institute's Computer-Aided Drug Design (CADD) Group hosts the site.

The site is open to the general public; however, the About section of the website states, "The information is not geared toward the general public, and will probably be most useful for researchers working with, or interested in, chemical information."

Subject(s): Chemical Information

Earth Observing System (EOS)—NASA

https://eospso.gsfc.nasa.gov/

Description: EOS consists of a science component and a data system supporting a coordinated series of satellites for global observations of the land surface, biosphere, solid earth, atmosphere, and oceans. The main categories of this website are Missions, Data, Communications, People, and *The Earth Observer* Newsletter. The site also links to sources for images of the Earth from space.

Subject(s): Planetary Science

Earth Observing System—NOAA

http://www.noaa.gov/node16

Description: This NOAA site provides information about the emerging Global Earth Observation System of Systems (GEOSS). It links to related websites, such as the U.S. Group on Earth Observations (USGEO) site and the Intergovernmental Group on Earth Observations (GEO) site.

NASA also provides a webpage on Earth observing systems, and this is described in a separate entry.

Subject(s): Planetary Science

Earthquake Hazards Program

https://earthquake.usgs.gov/

Description: The mission of the Earthquake Hazards Program is to understand the characteristics and effects of earthquakes and to apply this knowledge to reduce deaths, injuries, and property damage from earthquakes. The website features reports and maps of current earthquakes, past earthquakes, and significant earthquakes in history. The site also has information on U.S. and global seismic networks for monitoring and recording quakes. The Research section of the site includes scientific data and software and reports of ongoing research projects. A section of interest to the general public is Learn, for children and teachers. The site also links to regional information from program sites in the Pacific Northwest, Northern California, Southern California, the Intermountain West, and the Central and Eastern U.S.

With everything from earthquake ShakeMaps and photos to research data to science fair project ideas, this USGS site is a good place to start an earthquake information search.

Subject(s): Earthquakes

Environmental Molecular Sciences Laboratory (EMSL)

https://www.emsl.pnl.gov/emslweb/

Description: The EMSL national research laboratory conducts fundamental research in molecular and computational sciences, particularly in relation to energy technologies. The Science section of the website describes lab research in the areas of biological interactions and dynamics, biogeochemistry, and the science of interfacial phenomena. The website also describes the lab's capabilities and cites science journal articles in which all or part of the research was carried out using EMSL resources.

Subject(s): Research Laboratories; Scientific Research

Geology Research and Information

https://geology.usgs.gov/

Description: This USGS website covers natural hazards, Earth resources, and geologic processes. The site provides a central point for geology-related publications and for links to all related USGS programs. The programs are grouped into four categories: Natural Resources includes Energy and Minerals programs; Hazards includes Earthquakes, Landslides, Geomagnetism, the Global Seismic Network, and Volcanoes; and Landscape and Coasts has Geologic Mapping and Coastal Marine Geology. A fourth category, Other, has Astrogeology and Data Preservation information. Each section leads to detailed information about the program and the science involved. The site also has geologic databases, software, and standards information.

Subject(s): Geology

Geophysical Fluid Dynamics Laboratory (GFDL)

https://www.gfdl.noaa.gov/

Description: GFDL is a research laboratory focusing on the physical processes influencing the behavior of the atmosphere and the oceans as complex fluid systems. The Research section of the site includes resources from project groups for Atmospheric Physics, Chemistry, and Climate; Climate and Ecosystems; Climate Diagnostics; Climate Change, Variability, and Predictions; Oceans and Climate; and Weather and Atmospheric Dynamics. The site also provides bibliographies of GFDL published articles and presentations.

Subject(s): Atmospheric Sciences—Research; Climatology—Research

Harvard-Smithsonian Center for Astrophysics

https://www.cfa.harvard.edu/

Description: The Harvard-Smithsonian Center for Astrophysics is a collaboration between the Smithsonian Astrophysical Observatory and the Harvard College Observatory to study the basic physical processes that determine the nature and evolution of the universe. The website has information about the center, its research, and its facilities.

Subject(s): Astrophysics—Research

Hawaiian Volcano Observatory (HVO)

https://volcanoes.usgs.gov/observatories/hvo/

Description: HVO conducts research on the volcanoes of Hawaii and works with emergency-response officials to protect people and property from earthquakes and volcano-related hazards. The site has information on current activity, history, and hazards for the Mauna Loa and Kilauea volcanoes. Other sections cover earthquakes, other volcanoes, and volcanic hazards. The site also features *Volcano Watch*, a weekly newsletter for the general public that is written by scientists at HVO.

This site will be of great interest to anyone living on or visiting Hawaii, and it provides educational information for anyone else interested in volcanoes and volcanology.

Subject(s): Volcanoes

High Energy Astrophysics Science Archive Research Center (HEASARC)

https://heasarc.gsfc.nasa.gov/

Description: The purpose of HEASARC is to support a multimission archive facility in high energy astrophysics for scientists all over the world.

HEASARC has data from multiple observatories covering 30 years of X-ray and gamma-ray astronomy. The data from space-borne instruments are provided along tools to analyze multiple datasets. The HEASARC website also has astronomy information for the public, students, and teachers.

Primarily intended for professional astronomers and astrophysicists, the HEASARC website does offer some content for the general public and the educational community.

Subject(s): Astrophysics—Research

Jefferson Lab

https://www.jlab.org/

Description: The Thomas Jefferson National Accelerator Facility (Jefferson Lab) is a nuclear physics research laboratory built to probe the nucleus of an atom to learn more about the quark structure of matter. The lab is funded by the Energy Department's Office of Science, the City of Newport News, and the state of Virginia. The Jefferson Lab's website features information about its scientific program as well resources for K–12 education.

Subject(s): Nuclear Physics—Research; Particle Accelerators; Research Laboratories

NASA Astrophysics Data System (ADS)

http://adswww.harvard.edu

Description: ADS is a NASA-funded project maintaining three sets of bibliographic databases: Astronomy and Astrophysics, Physics, and preprints in Astronomy (ArXiv e-prints). All are available to search or browse at this site. The site also has a current awareness e-mail service called myADS.

Subject(s): Astrophysics

NASA Goddard Institute for Space Studies (GISS)

https://www.giss.nasa.gov/

Description: GISS is a NASA research institute that emphasizes a broad, interdisciplinary study of global environmental change. A key objective of its research is the prediction of atmospheric and climate changes in the 21st century. Research themes described on the website include global climate modeling, planetary atmospheres, and atmospheric chemistry. The site's sections include Datasets & Images, Publications, Software, Education, and About GISS.

Subject(s): Climate Change—Research

National Earthquake Information Center (NEIC)

https://earthquake.usgs.gov/contactus/golden/neic.php

Description: NEIC identifies its mission as "to provide and apply relevant earthquake science information and knowledge for reducing deaths, injuries, and property damage from earthquakes through understanding of their characteristics and effects and by providing the information and knowledge needed to mitigate these losses." (from the website) The site includes earthquake catalogs and bulletins, and the *International Registry of Seismograph Stations*.

Subject(s): Earthquakes

National Centers for Environmental Information (NCEI)

https://www.ncei.noaa.gov/

Description: NOAA's National Centers for Environmental Information are "responsible for hosting and providing access to one of the most significant archives on earth, with comprehensive oceanic, atmospheric, and geophysical data." (from the website) The site allows users to find data by category, such as Climate Monitoring & Extremes, Coastal & Regional, Ocean Data, Paleoclimatology, and Space Weather.

Subject(s): Data Products; Environmental Science

National Radio Astronomy Observatory (NRAO)

https://public.nrao.edu/

Description: The NRAO designs, builds, and operates state-of-the-art radio telescope facilities for use by the scientific community. The NRAO website has extensive information about each of its sites in Virginia, West Virginia, Arizona, Chile, and New Mexico. The Image Gallery section includes galaxies, stars, comets, black holes, telescopes, and historical photographs of telescopes and astronomers.

Subject(s): Astronomy; Observatories

Naval Oceanography Portal

http://www.usno.navy.mil

Description: This portal website links to sites available from the component commands of the United States Naval Meteorology and Oceanography Command. Linked sites include the U.S. Naval Observatory, the Joint Typhoon Warning Center, the Naval Oceanography Operations Command, the Fleet Numerical Meteorology and Oceanography Center, and the Naval Oceanographic Office. Topical sections of the site include Time, Earth Orientation, Astronomy, Meteorology, Oceanography, and Ice.

Subject(s): Oceanography

New Brunswick Laboratory

https://science.energy.gov/nbl/

Description: The New Brunswick Laboratory is a federal lab specializing in the science of measuring nuclear materials. This site describes the mission and programs of the lab. Programs include Nuclear Safeguards and Nonproliferation Support, Measurement Development, Measurement Evaluation, Measurement Services, and Certified Reference Materials.

Subject(s): Chemistry Research; Standards and Specifications

NIST Physical Measurement Laboratory

https://www.nist.gov/pml

Description: The Physical Measurement Laboratory supports industry by providing measurement services and research for electronic, optical, and radiation technologies. The site links to detailed information from each of the research divisions: Radiation Physics, Sensor Science, Time and Frequency, Semiconductor and Dimensional Metrology, Applied Physics, Quantum Physics, Quantum Measurement, Quantum Electromagnetics, and Office of Weights and Measures. The Product/Services section of the site features the following subsections: Measurements & Calibrations, General Interest, Special Publications & Tutorials, The Official U.S. Time, and Physical Reference Data.

Subject(s): Physics—Research; Standards and Specifications

Ocean Surface Topography from Space

https://sealevel.jpl.nasa.gov/

Description: This site describes NASA research and missions related to ocean topography. It has information on the TOPEX/Poseidon Mission, a partnership between the United States and France to monitor global ocean topography, discover the links between ocean and atmosphere, and improve global climate predictions. The follow-on missions, called Jason-1 and Jason-2, are also described in detail.

The website is a rich source of educational information on the effects of oceans on our climate, weather events such as El Niño/La Niña, and NASA's satellite missions. The site's Sea Level Viewer presents images of the Earth during events such as El Niño/La Niña, the Indian Ocean tsunami in 2004, and Hurricane Katrina in 2005.

Subject(s): Climate Research; Oceans—Research

Princeton Plasma Physics Laboratory (PPPL)

https://www.pppl.gov/

Description: PPPL is concerned with fusion energy and plasma physics research. PPPL is managed by Princeton University for the Department of Energy. The site features information about the lab, such as its research and equipment. The Fusion Basics section (under About) provides extensive information for the interested public. The Research section describes current projects.

Subject(s): Plasma Physics—Research

SOHO: The Solar and Heliospheric Observatory

https://soho.nascom.nasa.gov/

Description: SOHO is a cooperative project of NASA and the European Space Agency to study the sun and solar wind. Major sections of the SOHO website are Data/Archive and a solar image gallery. The About section discusses the SOHO project's history. The site's Publications page includes a SOHO bibliography and publications database, SOHO documentation, and links to privately published online journals that cover solar physics research.

Subject(s): Solar-Terrestrial Physics; Sun

SLAC National Accelerator Laboratory

https://www6.slac.stanford.edu/

Description: SLAC, operated by Stanford University for the Department of Energy, conducts high-energy physics research. This site provides an introduction to SLAC and its programs. The Research section provides detail on the center's research in accelerator physics, astrophysics and cosmology, materials and nanoscience, and other areas.

Subject(s): Particle Accelerators; Physics—Research; Research Laboratories

T-2 Nuclear Information Service

http://t2.lanl.gov/

Description: Run by the Nuclear, Particle, Astrophysics and Cosmology Group of the Theoretical Division of the Los Alamos National Lab, this site covers nuclear modeling, nuclear data, cross sections, nuclear masses, nuclear astrophysics, radioactivity, radiation shielding, data for medical radiotherapy, data for high-energy accelerator applications, data and codes for fission and fusion systems, and more.

The very technical nature of this data means that the site will primarily be of interest to nuclear physicists.

Subject(s): Nuclear Physics

U.S. Naval Observatory (USNO)

http://www.usno.navy.mil/usno/

Description: USNO is responsible for measuring the positions and motions of Earth, the sun, the moon, planets, stars, and other celestial objects; providing astronomical data; determining precise time; measuring the Earth's rotation; and maintaining the Master Clock for the United States. The Astronomical Applications section of the website includes popular reference information, such as daily sun and moon rise and set times for locations worldwide, a map of world time zones, solar and lunar eclipse information, and an online astronomical almanac. Other sections of the site provide USNO information in the areas of astrometry, Earth orientation, and precise time. The site also links to the James M. Gilliss Library and to tour information.

Subject(s): Astronomy; Observatories

Volcano Hazards Program

https://volcanoes.usgs.gov/index.html

Description: This central site for the USGS Volcano Hazards Program includes information on the status of volcanic activity in the United States, including a volcanic status map and a list of current alerts. The Hazards section of the site discusses aspects of volcanic eruptions, including volcanic gases and volcanic ash. The Observatories section links to extensive information from the regional observatories in Washington State/Oregon, Hawaii, Alaska, and the Mariana Islands. It also links to information on the Volcano Disaster Assistance Program (VDAP). The website also has a Learn section with information for teachers and students.

For checking either current activity or historical eruptions, this website is a great starting point for finding information on volcanoes.

Subject(s): Volcanoes

SCIENCE AGENCIES AND POLICY

National Aeronautics and Space Administration (NASA)

https://www.nasa.gov/

Description: The central NASA website provides information about the agency and its activities as well as links to the numerous other websites and resources NASA maintains. The NASA homepage highlights current news and popular features such as the Launch Schedule. The Missions section features detailed information about past, present, and future NASA missions. Audience-specific views of NASA's online content are available for the general public (the default), educators, students, and the media.

Subject(s): Space

National Science Advisory Board for Biosecurity (NSABB)

https://osp.od.nih.gov/biotechnology/nsabb-faq/

Description: The NSABB is an interagency board chartered with minimizing the risk of the misuse of life sciences research technologies, particularly as a threat to public health and national security. The website has NSABB news, information about its members, and meeting schedules and webcasts.

Subject(s): Scientific Research—Policy; Life Sciences—Policy

National Science and Technology Council (NSTC)

https://www.whitehouse.gov/administration/eop/ostp/nstc/

Description: The NSTC was formed in 1993 to coordinate science and technology policy across multiple White House and Executive branch departments. The website has information on council members, meetings, and reportsbut was still in the process of being updated as this book went to press.

Subject(s): Science and Technology Policy

National Science Board (NSB)

https://www.nsf.gov/nsb/

Description: The NSB is the governing board for NSF and serves as national science policy adviser to the president and Congress. The website has information on NSB membership, meetings, and the honorary science awards it bestows.

Subject(s): Science—Policy

National Science Foundation (NSF)

https://www.nsf.gov/

Description: As one of the government's major scientific agencies, NSF promotes science and engineering research and education. NSF supports scientists, engineers and educators directly through their own home institutions (typically universities and colleges). The site's main sections provide information about funding opportunities and awards. The site also includes a wealth of publications and data from NSF, particularly on science and engineering education, funding, and the workforce. A Discoveries section profiles discoveries and innovations that began with NSF support.

Subject(s): Science Education; Scientific Research—Grants

Office of Science

https://science.energy.gov/

Description: The Department of Energy's Office of Science is the gateway to the agency's scientifically focused research, analysis, and information. Its core programs include Advanced Scientific Computing Research, Basic Energy Sciences, Biological and Environmental Research, Fusion Energy Sciences, High Energy Physics, and Nuclear Physics. An interactive grants map can be found under the Universities heading, and a list of related facilities is located in the Laboratories section.

Subject(s): Science

Office of Science and Technology Policy (OSTP)

https://www.whitehouse.gov/ostp

Description: Established in 1976, OSTP serves as a source of scientific and technological analysis and judgment for the president with respect to major policies, plans, and programs of the federal government. The website offers general information on the organization and activities of OSTP. Along with current news and the OSTP Blog, the site has information on the administration's policy on science and technology issues and on the federal research and development budget.

Subject(s): Science and Technology Policy

Office of Science and Technology Policy (OSTP) Blog

https://obamawhitehouse.archives.gov/administration/eop/ostp/blog

Description: This blog was maintained by the Obama administration. The OSTP blog discussed policy making from a science and technology perspective. An RSS subscription feed is available.

Subject(s): Science and Technology Policy; Blogs

President's National Medal of Science

https://www.nsf.gov/od/nms/medal.jsp

Description: The National Medal of Science was established by Congress in 1959 as a Presidential Award to be given to individuals "deserving of special recognition by reason of their outstanding contributions to knowledge in the physical, biological, mathematical, or engineering sciences." (from the website) In 1980, Congress expanded this recognition to include the social and behavioral sciences. This site features information on nomination procedures, new award announcements, former medalists, and members of the President's Committee. The site also links to information on the National Medal of Technology and Innovation, administered by the Patent and Trademark Office.

Subject(s): Science—Awards and Honors

Research.gov

https://www.research.gov

Description: Research.gov has information for and about researchers working under a federal grant. The Research.gov program is led by the National Science Foundation; NSF partners include NASA and Defense Department research agencies. The site's Research Spending & Results database has information on research awards active in fiscal year 2007 and beyond with total obligations of $25,000 or more. The site also provides online tools specifically for federal research grant recipients.

Subject(s): Scientific Research—Grants

Science of Science and Innovation Policy (SOSP)

https://www.nsf.gov/funding/pgm_summ.jsp?pims_id=501084

Description: The Science of Science and Innovation Policy (SciSIP) program supports research designed to advance the scientific basis of science and innovation policy. The program funds research to develop models, analytical tools, data and metrics that can be applied in the science policy decision making process and concern the use and allocation of scarce scientific resources.

Subject(s): Scientific Research—Policy

U.S. Arctic Research Commission (USARC)

https://www.arctic.gov/

Description: The Arctic Research Commission was established to set the national goals and priorities for the federal basic and applied scientific research plan for the Arctic. This website has information on current commission news, meetings, and publications. Publications include research goals reports and Arctic boundary maps.

Subject(s): Scientific Research—Policy

U.S. Geological Survey (USGS)

https://www.arctic.gov/

Description: As one of the government's primary scientific agencies, USGS offers a broad range of scientific material on its website. USGS provides scientific and safety information about such natural hazards as landslides, earthquakes, and volcanoes. USGS also studies natural resources, such as minerals. Science in Your Backyard links to USGS information—such as flood or drought watches—for each state, the District of Columbia, Puerto Rico, and the U.S. Virgin Islands. The Social Media section includes a consolidated list of USGS podcasts and RSS newsfeeds on topics such as earthquake news, volcano watches, and satellite imagery updates. The Maps, Imagery, and Publications section centralizes access to the many USGS webpages that provide catalogs or collections of USGS information products. The website also has a substantial science-related Education section.

The USGS homepage provides multiple access points to its rich collection of scientific resources and publications.

Subject(s): Geography; Geology; Natural Resources; Scientific Research

SCIENTIFIC AND TECHNICAL INFORMATION

DOEpatents

https://www.osti.gov/doepatents/

Description: DOEpatents is a database providing information on patents resulting from research and development funded by the Department of Energy. When possible, the database records provide the full text of the patent from the DOE or link to the information at the United States Patent and Trademark Office. The site is intended to demonstrate the Energy Department's contributions to the sciences.

Subject(s): Inventions; Research and Development

NASA Scientific and Technical Information (STI) Program

https://www.sti.nasa.gov/

Description: NASA defines STI as basic and applied research results from the work of scientists, engineers, and others. The NASA Scientific and Technical Information Program disseminates STI from NASA research and other sources to the public. This site offers databases, documents, and new reports announcements. The major asset on the site is the NASA Technical Reports Server (NTRS), which covers NASA materials such as reports, journal articles, conference and meeting papers, and technical videos. NTRS also includes records from the National Advisory Committee for Aeronautics (NACA) database; NACA, NASA's predecessor, was operational from 1917 to 1958. In addition, NTRS includes the NASA Image eXchange (NIX) collection and material from outside organizations, such as the European Space Agency (ESA).

Other free STI resources on the site include NASA's *Spinoff* magazine and a database of abstracts for every successfully commercialized NASA technology published in *Spinoff*. The site also offers two current awareness services announcing newly released and newly acquired STI: the Selected Current Aerospace Notices (SCAN) service and Scientific and Technical Aerospace Reports (STAR). An RSS feed is available for tracking new STI from NASA and for the STI blog.

NTRS is a major bibliographic database of broad interest to the engineering and scientific communities. NTRS and the other services offered by NASA's STI Program make this site a key resource for scientific and technical literature.

Subject(s): Scientific and Technical Information; Databases

National Science Digital Library (NSDL)

https://nsdl.oercommons.org/

Description: NSDL is a National Science Foundation program. The NSDL goal is to provide "high quality online educational resources for teaching and learning, with current emphasis on the sciences, technology, engineering, and mathematics (STEM) disciplines—both formal and informal, institutional and individual, in local, state, national, and international educational settings." (from the website) NSDL collections focus on science portal sites that provide material for educators or students. In addition to the NSDL contents, the site provides a wealth of related resources for teachers.

Subject(s): Science Education

National Technical Reports Library (NTRL)

https://ntrl.ntis.gov/NTRL/

Description: Launched in 2009, this site offers web-based subscription access to an electronic library over three million bibliographic records. The coverage is from the late 1890s to the present although most reports are from the 1970s onward. While it is not free of charge like most of the sites mentioned in this book, it does mention that it offers "affordable fixed fee subscription pricing."

Subject(s): Scientific and Technical Information

NIST Data Gateway

https://srdata.nist.gov/gateway/

Description: The NIST Data Gateway links to over 80 databases from the National Institute of Standards and Technology. As stated on the site, "these data cover a broad range of substances and properties from many different scientific disciplines." Specific resources include the Atomic Spectra Database (ASD), *Engineering Statistics Handbook*, CODATA Fundamental Physical Constants, and the *NIST Chemistry WebBook*. The site also lists NIST databases that are available for purchase or subscription.

Subject(s): Engineering Research; Scientific and Technical Information; Databases

Public Technical Reports

http://www.dtic.mil/dtic/search/tr/tr.html

Description: The scope of the Public Technical Reports database includes defense research topics, the basic sciences, and specific documents such as conference papers and patent applications. It provides access to citations to unclassified, unlimited documents entered into DTIC's Technical Reports Collection since 1960 and to online copies of many documents published after 1990.

Subject(s): Scientific and Technical Information; Databases

Science Inventory

https://cfpub.epa.gov/si/

Description: The EPA's Science Inventory site is a database of EPA scientific and technical projects and scientific activities. Database entries include project descriptions, products produced, types of peer review, links to related work, and contacts for additional information. The database can be searched by word. Researchers can subscribe to an RSS feed of all new entries or set up a customized RSS feed based on a word search or topic.

Subject(s): Research and Development

Science Tracer Bullets Online

http://www.loc.gov/rr/scitech/tracer-bullets/

Description: The Library of Congress *Science Tracer Bullet Series* contains research guides for finding books, journal articles, Internet resources, and other literature on specific science and technology topics. The guides cover such topics as careers in science, earthquakes and earthquake engineering, introductory physics, global warming and climate change, and science fair projects.

The Tracer Bullets range from one year to over ten years old; only the newest include Internet resources. While much of the research guidance is still worthwhile, researchers should remember that more current resources are probably available. Consult the homepage of Science Reference Services at http://www.loc.gov/rr/scitech/ for additional science research guides.

Subject(s): Science—Research

Science.gov

https://www.science.gov/

Description: Science.gov represents a collaborative effort by a group of government agencies to select and share the best of their online science information. Science.gov accesses over 60 databases and more than 2,200 science websites. The Energy Department's Office of Scientific and Technical Information (OSTI) hosts the site. The science resources can be browsed by topic or searched by word. The search feature allows users to select a combination of government science websites and databases to search. Users can also set up e-mail alerts based on search topics. Indexed resources in Science.gov include the Energy Citations Database, the NASA Technical Reports Server, PubMed, and National Science Foundation publications. Science.gov also has science news and special collections of links on topics such as science conferences and internships and fellowships.

Science.gov allows for easy discovery of science and technical information that is distributed through government websites.

Subject(s): Scientific and Technical Information; Databases

SPACE

Aeronautics Research Mission Directorate (ARMD)

https://www.nasa.gov/aeroresearch

Description: ARMD is concerned with cutting-edge aeronautics research. The Programs section of the ARMD website lists the directorate's three mission programs: the Airspace Operations and Safety Program, the Advanced Air Vehicles Program, and the Integrated Aviation Systems Program. The Reference Materials section has ARMD publications and related NASA publications. The Education section has resources on aeronautics for all levels of students.

Subject(s): Aerospace Engineering—Research

Ames Research Center

https://www.nasa.gov/centers/ames/

Description: NASA's Ames Research Center in California specializes in researching and developing new technologies in such fields as supercomputing, nanotechnology, fundamental space biology, biotechnology, and human factors. The Research section of the site provides information on current projects. The Research section also links to information on collaborative efforts such as NASA Research Park and the NASA Astrobiology Institute.

Subject(s): Space Sciences—Research; Space Technology—Research

Astronomy Resources at STScI

http://www.stsci.edu

Description: The Space Telescope Science Institute (STScI) is one of the astronomy centers operated for NASA by the Association of Universities for Research in Astronomy, Inc. (AURA). It is responsible for the scientific operation of the Hubble Space Telescope and will be supporting the James Webb Space Telescope (JWST); each one is described in detail at this site. Other main categories on this website include News and Education, Data Archives, News and Education, Events, and Future Missions and Initiatives Support.

Subject(s): Astronomy; Telescopes

Cassini Solstice Mission

https://saturn.jpl.nasa.gov/

Description: The Cassini spacecraft orbiting Saturn has completed both its initial mission and first extended mission to explore the Saturn System. Its second extended mission, called the Solstice Mission, has a projected end date of 2017. The website has mission news, Saturn images, and information about Cassini. It also has educational materials and a link to the mission's Twitter feed.

Subject(s): Spacecraft; Saturn

Chandra X-Ray Observatory

http://chandra.harvard.edu/

Description: Chandra X-Ray Observatory is an orbiting space telescope launched in 1999. Chandra captures X-ray images from high-energy regions of the universe, such as the remnants of exploded stars. This website serves as a center for information on Chandra's status and discoveries.

Subject(s): Astrophysics; Telescopes

Columbia Accident Investigation Board (CAIB)

http://govinfo.library.unt.edu/caib/

Description: The Columbia Accident Investigation Board (CAIB) was established to determine actual or probable causes of the failure of NASA's Columbia space shuttle on February 1, 2003. The website includes the final report, information on board members, the board charter, press releases, transcripts of press briefings, and minutes of any public meetings. It is archived at the University of North Texas Libraries' CyberCemetery.

Subject(s): Space Shuttle

Compton Gamma Ray Observatory Science Support Center (CGRO)

https://heasarc.gsfc.nasa.gov/docs/cgro/

Description: CGRO, in service from 1991 to 2000, was the second of NASA's four Great Observatories. The website has sections for the CGRO data archive, data analysis, and the CGRO instruments. It also has an Education & Public Info section that details CGRO discoveries.

Subject(s): Astronomy; Telescopes

Crustal Dynamics Data Information System (CDDIS)

https://cddis.nasa.gov/

Description: According to the website, CDDIS "continues to support the space geodesy and geodynamics community through NASA's Space Geodesy Project as well as NASA's Earth Science Enterprise." This site offers access to CDDIS data sets, programs, and reports.

This site will primarily be of interest to researchers in this field.

Subject(s): Geodesy

NASA Eclipse

https://eclipse.gsfc.nasa.gov/eclipse.html

Description: This site provides details on total and partial solar and lunar eclipses around the world. It includes eclipse maps, listings, path coordinates, explanations, and predication information. The site also has information on lunar eclipses and planetary transits across the sun.

The clear organization of this site makes it an excellent reference source on the topic.

Subject(s): Eclipses; Sun

Galileo Legacy Site

https://solarsystem.nasa.gov/missions/galileo/in-depth/

Description: NASA's Galileo mission ended when the spacecraft impacted Jupiter on September 2003 as planned. The Galileo site provides an extensive collection of information on the Galileo spacecraft and the planet Jupiter. The site also includes images, mission details, and educational resources.

Subject(s): Jupiter; Spacecraft

Glenn Research Center

https://www.nasa.gov/centers/glenn/

Description: Formerly known as the Lewis Research Center, the Glenn Research Center was renamed after John H. Glenn, former astronaut and U.S. senator. Spaceflight systems, aeronautics, and aeropropulsion technologies are the center's focus. The website describes the center's work related to the space station and shuttle, moon and Mars missions, technology, and aeronautics. The site also has sections on education and on doing business with the center.

Subject(s): Aerospace Engineering—Research; Space Technology—Research

Goddard Space Flight Center (GSFC)

https://www.nasa.gov/goddard

Description: GSFC specializes in developing and operating unmanned scientific spacecraft conducting research on the Earth, sun, and universe. The website describes past, present, and future missions supported by Goddard. It includes feature stories and videos highlighting Earth and space observations. Other sections of the site cover Goddard's educational programs and business opportunities.

Subject(s): Space Sciences; Space Technology

GRIN: Great Images in NASA

https://www.flickr.com/photos/nasacommons

Description: The Great Images in NASA(GRIN) site was recently retired in favor of the improved NASA Commons site mentioned above. This sitea collection of over a thousand photographs of significant historical interest from both NASA and its predecessor, the National Advisory Committee for Aeronautics (NACA). The images can be searched by a variety of factors, such as keyword, date range, and GRIN number. While most of the images are not protected by copyright, the Copyright Information section (under How to Use GRIN) should be reviewed for information on usage restrictions.

The emphasis of this selective collection is on NASA history. Researchers looking for a broader collection of images may wish to check the NASA Image eXchange (NIX) and NASA Multimedia Gallery websites. Both are linked to from the GRIN homepage.

Subject(s): Aerospace Engineering—History; Photography; Space—History

International Space Station (ISS)

https://www.nasa.gov/mission_pages/station/main/index.html

Description: This central website for the ISS has news, mission and crew profiles, images, interactive features, and science information. The News & Media Resources section includes press kits, briefing materials, and documents related to the station. Interactive features on the site include an animated reference guide. Links to ISS social media pages are also provided.

Subject(s): Space Stations

James Webb Space Telescope (JWST)

https://www.jwst.nasa.gov/

Description: JWST is the planned successor to the Hubble Space Telescope. This website gives an overview of the project, news, science goals, and mission hardware. The For Scientists section includes the *Webb Update* newsletter and has information for astronomers who would like to learn more about using JWST for their research programs. The website also has images, videos, animations, and educational games about the telescope.

Subject(s): Astronomy; Telescopes—Research

Jet Propulsion Laboratory (JPL)

https://www.jpl.nasa.gov/

Description: JPL is the lead U.S. center for robotic exploration of the solar system. Major subject links on the JPL website include News, Missions, Galleries, Public Events, Education, and About. The Missions page profiles specific robotic spacecraft, such as the Voyager and the Mars Global Surveyor, and the accomplishments of their missions. It includes current, past, present, and proposed missions with JPL involvement. The News section provides press releases, mission fact sheets, and a JPL blog. The site has a well-stocked Education section, with information for teachers and students.

Subject(s): Planets; Space technology

Johnson Space Center (JSC)

https://www.nasa.gov/centers/johnson/home/index.html

Description: Programs at the JSC in Texas focus on human spaceflight, the International Space Station (ISS), the Mission Control Center, and astronaut training. The About Johnson section links to information on each of these topics, including the NASA Astronaut Corps. The Johnson News section includes status reports for the ISS. The Education section provides news and information about JSC education programs and about internships at JSC.

Most of the material on this site is geared toward the public, the press, and business. It is also an excellent site for students and teachers to find material for education related to humans in space, manned space flights, and basic astronomy.

Subject(s): Astronauts; Human Space Exploration; Spacecraft

Kennedy Space Center (KSC)

https://www.nasa.gov/centers/kennedy/home/index.html

Description: NASA's Kennedy Space Center in Florida has primary responsibility for ground turnaround, support, and launch of the space shuttle and its payloads, including elements for the International Space Station (ISS). The website has information on shuttle and KSC history. The site provides status reports for these and other rockets that launch from the center.

Subject(s): Space Shuttle; Space Stations; Rockets

Lunar and Planetary Science at the NSSDCA

https://nssdc.gsfc.nasa.gov/planetary/

Description: The NASA Space Science Data Center Archive (NSSDCA) is responsible for the collection and storage and distribution of lunar and planetary images and other data to scientists, educators, and the general public. The site offers a separate page for each planet and for the moon, asteroids, and comets. Each of these separate pages features fact sheets, images, a Frequently Asked Questions file, other resources, and information on spacecraft missions to that specific astral body.

This site offers a substantial body of textual and pictorial information for all the planets in our solar system. Information is available at many levels and for many audiences, from children to research scientists. It is worth a visit from anyone in search of basic information on or images of the planets, the moon, asteroids, or comets.

Subject(s): Planetary Science; Planets

Marshall Space Flight Center (MSFC)

https://www.nasa.gov/centers/marshall/home/index.html

Description: The Marshall Space Flight Center in Alabama develops space transportation and propulsion systems and oversees science and hardware development for the International Space Station. Its website provides a broad range of technical and background information on the many projects, scientific disciplines, and specific space flight missions with which the center is involved. Major sections of the website include Propulsion, Living in Space, Solar System, and Technology. The site also has a history of the center.

Subject(s): Microgravity; Propulsion Technology; Space Technology

NASA Armstrong Flight Research Center (AFRC)

https://www.nasa.gov/centers/armstrong/home/index.html

Description: Armstrong Flight Research Center, located on Edwards Air Force Base in California, is responsible for flight research and flight testing. Website sections include Overview, Capabilities and Facilities, Aircraft, Education, and Doing Business with AFRC. The Images and Videos sections feature digitized photos, movies, and drawings of many of the unique research aircraft flown at the facility from the 1940s to the present.

Subject(s): Aerospace Engineering—Research; Aircraft—Research

NASA Human Exploration and Operations (HEO) Mission Directorate

https://www.nasa.gov/directorates/heo/index.html

Description: HEO leads the agency's human space exploration programs. The site has information about human health and safety on long space missions and research about the best methods for safe human space travel. The site links to several social media pages.

Subject(s): Human Space Exploration; Space Technology

NASA Headquarters

https://www.nasa.gov/centers/hq/

Description: NASA Headquarters in Washington, D.C., manages the agency's space flight centers and research centers and other installations. Under the heading Organization, the site links to headquarters leaders and NASA mission directorates, agency financial reports, and business and research opportunities.

Subject(s): Space

NASA History Division

https://history.nasa.gov/

Description: The NASA History Division, dating back to 1958, documents and preserves the agency's history. The site includes a brief history of NASA—including that of its predecessor, NACA—and an extensive topical index to historical information distributed on the many NASA websites. The Publications section lists print publications about NASA history, many of which are also available online, and links to NASA's own electronic publications about the agency's history.

Subject(s): Spacecraft—History

NASA Langley Research Center (LaRC)

https://www.nasa.gov/langley

Description: NASA's Langley Research Center, located in Virginia, has long been a major center for aeronautics research. The website provides news, images, and information related to this research and also highlights the center's contributions to space exploration and science. The Business section has information on procurement and technology transfer.

Subject(s): Aerospace Engineering—Research

NASA Solar System Exploration Research Virtual Institute (SSERVI)

https://lunarscience.arc.nasa.gov/

Description: SSERVI is managed by the NASA Ames Research Center but has dispersed teams across the nation. As stated on the website, the institute's research activities focus on "understanding the Moon, Near Earth Asteroids, the Martian moons Phobos and Deimos, and the near space environments of these large target bodies." The website provides information on the research teams and lunar science. It also has a section for the Lunar Science Forum.

Subject(s): Moon—Research

NASA Science

https://science.nasa.gov/

Description: NASA's Science Mission Directorate offers this website with detailed information on the agency's science strategy and science missions. The website describes each science mission and organizes science topics in sections for Earth, Heliophysics, Planets, and Astrophysics. The site has audience-specific sections for researchers, educators, kids, teens, and "citizen scientists." The website also has science news.

Subject(s): Space Sciences

NASA Shuttle

https://www.nasa.gov/mission_pages/shuttle/main/index.html

Description: The final Space Shuttle mission took place in July 2011, and the Space Shuttle Discovery was turned over to the Smithsonian in April 2012. The website has information on the final flights and on past missions. Under several Missions subheadings, the Shuttle Archives section documents the crew, payloads, and timeline for previous missions back to 1981. Other subsections include Behind the Scenes, Launch & Landing, and Vehicle Structure.

Subject(s): Space Shuttle

NASA Tech Briefs

https://www.techbriefs.com/Briefs/

Description: *NASA Tech Briefs* feature information on commercially significant technologies developed in the course of NASA research and development. Their publication is a joint publishing venture of NASA and Tech Briefs Media Group, which runs this website. The site also offers free downloadable Technical Support Packages (TSPs) with further information on the innovations described in the *NASA Tech Briefs*.

Subject(s): Space Technology; Technology Transfer

NASA Technical Reports Server

https://ntrs.nasa.gov/advSearch.jsp

Description: This site provides access to aerospace-related citations, full-text online documents, images and videos. The types of information available for search also include research reports, movies, journal articles, patents, and conference papers.

NASA White Sands Test Facility (WSTF)

https://www.nasa.gov/centers/wstf/index_new.html

Description: NASA's White Sands Test Facility (WSTF) in New Mexico is operationally part of the NASA Johnson Space Center. The facility tests rocket propulsion systems, propellants and hazardous fluids, and materials and components used in spaceflight. It also serves as the primary training area for space shuttle pilots practicing landings. The website describes WSTF capabilities in each of these areas.

Subject(s): Aerospace Engineering; Propulsion Technology

NASA Space Science Data Coordinated Archive (NSSDCA)

https://nssdc.gsfc.nasa.gov/

Description: NASA Space Science Data Coordinated Archive serves as the permanent archive for space science data from NASA spaceflight missions. The data are related to the fields of astronomy and astrophysics, solar and space plasma physics, and planetary and lunar science. The site has an online Master Catalog of available data and resources. Some resources are available online; others must be ordered. The data are intended for use by the professional scientific community.

Subject(s): Space Sciences

NSPIRES—NASA Research Opportunities

https://nspires.nasaprs.com/external/

Description: NSPIRES stands for NASA Solicitation and Proposal Integrated Review and Evaluation System. The website is an online service center for each stage in the NASA research solicitation and award process. Users can search for open, closed, past, and future NASA research announcements; and view the list of proposals selected to conduct NASA research, including the principal investigator, institution, and proposal title. Extensive guidance is provided in the NSPIRES Help section.

Subject(s): Scientific Research—Grants; Space—Research

Office of Space Commerce

http://www.space.commerce.gov/

Description: "The Office of Space Commerce is the principal unit for space commerce policy activities within the Department of Commerce. Its mission is to foster the conditions for the economic growth and technological advancement of the U.S. commercial space industry." (from the website) The website outlines space commerce policy, particularly in the areas of remote sensing and space transportation. Topical sections bring together information on various specializations, such as satellite navigation and new entrepreneurial initiatives.

Subject(s): Space Technology

Planetary Data System (PDS)

https://pds.jpl.nasa.gov/

Description: PDS is an archive of peer-reviewed data products from NASA planetary missions, astronomical observations, and laboratory measurements. The site includes sections for data services information, tools to manage the downloaded data, and documentation and manuals. PDS is managed by a system of nodes—NASA offices and university consortia—with specialties in the planetary disciplines. Links to each node's specialized website are in the left column of the PDS homepage. While most of the content is for scientists, the site also has a section with resources for students and educators.

Subject(s): Planetary Science—Research

Solar System Exploration

https://solarsystem.nasa.gov/

Description: The Jet Propulsion Lab's Solar System Exploration website is a public outreach effort with a wealth of information on the Earth's solar system and on planetary science. It profiles current and past planetary missions and includes a multimedia section with images. Most of the site is written for the general public of high school or adult age, but it also provides sections for kids and for educators.

This is a colorful and well-designed site with fresh content for space enthusiasts and amateur astronomers.

Subject(s): Planetary Science

Space Calendar

https://www2.jpl.nasa.gov/calendar/

Description: JPL's Space Calendar covers space-related activities and historical anniversaries for the coming year, with more than 5,200 links to related webpages. The calendar includes launch dates, conferences, and celestial events such as eclipses. The site also offers calendar archives for the past several years.

This is an excellent resource for amateur astronomers and those interested in the history of space exploration.

Subject(s): Space—History

Space Weather Prediction Center

https://www.swpc.noaa.gov/

Description: As stated on the website, "Space Weather impacts numerous facets of everyday life, from where airplanes can safely fly, to how accurately a farmer plows his field. In addition, there are a large variety of phenomena that are driven by the variability of the sun over periods ranging from hours to years. SWPC provides information for novices and experts alike about the impacts and phenomena of Space Weather." The website's About Space Weather section reports on geomagnetic storms, solar radiation storms, radio blackouts, and the latest alerts and advisories. The Education and Outreach section (under Media and Resources) has classroom materials, brief papers on topics such as the ionosphere and radio wave propagation, and general information on space weather, including a webpage in Spanish.

Subject(s): Space Environment; Sun

Spitzer Space Telescope

http://www.spitzer.caltech.edu

Description: The Spitzer Space Telescope is a cryogenically-cooled infrared observatory. It is the final element of what are called NASA's four "Great Observatories," the others being the Hubble Space Telescope, Compton Gamma-Ray Observatory, and Chandra X-Ray Observatory. The Mission section of the site provides detailed information on project's history, mission, science, and technology. The site also has project news and a large image gallery.

Subject(s): Astronomy; Telescopes

Stennis Space Center (SSC)

https://www.nasa.gov/centers/stennis/home/index.html

Description: SSC is NASA's primary center for testing large rocket propulsion systems and for developing remote sensing technology. These programs are detailed in the Propulsion section of the website. Under Images, the site features images related to work at SSC. The site also has information about Stennis education and business opportunities.

Subject(s): Propulsion Technology; Remote Sensing; Rockets

Voyager

https://voyager.jpl.nasa.gov/

Description: This site covers the missions of the Voyager-1 and Voyager-2 spacecraft, both launched in 1977 and now heading out of the solar system. The site has information on the science, spacecraft, and images of the Voyager missions.

Subject(s): Spacecraft

Wallops Flight Facility

https://www.nasa.gov/centers/wallops/home

Description: Wallops Flight Facility is responsible for the launch and operation of suborbital and small orbital payloads that support space-based research focused on Earth. It supports NASA's Sounding Rocket and Scientific Balloon Programs. The website describes the Wallops programs, facilities, business opportunities, education outreach, and history.

Subject(s): Rockets

Chapter Nineteen

Social Welfare

The federal government develops programs and policies and administers grants in areas such as housing, community development, volunteer services, and welfare. This chapter includes agency websites that either serve the customers of such programs, or compile information on such programs.

Subsections in this chapter are Child Welfare, Economic Development, Housing, Social Services, and Volunteerism and Charities.

CHILD WELFARE

Administration for Children and Families (ACF)

https://www.acf.hhs.gov/

Description: ACF is a federal agency that funds state, local, and tribal organizations that provide family assistance (welfare), child support, child-care, Head Start, child welfare, and other services related to children and families. Its website presents program and agency information under sections including About, Find Help, Topics, Grants & Funding, and Data & Research. Program information and resources organized under the Topics heading include information about children and youths, families, and emergency response and recovery.

The ACF website is a well-organized and informative resource for child and family federal welfare programs. The agency's research, data, and statistics information should be of interest to social service researchers.

Subject(s): Child Welfare; Early Childhood Education; Families; Welfare

Child Welfare Information Gateway

https://www.childwelfare.gov/

Description: The Child Welfare Information Gateway is a web portal to information on such topics as child abuse and neglect, out-of-home care, and adoption. Resources include the National Foster Care & Adoption Directory, statistics on child neglect issues, summaries of state laws, and links to relevant national organizations. Core information and some publications are available in Spanish.

Subject(s): Child Welfare

Child Care

https://www.usa.gov/child-care/

Description: This USA.gov webpage links to information about child care and early learning from federal government and government-sponsored sources. The site is designed for the general public, with special sections for parents, child care providers, researchers, and policy makers. It includes information on finding, choosing, and paying for child care; running a child care business; and topics such as the Head Start program and childproofing. Information is available in Spanish.

Subject(s): Child Care; Early Childhood Education

Family and Youth Services Bureau (FYSB)

https://www.acf.hhs.gov/fysb

Description: FYSB provides runaway and homeless youth service grants to local communities. It also funds research and demonstration projects. The FYSB divisions described on the website include Family Violence Prevention and Services, Special Projects for Runaway and Homeless Youth, and Adolescent Pregnancy Prevention. Links to resources and funding opportunities are also provided.

Subject(s): Adolescents; Social Services—Grants

Intercountry Adoption

https://travel.state.gov/content/adoptionsabroad/en.html

Description: This site provides information on the international adoption process for Americans wishing to adopt a child from another country. It has sections on the Hague Convention on Intercountry Adoption, visas, country information, and the adoption process.

Subject(s): Adoption—International

National Clearinghouse on Families and Youth (NCFY)

https://ncfy.acf.hhs.gov/

Description: NCFY provides information on youth development, family violence prevention, abstinence education, and mentoring children of prisoners. The site is intended to support Family and Youth Service Bureau grantees and organizations interested in youth programming and policy. NCFY links to its own publications and an online database of summaries of publications from other sources. The site also has an online newsletter, *Youth Initiatives Update*.

Subject(s): Adolescents; Families

National Responsible Fatherhood Clearinghouse (NRFC)

https://www.fatherhood.gov/

Description: NRFC collects, organizes, and provides access to research, policies, best practices, and other information to support ACF-funded grantees in the Promoting Responsible Fatherhood program. Some information is available in Spanish, including information on the president's Fatherhood and Mentoring Initiative. The site also links to the DadTalk blog.

Subject(s): Families

Office of Child Care

https://www.acf.hhs.gov/occ

Description: The Office of Child Care administers federal funds to states, territories, and tribes to help low-income families obtain quality child care. The site has policy and regulatory guidance documents and technical assistance information for the local governments administering the funds. It links to resources for childcare providers and for parents seeking quality child care. The site provides statistics on the Child Care and Development Fund.

Subject(s): Child Care

Women, Infants, and Children (WIC)

https://www.fns.usda.gov/wic/women-infants-and-children-wic

Description: "WIC provides Federal grants to States for supplemental foods, health care referrals, and nutrition education for low-income pregnant, breastfeeding, and non-breastfeeding postpartum women, and to infants and children who are found to be at nutritional risk." (from the website) The website serves multiple audiences, including WIC applicants, state program administrators, and food manufacturers wishing to participate in the program.

Subject(s): Nutrition—Grants; Pregnancy

ECONOMIC DEVELOPMENT

Administration for Native Americans (ANA)

https://www.acf.hhs.gov/ana

Description: As stated on the website, the Administration for Native Americans (ANA) has a mission to promote "self-sufficiency for Native Americans by providing discretionary grant funding for community based projects, and training and technical assistance to eligible tribes and native organizations." The site has information on grant programs and awards, emergency preparedness, and funding opportunities. Special initiatives include the Social and Economic Development Strategies (SEDS) and Native American Language Preservation and Maintenance projects.

Subject(s): Indigenous Peoples; Social Welfare; American Indians

Appalachian Regional Commission (ARC)

https://www.arc.gov/index.asp

Description: ARC supports economic and social development in the Appalachian region, which spans the spine of the Appalachian Mountains from southern New York to northern Mississippi. It includes all of West Virginia and parts of 12 other states: Alabama, Georgia, Kentucky, Maryland, Mississippi, New York, North Carolina, Ohio, Pennsylvania, South Carolina, Tennessee, and Virginia. The ARC website lists the individual counties that make up Appalachia. The site also features news about ARC and the Appalachian region and ARC's now-discontinued *Appalachia Magazine*.

Subject(s): Rural Development

Consumer Financial Protection Bureau (CFPB)

https://www.consumerfinance.gov/

Description: CFPB is an independent Federal Reserve agency. According to its website, its mission is "to make markets for consumer financial products and services work for Americans—whether they are applying for a mortgage, choosing among credit cards, or using any number of other consumer financial products," through the application of education, enforcement, and research. The Get Assistance section informs consumers about protecting against credit discrimination, getting mortgage help, and other procedures. Information is available in several languages including Spanish, Chinese, Russian, and Arabic. The homepage provides links to the bureau's Facebook page and Twitter feed.

Subject(s): Consumer Information; Finance

Economic Development Administration (EDA)

https://www.eda.gov/

Description: The EDA gives grants to local communities for infrastructure and business development. Its website provides a full list of EDA contacts and links to the administration's social media pages. The Newsroom section lists press releases in reverse chronological order and links to the EDA's blog.

Subject(s): Economic Development—Grants

Office of Economic Adjustment (OEA)

http://www.oea.gov

Description: OEA provides adjustment assistance to communities affected by a military base closure, a base expansion, or contract and program cancellations. The website has assistance information and resources related to planning for local development authorities, for growth management organizations, and for supporting compatible uses. The About Us section includes news, project highlights, and information on the Economic Adjustment Committee, an interagency group that helps to coordinate federal intergovernmental assistance to local communities.

Subject(s): Economic Development

Rural Information Center (RIC)

https://www.nal.usda.gov/ric

Description: RIC is a specialized information and referral service within the National Agricultural Library. In the About RIC section, the RIC site links to information on rural resources and funding sources and RIC's own database, Federal Funding Sources for Rural Areas Database. The RIC website also provides a documented definition of "rural" for major federal programs.

The RIC website is an excellent starting point for those researching rural development topics for grant-writing or other purposes. It can be of assistance to rural governments, grant-seekers, small farms, and nonprofit organizations.

Subject(s): Rural Development—Research

USDA Rural Development

https://www.rd.usda.gov/

Description: The Rural Development website links to information on its major program areas: businesses, cooperatives, community development, energy, utilities, and housing. It includes current notices of funding availability and program news. The site also carries regulations, forms, and publications. Some publications are available in Spanish, and a version of the site is also available in Spanish.

Subject(s): Rural Development

HOUSING

Department of Housing and Urban Development (HUD)

https://www.hud.gov/

Description: HUD's website describes the agency's programs in housing and community development. Under the heading State Info, the site has information for residents of each of the 50 states, the District of Columbia,

Puerto Rico, and the Virgin Islands. Another main section of the site, Topic Areas, provides information on numerous topics, including avoiding foreclosure, buying a home, fair lending practices, homes for sale, housing discrimination, housing research and data sets, rental assistance, and veterans information. Under Resources, the site has an extensive online library of information and tools including a Loan Estimator Calculator, a Lender Locator, and a database of HUD-approved appraisers. The site also has an A–Z index and is available in Spanish.

As with other Cabinet agencies, HUD has Recovery Act and Open Government sections on its website.

This site provides valuable resources on housing to the general public.

Subject(s): Community Development; Housing

Federal Housing Administration (FHA)

https://www.hud.gov/program_offices/housing/fhahistory

Description: According to the website, FHA provides mortgage insurance on "single-family and multifamily homes including manufactured homes and hospitals." Under Resources, the website has sections for consumers, lenders, real estate professionals, appraisers, builders, inspectors, and counseling services. The site also includes information on the FHA National Servicing Center, which helps homeowners by working with lenders to find solutions to avoid foreclosure. The FHA website provides detailed information on its programs, products, services, and rules. It also links to state websites.

Subject(s): Home Mortgages

Federal Housing Finance Agency (FHFA)

https://www.fhfa.gov/

Description: Created in 2008, FHFA oversees Fannie Mae, Freddie Mac, and the Federal Home Loan Banks. It replaces Office of Federal Housing Enterprise Oversight (OFHEO), the Federal Housing Finance Board (FHFB), and the government-sponsored enterprise team (GSE) mission office at the Department of Housing and Urban Development (HUD). The website includes FHFA regulations and agency guidance. The House Price Index (HPI) section of the site includes current HPI data reports, downloadable data in text and spreadsheet formats, and historical reports.

Subject(s): Housing Finance

Foreclosure Resource Center

https://www.stlouisfed.org/community-development/housing-and-foreclosure-resources/foreclosure-resource-center/

Description: The Foreclosure Resource Center of the Federal Reserve Bank of St. Louis provides a *Foreclosure Survival Guide* for consumers and a *Mitigation Toolkit* for communities. The site provides additional links to home foreclosure information for consumers, communities, and financial institutions.

Subject(s): Home Mortgages

Ginnie Mae

https://www.ginniemae.gov/pages/default.aspx

Description: Ginnie Mae (Government National Mortgage Association), a wholly owned government corporation within the HUD, aims to help provide affordable, government-insured mortgages to American families. Its website includes information for investors, homeowners, and mortgage-backed securities issuers, as well as information about Ginnie Mae. The site also has information on the history of Ginnie Mae and on relevant statutes and regulations.

Subject(s): Housing Finance

Home Loans—VA

https://www.benefits.va.gov/homeloans/

Description: The VA helps veterans finance the purchase of homes through favorable loan terms and competitive interest rates. The website provides information for home buyers, lenders, loan servicers, and real estate professionals. It has online videos, pamphlets, and disaster advice for VA borrowers. The site also has information on grants for specially adapted housing.

Subject(s): Housing Finance; Veterans

HUD User

https://www.huduser.gov/portal/home.html

Description: HUD User is the primary source for federal government reports and information about housing policy and programs, building technology, economic development, urban planning, and other housing-related topics. Website sections include About PD&R, Research & Publications, Data Sets, Initiatives, and Quick Links. The Bibliographic Database links to information on thousands of reports, articles, case studies, and other research literature related to housing and community development. The Data Sets section includes the original electronic data sets from the American Housing Survey and other housing research initiatives. The About PD&R section features the current research and initiatives of the Office of Policy Development and Research.

Subject(s): Community Development—Research; Housing—Research; Databases

HUDCLIPS

https://portal.hud.gov/hudportal/HUD?src=/program_offices/administration/hudclips/

Description: HUDCLIPS (HUD's Client Information Policy Systems) is a searchable online database that contains the entire inventory of official HUD policies, procedures, announcements, forms, and other materials. The site provides HUD forms in PDF format; some of these forms are also available in Spanish. Other documents on HUDCLIPS include HUD handbooks, letters, guidebooks, notices, bulletins, housing policy documents, and legal opinions.

Subject(s): Housing; Publication Catalogs

Making Home Affordable

https://www.makinghomeaffordable.gov/pages/default.aspx

Description: Making Home Affordable is the central website for information on government programs to help homeowners afford their mortgages to promote financial stability. Major sections of the site cover eligibility, finding an HUD-approved housing counselor, and applying for the Home Affordable Modification Program (HAMP). The Learning Center section provides practical information for borrowers, including information about avoiding scams. The site is available in languages other than English, including Spanish, Chinese, Korean, Russian, and Vietnamese.

Subject(s): Housing—Financial Programs

United States Interagency Council on Homelessness

https://www.usich.gov/

Description: Nineteen federal departments and agencies are members of the Interagency Council on Homelessness. The council coordinates federal policy and programs on homelessness and employs regional coordinators to work with state and local governments. The website provides information on the council's activities, programs to reduce homelessness, and state and local initiatives, as well as news about funding and technical assistance. The council's fact sheets are in the Resources section.

Subject(s): Homelessness

SOCIAL SERVICES

Administration on Developmental Disabilities (AIDD)

https://acl.gov/programs/aidd/

Description: AIDD coordinates service programs for those with developmental disabilities (defined as physical or mental impairments that begin before age 22 and restrict a person's ability to perform basic tasks for self-sufficiency). The site provides AIDD publications and program guidance and describes AIDD's major programs and program outcomes. The AIDD Programs section of the site links to institutional resources such as state councils on developmental disabilities and state protection and advocacy systems.

Subject(s): Disabilities

Benefits.gov

https://www.benefits.gov/

Description: Benefits.gov is a multi-agency effort to provide a single website for users with questions about government benefits. The site can help users find benefits information without having to know which agency to contact. One of its major features is its Benefit Finder; the user answers a series of questions to determine eligibility for specific government benefits. (The site does not ask for identifying information, such as name or Social Security number.) A Spanish-language version of the site is available.

Although the site is managed by a multi-agency partnership, the Department of Labor takes the "managing partner" role.

Subject(s): Social Welfare

Campaign to Rescue and Restore Victims of Human Trafficking

https://www.acf.hhs.gov/otip/resource/about-rescue-restore

Description: The Health and Human Services Department is responsible for helping victims of human trafficking become eligible to receive benefits and services. This website provides information on the department's campaign to locate human trafficking victims. It provides campaign toolkits for social service organizations, health care providers, and law enforcement officers. The site also links to other agency program websites concerned with human trafficking.

Subject(s): International Crimes

***Catalog of Federal Domestic Assistance* (*CFDA*)**

https://www.cfda.gov/

Description: This website features an online, searchable version of the *Catalog of Federal Domestic Assistance* (*CFDA*). *CFDA* describes a broad range of federal assistance programs, including formula-based grants, guaranteed loans, insurance, counseling, training, information services, and donation of goods. The site has a separate database to highlight Recovery Act programs. Most of the programs are not for direct assistance to individuals, but rather for state and local governments, Indian tribal governments, or other organizations that administer the distribution of aid. Catalog entries include a program identifier number, a description, eligibility requirements, program contact information, and details on the application and awards process.

With the advanced search feature, users of the catalog can search programs by keyword, type of assistance, type of entity eligible for the assistance, descriptive subject area or function, deadline for application, and more. Programs can be listed by agency or easily retrieved by *CFDA* program number. The General Info section of the site includes important resources such as a guide to writing grant proposals, explanations of the types of assistance in the *CFDA*, and a link for those who want to store and use the *CFDA* data at their own site.

Subject(s): Government Loans; Grants

Center for Faith-Based and Neighborhood Partnerships (DOL)

https://www.dol.gov/cfbnp/

Description: This website carries news on worker issues, the Labor Department's grants, and recent grant awards. Information is available in Spanish, Chinese, and Vietnamese.

Subject(s): Employment—Policy; Grants

Center for Faith-Based and Neighborhood Partnerships (ED)

https://sites.ed.gov/fbnp/

Description: This is one of the Centers for Faith-Based and Neighborhood Partnerships, which work with 13 federal agencies; these centers were created to encourage new participation in federal grant programs. The website includes information on program goals, news, and partnership funding.

Subject(s): Education Funding; Grants

Center for Faith-Based and Neighborhood Partnerships (HUD)

https://portal.hud.gov/hudportal/HUD?src=/program_offices/faith_based

Description: The HUD's Center for Faith-Based and Community Initiatives website has information on grants and technical assistance for nonprofits, as well as other housing-related resources.

Subject(s): Grants; Social Services

Department of Health and Human Services (HHS)

https://www.hhs.gov/

Description: The HHS website is a gateway to information on all of the health and social services programs overseen by the department. Major sections of the site cover federal grants and funding, services for families, disease prevention, disease information, and public health emergency preparedness. The site also links to regulations, policies, and guidelines relevant to HHS. The About HHS section links to HHS regional offices, and the HHS Secretary section links to speeches and testimony. The site's homepage features links to the websites for major initiatives, such as HealthCare.gov and FoodSafety.gov. For navigating the abundance of information on HHS.gov, the site has a search engine, frequently asked questions section, and an A–Z index. Like other Cabinet agencies, HHS has Open Government and Recovery Act information on its site.

This site is a good starting point for learning about HHS programs and initiatives.

Subject(s): Public Health; Social Services

Coordinating Council on Access and Mobility

https://www.transit.dot.gov/ccam

Description: The Coordinating Council on Access and Mobility (CCAM) is a partnership of federal agencies working to improve the availability, quality, and efficient delivery of transportation services to people with disabilities, older adults, and people with low incomes. It was established by an Executive Order in 2014.

Subject(s): Transportation; disabilities

Disability Resources

https://www.dol.gov/odep/topics/disability.htm

Description: Disability Resources is a portal to federal websites and programs of concern to persons with disabilities. The site is divided into topical sections, including Benefits, Community Life, Civil Rights, Emergency Preparedness, Employment, Education, Health, Housing, Transportation, and Technology.

Subject(s): Disabilities

Youth.gov

https://youth.gov/

Description: Youth.gov is designed to help community organizations in their efforts to support youth. It provides tools to find existing federal and local resources and to develop local programs and partnerships. The site is sponsored by a working group of 12 federal agencies, including the White House Office of National Drug Control Policy, the Corporation for National and Community Service, the Department of Justice, and the Department of Housing and Urban Development.

Subject(s): Adolescents

Food and Nutrition Service (FNS)

https://www.fns.usda.gov/

Description: FNS manages programs including School Meals; the Women, Infants, and Children (WIC) program; the Supplemental Nutrition Assistance Program (SNAP, formerly the Food Stamp Program); Food Assistance for Disaster Relief; and Food Distribution Programs. The website provides information on the regulations, statistics, and forms related to the programs.

A Nutrition Education section, under Research, highlights federal programs and resources in this area. The Newsroom section includes links to each program's publications. Other sections cover Forms, Programs, and Data. The site also has a Spanish-language version.

Subject(s): Food Stamps; Nutrition; School Meal Programs

Food Distribution Programs

https://www.fns.usda.gov/fdd/food-distribution-programs

Description: The Food Distribution Programs provide commodity distribution and other nutrition assistance to low-income families, emergency feeding programs, Indian Reservations, and the elderly. The website offers information primarily for food commodity providers. The Help section includes a site map and an A–Z index for the site. The site is also available in Spanish.

Subject(s): Food Aid

HIV/AIDS Programs

https://hab.hrsa.gov/

Description: This site focuses on the federal programs funded under the Ryan White Comprehensive AIDS Resources Emergency (CARE) Act. CARE Act programs are designed to help individuals with HIV who lack the health insurance and financial resources necessary for their care. The programs include health care and support, grants, training, and technical assistance. This site provides detailed information on the CARE Act and on applying for and managing the program grants. It also provides program data, including state profiles.

Subject(s): AIDS; HIV Infections

Low Income Home Energy Assistance Program (LIHEAP)

https://www.acf.hhs.gov/ocs/programs/liheap

Description: LIHEAP is a federally funded program that helps low-income households with their home energy bills for heating or cooling. Its website provides information for consumers who may be eligible for LIHEAP, as well as for professionals who coordinate LIHEAP programs in states, tribal areas, and localities. The site has information on funding and on applying for assistance. Instructions on applying are available in Spanish and English. The website also has regulatory guidance, policy information, and program statistics.

The LIHEAP Clearinghouse, a network for parties interested in low-income energy issues and a repository for information on the topic, can be accessed at https://liheapch.acf.hhs.gov/.

Subject(s): Energy Prices and Costs

Migrant and Seasonal Farmworkers

https://www.doleta.gov/farmworker/

Description: The Department of Labor maintains this website for their National Farmworker Jobs Program (NFJP). The program provides funding to community-based organizations and public agencies that assist migrant and seasonal farmworkers with job skills training, housing, and health care. The website has information on the program, grant awards, and state allocations, as well as information on the Monitor Advocate System.

Subject(s): Farms and Farming; Job Training—Grants

Office of Faith-Based and Neighborhood Partnerships

https://obamawhitehouse.archives.gov/administration/eop/ofbnp

Description: This site was maintained by the Obama administration. This White House office coordinated the work of the Federal Centers for Faith-Based and Community Initiatives. The centers helped community organizations find and apply for federal grants and implement grant awards to serve their communities.

Subject(s): Grants; Social Services

Office of Family Assistance (OFA)

https://www.acf.hhs.gov/ofa

Description: OFA administers the Temporary Assistance for Needy Families (TANF) welfare program. Along with non-technical overviews of how TANF works, the site provides legislative, regulatory, and technical documents related to the program. The TANF Program section links to data on TANF finances, demographics of recipients, and work participation rates of recipients.

OFA also administers the Healthy Marriage and Responsible Fatherhood program. The website provides information for funding information and research.

Subject(s): Welfare

Office of University Partnerships (OUP)

https://www.huduser.gov/portal/oup/home.html

Description: OUP functions as a national clearinghouse for disseminating information about HUD's Community Outreach Partnership Centers Program. HUD established OUP in 1994 to encourage university-community partnerships. The website's grantee database lists current and past grant recipients by state. The Research & Publications section includes more information on research and links to related websites. Other sections cover data, initiatives, and events.

Subject(s): Community Development—Grants

Poverty Guidelines, Research, and Measurement

https://aspe.hhs.gov/poverty-guidelines

Description: This site provides the text of the current HHS poverty guidelines, as published annually in the Federal Register. A table lists the actual dollar figures going back to 1982 and links to the guidelines going back to 1996. The site explains the difference between the "poverty threshold" issued by the Census Bureau and the "poverty guidelines" issued by HHS. The site includes papers and articles about how poverty can be measured and how it has been measured over time. It also links to academic research centers studying poverty.

This is an essential site for checking the current poverty guidelines, particularly since it includes additional explanatory information and context.

Subject(s): Poverty

Social Security Administration (SSA)

https://www.ssa.gov/

Description: The SSA's central website leads to a wealth of information and online services from the agency. Major programs involve such subjects as retirement, survivors, disability, Supplemental Security Income (SSI), and Medicare. Other sections on the homepage link to SSA's online services, tools for calculating benefits, a directory of local Social Security Offices, forms and publications, and program news. The homepage also features a menu to select answers to common questions and information tailored to specific groups (such as attorneys, press, and veterans).

Other Languages, located on the top menu of the homepage, links to the SSA Multilanguage Gateway. Consumer information is available there in 17 languages, including Spanish, Arabic, Chinese, French, Portuguese, Farsi, Korean, and Russian. Each section also has information on interpreter services. A Spanish-language version of the site is available directly on the homepage.

The design of the SSA's main webpage makes it easy to find information on popular topics. The site also has a search engine. For specific topics, one of the most helpful tools may be the FAQs menu on the homepage. The FAQs section can also be accessed directly at https://faq.ssa.gov/.

Subject(s): Social Security

Social Security Advisory Board

https://www.ssab.gov

Description: The Social Security Advisory Board is an independent, bipartisan board whose purpose is to advise the president, Congress, and the commissioner of Social Security on the Social Security and Supplemental Security Income programs. Its website has information on the board's authority and operations and has brief biographies of its members. The board's reports are online in full text back to 1997.

Subject(s): Social Security

Social Security Online for Women

https://www.ssa.gov/people/women/

Description: This site provides SSA program information on retirement, survivors, disability, and Supplemental Security Income benefits relevant to women. Information is organized into categories that correspond to the various life stages of women: Working Women, Women Who Receive Social Security Benefits, Brides, New Mothers, Wives, Divorced Women, Caregivers, and Widows.

Subject(s): Social Security; Women

Supplemental Nutrition Assistance Program (SNAP)

https://www.fns.usda.gov/snap/supplemental-nutrition-assistance-program-snap

Description: SNAP, formerly known as the Food Stamp Program, helps low-income people and families buy food. The website has program application forms and information for recipients and for retail stores. The site also has nutrition education materials, regulations and policy information, and data such as state-level participation. The site is also available in Spanish.

Subject(s): Food Stamps

The Work Site

https://www.ssa.gov/work/

Description: This site describes the voluntary Ticket to Work program and other programs useful to persons with disabilities who want to try to work. The site has information and documents for both beneficiaries and service providers.

Subject(s): Disabilities; Employment

Title V Information System (TVIS)

https://mchb.tvisdata.hrsa.gov/

Description: TVIS electronically captures data from annual Title V Block Grant applications and reports. Title V of the Social Security Act covers a major federal block grant program funding health promotion efforts for mothers, infants, and children. Reports available on the site include *Financial Data for the Most Recent Year*, *Program Data for the Most Recent Year*, and *Measurement and Indicator Data*.

Subject(s): Reproductive Health—Statistics; Child Health and Safety—Statistics

Unemployment Insurance

https://www.dol.gov/general/topic/unemployment-insurance

Description: Each state administers a separate unemployment insurance (UI) program within guidelines established by federal law. This Department of Labor website provides a centralized location for information on the federal-state program. The site provides extensive information on available programs, laws and regulations, statistics, budget, and reemployment services. The site also links to each state office responsible for administering unemployment insurance.

Subject(s): Unemployment Insurance

USAID Faith-Based and Community Initiatives

https://www.usaid.gov/who-we-are/organization/independent-offices/office-faith-based-and-community-initiatives/

Description: The Office of Faith-Based and Community Initiatives at USAID uses this page to highlight relevant information and to provide resources for interested organizations. USAID works in such areas as global health, disaster response, and food aid.

Subject(s): Foreign Assistance; Grants

USDA Faith-Based and Neighborhood Partnerships

https://www.rd.usda.gov/about-rd/initiatives/faith-based-and-neighborhood-partnerships-fbnp

Description: This USDA site highlights opportunities for faith-based and community organizations in USDA grant programs. The site highlights opportunities in the areas of reducing hunger, revitalizing rural communities, and helping to conserve natural resources.

Subject(s): Grants; Social Services

VOLUNTEERISM AND CHARITIES

AmeriCorps

https://www.nationalservice.gov/programs/americorps

Description: AmeriCorps is a program of the Corporation for National and Community Service. AmeriCorps volunteers serve on education, public safety, health, and environmental assistance projects and are eligible for an education-related stipend. The website has news and information for potential volunteers and for organizations seeking AmeriCorps assistance. Major sections of the site describe AmeriCorps VISTA (Volunteers in Service to America), AmeriCorps NCCC (National Civilian Community Corps), and AmeriCorps State and National.

Subject(s): Volunteerism

Citizen Corps

https://www.ready.gov/citizen-corps

Description: Citizen Corps was created to help coordinate volunteer activities that work to prepare communities to respond to emergency situations. Under Our Partners (which can be found under the Citizen Corps tab on the homepage), the website describes the major programs that Citizen Corps supports: CERT (Community Emergency Response Teams), VIPs (Volunteers in Police Service), USAonWatch, the Fire Corps, the Corporation for National and Community Service (CNCS), and the Medical Reserve Corps (MRC). The site also links to emergency preparedness guidance.

Subject(s): Volunteerism

Corporation for National and Community Service (CNCS)

https://www.nationalservice.gov/

Description: CNCS is a federal corporation governed by a board of directors. CNCS programs include AmeriCorps, Learn and Serve America, Senior Corps, and a number of special initiatives. The website has prominent links to the websites for its programs and information about how to volunteer. The About Us section has information on staff and organizational structure, fact sheets, relevant laws and regulations, and the annual report to Congress. Other sections are directed toward organizations needing assistance and individuals seeking to volunteer. The site also covers developments such as Recovery Act funding and the Edward M. Kennedy Serve America Act.

Subject(s): Volunteerism

Search for Charities

https://www.irs.gov/charities-non-profits/search-for-charities/

Description: This site began an online version of the IRS's *Cumulative List of Organizations described in Section 170(c) of the Internal Revenue Code*, which is no longer published by the IRS. To get information about tax-exempt organizations including those eligible to receive tax deductible charitable contribution , please click here: https://www.irs.gov/charities-non-profits/exempt-organizations-select-check

Subject(s): Charities

Senior Corps

https://www.nationalservice.gov/programs/senior-corps

Description: Senior Corps is a program of the Corporation for National and Community Service involving volunteers ages 55 and older. The website describes its major programs, such as Senior Companions and the Retired and Senior Volunteer Program (RSVP). The site has information for potential volunteers and for organizations seeking assistance from Senior Corps.AA

Subject(s): Senior Citizens; Volunteerism

Volunteer.gov

https://www.volunteer.gov/

Description: The goal of Volunteer.gov is to connect people with public service volunteer opportunities. Users can view descriptions of volunteer opportunities by type, city, and state and apply for positions online. Volunteer.gov is an interagency effort. The Department of the Interior manages the website.

Subject(s): Volunteerism

Chapter Twenty

Transportation

Although some aspects of transportation are handled at the state and local levels, the federal government still plays a major role in transportation funding, policy, regulation, and research. This chapter covers many modes of transportation, and includes websites that are intended for consumers as well as sites for transportation operators and makers of transportation policy. Websites concerning transportation security are listed in the Homeland Security section of the Defense and Intelligence chapter.

Subsections in this chapter are Aviation, Maritime Transportation, Mass Transit, Surface Transportation, Transportation Policy and Research, and Transportation Safety.

AVIATION

Federal Aviation Administration (FAA)

https://www.faa.gov/

Description: The FAA is responsible for the safety of civil aviation. Its website includes the following sections: Aircraft, Airports, Air Traffic (with airport status and airline on-time statistics), Data & Research (aviation and commercial space statistics and research funding), Licenses & Certificates, Regulations & Policies, and Training & Testing (aviation schools). The About FAA section links to field and regional offices and information on current FAA initiatives. The site has audience-specific sections for airline pilots, pilots, mechanics, and others, and an A–Z index for locating specific information on the site.

Subject(s): Aviation—Regulations; Aviation Safety—Regulations

Flight Delay Information

http://www.fly.faa.gov

Description: The Air Traffic Control System Command Center provides this interactive U.S. map for information on flight delays. As stated on the website, "the status information provided on this site indicates general airport conditions; it is not flight-specific."

Subject(s): Air Traffic Control

Flight Standards Service

https://www.faa.gov/about/office_org/headquarters_offices/avs/offices/afx/

Description: The FAA's Flight Standards Service maintains this website to provide FAA safety-related information for pilots and others regarding flying, airlines, and aircraft. The site has information on its safety programs and the Civil Aviation Registry, which is responsible for the registration of United States civil aircraft and certification of airmen.

Subject(s): Aviation Safety

William J. Hughes Technical Center

https://www.faa.gov/about/office_org/headquarters_offices/ang/offices/tc/

Description: The William J. Hughes Technical Center is an aviation research, development, engineering, testing, and evaluation facility located in New Jersey. Center activities involve testing and evaluation in air traffic control, communications, navigation, airports, and aircraft safety and security, as well as long-range R&D projects. This website includes an overview of the center's work and facility.

Subject(s): Aviation Safety—Research

MARITIME TRANSPORTATION

Federal Maritime Commission (FMC)

https://www.fmc.gov/

Description: The FMC is responsible for the regulation of shipping in the foreign trades of the United States. Its website is designed for providers and consumers of international shipping services. The Agreement Notices & Library section, under Databases & Services, allows for browsing Agreement Notices by carrier, country, type of agreement, and more. The website also links to SERVCON, the commission's electronic filing system, and provides commonly used FMC forms and applications.

Subject(s): Shipping—Regulations

Maritime Administration (MARAD)

https://www.marad.dot.gov/

Description: The Department of Transportation's MARAD promotes the U.S. Merchant Marine for waterborne commerce and as a naval and military auxiliary in time of war or national emergency. The Ports section of the site covers port security, infrastructure, conveyance, and licensing. The Education section features maritime career information, the Adopt a Ship program, and a page for kids. Statistics provided in the Resources section of the site cover the cruise industry, waterborne foreign trade, flags of registry, and vessel calls at US. port by vessel type. This section also has publications, including forms, policy papers, a *Glossary of Shipping Terms*, and *Maritime Laws*.

Subject(s): Merchant Marine; Shipping—Statistics

National Maritime Center

http://www.dco.uscg.mil/Our-Organization/Assistant-Commandant-for-Prevention-Policy-CG-5P/National-Maritime-Center/

Description: This website serves as a central location for information on merchant marine licenses, certificates of registry, and merchant mariner documents (issued to unlicensed personnel who support the operation of a vessel). It includes background information and checklists, applications and forms, and a user fee schedule.

Subject(s): Merchant Marine—Regulations

Saint Lawrence Seaway Development Corporation (SLSDC)

https://www.seaway.dot.gov/

Description: SLSDC works to ensure the safe transit of vessels through the two U.S. locks and navigation channels of the Saint Lawrence Seaway System. SLSDC works cooperatively with the Canadian Saint Lawrence Seaway Management Corporation, and many of the links on this site lead to a binational website run by both corporations (http://www.greatlakes-seaway.com/). The site includes press releases, *Seaway Notices*, and the toll schedule. Annual reports from 1997 onward are available under a separate heading.

Subject(s): Shipping

USCG Navigation Center

https://www.navcen.uscg.gov/

Description: The U.S. Coast Guard Navigation Center provides navigation services that promote safe transportation and support the commerce of the United States. The site features information on navigation rules, maritime telecommunications, global positioning systems (GPS), differential global positioning systems (DGPS), *Local Notices to Mariners (LMNs)*, and the

LORAN C service. The site also provides the *Light List*, a list of U.S. lights, sound signals, buoys, day beacons, and other aids to navigation.

Subject(s): Maritime Transportation

MASS TRANSIT

Federal Transit Administration (FTA)

https://www.transit.dot.gov/

Description: FTA assists in the planning, development, and financing of public transportation. Its website provides information on transit planning, safety, and security programs. The site also has major sections on FTA grant programs, including Recovery Act information, and on research and technical assistance. The About FTA section has agency budget and contracting information. The News section provides press releases, procurement news, congressional testimony, and policy letters. The site also provides transit laws and regulations, as well as regulatory guidance. The Publications section includes FTA reports to Congress, other publications, and a transit glossary.

Subject(s): Mass Transit; Transportation—Grants

National Transit Database

https://www.transit.dot.gov/ntd

Description: The *National Transit Database* is the Federal Transit Administration's primary national database for statistics on the transit industry. Information is available in spreadsheet and PDF formats and includes financial data, ridership counts, and safety reports. The data is intended for transit planning purposes and is also used in the formula allocations of federal transit funds.

Subject(s): Mass Transit—Statistics

SURFACE TRANSPORTATION

Amtrak

https://www.amtrak.com/home

Description: Passengers can use the Amtrak website to plan rail excursions, book trips, and check on train schedules. Main sections and tabs include Tickets, Timetables, Stations, and Routes. Amtrak, officially named the National Passenger Railroad Corporation, is a federally chartered for-profit public corporation. For information about its operations and finances, see the About Amtrak (with the employee newsletter *Amtrak Ink*) and News and Media sections, linked at the bottom of each page. The site is also available in Spanish, French, German, and Chinese.

Subject(s): Amtrak; Railroads

Office of Federal Lands Highway (FLH)

https://flh.fhwa.dot.gov/

Description: The FLH administers highway programs in cooperation with other federal agencies and provides transportation engineering services for highways and bridges that are on (or provide access to) federally owned lands. The office is comprised of three divisions: Eastern, Central, and Western. This site contains detailed information in its Projects, Programs, Business, Resources, and Careers sections. The Projects section lists projects by state and provides links to construction documents.

Subject(s): Highways and Roads; West (United States)

Federal Highway Administration (FHWA)

https://www.fhwa.dot.gov/

Description: The FHWA website offers a wide range of information related to the nation's highways and roads. The home page highlights Recovery Act information, monthly traffic volume trends, and the Fast Lane blog from the secretary of transportation. Also highlighted are FHWA's Facebook page and YouTube channel. The site links to information about roads and bridges, highway funding, the environment, road operations and congestion, road users (bicyclists, motorcycles), safety, international issues, and federal and Indian lands. Other major sections of the site cover legislation, regulations and regulatory guidance, statistics, publications, business opportunities, and news. The Briefing Room section displays press releases, speeches, and testimony.

Subject(s): Highways and Roads

Federal Railroad Administration (FRA)

https://www.fra.dot.gov/Page/P0001

Description: FRA consolidates government support of railroad activities and provides regulation and research for improved railroad safety. The site includes sections for Railroad Safety, Rail Network Development, Research & Development, and Grants & Loans.

Subject(s): Railroad Safety; Railroads—Regulations

Highways for LIFE

https://www.fhwa.dot.gov/hfl/

Description: Highways for LIFE is a Federal Highway Administration grant program for states to build "longer-lasting highway infrastructure using innovations to accomplish the fast construction of efficient and safe highways and bridges." (from the website) This site describes the program, projects, technology transfer, and funding opportunities.

Subject(s): Highways and Roads

National Traffic and Road Closure Information

https://www.fhwa.dot.gov/trafficinfo/

Description: This FHWA site centralizes access to government and commercial road condition and traffic information websites nationwide. It also links to each state's 511 travel conditions website and to sites reporting on weather and conditions.

Subject(s): Highways and Roads

Surface Transportation Board (STB)

https://www.stb.gov/stb/index.html

Description: STB is an independent adjudicatory body within the Department of Transportation. The board is responsible for the economic regulation of interstate surface transportation, primarily railroads. Its website features sections including Rail Consumers (shippers, receivers, rail car owners, and rail car manufacturers), Industry Data (economic and merger data), and Environmental Matters (regulations, cases, and correspondence). The site also has STB decisions and notices, transcripts and statements from STB hearings, and relevant correspondence.

Subject(s): Railroads

Vehicle Technologies Office

https://energy.gov/eere/vehicles/vehicle-technologies-office

Description: The Vehicle Technologies Office focuses on technologies for cleaner and more fuel-efficient cars and other road vehicles. The site describes technology developments related to hybrid vehicles, energy storage, power electronics, advanced combustion engines, fuels and lubricants, and materials technologies. The About the Vehicles Technology Office section provides organizational contacts and links to the national laboratories working on vehicle technologies. Grants are described in the Financial Opportunities section, and publications are listed in the News section.

Subject(s): Motor Vehicles—Research

TRANSPORTATION POLICY AND RESEARCH

Bureau of Transportation Statistics (BTS)

https://www.bts.gov/

Description: The BTS website is a central source for U.S. transportation data collected by BTS and other agencies. The home page features current news and data releases. The Data and Statistics section covers numerous areas, including airlines, border crossings, freight data, household commuting and travel, and bridge data. The BTS Publications section (under Library) links to many free, online statistical reports. The External Links section (under Library) links to other government and private sources of statistics. Under Subject Areas, the site provides background information and reports on key areas such as congestion, connectivity, and safety.

A major portal to transportation statistics, *TranStats*, is in the Data and Statistics section of the BTS website. *TranStats* is described in a separate entry in this chapter.

Subject(s): Transportation—Statistics

Center for Transportation Analysis (CTA)

https://cta.ornl.gov/cta/

Description: CTA conducts research and development for many aspects of transportation. The Research Areas section on the CTA website includes subsections on Aviation Safety and Air Traffic Management Analysis, Defense Transportation, Energy and Environmental Policy Analysis, Intelligent Transportation Systems, and many other topics. The site also has a publications directory and an extensive list of links to related websites.

Subject(s): Energy Consumption—Research; Transportation—Research

Department of Transportation (DOT)

https://www.transportation.gov/

Description: DOT is concerned with the safety and efficiency of the nation's transportation systems. The DOT website home page links to its component agencies, including the Federal Aviation Administration, Federal Transit Administration, Federal Railroad Administration, Maritime Administration, and others. The home page highlights popular search topics, such as DOT numbers for motor carriers, airline complaints, trucking company complaints, and car safety information. As with other departments, DOT provides an online section with Recovery Act information.

The home page of the DOT site provides quick access to major issues and to its component agencies.

Subject(s): Transportation

Intelligent Transportation Systems (ITS)

https://www.its.dot.gov/

Description: According to the website, "The U.S. Department of Transportation's (U.S. DOT) Intelligent Transportation Systems (ITS) Program aims to bring connectivity to transportation through the application of advanced wireless technologies—powerful technologies that enable transformative change." The ITS website also discusses the specific role of its Joint Program Office, which coordinates ITS initiative with other Transportation Department offices, such as the Federal Highway Administration and the

Federal Transit Administration. The ITS website provides information about the office's research and projects. The Press Room section contains news and information about public meetings and events.

Subject(s): Transportation Policy and Research

John A. Volpe National Transportation Systems Center

https://www.volpe.dot.gov/

Description: The John A. Volpe National Transportation Systems Center conducts research and development, engineering, and analysis on transportation and logistics topics. The center's expertise includes environmental issues, safety engineering, noise and vibration, and Global Positioning Systems (GPS). The Information Resources section includes reports, technical papers, and articles published by Volpe Center staff. The Volpe Center receives no federal appropriations and works on a fee-for-service basis. Its site also has information about doing business with the center for clients and for vendors.

Subject(s): Engineering Research; Transportation—Research

Office of Research, Development & Technology (RDT)

https://www.transportation.gov/administrations/assistant-secretary-research-and-technology/office-research-development-technology-0

Description: RDT is responsible for hosting and moderating the collaboration between the Transportation Department's research clusters, awarding and overseeing grant administration, and coordinating the department's research, development activities, and investments. The site provides links to current research topics and maps of research facilities, including those involved in alternative fuel, hydrogen, remote sensing, and cold region rural transportation research. The University Transportation Centers section links to lists of national and regional centers and related news and publications.

Subject(s): Transportation Policy and Research

Research andTechnology—Department of Transportation

https://www.transportation.gov/research-technology

Description:This website contains the latest information on research and technology from the Department of Transportation. It includes formation on safety and innovation, tools for researchers, grants and opportunities, and it provides a link to the National Transportation Library.

Subject(s): Transportation—Research

Transportation and Climate Change Clearinghouse

https://www.transportation.gov/climate-change-clearinghouse

Description: This clearinghouse website provides access to reports and information on the relationship between transportation practices—particularly greenhouse gas emissions—and climate change. Reports are from state and federal government, international organizations, and the private sector.

Subject(s): Greenhouse Gases; Transportation—Research; Climate Change

TranStats

https://www.transtats.bts.gov/

Description: TranStats offers organized access to over 100 transportation-related databases, as well as the social and demographic data sets commonly used in transportation analysis. The data comes from federal agencies and several transportation-related organizations. The data sets are packaged with basic documentation. The TranStats website offers downloading in comma-separated file format and provides some interactive mapping applications. Transportation modes covered by the data sets include aviation, highway, mass transit, rail, bike/pedestrian, pipeline, and others. The site also has a schedule of upcoming data releases.

Subject(s): Transportation—Statistics; Databases

TRANSPORTATION SAFETY

ATV Safety Information Center

https://www.cpsc.gov/Safety-Education/Safety-Education-Centers/ATV-Safety-Information-Center/

Description: This site provides safety tips for using all-terrain vehicles (ATVs). It has national and state injury statistics and information on state laws regarding ATVs.

Subject(s): Vehicle Safety

Distracted Driving

https://www.distraction.gov/

Description: This site is part of a safety campaign warning against visual, manual, and cognitive distractions for drivers, particularly the use of handheld electronic devices while driving. The site provides information on relevant state laws, research, and Department of Transportation initiatives.

Subject(s): Traffic Safety

FARS Encyclopedia

https://www-fars.nhtsa.dot.gov/

Description: The *FARS Encyclopedia* presents data from the Fatality Analysis Reporting System (FARS). FARS collects data on all vehicle crashes in the United States that occur on a public roadway and involve a fatality. The website provides statistics from 1994 to the most current year available, including state-by-state statistics and maps.

Subject(s): Accidents (Motor Vehicles)—Statistics

Federal Motor Carrier Safety Administration (FMCSA)

https://www.fmcsa.dot.gov/

Description: FMCSA's mission is to "reduce crashes, injuries and fatalities involving large trucks and buses." (from the website) For regulated carriers the site has online registration for USDOT Numbers and Operating Authority and the relevant registration requirements. The Safety section has company safety records and information on cargo securement and hazardous material security. The Data and Statistics subsection has a variety of motor carrier safety statistics, including a table on the costs of accidents, and a schedule of free webinars.

Subject(s): Trucking; Transportation Safety

FHWA Office of Safety

https://safety.fhwa.dot.gov/

Description: FHWA's Office of Safety focuses on highway engineering to promote road safety. The website covers road design research and other topics, such as public education, accident statistics, laws and guidelines, and safety technologies. Special sections discuss the safety of pedestrians, bicyclists, older drivers, intersections, and routes to school. The site also links to resources for states and localities.

Subject(s): Accidents (Motor Vehicles); Highways and Roads; Safety

National Highway Traffic Safety Administration (NHTSA)

https://www.nhtsa.gov/

Description: NHTSA sets and enforces safety performance standards for motor vehicles and assists state and local governments with grants for local highway safety programs. The NHTSA website has information about product recalls, crash test results, consumer complaints, technical service bulletins, and defects investigations for cars, child seats, tires, and auto equipment. There are car and tire safety tips, as well as regulatory information on such topics as fuel economy, child seats, safety standards, and air bags. The Driving Safety section covers topics such as distracted driving, driver education, impaired driving, child passengers, school buses, and pedestrian and bicycle safety. The NHTSA site also includes extensive data related to traffic safety.

This site offers a substantial collection of information about the government's testing of vehicles and its auto safety ratings and makes it accessible for consumers. The site also brings together grants, regulatory, and state and national legislative information concerning motor vehicle standards and traffic safety.

Subject(s): Motor Vehicles—Regulations; Traffic Safety; Vehicle Safety

National Transportation Safety Board (NTSB)

https://www.ntsb.gov

Description: The NTSB website features information about its programs and the primary areas of safety in which the NTSB works. These programs include aviation, highway, marine, railroad, pipeline, and hazardous materials. The News & Events section includes documents from recent major investigations and information about board meetings and public hearings. The Safety Advocacy section provides the agency's Most Wanted List, safety alerts, safety recommendations, and safety studies. The Disaster Assistance section explains the role of the NTSB in coordinating responses from federal, state, and local governments and the airlines to meet the needs of disaster victims and their families.

Subject(s): Accidents (Motor Vehicles)—Statistics; Safety; Transportation

NHTSA Parents Central

https://www.safercar.gov/parents/

Description: This website provides comprehensive information on keeping children safe on the road. It focuses on seat belts, car seats, teen driving, and dangers such as heatstroke. Among much else, the site features a Find a Car Seat page and a video guide on car seat installation. Some information is available in Spanish.

Subject(s): Child Health and Safety

Pipeline and Hazardous Materials Safety Administration (PHMSA)

https://www.phmsa.dot.gov/

Description: PHMSA is responsible for the safe and secure movement of hazardous materials shipments by all modes of transportation, including through pipeline infrastructure. The Pipeline Safety section includes information on compliance and enforcement, safety training, data and statistics, and more.

Subject(s): Toxic Substances; Transportation Safety

SaferCar.gov

https://www.safercar.gov/

Description: SaferCar.gov provides information about vehicle safety for drivers and car shoppers. Topics covered include tires, air bags, and rollover prevention. Also provided is information about the government's "5-star safety ratings" as well as reported defects and recalls.

Subject(s): Motor Vehicles

Transportation Safety Institute

https://www.transportation.gov/transportation-safety-institute

Description: The Transportation Safety Institute is a self-funding federal agency that provides safety and security training to both the public and private sectors. The institute provides training related to mass transit, aviation, multi-modal safety, and traffic safety. Its website provides a course catalog and detailed information about each of its program areas.

Subject(s): Transportation Security; Transportation Safety

TSA Blog

https://www.tsa.gov/blog

Description: The TSA uses its blog "to communicate with the public about all things TSA related." (from the website) Bloggers are TSA employees. Comments are encouraged.

Subject(s): Homeland Security; Blogs

USCG Boating Safety Resource Center

http://www.uscgboating.org

Description: This website, provided by the Coast Guard, is a resource for boaters and those who keep the waterways safe. Links are provided for reporting boating accidents and for navigation rules. The Recalls and Safety Defects section links to tools for reporting defects in boating products and notices of recalls. Boating laws can be found under the Regulations section. The NBSAC section provides information about joining the National Boating Safety Advisory Council. The Statistics section presents information on such topics as accident rates and the prevalence of life jackets and their use.

Subject(s): Boating Safety

Chapter Twenty-One

Beyond the Federal Web—Nongovernmental Websites

While the preceding chapters have provided information about government Internet sites, this final chapter takes a look at related, but no less valuable, non-federal sources. These resources cover a wide range of topics—in fact, their scope mirrors that of all of the preceding chapters—and come from a multitude of different types of organizations. The common thread between these sites is their relevance to the subjects published by the federal agencies.

Sources for the websites include nongovernmental organizations, advocacy organizations and "think tanks," social welfare and justice organizations, multinational and binational initiatives, science and technology cooperatives, and international organizations.

Africa Fighting Malaria (AFM)
http://www.fightingmalaria.org
Description: AFM, founded in 2000, works to increase the efficiency and effectiveness of malaria treatment. The What We Do section contains editorials, papers, and testimony, while the Initiatives section has information about malarial countries and donor programs. This website was currently down for maintenance when this book went to press.
Subject(s): Malaria

American Aging Association
https://www.americanagingassociation.org/
Description: According to the website, "The American Aging Association is a group of experts dedicated to understanding the basic mechanisms of aging and the development of interventions in age-related disease to increase healthy lifespan for all." This site has information about the association's

history and initiatives. It also provides access to the association's journal, *AGE: Journal of the American Aging Association.*

Subject(s): Senior citizens

American Association of Retired People (AARP)

https://www.aarp.org/

Description: AARP was established to help older Americans (age 50 and above) improve their quality of life. The homepage features a long list of links with information about such subjects as caregiving, job hunting, Social Security and Medicare, and AARP discounts. News, videos, and opinion pieces are also accessible from the homepage. Sections toward the top of the page break down the subjects even further, with links for Health, Work & Retirement, Money, Home & Family, Entertainment, Food, Travel, Politics, and Games. Links at the top of the page lead to *AARP The Magazine* and the *AARP Bulletin.*

Subject(s): Senior citizens

American Bar Association (ABA)

https://www.americanbar.org/aba.html

Description: The ABA has nearly 400,000 members nationwide. Its website includes information about the association, information about membership, and other resources for lawyers. The Advocacy section has information about ABA's policy initiatives and its governmental and legislative work. Amicus curiae briefs are also available in this section.

Subject(s): Law and legal information

American Civil Liberties Union (ACLU)

https://www.aclu.org/

Description: Much of the ACLU website's information can be found right on its homepage. Recent news stories and blog postings are highlighted, while toward the bottom of the page, topic sections for issues such as capital punishment, free speech, human rights, HIV/AIDS, racial justice, and religion and belief each provide multiple links to related content. A drop-down menu is available to help users find issues of interest.

Subject(s): Civil rights

American Heart Association

http://www.heart.org

Description: The homepage of the American Heart Association's website provides insight into its initiatives and programs, with a tabbed menu for new topics, most searched topics, and most popular topics. Also included is an online "Heart and Stroke Encyclopedia" reference tool, as well as a section for the warning signs of these diseases. Sections for educators and caregivers can be found toward the top of the page. The Healthcare/Research section has membership information and documents for health care professionals.

Subject(s): Health promotion; Heart disease

American Lung Association

http://www.lung.org

Description: This website contains informative sections about lungs and lung disease. Under Your Lungs, users can find anatomical information and warning signs of lung disease. The section also discusses lung issues in the context of the Affordable Care Act. The Healthy Air section discusses the subject in the contexts of schools, homes, workplaces, and the outdoors.

Subject(s): Air Quality; Diseases and Conditions

American Medical Association

https://www.ama-assn.org/

Description: According to the website, AMA's mission is "to promote the art and science of medicine and the betterment of public health." The Resources section provides links to information about such topics as continuing medical education, medical ethics, the Physician Consortium for Performance Improvement, legal issues, and health information technology. In this section, resources are also organized for audiences, including patients, physicians, residents, and medical students. Newsletters and events can be found in the Advocacy section. A link to the JAMA Network, which is described in a separate entry, can be found in the Publications section. The Education section contains a multitude of information for students on such topics as careers in health care, becoming a physician, and finding a position.

Subject(s): Health and Safety; Health Care; Public Health

American Psychiatric Association

https://www.psychiatry.org/

Description: The American Psychiatric Association, with more than 36,000 members worldwide, is the largest organization of its kind in the world. The website has sections for Physicians, Residents, Medical Students, Researchers, and the general public. The Mental Health section has a drop-down menu for finding further information on psychiatric topics and people in psychiatry. The Advocacy & Newsroom section has links to news, videos, and position statements.

Subject(s): Psychiatry

American Red Cross

http://www.redcross.org

Description: The American Red Cross's website contains extensive information about its initiatives and activities. Under What We Do, the site links to sections on disaster relief, supporting military families, health and safety training and education, and the lifesaving benefits of blood. The News & Events section has a calendar of events, local and national Twitter feeds, Facebook postings, and recent press releases. The homepage has direct links for donating blood, obtaining assistance, and volunteering.

Subject(s): Disaster Assistance; Health and Safety

Amnesty International

https://www.amnestyusa.org/

Description: Amnesty International is an organization that works to assert human rights throughout the global community. The Our Work section has information about the organization's issues and campaigns, countries in which it works, and cases and victories. Under About Us, two initiatives are featured: advocacy for the Arms Trade Treaty and an analysis of the human rights situation in Aleppo, Syria. The homepage includes links to Amnesty International's Facebook and Twitter pages, as well as to its blog. The site is available in Spanish.

Subject(s): Human Rights

Anti-Defamation League

https://www.adl.org/

Description: As stated on the website, the Anti-Defamation League "fights anti-Semitism and all forms of bigotry, defends democratic ideals and protects civil rights for all." The homepage links to sections including Anti-Semitism, Combating Hate, Israel & International, Civil Rights, and Education & Outreach. The site also has a Newsroom section featuring relevant news stories and opinions.

Subject(s): Civil Rights; Anti-defamation

Asia-Pacific Economic Cooperation

https://www.apec.org/

Description: APEC is an international forum promoting open trade and economic cooperation. Established in 1989 in response to the growing interdependence among Asia-Pacific economies, its members are located in the Pacific Rim and include the United States. The website provides links to relevant topics and publications. Its Topics section links to APEC's work in specific fields, such as agriculture, health, and trade facilitation.

Subject(s): Military Training and Education; Asia—Policy; Defense Research

Association of Southeast Asian Nations (ASEAN)

http://www.asean.org

Description: ASEAN was established in 1967, and its member states currently include Brunei, Cambodia, Indonesia, Laos, Malaysia, Myanmar (Burma), the Philippines, Singapore, Thailand, and Vietnam. Under ASEAN Member States, the website provides country information and links to each one's relevant international ministry or office. The Resources section provides users with access to relevant ASEAN and ASEAN-related statistics, publications, and speeches. The Calendar section lists public holidays and official meetings.

Subject(s): International Economic Relations

Association of Universities for Research in Astronomy (AURA)

http://www.aura-astronomy.org

Description: AURA is comprised of 40 national institutions and 4 international entities. The organization's mission, according to the website, is "to establish, nurture, and promote public observatories and facilities that advance innovative astronomical research." Its homepage features links to major initiatives, such as the James Webb Space Telescope, as well as community projects, such as the NSF Science Folio Review. AURA's facilities include the Gemini Observatory, the Large Synoptic Survey Telescope (LSST), the National Optical Astronomical Observatory (NOAO), the National Solar Observatory (NSO), and the Space Telescope Science Institute (STScI), which are all described in this publication.

Subject(s): Astronomy; Space

CARE International

https://www.care-international.org/

Description: CARE's member countries have helped the organization work to fight poverty in 90 countries around the world. In addition to participating in relief during emergencies such as conflict or natural disasters, CARE works on the following issues: agriculture and natural resources, climate change, education, health, HIV/AIDS, nutrition, economic development, water, sanitation, and environmental health. More information about the topics can be found in the site's Work section. Media releases and featured articles can be found in the News section. The United States' country-specific CARE website can be accessed at http://www.care.org/.

Subject(s): Poverty

Center for International Trade & Security

http://spia.uga.edu/departments-centers/center-for-international-trade-and-security-cits/

Description: This University of Georgia facility's mission is to research issues related to trade technologies and security. Its homepage links to a list of current issues of interest and news. A Student Opportunities section links to application materials for the center's programs.

Subject(s): Security

Center for Restorative Justice and Peacemaking

http://www.cehd.umn.edu/ssw/rjp/

Description: The Center for Restorative Justice and Peacemaking's mission, according to the website, is "to provide support and resources to program leaders, practitioners, and workshop participants so they can maintain and strengthen restorative dialogue on all levels. To do this in a comprehensive way, our center does a variety of activities and services." The center's Community Peacemaking Project combats hate crimes and political intolerance, and it has partnered on similar issues with Northern Ireland's Seeds of Hope organization. The website contains information about the center's initiatives and training programs.

Subject(s): Peace; Crime Prevention

Commission on Security and Cooperation in Europe (CSCE)

https://www.csce.gov/

Description: CSCE, better known as the U.S. Helsinki Commission, is an independent government agency created by Congress. It monitors and encourages compliance with the Helsinki Accords and other commitments of the countries participating in the Organisation for Security and Co-operation in Europe (OSCE). The commission's website includes information about the CSCE and OSCE and the full texts of the commission's press releases, hearings, briefings, and statements.

Subject(s): Human Rights

Congressional Quarterly Roll Call

http://www.cqrollcall.com

Description: CQ Roll Call is a subscription-based service that provides users with legislation and policy tracking. Major sections include News, Analysis & Schedules; Legislative Tracking; and Advocacy & Engagement Solutions. Related products, including *CQ Weekly* and subscriptions to the congressionally oriented *Roll Call* newspaper, which is described in a separate entry, are available for purchase.

Subject(s): News Services

Corporation for Public Broadcasting (CPB)

https://www.cpb.org/

Description: CPB is a private, nonprofit corporation that was created by Congress in 1967. It receives partial funding through annual congressional appropriations and, in turn, funds public television and radio programming.

The About CPB section of this website includes leadership profiles, CPB's annual reports, and financial information. The Programs & Projects section has a directory of CPB-funded programs for television, radio, and the Web.

Subject(s): Broadcasting

Democratic Congressional Campaign Committee (DCCC)

https://dccc.org/

Description: The DCCC is the official campaign arm of the Democrats in the House of Representatives. The Actions section features information on the committee's community-oriented outreach efforts as well as information on how to volunteer and register to vote. The News section offers timely commentary on national politics, often linking to outside articles.

Subject(s): Political Parties

Democratic Senatorial Campaign Committee (DSCC)

http://www.dscc.org

Description: The DSCC website features news, recent Tweets, and a race tracker (for election season). A map on the homepage provides information on campaigns for the 2016 elections. Job and internship information can be found in the About section.

Subject(s): Political Parties

Doctors Without Borders / Médecins Sans Frontières

https://www.doctorswithoutborders.org/

Description: Doctors Without Borders/Médecins Sans Frontières has a presence in more than 60 countries, where they provide medical relief to regions facing issues such as epidemics, armed conflicts, malnutrition, natural disasters, and lack of access to health care. Stories from the field and aid worker blogs can be found in the Our Work section. Another section discusses working with the organization. The News & Stories section contains research articles, opinions, and reports.

Subject(s): Medicine; Physicians

Export-Import Bank of the United States

https://www.exim.gov/

Description: The Export-Import Bank offers export financing for U.S. businesses. The Products section of its website provides information about the bank's working capital financing, export credit insurance, loan guarantees, and direct loans. Application forms and instructions on applying are included with the information. The site also features sections for specific audiences, including small businesses.

Subject(s): Finance; International Trade

Federation of American Scientists (FAS)

https://fas.org/

Description: FAS is a private, nonprofit group concerned with public policy. While this website is not an official government source of information, the information offered is valuable for its ease of access. Featured issue areas include biosecurity, Earth systems, government secrecy, and nuclear information. The Policy Action section provides links to FAS's social media pages, video clips, and an e-mail signup for news releases.

FAS sponsors a Presidential Directives and Executive Orders page that is described elsewhere in this publication. This page, which can be found at https://fas.org/irp/offdocs/direct.htm contains related documents from the Truman administration through to the Obama administration.

Subject(s): Presidential Documents; Security

G8 Information Centre

http://www.g8.utoronto.ca

Sponsor(s): University of Toronto

Description: This site organizes and provides access to materials and sites related to the G8, its summits, and other meetings. The G8 refers to a group of eight major market-oriented democracies. The site's homepage features recent news and social media posts (from sites such as Twitter), as well as links to frequently asked questions, such as "What is the G8?" Links to its sponsoring institutions and to publications can be found toward the bottom of the homepage. Publications offered include governance working papers and the *Ashgate Series*. The homepage also offers resources for teaching.

Subject(s): International Economic Relations

Gemini Observatory

http://www.gemini.edu

Description: The Gemini Observatory consists of twin telescopes located in Hawaii and Chile. The observatory is the creation of a six-country partnership, including the United States, Canada, Chile, Australia, Brazil, and Argentina. A Science section provides more information about Gemini's technology, science, operation, and data. Under Public/Images, access is provided to podcasts, education and outreach materials, and an image gallery.

Subject(s): Astronomy; Telescopes

Government and Geographic Information Collection

http://www.library.northwestern.edu/libraries-collections/evanston-campus/government-information/international-documents/

Description: According to the website, this organization contains " materials produced by the U.S. Federal government, the State of Illinois, the City of Chicago and several international governmental organizations, including the United Nations. Our extensive map collection is complemented by geospatial services supporting the use of GIS software for data analysis and visualization."

Subject(s): Finding Aids; International Organizations

Habitat for Humanity® International

https://www.habitat.org/

Description: Habitat for Humanity is dedicated to providing low-income families worldwide with safe and affordable housing by either building or renovating dwellings. Habitat trains volunteers and the prospective homeowner families to assist in the building and renovation tasks. Under Where We Build, website users can find a map and directory of Habitat sites by region. The Stories section links to the organization's magazine, *Habitat World*, and blog.

Subject(s): Housing; Housing Subsidies

Hague Conference on Private International Law (HCCH)

https://www.hcch.net/

Description: HCCH, which consists of 78 members (77 countries and the European Union), works to develop means of unifying counties in the context of private international law. One of its major functions is to have its Conventions ratified and enacted. HCCH adopted 38 Conventions between 1951 and 2008. The United States ratified the Hague Convention on Intercountry Adoptions in 2007. The website's FAQ section presents a wealth of introductory information on topics ranging from "What is a Special Commission of the Hague Conference?" to "How does a State become a Member of the Hague Conference?" The site is available in 24 languages, including French, Spanish, Polish, and Dutch.

Subject(s): International Law

Homeland Security Studies & Analysis Institute

http://www.anser.org/hssai/

Description: The Homeland Security Studies & Analysis Institute, an FFRDC (federally funded research and development center) operated on behalf of the Department of Defense, is concerned with the following areas: Counterterrorism, Borders, and Immigration; Resilience and Emergency Preparedness/Response; and Departmental Integration/Unification. The Project Spotlights and Featured Work sections have publications and news articles.

Subject(s): Homeland Security

Humane Society of the United States

http://www.humanesociety.org

Description: Animal welfare is the focus of the Humane Society, and this site has a plethora of information about its activities. The homepage includes top news stories and feeds from the Humane Society's Facebook and Twitter pages. A drop-down menu on the homepage allows users to learn facts about specific animals and adoption. The Animals section includes information about pets and wild animals, as well as information about animal care. The Magazines section includes links to publications including *All Animals* and *Animal Sheltering*.

Subject(s): Animals

Inter-American Development Bank (IDB)

https://www.iadb.org/en

Description: The Inter-American Development Bank was established to help accelerate economic and social development in Latin America and the Caribbean. Its website features categories including Doing Business, Accountability, Our Organization, and Resources. Under Data, the site offers searchable statistics and indicators for Latin American and Caribbean countries. The Publications section includes technical notes, working papers, and policy briefs. The site has a Spanish-language version.

Subject(s): International Economic Development; South America; Caribbean

International Bureau of Education (IBE)

http://www.ibe.unesco.org

Description: IBE is a UNESCO center for information and research in the field of education, focusing currently on the management of curricula change for the 21st century. This website features sections including Themes, Areas of Action, and Services. The site is available in Spanish, French, and other languages.

Subject(s): Education Research—International

International Criminal Court (ICC)

https://www.icc-cpi.int/

Description: According to the website, the ICC is "the first permanent, treaty based, international criminal court established to help end impunity for the perpetrators of the most serious crimes of concern to the international community." Its seat is at the Hague in the Netherlands. The Situations and Cases section breaks down the court's cases by country.

Subject(s): International Crimes; International Law

International Monetary Fund (IMF)

http://www.imf.org

Description: The IMF is an international organization established to promote international monetary cooperation, exchange stability, and economic growth. Its website features sections such as About the IMF, News, Data, Publications, Research, and Countries. The Publications page provides search and browse access to IMF print and online publications. A fair number of publications are accessible online. The Research tab links users to a variety of indicators and reports. Available material includes the *World Economic Outlook (WEO) Reports*, *Global Financial Stability Reports (GFSRs)*, and WEO Databases. The Country Info section arranges publications and reports by country. Also in this section, the IMF DataMapper® comprises a clickable, interactive map that displays the findings of IMF Datasets.

Subject(s): International Economic Relations; Monetary Policy—International

JAMA Network

https://jamanetwork.com/

Description: The JAMA (Journal of the American Medical Association) Network, a subscription-based service, provides search tools for finding videos, articles, and other journal products. A mobile version is available.

Subject(s): Health and Safety; News Services

James Martin Center for Nonproliferation Studies (CNS)

https://www.nonproliferation.org/

Description: CNS's research focuses on weapons of mass destruction (WMD) and the training of individuals to prevent their dissemination. The Publications section includes the center's *Nonproliferation Review* and *WMD Junction* products. The Students section provides information about obtaining a master's degree and about internships, while the Programs section has links to such components as the Chemical and Biological Weapons Nonproliferation Program (CBWNP) and the East Asia Nonproliferation Program (EANP).

Subject(s): Arms Control; Nonproliferation; Trade Laws and Regulations; Weapons of Mass Destruction

Large Synoptic Survey Telescope (LSST)

https://www.lsst.org/

Description: The LSST, subtitled on the website as "the widest, fastest, deepest eye of the new digital age," uses a three-billion pixel digital camera to study objects such as near-Earth asteroids. Information sections on the site include areas for the public and for scientists. A Gallery section provides both photos and videos, and an FAQ section answers questions about the technology for the public. This section also has a link to a scientist FAQ.

Subject(s): Astronomy; Telescopes

League of Conservation Voters (LCV)

https://www.lcv.org/

Description: According to the website, "LCV works to turn environmental values into national, state and local priorities. LCV, in collaboration with [its] state LCV partners, advocates for sound environmental laws and policies, holds elected officials accountable for their votes and actions, and elects pro-environment candidates who will champion our priority issues." Information about its initiatives is broken down by topic in the Issues section, with topics ranging from hardrock mining to toxic chemicals. A States section has local contact information.

Subject(s): Conservation (Natural Resources); Environmental Protection

Millennium Challenge Corporation (MCC)

https://www.mcc.gov/

Description: MCC, a government corporation, works with countries to promote sustainable economic growth and reduce poverty through investments in areas such as agriculture, education, and private sector development. Countries are selected to receive aid based on their performance in governing justly, investing in their citizens, and encouraging economic freedom. The website provides information on MCC and its leadership, selection criteria, country activities, and business and procurement.

Subject(s): International Economic Development

Mothers Against Drunk Driving (MADD)

https://www.madd.org/

Description: MADD, formed to combat drunk driving and underage drinking, provides a wealth of information on its site. The homepage links to its social media profiles and provides information about its initiatives, such as Walk Like MADD and the Victim/Survivor Tributes. Under Victim Services, users can find information about victims' compensation and funding, links to other victims, and *MADDvocate Magazine*. The Get Involved section describes how uses can donate, volunteer, and find a local chapter of MADD.

Subject(s): Alcohol Abuse

National American Indian Court Judges Association (NAICJA)

https://naicja.wildapricot.org/

Description: NAICJA, founded in 1969, was established to help strengthen the tribal justice system. The organization's focus includes education about tribal justice, national advocacy, providing networking and membership opportunities, and improving cooperation between the state, federal, and tribal judicial systems. The website has information about membership, training, and events, as well as links to NAICJA's Facebook and YouTube accounts.

Subject(s): Judicial System; Tribal Governments

National Association for the Advancement of Colored People (NAACP)

http://www.naacp.org

Description: NAACP, which celebrated its centennial in 2009, was founded in order to fight racial discrimination. Its website has a plethora of information about its causes and programs. Under Advocacy & Issues, users can find information on topics such as civic engagement, climate justice, and media diversity. A richly detailed History section provides users with background on the association. Publications, financial reports, legal dockets, and amicus briefs can be found under Resources. A menu on the right-hand side of the homepage allows users to look up their local NAACP chapters.

Subject(s): Civil Rights

National Center for Missing and Exploited Children (NCMEC)

http://www.missingkids.org

Description: Founded in 1984, NCMEC serves as a clearinghouse of information on missing children and child exploitation. The top of the homepage has a link to active AMBER Alerts (described in a separate entry). Under How You Can Help, information about a 24-hour hotline is provided for users to report a missing child or a case of possible child exploitation. RSS feeds and an eNews signup can be found in the Stay Informed section.

Subject(s): Child Abuse; Children

National Center for Victims of Crime (NCVC)

http://www.victimsofcrime.org

Description: NCVC works to advocate for the rights and protections of crime victims and to supply them with information, services, and advocacy. Its mission also encompasses related education and training. The NCVC website provides information on the center's programs and initiatives. Under Help for Crime Victims, national hotlines, information on coping with trauma and grief, and a local assistance directory are provided. The Library section contains publications and relevant statistics.

Subject(s): Victims of Crime

National Indian Justice Center (NIJC)

http://www.nijc.org

Description: NIJC was founded "in order to establish an independent national resource for Native communities and tribal governments." (from the website) The Projects/Surveys section provides links to current initiatives, such as Communities Empowering Native Youth and the Tribal Traffic Safety Justice Liaison Project. Training manuals and videos are available in the Publications section, and the Resources section links to outside organizations that might be of interest to users, including the California Indian Museum and the Native American Bar Association.

Subject(s): Judicial System; Tribal Governments

National Journal

https://www.nationaljournal.com/

Description: The *National Journal* is a publication focused on politics and policy. Its website offers sections for the topics of which the publication offers the most coverage: White House, Politics, Congress, Health Care, Energy, Defense, and Tech.

Subject(s): News Services

National Optical Astronomy Observatory (NOAO)

https://www.noao.edu/

Description: As stated on the website, "NOAO is the US national research & development center for ground-based night-time astronomy. Our mission is to provide public access to qualified professional researchers to forefront scientific capabilities on telescopes operated by NOAO as well as other optical and infrared telescopes. Today, these telescopes range in aperture size from 2-m to 10-m." Its observatories are located in Chile and Arizona, and it is involved with the Gemini telescopes, which are described elsewhere in this publication. It has a special section for astronomers, an image gallery, and an education- and outreach-oriented section with information for such audiences as middle school teachers, undergraduates, and citizens.

Subject(s): Astronomy; Telescopes

National Organization for Women (NOW)

https://now.org/

Description: NOW, which has half a million contributing members and 550 chapters nationwide, was founded in 1966 to advocate for issues pertaining to women's rights. A history of the organization and a section of frequently asked questions can be found by accessing the About the Foundation link. An issues tab on the homepage links to major initiatives, such as ending gender discrimination and promoting diversity. The site has links to blog posts and a tool for finding one's local chapter.

Subject(s): Women

National Republican Congressional Committee (NRCC)

https://www.nrcc.org/

Description: The NRCC website features news and opinions relevant to the committee's mission and focus. Links for blog entries and videos can be found in the upper right-hand part of the homepage.

Subject(s): Political Parties

National Republican Senatorial Committee (NRSC)

https://www.nrsc.org/

Description: The NRSC website features current news stories and links to the NRSC's social media pages.

Subject(s): Political Parties

National Security Archive

https://nsarchive.gwu.edu/

Description: The National Security Archive is a private, independent research institute and library located at George Washington University in Washington, D.C. Despite the official-sounding name, it is not a government agency. The archive collects and publishes declassified documents acquired through the Freedom of Information Act (FOIA). Only a fraction of the archive's holdings are online; nevertheless, the online offerings are significant.

The Documents section of the site includes Electronic Briefing Books (EBBs) and collections of scanned declassified documents along with National Security Archive analysis. The collections are grouped by topic, such as nuclear history. These online briefing books are free; other formal collections and analysis are available for purchase. The FOIA section of the site includes the downloadable guide *Effective FOIA Requesting for Everyone* and information on document classification.

The National Security Archive provides a valuable research service offline, with its archive of declassified U.S. documents obtained through FOIA and its own print and microform publications. The online collections meet some popular information needs and present documents with contextual commentary identifying relevant people and events.

Subject(s): Declassified Documents; Foreign Policy—Research; Freedom of Information Act

National Solar Observatory (NSO)

https://www.nso.edu/

Description: The prime objective of the NSO is to study the sun, with facilities located in Arizona and New Mexico. A Current Images section provides views of the sun, as well as relevant NSO data. Data sets are provided in the Digital Library section. The data, according to the website, consist of "the Kitt Peak Vacuum telescope magnetograms and spectroheliograms, the Fourier Transform Spectrometer transformed spectra, the Sacramento Peak Evans Facility spectroheliograms and coronal scans, and solar activity indices."

Subject(s): Space; Sun

North Atlantic Treaty Organization (NATO)

https://www.nato.int/

Description: NATO is an alliance of independent nations committed to each other's defense. The NATO website features news, speeches, and videos on current NATO activities. The Organization section features information on the structure of NATO and links to the national information servers of member countries. The NATO A–Z index contains a thematic index that links to information about such topics as human trafficking, NATO in Afghanistan, and NATO and the fight against terrorism.

While only a small subset of NATO's printed publications are available online, the website provides a significant collection of documents from and about NATO. It is an excellent source of information on the organization.

Subject(s): Military Forces—International

Nuclear Threat Initiative (NTI)

http://www.nti.org

Description: According to the website, "The Nuclear Threat Initiative (NTI) is a nonprofit, nonpartisan organization with a mission to strengthen global security by reducing the risk of use and preventing the spread of nuclear, biological, and chemical weapons and to work to build the trust, transparency, and security that are preconditions to the ultimate fulfillment of the Non-Proliferation Treaty's goals and ambitions." In this capacity, NTI has created the now-independent World Institute for Nuclear Security (WINS) and the Middle East Consortium on Infectious Disease Surveillance. The institute also provides support to Kazakhstan for the securing and dispersal of its uranium stores. The Threats section of the website breaks down issues topically, with sections for nuclear, biological, chemical, and radiological threats.

Subject(s): Nonproliferation; Nuclear Weapons

Open Secrets

http://www.opensecrets.org

Description: According to the website, Open Secrets, which was launched after the 1996 elections, "is the nation's premier research group tracking money in U.S. politics and its effect on elections and public policy." Frequently cited in Washington, D.C., and national media outlets, the website serves as a clearinghouse of information regarding many of the different roles that money plays in politics. The site also provides access to the Open Secrets Blog, which is described in a separate entry. Issue profiles can be found in the News & Analysis section, while information about PACs and lobbying can be found in the Influence & Lobbying section. The Take Action section provides users with a list of issues on which the Center for Responsive Politics is currently working. The Community link under Resources provides access to the organization's social media pages.

Subject(s): Campaign Finance

Open Secrets Blog

http://www.opensecrets.org/news/

Description: This blog, subtitled "Investigating Money in Politics," examines both politicians and organizations under the scope of its mission. Comments are allowed.

Subject(s): Campaign Finance; Blogs

Organisation for Economic Co-operation and Development (OECD) Online

http://www.oecd.org

Description: OECD Online contains descriptive information about the OECD, its activities, and its member countries. Major categories include About OECD, Countries, Topics, Data, and Publications. Key topics available on the homepage include restoring public finance, boosting jobs and skills, restoring public trust, and new sources of growth. There is free access to many online documents including the *OECD Observer* and *OECD Outlooks*. The site contains useful descriptive information about the OECD and a useful collection of free online publications and statistics.

Subject(s): International Economic Development

Organisation for Security and Co-operation in Europe (OSCE)

https://www.osce.org/

Description: OSCE is a regional security organization that consists of 57 European, North American, and Central Asian member states. Its security issues portfolio includes such topics as arms control, border management, combating human trafficking, counterterrorism, conflict resolution, education, good governance, and environmental activities. OSCE news can be found in the Newsroom section.

Subject(s): International Organizations; Security

Organization of American States (OAS)

http://www.oas.org

Description: The OAS website features information on the organization and its involvements. Major sections include About the OAS, Topics, Strategic Partners, Member States, Media Center, Documents, and Calendar. The Strategic Partners section links to information about the Trust for the Americas, Consortium of Universities, Pan American Development Foundation (PADF), Joint Summit Working Group, and Young Americas Business Trust (YABT). The site is available in English, Spanish, French and Portuguese.

Subject(s): South America; Caribbean

Organization of the Petroleum Exporting Countries (OPEC)

http://www.opec.org

Description: OPEC is an organization of oil-exporting nations dedicated to the stability and prosperity of the petroleum market. The OPEC website features sections such as About Us, Press Room, Data/Graphs, Publications, 50th Anniversary, and Multimedia. The Publications section highlights major reports and bulletins.

Subject(s): Petroleum—International

Pantex Plant

https://pantex.energy.gov/

Description: As stated on the website, "Pantex Plant's key role is to ensure the safety, security and reliability of the nation's nuclear stockpile…excess weapons are dismantled, surveillance is conducted on the stockpile and aging weapons are maintained through the Life Extension Programs." Community involvement and emergency preparation information is available under the About Pantex heading. The site also has procurement information, as well as a section for employment.

Subject(s): Nuclear Weapons

Partners in Health

https://www.pih.org/

Description: Partners in Health, which was created to provide health care to people living in poverty worldwide, features resources and tools for health care professionals. The Our Work section has links to the organization's priority health programs: Cancer & Chronic Diseases, Child Health, Cholera, Ebola, Community Health Workers, HIV/AIDS, Mental Health, Nursing, Surgery, Tuberculosis, and Women's Health. The News section features recent articles. Links to the organization's social media pages are also provided on the site.

Subject(s): Health Care; Poverty

Partnership for the National Trails System

http://pnts.org/new/

Description: PNTS is a collective of nonprofit trail organizations and federal agencies working together in order to preserve, complete, protect, and oversee 30 National Scenic and Historic Trails contained within the National Trails System. Its website includes news and a quarterly publication about recent relevant events. A Youth Gateway section has a blog for young adults and related job postings.

Subject(s): National Parks and Reserves

Politico

https://www.politico.com

Description: *Politico* is a multimedia journalism company that focuses on Washington-based news, particularly Congress, public policy, and the White House. Its newspaper, *The Politico*, was first published in 2007. Its website features current news articles and links to Politico Pro, a subscription-based service that offers enhanced access to coverage.

Subject(s): News Services

Presidential Directives and Executive Orders

https://fas.org/irp/offdocs/direct.htm

Description: This website, maintained by a nonprofit research organization, focuses on intelligence-related presidential directives and Executive orders from the Truman administration to the present. Copies of documents that are not still classified are available on this site. The site also links to helpful background information on presidential directives.

Subject(s): Intelligence; Presidential Documents

RAND Corporation

https://www.rand.org/

Description: Founded more than 60 years ago, RAND's mission is to improve policymaking and decision making through research and analysis. The Research section denotes topics with which the corporation works, including public safety, health and health care, and terrorism and homeland security. News releases, announcements, a calendar, and the blog can be found in the Press Room section.

Subject(s): Education; Health and Safety; Homeland Security

Roll Call

http://www.rollcall.com

Description: *Roll Call* is a newspaper dedicated to coverage of the workings of Capitol Hill. The site's homepage links to news, opinions, and blogs. The newspaper also publishes its annual "*Roll Call* Fabulous 50," a list of what it dubs "Capitol Hill's leading staffers."

Subject(s): News Services

Sierra Club

https://www.sierraclub.org/

Description: The motto of the Sierra Club is "explore, enjoy and protect the planet." Users can find information about some of the organization's issues, including protecting America's waters and facilitating resilient habitats. The homepage links to the Sierra Club's blogs, e-mail newsletters, and other publications. The Local Chapters & Events section has state-by-state chapter information.

Subject(s): Environmental Protection

Southern Poverty Law Center (SPLC)

https://www.splcenter.org/

Description: Founded in 1971, SPLC's mission is to eradicate hate crimes and bigotry-motivated violence. Its website provides information about the center's history and its target issues (at-risk children, hate and extremism, immigrant justice, and LGBT rights). The Teaching Tolerance section describes this program, an anti-prejudice education-oriented program that takes place in school classrooms. A link to *Teaching Tolerance* magazine is also provided.

Subject(s): Law—Public Interest

Stimson Center

https://www.stimson.org/

Description: The Stimson Center's research and outreach work toward the goals of establishing international peace and security, building stability throughout the regions of the world, and reducing the presence of weapons of mass destruction. In its Programs section, topical initiatives are grouped into three categories: Transnational Threats, Regional Security, and Effective Institutions. The Topics section provides further information about its research and analysis in such areas as border security, biological and chemical weapons, energy, and humanitarian issues.

Subject(s): Nonproliferation; Peace

Stockholm International Peace Research Institute (SIPRI)

https://www.sipri.org/

Description: SIPRI, established in 1996, "is an independent international institute dedicated to research into conflict, armaments, arms control and disarmament." Issues are organized topically on the homepage, with sections for Regional and Global Security, Armed Conflict and Conflict Management, and Military Spending and Armaments. Available databases include the SIPRI Multilateral Peace Operations Database and the SIPRI Arms Transfers Database.

Subject(s): Nonproliferation; Arms Control; Security

The Hill

http://www.thehill.com

Sponsor(s): News Communications, Inc.

Description: *The Hill* is a daily newspaper focusing on Capitol Hill and Congress. An online subscription service is available. The website's homepage links to related blogs.

Subject(s): News Services

U.S-Mexico Border 2020

https://www.epa.gov/border2020

Sponsor(s): Environmental Protection Agency (EPA)

Description: U.S.-Mexico Border 2020 Program is a U.S-Mexico binational program focusing on cleaning the air, providing safe drinking water, reducing the risk of exposure to hazardous waste, and ensuring emergency preparedness along the U.S-Mexico border. The website has information on regional and border-wide working groups and on measuring conditions and progress in the border region. The site is also available in Spanish, Chinese, Vietnamese, and Korean.

Subject(s): Environmental Protection; Mexico

UN Refugee Agency (UNHCR)

http://www.unhcr.org

Description: Established in 1950, UNHCR is charged with protecting refugees and resolving refugee situations. The Who We Help section provides clarity on the groups of refugees assisted, and information about refugees is broken down into topical demographic groups, such as stateless people and internally displaced people. A photo gallery can be found in the News & Views section, and research, statistics, and publications are available in the Resources section. The site is available in Arabic, Chinese, Spanish, French, and Russian.

Subject(s): Refugees

UNESCO World Heritage Centre

http://whc.unesco.org/

Description: The UNESCO World Heritage Centre is committed to the preservation of places of significant natural and/or cultural importance. This website provides information about the initiative, a list of UNESCO World Heritage sites (complete with a map), a list of sites potentially in danger of damage or eradication, and information about its activities and volunteer organizations.

Subject(s): Cultural Artifacts; Culture

UNICOR: Federal Prison Industries, Inc.

https://www.unicor.gov/index.aspx

Description: The UNICOR website allows the federal government and contractors to buy goods and services from Federal Prison Industries (FPI), Inc., whose primary mission is the productive employment of inmates. The site has an online product catalog with browsing and ordering capabilities. It also provides substantial background information on the Inmate Training Programs.

Subject(s): Government Procurement; Prisoners

Union of Concerned Scientists (UCS)

https://www.ucsusa.org/

Description: UCS's mission, according to the website, is to "develop and implement innovative, practical solutions to some of our planet's most pressing problems—from combating global warming and developing sustainable ways to feed, power, and transport ourselves, to fighting misinformation and reducing the threat of nuclear war." The Take Action section of the site provides science-related "Action Alerts" and tips and tools for activists seeking to connect with policy makers and media outlets. The top of the page offers a link to UCS's blog, and the Publications section includes documents on a variety of topics, such as *Catalyst* magazine and the *Earthwise* newsletter.

Subject(s): Government Procurement; Prisoners

United Nations (UN)

http://www.un.org

Description: This main United Nations site features information and documents about the UN. Aside from organization and program information, the site includes an extensive news center, a UN Webcast section, and an educational section. Other sections link to the main bodies of the UN, such as the General Assembly, Security Council, and Economic and Social Council. A section called Global Issues organizes UN resources by topic, such as AIDS, Climate Change, Disarmament, Human Rights, Peace and Security, Refugees, and Terrorism. The Member States section includes a list with date of admission to the UN, as well as links to Permanent Missions and to nonmember states maintaining Permanent Observer Missions at UN Headquarters. The Publications section of the site includes sales publications and online versions of popular UN publications. The Documents section has meeting records, Security Council resolutions, the *Journal of the United Nations*, press releases, and other documents.

Subject(s): International Relations

United Nations Children's Fund Works for Children Worldwide (UNICEF)

https://www.unicef.org/

Description: UNICEF presents a site filled with information on international children's rights, the health and well-being of children, the abuse of children, and other material related to children. The site features the following main categories: What We Do, Who We Are, Focus Areas, Where We Work, and Press Centre. Links to UNICEF's Facebook, Twitter, and YouTube pages are provided. Focus areas include such topics as child survival and development, basic education and gender equality, children and HIV/AIDS, and child protection. The UNICEF sites are a treasure trove of information about children and UNICEF's activities on behalf of children.

Subject(s): Child Welfare; International

United Nations Climate Change Portal

http://www.un.org/climatechange/

Description: This page discusses the UN's actions regarding climate change. The UN Climate Voices section features interviews with UN officials involved with climate change initiatives, and the Publications section links to related UN-issued reports.

Subject(s): Climate Change

United Nations Educational, Scientific and Cultural Organization (UNESCO)

https://en.unesco.org/

Description: UNESCO, founded in 1945, has 195 members and 10 associate members, with more than 50 field offices around the world. UNESCO's slate of topics is diverse, with major programs including natural sciences, education, social and human sciences, and communications and information. Each topical section links to news, events, and other related materials. The Media subsection includes press releases, advisories, and multimedia content, such as photos and videos. The site is available in Spanish, French, Russian, Chinese, Arabic, and Portuguese. One of UNESCO's major initiatives is its World Heritage Centre program, which is described in a separate entry.

Subject(s): Culture; Education; Science

Wisconsin Project on Nuclear Arms Control

https://www.wisconsinproject.org/

Description: The aim of the Wisconsin Project on Nuclear Arms Control is to control and prevent the spread of long-rage missiles and weapons of mass destruction. Its products include the Risk Report database, which compiles information on companies around the world suspected of contributing to the creation and building of weapons of mass destruction; the Iran Watch, which tracks that country's weapons capabilities; and the Iraq Watch, which was active from 2000–2006.

Subject(s): Arms Control; Nuclear Weapons; Weapons of Mass Destruction

Woodrow Wilson International Center for Scholars

https://www.wilsoncenter.org/

Description: The Wilson Center supports scholarship linked to public policy. The center offers fellowships and special opportunities for research and writing with a focus on history, political science, and international relations. As a public/private partnership, the center receives roughly one-third of its operating funds from federal appropriations. The website has information about current Wilson Center projects and publications, and audio files of its weekly radio program, "Dialogue." The site also carries essays and other items from the center's journal, *The Wilson Quarterly*. In the About section, the site offers information on applying for a fellowship or internship with the center.

Subject(s): Fellowships; Public Policy—Research; Social Science Research

World Bank

http://www.worldbank.org

Description: This site concentrates on information about the World Bank, its programs, and constituent organizations. Sections include Data, Research, Learning, News, Projects & Operations, and Publications. A Countries section provides detailed data on countries of the world. The Projects & Operations section allows users to browse topics and issues by country/area, sector, and theme.

Subject(s): International Economic Development

World Health Organization (WHO)

http://www.who.int

Description: WHO is a UN agency focusing on global health issues. The WHO site features the major categories: Health Topics, Data, Media Centre, Publications, Countries, Programmes, Governance, and About WHO. The Countries section gives a health profile of member nations. The Media Centre section links to fact sheets on global health topics such as African trypanosomiasis (sleeping sickness), Chagas disease, dengue, malaria, and tobacco use.

Subject(s): Health and Safety—International

World Intellectual Property Organization (WIPO)

http://www.wipo.int

Description: The site, subtitled "Encouraging Creativity and Innovation," includes sections such as About IP, Inside WIPO, IP Services, Policy, Cooperation, and Reference. The IP Services section has information on such topics as developing laws and standards, copyright issues, and the economics of IP, or intellectual property. Case studies, country profiles, databases, documents, and publications can be found in the Reference section. The site is available in Spanish, French, Russian, Arabic, and Chinese.

Subject(s): Intellectual Property— International

World Meteorological Organization (WMO)

https://www.wmo.int/pages/index_en.html

Description: The World Meteorological Organization is a United Nations agency that promotes the effective use worldwide of meteorological and hydrological information, notably in weather and water resource prediction and in climatology. The homepage features current news, weather forecasts and warnings, recent and upcoming events, and a link to the MyWorld-Weather app for iPhone and Android. The site's Media Centre section has news, press releases, and podcasts. The site is available in Arabic, Chinese, French, Russian, and Spanish.

Subject(s): Meteorology—International

World Trade Organization (WTO)

https://www.wto.org/

Description: The WTO website features Trade Topics; About WTO; Documents, Data and Resources; and News and Events. Under Trade Topics, the page organizes information under the headings Goods, Services, Intellectual Property, Building Trade Capacity, Doha Development Agenda, Trade Monitoring, and Dispute Settlement. The Documents, Data and Resources section links to an online bookstore and key WTO publications.

Subject(s): International Trade

World Wildlife Fund (WWF)

https://www.worldwildlife.org/

Description: With a presence in over 100 countries, the WWF strives to support conservation and natural protection issues. Under About Us, the News & Press section includes news articles, press releases, and contact information for the media. The Places section breaks down WWF initiatives by region/area. Information about partnerships and projects can be found in Our Work.

Subject(s): Animals; Conservation (Natural Resources)

XML

US Government Web Services and XML Data Sources

http://www.usgovxml.com/

Description: This website is an index to publicly available web services and XML data sources that are provided by the US government. USGovXML is a non-governmental effort to index publicly available web services and XML data sources. USGovXML documents, in one place and in a uniform manner, the web services and XML data sources that are provided by the US government

Subject(s): World Wide Web

Appendix A

List of Members of the 115th Congress

Alabama

Sen. Richard C. Shelby (R)
https://www.shelby.senate.gov/public/

Sen. Doug Jones (D)
https://www.jones.senate.gov/

Rep. Bradley Byrne (R-01)
https://byrne.house.gov/

Rep. Martha Roby (R-02)
https://roby.house.gov/

Rep. Mike Rogers (R-03)
https://mikerogers.house.gov/

Rep. Robert Aderholt (R-04)
https://aderholt.house.gov/

Rep. Mo Brooks (R-05)
https://brooks.house.gov/

Rep. Gary Palmer (R-06)
https://palmer.house.gov/

Rep. Terri A. Sewell (D-07)
http://sewell.house.gov

Alaska

Sen. Lisa Murkowski (R)
https://www.murkowski.senate.gov/

Sen. Daniel Sullivan (R)
https://www.sullivan.senate.gov/

Rep. Don Young (R-At Large)
https://donyoung.house.gov/

American Samoa

Del. Aumua Amata Coleman Radewagen (R-At Large)
https://radewagen.house.gov/

Arizona

Sen. John McCain (R)
https://www.mccain.senate.gov/public/

Sen. Jeff Flake (R)
https://www.flake.senate.gov/public/

Rep. Tom O'Halleran (D-01)
https://ohalleran.house.gov/

Rep. Martha McSally (R-02)
https://mcsally.house.gov/

Rep. Raul Grijalva (D-03)
https://grijalva.house.gov/

Rep. Paul A. Gosar (R-04)
https://gosar.house.gov/

Rep. Andy Biggs (R-05)
https://biggs.house.gov/

Rep. David Schweikert (R-06)
https://schweikert.house.gov/

Rep. Ruben Gallego (D-07)
https://rubengallego.house.gov/

Debbie Lesko (R-09)
https://lesko.house.gov

Rep. Kyrsten Sinema (D-09)
https://sinema.house.gov/

Arkansas

Sen. John Boozman (R)
https://www.boozman.senate.gov/public/

Sen. Tom Cotton (R)
https://www.cotton.senate.gov/

Rep. Rick Crawford (R-01)
https://crawford.house.gov/

Rep. French Hill (R-02)
https://hill.house.gov/

Rep. Steve Womack (R-03)
https://womack.house.gov/

Rep. Bruce Westerman (R-04)
https://westerman.house.gov/

California

Sen. Dianne Feinstein (D)
https://www.feinstein.senate.gov/public/

Sen. Kamala Harris (D)
https://www.harris.senate.gov/

Rep. Doug LaMalfa (R-01)
https://lamalfa.house.gov/

Rep. Jared Huffman (D-02)
https://huffman.house.gov/

Rep. John Garamendi (D-03)
https://garamendi.house.gov/

Rep. Tom McClintock (R-04)
https://mcclintock.house.gov/

Rep. Mike Thompson (D-05)
https://mikethompson.house.gov/

Rep. Doris O. Matsui (D-06)
https://matsui.house.gov/

Rep. Ami Bera (D-07)
https://bera.house.gov/

Rep. Paul Cook (R-08)
https://cook.house.gov/

Rep. Jerry McNerney (D-09)
https://mcnerney.house.gov/

Rep. Jeff Denham (R-10)
https://denham.house.gov/

Rep. Mark DeSaulnier (D-11)
https://desaulnier.house.gov/

Rep. Nancy Pelosi (D-12)
https://pelosi.house.gov/

Rep. Barbara Lee (D-13)
https://lee.house.gov/

Rep. Jackie Speier (D-14)
https://speier.house.gov/

Rep. Eric Swalwell (D-15)
https://swalwell.house.gov/

Rep. Jim Costa (D-16)
https://costa.house.gov/

Rep. Ro Khanna (D-17)
https://khanna.house.gov/

Rep. Anna G. Eshoo (D-18)
https://eshoo.house.gov/

Rep. Zoe Lofgren (D-19)
https://lofgren.house.gov/

Rep. Jimmy Panetta (D-20)
https://panetta.house.gov/

Rep. David Valadao (R-21)
https://valadao.house.gov/

Rep. Devin Nunes (R-22)
https://nunes.house.gov/

Rep. Kevin McCarthy (R-23)
https://kevinmccarthy.house.gov/

Rep. Salud O. Carbajal (D-24)
https://carbajal.house.gov/

Rep. Steve Knight (R-25)
https://knight.house.gov/

Rep. Julia Brownley (D-26)
http://juliabrownley.house.gov/

Rep. Judy Chu (D-27)
https://chu.house.gov/

Rep. Adam Schiff (D-28)
http://schiff.house.gov/

Rep. Tony Cardenas (D-29)
https://cardenas.house.gov/

Rep. Brad Sherman (D-30)
https://sherman.house.gov/

Rep. Pete Aguilar (D-31)
https://aguilar.house.gov/

Rep. Grace Napolitano (D-32)
https://napolitano.house.gov/

Rep. Ted Lieu (D-33)
https://lieu.house.gov/

Rep. Jimmy Gomez (D-34)
https://gomez.house.gov/

Rep. Norma Torres (D-35)
https://torres.house.gov/

Rep. Raul Ruiz (D-36)
https://ruiz.house.gov/

Rep. Karen Bass (D-37)
https://bass.house.gov/

Rep. Linda Sanchez (D-38)
https://lindasanchez.house.gov/

Rep. Ed Royce (R-39)
https://royce.house.gov/

Rep. Lucille Roybal-Allard (D-40)
https://roybal-allard.house.gov/

Rep. Mark Takano (D-41)
http://takano.house.gov/

Rep. Ken Calvert (R-42)
https://calvert.house.gov/

Rep. Maxine Waters (D-43)
https://waters.house.gov/

Rep. Nanette Diaz Barragan (D-44)
https://barragan.house.gov/

Rep. Mimi Walters (R-45)
https://walters.house.gov/

Rep. J. Luis Correa (D-46)
https://correa.house.gov/

Rep. Alan Lowenthal (D-47)
https://lowenthal.house.gov/

Rep. Dana Rohrabacher (R-48)
https://rohrabacher.house.gov/

Rep. Darrell Issa (R-49)
https://issa.house.gov/

Rep. Duncan D. Hunter (R-50)
https://hunter.house.gov/

Rep. Juan Vargas (D-51)
https://vargas.house.gov/

Rep. Scott Peters (D-52)
https://scottpeters.house.gov/

Rep. Susan Davis (D-53)
https://susandavis.house.gov/

Colorado

Sen. Michael F. Bennet (D)
https://www.bennet.senate.gov/

Sen. Cory Gardner (R)
https://www.gardner.senate.gov/

Rep. Diana DeGette (D-01)
https://degette.house.gov/

Rep. Jared Polis (D-02)
https://polis.house.gov/

Rep. Scott Tipton (R-03)
https://tipton.house.gov/

Rep. Ken Buck (R-04)
https://buck.house.gov/

Rep. Doug Lamborn (R-05)
https://lamborn.house.gov/

Rep. Mike Coffman (R-06)
https://coffman.house.gov/

Rep. Ed Perlmutter (D-07)
https://perlmutter.house.gov/

Connecticut

Sen. Richard Blumenthal (D)
https://www.blumenthal.senate
.gov/

Sen. Christopher Murphy (D)
https://www.murphy.senate.gov/

Rep. John B. Larson (D-01)
https://larson.house.gov/

Rep. Joe Courtney (D-02)
https://courtney.house.gov/

Rep. Rosa L. DeLauro (D-03)
https://delauro.house.gov/

Rep. Jim Himes (D-04)
https://himes.house.gov/

Rep. Elizabeth Esty (D-05)
https://esty.house.gov/

Delaware

Sen. Thomas R. Carper (D)
https://www.carper.senate.gov/public/

Sen. Christopher A. Coons (D)
https://www.coons.senate.gov/

Rep. Lisa Blunt Rochester (D-At Large)
https://bluntrochester.house.gov/

District of Columbia

Del. Eleanor Holmes Norton (D-At Large)
https://norton.house.gov/

Florida

Sen. Bill Nelson (D)
https://www.billnelson.senate.gov/

Sen. Marco Rubio (R)
https://www.rubio.senate.gov/public/

Rep. Matt Gaetz (R-01)
https://gaetz.house.gov/

Rep. Neal P. Dunn (R-02)
https://dunn.house.gov/

Rep. Ted Yoho (R-03)
https://yoho.house.gov/

Rep. John H. Rutherford (R-04)
https://rutherford.house.gov/

Rep. Al Lawson Jr. (D-05)
https://lawson.house.gov/

Rep. Ron DeSantis (R-06)
https://desantis.house.gov/

Rep. Stephanie Murphy (D-07)
https://stephaniemurphy.house.gov/

Rep. Bill Posey (R-08)
https://posey.house.gov/

Rep. Darren Soto (D-09)
https://soto.house.gov/

Rep. Val Butler Demings (D-10)
https://demings.house.gov/

Rep. Daniel Webster (R-11)
https://webster.house.gov/

Rep. Gus M. Bilirakis (R-12)
https://bilirakis.house.gov/

Rep. Charlie Crist (D-13)

https://crist.house.gov/

Rep. Kathy Castor (D-14)
https://castor.house.gov/

Rep. Dennis Ross (R-15)
https://dennisross.house.gov/

Rep. Vern Buchanan (R-16)
https://buchanan.house.gov/

Rep. Tom Rooney (R-17)
https://rooney.house.gov/

Rep. Brian J. Mast (R-18)
https://mast.house.gov/

Rep.Francis Rooney (R-19)
https://rooney.house.gov/

Rep. Alcee L. Hastings (D-20)
https://alceehastings.house.gov/

Rep. Lois Frankel (D-21)
https://frankel.house.gov/

Rep. Ted Deutch (D-22)
https://teddeutch.house.gov/

Rep. Debbie Wasserman Schultz (D-23)
https://wassermanschultz.house.gov/

Rep. Frederica Wilson (D-24)
https://wilson.house.gov/

Rep. Mario Diaz-Balart (R-25)
https://mariodiazbalart.house.gov/

Rep. Carlos Curbelo (R-26)
https://curbelo.house.gov/

Rep. Ileana Ros-Lehtinen (R-27)
https://ros-lehtinen.house.gov/

Georgia

Sen. Johnny Isakson (R)
https://www.isakson.senate.gov/public/

Sen. David Perdue (R)
https://www.perdue.senate.gov/

Rep. Buddy Carter (R-01)
https://buddycarter.house.gov/

Rep. Sanford D. Bishop, Jr. (D-02)
https://bishop.house.gov/

Rep. A. Drew Ferguson IV (R-03)
https://ferguson.house.gov/

Rep. Henry C. "Hank" Johnson, Jr. (D-04)
https://hankjohnson.house.gov/

Rep. John Lewis (D-05)
https://johnlewis.house.gov/

Rep. Karen Handel (R-06)
https://handel.house.gov/

Rep. Robert Woodall (R-07)
https://woodall.house.gov/

Rep. Austin Scott (R-08)
https://austinscott.house.gov/

Rep. Doug Collins (R-09)
https://dougcollins.house.gov/

Rep. Jody Hice (R-10)
https://hice.house.gov/

Rep. Barry Loudermilk (R-11)
https://loudermilk.house.gov/

Rep. Rick Allen (R-12)
https://allen.house.gov/

Rep. David Scott (D-13)
https://davidscott.house.gov/

Rep. Tom Graves (R-14)
https://tomgraves.house.gov/

Guam

Del. Madeleine Bordallo (D-At Large)
https://bordallo.house.gov/

Hawaii

Sen. Brian Schatz (D)
https://www.schatz.senate.gov/

Sen. Mazie K. Hirono (D)
https://www.hirono.senate.gov/

Rep. Colleen Hanabusa (D-01)
https://hanabusa.house.gov/

Rep. Tulsi Gabbard (D-02)
https://gabbard.house.gov/

Idaho

Sen. Mike Crapo (R)
https://www.crapo.senate.gov/

Sen. James E. Risch (R)
https://www.risch.senate.gov/public/

Rep. Raul R. Labrador (R-01)
https://labrador.house.gov/#di-alog

Rep. Mike Simpson (R-02)
https://simpson.house.gov/

Illinois

Sen. Richard J. Durbin (D)
https://www.durbin.senate.gov/

Sen. Tammy Duckworth (D)
https://www.duckworth.senate.gov/

Rep. Bobby L. Rush (D-01)
https://rush.house.gov/

Rep. Robin Kelly (D-02)
https://robinkelly.house.gov/

Rep. Daniel Lipinski (D-03)
https://lipinski.house.gov/

Rep. Luis Gutierrez (D-04)
https://gutierrez.house.gov/

Rep. Mike Quigley (D-05)
https://quigley.house.gov/

Rep. Peter J. Roskam (R-06)
https://roskam.house.gov/

Rep. Danny K. Davis (D-07)
https://davis.house.gov/

Rep. Raja Krishnamoorthi (D-08)
https://krishnamoorthi.house.gov/

Rep. Jan Schakowsky (D-09)
https://schakowsky.house.gov/

Rep. Bradley Scott Schneider (D-10)

https://schneider.house.gov/

Rep. Bill Foster (D-11)
https://foster.house.gov/

Rep. Mike Bost (R-12)
https://bost.house.gov/

Rep. Rodney Davis (R-13)
https://rodneydavis.house.gov/

Rep. Randy Hultgren (R-14)
https://hultgren.house.gov/

Rep. John Shimkus (R-15)
https://shimkus.house.gov/

Rep. Adam Kinzinger (R-16)
https://kinzinger.house.gov/

Rep. Cheri Bustos (D-17)
http://bustos.house.gov/

Rep. Darin LaHood (R-18)
https://lahood.house.gov/

Indiana

Sen. Joe Donnelly (D)
https://www.donnelly.senate.gov/

Sen. Todd Young (R)
https://www.young.senate.gov/

Rep. Peter Visclosky (D-01)
https://visclosky.house.gov/

Rep. Jackie Walorski (R-02)
https://walorski.house.gov/

Rep. Jim Banks (R-03)
https://banks.house.gov/

Rep. Todd Rokita (R-04)
https://rokita.house.gov/

Rep. Susan W. Brooks (R-05)
https://susanwbrooks.house.gov/

Rep. Luke Messer (R-06)
https://messer.house.gov/

Rep. Andre Carson (D-07)
https://carson.house.gov/

Rep. Larry Bucshon (R-08)
https://bucshon.house.gov/

Rep. Trey Hollingsworth (R-09)
https://hollingsworth.house.gov/

Iowa

Sen. Chuck Grassley (R)
https://www.grassley.senate.gov/

Sen. Joni Ernst (R)
https://www.ernst.senate.gov/
public/

Rep. Rod Blum (R-01)
https://blum.house.gov/

Rep. David Loebsack (D-02)
https://loebsack.house.gov/

Rep. David Young (R-03)
https://davidyoung.house.gov/

Rep. Steve King (R-04)
https://steveking.house.gov/

Kansas

Sen. Pat Roberts (R)

https://www.roberts.senate.gov/public/

Sen. Jerry Moran (R)
https://www.moran.senate.gov/public/

Rep. Roger W. Marshall (R-01)
https://marshall.house.gov/

Rep. Lynn Jenkins (R-02)
https://lynnjenkins.house.gov/

Rep. Kevin Yoder (R-03)
https://yoder.house.gov/

Rep. Ron Estes (R-04)
http://estes.house.gov

Kentucky

Sen. Mitch McConnell (R)
https://www.mcconnell.senate.gov/public/

Sen. Rand Paul (R)
https://www.paul.senate.gov/

Rep. James Comer (R-01)
https://comer.house.gov/

Rep. S. Brett Guthrie (R-02)
https://guthrie.house.gov/#dialog

Rep. John A. Yarmuth (D-03)
https://yarmuth.house.gov/

Rep. Thomas Massie (R-04)
https://massie.house.gov/

Rep. Harold "Hal" Rogers (R-05)
https://halrogers.house.gov/

Rep. Andy Barr (R-06)
https://barr.house.gov/

Louisiana

Sen. Bill Cassidy (R)
https://www.cassidy.senate.gov/

Sen. John Kennedy (R)
http://kennedy.senate.gov

Rep. Steve Scalise (R-01)
https://scalise.house.gov/

Rep. Cedric Richmond (D-02)
https://richmond.house.gov/

Rep. Clay Higgins. (R-03)
https://clayhiggins.house.gov/

Rep. Mike Johnson (R-04)
https://mikejohnson.house.gov/

Rep. Ralph Abraham (R-05)
https://abraham.house.gov/

Rep. Garret Graves (R-06)
https://garretgraves.house.gov/

Maine

Sen. Susan M. Collins (R)
https://www.collins.senate.gov/

Sen. Angus S. King, Jr. (I)
https://www.king.senate.gov/

Rep. Chellie Pingree (D-01)
https://pingree.house.gov/

Rep. Bruce Poliquin (R-02)
https://poliquin.house.gov/

Maryland

Sen. Benjamin L. Cardin (D)
https://www.cardin.senate.gov/

Sen. Chris Van Hollen (D)
https://www.vanhollen.senate.gov/

Rep. Andy Harris (R-01)
https://harris.house.gov/

Rep. C.A. Dutch Ruppersberger (D-02)
https://ruppersberger.house.gov/

Rep. John P. Sarbanes (D-03)
https://sarbanes.house.gov/

Rep. Anthony G Brown (D-04)
https://anthonybrown.house.gov/

Rep. Steny H. Hoyer (D-05)
https://hoyer.house.gov/

Rep. John Delaney (D-06)
https://delaney.house.gov/

Rep. Elijah Cummings (D-07)
https://cummings.house.gov/

Rep. Jamie Raskin (D-08)
https://raskin.house.gov/

Massachusetts

Sen. Elizabeth Warren (D)
https://www.warren.senate.gov/

Sen. Edward J. Markey (D)
https://www.markey.senate.gov/

Rep. Richard E. Neal (D-01)
https://neal.house.gov/

Rep. James McGovern (D-02)
https://mcgovern.house.gov/

Rep. Niki Tsongas (D-03)
https://tsongas.house.gov/

Rep. Joseph P. Kennedy III (D-04)
https://kennedy.house.gov/

Rep. Katherine Clark (D-05)
https://katherineclark.house.gov/

Rep. Seth Moulton (D-06)
https://moulton.house.gov/

Rep. Michael E. Capuano (D-07)
http://capuano.house.gov/

Rep. Stephen F. Lynch (D-08)
https://lynch.house.gov/

Rep. William Keating (D-09)
https://keating.house.gov/

Michigan

Sen. Debbie Stabenow (D)
https://www.stabenow.senate.gov/

Sen. Gary Peters (D)
https://www.peters.senate.gov/

Rep. Jack Bergman (R-01)
https://bergman.house.gov/

Rep. Bill Huizenga (R-02)
https://huizenga.house.gov/

Rep. Justin Amash (R-03)
https://amash.house.gov/

Rep. John Moolenaar (R-04)
https://moolenaar.house.gov/

Rep. Daniel Kildee (D-05)
https://dankildee.house.gov/

Rep. Fred Upton (R-06)
https://upton.house.gov/

Rep. Tim Walberg (R-07)
https://walberg.house.gov/

Rep. Mike Bishop (R-08)
https://mikebishop.house.gov/

Rep. Sander "Sandy" Levin (D-09)
https://levin.house.gov/

Rep. Paul Mitchell (R-10)
https://mitchell.house.gov/

Rep. Dave Trott (R-11)
https://trott.house.gov/

Rep. Debbie Dingell (D-12)
https://debbiedingell.house.gov/

Vacant (District 13)

Rep. Brenda Lawrence (D-14)
https://lawrence.house.gov/

Minnesota

Sen. Amy Klobuchar (D)
https://www.klobuchar.senate.gov/public/

Sen. Tina Smith (D)
https://www.smith.senate.gov/

Rep. Timothy J. Walz (D-01)
https://walz.house.gov/

Rep. Jason Lewis (R-02)
https://jasonlewis.house.gov/

Rep. Erik Paulsen (R-03)
https://paulsen.house.gov/

Rep. Betty McCollum (D-04)
https://mccollum.house.gov/

Rep. Keith Ellison (D-05)
https://ellison.house.gov/

Rep. Tom Emmer (R-06)
https://emmer.house.gov/

Rep. Collin C. Peterson (D-07)
https://collinpeterson.house.gov/

Rep. Rick Nolan (D-08)
https://nolan.house.gov/

Mississippi

Sen. Cindy Hyde-Smith (R)
https://www.hydesmith.senate.com

Sen. Roger F. Wicker (R)
https://www.wicker.senate.gov/public/

Rep. Trent Kelly (R-01)
https://trentkelly.house.gov/

Rep. Bennie G. Thompson (D-02)
https://benniethompson.house.gov/

Rep. Gregg Harper (R-03)
https://harper.house.gov/

Rep. Steven Palazzo (R-04)
https://palazzo.house.gov/

Missouri

Sen. Claire McCaskill (D)
https://www.mccaskill.senate.gov/

Sen. Roy Blunt (R)
https://www.blunt.senate.gov/public/

Rep. William "Lacy" Clay, Jr. (D-01)
https://lacyclay.house.gov/

Rep. Ann Wagner (R-02)
https://wagner.house.gov/

Rep. Blaine Luetkemeyer (R-03)
https://luetkemeyer.house.gov/

Rep. Vicky Hartzler (R-04)
https://hartzler.house.gov/

Rep. Emanuel Cleaver II (D-05)
https://cleaver.house.gov/

Rep. Sam Graves (R-06)
https://graves.house.gov/

Rep. Billy Long (R-07)
https://long.house.gov/

Rep. Jason Smith (R-08)
https://jasonsmith.house.gov/

Montana

Sen. Jon Tester (D)
https://www.tester.senate.gov/

Sen. Steve Daines (R)
https://www.daines.senate.gov/

Rep. Greg Gianforte (R)
https://gianforte.house.gov/

Nebraska

Sen. Deb Fischer (R)
https://www.fischer.senate.gov/public/

Sen. Ben Sasse (R)
https://www.sasse.senate.gov/public/

Rep. Jeff Fortenberry (R-01)
https://fortenberry.house.gov/

Rep. Don Bacon (R-02)
https://bacon.house.gov/

Rep. Adrian Smith (R-03)
https://adriansmith.house.gov/

Nevada

Sen. Dean Heller (R)
https://www.heller.senate.gov/public/

Sen. Catherine Cortez Masto (D)
https://www.cortezmasto.senate.gov

Rep. Dina Titus (D-01)
https://titus.house.gov/

Rep. Mark Amodei (R-02)
https://amodei.house.gov/#dialog

Rep. Jacky Rosen (D-03)
https://rosen.house.gov/

Rep. Ruben Kihuen (D-04)
https://kihuen.house.gov/

New Hampshire

Sen. Jeanne Shaheen (D)
https://www.shaheen.senate.gov/

Sen. Margaret Wood Hassan (D)
https://www.hassan.senate.gov/

Rep. Carol Shea-Porter (D-01)
https://shea-porter.house.gov/

Rep. Ann Kuster (D-02)
https://kuster.house.gov/

New Jersey

Sen. Robert "Bob" Menendez (D)
https://www.menendez.senate.gov/

Sen. Cory A. Booker (D)
https://www.booker.senate.gov/

Rep. Donald Norcross (D-01)
https://norcross.house.gov/

Rep. Frank LoBiondo (R-02)
https://lobiondo.house.gov/

Rep. Tom MacArthur (R-03)
https://macarthur.house.gov/

Rep. Chris Smith (R-04)
https://chrissmith.house.gov/

Rep. Josh Gottheimer (D-05)
https://gottheimer.house.gov/

Rep. Frank Pallone, Jr. (D-06)
https://pallone.house.gov/

Rep. Leonard Lance (R-07)
https://lance.house.gov/

Rep. Albio Sires (D-08)
https://sires.house.gov/

Rep. Bill Pascrell, Jr. (D-09)
https://pascrell.house.gov/

Rep. Donald Payne, Jr. (D-10)
https://payne.house.gov/

Rep. Rodney Frelinghuysen (R-11)
https://frelinghuysen.house.gov/

Rep. Bonnie Watson Coleman (D-12)
https://watsoncoleman.house.gov/

New Mexico

Sen. Tom Udall (D)
https://www.tomudall.senate.gov/

Sen. Martin Heinrich (D)
https://www.heinrich.senate.gov/

Rep. Michelle Lujan Grisham (D-01)
https://lujangrisham.house.gov/

Rep. Steve Pearce (R-02)
https://pearce.house.gov/

Rep. Ben R. Lujan (D-03)
https://lujan.house.gov/

New York

Sen. Charles E. Schumer (D)

https://www.schumer.senate.gov/

Sen. Kirsten E. Gillibrand (D)
https://www.gillibrand.senate.gov/

Rep. Lee Zeldin (R-01)
https://zeldin.house.gov/

Rep. Pete King (R-02)
https://peteking.house.gov/

Rep. Thomas Suozzi (D-03)
https://suozzi.house.gov/

Rep. Kathleen Rice (D-04)
https://kathleenrice.house.gov/

Rep. Gregory W. Meeks (D-05)
https://meeks.house.gov/

Rep. Grace Meng (D-06)
https://meng.house.gov/

Rep. Nydia M. Velazquez (D-07)
https://velazquez.house.gov/

Rep. Hakeem Jeffries (D-08)
https://jeffries.house.gov/

Rep. Yvette D. Clarke (D-09)
http://clarke.house.gov/

Rep. Jerrold Nadler (D-10)
https://nadler.house.gov/

Rep. Daniel Donovan (R-11)
https://donovan.house.gov/

Rep. Carolyn Maloney (D-12)
https://maloney.house.gov/

Rep. Adriano Espaillat (D-13)
https://espaillat.house.gov/

Rep. Joseph Crowley (D-14)
https://crowley.house.gov/

Rep. Jose E. Serrano (D-15)
https://serrano.house.gov/

Rep. Eliot Engel (D-16)
https://engel.house.gov/

Rep. Nita Lowey (D-17)
https://lowey.house.gov/

Rep. Sean Patrick Maloney (D-18)
https://seanmaloney.house.gov/

Rep. John J. Faso (R-19)
https://faso.house.gov/

Rep. Paul D. Tonko (D-20)
https://tonko.house.gov/

Rep. Elise Stefanik (R-21)
https://stefanik.house.gov/

Rep. Claudia Tenney (R-22)
https://tenney.house.gov/

Rep. Tom Reed (R-23)
https://reed.house.gov/

Rep. John Katko (R-24)
https://katko.house.gov/

Vacant (District 25)

Rep. Brian Higgins (D-26)
https://higgins.house.gov/

Rep. Chris Collins (R-27)
https://chriscollins.house.gov/

North Carolina

Sen. Richard Burr (R)
https://www.burr.senate.gov/

Sen. Thom Tillis (R)
https://www.tillis.senate.gov/public/

Rep. G. K. Butterfield (D-01)
https://butterfield.house.gov/

Rep. George Holding (R-02)
https://holding.house.gov/

Rep. Walter B. Jones (R-03)
https://jones.house.gov/

Rep. David Price (D-04)
https://price.house.gov/

Rep. Virginia Foxx (R-05)
https://foxx.house.gov/

Rep. Mark Walker (R-06)
https://walker.house.gov/

Rep. David Rouzer (R-07)
https://rouzer.house.gov/

Rep. Richard Hudson (R-08)
https://hudson.house.gov/

Rep. Robert Pittenger (R-09)
https://pittenger.house.gov/

Rep. Patrick T. McHenry (R-10)
https://mchenry.house.gov/

Rep. Mark Meadows (R-11)
https://meadows.house.gov/

Rep. Alma Adams (D-12)
https://adams.house.gov/

Rep.Tedd Budd (R-13)
https://holding.house.gov/

North Dakota

Sen. John Hoeven (R)
https://www.hoeven.senate.gov/

Sen. Heidi Heitkamp (D)
https://www.heitkamp.senate.gov/public/

Rep. Kevin Cramer (R-At Large)
https://cramer.house.gov/

Northern Mariana Islands

Del. Gregorio Sablan (D-At Large)
https://sablan.house.gov/

Ohio

Sen. Sherrod Brown (D)
https://www.brown.senate.gov/

Sen. Rob Portman (R)
https://www.portman.senate.gov/public/

Rep. Steve Chabot (R-01)
https://chabot.house.gov/

Rep. Brad Wenstrup (R-02)
https://wenstrup.house.gov/

Rep. Joyce Beatty (D-03)
https://beatty.house.gov/

Rep. Jim Jordan (R-04)
https://jordan.house.gov/

Rep. Robert E. Latta (R-05)
https://latta.house.gov/

Rep. Bill Johnson (R-06)
https://billjohnson.house.gov/

Rep. Bob Gibbs (R-07)
https://gibbs.house.gov/

Warren Davidson, (R-08)
https://davidson.house.gov/

Rep. Marcy Kaptur (D-09)
https://kaptur.house.gov/

Rep. Michael Turner (R-10)
https://turner.house.gov/

Rep. Marcia L. Fudge (D-11)
https://fudge.house.gov/#dialog

Vacant (District 12)

Rep. Tim Ryan (D-13)
https://timryan.house.gov/

Rep. David Joyce (R-14)
https://joyce.house.gov/#dialog

Rep. Steve Stivers (R-15)
https://stivers.house.gov/

Rep. Jim Renacci (R-16)
http://renacci.house.gov/

Oklahoma

Sen. James M. Inhofe (R)
https://www.inhofe.senate.gov/

Sen. James Lankford (R)
https://www.lankford.senate.gov/

Vacant (District 1)

Rep. Markwayne Mullin (R-02)
https://mullin.house.gov/

Rep. Frank Lucas (R-03)
https://lucas.house.gov/

Rep. Tom Cole (R-04)
https://cole.house.gov/

Rep. Steve Russell (R-05)
https://russell.house.gov/

Oregon

Sen. Ron Wyden (D)
https://www.wyden.senate.gov/

Sen. Jeff Merkley (D)
https://www.merkley.senate.gov/

Suzanne Bonamici (D-01)
https://bonamici.house.gov/

Rep. Greg Walden (R-02)
https://walden.house.gov/

Rep. Earl Blumenauer (D-03)
https://blumenauer.house.gov/

Rep. Peter DeFazio (D-04)
https://defazio.house.gov/

Rep. Kurt Schrader (D-05)
https://schrader.house.gov/

Pennsylvania

Sen. Robert P. Casey, Jr. (D)
https://www.casey.senate.gov/

Sen. Patrick J. Toomey (R)

https://www.toomey.senate.gov/

Rep. Robert Brady (D-01)
https://brady.house.gov/

Rep. Dwight Evans (D-02)
https://evans.house.gov/

Rep. Mike Kelly (R-03)
https://kelly.house.gov/

Rep. Scott Perry (R-04)
https://perry.house.gov/

Rep. Glenn W. Thompson (R-05)
https://thompson.house.gov/

Rep. Ryan Costello (R-06)
https://costello.house.gov/

Vacant (District 7)

Rep. Brian K. Fitzpatrick (R-08)
https://fitzpatrick.house.gov/

Rep. Bill Shuster (R-09)
https://shuster.house.gov/

Rep. Tom Marino (R-10)
https://marino.house.gov/

Rep. Lou Barletta (R-11)
https://barletta.house.gov/

Rep. Keith Rothfus (R-12)
https://rothfus.house.gov/

Rep. Brendan Boyle (D-13)
https://boyle.house.gov/

Rep. Mike Doyle (D-14)
https://doyle.house.gov/

Vacant (District 15)

Rep. Lloyd Smucker (R-16)
https://smucker.house.gov/

Rep. Matthew Cartwright (D-17)
https://cartwright.house.gov/

Conor Lamb (D-18)
https://lamb.house.gov

Puerto Rico

Jenniffer González-Colón (R-At Large)
https://gonzalez-colon.house.gov/

Rhode Island

Sen. Jack Reed (D)
https://www.reed.senate.gov/

Sen. Sheldon Whitehouse (D)
https://www.whitehouse.senate.gov/

Rep. David Cicilline (D-01)
https://cicilline.house.gov/

Rep. Jim Langevin (D-02)
https://langevin.house.gov/

South Carolina

Sen. Lindsey Graham (R)
https://www.lgraham.senate.gov/public/

Sen. Tim Scott (R)
https://www.scott.senate.gov/

Rep. Mark Sanford (R-01)
https://www.scott.senate.gov/

Rep. Joe Wilson (R-02)
https://joewilson.house.gov/

Rep. Jeff Duncan (R-03)
https://jeffduncan.house.gov/

Rep. Trey Gowdy (R-04)
https://gowdy.house.gov/

Rep. Ralph Norman (R-05)
https://norman.house.gov/

Rep. James E. Clyburn (D-06)
https://clyburn.house.gov/

Rep. Tom Rice (R-07)
https://rice.house.gov/

South Dakota

Sen. John Thune (R)
https://www.thune.senate.gov/public/

Sen. Mike Rounds (R)
https://www.rounds.senate.gov/

Rep. Kristi Noem (R-At Large)
http://noem.house.gov/

Tennessee

Sen. Lamar Alexander (R)
https://www.alexander.senate.gov/public/

Sen. Bob Corker (R)
https://www.corker.senate.gov/public/

Rep. David P. Roe (R-01)
https://roe.house.gov/

Rep. John J. Duncan, Jr. (R-02)
https://duncan.house.gov/

Rep. Chuck Fleischmann (R-03)
https://fleischmann.house.gov/

Rep. Scott DesJarlais (R-04)
https://desjarlais.house.gov/

Rep. Jim Cooper (D-05)
https://cooper.house.gov/

Rep. Diane Black (R-06)
https://black.house.gov/

Rep. Marsha Blackburn (R-07)
https://blackburn.house.gov/

Rep. David Kustoff (R-08)
https://kustoff.house.gov/

Rep. Steve Cohen (D-09)
https://cohen.house.gov/

Texas

Sen. John Cornyn (R)
https://www.cornyn.senate.gov/

Sen. Ted Cruz (R)
https://www.cruz.senate.gov/

Rep. Louie Gohmert (R-01)
https://gohmert.house.gov/

Rep. Ted Poe (R-02)
https://poe.house.gov/

Rep. Sam Johnson (R-03)
https://samjohnson.house.gov/

Rep. John Ratcliffe (R-04)

https://ratcliffe.house.gov/

Rep. Jeb Hensarling (R-05)
https://hensarling.house.gov/

Rep. Joe Barton (R-06)
https://joebarton.house.gov/

Rep. John Culberson (R-07)
https://culberson.house.gov/

Rep. Kevin Brady (R-08)
https://kevinbrady.house.gov/

Rep. Al Green (D-09)
https://algreen.house.gov/

Rep. Michael T. McCaul (R-10)
https://mccaul.house.gov/

Rep. K. Michael Conaway (R-11)
https://conaway.house.gov/

Rep. Kay Granger (R-12)
https://kaygranger.house.gov/

Rep. Mac Thornberry (R-13)
https://thornberry.house.gov/

Rep. Randy Weber (R-14)
https://weber.house.gov/

Rep. Vicente Gonzalez (D-15)
https://gonzalez.house.gov/

Rep. Beto O'Rourke (D-16)
http://orourke.house.gov/

Rep. Bill Flores (R-17)
https://flores.house.gov/

Rep. Sheila Jackson Lee (D-18)
https://jacksonlee.house.gov/

Rep. Jodey C. Arrington (R-19)
https://arrington.house.gov/

Rep. Joaquin Castro (D-20)
https://castro.house.gov/

Rep. Lamar Smith (R-21)
https://lamarsmith.house.gov/

Rep. Pete Olson (R-22)
https://olson.house.gov/

Rep. Will Hurd (R-23)
https://hurd.house.gov/

Rep. Kenny Marchant (R-24)
https://marchant.house.gov/

Rep. Roger Williams (R-25)
https://williams.house.gov/

Rep. Michael Burgess (R-26)
https://burgess.house.gov/

Vacant (District 27)

Rep. Henry Cuellar (D-28)
https://cuellar.house.gov/

Rep. Gene Green (D-29)
https://green.house.gov/

Rep. Eddie Bernice Johnson (D-30)
https://ebjohnson.house.gov/

Rep. John Carter (R-31)
https://carter.house.gov/

Rep. Pete Sessions (R-32)
https://sessions.house.gov/

Rep. Marc Veasey (D-33)

https://veasey.house.gov/

Rep. Filemon Vela (D-34)
https://vela.house.gov/

Rep. Lloyd Doggett (D-35)
https://doggett.house.gov/

Rep. Brian Babin (R-36)
https://babin.house.gov/

Utah

Sen. Orrin G. Hatch (R)
https://www.hatch.senate.gov/public/

Sen. Mike Lee (R)
https://www.lee.senate.gov/public/

Rep. Rob Bishop (R-01)
https://robbishop.house.gov/

Rep. Chris Stewart (R-02)
https://stewart.house.gov/

Rep. John R. Curtis (R-03)
https://curtis.house.gov/

Rep. Mia Love (R-04)
https://love.house.gov/

Vermont

Sen. Patrick J. Leahy (D)
https://www.leahy.senate.gov/

Sen. Bernard Sanders (I)
https://www.sanders.senate.gov/

Rep. Peter Welch (D-At Large)
https://welch.house.gov/

Virgin Islands

Del. Stacey Plaskett (D-At Large)
https://plaskett.house.gov/

Virginia

Sen. Mark R. Warner (D)
https://www.warner.senate.gov/public/

Sen. Tim Kaine (D)
https://www.kaine.senate.gov/

Rep. Robert J. Wittman (R-01)
https://wittman.house.gov/

Rep. Scott Taylor (R-02)
https://taylor.house.gov/

Rep. Robert C. "Bobby" Scott (D-03)
https://bobbyscott.house.gov/

Rep. A. Donald McEachin (D-04)
https://mceachin.house.gov/

Rep. Thomas A. Garrett Jr. (R-05)
https://tomgarrett.house.gov/

Rep. Bob Goodlatte (R-06)
https://goodlatte.house.gov/

Rep. Dave Brat (R-07)
https://brat.house.gov/

Rep. Don Beyer (D-08)
https://beyer.house.gov/

Rep. Morgan Griffith (R-09)
https://morgangriffith.house.gov/

Rep. Barbara Comstock (R-10)
https://comstock.house.gov/

Rep. Gerald E. "Gerry" Connolly (D-11)
https://connolly.house.gov/

Washington

Sen. Patty Murray (D)
https://www.murray.senate.gov/public/

Sen. Maria Cantwell (D)
https://www.cantwell.senate.gov/

Rep. Suzan DelBene (D-01)
https://delbene.house.gov/

Rep. Rick Larsen (D-02)
https://larsen.house.gov/

Rep. Jaime Herrera Beutler (R-03)
https://herrerabeutler.house.gov/

Rep. Dan Newhouse (R-04)
https://newhouse.house.gov/

Rep. Cathy McMorris Rodgers (R-05)
https://mcmorris.house.gov/

Rep. Derek Kilmer (D-06)
http://kilmer.house.gov/

Pramila Jayapal (D-07)
https://jayapal.house.gov/

Rep. David G. Reichert (R-08)
https://reichert.house.gov/

Rep. Adam Smith (D-09)
https://adamsmith.house.gov/

Rep. Denny Heck (D-10)
https://dennyheck.house.gov/

West Virginia

Sen. Joe Manchin III (D)
https://www.manchin.senate.gov/

Sen. Shelley Moore Capito (R)
https://www.capito.senate.gov/

Rep. David McKinley (R-01)
https://mckinley.house.gov/

Rep. Alex Mooney (R-02)
https://mooney.house.gov/

Rep. Evan Jenkins (R-03)
https://evanjenkins.house.gov/

Wisconsin

Sen. Ron Johnson (R)
https://www.ronjohnson.senate.gov/public/

Sen. Tammy Baldwin (D)
https://www.baldwin.senate.gov/

Rep. Paul D. Ryan (R-01)
https://paulryan.house.gov/

Rep. Mark Pocan (D-02)
https://pocan.house.gov/

Rep. Ron Kind (D-03)
https://kind.house.gov/

Rep. Gwen Moore (D-04)
https://gwenmoore.house.gov/

Rep. F. James Sensenbrenner (R-05)

https://sensenbrenner.house.gov/

Rep. Glenn Grothman (R-06)
https://grothman.house.gov/

Rep. Sean P. Duffy (R-07)
https://duffy.house.gov/

Rep. Mike Gallagher (R-08)
https://gallagher.house.gov/

Wyoming

Sen. Michael B. Enzi (R)
https://www.enzi.senate.gov/public/

Sen. John Barrasso (R)
https://www.barrasso.senate.gov/public/

Rep. Liz Cheney (R-At Large)
https://cheney.house.gov/

Appendix B

Congressional Committees

This appendix lists the committees and related websites for the 115th Congress's House, Senate, and Joint committees.

United States House of Representatives
https://www.house.gov/

Standing Committees

Committee on Agriculture
https://agriculture.house.gov/
Chairman: K. Michael Conway (R), Texas
Ranking Member: Collin C. Peterson (D), Minnesota

Committee on Appropriations
https://appropriations.house.gov/
Chairman: Rodney P. Frelinghuysen, (R), New Jersey
Ranking Member: Nita Lowey (D), New York

Committee on Armed Services
https://armedservices.house.gov/
Chairman: Mac Thornberry (R), Texas
Ranking Member: Adam Smith (D), Washington

Committee on the Budget
http://budget.house.gov/

Chairman: Steve Womack, (R), Arkansas
Ranking Member: John A. Yarmuth, (D), Kentucky

Committee on Education and the Workforce
https://edworkforce.house.gov/
Chairman: Virginia Foxx, (R) North Carolina
Ranking Member: Robert C. "Bobby" Scott (D), Virginia

Committee on Energy and Commerce
https://energycommerce.house.gov/
Chairman: Greg Walden (R), Oregon
Ranking Member: Frank Pallone, Jr. (D), New Jersey

Committee on Ethics
https://ethics.house.gov/
Chairman: Susan W. Brooks, (R), Indiana
Ranking Member: Theodore E. Deutch, (D), Florida

Committee on Financial Services
https://financialservices.house.gov/
Chairman: Jeb Hensarling (R), Texas
Ranking Member: Maxine Waters (D), California

Committee on Foreign Affairs
https://foreignaffairs.house.gov/
Chairman: Ed Royce (R), California
Ranking Member: Eliot Engel (D), New York

Committee on Homeland Security
https://homeland.house.gov/
Chairman: Michael T. McCaul (R), Texas
Ranking Member: Bennie G. Thompson (D), Mississippi

Committee on House Administration
https://cha.house.gov/
Chairman: Gregg Harper (R), Mississippi
Ranking Member: Robert Brady (D), Pennsylvania

Committee on the Judiciary
https://judiciary.house.gov/
Chairman: Bob Goodlatte (R), Virginia
Ranking Member: Jerrold Naddler (D), New York

Committee on Natural Resources
https://naturalresources.house.gov/
Chairman: Rob Bishop (R), Utah
Ranking Member: Raul Grijalva (D), Arizona

Committee on Oversight and Government Reform
https://oversight.house.gov/
Chairman: Trey Gowdy (R), South Carolina
Ranking Member: Elijah Cummings (D), Maryland

Committee on Rules
https://rules.house.gov/
Chairman: Pete Sessions (R), Texas
Ranking Member: James P. McGovern (D), Massachusetts

Committee on Science, Space, and Technology
https://science.house.gov/
Chairman: Lamar Smith (R), Texas
Ranking Member: Eddie Bernice Johnson (D), Texas

Committee on Small Business
https://smallbusiness.house.gov/
Chairman: Steve Chabot (R), Ohio
Ranking Member: Nydia M. Velazquez (D), New York

Committee on Transportation and Infrastructure
https://transportation.house.gov/
Chairman: Bill Shuster (R), Pennsylvania
Ranking Member: Peter DeFazio (D), Oregon

Committee on Veterans' Affairs
https://veterans.house.gov/
Chairman: David P. Roe, (R), Tennessee
Ranking Member: Timothy J. Walz, (D), Minnesota

Committee on Ways and Means
https://waysandmeans.house.gov/
Chairman: Kevin Brady (R), Texas
Ranking Member: Richard E. Neal, (D), Massachusetts

Select and Special Committees

House Permanent Select Committee on Intelligence
https://intelligence.house.gov/

Chairman: K. Michael Conaway, (R), Texas
Ranking Member: Adam Schiff (D), California

United States Senate
https://www.senate.gov/

Standing Committees

Committee on Agriculture, Nutrition, and Forestry
https://www.agriculture.senate.gov/
Chairman: Pat Roberts (R), Kansas
Ranking Member: Debbie Stabenow (D), Michigan

Committee on Appropriations
https://www.appropriations.senate.gov/
Chairman: Richard Shelby (R), Alabama
Vice Chairman: Patrick J. Leahy (D), Vermont

Committee on Armed Services
https://www.armed-services.senate.gov/
Chairman: John McCain (R), Arizona
Ranking Member: Jack Reed (D), Rhode Island

Committee on Banking, Housing, and Urban Affairs
https://www.banking.senate.gov/public/
Chairman: Mike Crapo (R), Idaho
Vice Chairman: Sherrod Brown (D), Ohio

Committee on the Budget
https://www.budget.senate.gov/
Chairman: Michael B. Enzi (R), Wyoming
Vice Chairman: Bernie Sanders (I), Vermont

Committee on Commerce, Science, and Transportation
https://www.commerce.senate.gov/public/
Chairman: John Thune (R), South Dakota
Ranking Member: Bill Nelson (D), Florida

Committee on Energy and Natural Resources
https://www.energy.senate.gov/public/
Chairman: Lisa Murkowski (R), Alaska
Ranking Member: Maria Cantwell (D), Washington

Committee on Environment and Public Works
https://www.epw.senate.gov/public/
Chairman: John Barraso (R), Wyoming
Ranking Member: Tom Carper (D), Delaware

Committee on Finance
https://www.finance.senate.gov/
Chairman: Orrin G. Hatch (R), Utah
Ranking Member: Ron Wyden (D), Oregon

Committee on Foreign Relations
https://www.foreign.senate.gov/
Chairman: Bob Corker (R), Tennessee
Ranking Member: Bob Menendez (D), New Jersey

Committee on Health, Education, Labor, and Pensions
https://www.help.senate.gov/
Chairman: Lamar Alexander (R), Tennessee
Ranking Member: Patty Murray, (D), Washington

Committee on Homeland Security and Governmental Affairs
https://www.hsgac.senate.gov/
Chairman: Ron Johnson (R), Wisconsin
Ranking Member: Claire McCaskill (D), Missouri

Committee on the Judiciary
https://www.judiciary.senate.gov/
Chairman: Chuck Grassley (R), Iowa
Ranking Member: Diane Feinstein, (D) California

Committee on Rules and Administration
https://www.rules.senate.gov/
Chairman: Roy Blunt (R), Missouri
Ranking member: Amy Klobuchar (D), Minnesota

Committee on Small Business and Entrepreneurship
https://www.sbc.senate.gov/public/
Chairman: James E. Risch (R), Idaho
Ranking Member: Bob Cardin (D), Maryland

Committee on Veterans' Affairs
https://www.veterans.senate.gov/
Chairman: Johnny Isakson (R), Georgia

Ranking Member: Jon Tester (D), Montana

Special, Select, and Other Committees

Committee on Indian Affairs
https://www.indian.senate.gov/
Chairman: John Hoeven (R), North Dakota
Ranking Member: Tom Udall (D), New Mexico

Select Committee on Ethics
https://www.ethics.senate.gov/public/
Chairman: Johnny Isakson (R), Georgia
Vice Chariman: Christopher Coons (D), Delaware

Select Committee on Intelligence
https://www.intelligence.senate.gov/
Chairman: Richard Burr (R), North Carolina
Vice Chairman: Mark Warner (D), Virginia

Special Committee on Aging
https://www.aging.senate.gov/
Chairman: Susan M. Collins (R), Maine
Ranking Member: Robert P. Casey (D), Pennsylvania

Joint Committees

Joint Committee on Printing
https://cha.house.gov/jointcommittees/joint-committee-on-printing/
Chairman: Roy Blunt (R), Missouri
Vice Chairman: Rodney Davis (R), Illinois

Joint Committee on Taxation
https://www.jct.gov/
Chairman: Orrin G. Hatch (R), Utah
Vice Chairman: Kevin Brady (R), Texas

Joint Committee on the Library
https://cha.house.gov/jointcommittees/joint-committee-library/
Chairman: Gregg Harper (R), Mississippi
Vice Chairman: Roy Blunt (R), Missouri

Joint Economic Committee
https://www.jec.senate.gov/public/
Chairman: Erik Paulsen (R), Minnesota

Ranking Member: Martin Heinrich (D), New Mexico

Appendix C

U.S. Embassies Abroad

Please note: Consulate offices are not included. Countries that share an embassy have the embassy country location clearly marked.

The information in this section is from https://www.usembassy.gov/, a State Department website.

A

Afghanistan (Kabul)
https://af.usembassy.gov/

Albania (Tirana)
https://al.usembassy.gov/

Algeria (Algiers)
https://dz.usembassy.gov/

Andorra (Madrid, Spain)
https://es.usembassy.gov/

Angola (Luanda)
https://ao.usembassy.gov/

Antigua and Barbuda (Barbados and the Eastern Caribbean)
https://bb.usembassy.gov/

Argentina (Buenos Aires)
https://ar.usembassy.gov/embassy/

Armenia (Yerevan)
https://am.usembassy.gov/

Australia (Canberra)
https://au.usembassy.gov/

Austria (Vienna)
https://at.usembassy.gov/

Azerbaijan (Baku)
https://az.usembassy.gov/

B

Bahamas, The (Nassau)
https://bs.usembassy.gov/

Bahrain (Manama)
https://bh.usembassy.gov/

Bangladesh (Dhaka)
https://bd.usembassy.gov/

Barbados (Barbados and the Eastern Caribbean)
https://bb.usembassy.gov/

Belarus (Minsk)
https://by.usembassy.gov/

Belgium (Brussels)
https://be.usembassy.gov/

Belize (Belmopan)
https://bz.usembassy.gov/

Benin (Cotonou)
https://bj.usembassy.gov/

Bolivia (La Paz)
https://bo.usembassy.gov/

Bosnia and Herzegovina (Sarajevo)
https://ba.usembassy.gov/

Botswana (Gaborone)
https://bw.usembassy.gov/

Brazil (Brasilia)
https://br.usembassy.gov/embassy-consulates/embassy/

Brunei (Bandar Seri Begawan)
https://bn.usembassy.gov/

Bulgaria (Sofia)
https://bg.usembassy.gov/

Burkina Faso (Ouagadougou)
https://bf.usembassy.gov/

Burma (Rangoon)
https://mm.usembassy.gov/

Burundi (Bujumbura)
https://bi.usembassy.gov/

C

Cambodia (Phnom Penh)
https://kh.usembassy.gov/

Cameroon (Yaounde)
https://cm.usembassy.gov/

Canada (Ottawa)
https://ca.usembassy.gov/embassy-and-consulates-to-mark-black-history-month-through-the-arts/

Cape Verde (Praia)
https://cv.usembassy.gov/

Central African Republic (Bangui)
https://cf.usembassy.gov/

Chad (N'Djamena)
https://td.usembassy.gov/

Chile (Santiago)
https://cl.usembassy.gov/

China (Beijing)
https://china.usembassy-china.org.cn/

Colombia (Bogota)
https://co.usembassy.gov/

Congo, Democratic Republic of the (Kinshasa)
https://cd.usembassy.gov/

Congo, Republic of the (Brazzaville)
https://cg.usembassy.gov/

Costa Rica (San Jose)
https://cr.usembassy.gov/

Cote d'Ivoire (Abidjan)
https://ci.usembassy.gov/

Croatia (Zagreb)
https://hr.usembassy.gov/

Cuba (Havana)
https://cu.usembassy.gov/

Curacao (U.S. Consulate General in Curacao and U.S. Chief Mission to the Dutch Caribbean)
https://cw.usconsulate.gov/

Cyprus (Nicosia)
https://cy.usembassy.gov/

Czech Republic (Prague)
https://cz.usembassy.gov/

D

Denmark (Copenhagen)
https://dk.usembassy.gov/

Djibouti (Djibouti)
https://dj.usembassy.gov/

Dominica (Barbados and the Eastern Caribbean)
https://bb.usembassy.gov/

Dominican Republic (Santo Domingo)
https://do.usembassy.gov/

E

Ecuador (Quito)
https://ec.usembassy.gov/

Egypt (Cairo)
https://eg.usembassy.gov/

El Salvador (San Salvador)
https://sv.usembassy.gov/

Equatorial Guinea (Malabo)
https://gq.usembassy.gov/

Eritrea (Asmara)
https://er.usembassy.gov/

Estonia (Tallinn)
https://ee.usembassy.gov/

Ethiopia (Addis Ababa)
https://et.usembassy.gov/

F

Fiji (Suva)
https://fj.usembassy.gov/

Finland (Helsinki)
https://fi.usembassy.gov/

France (Paris)
https://fr.usembassy.gov/embassy-consulates/

G

Gabon (Libreville)
https://ga.usembassy.gov/

Gambia, The (Banjul)
https://gm.usembassy.gov/

Georgia (Tbilisi)
https://ge.usembassy.gov/

Germany (Berlin)

https://de.usembassy.gov/embassy-consulates/embassy/

Ghana (Accra)
https://www.usembassy.gov/ghana/

Greece (Athens)
https://gr.usembassy.gov/

Grenada (Barbados and the Eastern Caribbean)
https://bb.usembassy.gov/ v/

Guatemala (Guatemala City)
https://gt.usembassy.gov/

Guinea (Conakry)
https://gn.usembassy.gov/

Guinea-Bissau (Virtual Presence Post)
https://gw.usmission.gov/

Guyana (Georgetown)
https://gy.usembassy.gov/

H

Haiti (Port-au-Prince)
https://ht.usembassy.gov/

Honduras (Tegucigalpa)
https://hn.usembassy.gov/

Hong Kong (Hong Kong and Macau)
https://hk.usconsulate.gov/

Hungary (Budapest)
https://hu.usembassy.gov/

I

Iceland (Reykjavik)
https://is.usembassy.gov/

India (New Delhi)
https://in.usembassy.gov/

Indonesia (Jakarta)
https://id.usembassy.gov/

Iran (Virtual Embassy)
https://ir.usembassy.gov/
Please note: The United States does not currently have diplomatic relations with Iran.

Iraq (Baghdad)
https://iq.usembassy.gov/

Ireland (Dublin)
https://ie.usembassy.gov/embassy/

Israel (Tel Aviv)
https://il.usembassy.gov/

Italy (Rome)
https://it.usembassy.gov/

J

Jamaica (Kingston)

Japan (Tokyo)
https://jp.usembassy.gov/

Jordan (Amman)
https://jo.usembassy.gov/

K

Kazakhstan (Astana)
https://kz.usembassy.gov/

Kenya (Nairobi)
https://ke.usembassy.gov/

Korea, South
https://kr.usembassy.gov/

Kosovo (Pristina)
https://xk.usembassy.gov/

Kuwait (Kuwait City)
https://kw.usembassy.gov/

Kyrgyz Republic (Bishkek)
https://kg.usembassy.gov/

L

Laos (Vientiane)
https://la.usembassy.gov/

Latvia (Riga)
https://lv.usembassy.gov/

Lebanon (Beirut)
https://lb.usembassy.gov/

Lesotho (Maseru)
https://ls.usembassy.gov/

Liberia (Monrovia)
https://lr.usembassy.gov/

Libya (Tripoli)
https://ly.usembassy.gov/

Lithuania (Vilnius)
https://lt.usembassy.gov/

Luxembourg (Luxembourg)
https://lu.usembassy.gov/

M

Macau (Hong Kong and Macau)
https://hk.usconsulate.gov/

Macedonia (Skopje)
https://mk.usembassy.gov/

Madagascar (Antananarivo)
https://mg.usembassy.gov/

Malawi (Lilongwe)
https://mw.usembassy.gov/

Malaysia (Kuala Lumpur)
https://my.usembassy.gov/embassy/

Mali (Bamako)
https://ml.usembassy.gov/

Malta (Valletta)
https://ml.usembassy.gov/

Marshall Islands (Majuro)
https://mh.usembassy.gov/

Mauritania (Nouakchott)
https://mr.usembassy.gov/

Mauritius (Port Louis)
https://mu.usembassy.gov/

Mexico (Mexico City)
https://mx.usembassy.gov/embassy-consulates/embassy/

Micronesia, Federated States of (Kolonia)
https://fm.usembassy.gov/

Moldova (Chisinau)
https://md.usembassy.gov/

Mongolia (Ulaanbaatar)
https://mn.usembassy.gov/

Montenegro (Podgorica)
https://me.usembassy.gov/

Morocco (Rabat)
https://ma.usembassy.gov/

Mozambique (Maputo)
https://mz.usembassy.gov/

N

Namibia (Windhoek)
https://na.usembassy.gov/

Nepal (Kathmandu)
https://np.usembassy.gov/

Netherlands (The Hague)
https://nl.usembassy.gov/

New Zealand (Wellington)
https://nz.usembassy.gov/embassy-consulates/

Nicaragua (Managua)
https://ni.usembassy.gov/

Niger (Niamey)
https://ne.usembassy.gov/

Nigeria (Abuja)
https://ng.usembassy.gov/

Norway (Oslo)
https://no.usembassy.gov/

O

Oman (Muscat)
https://om.usembassy.gov/

P

Pakistan (Islamabad)
https://pk.usembassy.gov/

Palau, Republic of (Koror)
https://pw.usembassy.gov/

Panama (Panama City)
https://pa.usembassy.gov/

Papua New Guinea (Papua New Guinea, Solomon Islands, and Vanuatu)
https://pg.usembassy.gov/

Paraguay (Asuncion)
https://py.usembassy.gov/

Peru (Lima)
https://pe.usembassy.gov/

Philippines (Manila)
https://ph.usembassy.gov/

Poland (Warsaw)
https://pl.usembassy.gov/embassy-consulate/embassy/

Portugal (Lisbon)
https://pt.usembassy.gov/

Q

Qatar (Doha)
https://qa.usembassy.gov/

R

Romania (Bucharest)
https://ro.usembassy.gov/

Russia (Moscow)
https://ru.usembassy.gov/

Rwanda (Kigali)
https://rw.usembassy.gov/

S

Saint Kitts and Nevis (Barbados and the Eastern Caribbean)
https://bb.usembassy.gov/

Saint Lucia (Barbados and the Eastern Caribbean)
https://bb.usembassy.gov/

Saint Vincent and the Grenadines (Barbados and the Eastern Caribbean)
https://bb.usembassy.gov/

Samoa (Apia)
https://ws.usembassy.gov/embassy/

Saudi Arabia (Riyadh)
https://sa.usembassy.gov/

Senegal (Dakar)
https://sn.usembassy.gov/

Serbia (Belgrade)
https://rs.usembassy.gov/

Sierra Leone (Freetown)
https://sl.usembassy.gov/u-s-citizen-services/

Singapore (Singapore)
https://sg.usembassy.gov/

Slovakia (Bratislava)
https://sk.usembassy.gov/

Slovenia (Ljubljana)
https://si.usembassy.gov/

Solomon Islands (Papua New Guinea, Solomon Islands, and Vanuatu)
https://pg.usembassy.gov/

Somalia (U.S. Mission to Somalia)
https://so.usmission.gov/

South Africa (Pretoria)
https://za.usembassy.gov/embassy-consulate-social-media-properties/

South Sudan (Juba)
https://ss.usembassy.gov/

Spain(Madrid)
https://es.usembassy.gov/

Sri Lanka
https://lk.usembassy.gov/

Sudan (Khartoum)
https://sd.usembassy.gov/

Suriname (Paramaribo)
https://sr.usembassy.gov/

Swaziland(Mbabane)
https://sz.usembassy.gov/

Sweden (Stockholm)
https://se.usembassy.gov/embassy/

Switzerland (Bern)
https://ch.usembassy.gov/

Syria (Damascus)
https://sy.usembassy.gov/

T

Tajikistan (Dushanbe)
https://tj.usembassy.gov/

Tanzania (Dar es Salaam)
https://tz.usembassy.gov/

Thailand(Bangkok)
https://th.usembassy.gov/

Timor-Leste (Dili)
https://tl.usembassy.gov/

Togo (Lome)
https://tg.usembassy.gov/

Togo
https://tg.usembassy.gov/

Tunisia (Tunis)
https://tn.usembassy.gov/

Turkey (Ankara)
https://tr.usembassy.gov/

Turkmenistan (Ashgabat)
https://tm.usembassy.gov/

U

Uganda (Kampala)
https://ug.usembassy.gov/embassy/kampala/

Ukraine (Kyiv)
https://ua.usembassy.gov/

United Arab Emirates (Abu Dhabi)
https://ae.usembassy.gov/

United Kingdom (London)
https://uk.usembassy.gov/embassy-consulate-closures-christmas-holidays/

Uruguay (Montevideo)
https://uy.usembassy.gov/

U.S. Mission to the African Union
https://www.usau.usmission.gov/

U.S. Mission to ASEAN
https://asean.usmission.gov/

U.S. Mission to the ICAO
https://icao.usmission.gov/

U.S. Mission to the International Organizations in Vienna
https://vienna.usmission.gov/

U.S. Mission to the EU
https://useu.usmission.gov/

U.S. Mission to NATO
https://nato.usmission.gov/

U.S. Mission to the OAS
https://usoas.usmission.gov/

U.S. Mission to the OECD
https://usoecd.usmission.gov/

U.S. Mission to the OSCE
https://osce.usmission.gov/

U.S. Mission to the U.N.: Geneva
https://geneva.usmission.gov/

U.S. Mission to the U.N.: Rome
https://usunrome.usmission.gov/

U.S. Mission to UNESCO
https://unesco.usmission.gov/

Uzbekistan (Tashkent)
https://uz.usembassy.gov/

V

Vanuatu (Papua New Guinea, Solomon Islands, and Vanuatu)
https://pg.usembassy.gov/

Vatican, The (Holy See)
https://va.usembassy.gov/

Venezuela (Caracas)
https://ve.usembassy.gov/

Vietnam (Hanoi)
https://vn.usembassy.gov/

Y

Yemen (Sana'a)
https://ye.usembassy.gov/

Z

Zambia (Lusaka)
https://zm.usembassy.gov/embassy/

Zimbabwe (Harare)
https://zw.usembassy.gov/

Appendix D

Foreign Embassies in the United States

A

Afghanistan
https://www.afghanembassy.us/

Algeria
http://www.algerianembassy.org/

Angola
http://www.angola.org/

Argentina
http://www.embassyofargentina.us/

Armenia
http://www.usa.mfa.am/en/

Australia
https://usa.embassy.gov.au/

Austria
http://www.austria.org/

Azerbaijan
http://washington.mfa.gov.az/

B

Bahrain
http://www.bahrainembassy.org/

Bangladesh
http://www.bdembassyusa.org/

Belarus
http://usa.mfa.gov.by/en/

Belize
https://www.belizeembassyusa.mfa.gov.bz/

Benin
http://beninembassy.us/

Bosnia and Herzegovina
http://www.bhembassy.org/

Botswana
http://www.botswanaembassy.org/

Brazil

http://washington.itamaraty.gov.br/pt-br/

Brunei
http://www.bruneiembassy.org/

Bulgaria
www.bulgaria-embassy.org/en/homepage/

Burkina Faso
https://burkina-usa.org/

Burundi
http://www.burundiembassydc-usa.org/

C

Cambodia
http://www.embassyofcambodia.org/

Cameroon
http://cameroonembassyusa.org/ca-musa/

Canada
http: www.canadianembassy.org

Cape Verde
http://www.embcv-usa.gov.cv/

Central African Republic
http://rcawashington.org/

Chad
http://www.chadembassy.us/

Chile
https://chile.gob.cl/en/

China
http://www.china-embassy.org/chn/

Colombia
http://www.colombiaemb.org/

Comoros
http://www.comorosembassy.org/

Congo, Democratic Republic of the
https://ambardcusa.org/

Congo, Republic of the
http://www.ambacongo-us.org/

Costa Rica
http://www.costarica-embassy.org/

Cote d'Ivoire
http://www.ambaciusa.org/Site/

Croatia
http://us.mvep.hr/

Cyprus
http://www.cyprusembassy.net/home/

Czech Republic
http://www.mzv.cz/jnp/

D

Denmark
http://usa.um.dk/

Dominican Republic
http://www.domrep.org/

E

Ecuador
http://www.ecuador.org/nuevosite/

Egypt
http://www.egyptembassy.net/

El Salvador

http://www.elsalvador.org/

Equatorial Guinea
https://www.egembassydc.com/

Eritrea
http://www.embassyeritrea.org/

Estonia
http://www.estemb.org/

Ethiopia
http://www.ethiopianembassy.org/

European Union
https://eeas.europa.eu/delegations/united-states-america_en/

F

Fiji
https://www.fijiembassydc.com/

Finland
http://www.finland.org/Public/Default.aspx

France
https://www.info-france-usa.org/

G

Gabon
https://www.gabonembassyusa.org/

Georgia
http://georgiaembassyusa.org/

Germany
https://www.germany.info/

Ghana
https://www.ghanaembassydc.org/

Greece
https://www.mfa.gr/

Grenada
http://www.grenadaembassyusa.org/

Guatemala
http://guatemalaembassyusa.org/

Guinea
http://www.guineaembassyusa.com/

Guyana
http://www.guyana.org/

H

Haiti
http://haiti.org/

Holy See
https://holyseemission.org/

Honduras
http://www.hondurasemb.org/site/

Hungary
http://washington.kormany.hu/

I

Iceland
https://www.iceland.is/

India
https://www.indianembassy.org/

Indonesia
http://www.embassyofindonesia.org/

Iraq
http://www.iraqiembassy.us/

Ireland
https://www.dfa.ie/irish-embassy/USA/

Israel
http://www.israelemb.org/washington/pages/default.aspx

Italy
https://ambwashingtondc.esteri.it/ambasciata_washington/it

J

Jamaica
http://www.embassyofjamaica.org/

Japan
http://www.us.emb-japan.go.jp/itprtop_ja/index.html

Jordan
http://www.jordanembassyus.org/

K

Kazakhstan
https://www.kazakhembus.com/

Kenya
http://www.kenyaembassy.com/

Korea, South
http://overseas.mofa.go.kr/us-ko/index.do/

Kosovo
http://ambasada-ks.net/

Kuwait
http://www.kuwaitembassy.us/

Kyrgyz Republic
https://www.kgembassy.org/en/

L

Laos
http://www.laoembassy.com/

Latvia
http://www.mfa.gov.lv/

Lebanon
http://www.lebanonembassyus.org/

Liberia
http://www.liberianembassyus.org/

Liechtenstein
http://www.liechtensteinusa.org/

Lithuania
http://usa.mfa.lt/

Luxembourg
http://washington.mae.lu/en

M

Madagascar
http://www.madagascar-embassy.org/en/

Malawi
http://www.malawiembassy-dc.org/

Malaysia
http://www.kln.gov.my/web/guest/home

Mali
http://www.maliembassy.us/

Malta
https://foreignaffairs.gov.mt/en/Pages/Home.aspx

Marshall Islands
http://www.rmiembassyus.org/

Mauritius

http://www1.govmu.org/portal/sites/mfamission/washington/index.htm

Mexico
https://embamex.sre.gob.mx/eua/index.php/es/

Micronesia, Federated States of
http://www.fsmembassydc.org/

Moldova
http://www.sua.mfa.md/

Monaco
http://monacodc.org/

Mongolia
http://mongolianembassy.us/

Morocco
http://www.embassyofmorocco.us/

Mozambique
http://www.embamoc-usa.org/

Myanmar
http://www.mewashingtondc.org/

N
Namibia
http://www.namibiaembassyusa.org/

Nepal
http://us.nepalembassy.gov.np/

Netherlands
https://www.netherlandsworldwide.nl/countries/united-states/

New Zealand
https://www.mfat.govt.nz/en/embassies/

Niger
http://www.embassyofniger.org/

Nigeria
http://www.nigeriaembassyusa.org/

Norway
https://www.norway.no/en/usa

O

P
Pakistan
http://embassyofpakistanusa.org/

Palau
http://www.palauembassy.com/

Panama
http://www.embassyofpanama.org/

Papua New Guinea
http://www.pngembassy.org/

Paraguay
http://www2.mre.gov.py/

Peru
https://www.embassyofperu.org/

Philippines
http://www.philippineembassy-usa.org/

Poland
http://washington.mfa.gov.pl/en/

Portugal
http://www.embassyportugal-us.org/

Q
R
Romania

http://washington.mae.ro/

Russia
http://www.russianembassy.org/

Rwanda
https://rwandaembassy.org/

S

Saint Vincent and the Grenadines
http://wa.embassy.gov.vc/washington/

Saudi Arabia
https://www.saudiembassy.net/

Senegal
http://www.ambasenegal-us.org/

Serbia
http://www.washington.mfa.gov.rs/index.php

Seychelles
http://www.mfa.gov.sc/

Sierra Leone
http://embassyofsierraleone.net/

Singapore
https://www.mfa.gov.sg/content/mfa/index.html/

Slovakia
http://www.mzv.sk/

Slovenia
http://www.washington.embassy.si/

South Africa
http://www.saembassy.org/

South Sudan
http://www.southsudanembassyusa.org/

Spain
http://www.exteriores.gob.es/Embajadas/WASHINGTON/en/Pages/inicio2.aspx

Sri Lanka
http://slembassyusa.org/

Suriname
http://www.surinameembassy.org/

Swaziland
http://www.gov.sz/

Sweden
https://www.swedenabroad.se/

Switzerland
https://www.eda.admin.ch/countries/usa/en/home.html

T

Taiwan

Tajikistan
http://www.tjus.org/

Tanzania
http://tanzaniaembassy-us.org/

Thailand
http://thaiembdc.org/

Timor-Leste
http://www.timorlesteembassy.org/

Togo
http://embassyoftogousa.com/

Trinidad and Tobago

https://foreign.gov.tt/missions-consuls/tt-missions-abroad/diplomatic-missions/embassy-washington-dc-us/

Tunisia
https://www.tunisianembassy.org/

Turkey
http://vasington.be.mfa.gov.tr/Mission/

Turkmenistan
http://turkmenistanembassy.us/

U

Uganda
https://washington.mofa.go.ug/

Ukraine
http://usa.mfa.gov.ua/ua

United Arab Emirates
https://www.uae-embassy.org/

United Kingdom
https://www.gov.uk/

Uruguay
http://www.mrree.gub.uy/

Uzbekistan
http://www.uzbekistan.org/

V

Venezuela
http://eeuu.embajada.gob.ve/

Vietnam
http://vietnamembassy-usa.org/

Y

Yemen
http://www.yemenembassy.org/

Z

Zambia
http://www.zambiaembassy.org/

Zimbabwe
http://ww1.zimbabwe-embassy.us/

Index

AbilityOne, 252
Access Board, 345
Access to Archival Databases (AAD), 62
Accounts and Accounting: Federal Accounting Standards Advisory Board, 262
Acquisition.gov, 253
Acquisition One Source, 253
Actuaries: Joint Board for the Enrollment of Actuaries, 41
ADA Homepage, 339
Administration: Current administration, 385
Administration for Children and Families (ACF), 423; Child Welfare Information Gateway, 423; Developmental Disabilities Administration, 430; Family and Youth Services Bureau, 424; Low Income Home Energy Assistance Program, 434; Native Americans Administration, 425; Office of Child Care, 425; Office of Family Assistance, 435
Administration for Native Americans (ANA), 425
Administration on Aging (AoA), 286; Eldercare Locator, 278
Administration on Developmental Disabilities (AIDD), 430
Administrative Conference of the United States (ACUS), 248
Administrative Law: Administrative Decisions and Other Actions, 340
Administrative Office of the U.S. Courts: PACER: Public Access to Court Electronic Records, 350; U.S. Courts: The Federal Judiciary, 351
Admongo.gov, 158
Adolescent and School Health, 287
Adoption, Intercountry, 424
Adult Education: Defense Activity for Non-Traditional Education Support, 137; Office of Career, Technical, and Adult Education, 137; USA Learns, 138
Advanced Counterfeit Deterrence (ACD) Program, 52
Advancing Translational Sciences, National Center for, 298
Advisory Commission on Intergovernmental Relations (ACIR), 271
Advisory Council on Historic Preservation (ACHP), 62
Aeronautics Research Mission Directorate (ARMD), 411
Afghanistan: National Center for PTSD, 280; Wartime Contracting Commission, 253
Africa Command (AFRICOM), 96
Africa Fighting Malaria (AFM), 453
African Affairs, Bureau of, 330

African American History and Culture: National Museum, 83; National Museum of African Art, 83
African Growth and Opportunity Act (AGOA), 44
Agency for Healthcare Research and Quality (AHRQ), 295
Agency for International Development (USAID), 327; Faith-Based and Community Initiatives, 438; Famine Early Warning Systems Network, 336; President's Malaria Initiative, 282; USAID Knowledge Management (KM) Support, 80
Aging, National Institute on, 302
AgingStats.gov, 134
AGRICOLA: NAL Catalog, 13
Agricultural Marketing Service (AMS), 5
Agricultural Research Service (ARS), 5
Agriculture Department (USDA), 8; Agricultural Research Service, 5; *Amber Waves*, 7; Animal and Plant Health Inspection Service, 7; Animal Disease Traceability, 7; Animal Welfare, 228; Animal Welfare Information Center, 228; Beltsville Agricultural Research Center, 8; Carl Hayden Bee Research Center, 8; Census of Agriculture, 9; ChooseMyPlate.gov, 316; ChooseMyPlate for Kids, 159; Civil Rights, Office of the Assistant Secretary for, 345; Crop Explorer, 8; Economic Research Service, 9; Economics, Statistics, and Market Information System, 9; Faith-Based and Neighborhood Partnerships, 438; Farm Service Agency, 10; Food and Nutrition Information Center, 316; Food and Nutrition Service, 433; Food Distribution Programs, 434; Food Safety, 319; Food Safety and Inspection Service, 319; Foreign Agricultural Service, 11; Forestry Technical Resources, 20; Forest Service Recreational Activities, 85; Germplasm Resources Information Network, 11; GrainGenes, 11; Grain Inspection, Packers & Stockyards Administration, 12; Integrated Taxonomic Information System, 392; Joint Agricultural Weather Facility, 12; NAL Catalog (AGRICOLA), 13; NAL Digital Collections, 13; National Agricultural Law Center, 13; National Agricultural Library, 74; National Agricultural Library Digital Collections, 13; National Agricultural Statistics Service, 14; National Agroforestry Center, 20; National Arboretum, 14; National Institute of Food and Agriculture, 14; National Organic Program, 15; Natural Resources Conservation Service, 217; NRCS Soils, 15; Nutrition.gov, 317; Office of Public Health Science, 15; Office of the Assistant Secretary for Civil Rights, 345; Plants & Animals, 15; PLANTS Database, 16; Procurement, 258; Production, Supply and Distribution (PSD) Online, 16; Risk Management Agency, 16; Rural Development, 427; Rural Information Center, 427; Rural Utilities Service, 192; Small and Disadvantaged Business Utilization, 257; State Fact Sheets-ERS, 16; Supplemental Nutrition Assistance Program, 437; Telecommunications Program, 199; WIC Works Resource System, 318; World Agricultural Outlook Board, 17
Agriculture-EPA, 6
Agriculture Network Information Collaborative (AgNIC), 6
A Guide to the War of 1812, 64
AIDS Global Coordinator, 293
AIDSinfo, 275
AIDS Policy, Office of National, 291
AIDS Relief Emergency Plan, 293
Air and Space Museum, 82
AirCompare, 234
Air Education and Training Command (AETC), 89
Air Force, 90; Air Education and Training Command, 89; AirForce.com, 91; Air Mobility Command (AMC), 91; Air Reserve Personnel Center (ARPC), 91; Bands, 123; Civil Air Patrol (CAP), 110; D'Azzo Research Library, 69;

Exchange Service, 124; Los Angeles Air Force Base, 93; Materiel Command (AFMC), 90; Medical Service, 123; Office of Scientific Research, 105; Personnel Center (AFPC), 90; Rescue Coordination Center, 318; Research Laboratory (AFRL), 105; Reserve Command (AFRC), 90; Reserve Employer Support, 125; Space Command (AFSPC), 90; Twenty-Fifth Air Force (25 AF), 122; U.S. Air Force Live, 96; Wright-Patterson Air Force Base, 100
Air Force Academy, 155
Air Force Institute of Technology (AFIT), 151; D'Azzo Research Library, 69
Air Force Research Laboratory (AFRL), 105
AirNow, 239
Air Resources Laboratory (ARL), 219
Air University, 151; Library Index to Military Periodicals, 68; Muir S. Fairchild Research Information Center, 74
Alaska Natives: American Indian and Alaska Native Resources, 135
Alaska Science Center, 228
Alaska Volcano Observatory (AVO), 397
Alcohol, Tobacco, Firearms, and Explosives, Bureau of (BATFE), 354
Alcohol Abuse and Alcoholism, National Institute on (NIAAA), 303
Alcohol and Tobacco Tax and Trade Bureau (TTB), 21
Alcohol Policy Information System (APIS), 340
ALFRED: Archival Federal Reserve Economic Data, 30
Allergy and Infectious Diseases, National Institute of (NIAID), 299
Alternative and Renewable Fuels: Alternative Fuels and Data Center, 183; Bioenergies Technology Office, 183; Biomass Research, 184; Clean Cities, 184; Energy Efficiency and Renewable Energy Office, 185; Hydrogen and Fuel Cells Interagency Working Group, 184; National Renewable Energy Laboratory, 185
Alternative Farming Systems Information Center (AFSIC), 6
Alzheimer's Disease Education and Referral (ADEAR) Center, 276
AMBER Alert, 354
Amber Waves, 7
American Aging Association, 453
American Art Museum, Smithsonian (SAAM), 84
American Association of Retired People (AARP), 454
American Bar Association (ABA), 454
American Civil Liberties Union (ACLU), 454
American Community Survey (ACS), 129
American FactFinder, 130
American Folklife Center, 57
American Heart Association, 454
American History: National Museum, 83
American Indians: American Indian Health, 287; National Museum of the American Indian, 83
American Lung Association, 455
American Medical Association (AMA), 455
American Memory, 63
American Presidency Project, 388
American Psychiatric Association, 455
American Red Cross, 455
Americans with Disabilities Act (ADA), 339
America's Byways, 85
America's Heroes at Work (AHAW), 123
America's Historical Documents, 62
America's Most Wanted Criminals, 354
America's National Wildlife Refuge System, 214
America's Story from America's Library, 159
AmeriCorps, 438
Ames Educator Resource Center (ERC), 165
Ames Research Center, 412
Amnesty International, 456
Amtrak, 444
Anacostia Community Museum, 81
Animal & Veterinary-Center for Veterinary Medicine (CVM), 7

Animal and Plant Health Inspection Service (APHIS), 7
Animal Care and Use, Office of, 306
Animal Disease Traceability, 7
Animal Welfare, 228; Information Center, 228
Annapolis: Naval Academy at Annapolis, 156
Annual & Quarterly Services, 30
Anti-Defamation League, 456
Antitrust Division, 340
Appalachian Regional Commission (ARC), 426
Apparel: Office of Textiles and Apparel, 50
Archeology Program, 57
Architect of the Capitol (AOC), 377
Archives Library Information Center (ALIC), 68
Arctic Health, 295
Arctic Research Commission, 408
Argonne National Laboratory (ANL), 394
Arlington National Cemetery, 124
Armed Forces Court of Appeals, 351
Armed Forces Medical Examiner System (AFMES), 296
Armed Forces Retirement Home (AFRH), 124
Arms Control: Chemical Weapons Convention, 323; Nonproliferation and Disarmament Fund, 324; Verification and Compliance, 323
Armstrong Flight Research Center (AFRC), 416
Army, 97; Army Live, 91; Army Music, 127; Center for Army Lessons Learned (CALL), 92; Center of Military History, 66; Defense Forensics & Biometrics Agency (DFBA), 106; Exchange Service, 124; Financial Management, 100; GoArmy.com, 92; Heritage and Education Center, 67; Medical Research Institute of Infectious Diseases, 109; Military Academy at West Point, 156; OAC-SIM (Installation Management), 95; OASA(ALT) (Acquisition, Logistics, and Technology), 95; Publishing Directorate, 91; Redstone Arsenal, 95; Reserve Employer Support, 125; *Soldiers*, 96
Army Command and General Staff College (CGSC), 155
Army Corps of Engineers, 202; Coastal and Hydraulics Laboratory, 199; Cold Regions Research and Engineering Laboratory, 202; Construction Engineering Research Laboratory, 200; Engineer Research and Development Center, 200; Lakes Gateway, 85
Army Financial Management, 100
Army Intelligence and Security Command (INSCOM), 123
Army Logistics University, 152
Army Medical Research Institute of Infectious Diseases (USAMRIID), 109
Army Research Laboratory (ARL), 106
Army War College, 155
Arthritis and Musculoskeletal and Skin Diseases, National Institute (NIAMS), 300
Arts: Indian Arts and Crafts Board, 55; National Endowment for the Arts, 55; National Film Preservation Board, 56; National Gallery of Art, 82; Poetry and Literature Center of the Library of Congress, 56; U.S. Commission of Fine Arts, 56
ArtsEdge: The Kennedy Center's Arts Education Network, 138
Asia-Pacific Economic Cooperation, 456
Association of Southeast Asian Nations (ASEAN), 456
Association of Universities for Research in Astronomy (AURA), 457
Astrobiology: NASA, 393
Astronomy Resources at STScI, 412
Astrophysics Data System (ADS), 401
Atlantic Oceanographic and Meteorological Laboratory (AOML), 219
Atlantic States Marine Fisheries Commission (ASMFC), 17
Attorney General, Office of the, 362
ATV Safety Information Center, 449
Autism Coordinating Committee, Interagency, 290
Autism Information, 276

Automated Export System Direct (AESDirect), 45
Aviation Consumer Protection Division, 27
Aviation Weather Center (AWC), 239

Baby Names: Popular Baby Names, 88
Baldrige Performance Excellence Program (BPEP), 22
Bankruptcy Courts: United States Courts, 345
Banks and Financial Institutions: Export-Import Bank of the United States, 47, 459; Federal Financial Institutions Examination Council, 40; Federal Financing Bank, 263; HelpWithMyBank.gov, 28; National Credit Union Administration, 42
Barry Goldwater Scholarship Program, 152
Behavioral and Social Sciences Research, Office of (OBSSR), 306
Beltsville Agricultural Research Center (BARC), 8
Benefits.gov, 431
Benefits Review Board (BRB), 169
Ben's Guide to U.S. Government, 159
Bilateral Relations Fact Sheets, 324
Bioenergies Technology Office (BETO), 183
Bioethics Department, 288
Biographical Directory of the United States Congress, 371
Biomass Research, 184
Biomedical Communications, Lister Hill National Center for, 308
Biomedical Imaging and Bioengineering, National Institute of, 300
Biometrics, 202
Biometrics Resource Center, 203
Biosecurity Advisory Board (NSABB), 405
Black Americans in Congress, 372
BLS Career Information, 159
Blue Angels, 91
Blue Ribbon Commission on America's Nuclear Future, 188
Board of Governors of the Federal Reserve System (FRB), 33
Boating Safety Resource Center, 452
Borders: U.S.-Mexico Border 2020 Program, 219
Botanic Garden, 84
Broadband: National Broadband Plan, 198; USDA Telecommunications Program, 199
Broadcasting Board of Governors (BBG), 325
Brookhaven National Laboratory (BNL), 395
Budget of the United States Government, 262
Building America, 185
Building Energy Codes Program (BECP), 185
Bureau of African Affairs, 330
Bureau of Alcohol, Tobacco, Firearms, and Explosives (BATFE), 354
Bureau of Arms Control, Verification, and Compliance (AVC), 323
Bureau of Counterterrorism (CT), 334
Bureau of Diplomatic Security (DS), 325
Bureau of Economic Analysis (BEA), 30
Bureau of Economic and Business Affairs, 330
Bureau of Educational and Cultural Affairs (ECA), 156
Bureau of Engraving and Printing (BEP), 53
Bureau of Health Workforce (BHW), 285
Bureau of Indian Education (BIE), 143
Bureau of Industry and Security (BIS), 45
Bureau of Intelligence and Research (INR), 118
Bureau of Justice Assistance (BJA), 355
Bureau of Justice Statistics (BJS), 355
Bureau of Labor Statistics (BLS), 175
Bureau of Land Management (BLM), 229; General Land Office Records Automation, 63; Learning Landscapes, 138; Library, 68; National Wild Horse and Burro Program, 231
Bureau of Near Eastern Affairs, 331
Bureau of Ocean Energy Management (BOEM), 219
Bureau of Oceans and International Environmental and Scientific Affairs, 211

Bureau of Population, Refugees, and Migration (PRM), 332
Bureau of Reclamation, 229
Bureau of Safety and Environmental Enforcement (BSEE), 212
Bureau of South and Central Asian Affairs, 331
Bureau of the Fiscal Service, 262
Bureau of Transportation Statistics (BTS), 446
Bureau of Western Hemisphere Affairs, 331
Business & Industry, 22
Business and Economics: Alcohol and Tobacco Tax and Trade Bureau, 21; Aviation Consumer Protection Division, 27; Baldrige Performance Excellence Program, 22; Business USA, 22; Census Bureau Business & Industry, 22; Center for Verification and Evaluation, 23; Commerce Department, 23; Committee on Foreign Investments in the U.S., 23; Consumer Information-FTC, 27; Consumer Product Safety Commission, 27; econsumer.gov, 28; E-Stats: Measuring the Electronic Economy, 24; Federal Trade Commission, 24; Federal Trade Commission Business Center, 22; HelpWithMyBank.gov, 28; Manufacturing & Construction Statistics, 25; Manufacturing.gov, 24; MBDA Web Portal, 25; MyMoney.gov, 28; NAICS-North American Industry Classification System, 25; National Consumer Protection Week, 29; National Women's Business Council, 25; Office of Women's Business Ownership, 26; Patent and Trademark Office, 26; Small Business Administration, 26; STOPfakes.gov, 22, 51
Business Center: FTC Business Center, 22
Business USA, 22

CADRE: Center for Aerospace-Defense Research and Engineering, 199
Campaign Finance Reports and Data, 245
Campaign to Rescue and Restore Victims of Human Trafficking, 431
Cancer.gov Clinical Trials, 296
Cancer Control P.L.A.N.E.T., 276
Cancer Information Service (CIS), 276
Cancer Institute and Frederick, 305
Cancer Prevention and Control, 276
Cancer Research Network, 296
Cancer Survivorship, Office of, 281
Capital: National Capital Planning Commission, 59
Capitol, History of, 373
Capitol Architect, 377
Capitol Visitor Center, 380
CARE International, 457
Carl Hayden Bee Research Center (CHBRC), 8
Cascades Volcano Observatory (CVO), 397
CASSIDI: Competitive Analysis and Structure Source Instrument for Depository Institutions, 34
Cassini Solstice Mission, 412
Catalog of Federal Domestic Assistance (CFDA), 431
Catalog of U.S. Government Publications (CGP), 1
CENDI, 265
Census Bureau, 131; American Community Survey, 129; American FactFinder, 130; Annual & Quarterly Services, 30; Business & Industry, 22; *Census 2000*Gateway, 130; *Census 2010*, 130; DataFerrett, 131; *Economic Census*, 31; E-Stats: Measuring the Electronic Economy, 24; Federal, State, and Local governments, 272; Foreign Trade Statistics, 47; Income-Census Bureau, 176; International Programs Center, 131; Manufacturing & Construction Statistics, 25; My Congressional District, 132; QuickFacts, 133; Regional Offices, 131; Selected Historical Decennial Census Counts, 132; State Data Center Program, 133; TIGER Products, 134; U.S. and World Population Clock, 133
Census of Agriculture, 9

Center for Army Lessons Learned (CALL), 92
Center for Food Safety and Applied Nutrition (CFSAN), 315
Center for Homeland Defense and Security (CHDS), 109
Center for Information Technology (CIT), 296
Center for International Trade & Security, 457
Center for Legislative Archives, 381
Center for Nutrition Policy and Promotion (CNPP), 316
Center for Restorative Justice and Peacemaking, 458
Center for Scientific Review (NIH), 305
Center for Sponsored Coastal Ocean Research (CSCOR), 220
Center for the Book in the Library of Congress, 57
Center for Transportation Analysis (CTA), 447
Center for Verification and Evaluation (CVE), 23
Centers for Disease Control and Prevention (CDC), 277; Adolescent and School Health, 287; Cancer Prevention and Control, 276; CDC WONDER, 307; Chronic Disease Prevention, 287; Community Health Division, 288; Emergency Preparedness and Response, 318; Epidemic Intelligence Service, 297; Flu.gov, 278; Global Health Center, 287; Health Statistics, National Center for, 309; *HIV/AIDS Surveillance Reports*, 279; HIV and STD Testing Resources, 281; Influenza (Flu), 279; Injury Prevention and Control, National Center for, 321; *Morbidity and Mortality Weekly Report*, 309; National Ag Safety Database, 13; National Center for HIV/AIDS, Viral Hepatitis, STD, and TB Prevention, 280; National Prevention Information Network, 277; Travel Information, 332; Vaccines and Immunizations, 315; VetoViolence, 366; VitalStats, 312
Centers for Medicare & Medicaid Services (CMS), 283
Central Command (CENTCOM), 97
Central Intelligence Agency (CIA), 116; CIA FOIA Electronic Reading Room, 117; CREST Records Search Tool, 118; Directorate of Operations, 117; In-Q-Tel, 119; Open Source Center, 122; *World Factbook*, 325
Chandra X-Ray Observatory, 412
Charities Search, 439
Chemical Weapons Convention, 323
Chemoinformatics Tools and Services, 398
Chief Information Officers Council, 249
Child Care, 424
Child Health and Human Development, National Institute of, 300
Children and Families, Administration for (ACF), 423; Office of Child Support Enforcement, 362
Children's Health Insurance Program (CHIP), 283
ChildStats.gov, 135
Child Support Enforcement, Office of, 362
Child Welfare Information Gateway, 423
China: Congressional-Executive Commission on China, 335; U.S.-China Economic and Security Review Commission, 338
ChooseMyPlate.gov, 316
ChooseMyPlate for Kids, 159
Chronic Disease Prevention, 287
CIA Kids' Zone, 159
Citizen Corps, 439
Citizen Services and Communications Office: U.S. Government Blog, 269
Citizens' Stamp Advisory Committee (CSAC), 269
Civics and Citizenship Toolkit, 245
Civil Air Patrol (CAP), 110
Civil Division, 346
Civilian Board of Contract Appeals (CBCA), 253
Civil Rights Commission (USCCR), 345; Historical Publications of the Commission, 343
Civil Rights Division, 341
Civil War: The Civil War, 63
Clean Cities, 184

Clearinghouse on Families and Youth, 424
Clerk of the House of Representatives, 372
Climate Analysis Branch (CAB), 239
Climate Change, 220; Transportation and Climate Change Clearinghouse, 448
Climate Prediction Center, 240
Clinical Center at NIH, 305
Clinical Trials: Cancer.gov, 296; ClinicalTrials.gov, 297
Coastal and Hydraulics Laboratory (CHL), 199
Coastal and Marine Geology Program (CMGP), 220
Coastal Ocean Research, Center for, 220
Coastal Program, 214
Coast Guard (USCG), 92; Boating Safety Resource Center, 452; National Maritime Center, 443; Navigation Center, 443; RestoreTheGulf.gov, 237
Code of Federal Regulations (CFR), 366
Codetalk, 271
Cold Regions Research and Engineering Laboratory (CRREL), 202
College Navigator, 152
Columbia Accident Investigation Board (CAIB), 412
Combating Terrorism Center (CTC) at West Point, 106
Combating Terrorism Technical Support Office (CTTSO), 100
Combined Arms Research Library (CARL), 71
Command and General Staff College (CGSC)
Commerce Department (DOC), 23; Baldrige Performance Excellence Program, 22; Business USA, 22; Chemical Weapons Convention, 323; Economic Development Administration, 426; Engineering Laboratory, 201; E-Stats: Measuring the Electronic Economy, 24; Estuary Education, 215; Hollings Manufacturing Extension Partnership, 200; Institute for Telecommunication Sciences, 198; Manufacturing.gov, 24; National Institute of Standards and Technology, 201; National Telecommunications and Information Administration, 198; Standards.gov, 202; Statistics in Schools, 142; STOPfakes.gov, 22, 51; TradeStats Express, 52
Commercial Service, 45
Commercial Service in China, 45
Commission on Intelligence Capabilities Regarding WMD, 117
Commission on Security and Cooperation in Europe (CSCE), 335, 458
Commission on Wartime Contracting in Iraq and Afghanistan, 253
Committee on Foreign Investments in the U.S. (CFIUS), 23
Commodity Futures Trading Commission (CFTC), 39
Common Core of Data (CCD): National Center for Education Statistics, 148
Community Development Financial Institutions (CDFI) Fund, 39
Community Health Division, 288
Community Relations Service (CRS), 355
Competition and Real Estate, 23
Complementary and Integrative Health, National Center for, 298
Compliance Office, 260
Compton Gamma Ray Observatory Science Support Center (CGRO), 413
Comptroller General Decisions and Opinions, 341
Comptroller of the Currency, Office of (OCC), 42
Computational Bioscience and Engineering Laboratory (CBEL), 391
Computer Crime and Intellectual Property Section (CCIPS), 355
Computers: OnGuard Online, 29
Computers for Learning, 148
Congress: *Biographical Directory of the United States Congress*, 371; Black Americans in Congress, 372; Capitol Visitor Center, 380; My Congressional District, 132; Office of Congressional Ethics, 380; Women in Congress, 377
Congress.gov, 382
Congressional Budget Office (CBO), 378
Congressional Directory, 372
Congressional Documents and Debates, 380

Congressional-Executive Commission on China (CECC), 335
Congressional Oversight Panel, 378
Congressional Quarterly Roll Call, 458
Congressional Research Service (CRS): Employment Opportunities, 379
Conservation Library, 68
Construction Engineering Research Laboratory (CERL), 200
Consumer and Governmental Affairs Bureau (CGB), 27
Consumer Financial Protection Bureau (CFPB), 426
Consumer Health Information, 288
Consumer Information: Aviation Consumer Protection Division, 27; Consumer and Governmental Affairs Bureau (CGB), 27; Consumer Product Safety Commission, 27; econsumer.gov, 28; FTC Consumer Information, 27; HelpWithMyBank.gov, 28; MyMoney.gov, 28; National Consumer Protection Week, 29; National Do Not Call Registry, 29; OnGuard Online, 29; SaferProducts.gov, 29
Consumer Product Safety Commission (CPSC), 27; ATV Safety Information Center, 449; SaferProducts.gov, 29
Consumer Protection Week, 29
Contact Your Government, 2
Contaminated Site Clean-Up Information (CLU-IN), 234
Cooper Hewitt, Smithsonian Design Museum, 81
Coordinating Council on Access and Mobility, 433
Coordinating Council on Juvenile Justice and Delinquency Prevention, 355
COPS Office: Grants and Resources for Community Policing, 356
Copyright Office, 341
Copyright Royalty Board (CRB), 341
Coral Reef Information System (CoRIS), 232
Coral Reef Task Force, 218
Core Documents of U.S. Democracy, 246
Cornell University Law School: Economics, Statistics, and Market Information System, 9; *U.S. Code*, 369
Corporation for National and Community Service (CNCS), 439; AmeriCorps, 438; Senior Corps, 439
Corporation for Public Broadcasting (CPB), 57, 458
Corps Lakes Gateway, 85
Corrections, National Institute of (NIC), 361
Council on Environmental Quality (CEQ), 212
Counterfeiting: Advanced Counterfeit Deterrence Program, 52; STOPfakes.gov, 22, 51
Counterterrorism: National Counterterrorism Center, 119
Counterterrorism Bureau, 334
Country Studies Series, 324
Court of Federal Claims, 352
Court of International Trade, 352
Courts of Appeal: Armed Forces Court of Appeals, 351; District of Columbia Circuit, 348; Eighth Circuit, 348; Eleventh Circuit, 348; Federal Circuit, 349; Fifth Circuit, 347; FindLaw: Cases and Codes, 349; First Circuit, 346; Fourth Circuit, 347; Ninth Circuit, 348; Second Circuit, 346; Seventh Circuit, 347; Sixth Circuit, 347; Tenth Circuit, 348; Third Circuit, 346; Veterans Claims Court of Appeals, 351
Credit Unions: National Credit Union Administration, 42
CREST: CIA Records Search Tool, 118
Criminal Division, 356
Crop Explorer, 8
CRS Reports-UNT Libraries, 379
Crustal Dynamics Data Information System (CDDIS), 413
CryptoKids, 160
C-SPAN, 382
Cultural Heritage Center, 58
Culture: American Folklife Center, 57; Archeology Program, 57; Center for the Book in the Library of Congress, 57; Corporation for Public Broadcasting, 57, 458; Cultural Heritage Center, 58; Institute of Museum and Library Services, 58; John W. Kluge Center at

the Library of Congress, 58; National Archeological Database, 58; National Capital Planning Commission, 59; National Center for Preservation Technology and Training, 59; National Endowment for the Humanities, 59; National NAGPRA, 60; National Recording Preservation Board, 60; Preserve America, 60; Read.gov, 60; Smithsonian Center for Folklife and Cultural Heritage, 61; Smithsonian Institution, 61; Smithsonian Institution Research Information System, 61; Smithsonian Magazine, 62
Current Population Survey (CPS), 176
Customs and Border Protection (CBP), 364
CyberCemetery, 4
CyberCorps Scholarship for Service (SFS), 143
Cyber Crime, 356

DailyMed, 312
DANTES: Defense Activity for Non-Traditional Education Support, 137
DARPA, 106
Data.gov, 265
DataFerrett, 131
Data Gateway, 410
Davis-Bacon and Related Acts, 169
D'Azzo Research Library, 69
Deafness and Other Communication Disorders, Institute of (NIDCD), 303
Defense Activity for Non-Traditional Education Support (DANTES), 137
Defense Civilian Personnel Advisory Service (DCPAS), 101
Defense Department (DoD), 103; Africa Command (AFRICOM), 96; Armed Forces Medical Examiner System, 296; Central Command (CENTCOM), 97; Civilian Personnel Advisory Service (DCPAS), 101; Combating Terrorism Technical Support Office (CTTSO), 100; Defense Advanced Research Projects Agency (DARPA), 106; Defense Finance and Accounting Service (DFAS), 101; Defense Science Board (DSB), 107; Defense Systems Information Analysis Center (DSIAC), 107; Defense Technical Information Center (DTIC), 107; Defense Technology Security Administration, 46; Defense Threat Reduction Agency (DTRA), 110; Dictionary of Military Terms, 103; Education Activity (DoDEA), 124; Environmental and Sustainable Programs, 236; European Command (EUCOM), 98; Federal Voting Assistance Program, 247; Information Analysis Centers (IACs), 108; Information Systems Agency (DISA), 101; Institute for National Strategic Studies (INSS), 108; Joint Chiefs of Staff, 93; Joint Electronic Library (JEL), 104; Learning Registry, 140; Logistics Agency (DLA), 101; Logistics Agency (DLA) Energy, 102; Manufacturing Technology Program, 201; Media Activity (DMA), 102; National Defense University Library, 75; Northern Command (NORTHCOM), 98; Office of Economic Adjustment, 426; Office of the Under Secretary (Acquisition, Technology, and Logistics), 104; Office of the Under Secretary (Comptroller), 104; Overseas Basing Commission, 104; Pacific Command (PACOM), 99; Pentagon Digital Library, 79; Pentagon Force Protection Agency (PFPA), 104; Security Service (DSS), 103; SENSIAC: Military Sensing Information Analysis Center, 109; Southern Command (SOUTHCOM), 99; Strategic Command (STRATCOM), 99; System for Award Management, 257; Today's Military, 96; Transportation Command (TRANSCOM), 100; TRICARE, 284; U.S. Mission to NATO, 338; Uniformed Services University of the Health Sciences, 286; USA4 Military Families, 128
Defense Finance and Accounting Service (DFAS), 101
Defense Forensics & Biometrics Agency (DFBA), 106

Defense Information Systems Agency (DISA), 101
Defense Intelligence Agency (DIA), 118
Defense Language Institute Foreign Language Center (DLIFLC), 152
Defense Logistics Agency (DLA), 101; Disposition Services, 254; Land and Maritime, 254
Defense Logistics Agency (DLA) Energy, 102
Defense Media Activity (DMA), 102
Defense Nuclear Facilities Safety Board (DNFSB), 110
Defense Prisoner of War/Missing in Action Accounting Agency, 102
Defense Procurement and Acquisition Policy (DPAP), 102
Defense Research: Air Force Office of Scientific Research, 105; Army Medical Research Institute of Infectious Diseases, 109; Army Research Laboratory, 106; Combating Terrorism Center at West Point, 106; Defense Advanced Research Projects Agency, 106; Defense Science Board, 107; Foreign Military Studies Office, 107; High Performance Computing Modernization Program, 108; Information Analysis Centers, 108; Institute for National Strategic Studies, 108; Naval Research Laboratory, 109
Defense Science Board (DSB), 107
Defense Security Cooperation Agency (DSCA), 335
Defense Security Service (DSS), 103
Defense Systems Information Analysis Center (DSIAC), 107
Defense Technical Information Center (DTIC), 107; Public Technical Reports, 410
Defense Technology Security Administration (DTSA), 46
Defense Threat Reduction Agency (DTRA), 110
Democratic Congressional Campaign Committee (DCCC), 459
Democratic National Committee, 246
Democratic Senatorial Campaign Committee (DSCC), 459
Demographic Groups: AgingStats.gov, 134; American Indian and Alaska Native Resources, 135; ChildStats.gov, 135
DENIX: DoD Environment, Safety, and Occupational Health Network, 212
Dental and Craniofacial Research, National Institute of (NIDCR), 301
Depleted UF6 Management Information Network, 189
Deputy Attorney General, Office of the, 363
Developmental Disabilities Administration (AIDD), 430
Devices and Radiological Health, Center for (CDRH): Medical Devices, 314
Diabetes and Digestive and Kidney Diseases, National Institute of, 301
Diabetes Education Program (NDEP), 280
Diabetes Public Health Resource, 278
Dictionary of Military Terms (DoD), 103
Dietary Supplements, Office of (ODS), 317
Dietary Supplements Label Database (DSLD), 316
Digital Preservation, 203
Digital Television, 203
Diplomatic Security, Bureau of, 325
DipNote, 326
Directorate for Education and Human Resources (EHR), 145
Directorate of Defense Trade Controls (DDTC), 46
Disability, Independent Living, and Rehabilitation Research, 303
Disability, National Council on, 299
Disability Employment Policy, Office of (ODEP), 172
Disability Resources, 433
Disability Rights Section, 342
Disabled Persons: AbilityOne, 252; Access Board, 345; Americans with Disabilities Act, 339; Coordinating Council on Access and Mobility, 433; The Work Site, 437
DisasterAssistance.gov, 319
Disaster Information Management Research Center, 319

Discover History and Historic Preservation, 64
Disease Prevention, Office of (ODP), 306
Diseases: Army Medical Research Institute of Infectious Diseases, 109
Distracted Driving, 449
District of Columbia Circuit Court of Appeals, 348
Division of Community Health (DCH), 288
Division of Research on Learning in Formal and Informal Settings, 146
DocsTeach, 139
Doctors Without Borders/Medecins Sans Frontieres, 459
Domestic Policy Council, 386
Do Not Call Registry, 29
Draft: Selective Service System, 105
Drug Abuse: NIDA for Teens: The Science Behind Drug Abuse, 291
Drug Abuse, National Institute on (NIDA), 303
Drug Enforcement Administration (DEA), 357
Drug Information Portal, 312
Drugs, 313
Drugs@FDA, 313
Dru Sjodin National Sex Offender Public Website, 357

Early Childhood Education: Early Childhood Learning and Knowledge Center, 142; Head Start, 143
Early Childhood Learning and Knowledge Center (ECLKC), 142
Earth Day, 215
EarthExplorer, 225
Earth Observatory, 220
Earth Observing System (EOS): NASA, 398; NOAA, 398
Earthquake Hazards Program, 399
Earth Resources Observation and Science (EROS) Center, 225
Earth System Research Laboratory (ESRL), 223
Economic and Business Affairs, Bureau of, 330
Economic Census, 31
Economic Development Administration (EDA), 426
Economic Indicators, 31
Economic Research Service (ERS), 9
Economics: ALFRED: Archival Federal Reserve Economic Data, 30; Annual & Quarterly Services, 30; Bureau of Economic Analysis, 30; *Economic Census*, 31; *Economic Indicators*, 31; Economics & Statistics Administration, 32; FRASER: Federal Reserve Archival System for Economic Research, 32; FRED: Federal Reserve Economic Data, 32; GeoFRED: Geographical Federal Reserve Economic Data, 32; Office of Economic Policy, 33; *Page One Economics*, 33
Economics & Statistics Administration (ESA), 32
Economics, Statistics, and Market Information System (ESMIS), 9
econsumer.gov, 28
Ecosystem Management Coordination (EMC), 19
ED Data Express, 147
EDGAR: SEC Filings & Forms, 39
EDSITEment, 139
Education: ArtsEdge: The Kennedy Center's Arts Education Network, 138; Bureau of Indian Education, 143; Defense Department Education Activity, 124; DocsTeach, 139; Early Childhood Learning and Knowledge Center, 142; EDSITEment, 139; Energy Education and Workforce Development, 139; English Language Acquisition Office, 141; Environmental Health Science Education: Teachers, 139; Every Student Succeeds Act, 146; Federal Reserve Education, 38; GLOBE Program, 140; Learning Landscapes, 138; Learning Registry, 140; NASA-Education, 140; National Archives-Teachers' Resources, 140; National Library of Education, 76; National Marine Sanctuaries-Education, 141; NOAA-Education Resources, 141; NSF Classroom Resources, 141; Picturing America,

142; Research on Learning in Formal and Informal Settings, 146; Statistics in Schools, 142; USA Science and Engineering Festival, 151; USGS and Science Education, 142
Education Department, 145; College Navigator, 152; ED Data Express, 147; Emergency Planning, 148; ERIC: Educational Resources Information Center, 147; Faith-Based and Neighborhood Partnerships, Center for, 432; Foreign Medical Education and Accreditation, 157; Institute of Education Sciences, 147; International Activities Program, 157; International Affairs Office, 157; Library Statistics Program, 73; Office of Career, Technical, and Adult Education, 137; Office of Innovation and Improvement, 146; Office of Postsecondary Education, 154; Office of Safe and Healthy Students, 150; Presidential Scholars Program, 150; State Contracts-Education Department, 151; U.S. Network for Education Information, 158
Education Funding: Bureau of Indian Education, 143; CyberCorps Scholarship for Service, 143; Department of Education, 145; Directorate for Education and Hunan Resources, 145; Education and Training-Department of Veterans Affairs, 145; Education Finance Statistics Center, 143; Every Student Succeeds Act (ESSA), 146; FAFSA4caster, 144; Federal Student Aid, 144; Federal Student Aid Gateway, 144; Free Application for Federal Student Aid, 144; Information for Financial Aid Professionals, 145
Education Policy: Directorate for Education and Human Resources, 145; White House Initiative on Educational Excellence for Hispanics, 146
Education Research and Statistics: Common Core of Data (CCD), 148; Division of Research on Learning in Formal and Informal Settings, 146; ED Data Express, 147; ERIC: Educational Resources Information Center, 147; Institute of Education Sciences, 147; National Center for Education Statistics, 147, 148
Eighth Circuit Court of Appeals, 348
elaws: Employment Laws Assistance for Workers and Small Businesses, 170
Elder Abuse, National Center on, 360
Eldercare Locator, 278
Election Assistance Commission (EAC), 246
Electioneering Communications Database (ECD), 247
Electoral College, 247
Electronic Orange Book, 313
Elementary and Secondary Education: Computers for Learning, 148; Emergency Planning, 148; NAEP Data Explorer, 149; Nation's Report Card, 149; Office of Elementary and Secondary Education, 149; Office of Safe and Healthy Students, 150; Office of Special Education Programs, 150; School District Demographics System, 150; State Contracts-Education Department, 151
Eleventh Circuit Court of Appeals, 348
Emergency Preparedness and Response (CDC), 318
Employee Benefits Security Administration (EBSA), 171
Employer Support of the Guard and Reserve (ESGR), 125
Employment and Training Administration (ETA), 177; Unemployment Insurance, 438
Employment Law: Benefits Review Board, 169; Davis-Bacon and Related Acts, 169; elaws: Employment Laws Assistance for Workers and Small Businesses, 170; Employee Benefits Security Administration, 171; Equal Employment Opportunity Commission, 171; E-Verify, 172; Foreign Labor Certification, 172; Job Accommodation Network, 172; Labor Department, 170; Labor Department Data Enforcement, 170; Office of Disability Employment

Policy, 172; Office of Special Counsel for Immigration-Related Unfair Employment Practices, 173; Pension Benefit Guaranty Corporation, 173; Railroad Retirement Board, 173; Veterans' Employment and Training Service, 174; Wage and Hour Division, 174; Wage Determinations OnLine.gov, 174; Youth at Work, 175; YouthRules!, 175
Employment Statistics: Bureau of Labor Statistics, 175; Current Population Survey, 176; Income-Census Bureau, 176; Longitudinal Employer-Household Dynamics, 176
Endangered Species, 230
Energy and the Environment, 186
Energy Department (DOE), 186; Argonne National Laboratory, 394; Center for Transportation Analysis, 447; DOEpatents, 408; EIA Energy Kids, 160; Energy Education and Workforce Development, 139; Fermilab Library, 70; genomics.energy.gov, 392; Hanford Site, 234; Jefferson Lab, 401; Joint Genome Institute, 391; Los Alamos National Laboratory Research Library, 73; New Brunswick Laboratory, 402; Office of Environmental Management, 235; Office of Fossil Energy, 191; Office of Nuclear Energy, 191; Office of Science, 406; OpenNet, 122; Savannah River National Laboratory, 397; SLAC National Accelerator Laboratory, 404; Southeastern Power Administration, 192; Southwestern Power Administration, 193; Vehicle Technologies Office, 446; Western Area Power Administration, 193; Y-12 National Security Complex, 116
Energy Information Administration (EIA), 186
Energy Policy and Information: Building America, 185; Building Energy Codes Program, 185; Department of Energy, 186; Energy and the Environment, 186; Energy Information Administration, 186; Energy Saver, 187; Energy Savers Blog, 187; ENERGY STAR, 187; Federal Energy Regulatory Commission, 187; Saving Energy at Home, 188; Weatherization and Intergovernmental Program, 188
Energy Resources Program, 189
Energy Saver, 187
Energy Savers Blog, 187
Energy Science and Technology Software Center (ESTSC), 203
Energy Sciences Network (ESnet), 204
ENERGY STAR, 187
Enforcement and Compliance (E&C), 46
Enforcement and Compliance History Online (ECHO), 209
Engineering: Army Corps of Engineers, 202; Coastal and Hydraulics Laboratory, 199; Cold Regions Research and Engineering Laboratory, 202; Construction Engineering Research Laboratory, 200; Engineering at LLNL, 200; Engineering Laboratory, 201; Engineer Research and Development Center, 200; Engineer Research and Development Center Library, 69; Hollings Manufacturing Extension Partnership, 200; Manufacturing Technology Program, 201; National Institute of Standards and Technology, 201; Standards.gov, 202
Engineering Laboratory, 201
Engineer Research and Development Center (ERDC) Library, 69
English Language Acquisition Office (OELA), 141; National Clearinghouse for English Language Acquisition, 166
Envirofacts Data Warehouse, 235
Environmental and Sustainable Programs, 236
Environmental Health Perspectives: EHP Online, 297
Environmental Health Sciences, National Institute of, 301
Environmental Information, Nation Centers for, 402
Environmental Molecular Sciences Laboratory (EMSL), 399
Environmental Policy: American Indian Tribal Portal, 211; Bureau of Oceans and International Environmental and

Scientific Affairs, 211; Council on Environmental Quality, 212; DENIX: DoD Environment, Safety, and Occupational Health Network, 212; National Center for Environmental Economics, 213; National Environmental Policy Act-CEQ, 210; National Environmental Policy Act-EPA, 210; Office of Natural Resources Revenue, 213; Tribal Energy and Environmental Information Clearinghouse, 214; Udall Foundation, 214
Environmental Prediction Centers, 221
Environmental Protection Agency (EPA), 215; Agriculture-EPA, 6; Appeals Board, 210; Contaminated Site Clean-Up Information, 234; Earth Day, 215; Enforcement and Compliance History Online, 209; EPA Blog, 212; Federal Advisory Committee at EPA, 213; Laws & Regulations, 210; Lead-EPA, 320; National Library Network, 69; Office of Air and Radiation, 235; Office of Chemical Safety and Pollution Prevention, 236; Office of Land and Emergency Management, 236; Office of Pollution Prevention and Toxics, 237; Office of Water, 230; Protecting Children's Environmental Health, 293; Regulatory Development and Retrospective Review Tracker, 211; Science Inventory, 410; Student's Guide to Global Climate Change, 163; Superfund Program, 237; U.S.-Mexico Border 2020 Program, 219
Environmental Science: Air Resources Library, 219; Atlantic Oceanographic and Meteorological Laboratory, 219; Climate Change, 220; Coastal and Marine Geology Program, 220; Coastal Ocean Science Centers, 224; Earth Observatory, 220; Earth System Research Laboratory, 223; Environmental Prediction Centers, 221; Global Change Research Program, 221; National Centers for Coastal Ocean Science, 224; National Environmental Satellite, Data, and Information Service, 221; National Oceanic and Atmospheric Administration, 222; National Ocean Service, 222; National Service Center for Environmental Publications, 224; National Water and Climate Center, 222; National Wetlands Inventory Center, 223; NOAA Commissioned Officers Corps, 223; NOAA Research, 223; Pacific Marine Environmental Laboratory, 224; Physical Oceanography Distributed Active Archive Center, 224; Smithsonian Tropical Research Institute, 224; Upper Midwest Environmental Sciences Center, 225
EPA Blog, 212
EPA National Library Network, 69
Epidemic Intelligence Service (EIS), 297
Equal Employment Opportunity Commission (EEOC), 171
ERIC: Educational Resources Information Center, 147
eSRS: Electronic Subcontracting Reporting System, 254
E-Stats: Measuring the Electronic Economy, 24
Estuarine Research Reserve System, 216
Estuary Education, 215
Estuary Restoration Act & NOAA, 215
Ethics: Office of Government Ethics, 250
European Command (EUCOM), 98
European Union: Commission on Security and Cooperation in Europe, 335, 458
Evaluating Internet Health Information, 307
E-Verify, 172
Every Student Succeeds Act (ESSA), 146
eVetRecs, 125
Exchange Rates: Foreign Exchange Rates, 53
Executive Office for Immigration Review (EOIR), 333
Executive Orders, 389, 471; *Codification of Presidential Proclamations and Executive Orders*, 388; Disposition Tables, 389
Export.gov, 46
Export Administration Regulations (EAR), 47

Export-Import Bank of the United States (EXIM), 47, 459
Export USA, 47

FAFSA4caster, 144
Family and Youth Services Bureau (FYSB), 424
Famine Early Warning Systems Network (FEWS NET), 336
Farm Credit Administration (FCA), 10
Farm Service Agency (FSA), 10
FARS Encyclopedia, 449
Fatality Analysis Reporting System (FARS): *FARS Encyclopedia*, 449
FedBizOpps.gov, 254
Federal, State, and Local Governments, 272
Federal Accounting Standards Advisory Board (FASAB), 262
Federal Acquisition Jumpstation, 255
Federal Acquisition Regulation (FAR), 255
Federal Acquisition Service (FAS), 255
Federal Advisory Committee at EPA, 213
Federal Aviation Administration (FAA), 441; Flight Delay Information, 441; Flight Standards Service, 442; William J. Hughes Technical Center, 442
Federal Bureau of Investigation (FBI), 357; Cyber Crime, 356; Internet Crime Complaint Center, 359; Kids' Page, 160; National Security Branch, 111
Federal Bureau of Prisons (BOP), 358; Library, 70
Federal Circuit Court of Appeals, 349
Federal Communications Commission (FCC), 197; Consumer and Governmental Affairs Bureau, 27; Electioneering Communications Database, 247; Enforcement Bureau, 195; International Bureau, 196; Kids Zone, 160; Media Bureau, 196; National Broadband Plan, 198; Office of Engineering and Technology, 196; Office of Native Affairs and Policy, 196; Parents' Place, 197; Public Safety & Homeland Security Bureau, 197; Wireless Telecommunications Bureau, 197
Federal Deposit Insurance Corporation (FDIC), 40; Financial Regulatory Reform, 40
Federal Depository Library Program (FDLP), 70
Federal Digital System (FDsys), 265
Federal Election Commission (FEC), 247; Campaign Finance Reports and Data, 245
Federal Emergency Management Agency (FEMA), 269; Fire Administration, 321; FloodSmart.gov, 270
Federal Energy Regulatory Commission (FERC), 187
Federal Executive Boards (FEBs), 249
Federal Financial Institutions Examination Council (FFIEC), 40
Federal Financing Bank (FFB), 263
Federal Geographic Data Committee (FGDC), 226
Federal Highway Administration (FHWA), 445; Highways for LIFE, 445; National Traffic and Road Closure Information, 446; Office of Safety, 450
Federal Housing Administration (FHA), 428
Federal Housing Finance Agency (FHFA), 428
Federal Judicial Center (FJC), 349; History of the Federal Judiciary, 350
Federal Laboratory Consortium for Technology Transfer, 255
Federal Labor Relations Authority, 258
Federal Lands Highway, Office of, 445
Federal Law Enforcement Training Centers (FLETC), 358
Federal Library and Information Network (FEDLINK), 70
Federal Maritime Commission (FMC), 442
Federal Mediation & Conciliation Service (FMCS), 179
Federal Mine Safety and Health Review Commission, 342
Federal Motor Carrier Safety Administration (FMCSA), 450
Federal Occupational Health (FOH), 181
Federal Prison Industries, Inc.: UNICOR, 258, 473

Federal Procurement Data System-Next Generation, 255
Federal Railroad Administration (FRA), 445
FederalRegister.gov, 367
Federal Register, 366; Office of the Federal Register, 268
Federal Remediation Technologies Roundtable (FRTR), 235
Federal Reserve: ALFRED: Archival Federal Reserve Economic Data, 30; Bank of Atlanta, 34; Bank of Boston, 35; Bank of Chicago, 35; Bank of Cleveland, 35; Bank of Dallas, 35; Bank of Kansas City, 36; Bank of Minneapolis, 36; Bank of New York, 36; Bank of Philadelphia, 37; Bank of Richmond, 37; Bank of San Francisco, 37; Bank of St. Louis, 37; Board of Governors of the Federal Reserve System, 33; CASSIDI: Competitive Analysis and Structure Source Instrument for Depository Institutions, 34; Consumer Financial Protection Bureau, 426; Federal Reserve Education, 38; Federal Reserve System Online, 38; Fed in Print, 34; Financial Crisis Timeline, 41; Foreclosure Resource Center, 428; FRASER: Federal Reserve Archival System for Economic Research, 32; FRED: Federal Reserve Economic Data, 32; GeoFRED: Geographical Federal Reserve Economic Data, 32; National Information Center, 38
Federal Retirement Thrift Investment Board (FRTIB), 258; Thrift Savings Plan, 261
Federal Student Aid, 144
Federal Student Aid Gateway, 144
Federal Trade Commission (FTC), 24; Business Center, 22; econsumer.gov, 28; FTC Consumer Information, 27; Identity Theft, 358
Federal Transit Administration (FTA), 444
Federal Voting Assistance Program (FVAP), 247
Federation of American Scientists (FAS), 460; Presidential Directives and Executive Orders, 389, 471
Fed in Print, 34
FEDLINK, 70
FedScope, 259
FedsHireVets.gov, 259
Fellows Program, 387
Fermilab, 395
Fermi National Accelerator Laboratory (Fermilab) Library, 70
Fifth Circuit Court of Appeals, 347
Films: National Film Preservation Board, 56
Finance: Commodity Futures Trading Commission, 39; Community Development Financial Institutions Fund, 39; EDGAR: SEC Filings & Forms, 39; FDIC and Financial Regulatory Reform, 40; Federal Deposit Insurance Corporation, 40; Federal Financial Institutions Examination Council, 40; Financial Crisis Inquiry Commission, 41; Financial Crisis Timeline, 41; Investor.gov, 41; Joint Board for the Enrollment of Actuaries, 41; Money Services Businesses, 41; National Credit Union Administration, 42; Office of Domestic Finance, 42; Office of the Comptroller of the Currency, 42; SIGTARP, 43; STOPfraud.gov, 44; XBRL.sec.gov, 44
Financial Crimes Enforcement Network (FinCEN), 358
Financial Crisis Inquiry Commission (FCIC), 41
Financial Crisis Timeline, 41
Financial Fraud Enforcement Task Force: STOPfraud.gov, 44
Financial Literacy and Education Commission: MyMoney.gov, 28
Find Government Forms, 2
FindLaw: Cases and Codes: Circuit Courts, 349; Supreme Court, 350
Fine Arts: U.S. Commission of Fine Arts, 56
Fire Administration, 321
First Circuit Court of Appeals, 346

First Ladies: Biographies of First Ladies, 389; First Lady Melania Trump, 386
Fish and Aquatic Conservation, 17
Fish and Wildlife Service (FWS), 230; Coastal Program, 214; Conservation Library, 68; Fishing, 85; Migratory Bird Conservation Commission, 216; Migratory Bird Program, 216; National Wildlife Refuge System, 214
Fishing, 85; Atlantic States Marine Fisheries Commission, 17; Fish and Aquatic Conservation, 17; FishWatch, 17; Gulf States Marine Fisheries Commission, 18; NOAA Fisheries, 18; NOAA Office of Aquaculture, 18; Northwest Fisheries Science Center, 19; Pacific States Marine Fisheries Commission, 19; Your Guide to Fishing on National Wildlife Refuges, 87
FishWatch, 17
Flight Delay Information, 441
Flight Standards Service, 442
FloodSmart.gov, 270
Flu.gov, 278
Fogarty International Center (FIC), 297
Folklife: American Folklife Center, 57; Smithsonian Center for Folklife and Cultural Heritage, 61
Following the Money: GAO's Oversight of the Recovery Act, 263
Food and Drug Administration (FDA), 314; Animal & Veterinary-Center for Veterinary Medicine, 7; Consumer Health Information, 288; Drugs@FDA, 313; MedWatch: FDA Safety Information and Adverse Event Reporting Program, 315; Notices of Judgment Collection, 314; *Orange Book*, 313; Toxicological Research, National Center for, 299
Food and Nutrition Information Center (FNIC), 316
Food and Nutrition Service (FNS), 433; Food Distribution Programs, 434; Food Safety, 319; Women, Infants, and Children, 425
Food Distribution Programs, 434
FoodSafety.gov, 320
Food Safety, 319
Food Safety and Applied Nutrition, Center for (CFSAN), 315
Food Safety and Inspection Service (FSIS), 319
Foreclosure Resource Center, 428
Foreign Agents Registration Act (FARA), 336
Foreign Agricultural Service (FAS), 11; Crop Explorer, 8; Production, Supply and Distribution (PSD) Online, 16
Foreign Claims Settlement Commission (FCSC), 343
Foreign Exchange Rates, 53
Foreign Investments: Committee on Foreign Investments in the U.S., 23
Foreign Labor Certification, 172
Foreign Military Studies Office (FMSO), 107
Foreign Relations of the United States (FRUS), 332
Foreign Trade Statistics, 47
Forestry Technical Resources, 20
Forests and Rangelands, 20
Forest Service (USFS), 19; National Avalanche Center, 86; Recreational Activities, 85
Fort Collins Science Center (FORT), 231
Fossil and Nuclear Fuels: Blue Ribbon Commission on America's Nuclear Future, 188; Depleted UF6 Management Information Network, 189; Energy Resources Program, 189; fueleconomy.gov, 189; Idaho National Laboratory, 190; National Energy Technology Laboratory, 190; Nuclear Regulatory Commission, 190; Office of Fossil Energy, 191; Office of Nuclear Energy, 191; Oil and Gas Industry Initiatives, 191; Petroleum Reserves, 192
Fourth Circuit Court of Appeals, 347
FRASER: Federal Reserve Archival System for Economic Research, 32
FRED: Federal Reserve Economic Data, 32
Free Application for Federal Student Aid (FAFSA), 144

Freedom of Information Act (FOIA): CIA FOIA Electronic Reading Room, 117; Office of Information and Privacy, 267
Frontline Diplomacy: Foreign Affairs Oral History Collection, 326
fueleconomy.gov, 189
Futures: Commodity Futures Trading Commission, 39

G8 Information Centre, 460
Galileo Legacy Site, 413
Gemini Observatory, 460
General Medical Sciences, National Institute of (NIGMS), 394
General Services Administration (GSA), 249; Acquisition.gov, 253; *Catalog of Federal Domestic Assistance*, 431; Civilian Board of Contract Appeals, 253; Electronic Subcontracting Reporting System, 254; Federal Acquisition Regulation, 255; Federal Acquisition Service, 255; Find Government Forms, 2; GSA Advantage!, 256; IDManagement.gov, 250; Office of Government-wide Policy, 250; Section 508, 207; USA.gov, 3
Genetic and Rare Diseases Information Center (GARD), 278
Genome Integrity & Structural Biology Laboratory, 392
genomics.energy.gov, 392
GeoFRED: Geographical Federal Reserve Economic Data, 32
Geographic Names Information System (GNIS), 226
Geography: Federal Geographic Data Committee, 226; Geographic Names Information System, 226; GEONet Names Server, 226; GeoPlatform.gov, 227; National Geodetic Survey, 227; National Geospatial Program, 227; *National Map*, 227; Office of Coast Survey, 228
Geological and Geophysical Data Preservation Program, 206
Geological Survey (USGS) Libraries Program, 70
Geology Research and Information, 399
GEONet Names Server (GNS), 226
Geophysical Fluid Dynamics Laboratory (GFDL), 400
GeoPlatform.gov, 227
Geospatial-Intelligence Agency (NGA), 120
Germplasm Resources Information Network (GRIN), 11
Ginnie Mae, 429
girlshealth.gov, 288
Glenn Research Center, 414
Global Change Research Program, 221
Global Health Center, 287
Global Legal Monitor (GLM), 367
Global Systems Division (GSD), 240
GLOBE Program, 140
GoArmy.com, 92
GobiernoUSA.gov, 2
Goddard Institute for Space Studies (GISS), 401
Goddard Library Repository, 71
Goddard Space Flight Center (GSFC), 414; Lunar and Planetary Science at the NSSDCA, 416; NASA Eclipse, 413; Space Science Data Coordinated Archive, 419
GOVDOC-L, 71
Government Accountability Office (GAO), 379; Comptroller General Decisions and Opinions, 341; Following the Money: GAO's Oversight of the Recovery Act, 263
Government and Geographic Information Collection, 460
Government Publishing Office (GPO), 265; Catalog of U.S. Government Publications, 1; Core Documents of U.S. Democracy, 246; CyberCemetery, 4; Federal Depository Library Program, 70; Federal Digital System (FDsys), 265; Legislative Resources on FDsys, 383; Public and Private Laws, 368; U.S. Government Bookstore, 269
Government Sources: Catalog of U.S. Government Publications, 1; Contact Your Government, 2; Find Government Forms, 2; GobiernoUSA.gov, 2; Grants.gov, 2; Registry of U.S. Government Publication Digitization

Projects, 2; U.S. Government Photos and Images, 3; U.S. Government YouTube Channel, 3; USA.gov, 3
Government-wide Policy, Office of, 250
GovLoans.gov, 270
GovSales.gov, 256
GrainGenes, 11
Grain Inspection, Packers & Stockyards Administration (GIPSA), 12
Grants.gov, 2
Green Book (FDA Approved Animal Drug Products), 12
Green Vehicle Guide, 236
GRIN: Great Images in NASA, 414
GulfLINK, 278
Gulf States Marine Fisheries Commission (GSMFC), 18

Habitat for Humanity International, 461
Hague Conference on Private International Law (HCCH), 461
Handicapped Persons: National Library Services for the Blind and Physically Handicapped, 76
Hanford Site, 234
Harry S. Truman Scholarship Foundation, 153
Harvard-Smithsonian Center for Astrophysics, 400
Hawaiian Volcano Observatory (HVO), 400
Head Start, 143
Health.gov, 289
Health and Human Services Department (HHS), 432; Administration for Children and Families, 423; AIDSinfo, 275; Autism Coordinating Committee, 290; Autism Information, 276; Campaign to Rescue and Restore Victims of Human Trafficking, 431; Cancer Control P.L.A.N.E.T., 276; Committee on Vital and Health Statistics, 290; Diabetes Public Health Resource, 278; Drugs, 313; FDA Kids' Site, 160; Flu.gov, 278; HealthIT.gov, 308; *Healthy People 2020*, 289; HIV/AIDS Programs, 434; *HIV/AIDS Surveillance Reports*, 279; Medical Reserve Corps, 285; National Ag Safety Database, 13; National Center for HIV/AIDS, Viral Hepatitis, STD, and TB Prevention, 280; National Health Service Corps, 285; NCEH Kids Page, 162; Office of Population Affairs, 292; Office of the Assistant Secretary for Planning and Evaluation, 291; Organ Donation, 282; Poverty Guidelines, Research, and Measurement, 436; Women's Health.gov, 295
Health Care: Navy and Marine Corps Public Health Center, 126; Navy Medicine, 126; Veterans Health Administration, 285
HealthCare.gov, 283
Health Care Benefits: TRICARE: Military Health System, 284
Health Center Program, 289
healthfinder.gov, 308
Health Information Center, National, 310
Health Insurance: Children's Health Insurance Program, 283; Insure Kids Now, 284
HealthIT.gov, 308
Health Public Access, National Institutes of, 304
Health Resources and Services Administration (HRSA), 289; Bureau of Health Workforce, 285; Health Center Program, 289; National Health Service Corps, 285; National Practitioner Data Bank, 286; Rural Health Policy, Office of, 292; Telehealth, 290; Title V Information System, 437
Health Statistics, National Center for (NCHS), 309
Health Workforce, Bureau of, 285
Healthy Homes and Lead Hazard Control, 320
Healthy Meals Resource System, 317
Healthy People 2020, 289
Heart, Lung, and Blood Institute (NHLBI), 281
Heat Island Effect, 240
HelpWithMyBank.gov, 28
Heritage Documentation Programs (HDP), 64

High Energy Astrophysics Science Archive Research Center (HEASARC), 400
Higher Education: Air Force Academy, 155; Air Force Institute of Technology, 151; Air University, 151; Army Command and General Staff College, 155; Army Logistics University, 152; Army War College, 155; Barry Goldwater Scholarship Program, 152; College Navigator, 152; Defense Language Institute Foreign Language Center, 152; Harry S. Truman Scholarship Foundation, 153; Initiative on Historically Black Colleges and Universities, 156; Marine Corps University, 153; Merchant Marine Academy, 155; Military Academy at West Point, 156; National Defense University, 153; Naval Academy, 156; Naval Postgraduate School, 153; NSF Division of Graduate Education, 154; NSF Division of Undergraduate Education, 154; Office of Postsecondary Education, 154; Presidential Scholars Program, 150; Smithsonian Office of Fellowships and Internships, 155
High Performance Computing Modernization Program (HPCMP), 108
Highways for LIFE, 445
Highway Traffic Safety Administration (NHTSA), 450
Hill Aerospace Museum, 81
Hispanics: White House Initiative on Educational Excellence for Hispanics, 146
Historical Publications of the Civil Rights Commission, 343
History and Historic Preservation: Access to Archival Databases, 62; Advisory Council on Historic Preservation, 62; A Guide to the War of 1812, 64; American Memory, 63; America's Historical Documents, 62; Discover History and Historic Preservation, 64; General Land Office Records Automation-BLM, 63; Heritage Documentation Programs, 64; JFK Assassination Records, 64; National Historical Publications and Records Commission, 65; National Register of Historic Places, 65; Naval History and Heritage Command, 65; Social Security History, 66; Social Security History, 66; The Civil War, 63; U.S. Army Center of Military History, 66; U.S. Army Heritage and Education Center, 67; Veterans History Project, 67; Vietnam-Era Prisoner-of-War/Missing-in-Action Database, 67
History of the United States Capitol, 373
HIV.gov, 279
HIV.gov Blog, 279
HIV/AIDS Programs, 434
HIV/AIDS Surveillance Reports, 279
HIV and STD Testing Resources, 281
Hollings Manufacturing Extension Partnership (MEP), 200
Holocaust Memorial Museum, 81
Homeland Security: Advisory Council, 112; Center for Homeland Defense and Security, 109; Digital Library, 112; FBI National Security Branch, 111; Information Sharing Environment, 112; Missile Defense Agency, 113; National Homeland Security Research Center, 113; National Nuclear Security Administration, 113; Ready.gov, 114; SAFETY Act, 114; Transportation Security Administration, 115; United States Secret Service, 115; USDOJ National Security Division, 115
Homeland Security Department (DHS), 111; Advisory Council, 112; Customs and Border Protection, 364; Federal Law Enforcement Training Centers, 358; Immigration and Customs Enforcement, 359; Immigration Data and Statistics, 333; SAFETY Act, 114; US-CERT, 207
Homeland Security Studies & Analysis Institute, 461
Homelessness, Interagency Council on, 430
Home Loans-VA, 429
House Democracy Partnership (HDP), 336
Household Products Database, 320

House of Representatives, 376; Clerk of the House, 372; Committee on House Administration, 372; Committees, 374; Congress.gov, 382; *Guide to House and Senate Members*, 373; House Democratic Leader, 374; Kids in the House, 161; Lobbying Disclosure, 374; Majority Whip, 375; Office of Congressional Ethics, 380; Office of the Clerk, 372; Office of the Law Revision Counsel, 367; Speaker.gov, 376; Speaker's Blog, 376; *Statement of Disbursements (SOD)*, 374
Housing and Urban Development, Department of (HUD), 427; Faith-Based and Neighborhood Partnerships, Center for, 432; Healthy Homes and Lead Hazard Control, 320; HUDCLIPS, 429; HUD User, 429; Making Home Affordable, 430; Office of Lead Hazard Control and Healthy Homes, 291; Office of University Partnerships, 435
How Our Laws Are Made, 382
HUDCLIPS, 429
HUD User, 429
Humane Society of the United States, 461
Human Exploration and Operations Mission Directorate, 417
Humanities: National Endowment for the Humanities, 59
Hydrogen and Fuel Cells Interagency Working Group, 184

IARPA, 118
Idaho National Laboratory (INL), 190
Identity Theft, 358
IDManagement.gov, 250
iEdison, 256
IGNET-Federal Inspectors General, 250
Ike Skelton Combined Arms Research Library (CARL), 71
Immigration and Customs Enforcement (ICE), 359
Immigration Data and Statistics, 333
Immigration Review, Executive Office for, 333
Immigration Services: Citizenship and Immigration Services, 334
Improving U.S. Voting Systems, 248
Income-Census Bureau, 176
Indian Affairs, 272
Indian Arts and Crafts Board, 55
Indian Gaming Commission, 343
Indian Health Service (IHS), 290
Industry & Analysis (I&A), 48
Infectious Diseases: U.S. Army Medical Research Institute of Infectious Diseases, 109
Influenza (Flu), 279
Information Analysis Centers (IACs), 108
Information for Financial Aid Professionals (IFAP), 145
Information Security Oversight Office (ISOO), 266
Information Sharing Environment (ISE), 112
Information Technology, Center for, 296
Information Technology Laboratory (ITL), 204
Information Technology Portal, 204
Injury Prevention and Control, National Center for (NCIPC), 321
In-Q-Tel, 119
INSCOM, 123
Inspector General for Tax Administration (TIGTA), 252
Institute for National Strategic Studies (INSS), 108
Institute for Telecommunication Sciences (ITS), 198
Institute of Education Sciences (IES), 147
Institute of Museum and Library Services (IMLS), 58
Institute of Peace, 328
Institute on Drug Abuse: NIDA for Teens: The Science Behind Drug Abuse, 291
Insure Kids Now, 284
Integrated Taxonomic Information System (ITIS), 392
Intellectual Property: STOPfakes.gov, 22, 51
Intelligence: Advanced Research Projects Activity, 118; Army Intelligence and Security Command, 123; Bureau of Intelligence and Research, 118; Central Intelligence Agency, 116; CIA FOIA Electronic Reading Room, 117;

Commission on Intelligence Capabilities Regarding WMD, 117; CREST Records Search Tool, 118; Defense Intelligence Agency, 118; IARPA, 118; In-Q-Tel, 119; Marine Corps Intelligence Department, 119; National Counterintelligence and Security Center, 119; National Counterterrorism Center, 119; National Geospatial-Intelligence Agency, 120; National Reconnaissance Office, 120; National Security Agency/Central Security Service, 120; National Security Archive, 120, 467; National Virtual Translation Center, 121; Office of Naval Intelligence, 122; Office of the Director of National Intelligence, 121; OpenNet, 122; Open Source Center, 122

Intelligence and Security Command (INSCOM), 123

Intelligence Careers, 177

Intelligent Transportation Systems (ITS), 447

Interactive Tariff and Trade DataWeb, 48

Interagency Autism Coordinating Committee (IACC), 290

Interagency Working Group on Limited English Proficiency, 270

Inter-American Development Bank (IDB), 462

Inter-American Foundation (IAF), 336

Intercountry Adoption, 424

Intergovernmental Relations Advisory Commission, 271

Interior Department (DOI), 229; Bureau of Ocean Energy Management, 219; Bureau of Reclamation, 229; Bureau of Safety and Environmental Enforcement, 212; EarthExplorer, 225; Earth Resources Observation and Science (EROS) Center, 225; Forests and Rangelands, 20; Heritage Documentation Programs, 64; Library, 69; National Register of Historic Places, 65; Office of the Special Trustee for American Indians, 272; Volunteer.gov, 440; Wetland and Aquatic Research Center, 234

Internal Revenue Service (IRS), 263; Charities Search, 439; Joint Board for the Enrollment of Actuaries, 41; Tax Information for Indian Tribal Governments, 273

International Bureau of Education (IBE), 462

International Criminal Court (ICC), 462

International Education: Bureau of Educational and Cultural Affairs, 156; EducationUSA, 156; Foreign Medical Education and Accreditation, 157; International Activities Program, 157; International Affairs Office, 157; STEM: Science, Technology, Engineering, and Math, 157; U.S. Network for Education Information, 158

International Monetary Fund (IMF), 462

International Programs Center (IPC), 131

International Programs Center (IPC)-Census Bureau, 131

International Space Station (ISS), 414

International Trade: AESDirect, 45; African Growth and Opportunity Act (AGOA), 44; Bureau of Industry and Security, 45; Commercial Service, 45; Commercial Service in China, 45; Defense Technology Security Administration, 46; Directorate of Defense Trade Controls, 46; Enforcement and Compliance, 46; Export.gov, 46; Export Administration Regulations, 47; Export-Import Bank of the United States, 47, 459; Foreign Exchange Rates, 53; Foreign Trade Statistics, 47; Industry & Analysis, 48; Interactive Tariff and Trade DataWeb, 48; Interactive Tariff and Trade DataWeb, 48; International Trade Administration, 48; International Trade Commission, 49; Market Research Library, 49; Notify U.S., 49; Office of Textiles and Apparel, 50; Office of the U.S. Trade Representative, 50; Office of Trade Agreements Negotiations and Compliance, 50; Office of Trade Policy & Analysis, 50; Overseas Private Investment Corporation, 51; Special

American Business Internship Training Program, 51; STOPfakes.gov, 22, 51; Trade and Development Agency, 52; TradeStats Express, 52; United States Court of International Trade, 352
International Trade Administration (ITA), 48; Industry & Analysis, 48; Special American Business Internship Training Program, 51
International Trade Commission (ITC), 49; *Export USA*, 47; Interactive Tariff and Trade DataWeb, 48
Internet Crime Complaint Center (IC3), 359
Internet Service: NASA Acquisition Internet Service, 256
INTERPOL Washington, 359
Investor.gov, 41
IPUMS USA: Integrated Public Use Microdata Series, 132
Iraq: GulfLINK, 278; Justice Department Activities in Iraq, 335; National Center for PTSD, 280; Wartime Contracting Commission, 253

JAMA Network, 463
James Madison Graduate Fellowships, 166
James Martin Center for Nonproliferation Studies (CNS), 463
James Melville Gilliss Library, 79
James Webb Space Telescope (JWST), 415
Japan-United States Friendship Commission (JUSFC), 327
Jefferson Lab, 401
Jet Propulsion Laboratory (JPL), 415; Cassini Solstice Mission, 412; Ocean Surface Topography from Space, 403; Solar System Exploration, 420; Space Calendar, 420; Voyager, 421
JFK Assassination Records, 64
Job Accommodation Network (JAN), 172
Jobs: Employment and Training Administration, 177; Intelligence Careers, 177; O*NET OnLine: Occupational Information Network, 177; *Occupational Outlook Handbook*, 178; Standard Occupational Classification System, 178; Student and Recent Graduate Jobs-USAJOBS, 178; USAJOBS, 178, 179; Women's Bureau, 179
John A. Volpe Transportation Systems Center, 448
John C. Stennis Center for Public Service, 273
Johnson Space Center, 415
John W. Kluge Center at the Library of Congress, 58
Joint Agricultural Weather Facility (JAWF), 12
Joint Board for the Enrollment of Actuaries, 41
Joint Chiefs of Staff, 93
Joint Electronic Library (JEL), 104
Joint Genome Institute (JGI), 391
Journal of Extension (JOE), 12
Justice, National Institute of, 361
Justice Assistance, Bureau of, 355
Justice Department (DOJ), 342; Activities in Iraq, 335; Americans with Disabilities Act, 339; Antitrust Division, 340; Bureau of Alcohol, Tobacco, Firearms, and Explosives, 354; Civil Division, 346; Civil Rights Division, 341; Community Relations Service, 355; Competition and Real Estate, 23; Computer Crime and Intellectual Property Section, 355; COPS Office: Grants and Resources for Community Policing, 356; Criminal Division, 356; Criminal Justice Reference Service, 360; Disability Rights Section, 342; Executive Office for Immigration Review, 333; Federal Bureau of Investigation, 357; Foreign Agents Registration Act, 336; Foreign Claims Settlement Commission, 343; Justice Information Sharing, 360; Legal Policy Office, 350; Libraries, 69; National Security Division, 115; Office of Information and Privacy, 267; Office of Legal Counsel, 344; Office of Legal Policy, 350; Office of the Attorney General, 362; Office of the Deputy Attorney General, 363; Office of the Pardon Attorney, 389; Office of Tribal Justice, 273; Office on Violence

Against Women, 363; Parole Commission, 365; Privacy and Civil Liberties Office, 344; Project Safe Childhood, 364; Project Safe Neighborhoods, 364; Servicemembers and Veterans Initiative, 127; *Sourcebook of Criminal Justice Statistics*, 364; Trustee Program, 353; United States Attorneys, 352
Justice Programs, Office of (OJP), 362
Justice Statistics, Bureau of (BJS), 355
JUSTNET-Justice Technology Information Network, 360
Juvenile Justice and Delinquency Prevention, Office of, 363
Juvenile Justice and Delinquency Prevention Council, 355

Kennedy Space Center, 416
Kidney Disease Education Program (NKDEP), 281
Kids' Pages: Admongo.gov, 158; America's Story from America's Library, 159; Ben's Guide to U.S. Government, 159; BLS Career Information, 159; ChooseMyPlate for Kids, 159; CIA Kids' Zone, 159; CryptoKids, 160; EIA Energy Kids, 160; FBI Kids' Page, 160; FCC Kids Zone, 160; FDA Kids' Site, 160; Inside the White House, 161; Kids.gov, 161; Kids and Families-Social Security, 161; Kids in Parks, 161; Kids in the House, 161; Let's Go Outside!, 162; NASA for Students, 162; NASA Space Place, 162; NCEH Kids Page, 162; NGAkids Art Zone, 162; NIEHS Kids' Pages, 163; NRO Jr.gov, 163; Peace Corps Kids World, 163; Sci4Kids, 163; Science Education, 164; Smithsonian Education: Students, 164; State Facts for Students, 164; StopBullying.gov, 164; Students for the Environment, 164; Student's Guide to Global Climate Change, 163; The Student Corner-NRC, 163; ToxMystery, 165; United States Mint's Site for Kids: H.I.P. Pocket Change, 165; USPTO Kids, 165
Korean War: State-Level Lists of Fatal Casualties, 66

Laboratory of Neurosciences, 392
Labor Department, 170; America's Heroes at Work, 123; Benefits.gov, 431; Data Enforcement, 170; Davis-Bacon and Related Acts, 169; Faith-Based and Neighborhood Partnerships, Center for, 432; Migrant and Seasonal Farmworkers, 435; Wage and Hour Division, 174; Wirtz Labor Library, 81; Women's Bureau, 179
Labor-Management Relations: Federal Mediation & Conciliation Service, 179; National Labor Relations Board, 180; National Mediation Board, 180; Office of Labor-Management Standards, 180
Labor Relations Authority (FLRA), 258
Lakes Gateway, 85
Land and Maritime-DLA, 254
Langley Research Center (LaRC), 417
Large Synoptic Survey Telescope (LSST), 463
Law Librarians' Society of Washington, DC: *Legislative Source Book*, 383
Lawrence Berkeley National Laboratory (LBL), 395
Lawrence Livermore National Laboratory (LLNL), 395; Engineering at LLNL, 200
Lead-EPA, 320
Lead Hazard Control and Healthy Homes, Office of, 291
League of Conservation Voters (LCV), 464
Learning Landscapes (BLM), 138
Learning Registry, 140
Legal Policy Office, 350
Legal Services Corporation (LSC), 350
Legislative Resources on FDsys, 383
LEP.gov, 270
Let's Go Outside!, 162
Libraries: Air University Library Index to Military Periodicals, 68; Archives Library Information Center (ALIC), 68; Bureau of Land Management Library, 68; Combined Arms Research Library, 71; Conservation Library, 68; D'Azzo

Research Library, 69; Department of Justice Libraries, 69; Engineer Research and Development Center Library, 69; EPA National Library Network, 69; Federal Bureau of Prisons Library, 70; Federal Depository Library Program, 70; Federal Library and Information Network (FEDLINK), 70; Fermilab Library, 70; Geological Survey Libraries Program, 70; Goddard Library Repository, 71; GOVDOC-L, 71; Homeland Security Digital Library, 112; Institute of Museum and Library Services, 58; Interior Department Library, 69; Joint Electronic Library, 104; Justice Department Libraries, 69; Library Statistics Program, 73; Los Alamos National Laboratory Research Library, 73; Marine Corps Library, 73; MERLN (Military Educational Research Library Network), 73; Mine Safety and Health Administration Library Information, 74; Muir S. Fairchild Research Information Center, 74; NARA Locations Nationwide, 75; NASA Headquarters Library, 74; National Agricultural Library, 74; National Defense University Library, 75; National Institute of Corrections Library, 75; National Institute of Environmental Health Sciences Library, 75; National Institutes of Health Library, 77; National Library of Education, 76; National Library of Medicine, 76; National Library Services for the Blind and Physically Handicapped, 76; National Network of Libraries of Medicine, 77; National Radio Astronomy Observatory Library, 78; National Science Digital Library, 409; National Technical Reports Library, 409; National Transportation Library, 78; NIEHS Library, 75; NIH Library, 77; Nimitz Library, U.S. Naval Academy, 78; NIST Virtual Library, 76; NOAA Central Library, 77; NOAA Seattle Library, 78; Northwest and Alaska Fisheries Science Centers Library, 79; Patent and Trademark Resource Centers, 79; Pentagon Digital Library, 79; Presidential Libraries and Museums, 79; Ralph J. Bunche Library, 80; Scientific Library at the National Cancer Institute at Frederick, 80; Smithsonian Libraries, 80; Staff College Automated Military Periodicals Index (SCAMPI), 80; USAID Knowledge Management (KM) Support, 80; USNO James Melville Gilliss Library, 79; Wirtz Labor Library, 81

Library of Congress, 71; A Century of Lawmaking for a New Nation, 380; A Guide to the War of 1812, 64; American Memory, 63; Blog of the LOC, 72; Center for the Book, 57; Congressional Documents and Debates, 380; Copyright Office, 341; *Country Studies Series*, 324; FEDLINK, 70; Frontline Diplomacy: Foreign Affairs Oral History Collection, 326; Global Legal Monitor, 367; John W. Kluge Center, 58; Military Legal Resources, 343; Online Catalog, 72; Poetry and Literature Center, 56; Read.gov, 60; Science Tracer Bullets Online, 410; Teacher Resources, 165; Veterans History Project, 67; Web Archiving, 67

Library of Medicine: DailyMed, 312; Disaster Information Management Research Center, 319; Drug Information Portal, 312; Household Products Database, 320; National Center for Biotechnology Information, 393; NLM Gateway, 310; PubChem, 394; PubMed, 310; PubMed Central, 311; Visible Human Project, 312

Life Sciences Data Archive, 393

Lister Hill National Center for Biomedical Communications, 308

LLSDC's Legislative Source Book, 383

Lobbying Disclosure: House of Representatives, 374; Senate, 375

Longitudinal Employer-Household Dynamics (LEHD), 176

Los Alamos National Laboratory (LANL): Energy Department, 396; Research Library, 73; T-2 Nuclear Information

Service, 404
Los Angeles Air Force Base, 93
Low Income Home Energy Assistance Program (LIHEAP), 434
Lunar and Planetary Science at the NSSDCA, 416

Making Home Affordable, 430
Malaria Initiative, 282
Manufacturing & Construction Statistics, 25
Manufacturing.gov, 24
Manufacturing Technology Program (ManTech), 201
Marine Corps (USMC), 98; Intelligence Department, 119; Library of the Marine Corps (LoMC), 73; Manpower and Reserve Affairs (M&RA), 94; Marine Corps Forces Reserve (MARFORRES), 93; Public Health Center, 126; Recruiting, 93; Reserve Employer Support, 125; Wounded Warrior Regiment, 128
Marine Corps University (MCU), 153
Marine Protected Areas of the United States, 216
Maritime Administration (MARAD), 442
Maritime Commission (FMC), 442
Market Research Library, 49
Marshall Space Flight Center (MSFC), 416
Marshals Service, 365
MBDA Web Portal, 25
Medical Research Institute of Infectious Diseases (USAMRIID), 109
Medical Reserve Corps (MRC), 285
Medical Schools: National Committee on Foreign Medical Education and Accreditation, 157
Medicare & Medicaid Services, Centers for, 283
Medicare.gov, 284
Medicare Payment Advisory Commission (MedPAC), 284
Medicine and Medical Devices: Devices and Radiological Health, Center for, 314; General Medical Sciences, National Institute of, 394; National Library of Medicine, 76; National Museum of Health and Medicine, 83; National Network of Libraries of Medicine, 77
MedlinePlus, 309
MedWatch: FDA Safety Information and Adverse Event Reporting Program, 315
Mental Health, National Institute of (NIMH), 301
Mental Health, President's New Freedom Commission on, 293
Merchant Marine Academy, 155
Merit Systems Protection Board (MSPB), 259
MERLN, 73
MIAs: Vietnam-Era Prisoner-of-War/ Missing-in-Action Database, 67
Middle East Partnership Initiative (MEPI), 337
Migrant and Seasonal Farmworkers, 435
Migratory Bird Conservation Commission, 216
Migratory Bird Program, 216
Military Academy at West Point, 156; Combating Terrorism Center, 106
Military Commissions, 343
Military Educational Research Library Network (MERLN), 73
Military Legal Resources, 343
Military Morale and Welfare: Air Force Bands, 123; Air Force Medical Service, 123; America's Heroes at Work, 123; Arlington National Cemetery, 124; Armed Forces Retirement Home, 124; Army & Air Force Exchange Service, 124; Army Music, 127; Defense Department Education Activity, 124; Employer Support of the Guard and Reserve, 125; eVetRecs, 125; National Resource Directory, 126; Nationwide Gravesite Locator, 126; Navy and Marine Corps Public Health Center, 126; Navy Band, 127; Navy Medicine, 126; Returning Service Members, 127; Servicemembers and Veterans Initiative, 127; USA4 Military Families, 128; Veterans Affairs Department, 125; Veterans Benefits Administration, 128; Wounded Warrior Regiment, 128
Military Office, White House, 387

Military Resources: War of 1812, 65
Military Sensing Information Analysis Center (SENSIAC), 109
Millennium Challenge Corporation (MCC), 337, 464
Mine Safety and Health Administration (MSHA): Library Information, 74; Workplace conditions, 181
Mine Safety and Health Review Commission (FMSHRC), 342
Mines and Mining: Manufacturing & Construction Statistics, 25
Minority Business Development Agency (MBDA), 25
Minority Health and Health Disparities, National Institute on, 299
Mint: U.S. Mint, 53
Missile Defense Agency (MDA), 113
Missing and Unidentified Persons System (NamUs), 361
Money: Advanced Counterfeit Deterrence Program, 52; Bureau of Engraving and Printing, 53; Foreign Exchange Rates, 53; United States Mint, 53
Money Services Businesses (MSBs), 41
Morbidity and Mortality Weekly Report, 309
Mothers Against Drunk Driving (MADD), 464
Muir S. Fairchild Research Information Center (MSFRIC), 74
Museums: Anacostia Community Museum, 81; Cooper Hewitt, Smithsonian Design Museum, 81; Hill Aerospace Museum, 81; Institute of Museum and Library Services, 58; Museum Management Program, 82; National Air and Space Museum, 82; National Gallery of Art, 82; National Museum of African American History and Culture, 83; National Museum of African Art, 83; National Museum of American History, 83; National Museum of Health and Medicine, 83; National Museum of Natural History, 84; National Museum of the American Indian, 83; National Postal Museum, 84; Naval Undersea Museum, 84; Presidential Libraries and Museums, 79; Smithsonian American Art Museum, 84; Smithsonian Institution, 61; United States Holocaust Memorial Museum, 81
MyMoney.gov, 28

NAEP Data Explorer (NDE), 149
NAL Catalog (AGRICOLA), 13
NAL Digital Collections (NALDC), 13
Names: Popular Baby Names, 88
Nanotechnology at NIH, 204
Nanotechnology at NIOSH, 181
Nanotechnology Initiative, 206
National Aeronautics and Space Administration (NASA), 405; Acquisition Internet Service, 256; Advanced Supercomputing Division, 204; Aeronautics Research Mission Directorate, 411; Ames Research Center, 412; Armstrong Flight Research Center, 416; Astrobiology, 393; Astrophysics Data System, 401; Earth Observing System, 398; Eclipse, 413; Federal Acquisition Jumpstation, 255; Galileo Legacy Site, 413; Glenn Research Center, 414; GLOBE Program, 140; Goddard Institute for Space Studies, 401; Goddard Library Repository, 71; GRIN: Great Images in NASA, 414; Headquarters, 417; Headquarters Library, 74; High Energy Astrophysics Science Archive Research Center, 400; History Division, 417; Human Exploration and Operations Mission Directorate, 417; Independent Verification and Validation Facility, 205; International Space Station, 414; Internet Service, 256; James Webb Space Telescope, 415; Jet Propulsion Laboratory, 415; Johnson Space Center, 415; Kennedy Space Center, 416; Langley Research Center, 417; Life Sciences Data Archive, 393; Marshall Space Flight Center, 416; NASA-Education, 140; NASA for Students, 162; NASA Space Place, 162; NSPIRES-NASA Research Opportunities, 419; Ocean Surface Topography from Space, 403; Planetary

Data System, 420; Science, 418; Scientific and Technical Information Program, 409; Shuttle, 418; SOHO: The Solar and Heliospheric Observatory, 404; Solar System Exploration, 420; Solar System Exploration Research Virtual Institute, 418; Space Science Data Coordinated Archive, 419; Stennis Space Center, 421; Strategic Partnerships Office, 205; *Tech Briefs*, 418; Technical Reports Server, 418; Technology Transfer Portal, 205; Voyager, 421; Wallops Flight Facility, 422; White Sands Test Facility, 419

National Agricultural Law Center, 13

National Agricultural Library (NAL), 74

National Agricultural Library Digital Collections (NALDC), 13

National Agricultural Statistics Service (NASS), 14

National Agroforestry Center (NAC), 20

National Ag Safety Database (NASD), 13

National AIDS Policy, Office of (ONAP), 291

National Air and Space Museum (NASM), 82

National American Indian Court Judges Association (NAICJA), 464

National Arboretum, 14

National Archaeological Database (NADB), 58

National Archives and Records Administration (NARA), 266; Access to Archival Databases, 62; America's Historical Documents, 62; Archives Library Information Center (ALIC), 68; Center for Legislative Archives, 381; Compilation of Presidential Documents, 388; Declassification Center, 267; Electoral College, 247; eVetRecs, 125; Executive Orders Disposition Tables, 389; Information Security Oversight Office, 266; JFK Assassination Records, 64; Locations Nationwide, 75; Military Resources: War of 1812, 65; National Historical Publications and Records Commission, 65; Office of the Federal Register, 268; Personnel Records Center, 260; Presidential Libraries and Museums, 79; Public Interest Declassification Board, 268; Public Laws, 368; *Public Papers of the Presidents of the United States*, 390; Teachers' Resources, 140; *United States Government Manual*, 252

National Association for the Advancement of Colored People (NAACP), 465

National Avalanche Center (NAC), 86

National Broadband Plan, 198

National Cancer Institute (NCI), 298; Cancer Information Service, 276; Frederick, 305; Scientific Library at the NCI, 80; Surveillance, Epidemiology, and End Results (SEER) Program, 311; TOXNET, 311

National Capital Planning Commission (NCPC), 59

National Center for Advancing Translational Sciences (NCATS), 298

National Center for Biotechnology Information (NCBI), 393

National Center for Complementary and Integrative Health (NCCIH), 298

National Center for Education Statistics (NCES), 147, 148

National Center for Environmental Economics (NCEE), 213

National Center for Health Statistics (NCHS), 309

National Center for HIV/AIDS, Viral Hepatitis, STD, and TB Prevention, 280

National Center for Injury Prevention and Control (NCIPC), 321

National Center for Missing and Exploited Children (NCMEC), 465

National Center for Preservation Technology and Training (NCPTT), 59

National Center for PTSD, 280

National Center for Toxicological Research (NCTR), 299

National Center for Veterans Analysis and Statistics, 135

National Center for Victims of Crime (NCVC), 465

National Center on Elder Abuse (NCEA), 360

National Centers for Coastal Ocean Science (NCCOS), 224
National Centers for Environmental Information (NCEI), 240
National Centers for Environmental Prediction (NCEP), 221
National Clearinghouse on Families and Youth (NCFY), 424
National Commission on Terrorist Attacks Upon the United States, 113
National Committee on Foreign Medical Education and Accreditation, 157
National Committee on Vital and Health Statistics (NCVHS), 290
National Consumer Protection Week, 29
National Council on Disability (NCD), 299
National Counterintelligence and Security Center (NCSC), 119
National Counterterrorism Center (NCTC), 119
National Credit Union Administration (NCUA), 42
National Criminal Justice Reference Service (NCJRS), 360
National Data Buoy Center (NDBC), 241
National Declassification Center (NDC), 267
National Defense University (NDU), 153; Staff College Automated Military Periodicals Index (SCAMPI), 80
National Do Not Call Registry, 29
National Earthquake Information Center (NEIC), 401
National Endowment for the Arts (NEA), 55
National Endowment for the Humanities (NEH), 59
National Energy Research Scientific Computing Center (NERSC), 206
National Energy Technology Laboratory (NETL), 190
National Environmental Policy Act (NEPA)-CEQ, 210
National Environmental Policy Act (NEPA)-EPA, 210
National Environmental Satellite, Data, and Information Service, 221
National Estuarine Research Reserve System, 216
National Eye Institute (NEI), 299
National Film Preservation Board (NFPB), 56
National Gallery of Art (NGA), 82
National Genetic Resources Program: Germplasm Resources Information Network, 11
National Geodetic Survey (NGS), 227
National Geological and Geophysical Data Preservation Program, 206
National Geospatial-Intelligence Agency (NGA), 120
National Geospatial Program (NGP), 227
National Guard, 94; Employer Support of the Guard and Reserve, 125
National Health Information Center (NHIC), 310
National Health Service Corps (NHSC), 285
National Highway Traffic Safety Administration (NHTSA), 450; *FARS Encyclopedia*, 449; Parents Central, 451; SaferCar.gov, 451
National Historical Publications and Records Commission (NHPRC), 65
National Homeland Security Research Center (NHSRC), 113
National Human Genome Research Institute (NHGRI), 394
National Hurricane Center, 241
National Indian Gaming Commission (NIGC), 343
National Indian Justice Center (NIJC), 465
National Information Center (NIC), 38
National Institute of Allergy and Infectious Diseases (NIAID), 299
National Institute of Biomedical Imaging and Bioengineering (NIBIB), 300
National Institute of Child Health and Human Development (NICHD), 300
National Institute of Corrections (NIC), 361; Library, 75
National Institute of Dental and Craniofacial Research (NIDCR), 301
National Institute of Diabetes and Digestive and Kidney Diseases (NIDDK), 301
National Institute of Environmental Health Sciences (NIEHS), 301; Environmental

Health Perspectives: EHP Online, 297; Kids' Pages, 163; Library, 75; National Toxicology Program, 305
National Institute of Food and Agriculture (NIFA), 14
National Institute of General Medical Sciences (NIGMS), 394
National Institute of Justice (NIJ), 361
National Institute of Mental Health (NIMH), 301
National Institute of Neurological Disorders and Stroke (NINDS), 302
National Institute of Nursing Research (NINR), 302
National Institute of Occupational Safety and Health (NIOSH), 181
National Institute of Standards and Technology (NIST), 201; Computer Security Resource Center, 206; Data Gateway, 410; Improving U.S. Voting Systems, 248; Manufacturing.gov, 24; Notify U.S., 49; Physical Measurement Laboratory, 403; Virtual Library, 76
National Institute on Aging (NIA), 302
National Institute on Alcohol Abuse and Alcoholism (NIAAA), 308; Alcohol Policy Information System, 340
National Institute on Drug Abuse (NIDA), 303
National Institute on Minority Health and Health Disparities (NIMHD), 299
National Institutes of Health (NIH), 304; Advancing Translational Sciences, National Center for, 298; Aging, National Institute on, 302; Alcohol Abuse and Alcoholism, National Institute on, 303; Alcohol Policy Information System, 340; Allergy and Infectious Diseases, National Institute of, 299; Alzheimer's Disease Education and Referral (ADEAR) Center, 276; American Indian Health, 287; Animal Care and Use, Office of, 306; Arctic Health, 295; Arthritis and Musculoskeletal and Skin Diseases, National Institute of, 300; Behavioral and Social Sciences Research, Office of, 306; Bioethics Department, 288; Biomedical Imaging and Bioengineering, National Institute of, 300; Cancer Information Service, 276; Center for Information Technology, 296; Center for Scientific Review, 305; Chemoinformatics Tools and Services, 398; Child Health and Human Development, National Institute of, 300; Clinical Center, 305; Common Fund, 305; Computational Bioscience and Engineering Laboratory, 391; Deafness and Other Communication Disorders, 303; Dental and Craniofacial Research, National Institute of, 301; Diabetes and Digestive and Kidney Diseases, National Institute of, 301; Diabetes Education Program, 280; Disease Prevention, Office of, 306; Environmental Health Science Education: Teachers, 139; Fogarty International Center, 297; General Medical Sciences Institute, 394; Genetic and Rare Diseases Information Center, 278; Genome Integrity & Structural Biology Laboratory, 392; Health Public Access, National Institutes of, 304; Heart, Lung, and Blood Institute, 281; iEdison, 256; Laboratory of Neurosciences, 392; Library, 77; Lister Hill National Center for Biomedical Communications, 308; Mental Health, National Institute of, 301; Nanotechnology at NIH, 204; National Center for Complementary and Integrative Health, 298; National Eye Institute, 299; National Human Genome Research Institute, 394; National Institute of Environmental Health Sciences, 301; National Institute on Minority Health and Health Disparities, 299; National Kidney Disease Education Program, 281; Neurological Disorders and Stroke, National Institute of, 302; NIAID Biodefense and Related Programs, 114; NLM Gateway, 310; Nursing Research, National Institute of, 302; Office of the Director, 306; Profiles in Science, 306; PubChem, 394; *Reports of the Surgeon General*, 294; Research Portfolio

Online Reporting Tools, 307; Science Policy, Office of, 292; Senior Health, 281; Smokefree.gov, 294; Specialized Information Services Division, 294; Stem Cell Information, 307
National Interagency Fire Center (NIFC), 231
National Journal, 466
National Labor Relations Board (NLRB), 180
National Library of Education (NLE), 76
National Library of Medicine (NLM), 76
National Library Services for the Blind and Physically Handicapped, 76
National Map, 227
National Marine Sanctuaries, 217; Education, 141
National Maritime Center, 443
National Mediation Board (NMB), 180
National Missing and Unidentified Persons System (NamUs), 361
National Museum of African American History and Culture (NMAAHC), 83
National Museum of African Art, 83
National Museum of American History, 83
National Museum of Health and Medicine (NMHM), 83
National Museum of Natural History, 84
National Museum of the American Indian (NMAI), 83
National Nanotechnology Initiative (NNI), 206
National Native American Graves Protection and Repatriation Act Program, 60
National Network of Libraries of Medicine (NN/LM), 77
National Nuclear Security Administration (NNSA), 113
National Oceanic and Atmospheric Administration (NOAA), 222; Air Resources Laboratory, 219; Center for Sponsored Coastal Ocean Research, 220; Centers for Coastal Ocean Science, 224; Central Library, 77; Commissioned Officers Corps, 223; Coral Reef Information System, 232; Coral Reef Task Force, 218; Earth Observing System, 398; Earth System Research Laboratory, 223; Education Resources, 141; Estuarine Research Reserve System, 216; Estuary Restoration Act, 215; Geophysical Fluid Dynamics Laboratory, 400; Marine Protected Areas of the U.S., 216; National Centers for Environmental Information, 402; National Estuarine Research Reserve System, 216; National Marine Sanctuaries, 217; NOAA Fisheries, 18; Northwest Fisheries Science Center, 19; Office for Coastal Management, 217; Office of Aquaculture, 18; Office of Protected Resources, 218; Office of Response and Restoration, 218; Research, 223; Seattle Library, 78; Space Commerce, Office of, 419; Space Weather Prediction Center, 421; Tides & Currents, 242; Weather Radio, 242
National Oceanographic Data Center (NODC), 222
National Ocean Service (NOS), 222
National Optical Astronomy Observatory (NOAO), 466
National Organic Program (NOP), 15
National Organization for Women (NOW), 466
National Park Service (NPS), 86; Archeology Program, 57; Explore Nature, 232; Heritage Documentation Programs, 64; Kids in Parks, 161; National Archeological Database, 58; National Center for Preservation Technology and Training, 59; Native American Graves Protection and Repatriation Act Program, 60; United States Park Police, 365; Wild and Scenic Rivers System, 217
National Personnel Records Center (NPRC), 260
National Postal Museum, 84
National Practitioner Data Bank, 286
National Radio Astronomy Observatory (NRAO), 402; Library, 78
National Reconnaissance Office (NRO), 120
National Recording Preservation Board (NRPB), 60

National Register of Historic Places (NRHP), 65
National Rehabilitation Information Center (NARIC), 310
National Renewable Energy Laboratory (NREL), 185
National Republican Congressional Committee (NRCC), 466
National Republican Senatorial Committee (NRSC), 467
National Resource Directory, 126
National Responsible Fatherhood Clearinghouse (NRFC), 425
National Science Advisory Board for Biosecurity (NSABB), 405
National Science and Technology Center (NSTC), 405
National Science Board (NSB), 406
National Science Foundation (NSF), 406; Classroom Resources, 141; Directorate for Education and Human Resources, 145; Graduate Education Division, 154; National Science Board, 406; President's National Medal of Science, 407; Research.gov, 407; Research on Learning in Formal and Informal Settings, 146; Science Digital Library, 409; Undergraduate Education Division, 154
National Security Agency (NSA), 120
National Security Archive, 120, 467
National Security Council (NSC), 386
National Service Center for Environmental Publications (NSCEP), 224
National Severe Storms Laboratory (NSSL), 241
National Sex Offender Public Website, 357
National Solar Observatory (NSO), 467
National Technical Information Service (NTIS), 267; Technical Reports Library, 409
National Technical Reports Library (NTRL), 409
National Telecommunications and Information Administration (NTIA), 198
National Toxicology Program (NTP), 305
National Traffic and Road Closure Information, 446
National Trails System, 86
National Transit Database, 444
National Transportation Library (NTL), 78
National Transportation Safety Board (NTSB), 451
National Virtual Translation Center (NVTC), 121
National Vulnerability Database (NVD), 206
National Water and Climate Center, 222
National Weather Service (NWS), 241
National Weather Service Marine Forecasts, 242
National Wetlands Inventory Center (NWI), 223
National Wild and Scenic Rivers System, 217
National Wild Horse and Burro Program, 231
National Wildlife Health Center (NWHC), 231
National Women's Business Council (NWBC), 25
National Zoological Park, 87
Nation's Report Card, 149
Nationwide Gravesite Locator, 126
Native Americans: Administration for Native Americans, 425; American Indian and Alaska Native Resources, 135; American Indian Health, 287; American Indian Tribal Portal, 211; Bureau of Indian Education, 143; Codetalk, 271; FCC Office of Native Affairs and Policy, 196; Indian Affairs, 272; Indian Arts and Crafts Board, 55; Indian Gaming Commission, 343; Indian Health Service, 290; National Museum of the American Indian, 83; Native American Graves Protection and Repatriation Act Program, 60; Office of the Special Trustee for American Indians, 272; Office of Tribal Justice, 273; Tax Information for Indian Tribal Governments, 273; TribalAIR, 238; Tribal Energy and Environmental Information Clearinghouse, 214
NATO: U.S. Mission to NATO, 338
Natural History Museum, 84

Natural Resources: Alaska Science Center, 228; Animal Welfare, 228; Animal Welfare Information Center, 228; Bureau of Land Management, 229; Coral Reef Information System, 232; Endangered Species, 230; Explore Nature, 232; Fish and Wildlife Service, 230; Fort Collins Science Center, 231; Interior Department, 229; National Interagency Fire Center, 231; National Wild Horse and Burro Program, 231; National Wildlife Health Center, 231; Northern Prairie Wildlife Research Center, 232; Office of Water, 230; Patuxent Wildlife Research Center, 233; Surface Mining Reclamation and Enforcement Office, 232; Water Data for the Nation, 233; Water Resources of the United States, 233; Wetland and Aquatic Research Center, 234
Natural Resources Conservation Service (NRCS), 217; Forestry Technical Resources, 20; NRCS Soils, 15; Plants & Animals, 15; PLANTS Database, 16
Naval Academy, 156; Nimitz Library, 78
Naval History and Heritage Command (NHHC), 65
Naval Network Warfare Command (NETWARCOM), 94
Naval Observatory (USNO), 404; USNO James Melville Gilliss Library, 79
Naval Oceanography Portal, 402
Naval Postgraduate School (NPS), 153
Naval Research Laboratory (NRL), 109
Naval Sea Systems Command (NAVSEA), 94
Naval Undersea Museum, 84
Naval Warfare Centers (NWCs), 94
Navigation Center, USCG, 443
Navy, 98; Acquisition One Source, 253; Band, 127; Blue Angels, 91; Center for Homeland Defense and Security (CHDS), 109; History and Heritage Command, 65; Naval Oceanography Portal, 402; Naval Warfare Centers (NWCs), 94; Navy.com, 95; Navy Reserve (USNR), 95; Network Warfare Command (NETWARCOM), 94; Office of Naval Intelligence (ONI), 122; Personnel Command (NPC), 92; Public Health Center, 126; Research Laboratory (NRL), 109; Reserve Employer Support, 125; Sea Systems Command (NAVSEA), 94; Space and Naval Warfare Systems Command (SPAWAR), 96
Navy Medicine, 126
Navy Reserve (USNR), 95
NCELA: National Clearinghouse for English Language Acquisition, 166
Near Eastern Affairs, Bureau of, 331
Network for Education Information (USNEI), 158
Networking and Information Technology Research and Development Program, 205
Neurological Disorders and Stroke, National Institute of, 302
New Brunswick Laboratory, 402
New Freedom Commission on Mental Health, 293
NGAkids Art Zone, 162
NIAID Biodefense and Related Programs, 114
Nimitz Library, U.S. Naval Academy, 78
Ninth Circuit Court of Appeals, 348
NLM Gateway, 310
Nonproliferation and Disarmament Fund (NDF), 324
North American Industry Classification System (NAICS), 25
North Atlantic Treaty Organization (NATO), 468
Northern Command (NORTHCOM), 98
Northern Prairie Wildlife Research Center, 232
Northwest and Alaska Fisheries Science Centers Library, 79
Northwest Fisheries Science Center (NWFSC), 19
Notices of Judgment Collection (FDA), 314
Notify U.S., 49
NPS: Explore Nature, 232
NRCS Soils, 15
NSPIRES-NASA Research Opportunities, 419

Nuclear Facilities: Defense Nuclear Facilities Safety Board (DNFSB), 110
Nuclear Regulatory Commission (NRC), 190
Nuclear Threat Initiative (NTI), 468
Nursing: National Institute of Nursing Research, 302
Nutrition: Center for Nutrition Policy and Promotion, 316; Dietary Supplements, Office of, 317; Dietary Supplements Label Database, 316; Food and Nutrition Information Center, 316; Food Safety and Applied Nutrition, Center for, 315; Healthy Meals Resource System, 317; Nutrition.gov, 317; Nutrition Policy and Promotion, Center for, 316; SNAP-Ed Connection, 317; WIC Works Resource System, 318

O*NET OnLine: Occupational Information Network, 177
Oak Ridge National Laboratory (ORNL), 396
Occupational Outlook Handbook, 178
Occupational Safety and Health Administration (OSHA), 182
Occupational Safety and Health Review Commission (OSHRC), 344
Oceanographic Data Center (NODC), 222
Ocean Surface Topography from Space, 403
Office for Coastal Management, 217
Office for Victims of Crime (OVC), 362
Office of Air and Radiation (OAR), 235
Office of Animal Care and Use, 306
Office of Aquaculture (NOAA), 18
Office of Behavioral and Social Sciences Research (OBSSR), 306
Office of Cancer Survivorship, 281
Office of Career, Technical, and Adult Education (OCTAE), 137
Office of Chemical Safety and Pollution Prevention, EPA (OCSPP), 236
Office of Child Care, 425
Office of Child Support Enforcement (OCSE), 362
Office of Coast Survey (OCS), 228
Office of Commercial and Business Affairs (CBA), 49
Office of Compliance, 260
Office of Congressional Ethics (OCE), 380
Office of Dietary Supplements (ODS), 317
Office of Disability Employment Policy (ODEP), 172
Office of Disease Prevention (ODP), 306
Office of Domestic Finance, 42
Office of Economic Adjustment (OEA), 426
Office of Economic Policy, 33
Office of Elementary and Secondary Education (OESE), 149
Office of Energy Efficiency and Renewable Energy (EERE), 185
Office of Engineering and Policy (OET), 196
Office of English Language Acquisition (OELA), 141
Office of Environmental Management, 235
Office of Faith-Based and Neighborhood Partnerships, 435
Office of Family Assistance (OFA), 435
Office of Federal Lands Highway (FLH), 445
Office of Federal Sustainability Council, 213
Office of Fellowships and Internships, 155
Office of Financial Stability, 43
Office of Foreign Labor Certification (OFLC), 172
Office of Fossil Energy (FE), 191
Office of Global Criminal Justice (GCJ), 337
Office of Government Ethics (OGE), 250
Office of Government-wide Policy (OGP), 250
Office of Information and Privacy (OIP), 267
Office of Information and Regulatory Affairs (OIRA), 268
Office of Innovation and Improvement (OII), 146
Office of Justice Programs (OJP), 362
Office of Juvenile Justice and Delinquency Prevention (OJJDP), 363
Office of Labor-Management Standards (OLMS), 180
Office of Land and Emergency Management (OLEM), 236

Office of Lead Hazard Control and Healthy Homes (OLHCHH), 291
Office of Legal Policy, 350
Office of Management and Budget (OMB), 251; Blog, 251; Budget of the United States Government, 262; Office of Information and Regulatory Affairs, 268
Office of National AIDS Policy, 291
Office of Native Affairs and Policy (ONAP), 196
Office of Natural Resources Revenue (ONRR), 213
Office of Naval Intelligence (ONI), 122
Office of Nuclear Energy (NE), 191
Office of Personnel Management (OPM), 260; Federal Executive Boards, 249; FedScope, 259; Salaries and Wages, 260
Office of Pollution Prevention and Toxics (OPPT), 237
Office of Population Affairs (OPA), 292
Office of Postsecondary Education (OPE), 154
Office of Privacy and Civil Liberties, 344
Office of Protected Resources (OPR), 218
Office of Public Health Science (OPHS), 15
Office of Refugee Resettlement (ORR), 333
Office of Research, Development & Technology (RTD), 448
Office of Response and Restoration (OR&R), 218
Office of Rural Health Policy (ORHP), 292
Office of Safe and Healthy Students (OSHS), 150
Office of Science, 406
Office of Science and Technology Policy (OSTP), 406; Blog, 407; Science of Science and Innovation Policy, 407
Office of Science Policy, 292
Office of Space Commerce, 419
Office of Special Counsel (OSC), 261
Office of Special Counsel for Immigration-Related Unfair Employment Practices, 173
Office of Special Education Programs (OSEP), 150
Office of Surface Mining Reclamation and Enforcement (OSMRE), 232
Office of Technology Assessment: The OTA Legacy, 380
Office of Terrorism and Financial Intelligence, 363
Office of Textiles and Apparel (OTEXA), 50
Office of the Attorney General, 362
Office of the Chief of Protocol, 327
Office of the Comptroller of the Currency (OCC), 42
Office of the Director of National Intelligence (ODNI), 121
Office of the Federal Register, 268
Office of the Pardon Attorney, 389
Office of the Surgeon General, 292
Office of the U.S. Global AIDS Coordinator, 293
Office of the U.S. Trade Representative (USTR), 50
Office of Trade Agreements Negotiations and Compliance (TANC), 50
Office of Trade Policy & Analysis (TP&A), 50
Office of Tribal Justice (OTJ), 273
Office of University Partnerships (OUP), 435
Office of Water, 230
Office of Women's Business Ownership, 26
Office on Violence Against Women, 363
Official U.S. Time, 88
Oil and Gas Industry Initiatives, 191
OnGuard Online, 29
OpenNet, 122
Open Secrets, 468; Blog, 469
Open Source Center (OSC), 122
Open World Leadership Center, 327
Orange Book, 313
Organ Donation, 282
Organisation for Economic Co-operation and Development Online, 469
Organisation for Security and Co-operation in Europe, 469
Organization of American States (OAS), 469
Organization of the Petroleum Exporting Countries (OPEC), 470

Overseas Basing Commission, 104
Overseas Private Investment Corporation (OPIC), 51
Overseas Security Advisory Council (OSAC), 337

PACER: Public Access to Court Electronic Records, 350
Pacific Command (PACOM), 99
Pacific Marine Environmental Laboratory (PMEL), 224
Pacific Northwest National Laboratory (PNNL), 396
Pacific States Marine Fisheries Commission (PSMFC), 19
Page One Economics, 33
Pantex Plant, 470
Pardons: Office of the Pardon Attorney, 389
Parents Central (NHTSA), 451
Parents' Place, 197
Park Police, 365
Parole Commission, 365
Partnership for the National Trails System, 470
Partners in Health, 470
Patent and Trademark Office (PTO), 26; DOEpatents, 408; Resource Centers, 79; STOPfakes.gov, 22, 51
Patuxent Wildlife Research Center (PWRC), 233
Peace Corps Kids World, 163
Pension Benefit Guaranty Corporation (PBGC), 173
Pentagon Digital Library, 79
Pentagon Force Protection Agency (PFPA), 104
Performance.gov, 251
Petroleum Reserves, 192
Physical Fitness, Sports & Nutrition: President's Council, 293
Physical Measurement Laboratory, 403
Physical Oceanography Distributed Active Archive Center, 224
Picturing America, 142
Pipeline and Hazardous Materials Safety Administration (PHMSA), 451
Plain Language, 88
Planetary Data System (PDS), 420
Planning and Evaluation, Office of the Assistant Secretary for (ASPE), 291
Plants & Animals, 15
PLANTS Database, 16
Poetry and Literature Center of the Library of Congress, 56
Politico, 471
Pollutants and Waste: AirCompare, 234; Contaminated Site Clean-Up Information, 234; Envirofacts Data Warehouse, 235; Environmental and Sustainable Programs, 236; Green Vehicle Guide, 236; Hanford Site, 234; Office of Air and Radiation, 235; Office of Chemical Safety and Pollution Prevention, 236; Office of Environmental Management, 235; Office of Land and Emergency Management, 236; Office of Pollution Prevention and Toxics, 237; RadTown USA, 237; Remediation Technologies Roundtable, 235; RestoreTheGulf.gov, 237; Savannah River Site, 237; Superfund Program, 237; Tox Town, 238; TribalAIR, 238; TTN*Web*: Technology Transfer Network, 238; U.S. Chemical Safety Board, 238
Popular Baby Names, 88
Population, Refugees, and Migration, Bureau of, 332
Population Affairs, Office of, 292
Population Clock, 133
Postal Museum, 84
Postal Regulatory Commission (PRC), 270
Postal Service (USPS), 271; Citizens' Stamp Advisory Committee, 269
Post-Traumatic Stress Disorder (PTSD), National Center for, 280
Poverty Guidelines, Research, and Measurement, 436
Preserve America, 60
Presidency: Administration, 385; American Presidency Project, 388; *Codification of Presidential Proclamations and Executive Orders*, 388; Compilation of Presidential Documents, 388; Directives and Executive Orders, 389, 471; Emergency Plan for AIDS Relief, 293; Executive

Orders Disposition Tables, 389; National Medal of Science, 407; New Freedom Commission on Mental Health, 293; Physical Fitness, Sports & Nutrition, Council on, 293; *Public Papers of the Presidents of the United States*, 390
Presidential Directives and Executive Orders, 389, 471
Presidential Libraries and Museums, 79
Presidential Management Fellows Program, 260
Presidential Scholars Program, 150
President's Malaria Initiative (PMI), 282
Presidio, 87
Princeton Plasma Physics Laboratory (PPPL), 403
Prisoner of War/Missing in Action Accounting Agency, 102
Privacy and Civil Liberties Office, 344
Procurement and Acquisition Policy (DPAP), 102
Production, Supply and Distribution (PSD) Online, 16
Profiles in Science, 306
Project Safe Childhood, 364
Project Safe Neighborhoods, 364
Protecting Children's Environmental Health, 293
PubChem, 394
Public and Private Laws, 368
Public Broadcasting: Corporation for Public Broadcasting, 57, 458
Public Interest Declassification Board (PIDB), 268
Public Laws, 368
Public Technical Reports, 410
PubMed, 310
PubMed Central (PMC), 311

QuickFacts, 133

Radio Astronomy Observatory, 402
RadTown USA, 237
Railroad Retirement Board (RRB), 173
Ralph J. Bunche Library, 80
RAND Corporation, 471
Read.gov, 60
Ready.gov, 114
Real Estate: Competition and Real Estate, 23
Records and Recordings: National Recording Preservation Board, 60
Recovery Act: Following the Money: GAO's Oversight of the Recovery Act, 263
Recreation: America's Byways, 85; Fishing, 85; National Avalanche Center, 86; National Park Service, 86; National Trails System, 86; National Zoological Park, 87; Presidio, 87; Recreation.gov, 87; USDA Forest Service Recreational Activities, 85; Your Guide to Fishing on National Wildlife Refuges, 87
Recreation.gov, 87
Redstone Arsenal, 95
Reference: Official U.S. Time, 88; Plain Language, 88; Popular Baby Names, 88
Refugee Resettlement, Office of (ORR), 333
RegInfo.gov, 368
Registry of U.S. Government Publication Digitization Projects, 2
Regulations.gov, 368
Regulatory Development and Retrospective Review Tracker (RegDaRRT), 211
Rehabilitation Information Center (NARIC), 310
Religious Freedom: U.S. Commission on International Religious Freedom, 338
Religious Freedom in Focus, 344
Remediation Technologies Roundtable, 235
Renal Data System (USRDS), 311
Republican National Committee (RNC), 248
Research.gov, 407
Research and Technology, 448; Intelligent Transportation Systems, 447
Research on Learning in Formal and Informal Settings (DRL), 146
Research Portfolio Online Reporting Tools (RePORT), 307
Resources on Strategic Trade Management and Export Controls, 51

Responsible Fatherhood Clearinghouse, 425
RestoreTheGulf.gov, 237
Risk Management Agency (RMA), 16
Roll Call, 471
Rural Development, 427
Rural Health Policy, Office of (ORHP), 292
Rural Information Center (RIC), 427
Rural Utilities Service (RUS), 192

SaferCar.gov, 451
SaferProducts.gov, 29
SAFETY Act, 114
Saint Lawrence Seaway Development Corporation (SLSDC), 443
Salaries and Wages, 260
Sandia National Laboratories, 397
Savannah River National Laboratory (SRNL), 397
Savannah River Site (SRS), 237
Saving Energy at Home, 188
SCAMPI, 80
School District Demographics System (SDDS), 150
Sci4Kids, 163
Science.gov, 411
Science Digital Library (NSDL), 409
Science Inventory, 410
Science of Science and Innovation Policy (SOSP), 407
Science Policy, Office of, 292
Science Tracer Bullets Online, 410
Scientific and Technical Information Office: DOEpatents, 408; Science.gov, 411
Scientific and Technical Information Program, 409
Search for Charities, 439
Second Circuit Court of Appeals, 346
Securities and Exchange Commission (SEC), 43; EDGAR: SEC Filings & Forms, 39; Investor.gov, 41; XBRL.sec.gov, 44
Security and Cooperation in Europe, Commission on, 335, 458
Selective Service System (SSS), 105
Senate, 376; Committees Homepage, 377; Congress.gov, 382; *Guide to House and Senate Members*, 373; Lobbying Disclosure, 375; Majority Leader, 375; Minority Leader, 376
Senior Citizens: Administration on Aging, 286; National Center on Elder Abuse, 360; NIH Senior Health, 281
Senior Corps: Corporation for National and Community Service, 439
SENSIAC: Military Sensing Information Analysis Center, 109
Sentencing Commission (USSC), 353
Servicemembers and Veterans Initiative, 127
Seventh Circuit Court of Appeals, 347
Sex Offender Public Website, 357
Sexually Transmitted Diseases: HIV and STD Testing Resources, 281; National Center for HIV/AIDS, Viral Hepatitis, STD, and TB Prevention, 280
Sierra Club, 471
SIGTARP, 43
SIRIS: Smithsonian Institution Research Information System, 61
Sixth Circuit Court of Appeals, 347
SLAC National Accelerator Laboratory, 404
Small and Disadvantaged Business Utilization (OSDBU), 257
Small Business Administration (SBA), 26; Innovation Research Program, 114; SBIR and STTR Awards, 257; SUB-Net, 257
Small Business Innovation Research (SBIR) Program, 114
SmartGrid.gov, 192
Smithsonian Institution, 61; American Art Museum, 84; Center for Folklife and Cultural Heritage, 61; Cooper Hewitt, Smithsonian Design Museum, 81; Harvard-Smithsonian Center for Astrophysics, 400; Office of Fellowships and Internships, 155; Research Information System, 61; Smithsonian Education: Students, 164; Smithsonian Magazine, 62; Tropical Research Institute, 224
Smithsonian Libraries, 80
Smokefree.gov, 294
SNAP-Ed Connection, 317

Social Security Administration (SSA), 436; Advisory Board, 436; Kids and Families-Social Security, 161; Popular Baby Names, 88; Social Security Online for Women, 437; The Work Site, 437
Social Security History, 66
SOHO: The Solar and Heliospheric Observatory, 404
Solar System Exploration, 420
Solar System Exploration Research Virtual Institute, 418
Soldiers, 96
Sourcebook of Criminal Justice Statistics, 364
South and Central Asian Affairs, Bureau of, 331
Southeastern Power Administration (SEPA), 192
Southern Command (SOUTHCOM), 99
Southern Poverty Law Center (SPLC), 472
Southwestern Power Administration (SWPA), 193
Space and Naval Warfare Systems Command (SPAWAR), 96
Space Calendar, 420
Space Commerce, Office of, 419
Space Science Data Coordinated Archive, 419
Space Shuttle, 418
Space Telescope Science Institute (STScI), 412
Space Weather Prediction Center, 421
Special American Business Internship Training Program (SABIT), 51
Special Counsel Office (OSC), 261
Special Education Programs, Office of, 150
Specialized Information Services Division, 294
Spitzer Space Telescope, 421
Standard Occupational Classification (SOC) System, 178
Standards.gov, 202
Stanford Linear Accelerator Center (SLAC), 404
State Contracts-Education Department, 151
State Department, 326; Arms Control, Verification, and Compliance, Bureau of, 323; *Bilateral Relations Fact Sheets*, 324; Bureau of African Affairs, 330; Bureau of Counterterrorism, 334; Bureau of Diplomatic Security, 325; Bureau of Economic and Business Affairs, 330; Bureau of Educational and Cultural Affairs, 156; Bureau of Intelligence and Research (INR), 118; Bureau of Near Eastern Affairs, 331; Bureau of Population, Refugees, and Migration, 332; Bureau of South and Central Asian Affairs, 331; Bureau of Western Hemisphere Affairs, 331; Chief of Protocol, 327; Cultural Heritage Center, 58; Diplomacy Center, 328; DipNote, 326; Directorate of Defense Trade Controls, 46; EducationUSA, 156; *Foreign Relations of the United States*, 332; Global AIDS Coordinator, 293; Intercountry Adoption, 424; Middle East Partnership Initiative, 337; Mission to the United Nations, 329; Nonproliferation and Disarmament Fund, 324; Office of Commercial and Business Affairs, 49; Office of Global Criminal Justice (GCJ), 337; Office of the Historian, 331; Office to Monitor and Combat Trafficking in Persons, 364; Ralph J. Bunche Library, 80; Resources on Strategic Trade Management and Export Controls, 51; STEM: Science, Technology, Engineering, and Math, 157; Travel.State.gov, 333; U.S. Mission to International Organizations in Vienna, 329; U.S. Mission to NATO, 338; U.S. Mission to the OECD, 329; U.S. Mission to the OSCE, 329; USEmbassy.gov, 328; Youth and Education, 158
State Facts for Students, 164
State Fact Sheets-ERS, 16
State Justice Institute (SJI), 351
State-Level Lists of Fatal Casualties: Korean and Vietnam Wars, 66
Statistics in Schools, 142

STEM: Science, Technology, Engineering, and Math, 157
Stem Cell Information, 307
Stennis Space Center (SSC), 421
Stimson Center, 472
Stockholm International Peace Research Institute (SIPRI), 472
StopBullying.gov, 164
STOPfakes.gov, 22, 51
STOPfraud.gov, 44
Storm Prediction Center (SPC), 243
Strategic Command (STRATCOM), 99
Student and Recent Graduate Jobs-USAJOBS, 178
Students for the Environment, 164
SUB-Net, 257
Substance Abuse and Mental Health Services Administration (SAMHSA), 294; Publications Ordering, 282
Superfund Program, 237
Supplemental Nutrition Assistance Program (SNAP), 437
Supreme Court: FindLaw: Supreme Court Opinions, 350
Surface Mining Reclamation and Enforcement Office, 232
Surface Transportation Board (STB), 446
Surgeon General, Office of, 292; *Reports of the Surgeon General*, 293
Surveillance, Epidemiology, and End Results (SEER) Program, 311
System for Award Management (SAM), 257

T-2 Nuclear Information Service, 404
Tax Court, 353
Tax Information for Political Organizations, 248
Taxpayer Advocate Service, 264
Tax Statistics, 263
Teach.org, 166
Teachers and Teaching: Ames Educator Resource Center, 165; Environmental Health Science Education: Teachers, 139; James Madison Graduate Fellowships, 166; Library of Congress Teacher Resources, 165; National Clearinghouse for English Language Acquisition, 166; Teach.org, 166; Teachers' Resources, 140; What Works Clearinghouse, 166
Technical Reports Server (NASA), 418
Technology: Biometrics, 202; Biometrics Resource Center, 203; Digital Preservation, 203; Digital Television, 203; Energy Science and Technology Software Center, 203; Energy Sciences Network, 204; Federal Laboratory Consortium for Technology Transfer, 255; Information Technology Laboratory, 204; Information Technology Portal, 204; Nanotechnology at NIH, 204; NASA Advanced Supercomputing Division, 204; NASA Independent Verification and Validation Facility, 205; NASA Strategic Partnerships Office, 205; NASA Technology Transfer Portal, 205; National Energy Research Scientific Computing Center, 206; National Geological and Geophysical Data Preservation Program, 206; National Nanotechnology Initiative, 206; National Vulnerability Database, 206; Networking and Information Technology Research and Development Program, 205; NIST Computer Security Resource Center, 206; Section 508, 207; Technology Innovation Program, 207; Usability.gov, 207; US-CERT, 207
Telehealth, 290
Telephones and Telemarketing: National Do Not Call Registry, 29; OnGuard Online, 29
Telework.gov, 261
Tennessee Valley Authority (TVA), 193
Tenth Circuit Court of Appeals, 348
Terrorism: National Commission on Terrorist Attacks Upon the United States, 113; National Counterterrorism Center, 119; SAFETY Act, 114
Terrorism and Financial Intelligence, Office of (TFI), 363
Textiles: Office of Textiles and Apparel, 50
The Hill, 472
Third Circuit Court of Appeals, 346

Thrift Savings Plan (TSP), 261
Tides & Currents (NOAA), 242
TIGER Products, 134
Time and Clocks: Official U.S. Time, 88
Title V Information System (TVIS), 437
Tobacco Products: Alcohol and Tobacco Tax and Trade Bureau, 21; Smokefree.gov, 294; Youth Tobacco Prevention, 295
Today's Military, 96
ToxFAQs: Toxic Substances Portal, 238
Toxicological Research, National Center for (NCTR), 299
Toxicology, National Program, 305
Toxic Substances and Disease Registry: ToxFAQs: Toxic Substances Portal, 238
ToxMystery, 165
TOXNET, 311
Tox Town, 238
Trade and Development Agency (USTDA), 52
Trademarks: Patent and Trademark Office, 26
TradeStats Express, 52
Trafficking in Persons: Campaign to Rescue and Restore Victims of Human Trafficking, 431; Office to Monitor and Combat, 364
Trails System, 86
Transportation and Climate Change Clearinghouse, 448
Transportation Command (TRANSCOM), 100
Transportation Department (DOT), 447; Aviation Consumer Protection Division, 27; Bureau of Transportation Statistics, 446; Federal Highway Administration, 445; Federal Motor Carrier Safety Administration, 450; Federal Railroad Administration, 445; Federal Transit Administration, 444; Intelligent Transportation Systems, 447; John A. Volpe Transportation Systems Center, 448; Library, 78; Maritime Administration, 442; National Traffic and Road Closure Information, 446; *National Transit Database*, 444; Office of Federal Lands Highway, 445; Office of Research, Development & Technology, 448; Research and Technology, 448; Saint Lawrence Seaway Development Corporation, 443; Surface Transportation Board, 446; Traffic and Road Closure Information, 446
Transportation Safety Institute, 452
Transportation Security Administration (TSA), 115; TSA Blog, 452
TranStats, 449
Travel.State.gov, 333
Travel Information (CDC), 332
Treasury Department, 262; Alcohol and Tobacco Tax and Trade Bureau, 21; Bureau of Engraving and Printing, 53; Bureau of the Fiscal Service, 262; Community Development Financial Institutions Fund, 39; Federal Financing Bank, 263; Inspector General for Tax Administration, 252; Internal Revenue Service, 263; Money Services Businesses, 41; Office of Domestic Finance, 42; Office of Economic Policy, 33; Office of Financial Stability, 43; Office of the Comptroller of the Currency, 42; Taxpayer Advocate Service, 264; Tax Statistics, 263; Terrorism and Financial Intelligence, Office of, 363; TreasuryDirect, 264
TreasuryDirect, 264
Treasury International Capital (TIC) System, 44
TribalAIR, 236
Tribal Energy and Environmental Information Clearinghouse (TEEIC), 214
TRICARE: Military Health System, 284
Trustee Program
Tsunami, 243
TTN*Web*: Technology Transfer Network, 238
Tuberculosis: National Center for HIV/AIDS, Viral Hepatitis, STD, and TB Prevention, 280

U.S. Access Board, 345
U.S. Agency for International Development, 327

U.S. and World Population Clock, 133
U.S. Arctic Research Commission (USARC), 408
U.S. Army Center of Military History (CMH), 66
U.S. Army Heritage and Education Center (USAHEC), 67
U.S. Chemical Safety Board (CSB), 238
U.S. Chief Financial Officers Council (CFOC), 264
U.S.-China Economic and Security Review Commission (USCC), 338
U.S. Citizenship and Immigration Services (USCIS), 334; Civics and Citizenship Toolkit, 245
U.S. Code, 369
U.S. Commission of Fine Arts (CFA), 56
U.S. Commission on Civil Rights (USCCR), 345
U.S. Commission on International Religious Freedom, 338
U.S. Court Resources, 353
U.S. Diplomacy Center (USDC), 328
U.S. Fire Administration (USFA), 321
U.S. Geological Survey (USGS), 408; Cascades Volcano Observatory, 397; Earthquake Hazards Program, 399; Energy Resources Program, 189; Geology Research and Information, 399; Hawaiian Volcano Observatory, 400; Libraries Program, 70; National Earthquake Information Center, 401; Science Education, 142; Volcano Hazards Program, 405
U.S. Government Blog, 269
U.S. Government Photos and Images, 3
U.S. Government YouTube Channel, 3
U.S. Institute of Peace (USIP), 328
U.S. Marshals Service, 365
U.S.-Mexico Border 2020, 473
U.S. Mission to International Organizations in Vienna, 329
U.S. Mission to NATO, 338
U.S. Mission to the OECD, 329
U.S. Mission to the OSCE, 329
U.S. Mission to the United Nations, 329
U.S. Naval Observatory (USNO), 404
U.S. Parole Commission, 365
U.S. Petroleum Reserves, 192
U.S. Renal Data System (USRDS), 311
U.S. Sentencing Commission (USSC), 353
U.S. Tax Court, 353
U.S. Trustee Program, 353
Udall Foundation, 214
Unemployment Insurance, 438
UNESCO, 475
UNESCO World Heritage Centre, 473
UNICEF, 474
UNICOR: Federal Prison Industries, Inc., 258, 473
Uniformed Services University of the Health Sciences (USUHS), 286
Union of Concerned Scientists (UCS), 474
United Nations (UN), 474; U.S. Mission to the UN, 329
United Nations Children's Fund Works for Children Worldwide (UNICEF), 474
United Nations Climate Change Portal, 475
United Nations Educational, Scientific, and Cultural Organization, 475
United States Attorneys, 352
United States Botanical Garden (USBG), 84
United States Government Manual, 252
United States Holocaust Memorial Museum (USHMM), 81
United States Interagency Council on Homelessness, 430
United States Mint, 53; Kids' Site, 165
United States Park Police, 365
United States Postal Service (USPS), 271
United States Secret Service (USSS), 115
United States Supreme Court: FindLaw: Supreme Court Opinions, 350
United States Trade and Development Agency (USTDA), 52
University of Arkansas School of Law: National Agricultural Law Center, 13
University of Maryland Law Library: Historical Publications of the U.S. Commission on Civil Rights, 343
University of Minnesota: IPUMS USA: Integrated Public Use Microdata Series, 132
University of North Texas Libraries: Advisory Commission on Intergovernmental Relations, 271; CRS

Reports, 379; CyberCemetery, 4
University of Virginia: Administrative Decisions and Other Actions, 340
UN Refugee Agency (UNHCR), 473
Upper Midwest Environmental Sciences Center (UMESC), 225
Uranium Hexafluoride: Depleted UF6 Management Information Program, 189
USA.gov, 3
USA.gov Buying from the U.S. Government, 258
USA4 Military Families, 128
Usability.gov, 207
USAID, 327
USAID Knowledge Management (KM) Support, 80
USAJOBS, 178, 179
USA Learns, 138
USAMRIID: Army Medical Research Institute of Infectious Diseases, 109
USA Science and Engineering Festival, 151
US-CERT, 207
USEmbassy.gov, 328
USPTO Kids, 165
Utilities: Rural Utilities Service, 192; SmartGrid.gov, 192; Southeastern Power Administration, 192; Southwestern Power Administration, 193; Tennessee Valley Authority, 193; Western Area Power Administration, 193

Vaccines and Immunizations, 315
Vehicle Technologies Office, 446
Veterans Affairs Department (VA), 125; Education and Training, 145; Gravesite Locator, 126; Home Loans, 429; National Center for PTSD, 280; National Center for Veterans Analysis and Statistics, 135; Returning Service Members, 127
Veterans Benefits Administration (VBA), 128
Veterans Claims Court of Appeals, 351
Veterans' Employment and Training Service (VETS), 174
Veterans Employment Initiative, 259
Veterans Health Administration (VHA), 285
Veterans History Project, 67
VetoViolence, 366
Vice President Mike Pence, 386
Victims of Crime, Office for, 362
Vietnam Education Foundation (VEF), 330
Vietnam War: State-Level Lists of Fatal Casualties, 66; Vietnam-Era Prisoner-of-War/Missing-in-Action Database, 67
Violence Against Women, Office on, 363
Viral Hepatitis: National Center for HIV/AIDS, Viral Hepatitis, STD, and TB Prevention, 280
Visible Human Project, 312
Vital and Health Statistics Committee, 290
VitalStats, 312
Voice of America (VOA), 330
Volcano Hazards Program, 405
Volunteer.gov, 440
Voyager, 421

Wage and Hour Division (WHD), 174
Wage Determinations OnLine.gov, 174
Wallops Flight Facility, 422
War Crimes: Office of Global Criminal Justice, 337
War of 1812: A Guide to the War of 1812, 64; Military Resources: War of 1812, 65
Wartime Contracting Commission in Iraq and Afghanistan, 253
Washburn University School of Law: U.S. Court Resources, 353
Water Data for the Nation, 233
Water Resources of the United States, 233
Weapons of Mass Destruction: Commission on Intelligence Capabilities Regarding WMD, 117
Weather: AirNow, 239; Aviation Weather Center, 239; Climate Analysis Branch, 239; Climate Prediction Center, 240; Global Systems Division, 240; Heat Island Effect, 240; Joint Agricultural Weather Facility, 12; National Centers for Environmental Information, 240; National Data Buoy Center, 241; National Hurricane Center, 241; National Severe Storms Laboratory,

241; National Weather Service, 241; National Weather Service Marine Forecasts, 242; NOAA Tides & Currents, 242; NOAA Weather Radio, 242; Storm Prediction Center, 243; Tsunami, 243
Weatherization and Intergovernmental Program, 188
Weather Radio (NOAA), 242
Web Archiving: Library of Congress, 67
Western Area Power Administration (WAPA), 193
Western Hemisphere Affairs, Bureau of, 331
West Point: Military Academy at West Point, 156
Wetland and Aquatic Research Center (WARC), 234
What Works Clearinghouse (WWC), 166
White House, 386; 1600 Daily, 387; Administration, 385; Domestic Policy Council, 386; Fellows Program, 387; First Lady Melania Trump, 386; Global Change Research Program, 221; Initiative on Educational Excellence for Hispanics, 146; Initiative on Historically Black Colleges and Universities, 156; Inside the White House Kids' Page, 161; Military Office, 387; National Science and Technology Council, 405; National Security Council, 386; Office of Faith-Based and Neighborhood Partnerships, 435; Office of Federal Sustainability Council, 213; Office of Management and Budget, 251; Office of Science and Technology Policy, 406; Performance.gov, 251; Preserve America, 60; Science of Science and Innovation Policy, 407
White Sands Test Facility (WSTF), 419
WIC Works Resource System, 318
Wild and Scenic Rivers System, 217
William J. Hughes Technical Center, 442
Wireless Security: OnGuard Online, 29
Wireless Telecommunications Bureau, 197
Wirtz Labor Library, 81
Wisconsin Project on Nuclear Arms Control, 475
Women: Congress, Women in, 377; National Organization for Women, 466; National Women's Business Council, 25; Office of Women's Business Ownership, 26; Office on Violence Against Women, 363; Social Security Online for Women, 437
Women, Infants, and Children (WIC), 425
Women's Bureau, 179
Women's Health.gov, 295
Woodrow Wilson International Center for Scholars, 273, 476
Workplace Conditions: Federal Occupational Health, 181; Mine Safety and Health Administration, 181; Nanotechnology at NIOSH, 181; National Institute of Occupational Safety and Health, 181; Occupational Safety and Health Administration, 182
World Agricultural Outlook Board (WAOB), 17
World Bank, 476
World Factbook, 325
World Health Organization (WHO), 476
World Intellectual Property Organization (WIPO), 476
World Meteorological Organization (WMO), 477
World Trade Organization (WTO), 477
World Wildlife Fund (WWF), 477
Wounded Warrior Regiment, 128
Wright-Patterson Air Force Base, 100

XBRL.sec.gov, 44

Y-12 National Security Complex, 116
Your Guide to Fishing on National Wildlife Refuges, 87
Youth.gov, 433
Youth and Education, 158
Youth at Work, 175
YouthRules!, 175
Youth Tobacco Prevention, 295

Zoological Park, 87